A Companion to the Environmental History of Byzantium

Brill's Companions to the Byzantine World

Managing Editor

Wolfram Brandes

VOLUME 13

The titles published in this series are listed at *brill.com/bcbw*

A Companion to the Environmental History of Byzantium

Edited by

Adam Izdebski
Johannes Preiser-Kapeller

BRILL

LEIDEN | BOSTON

Cover illustration: Coring at Lake Pikrolimni, Greece. Raphael Gromig, 2019.

Library of Congress Cataloging-in-Publication Data

Names: Izdebski, Adam, editor. | Preiser-Kapeller, Johannes, editor.
Title: A companion to the environmental history of Byzantium / edited by
   Adam Izdebski, Johannes Preiser-Kapeller.
Description: Leiden : Boston : Brill, [2024] | Series: Brill's companions
   to the Byzantine world, 2212-7429 ; volume 13 | Includes bibliographical
   references and index.
Identifiers: LCCN 2023048613 (print) | LCCN 2023048614 (ebook) | ISBN
   9789004689282 (hardback : acid-free paper) | ISBN 9789004689350 (e-book)
Subjects: LCSH: Human ecology—Mediterranean Region—History. | Byzantine
   Empire—History. | Nature—Effect of human beings on—History—To 1500.
   | Climatic changes—Social aspects—History—To 1500.
Classification: LCC GF13.3.M47 C66 2024 (print) | LCC GF13.3.M47 (ebook)
   | DDC 304.209495/0902—dc23/eng/20231221
LC record available at https://lccn.loc.gov/2023048613
LC ebook record available at https://lccn.loc.gov/2023048614

Typeface for the Latin, Greek, and Cyrillic scripts: "Brill". See and download: brill.com/brill-typeface.

ISSN 2212-7429
ISBN 978-90-04-68928-2 (hardback)
ISBN 978-90-04-68935-0 (e-book)
DOI 10.1163/9789004689350

Copyright 2024 by Koninklijke Brill NV, Leiden, The Netherlands.
Koninklijke Brill NV incorporates the imprints Brill, Brill Nijhoff, Brill Schöningh, Brill Fink, Brill mentis, Brill Wageningen Academic, Vandenhoeck & Ruprecht, Böhlau and V&R unipress.
All rights reserved. No part of this publication may be reproduced, translated, stored in a retrieval system, or transmitted in any form or by any means, electronic, mechanical, photocopying, recording or otherwise, without prior written permission from the publisher. Requests for re-use and/or translations must be addressed to Koninklijke Brill NV via brill.com or copyright.com.

This book is printed on acid-free paper and produced in a sustainable manner.

Contents

List of Figures and Tables   IX
Notes on Contributors   XIII

Environmental History of Byzantium. An Introduction   1
   Adam Izdebski and Johannes Preiser-Kapeller

PART 1
The Basics: Methods and Evidence

1   Palaeoclimatology of Byzantine Lands (AD 300–1500)   27
      Jürg Luterbacher, Elena Xoplaki, Adam Izdebski and Dominik Fleitmann

2   Palynology and Historical Research   59
      Adam Izdebski

3   The Byzantine "Ecosystem": Evidence from the Bioarchaeological Record   83
      Chryssi Bourbou

4   Historical Epidemiology of the Medieval Eastern Mediterranean   109
      Costas Tsiamis

5   Animals and the Byzantine Environment: Zooarchaeological Approaches   137
      Henriette Baron

6   Historical Seismology   162
      Lee Mordechai

PART 2
Case Studies: Environmental History at Work

7   The Byzantines and Nature in the Christian Worldview   181
     Henry Maguire

8   Water and the Urban Environment of Constantinople
     and Thessaloniki   203
     James Crow

9   Continuities and Discontinuities in the Agriculture of the Levant in the
     Late Antique and Early Islamic Period   227
     Michael J. Decker

10 Sagalassos and Its Environs during Late Roman
     and Byzantine Times   251
     *Johan Bakker, Eva Kaptijn, Peter Talloen, Ralf Vandam and
     Jeroen Poblome*

11 Euchaïta, Landscape and Climate in the Byzantine Period   278
     Warren Eastwood and John Haldon

12 Ecology, Irrigation and Lordship in the Lake Van Region: A Long-Term
     View from Urartu to Vaspurakan   308
     Johannes Preiser-Kapeller

13 Sea of Agency: Islands and Coasts of the Byzantine Aegean in
     Environmental Perspective   346
     Myrto Veikou

14 "The Other Age of Justinian": Environment, Extreme Events, and the
     Transformation of the Mediterranean, 5th–7th Century   381
     Mischa Meier

15 The Medieval Climate Anomaly, the Oort Minimum, and Socio-Political
     Dynamics in the Eastern Mediterranean and the Byzantine Empire,
     10th to 12th Century   405
     Johannes Preiser-Kapeller

16 The Ecology of the Crusader States   489
    Abigail Sargent

17 The Little Ice Age in the Eastern Mediterranean, 14th–17th Centuries   512
    Sam White

Bibliography   533
Index of Place Names   539
Index of Names   548

Figures and Tables

Figures

1.1 Winter (December to February) mean climate in the Byzantine lands 1951–2016. Data stem from monthly CRU 4.01 with 0.5° × 0.5° spatial resolution (Harris et al. 2014, "Updated high-resolution grids of monthly climatic observations – the CRU TS3.10 Dataset") 29

1.2 Summer (June to August) mean climate in the Byzantine lands 1951–2016. Data stem from monthly CRU 4.01 with 0.5° × 0.5° spatial resolution (Harris et al. 2014, "Updated high-resolution grids of monthly climatic observations – the CRU TS3.10 Dataset") 31

1.3 Examples of documentary and natural proxies for palaeo climate and environmental research in the Mediterranean (Bradley et al. 1995) 32

1.4 Schematic diagram of the general methodology used to reconstruct past climates, including surface temperature reconstructions (From NRC, "Surface temperature reconstructions for the past 2,000 years") 34

1.5 Natural and documentary records resolving hydroclimate or temperature across the central and eastern Mediterranean, divided by proxy type that cover the full or a large part of the Byzantine period 43

1.6 Tree ring proxies together with documentary evidence and spatial distribution of proxy records used in the 2150 years summer temperature reconstructions for the central and eastern Mediterranean 48

1.7 Spatial Spearman correlation between detrended winter temperature around Constantinople and other areas across the central and eastern Mediterranean for the period 1951–2010 51

1.8 As Figure 1.7 but for decadal means covering the period 1901–2010 51

2.1 Microscope photographs of pollen grains of wheat (Triticum/Avena) and amaranth (Amaranthaceae) 62

2.2 Age-depth model for Lake Abant in NW Turkey (polynomial regression) 67

2.3 Pollen profile of Lake Pergusa in Central Sicily, with different groups of pollen taxa, depth, estimated age, and radiocarbon dates 70

2.4 Pollen sites in Anatolia that provide information on the course of the late antique–early medieval transition in agriculture 74

2.5 Aggregated trends in cereals' share of total vegetation structure (cerealia-type pollen, in %) in four major regions of the Byznatine world 76

3.1 Alikianos, skeleton 040. Massive concentration of calculus on the mandibular teeth 90

3.2 Alikianos, skeleton 057. Detail of cribra orbitalia 91

3.3	Alikianos, skeleton 011. Manifestation of scorbutic lesions in the form of dense hypervascularity on the endocranial of the frontal bone (a mixture of active and healed bone plaques, suggestive of a reaction to chronic hemorrhage)	93
4.1	Geographical distribution of epidemic outbreaks from AD 300 to 1453 (plague, dysentery, diphtheria, smallpox, unknown microbial origin)	130
5.1	Arithmetical mean of the main domestic mammal percentages (sheep/goat, cattle, and pig) in the regions of the Empire in comparison to Anthony King's results for the Roman Period (King, "Diet")	145
5.2	Arithmetical mean of identified bird family percentages in faunal materials from different regions, with the exception of the domestic chicken	150
5.3	Arithmetic mean of game percentages in different regions of the Byzantine Empire. In the north, a high share of deer; in the south, more bovids	151
5.4	Attribution of fish families found in Byzantine faunal materials to different water bodies	156
5.5	Small mammal finds on the North Plateau of Caričin Grad	158
6.1	SCEs and their effects	166
7.1	Ravenna, Arian Baptistery, dome mosaic: Baptism of Christ in the river Jordan	187
7.2	Thessaloniki, Hosios David, apse mosaic: Christ in Glory with river deity below	188
7.3	Umm al-Rasas, Church of St. Stephen, nave pavement, detail: iconoclastic erasures	192
7.4	Madaba, Church of the Apostles, nave pavement, detail: personification of the sea	195
7.5	Darmstadt, Landesmuseum, ivory box: personification of wealth with Adam and Eve laboring and grieving	198
8.1	Map showing the course of the long-distance aqueduct channels	205
8.2	Map showing the revised course of the low-level Hadrianic channel and the Valens channel	215
8.3	Map showing the distribution of 210 Byzantine period cisterns in Constantinople, the line of the two main channels and the approximate boundaries of the city's regions	217
9.1	Map of cities and sites mentioned in the chapter	228
10.1	Settlement patterns in the territory of ancient Sagalassos	252
10.2	a. Sagalassos seen from its southern entrance, b. the Bereket basin, c. Gravgaz marsh, d. fortified hilltop settlement KAA08, e./g. pattern burnished sherd (Early Byzantine Dark Age), f. Middle Byzantine pottery, h. press weight (Roman), i. monumental (funerary) architecture (Roman)	260
11.1	Physical relief of Çankırı-Çorum region	280

FIGURES AND TABLES XI

11.2 Simplified geology map of the Çankırı-Çorum Basin and surrounding region 281
11.3 Precipitation and temperature data for Çorum (average for 1930–2000) 284
11.4 Summary percentage pollen diagram for Abant 289
11.5 Summary percentage pollen diagram for Yeniçağa 290
11.6 Summary percentage pollen diagram for Kaz 291
11.7 Summary percentage pollen diagram for Lâdik 292
11.8 Summary percentage pollen diagram for Çöl 294
11.9 Nar Gölü (Cappadocia) & Tecer Gölü (Sivas) – a climate proxy for Avkat (after Kuzucuoğlu et al. 2011; Jones et al. 2006; England et al. 2008) 297
12.1 Map of selected localities mentioned in the chapter (J. Preiser-Kapeller, OEAW, 2021; base map: GoogleEarth) 309
12.2 Modern-day monthly average temperature (degree Celsius) and precipitation (mm) in the city of Van (J. Preiser-Kapeller, OEAW, 2021) 310
12.3 Map of irrigation installations in the region of the city of Van (J. Preiser-Kapeller, OEAW, 2021; base map: GoogleEarth) 312
12.4 Number of documented major construction works in the regions around Lake Van (Turkey) between the 6th and 16th centuries 318
12.5 Map of the area around the Arcruni residences of Ostan andAłtʻamar (J. Preiser-Kapeller, OEAW, 2021; base map: GoogleEarth) 323
12.6 Depiction of King Gagik Arcruni (904/908–943 CE) on the Church of the Holy Cross on the island of Ałtamar in Lake Van 325
12.7 Reconstruction of average humidity conditions in the Lake Van area based on oxygen isotope data 332
12.8 Reconstruction of average humidity and temperature conditions in the Lake Van area 333
13.1 Topographical and bathymetric map of the Aegean Sea area. Copyright Eric Gaba (Sting – fr:Sting) [GFDL (http://www.gnu.org/copyleft/fdl.html) or CC BY-SA 4.0-3.0-2.5-2.0-1.0 (https://creativecommons.org/licenses/by-sa/4.0-3.0-2.5-2.0-1.0)], via Wikimedia Commons from Wikimedia Commons: (https://commons.wikimedia.org/wiki/File:Aegean_Sea_map_bathymetry-fr.jpg) 348
13.2 Simplified map of the present-day geodynamic structure of the Hellenic Arc, showing the modern Aegean volcanic arc developed behind the Hellenic trench, the Peloponnese – Crete island arc and the Cretan back-arc basin 349
13.3 Satellite Image of the Aegean Sea Region 350
13.4 The active faults of the broader Aegean region on 2018.04.05 355
13.5 Ephesos deltaic area. J. Preiser-Kapeller, "Harbours and Maritime Networks as Complex Adaptive Systems – a Thematic Introduction", in: J. Preiser-Kapeller &

F. Daim (eds.), *Harbours and Maritime Networks as Complex Adaptive Systems*, RGZM Tagungen 23 (Mainz), 6: Fig. 3   359

15.1   Average summer temperatures in Western and Central Europe AD 500–1500, (in comparison with the average AD 1960–1990) reconstructed on the basis of tree rings   409

15.2   Map of selected climate patterns influencing weather dynamics in the Eastern Mediterranean: NAO (North Atlantic Oscillation), NCP (North Sea–Caspian Pattern), SH (Siberian High), ENSO (El Niño–Southern Oscillation), MLSH (Mid-Latitude Subtropical High-Pressure Systems); in red, territorial extent of the Byzantine Empire in AD c.1045 (J. Preiser-Kapeller, OEAW, 2022)   410

15.3   Map of selected cities and towns and proxy data sites mentioned in the chapter (J. Preiser-Kapeller, OEAW, 2022)   417

15.4   Cerealia pollen data indices for three regions in Asia Minor, AD 300–1200   418

15.5   Cerealia pollen data indices for two regions in Greece, AD 300–1600   419

15.6   Kuna Ba cave (Northern Iraq) oxygen isotopes record, AD 400–1500   433

15.7   Sofular Cave (northwestern Turkey) speleothem carbon isotopes record, AD 300–1600   437

15.8   Lake Nar (central Turkey) oxygen isotopes record, AD 500–1500   473

15.9   Reconstructed May/June precipitation in mm for the northern Aegean region based on tree rings, AD 1100–1500, 30-year average and long-term trend   474

16.1   Localities mentioned in the chapter   493

16.2   Pollen Variations: KIND4 (Sea of Galilee). Data for select pollen taxa from Baruch, "Late Holocene Vegetational History." Dates have been recalibrated as described above (note 23). See also Table 16.1   503

Tables

1.1   Proxy records and reconstructions of past climate conditions available for the Byzantine lands   44

2.1   Dates used for the calculation of Lake Abant age-depth model   66

2.2   Exemplary pollen data from Lake Abant, NW Turkey. Only the percentages of selected plants are reported   69

4.1   Comparison between the symptoms of the three Plague Pandemics   111

4.2   Chronological intervals of epidemic aggregations (AD 541–750/51)   121

10.1   An overview of the main changes in vegetation, climate, and settlement patterns, placed along a temporal axis   263

10.2   Byzantine sites in the territory of Sagalassos   258

16.1   Recalibrated dates for KIND4, using a cubic spline with 68 per cent certainty   504

Notes on Contributors

Johan Bakker
obtained his doctorate at the University of Leuven. Specializing in palynology, he studied environmental change from the Late Classical period to the present in the territory of Sagalassos.

Henriette Baron
is a post-doc researcher at the Leibniz-Zentrum für Archäologie (LEIZA) in Mainz (Germany) specializing in Byzantine Human–Animal Studies. Her book *Tiere im Byzantinischen Reich* reviews zooarchaeological research for the Byzantine Empire. Together with F. Daim she edited the conference volume *A Most pleasant Scene and an Inexhaustible Resource, Steps towards a Byzantine Environmental History*.

Chryssa Bourbou
is a bioarchaeologist at the Ephorate of Antiquities of Chania (Hellenic Ministry of Culture and Sports) and an External Scientific Collaborator at the University of Fribourg (Switzerland).

James Crow
teaches Roman and Byzantine archaeology at the University of Edinburgh. He studied at the Universities of Birmingham, Newcastle and Sofia. He was later based in Ankara and subsequently directed excavations on Hadrian's Wall. He lectured at Warwick and Newcastle Universities before his current post as professor of Classical Archaeology at Edinburgh. In Turkey he has directed survey projects on the Black Sea and from 1994 in the west hinterland of Istanbul, surveying and documenting the Anastasian Wall and the Water Supply of Byzantine Constantinople. He is the current chair of the British Institute at Ankara. His extensive publications include two books on Hadrian's Wall, a monograph on the water supply of Constantinople, an edited volume on Byzantine Naxos and the Aegean, and numerous articles on frontiers, fortifications, hydraulic infrastructure and landscape archaeology in the eastern Mediterranean including the Byzantine Cyclades and the Black Sea. He is currently part of a project investigating past and contemporary water issues in Istanbul with a focus on the Acropolis/Topkapi Saray area.

Michael J. Decker
is Maroulis Professor of Byzantine History and Orthodox Religion at the University of South Florida.

Warren J. Eastwood
is currently an Honorary Lecturer at the School of Geography, Earth and Environmental Sciences at the University of Birmingham. He is a biogeographer and palaeoecologist and researches past environmental change for the last 25,000 years or so in the eastern Mediterranean region where he has worked for the past 30 years. His main specialism is elucidating natural versus human-induced vegetation change using pollen analysis (palynology) and works closely with archaeologists and historians and is a core member of the University of Princeton's Climate Change and History Research Initiative (CCHRI). His research interests also include climate change and the impact of major volcanic eruptions and tephrochronology of volcanic ash layers preserved in lake and peat sediment archives. Warren is currently a member and Honorary Secretary of the British Institute of Archaeology at Ankara (BIAA).

Dominik Fleitmann
is a Quaternary geologist and palaeoclimatologist and professor at the Department of Environmental Sciences of the University of Basel, Switzerland.

John Haldon
is emeritus Shelby Cullom Davis '30 Professor of European History and Professor of Byzantine History and Hellenic Studies at Princeton University and a Co-Director of the Climate Change & History Research Initiative and Director of the Environmental History Lab within the Program in Medieval Studies.

Adam Izdebski
is Independent Research Group Leader at the Max Planck Institute of Geoanthropology in Jena, Germany and Professor of Human Ecology and Environmental History at the Institute of History of the Jagiellonian University in Krakow, Poland.

Eva Kaptijn
focuses on human–landscape interaction with a special interest in landscape archaeology, ancient water management, and the social aspects of subsistence economy. She is currently working for Erggoed Gelderland, the Netherlands.

Jürg Luterbacher
is Director Science and Innovation and Chief Scientist at the World Meteorological Organization (WMO) in Geneva, Switzerland and professor at the Justus-Liebig-Universität Gießen.

Henry Maguire
is Emeritus Professor at the Johns Hopkins University, Baltimore. He specializes in Early Medieval and Byzantine art. His most recent book is *Nectar and Illusion: Nature in Byzantine Art and Literature* (New York, 2012).

Mischa Meier
is Professor for Ancient History at the University of Tübingen. His research interests encompass Greek History (esp. Sparta), the early Principate and Late Antiquity. Among his monographs are *Das andere Zeitalter Justinians* (^{2}2004), *Anastasios I.* (^{2}2010) and *Geschichte der Völkerwanderung* (^{8}2021).

Lee Mordechai
is Senior Lecturer at the Department of History at the Hebrew University of Jerusalem. Lee has worked on historical disasters, including earthquakes and floods, and has focused his work in recent years on the 6th century Justinianic Plague and the 536 event.

Jeroen Poblome
is Professor of Archaeology at the University of Leuven. As director of the Sagalassos Archaeological Research project he coordinates research programmes into past and present socio-ecological systems, social innovation, governance, sustainable development, and resilience.

Johannes Preiser-Kapeller
is a researcher at the Institute for Medieval Research/Department for Byzantine Research, Austrian Academy of Sciences and lecturer in Byzantine and Global History at the University of Vienna. His research focuses on the history of Byzantium, the medieval Mediterranean and the Caucasus in a global perspective, as well as on historical network analysis, complexity studies, and environmental history. His recent publications include the monograph "Der Lange Sommer und die Kleine Eiszeit. Klima, Pandemien und der Wandel der Alten Welt von 500 bis 1500 n. Chr." (Vienna 2021).

Abigail Sargent
is a Ph.D. candidate at Princeton University. She focuses on the histories of rural societies in the high medieval West.

Peter Talloen
was a postdoctoral researcher at the University of Leuven. His research interests comprise the archaeology of cult, material culture, urbanisation, and

acculturation processes in ancient Anatolia from the late Iron Age to the Middle Byzantine period. He is currently working at the Suleyman Demirel University in Isparta, Turkey.

Costas Tsiamis
is Physician-Cytologist and Assistant Professor at the Department of Public and One Health of University of Thessaly (Greece). He received his Ph.D. in Historical Epidemiology at the Department of Hygiene, Epidemiology and Biostatistics, Medical School, National and Kapodistrian University of Athens. He specializes in Historical Epidemiology and Public Health. He teaches History of Public Health, Migrant and Refugee Health and Health Diplomacy.

Ralf Vandam
was a postdoctoral researcher at the University of Leuven. Landscape Archaeology, Human–environment Interactions, Material Culture Study, Late Prehistoric Archaeology, Early Complexity, Ancient Anatolia. He is currently working at the Vrije Universiteit, Brussel.

Myrto Veikou
specializes in Byzantine Studies (Archaeology, History, Philology) at Patras University, with particular interest in the investigation of the concepts of space and spatiality in Byzantium. She has been publishing on medieval settlement and spatial studies, based on Byzantine material culture and literary texts, since 2009. Her book *Byzantine Epirus, a topography of transformation. Settlements of the 7th–12th centuries in Southern Epirus and Aetoloacarnania, Greece* (Brill 2012), addressed the history of medieval settlement as a result of interaction between physical/social space and human agency, and set forth a new theory on the historicity of natural space.

Sam White
is professor of political history at the University of Helsinki, Finland, and formerly professor of history at the Ohio State University. His work specializes in environmental and climate history and the uses and politics of history. He has written books on the Ottoman Empire and colonial North America as well as articles on disease, disasters, climate reconstruction, and theory and methods in interdisciplinary history.

Elena Xoplaki
is researcher at the Department of Geography, Climatology, Climate Dynamics and Climate Change, Centre for International Development and Environmental Research, Justus-Liebig-University Giessen, Giessen, Germany.

Environmental History of Byzantium.
An Introduction

Adam Izdebski and Johannes Preiser-Kapeller

1   The Rationale and Genesis of the Present Volume

Let us begin this introduction with the characterization of environmental history in a recent synthesis by the French historian Grégory Quennet.[1] Instead of pointing out what environmental historians should do, as many earlier authors of introductions to environmental history had tried to do, Quennet sought to find the common denominator to all the works included in the research field. Quennet first drew attention to the fact that the field of research always begins from phenomena with their own concrete, material dimension. An environmental historian deals with the physical world, which includes plant growth, the lives of animals, the flows of river and ocean waters, energy conversion, and atmospheric phenomena. This leads to a duality that is atypical in humanistic thinking: on the one hand, the environment appears highly material, while on the other it must be seen as a cultural construct, as images "sitting" in the minds of people from the past; without taking these images into account it is not possible to understand the interdependence of man and nature. As a result, the story of the environment's role in history will always feature many actors, be they human, plant, animal, invisible to the eye (such as diseases), or inanimate. They will be connected by a web of dependencies, which environmental historians will almost all construct in their own individual ways depending on the topic at hand. This web, a complex historical ecosystem, is never stable: it is in an almost permanent state of disequilibrium. This is reflected in the imbalances between social groups and human institutions, in the painful differences in access to natural resources or in the threats to humans that the natural world harbours. This relationship between the vicissitudes of nature and social changes – which take place at a given time and location, and thus in a specific historical reality – is the starting point for all research into environmental history. It is also visible in the current companion, which begins with a series of introductions to the methods used to reconstruct different facets of the "material environment", and then moves on to demonstrate in selected

---

1 Quennet, *Qu'est-ce que l'histoire environnementale*, pp. 10–12.

case studies how these environmental realities became entangled in human experience, that of the people we call "Byzantine" and of their neighbours.

The story of this companion reaches back a decade. It began between 2012 and 2014, when an increasing number of lectures and publications indicated the beginning of a new trend in the study of the medieval environment of the Eastern Mediterranean. As a field of research, it had started much earlier (as we explain below), but, as the 2010s unrolled, what changed was the increasing consideration of the natural scientific data in relation to the written sources that had thus far dominated the field.[2] The original aims of the companion were thus firstly to introduce a wider readership of scholars to these various types of evidence and secondly to illustrate the potential and problems of this novel kind of research with a series of examples from several regions and periods.[3]

Various factors, however, delayed the finalization of the volume. Some were organizational or personal in nature, including the editors changing places and conditions of employment or authors withdrawing and new contributors being brought on board. This included Ronnie Ellenblum's tragic death, which robbed this book of his valuable perspective. Some emerged from the sheer dynamics of the growing field of environmental history, which became manifest in a rapid rise in the number of publications, both articles as well as monographs and collected volumes, and the associated necessity to update or modify chapters and to integrate (or evaluate) new findings and controversies.[4] On the one hand, this broadened the scientific basis for the present volume, which thus reflects a more mature stage of Byzantine environmental history's

---

2 See, for instance, McCormick et al., "Climate Change during and after the Roman Empire: Reconstructing the Past from Scientific and Historical Evidence", pp. 169–220; Ellenblum, *The Collapse of the Eastern Mediterranean. Climate Change and the Decline of the East, 950–1072*; Izdebski, *A Rural Economy in Transition. Asia Minor from Late Antiquity into the Early Middle Ages*; Raphael, *Climate and Political Climate. Environmental Disasters in the Medieval Levant*; Haldon et al., "The Climate and Environment of Byzantine Anatolia: Integrating Science, History, and Archaeology", pp. 113–61; Preiser-Kapeller, "A Collapse of the Eastern Mediterranean? New results and theories on the interplay between climate and societies in Byzantium and the Near East, ca. 1000–1200 AD", pp. 195–242.

3 For an overview of the "state of the art" of Byzantine environmental studies at that time, see Telelis, "Environmental History and Byzantine Studies. A Survey of Topics and Results", pp. 737–60. For an earlier overview on one aspect (climate history), see Stathakopoulos, "Reconstructing the Climate of the Byzantine World: State of the Problem and Case Studies", pp. 247–61.

4 For one relevant period in the history of the Eastern Mediterranean, that of Late Antiquity, a recent overview is provided in McMahon/Sargent, "The Environmental History of the Late Antique Eastern Mediterranean: a Bibliographic Essay", pp. 17–30. See also Telelis, "Byzantine Textual Sources" for a recent overview.

development; on the other hand, this required continuous revision and updating of the volume as it was taking its final shape.

What some readers (as well as reviewers) may miss in this volume is an overarching synthesis of the questions, methods and findings distributed among the various chapters. However, even if the amount of evidence and studies has significantly increased in the last decade, we are still far from presenting one coherent "environmental history" of the Byzantine Millennium (as they exist for diverse aspects of Byzantine history, such as political or church history, literature or law).[5] Many regions, periods, and phenomena are still massively underrepresented in our data, and where the latter exists, it still often poses more questions with regard to the actual entanglement between environmental and socio-economic or cultural dynamics than it provides answers. It seems questionable whether it will ever be possible to write a single synthesis that does justice to the various spatial and temporal scales of these dynamics, and, at the moment, collaborative works such as this provide the best approximations.[6]

At the same time, there is a growing interest in the environmental history of the Mediterranean[7] and of the Middle Ages.[8] It is in this trend that we need to embed the current activities in Byzantine studies, which in turn have profited enormously from developments that took off especially beginning in the 1960s.[9]

2   The Development of Environmental History

Environmental history as a field of historical research in its modern sense was born in the United States, and for its first decades focused on the history of that

---

5 Despite its main title, also the recent study of Olson, *Environment and Society in Byzantium, 650–1150. Between the Oak and the Olive*, confines itself to the two trees mentioned in the subtitle. See now also Izdebski, *Ein vormoderner Staat*.

6 See also Anagnostakis/Kolias/Papadopoulou, *Animals and Environment in Byzantium (7th–12th c.)*; Baron/Daim, *A Most Pleasant Scene and an Inexhaustible Resource. Steps Towards a Byzantine Environmental History*; Arentzen/Burrus/Peers, *Byzantine Tree Life: Christianity and the Arboreal Imagination*.

7 Luterbacher et al., "A Review of 2000 Years of Paleoclimatic Evidence in the Mediterranean", pp. 87–185; Walsh, *The Archaeology of Mediterranean Landscapes. Human-Environment Interaction from the Neolithic to the Roman Period*, and the new massive volume of Hofrichter, *Das Mittelmeer: Geschichte und Zukunft eines ökologisch sensiblen Raums*.

8 See Hoffmann, *An Environmental History of Medieval Europe*.

9 For an overview in connection with the general rise of the ecological movement, see Radkau, *The Age of Ecology: A Global History*, (originally in German: *Die Ära der Ökologie. Eine Weltgeschichte*).

country. The first works concerned nature conservation in the USA and the perception of the natural world in American culture. (The book later recognized as the first work in environmental history concerned what "wild nature" meant to American identity.[10]) Other topics appeared as new people educated in historical or environmental fields joined the group of environmental history pioneers. For many of them, the influence of an ideological involvement on their scientific interests, and on how they speak about the past, is evident.

Donald Worster, the author of one of the first books to describe not concepts but actual changes in the natural environment and their impacts on people, devoted his professional life to exploring capitalism's destructive influence on nature. In the first of his many works, which focused on the Dust Bowl – the decade of dust storms in the Great Plains of the United States in the 1930s – he tried to show how the capitalist exploitation of nature (in this case agriculture that ignores local natural resources) inevitably leads to ecological disaster.[11] Regardless of how right Worster was in declaring capitalism "guilty" of the ecological disaster experienced by the American prairies during the Great Depression, one thing is certain. His book was a breakthrough in the thinking of historians, who from then on began to realise that social and economic phenomena have a natural dimension that can sometimes completely change the course of events: as the pioneers of environmental history would say, "Nature can punch back."

At the same time, by highlighting the complex interplay between environmental and social dynamics, the pioneering authors such as Worster were rejecting deterministic scenarios developed in the late 19th and early 20th century. The American geographer Ellsworth Huntington (1876–1947), for instance, in his book *Civilization and Climate* (1915), assigned climate the prime role in historical developments.[12] In turn, the British historian William Henry Samuel Jones (1876–1963) claimed in 1907 that diseases such as malaria were the main cause of the decline of the Roman Empire, since they corrupted the morale of the Romans.[13] Such theories were often mixed with notions of the "racial" superiority or respective inferiority of specific ethnicities afforded by supposed environmental or climatic (dis)advantages.[14] This problematic heritage from earlier approaches to environmental history also burdened more

---

10   Nash, *Wilderness and the American Mind*.
11   Worster, *Dust Bowl: The Southern Plains in the 1930s*.
12   Huntington, *Civilization and Climate*.
13   Jones, *Malaria. A neglected factor in the history of Greece and Rome*, p. 85.
14   Such ideas already circulated in ancient ethnographic discourses, see Müller, *Geschichte der antiken Ethnologie*, pp. 131–7 and 189–91.

recent initiatives and among many historians contributed to scepticism towards attempts to bring environment and climate back into the discussion.[15]

Similarly controversial were works on the "biological advantages" of Europeans over the inhabitants of other continents: advantages that would ultimately allow them to dominate the whole world in the 19th and 20th centuries and to create a series of natural and social "new Europes" in various parts of the globe. The first work to address this topic in a fundamentally new way, from the perspective of environmental history, was *The Columbian Exchange* by Alfred Crosby.[16] It discusses the exchange of plants, animals, and microorganisms (diseases) that occurred between two previously isolated parts of the world – America and Eurasia – as a result of the conquests of Christopher Columbus. Of course, Europeans benefitted from this exchange, and not the natives of the Americas, where the overwhelming majority of the population died within a few decades as a result of previously unknown diseases brought from Europe.[17] Another important topic that the generation of environmental history pioneers took on was how social structure and culture penetrated the landscape – or, more broadly, how humanity shapes nature for its own use (or, one might say, "in its own image"). This issue was first raised in two works – one by William Cronon and one by Carolyn Merchant – that were published almost synchronously in the 1980s and that concerned the first period of the history of New England in the 17th and 18th centuries.[18]

Synthesizing systems of knowledge, mentality, gender roles, legal institutions, ecosystems and landscape into a single vision of the past led Merchant to formulate the concept of "the ecological revolution". This idea conceives of a holistic and simultaneous transformation of societal and natural structures. The concept of the ecological revolution points with full force to the histories of man and nature being inseparable. Of course, at first glance it may seem that nature is objectified in such a historical perspective – that it is subordinated

---

15 Preiser-Kapeller, *Die erste Ernte und der große Hunger. Klima, Pandemien und der Wandel der alten Welt bis 500 n. Chr.*, pp. 21–3, 39–40, also on the phenomenon of "neo-deterministic" scenarios of environmental history often presented by specialists coming from the natural sciences. On this problem, see also Collet, *Die doppelte Katastrophe. Klima und Kultur in der europäischen Hungerkrise 1770–1772*, pp. 7, 15–16. For examples of widely-read studies along "neo-deterministic" lines, see the works of Jared Diamond, such as *Collapse: How Societies Choose to Fail or Survive*.

16 Crosby, *The Columbian Exchange: Biological and Cultural Consequences of 1492*.

17 Which are currently beginning to be identified by researchers of ancient DNA: Vågene et al., *Salmonella Enterica Genomes from Victims of a Major Sixteenth-Century Epidemic in Mexico*, pp. 520–28.

18 Cronon, *Changes in the Land: Indians, Colonists, and the Ecology of New England*; Merchant, *Ecological revolutions: nature, gender, and science in New England*.

to man. Other key works by the pioneers of environmental history may make the same initial impression – those that show the mechanization of nature as industrialization progresses.[19] However, in fact, each of these works draws attention to the way in which ecosystems and the inanimate environment react to human activity. Nature never lies passive in the hands of man but responds to his or her actions in a way that accelerates or even directs changes in man's approach to nature, as well as changes at the very heart of society itself.

Although environmental history was born in North America and was initially primarily an attempt to rewrite US history, this does not mean that at the same time, or even earlier, European historians were not showing similar interests. The most important European equivalent to environmental history is the French Annales school, a new direction in historical research born in France in the interwar period that flourished in the 1960s and '70s (the name deriving from a journal in which representatives of the Annales school published their work, i.e., from the first version of the journal title, *Annales d'histoire économique et sociale*). The representatives of the new wave in French historiography were from the very outset interested in the spatial dimension of social changes, thus modifying the foundations of historical geography.[20] However, the breakthrough in this field of historical research was only made by a member of the second generation of the Annales school, Fernand Braudel (1902–85), in the famous work *The Mediterranean and the Mediterranean world in the times of Philip II* (King of Spain, Portugal, Naples and Sicily, 1556–98).[21] This several-hundred-pages-long book is unique for the fact that only the third part is dedicated to the conflicts and events of the reign of Philip II. The second part is a description of socio-economic transformations, which Braudel followed decade by decade and generation by generation, while the first, introductory part of the book deals with what he called "long-term processes". Braudel understood this concept as "almost stationary history" (*l'histoire presque immobile*): extraordinarily slow changes in the natural and spatial dimension of human activity, which can be observed only by looking at history from a "bird's eye" view – from the perspective of centuries or even longer periods of time.

The French historian's revolutionary approach consisted in making the study of the natural world a springboard to contemplating past social change

---

19   Steinberg, *Nature Incorporated: Industrialization and the Waters of New England*; White, *The Organic Machine. The Remaking of the Columbia River*.
20   Febvre, *La terre et l'évolution humaine. Introduction géographique à l'histoire*.
21   Braudel, *La Méditerranée et le monde méditerranéen à l'époque de Philippe II*.

and, ultimately, to thinking about the "surface level" of history – that is, events occurring in quick succession. In other words, Braudel understood the natural environment as frames that impose restrictions on, and provide opportunities to, historical societies – as the theatrical stage on which history plays out. With all the novelty of Braudel's approach, his perception of the place of nature in human history is actually the reverse of the view that underlies environmental history. In that approach, which this book adopts from the outset, the natural environment is a historical figure on a par with humanity; it changes at the same pace – according to various measures of historical time, be they short or long – as society in all aspects of its existence. For an environmental historian, nature cannot be relegated to the realm of the unchanging and "stationary". The human and natural world are constantly interacting and co-creating one another, building a common history.[22]

One far closer to the current understanding of nature's place in history was a younger member of the Annales school's second generation, Emmanuel Le Roy Ladurie (born in 1929). Preparing his first book on the history of the villages of Languedoc (in the French region on the Mediterranean Sea, to the west of Provence), he noticed that what should be unchanging and almost eternal – the annual rhythm of natural life and agricultural activity – is in fact subject to constant changes.[23] When he began to look more closely at the dates of the grape harvest from the end of the Middle Ages to the French Revolution, he discovered that they were closely related to the weather conditions in the summer of that year, and thus constituted a record of climate change, both from decade to decade and over a longer timeframe. This discovery led Le Roy Ladurie to make climate history and its impact on human history one of the mainstays of his scientific career, laying the foundations for a completely new field of historical and natural scientific knowledge (which is currently flourishing).[24] Moreover, the experience gained in studying the climate and the dependence of Languedoc peasants' way of life on the rhythms of nature sensitized Le Roy Ladurie to the historicity – in other words, the impermanence and variability – of all ecosystems and landscapes that humanity has a hand in. Hence, in another ground-breaking work, in the fascinating study of the heretical village of Montaillou, he devoted a great deal of space to the

---

22   Cf. the description of Braudel's approach in G. Quennet's foundational work on French environmental history, *Qu'est-ce que l'histoire environnementale?*, pp. 98–111.
23   Le Roy Ladurie, *Les paysans de Languedoc*.
24   Le Roy Ladurie, *Histoire et climat*, pp. 3–23; Idem, *Histoire du climat depuis l'an mil*; Soudière et al., *Devenir historien du climat? Entretien avec Emmanuel Le Roy Ladurie*, pp. 639–44.

ecological aspects of how this particular community that existed in the French Pyrenees in the late Middle Ages functioned.[25] In his understanding of the role of nature in history, Le Roy Ladurie was, in a word, "close" to the American pioneers of environmental history acting at the same time across the Atlantic and with whom he remained in frequent contact, as evidenced by the 1974 jointly-published thematic issue of the *Annales* journal.

Climate history itself grew over the following decades to become a European specialization within the wider field of environmental history. In addition to Le Roy Ladurie, the group that created this historical discipline included the British geographer Hubert Lamb (1913–97) and the still-active Nestor of Swiss environmental historians Christian Pfister (born in 1944). In his works, which mainly concerned the Early Modern period (16th–18th centuries), Pfister developed an approach that not only can reconstruct past climate changes, but also, above all, allows their impact on human life and activity to be studied – from agriculture, through understandings of the world, to superstitions and other phenomena of culture in its broader sense.[26] At the same time, historians from other European countries – Austria, Denmark, Germany, and Great Britain – have further attempted to transfer experiments in American environmental history to the European context, yielding works that present a new understanding of the key processes of socio-economic change in Europe at the beginning of Early Modern times.[27]

---

25   Le Roy Ladurie, *Montaillou: the promised land of error*; original French edition: idem, *Montaillou, village occitan de 1294 à 1324*.

26   Pfister, *Das Klima der Schweiz von 1525–1860 und seine Bedeutung in der Geschichte von Bevölkerung und Landwirtschaft*; Idem, *Wetternachhersage: 500 Jahre Klimavariationen und Naturkatastrophen (1496–1995)*; Idem, *Climatic Extremes, Recurrent Crises and Witch Hunts Strategies of European Societies in Coping with Exogenous Shocks in the Late Sixteenth and Early Seventeenth Centuries*, pp. 33–73. Christian Pfister's work was also crucial to how American environmental history was received in Europe; see at the very least the ground-breaking collective work under his editorship that reflects the contact and interests shared by European historians in the 1980s: *The Silent Countdown: Essays in European Environmental History*, ed. Brimblecombe/Pfister.

27   Kjærgaard, *The Danish Revolution, 1500–1800: An Ecohistorical Interpretation*; Radkau, *Natur und Macht: eine Weltgeschichte der Umwelt*; Warde, *Ecology, Economy and State Formation in Early Modern Germany*; an overview of studies of environmental history conducted in Europe around the turn of the 21st century can be found in an article written by historians from over 10 European nations: Winiwarter et al., *Environmental History in Europe from 1994 to 2004: Enthusiasm and Consolidation*, pp. 501–30; there are also worthwhile German and French introductions to environmental history: Winiwarter, Knoll, *Umweltgeschichte: eine Einführung*; Herrmann, *Umweltgeschichte. Eine Einführung in Grundbegriffe*; Quennet, *Qu'est-ce que l'histoire environnementale*.

3 Byzantine Studies and Environmental History

The field of Byzantine Studies has also long been engaged with environmental or geographical issues, and the "environmental interests" of byzantinists do map rather well onto how historical research into environment-related topics developed in different European countries.[28] The two key currents of environmental history *avant la lettre* within Byzantine Studies were inspired by historical geography, in both the French and the German version – the former closely connected with the *Annales* school and the latter focusing primarily on the reconstruction of settlement history and communication networks of the Byzantine world.[29] In France, we are thus faced with regional stories devoted to specific regions of the Byzantine world or neighbouring territories. One classic is Jean-Marie Martin's study of Apulia: in this case, the environment, which is discussed traditionally in the first part of the work, acts as the backdrop against which the region's history unfolds.[30] Meanwhile, research by a team led by Jacques Lefort and his work on Macedonia and Bithynia have already gone beyond the scope established by the Annales school. Representatives of the natural sciences collaborated on the work and undertook to reconstruct natural changes in the past (though to a limited extent), and the questions it posed concerned the landscape as much as settlement or the ecclesiastic network. Regrettably, Lefort's team managed to study only two regions of the Byzantine world – Macedonia and Bithynia.[31]

For the Viennese "school" of historical Byzantine geography, the *Tabula Imperii Byzantini* (TIB) project (first presented by Herbert Hunger at the International Congress of Byzantine Studies in Oxford in 1966) is of fundamental

---

28 For a detailed survey of the Byzantine Studies scholarship on topics related to environmental history, see Telelis, "Environmental History and Byzantine Studies: a Survey of Topics and Results".

29 In the German tradition, there is an interest in the historical geography of Byzantium dating back to the 19th century and pre-war times: Curtius, *Peloponnesos*; Philippson, *Das byzantinische Reich als geographische Erscheinung*; see also: Philippson, Lehmann, and Kirsten, *Die griechischen Landschaften*.

30 Martin, *La Pouille du VIe au XIIe siècle*. Michel Kaplan treated geographical issues similarly in a study of Byzantine agriculture and rural areas in which he collected modern data on the natural environment of the Byzantine world to indicate differences in agricultural potential between particular regions: Kaplan, *Les hommes et la terre à Byzance*. Similar "classic" geographic introductions can be found in the latest syntheses of Byzantium's economic history: Geyer, "Physical Factors in the Evolution of the Landscape and Land Use"; Laiou and Morrisson, *The Byzantine economy*.

31 Lefort, *Villages de Macédoine*; Lefort, *Paysages de Macédoine*; Geyer and Lefort, *La Bithynie au moyen âge*.

importance: successive volumes reconstruct the settlement and transport networks of a given region in successive periods of Byzantine history, from Late Antiquity to the end of the Middle Ages.[32] This large research project established a special framework for the methodological approach to historical geography. The research of the TIB aims to reconstruct the state of the Byzantine world at a certain moment in the past and to encapsulate the changes that its spatial organization has undergone. One of the most interesting works to have been created in this circle is Johannes Koder's introduction to the historical geography of Byzantium. It illustrates both the ambitions and the limitations of this approach. Even its title is significant: *Das Lebensraum der Byzantiner*, "The living space of the Byzantines".[33] This title reflects the author's ambition to reconstruct the space in which the Byzantines lived, in all its richness and diversity. The book contains chapters on landscapes and climate, but they are based on 20th-century (modern) data, rather than palaeoclimatic or palaeo-ecological data (which was, after all, hardly available in the 1980s). The historical analysis focuses on the transport network, state and church administration and the settlement network. It thus constitutes an overall synthesis of the *Tabula* approach but presented in relation to the Byzantine world. It should be emphasized that, even though the *Tabula Imperii Byzantini* team to this day largely continues to work along the methodological principles formulated in the 1960s and '70s, the group also seeks contact with researchers from within or beyond the world of Byzantology who deal with spatial phenomena of relevance to Byzantium.[34] These contacts spawned the works of a young generation of Viennese byzantinists who exceed the traditional bounds of historical geography, heading towards historical anthropology or digital humanities,

---

32   Project assumptions: Kelnhofer, *Die topographische Bezugsgrundlage der Tabula Imperii Byzantini*; vol. 1: Koder, *Hellas und Thessalia*. The latest discussion of the history and methodology of this undertaking can be found in: Popović, *Historische Geographie und Digital Humanities*, pp. 10–17.

33   Koder, *Der Lebensraum der Byzantiner*.

34   One of the most interesting outcomes of these contacts is a collective work published at the beginning of this century as a "supplement" to the TIB series and containing the work of Austrian and international researchers: Belke et al., *Byzanz als Raum. Zu Methoden und Inhalten der historischen Geographie des östlichen Mittelmeerraumes in Mittelalter*. It is worth mentioning the few but interesting works on the environmental aspects of the Byzantine world that have come out of Anglo-Saxon circles: Gerstel, *Rural Lives and Landscapes in Late Byzantium*; Thonemann, *The Maeander Valley*; Squatriti, *Water and Society in Early Medieval Italy, 400–1000*; Veikou, *Byzantine Epirus*; Squatriti, *Landscape and Change in Early Medieval Italy*; Della Dora, *Landscape, Nature, and the Sacred in Byzantium*. However, it is hard to speak of any "school" or approach common to all authors.

for instance.³⁵ In addition, research on environmental and climate historical aspects was integrated in Vienna into a new research programme on complexity and medieval global history.³⁶

In general, long-standing historiographic traditions – which, of course, do not represent the entirety of historical geography in Byzantine Studies – were joined by another very active research field, namely, the climate history of the Byzantine world. Although it had been raised as a research problem by the 1990s, for more than ten years it had enjoyed the interest of only two byzantinists: the Austrian historian and historical geographer Johannes Koder, who speculated as to the possible impact of climate change on the history of the Empire,³⁷ and Ioannis Telelis, a Greek philologist who gathered all mentions of weather phenomena scattered throughout Byzantine literary texts.³⁸ This situation changed in the 2010s, since Byzantium became a subject of interest

---

35   Popović, *Historische Geographie und Digital Humanities*; https://tib.oeaw.ac.at/index.php?seite=digtib. See for an overview on recent developments also Külzer/Polloczek/Popović/ with Koder (eds), *Raum und Geschichte. Der Historische Atlas "Tabula Imperii Byzantini" an der Österreichischen Akademie der Wissenschaften*.

36   https://www.oeaw.ac.at/en/byzantine-research/byzantium-and-beyond/mobility-and-intercultural-contacts/complexities-and-networks. See also Preiser-Kapeller, "A Collapse of the Eastern Mediterranean?"; Preiser-Kapeller/Mitsiou, "The Little Ice Age and Byzantium within the Eastern Mediterranean, ca. 1200–1350: An Essay on Old Debates and New Scenarios", pp. 190–220; Preiser-Kapeller, *Die erste Ernte und der große Hunger*; Preiser-Kapeller, *Der Lange Sommer und die Kleine Eiszeit*.

37   Koder, "Historical aspects of a recession of cultivated land at the end of the late antiquity in the east Mediterranean"; Koder, "Climatic Change in the Fifth and Sixth Centuries?". In an earlier work from the early 1980s, Koder only indicates that climate change "must have" occurred during the Byzantine millennium, which he asserts while discussing the climate diversity of the Balkans and Anatolia (based on modern data): Koder, *Der Lebensraum der Byzantiner*, pp. 40–41. Before Koder, Clive Foss lists climate change as having potential "divine agency" in the downfall of cities in early medieval Anatolia. Foss, "Archaeology and the 'Twenty Cities' of Byzantine Asia".

38   Telelis, *Meteōrologika phainomena*; Telelis, "Climatic Fluctuations in the Eastern Mediterranean and the Middle East AD 300–1500 from Byzantine Documentary and Proxy Physical Paleoclimatic Evidence – A Comparison"; Telelis, "Byzantine Textual Sources". A brief review article by Stathakopulos from the beginning of the 21st century is largely based on the results of research by Telelis: Stathakopoulos, "Reconstructing the Climate of the Byzantine World: State of the Problem and Case Studies". It is worth noting that Stathakopoulos is the author of a work that is similar to Telelis's monumental study and that uses the same method: a systematic collection of all mentions of subsistence crises and epidemics in the Late Antique East (up to and including AD 750): Stathakopoulos, *Famine and pestilence in the late Roman and early Byzantine Empire: a systematic survey of subsistence crises and epidemics*.

to Princeton's Climate Change and History Research Initiative.[39] This group is a forum bringing together historians and representatives of natural sciences (including palaeoclimatologists) investigating the Eastern Mediterranean. In recent years, the group has published or inspired a large number of studies on the climate history of Byzantium of Late Antiquity and the Middle Ages.[40] Thereby, Byzantine studies is also entangled within the wider and growing field of medieval environmental history, whose flourishing is also manifested in the choice of main thematic strands for major events such as the International Medieval Congress in Leeds (2021, on "Climates")[41] and a rapidly growing number of studies across periods and regions, from Late Antiquity to Early Modern, from the Atlantic to the Pacific, and from the Arctic to South Africa, in various languages.[42] As this volume makes clear, however, while climate history remains one of the main driving forces of the field of Byzantine environmental history, it is far from the only one, as the field is expanding to include a wide variety of environmental phenomena.

4   Byzantine Environmental History and Mediterranean Studies

Byzantium's environmental history can also not be discussed without mentioning the controversy about the Mediterranean world as a subject of historical research. The debate on this subject has been particularly reinvigorated in the last 20 years thanks to the monumental study by Peregerine Horden and Nicholas Purcell, *The Corrupting Sea* of the year 2000.[43] Written with the intention of taking its place as "the new Braudel", the work distinguishes between history that describes the Mediterranean world ("the history of the Mediterranean"), and history grounded in the realities of the Mediterranean, i.e. in which the Mediterranean is a historiographical category ("history in the Mediterranean"). The authors consider Braudel (and themselves as his

---

39   Haldon et al., "The climate and environment of Byzantine Anatolia: integrating science, history and archaeology".
40   Most of them appeared in the special issues of the "Quaternary Science Reviews" (vol. 136, 2016) and "Human ecology" (vol. 46, 2018).
41   https://www.imc.leeds.ac.uk/imc-2021/.
42   For an overview and some recent examples, see Hoffmann, *An Environmental History of Medieval Europe*; Zhang, *The River, the Plain, and the State*; White/Pfister/Mauelshagen, *The Palgrave Handbook of Climate History*; Nedkvitne, *Norse Greenland: Viking Peasants in the Arctic*; Devroey, *La Nature et le Roi*; Pikirayi, "Sustainability and an archaeology of the future", pp. 1669–71; Bauch/Schenk, *The Crisis of the 14th Century.*; Ebert, *Der Umwelt begegnen* (with a useful introduction to the field, pp. 11–69).
43   Horden/Purcell, *The Corrupting Sea*.

successors) a representative of this second tradition, unlike many other historians who, though they write about the Mediterranean world, are not interested in what makes it unique. Although this distinction may seem artificial, especially that it is expressed through the use of mere prepositions, it raises a significant problem that the authors of *The Corrupting Sea* had to grapple with and that, since the publication of their book, has been the subject of debate by historians: what makes the Mediterranean unique as a subject of historical research, what justifies writing about the history of the Mediterranean world, or what is to be the subject of a truly Mediterranean historiography?

Horden and Purcell pose this question because they have a suggested answer. Their position is that the Mediterranean world may be an almost timeless historiographical category, so their answer relates to essentially environmental phenomena (and not, for example, the socio-political: no empire or country, even one as long-lived as France, can accommodate a three-thousand-year history such as that which Horden and Purcell write about). Interestingly, the strategy of using arguments grounded "in nature" in this context is deeply rooted in the mode of thinking about nature and history that Braudel and the Annales school developed. As we have already explained, Braudel and his milieu saw geographical or environmental phenomena as the most stable element of reality and, because of this stability, geographical similarities can best be used to justify making a particular area the subject of long-term perspectives on history (as Braudel did in *La Méditerranée*).

It is worth exploring in more detail this justification, which in a way redefines the theme of *unité* that is repeated in the titles of successive chapters of the first part of *La Méditerranée*. Specifically, Horden and Purcell believe that what makes the Mediterranean world unique is its division into an infinite number of "microecologies" – small regions, sometimes consisting of a single valley or coastal plain, which differ in their environmental potential (climate, soils, vegetation) and have developed into a stunning mosaic of landscapes. At the same time, all these microregions are connected to one another by the sea on which they lie. According to Horden and Purcell, this interplay of fragmentation and connectivity should be the theme of every study of *history in the Mediterranean* (i.e., grounded in Mediterranean realities).

Besides Horden and Purcell, so too John McNeill has attempted to redefine the Mediterranean in the last quarter century by conducting a comparative study of mountain chains in various regions of the Mediterranean world.[44] His work has been innovative in many regards, especially in its attempt to apply the American environmental history model to a new geographical context,

---

44   McNeill, *The Mountains of the Mediterranean World*.

but it has had only a limited impact. Nor did McNeill avoid simplifications by allowing the influence of Worster and other pioneers of American environmental history to limit the scope of his historical analysis to the last two or three centuries. At the same time, his standpoint was that, in the pre-modern era, mountainous areas were subject to constant and repetitive rhythms, and that true changes occurred only with the advent of modernity (which is in keeping with Braudel's approach to the Mediterranean environment).[45]

More innovative were two other studies published at almost the same time as *The Corrupting Sea*. The first is a study of the historical ecology of Mediterranean Europe by Olivier Rackham and Alfred Grove,[46] based mainly on archaeological and environmental material. It focuses on the natural phenomena that historians and archaeologists usually take to be unchanging, but that do change over time and should be seen as dynamic actors of history rather than purely a set of relatively stable "geographical factors". To a large extent, the book contradicts Braudel's vision of the Mediterranean that Horden and Purcell, as well as McNeill, had adopted and developed. The second work is a monumental study by Michael McCormick[47] that focuses on economic phenomena, and that proves the durability of communication and trade in the Mediterranean world even in the centuries immediately following the fall of the Roman economic order at the end of Antiquity. Although McCormick does not attach such importance to the category of the Mediterranean, his research was an important reference point for the beginnings of the "Mediterranean debate", because it proved the endurance of a *sui generis* Mediterranean system of communication and exchange even through the most difficult conditions (somewhat confirming Horden and Purcell's thesis that a history grounded in Mediterranean realities can also be written beyond the context of the Roman Empire at peak power.)

While the work of Horden and Purcell garnered widespread admiration for the scale of the undertaking, the theses they presented were not widely accepted, but instead sparked a debate that continues to this day. It has strongly engaged ancient historians, which is not surprising considering that although Horden and Purcell look at the period from ancient Greece to the 19th century,

---

45 Interestingly, for the next 20 years, no one tried to relate the category of American environmental history to the ancient or medieval Mediterranean. The present author recently addressed this: Izdebski, "Setting the scene for an environmental history of Late Antiquity".
46 Grove/Rackham, *The nature of Mediterranean Europe*.
47 McCormick, *Origins of the European Economy*.

the bulk of their material relates to Greco-Roman antiquity.[48] This discussion has been approached from the perspectives of both traditional historiography and interdisciplinary research.[49] Two new book-size syntheses have also been published, one on the "prehistory" and the other on the "history" of the Mediterranean world.[50] However far from consensus we are, it is possible to talk of the Mediterranean as a historiographic category being reinstated – after a break of several decades; this is reflected by, for example, new textbooks on Mediterranean history, such as the *Companion to Mediterranean History*, whose editors include Horden.[51] Interestingly, even though it was published more than a decade after *The Corrupting Sea*, the in-depth understanding of the environmental aspect of Mediterranean history is provided not by Horden and Purcell, but by the Italian-American medievalist and environmental historian Paolo Squatriti. He argues that the ecological connectivity between the various regions and microregions of the Mediterranean world did not lead to a stable environmental structure, but that Mediterranean ecosystems were in a state of constant flux due to those connections, which needed to adapt to new socio-economic or ecological conditions and led to the spread of new species of plants and animals.[52]

Byzantine Studies do not hold back from the "Mediterranean debates" and try to address them in various ways. Byzantine historians are increasingly using the term "the Eastern Mediterranean" to designate their research subject. In one of the significant syntheses of Byzantine culture and history of recent decades, by Averil Cameron,[53] the last chapter is entitled, simply, "Byzantium and the Mediterranean" and begins by referencing *The Corrupting Sea*. But Cameron does not propose any innovative approach to Byzantium as part of the Mediterranean world in Horden and Purcell's meaning. The chapter concerns Byzantium's relations with the Islamic world and the place that Byzantium held in the complex political, religious, and cultural reality of the late antique and medieval "Eastern Mediterranean".

48 Squatriti, "Mohammed, the Early Medieval Mediterranean, and Charlemagne", particularly regarding an "early medieval" reading of *The Corrupting Sea*.
49 Harris, *Rethinking the Mediterranean*; Idem, *The Ancient Mediterranean. Environment between Science and History*. It should be emphasized that *The Corrupting Sea* has also revived the Braudel model among modern historians: Marino, *Early Modern History and the Social Sciences*; Piterberg/Ruiz/Symcox, *Braudel Revisited*. See also the recent summarization of the debate in: Greene, "The Mediterranean Sea".
50 "Prehistory": Broodbank, *The Making of the Middle Sea*; "history": Abulafia, *The Great Sea*; preceded by the collective work: Abulafia, *The Mediterranean in History*.
51 Horden/Kinoshita, *A companion to Mediterranean history*.
52 Squatriti, "The Vegetative Mediterranean".
53 Cameron, *The Byzantines*, pp. 179–96.

So, what might the Mediterranean category mean in relation to the environmental history of Byzantium? As all contributors to the "Mediterranean debate" admit, the days of the Roman Empire, Byzantium's predecessor, constitute the only historical period that affords a clear justification for thinking of the Mediterranean as a unified whole. After all, the Mediterranean concept is inspired by the existence of a unified Roman world surrounding the *Mare Nostrum*. Therefore, since some chapters in the present volume discuss the persistence of Roman features and elements in Byzantine socio-environmental structures, they also raise the question of the presence in the Byzantine world of a heritage of Mediterranean unity. This, however, does not mean adopting the concept of the "ever-lasting Mediterranean" that Horden and Purcell and Braudel all argue for. The Byzantine world co-created a particular Mediterranean, or rather only its Eastern part, which existed largely separately from the Western part. Byzantium co-created the Mediterranean, which had basically been formed by the late antique Roman Empire, and which was then transformed and consolidated by the Arab conquests and the coming into being of the Muslim world. According to Squatriti, it needs to be emphasized that the connectivity between micro-ecologies, or rather the ecological interdependence of individual regions of the Mediterranean world, is not permanent. They should instead be looked upon as a phenomenon that fluctuates, a kind of Mediterranean unity that constantly pulsates and morphs.[54] This perspective – the impermanent, variable structures of ecological interdependence – can also be taken to view the Romanness of the Byzantines. If the Roman world was the apex of Mediterranean unity dreamt of by subsequent empires, including fascist Italy and colonial France, it is appropriate to ask to what extent Byzantium carried this deep ecological interdependence of regions and microregions into the Middle Ages.

5 The Structure of the Volume

As we have already explained, the first section of our companion is devoted to the various "archives of society" and "archives of nature" for environmental

---

54 This statement goes back to the famous "Pirenne thesis" (on the collapse of the ancient Mediterranean world as a result of Arab conquests), which emphasises the historical changeability of the structural connections between the great Mediterranean regions: Pirenne, *Mahomet et Charlemagne*. The successive stages of the debate on the "Pirenne thesis" can be traced in the following review papers: Brown, "'Mohammed and Charlemagne' by Henri Pirenne"; Hodges/Whitehouse, *Mohammed, Charlemagne, and the Origins of Europe*; Squatriti, "Mohammed, the Early Medieval Mediterranean, and Charlemagne".

history, as Christian Pfister (see above) has called them,[55] with contributions from active (and often pioneering) scholars in the field. The chapter of Chryssi Bourbou discusses the evidence related to humans (bio-archaeology). Three other chapters look at the major agents entangled in the ecologies of the Byzantine Empire, such as animals (Henriette Baron), microbes (Costas Tsiamis), and plants (Adam Izdebski). Inanimate "forces of nature" are discussed in two more chapters dealing with climate dynamics (Jürg Luterbacher, Elena Xoplaki, Adam Izdebski, and Dominik Fleitmann) and seismic phenomena (Lee Mordechai).

The second section of our companion presents "environmental history at work" in various case studies. Two chapters are devoted to *longue durée* phenomena, such as the relationship between the Byzantines and nature (Henry Maguire) and the traditions and dynamics of agriculture in the Levant (Michael Decker). Other contributions focus on specific regions, such as the islands of the Aegean (Myrto Veikou), two important archaeological sites in Anatolia, Sagalassos (Johan Bakker, Eva Kaptijn, Jeroen Poblome) and Euchaïta (Warren Eastwood, John Haldon), or on the hydraulic infrastructures in a long-term perspective in Constantinople and Thessaloniki (James Crow) and in historical Armenia (Johannes Preiser-Kapeller).

The four last chapters in chronological sequence present major periods in the socio-political, environmental and climate history of Byzantium and the Eastern Mediterranean: Late Antiquity, with a focus on the 5th to 7th centuries (Mischa Meier), the "Medieval Climate Anomaly" and the apex and crisis of Byzantine power in the 10th to 12th centuries (Johannes Preiser-Kapeller, also tackling more general debates on the socio-political dynamics in this period, hence its length), the Crusader period (Abigail Sargent), and finally the Late Byzantine and Early Ottoman Period, characterized in climate historical terms as the "Little Ice Age" (Sam White).

Each chapter in this volume can be read separately, but together they create a valuable overview of the main aspects of the environmental history of Byzantium in its entirety, of course with significant lacunae (regarding periods, regions, or specific phenomena). Still, they provide a firm basis for an orientation in the field, enabling readers to evaluate claims and methods in the increasing number of relevant publications and, equally, to have a starting point for their own further research.

---

55 See also now Pfister/Wanner, *Climate and Society in Europe. The Last Thousand Years.*

Bibliography

Abulafia, D., *The Great Sea: A Human History of the Mediterranean*, Oxford 2011.

Abulafia, D. (ed.), *The Mediterranean in History*, Los Angeles 2003.

Anagnostakis, I./Kolias, T./Papadopoulou, E. (eds), *Animals and Environment in Byzantium (7th–12th c.)*, Athens 2011.

Arentzen, Th./Burrus, V./Peers, G., *Byzantine Tree Life: Christianity and the Arboreal Imagination*, Cham 2021.

Baron, H./Daim, F. (eds), *A Most Pleasant Scene and an Inexhaustible Resource. Steps Towards a Byzantine Environmental History*, Mainz 2017.

Bauch, M./Schenk, G.J. (eds), *The Crisis of the 14th Century. Teleconnections between Environmental and Societal Change?*, Berlin/Boston 2020.

Belke, K., et al., *Byzanz als Raum. Zu Methoden und Inhalten der historischen Geographie des östlichen Mittelmeerraumes in Mittelalter*, Vienna 2000.

Braudel, F., *La Méditerranée et le monde méditerranéen à l'époque de Philippe II*, Paris 1949 [2nd edition 1966].

Brimblecombe, P./Ch. Pfister (eds.), *The Silent Countdown: Essays in European Environmental History*, Berlin 1990.

Broodbank, C., *The Making of the Middle Sea: A History of the Mediterranean from the Beginning to the Emergence of the Classical* World, Oxford 2013.

Brown, P., '"Mohammed and Charlemagne" by Henri Pirenne'. *Daedalus* 103 (1974): 25–33.

Cameron, A., *The Byzantines*, Malden – Oxford 2006.

Collet, D., *Die doppelte Katastrophe. Klima und Kultur in der europäischen Hungerkrise 1770–1772*, Göttingen 2019.

Cronon, W., *Changes in the Land: Indians, Colonists, and the Ecology of New England*, New York 1983.

Crosby, A.W., *The Columbian Exchange: Biological and Cultural Consequences of 1492*, Westport CT 1972.

Curtius, E., *Peloponnesos: Eine Historisch-Geographische Beschreibung Der Halbinsel*. Gotha: Perthes, 1851.

Della Dora, V., *Landscape, Nature, and the Sacred in Byzantium*, Cambridge 2016.

Devroey, J.-P., *La Nature et le Roi. Environnement, pouvoir et société à l'âge de Charlemagne, 740–820*, Paris 2019.

Diamond, J., *Collapse: How Societies Choose to Fail or Survive*, London 2005.

Ebert, St. F., *Der Umwelt begegnen: Extremereignisse und die Verflechtung von Natur und Kultur im Frankenreich vom 8. Bis 10. Jahrhundert*, Stuttgart 2021.

Ellenblum, R., *The Collapse of the Eastern Mediterranean. Climate Change and the Decline of the East, 950–1072*, Cambridge 2012.

Febvre, L., *La terre et l'évolution humaine. Introduction géographique à l'histoire*, Paris 1922.

Foss, C., "Archaeology and the 'Twenty Cities' of Byzantine Asia", *American Journal of Archaeology* 81,4 (1977), 469–86.

Gerstel, Sh., *Rural Lives and Landscapes in Late Byzantium: Art, Archaeology, and Ethnography*, Cambridge 2015.

Geyer, B., 'Physical Factors in the Evolution of the Landscape and Land Use'. In *The Economic History of Byzantium: From the Seventh through the Fifteenth Century*, edited by Angeliki E Laiou, 1:31–45. Dumbarton Oaks Studies 39, Washington, DC 2002.

Geyer, B./Lefort, J. (eds.), *La Bithynie au moyen âge*, Paris 2003.

Greene, M., 'The Mediterranean Sea'. In *Oceanic Histories*, edited by David Armitage, Alison Bashford, and Sujit Sivasundaram, 134–55. Cambridge Oceanic Histories, New York 2018.

Grove, A. Th./Rackham, O., *The Nature of Mediterranean Europe: An Ecological History*, Yale 2003.

Haldon, J.F., et al., "The Climate and Environment of Byzantine Anatolia: Integrating Science, History, and Archaeology", *Journal of Interdisciplinary History* 45,2 (2014), 113–61.

Harris, W.V., *Rethinking the Mediterranean*. Oxford: Oxford University Press, 2005.

Harris, W.V. (ed.), *The Ancient Mediterranean. Environment between Science and History*. Leiden: Brill, 2013.

Herrmann, B., *Umweltgeschichte. Eine Einführung in Grundbegriffe*, Berlin 2013.

Hodges, R., and D. Whitehouse. *Mohammed, Charlemagne, and the Origins of Europe: The Pirenne Thesis in the Light of Archaeology*. Ithaca, NY: Cornell University Press, 1983.

Hoffmann, R.C., *An Environmental History of Medieval Europe* (Cambridge Medieval Textbooks), Cambridge 2014.

Hofrichter, R. (ed.), *Das Mittelmeer: Geschichte und Zukunft eines ökologisch sensiblen Raums*, Berlin 2020.

Horden, P., and Sh. Kinoshita (eds.), *A Companion to Mediterranean History*. Wiley Blackwell Companions to World History. Chichester: Wiley Blackwell, 2014.

Horden, P./Purcell, N., *The Corrupting Sea: A Study of Mediterranean* History, Malden – Oxford 2000.

Huntington, E., *Civilization and Climate*, New Haven 1915.

Izdebski, A., 'Setting the Scene for an Environmental History of Late Antiquity'. In *Environment and Society in the Long Late Antiquity*, edited by Adam Izdebski and Michael Mulryan, 3–13. Late Antique Archaeology 11–12. Leiden: Brill, 2018.

Izdebski, A., *A Rural Economy in Transition. Asia Minor from Late Antiquity into the Early Middle Ages* (Journal of Juristic Papyrology, Supplement vol. 18), Warsaw 2013.

Izdebski, A., *Ein vormoderner Staat als sozio-ökologisches System. Das oströmische Reich 300–1300 n.Chr.*, Dresden 2022.

Jones, W.H.S., *Malaria. A neglected factor in the history of Greece and Rome*, Cambridge 1907.

Kaplan, M., *Les hommes et la terre à Byzance du VIe au XIe siècle: Propriété et exploitation du sol*, Paris 1995.

Kelnhofer, F., *Die topographische Bezugsgrundlage der Tabula Imperii Byzantini*; Vienna 1976.

Kjærgaard, T., *The Danish Revolution, 1500–1800: An Ecohistorical Interpretation* (Studies in Environment and History), Cambridge 1994.

Koder, J. "Climatic Change in the Fifth and Sixth Centuries?", in: P. Allen/E. Jeffreys (eds.), The Sixth Century: End or Beginning?, Brisbane 1996, pp. 270–285.

Koder, J., 'Historical Aspects of a Recession of Cultivated Land at the End of the Late Antiquity in the East Mediterranean'. In *Evaluation of Land Surfaces Cleared from Forests in the Mediterranean Region during the Time of the Roman Empire*, 157–67. Paläoklimaforschung 10, Stuttgart 1994.

Koder, J., *Der Lebensraum der Byzantiner. Historisch-geographischer Abriss ihres mittelalterlichen Staates im östlichen Mittelmeerraum*, New edition, Vienna 2001.

Koder, J./Hild, F., *Hellas und Thessalia*, Tabula Imperii Byzantini 1, Vienna 1976.

Laiou, A. E,/Morrisson, C., *The Byzantine economy*, Cambridge 2007.

Le Roy Ladurie, E., *Histoire du climat depuis l'an mil*, Paris 1967.

Le Roy Ladurie, E., *Histoire et climat*, "Annales. Histoire, Sciences Sociales" 14,1 (1959), pp. 3–23.

Le Roy Ladurie, E., *Les paysans de Languedoc*, Paris 1966.

Le Roy Ladurie, E., *Montaillou: the promised land of error*, trans. B. Bray, New York 1978.

Lefort, J., *Villages de Macédoine: La Chalcidique occidentale*, Paris 1982.

Lefort, J., *Paysages de Macédoine: leurs caractères, leur évolution à travers les documents et les récits des* voyageurs, Paris 1986.

Luterbacher, J., et al., "A Review of 2000 Years of Paleoclimatic Evidence in the Mediterranean", in P. Lionello (ed.), *The Climate of the Mediterranean region: from the past to the future*, Amsterdam 2012, pp. 87–185.

Marino, J.A. (ed.), *Early Modern History and the Social Sciences: Testing the Limits of Braudel's Mediterranean*. Sixteenth Century Essays & Studies 61, Kirksville 2002.

Martin, J.-M., *La Pouille du VIe au XIIe siècle*. Collection de l'École française de Rome 179, Rome 1993.

McCormick, M., et al., "Climate Change during and after the Roman Empire: Reconstructing the Past from Scientific and Historical Evidence", *Journal of Interdisciplinary History* 43, 2 (2012), 169–220.

McCormick, M., *Origins of the European Economy. Communications and Commerce AD 300–900*, Cambridge 2001.

McMahon, L./Sargent, A., "The Environmental History of the Late Antique Eastern Mediterranean: a Bibliographic Essay", in A. Izdebski/M. Mulryan (eds), *Environment and Society in the Long Late Antiquity*, Leiden/Boston 2019, pp. 17–30.

McNeill, J.R., *The Mountains of the Mediterranean World. An Environmental History*, Cambridge 1992.

Merchant, C., *Ecological revolutions: nature, gender, and science in New England*, Chapel Hill NC 1989.

Müller, K.E., *Geschichte der antiken Ethnologie*, Reinbek 1997.

Nash, R., *Wilderness and the American Mind*, New Haven 1967.

Nedkvitne, A., *Norse Greenland: Viking Peasants in the Arctic*, London 2018.

Olson, A., *Environment and Society in Byzantium, 650–1150. Between the Oak and the Olive*, Cham 2020.

Pfister, Ch., "Climatic Extremes, Recurrent Crises and Witch Hunts Strategies of European Societies in Coping with Exogenous Shocks in the Late Sixteenth and Early Seventeenth Centuries", *The Medieval History Journal* 10, 1–2 (2006), 33–73.

Pfister, Ch., *Das Klima der Schweiz von 1525–1860 und seine Bedeutung in der Geschichte von Bevölkerung und Landwirtschaft*, Bern 1988.

Pfister, Ch., *Wetternachhersage: 500 Jahre Klimavariationen und Naturkatastrophen (1496–1995)*, Bern 1999.

Pfister, Ch./Wanner, H., *Climate and Society in Europe. The Last Thousand Years*, Bern 2021.

Philippson, A., *Das byzantinische Reich als geographische Erscheinung*, Leiden 1939.

Philippson, A./Lehmann, H./Kirsten, E., *Die griechischen Landschaften*, 4 vols, Frankfurt 1950–1959.

Pikirayi, I., "Sustainability and an archaeology of the future", *Antiquity* 93/372 (2019), 1669–671.

Pirenne, H., *Mahomet et Charlemagne*, Paris – Brussels 1937.

Piterberg, G., T.F. Ruiz, and G. Symcox, *Braudel Revisited: The Mediterranean World, 1600–1800*. UCLA Clark Memorial Library Series 13. Toronto: University of Toronto Press, 2010.

Popović, M., *Historische Geographie und Digital Humanities: Eine Fallstudie zum spätbyzantinischen und osmanischen Makedonien*, Wiesbaden 2014.

Külzer, A./Polloczek, V./Popović, M. St., with Koder J. (eds), *Raum und Geschichte. Der Historische Atlas "Tabula Imperii Byzantini" an der Österreichischen Akademie der Wissenschaften* (Studies in Historical Geography and Cultural Heritage 3), Vienna/Novi Sad 2020.

Preiser-Kapeller, J., "A Collapse of the Eastern Mediterranean? New results and theories on the interplay between climate and societies in Byzantium and the Near East, ca. 1000–1200 AD", *Jahrbuch der Österreichischen Byzantinistik* 65 (2015), 195–242.

Preiser-Kapeller, J., *Der Lange Sommer und die Kleine Eiszeit. Klima, Pandemien und der Wandel der Alten Welt von 500 bis 1500 n. Chr*, Vienna 2021.

Preiser-Kapeller, J./Mitsiou, E., "The Little Ice Age and Byzantium within the Eastern Mediterranean, ca. 1200–1350: An Essay on Old Debates and New Scenarios", in M. Bauch/G.J. Schenk (eds), *The Crisis of the 14th Century. Teleconnections between Environmental and Societal Change?*, Berlin/Boston 2020, pp. 190–220.

Quennet, G., *Qu'est-ce que l'histoire environnementale*, Seyssel 2014.

Radkau, J., *Natur und Macht: eine Weltgeschichte der Umwelt*, Munich 2000.

Radkau, J., *The Age of Ecology: A Global History*, Cambridge 2014 (originally in German: *Die Ära der Ökologie. Eine Weltgeschichte*, Munich 2011).

Raphael, S.K., *Climate and Political Climate. Environmental Disasters in the Medieval Levant* (Brill's Series in the History of the Environment 3), Leiden 2013.

Soudière, de la M., et al., *Devenir historien du climat? Entretien avec Emmanuel Le Roy Ladurie*, "Ethnologie Française" 39, 4 (2009), 639–644.

Squatriti, P., *Landscape and Change in Early Medieval Italy: Chestnuts, Economy, and Culture*, Cambridge 2013.

Squatriti, P., *Water and Society in Early Medieval Italy, 400–1000*, Cambridge 1998.

Squatriti, P., 'Mohammed, the Early Medieval Mediterranean, and Charlemagne'. *Early Medieval Europe* 11, no. 3 (2002): 263–79. https://doi.org/10.1046/j.0963-9462.2002.00111.x.

Squatriti, P., 'The Vegetative Mediterranean'. In *A Companion to Mediterranean History*, edited by Peregrine Horden and Sharon Kinoshita, 26–41. Wiley Blackwell Companions to World History, Chichester 2014.

Stathakopoulos, D., "Reconstructing the Climate of the Byzantine World: State of the Problem and Case Studies", in: J. Lazlovsky/P. Szabó (eds), *People and Nature in Historical Perspective*, Budapest 2003, pp. 247–61.

Stathakopoulos, D., *Famine and pestilence in the late Roman and early Byzantine Empire: a systematic survey of subsistence crises and epidemics*, Ashgate 2004.

Steinberg, T., *Nature Incorporated: Industrialization and the Waters of New England* (Studies in Environment and History), New York 1991.

Telelis, I., "Climatic Fluctuations in the Eastern Mediterranean and the Middle East AD 300–1500 from Byzantine Documentary and Proxy Physical Paleoclimatic Evidence – A Comparison". *Jahrbuch der Oesterreichischen Byzantinistik* 58 (2008), pp. 167–208.

Telelis, I., "Environmental History and Byzantine Studies: a Survey of Topics and Results", in: Kolias, T./Pitsakis, K. (eds), *Aureus. Volume dedicated to Professor Evangelos K. Chrysos*, Athens 2014, pp. 737–60.

Telelis, I., "Byzantine Textual Sources for Climatic and Environmental Developments", *Byzantine Symmeikta* 32 (2022), pp. 17–41.

Thonemann, P., *The Maeander Valley. A Historical Geography from Antiquity to Byzantium*, Cambridge 2011.

Vågene, Å.J., et al., *Salmonella Enterica Genomes from Victims of a Major Sixteenth-Century Epidemic in Mexico*, "Nature Ecology & Evolution" 2 (2018), 520–528.

Veikou, M., *Byzantine Epirus. A Topography of Transformation. Settlements of the Seventh-Twelfth Centuries in Southern Epirus and Aetoloacarnania*, Leiden 2012.

Walsh, K., *The Archaeology of Mediterranean Landscapes. Human-Environment Interaction from the Neolithic to the Roman Period*, Cambridge 2014.

Warde, P., *Ecology, Economy and State Formation in Early Modern Germany* (Cambridge Studies in Population, Economy, and Society in Past Time, 41), Cambridge 2006.

White, R., *The Organic Machine. The Remaking of the Columbia River*, New York 1995.

White, S./Pfister, Ch./Mauelshagen, F. (eds), *The Palgrave Handbook of Climate History*, London 2018.

Winiwarter, V., et al., "Environmental History in Europe from 1994 to 2004: Enthusiasm and Consolidation", *Environment and History* 10, 4 (2004), 501–530.

Winiwarter, V./Knoll, M., *Umweltgeschichte: eine Einführung*, Cologne 2007.

Worster, D., *Dust Bowl: The Southern Plains in the 1930s*, New York 1979.

Zhang, L., *The River, the Plain, and the State: An Environmental Drama in Northern Song China, 1048–1128*, Cambridge 2016.

PART 1

The Basics: Methods and Evidence

CHAPTER 1

Palaeoclimatology of Byzantine Lands (AD 300–1500)

Jürg Luterbacher, Elena Xoplaki, Adam Izdebski and Dominik Fleitmann

1   The Climate System

Although it is common to consider climate as simply a function of the atmospheric circulation over a period of time, this view tends to ignore the complex and interacting components of the climate system that determine the climate of a region. Climate is the result of various interactions between five principal subsystems – atmosphere, hydrosphere (oceans and other bodies of water), biosphere, land surface, and cryosphere (snow and ice), which collectively contribute to the climate system. Each subsystem interacts in different ways with the others such that changes in one subsystem can induce changes elsewhere. The atmosphere is the most variable subsystem, due to its low heat capacity (low specific heat), and thus responds most rapidly to external influences. It is coupled to other components of the climate system through energy exchanges at the Earth's surface (the atmospheric boundary layer) as well as through chemical interactions that affect the composition of the atmosphere, such as carbon dioxide, methane, etc., over many thousands of years.[1] Compared to the atmosphere, the oceans are a much slower subsystem of the climate system. Surface layers of the ocean respond to external influences on timescales ranging from months to decades, whereas changes in the deep oceans are much slower. Because water has a much higher heat capacity compared to air, oceans can store much larger quantities of energy and act as a buffer against large seasonal temperature changes. On a smaller spatial scale, proximity to the sea and oceans is a major factor affecting the climate of a region. Indeed, it is probably the single most important factor after latitude and elevation. On a large spatial scale, this is reflected in the differences between seasonal temperature ranges of the Northern and Southern Hemispheres.[2] The climate system is driven by solar radiation, and its temporal evolution is affected by its own internal dynamics and by changing external climate-forcing factors, such as

---

1   E.g., Overpeck et al., "Terrestrial Biosphere Dynamics in the Climate System".
2   Bradley, *Paleoclimatology: Reconstructing Climates of the Quaternary*.

volcanic eruptions, solar variations, and human-induced atmospheric composition changes.

2 Modern Climatology of the Byzantine Lands

The Byzantine Empire extended over a transitional climatic zone, the greater eastern Mediterranean Basin between the deserts of North Africa and the Middle East and the temperate areas of Central and Northern Europe. The climate of the eastern Mediterranean is influenced by subtropical and mid-latitude processes, which are mostly dry in summer, and in winter is also subject to continental influences as well as the large-scale mechanisms that act upon the entire global climate system. The region's topographical complexity, with peninsulas and islands, longitudinally and latitudinally aligned coasts, mountain ranges, and plateaus, together with the Mediterranean Sea, results in climatic conditions varying widely across a relatively small space. The Mediterranean Sea itself is an important source of energy and moisture and a key area for the development of rain-bearing cyclones, which are most frequent in winter and spring. Long, continuous and homogeneous meteorological observations are important for climate research and applications as they contribute to assessing variability, long-term trends, and past extreme events and comparing current conditions with the past. Widespread meteorological instrumental observations from the Mediterranean, however, are only available for ~70 years[3] with a few stations extending three centuries back in time.

In this section, we first characterize the winter (December–February) and summer (June–August) temperature and precipitation conditions covering the past decades in the Central and Eastern Mediterranean (30°–42° N and 11°–40° E). Monthly temperature and precipitation data are from CRU 4.01[4] and cover land areas on a 0.5° horizontal spatial resolution.

Precipitation is highest during the winter season (Fig. 1.1a) along the western coasts of Greece and Turkey and the southeastern Mediterranean coastal areas. There, the variability (expressed as the standard deviation in black lines around the mean values) is also the highest. Lower precipitation sums can be found over the rain shadow areas, the leeward side of the mountains and

---

3 See Fig. 3 in: Luterbacher et al., "A Review of 2000 Years of Paleoclimatic Evidence in the Mediterranean"; see also Noone et al., "Progress towards a holistic land and marine surface meteorological database".

4 Harris et al., "Version 4 of the CRU TS monthly high-resolution gridded multivariate climate dataset".

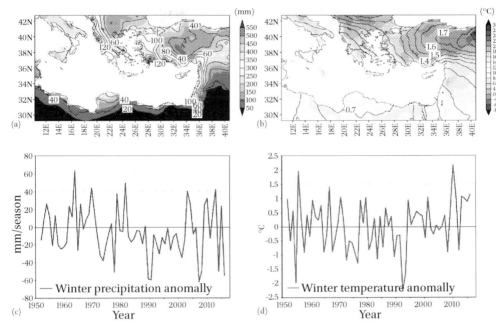

FIGURE 1.1 Winter (December to February) mean climate in the Byzantine lands 1951–2016. (a) Mean winter precipitation amount field (mm) and (c) temporal changes with respect to the 1951–1980 climatology. (b) Mean winter temperature field (°C) and (d) temporal changes with respect to the 1951–1980 climatology. Black contours on the map represent the standard deviation for each variable for the period 1951–2016 and gives an indication how variable seasonal temperature and precipitation are. Data stem from monthly CRU 4.01 with 0.5°× 0.5° spatial resolution (Harris et al. 2014, "Updated high-resolution grids of monthly climatic observations – the CRU TS3.10 Dataset")
Note: Harris et al., "Version 4 of the CRU TS monthly high-resolution gridded multivariate climate dataset".

generally south of 34° N. This very characteristic spatial distribution of winter precipitation in the eastern Mediterranean results from the combined effect of atmospheric circulation and the complex orography. Low-pressure systems of an Atlantic or Mediterranean origin move, generally, towards the eastern Mediterranean, where they are reinforced with energy and moisture as they pass over the warmer Mediterranean Sea, and, together with orographical forcing, they can cause high amounts of precipitation on the windward side of the mountains. The dry air masses in the lee of the mountains take up moisture again over the Aegean. Between 1950 and 2016, mean winter precipitation in the Central and Eastern Mediterranean (average over the geographical area 30°–42° N and 11°–40° E) shows a general decrease, though the trend is not statistically significant (Fig. 1.1c). The study region is characterized by a clear winter temperature gradient between the northern and southern parts (Fig. 1.1b). The highest temperatures are found over North Africa. The coastal regions experience generally milder winters, whereas temperatures are coldest in the more continental, inland areas in Northern Greece and Eastern Turkey. Sub-zero mean winter temperatures are associated with the combined influence of continentality and higher altitudes. The highest temperature variability around the mean, expressed as the standard deviation isolines, can be found over the northeastern area and Central Turkey (Fig. 1.1b). Winter temperature conditions in the south are very stable and show a low variability over the past ~70 years. The temperature amplitude of the coldest and mildest winter over the region is approximately 3.5 °C. Since the 1990s, winter temperatures have generally been rising and well above the mean temperature of the 1951–80 reference period (Fig. 1.1d).

During the summer months, precipitation is generally scarce (Fig. 1.2a) and mainly restricted to the northern regions, such as the Black Sea area in northern Turkey. Summer precipitation is connected with convective activity and thunderstorms. South of ~36° N, total summer precipitation is well below 50 mm and shows little variability. Furthermore, there is no visible trend in summer precipitation for recent decades (Fig. 1.2c). The temperature gradient between coastal areas and inland is also evident during the extended summer season (Fig. 1.2b) and strongly influenced by the orography.[5] The highest summer temperatures occur generally south of 36° N, whereas June to August temperature shows low variability, with the highest variability being less than 1 °C over the southeastern Balkans and stable summer temperatures of less than 0.4 °C over northeastern Africa. Since the 1980s, summer temperature over the area has shown a marked and significant upward trend (Fig. 1.2d). The seasonal temperature and precipitation patterns clearly indicate spatial and temporal variability, suggesting complex interactions and impacts that are connected to changes in climate conditions.

Evaluating the agricultural potential of the Byzantine lands, it is important to consider both precipitation and temperature changes. Higher temperatures will lead to higher evaporation rates, and thus soil moisture reserves from the winter are very important for winter crops such as wheat. The precipitation during spring is also crucial for agricultural production, although absolute precipitation is lower in spring than during winter. Reductions in winter precipitation and increases in summer evaporation reduce the precipitation as well as the evaporation balance, which sustains soil moisture, streamflow, and groundwater.

---

5 Xoplaki et al., "The Medieval Climate Anomaly and Byzantium: A Review of the Evidence on Climatic Fluctuations, Economic Performance and Societal Change".

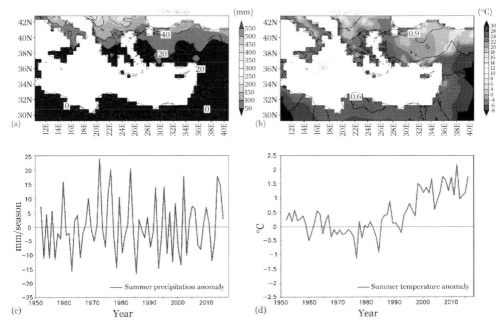

FIGURE 1.2   Summer (June to August) mean climate in the Byzantine lands 1951–2016. (a) Mean summer precipitation amount field (mm) and (c) temporal changes with respect to the 1951–1980 climatology. (b) Mean summer temperature field (°C) and (d) temporal changes with respect to the 1951–1980 climatology. Black contours on the map represent the standard deviation for each variable for the period 1951–2016 and gives an indication how variable seasonal temperature and precipitation are. Data stem from monthly CRU 4.01 with 0.5°× 0.5° spatial resolution (Harris et al. 2014, "Updated high-resolution grids of monthly climatic observations – the CRU TS3.10 Dataset")
Note: Harris et al., "Version 4 of the CRU TS monthly high-resolution gridded multivariate climate dataset".

3   How Is Proxy Information Used to Reconstruct Past Climate?

As mentioned above, the majority of instrumental meteorological records from the Mediterranean area are too short to capture the full range of climatic variations, trends, and extremes. Long climate records are therefore required to go further back in time. In this context, the term "proxy" has been extensively used in palaeoclimatology to refer to any line of evidence that provides an indirect measurement of past climatic conditions.[6] Information on past climatic and environmental conditions is commonly preserved in natural archives, such as marine and lacustrine sediments, ice, cave deposits

---

6   Ingram et al., "The use of documentary sources for the study of past climates".

FIGURE 1.3 Examples of documentary and natural proxies for palaeo climate and environmental research in the Mediterranean (Bradley et al. 1995)
Note: Bradley, *Paleoclimatology: Reconstructing Climates of the Quaternary.*

(speleothems), and subfossil biological material. In addition, some palaeoclimatological studies also use information on geomorphological features (glacial deposits, erosional features, palaeosols, and periglacial phenomena), loess, as well as weather phenomena described in the written documentary sources[7] (see Figure 1.3).

The principal approach to converting climate proxy information into quantitative and qualitative climate information is schematically shown in Figure 1.4.[8] The selection of a geographical site that includes a suitable archive represents the first crucial step in palaeoclimate investigations. Scientists look for locations such as lakes, old living or dead trees, or caves within a given region. One of the most important selection criteria is to find long, continuous, and well-preserved climate archives that cover several centuries to several millennia and allow the climate before the instrumental period to be studied at a high temporal resolution. Once the climate archive is sampled (e.g., sediment cores from a lake or speleothems from a cave), the selection of suitable climatic and environmental parameters that constitute valid proxies is based on the knowledge of the climate-related physical, chemical, physiological, and ecological processes that determine the reaction of a specific proxy (e.g., tree ring width/density, pollen assemblages) to local and regional environmental conditions. However, the type of proxy evidence at any given location is limited, as the relationship between proxy and climate is often complex and also influenced by non-climatic parameters. In practice, palaeoclimatologists follow well-established analytical techniques for the collection

---

7 Bradley, *Paleoclimatology: Reconstructing Climates of the Quaternary.*
8 National Research Council, *Surface temperature reconstructions for the past 2,000 years.*

and measurement of samples. The preferred locations are those where long, high-resolution, and continuous proxy records can be collected that allow the reconstruction of approximate target climatic variables (e.g., temperature, precipitation, soil moisture, water availability, drought, etc.). The second crucial step consists of dating the records, wherein the most common dating methods for geological and biological records are radiocarbon dating (e.g., of marine and lacustrine sediments), annual layer counting (e.g., of tree rings and varved sediment sequences) and uranium-series dating (e.g., of speleothems). Precise and accurate chronologies are a key prerequisite to synchronize and compare the records from different regions.

Records typically have different temporal resolutions, which can range from annual (e.g., tree rings, some speleothems) to decadal (see section below). Time series from different records stemming from the same area may also be averaged (e.g., tree rings) or put together to construct longer and more representative proxy records. However, the climate proxy records carry along a climatic signal that may be weak and embedded in extraneous "noise" produced by non-climatic effects such as biological, chemical, or geological processes. Extracting the environmental and palaeoclimatic signal from proxy records requires an understanding of the climatic and non-climatic processes influencing parameters in the proxy records (Fig. 1.4). This can be achieved either by continuous monitoring of sampling sites or by calibrating the proxy data obtained from the record with overlapping instrumental data. This is typically done using statistical techniques (linear or non-linear) to define the relationship between the measured parameters and the corresponding climatic variables obtained from instrumental climate records. Measured climate proxies are often seasonally biased as they represent climate conditions during a certain season. For instance, tree-ring widths in the Eastern Mediterranean are typically seasonally biased towards spring and summer, when trees grow. The fourth step (Fig. 1.4) of the procedure includes validation, which is the test of the empirical relationship derived in the previous step of calibration, and the quantitative assessment of its performance skill. Typically, the most recent part of the instrumental record is used for comparing and calibrating the proxy records, and linear regression coefficients (or other statistical measures) derived from the calibration are used for the reconstruction of the target climate time series from the proxy data during the validation period within the instrumental period. Various metrics are applied to assess the reconstruction skill during this validation step. The final step comprises the actual climate reconstruction. The statistical relationship between instrumental and proxy data developed during the calibration step and benchmarked for the validation period is applied to the proxy data to extend the quantitative reconstruction

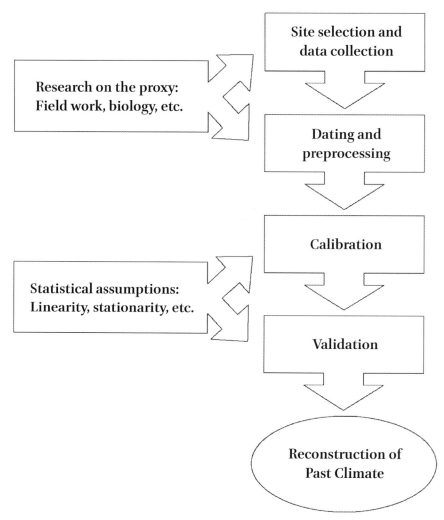

FIGURE 1.4 Schematic diagram of the general methodology used to reconstruct past climates, including surface temperature reconstructions (From NRC, "Surface temperature reconstructions for the past 2,000 years")
Note: From National Research Council, *Surface temperature reconstructions for the past 2,000 years*.

much further back in time. It is assumed that the modern relationships remain constant for the period of interest (the principle of uniformitarianism and stationarity; Fig. 1.4). Thus, palaeoclimatic research must build on studies of the modern-day climate dependency of natural phenomena. Although calibration against instrumental data is required to determine to what extent proxies reflect climate, proxy records are not thermometers or rainfall gauges, but rather measure some aspects of the proxies' reactions to the temperature or hydroclimatic conditions during a period of time. This means that the true relationship between the proxy and local climate is not known exactly. Proxies are also influenced by other non-climatic variables, or they are sensitive to multiple and interacting climate signals (e.g., precipitation, soil moisture, temperature, sea-level changes, sea surface temperature, water circulation and pH) and the length of their records vary. The complexity and interacting character of the effect of these factors make it harder to account for specific climate parameters. Moreover, it is often not possible to calibrate the proxy records due to age uncertainties, low temporal resolution, or lack of long instrumental data to calibrate. In this case, the proxy record can be used to determine warmer/colder or wetter/drier periods in at least a qualitative way. Uncertainties and error are usually assigned to the reconstruction based on how well it matches the observed temperature/hydroclimate or drought variations during the validation period in the fourth step (Figure 1.4). In general, the width of the error measures will vary in time according to the quantity and quality of the available proxy evidence.[9]

Natural archives can also provide a direct or indirect record of past climate forcings responsible for climatic fluctuations. Climate forcing factors include external forcings (changes in solar variability or volcanism) and internal forcings (e.g., the North Atlantic Oscillation, oceanic processes, sea ice dynamics, the El Niño Southern Oscillation). Therefore, palaeoclimatic data provide the basis for reconstructing climates of the past and for testing hypotheses about possible causes of past climatic changes. Detailed and accurate instrumental climate reconstructions enable us to identify the fundamental mechanisms responsible for climatic variations in the past.

The following section provides a short overview of the natural and documentary proxy information across the central and eastern Mediterranean during the Byzantine period.

4   Natural Proxy and Documentary Information for Byzantine Lands (AD 300–1500)

The Mediterranean region offers a relatively dense network of natural archives (lake and marine sediments, tree rings, and speleothems) and documentary evidence, allowing us to reconstruct climatic changes for the past centuries

---

9   National Research Council, *Surface temperature reconstructions for the past 2,000 years.*

to millennia.[10] Southeastern Europe has a high number of terrestrial archives from caves and lakes, which form the basis for understanding past environmental and climate changes and vegetation dynamics.[11] This is due to the geological features, geographical location, and related hydrological and climatic conditions that characterize the central and southeastern Mediterranean.[12] The study and interpretation of proxy records should use integrative approaches to disentangle the complex relationships between climate, land use, sea-level changes, human interactions, transformations of vegetation, and deforestation in the Mediterranean.[13] A network of highly-resolved palaeoclimatic records from historical, palaeo-ecological and archaeological archives is necessary, and the combined information is highly relevant for our understanding of climate sensitivity, environmental response, ecological processes, and human impact. Jones and colleagues[14] presented a 20,000-year overview of the palaeoclimate of the Fertile Crescent, a critical region for studying how climate has influenced societal changes. Labuhn et al.,[15] Finné et al.,[16] Xoplaki et al.,[17] and

---

10   See: Luterbacher et al., "A Review of 2000 Years of Paleoclimatic Evidence in the Mediterranean"; Labuhn et al., "Climatic changes and their impacts in the Mediterranean during the first millennium AD"; Finné et al., "Speleothem evidence for late Holocene climate variability and floods in Southern Greece"; Jones et al., "20,000 years of societal vulnerability and adaptation to climate change in southwest Asia"; Xoplaki et al., "The Medieval Climate Anomaly and Byzantium: A Review of the Evidence on Climatic Fluctuations, Economic Performance and Societal Change"; Xoplaki et al., "Modelling Climate and Societal Resilience in the Eastern Mediterranean in the Last Millennium"; Xoplaki et al., "Hydrological changes in Late Antiquity: spatio-temporal characteristics and socioeconomic impacts in the Eastern Mediterranean".

11   E.g., Masi et al., "Vegetation history and paleoclimate at Lake Dojran (FYROM/Greece) during the Late Glacial and Holocene"; Labuhn et al., "Climatic changes and their impacts in the Mediterranean during the first millennium AD".

12   Masi et al., "Vegetation history and paleoclimate at Lake Dojran (FYROM/Greece) during the Late Glacial and Holocene".

13   E.g., Luterbacher et al., "A Review of 2000 Years of Paleoclimatic Evidence in the Mediterranean".

14   Jones et al., "20,000 years of societal vulnerability and adaptation to climate change in southwest Asia".

15   Labuhn et al., "Climatic changes and their impacts in the Mediterranean during the first millennium AD".

16   Finné et al., "Holocene hydro-climatic variability in the Mediterranean: A synthetic multi-proxy reconstruction".

17   Xoplaki et al., "Hydrological changes in Late Antiquity: spatio-temporal characteristics and socioeconomic impacts in the Eastern Mediterranean".

Jacobson et al.[18] give recent overviews of the first millennium and Holocene hydro-climatic variability over the central and eastern Mediterranean.

Here, we give a short description of natural proxy records including speleothems, lake and marine sediments and tree rings that resolve annual to multidecadal hydroclimate variability and cover the Byzantine period between AD 300 and 1500 (Figure 1.5).

Speleothem (e.g., stalagmites, stalactites, and flowstones) is a general term for mineral deposits growing in caves. The majority of speleothems form when calcium carbonate precipitates from degassing solutions as they seep into limestone caves. Stalagmites are mainly used in palaeoclimate research due to their symmetric growth and better preservation of geochemical parameters. The formation of speleothems is a function of carbonate dissolution in the soil and bedrock and precipitation (deposition) in the underlying cave zone. Dissolution of the carbonate bedrock in the soil and epikarst is controlled by high CO_2 levels (high pCO_2) in the soil – a result of biological respiration and decomposition. The CO_2 dissolves in percolating meteoric water to form carbonic acid. The acidic water then dissolves the bedrock and the calcium concentration of the water increases. When the water enters the cave, the dissolved CO_2 degasses from the solution and calcite precipitates leading to the formation of speleothems.[19] Stalagmites can be dated by either counting annual bands (similar to tree rings) or by using uranium or thorium isotopes. The use of the so-called uranium-series dating methods allows stalagmites to be dated back to ~700,000 years before present and delivers very precise and absolute dates. The majority of stalagmites provide highly resolved records (1–10 years) of either precipitation or effective moisture; both are intrinsically linked to the hydrological cycle.[20] This climate archive can potentially provide long records at temporal resolutions as high as annual, reflecting a seasonal signal with very precise chronologies. Currently, a few absolutely-dated and well-replicated stalagmite $\delta^{18}O$ records with subannual to multi-decadal

---

18   Jacobson et al., "Heterogenous late Holocene climate in the Eastern Mediterranean – The Kocain Cave record from SW Turkey".

19   E.g., Fleitmann et al., "Holocene ITCZ and Indian monsoon dynamics recorded in stalagmites from Oman and Yemen (Socotra)"; Fleitmann et al., "Timing and climatic impact of Greenland interstadials recorded in stalagmites from northern Turkey".

20   E.g., Warken et al., "Reconstruction of late Holocene autumn/winter precipitation variability in SW Romania from a high-resolution speleothem trace element record"; Bini et al., "Hydrological changes during the Roman Climatic Optimum in northern Tuscany (Central Italy) as evidenced by speleothem records and archaeological data"; Regattieri et al., "Lateglacial to Holocene trace element record (Ba, Mg, Sr) from Corchia Cave (Apuan Alps, central Italy): paleoenvironmental implications"; Sinha et al., "Role of climate in the rise and fall of the Neo-Assyrian Empire".

resolution exist in the central and eastern Mediterranean and Middle East (Fig. 1.5).[21] Oxygen ($\delta^{18}O$) and carbon ($\delta^{13}C$) isotopes are the most frequent palaeoclimate proxies obtained from stalagmites. While $\delta^{18}O$ is often used as an indicator for the amount of precipitation above the cave (more negative $\delta^{18}O$ values indicate wetter climatic conditions) and changes in the seasonality of rainfall, carbon isotope values are mainly influenced by vegetation and soil microbial activity above the cave. Both of them are strongly governed by moisture and temperature. In addition, trace element concentrations (e.g., magnesium) in stalagmites can be also used as a proxy for the precipitation amount and groundwater recharge. Magnesium concentrations in stalagmites tend to be lower during wetter intervals.[22] However, it is very difficult to obtain quantitative records from stalagmites, and the vast majority of stalagmite-based reconstructions provides information on relative changes in the amount of precipitation (wetter/drier).

In the Mediterranean, marine and lacustrine sediments play an important role in the reconstruction of past hydroclimate variability over the last few millennia.[23] Sediments are composed of both biogenic materials (e.g.,

---

21   Bar-Matthews et al., "Sea-land oxygen isotopic relationships from planktonic foraminifera and speleothems in the Eastern Mediterranean region and their implication for paleorainfall during interglacial intervals"; Göktürk, "Climate on the southern Black Sea coast during the Holocene: implications from the Sofular Cave record"; Göktürk et al., "Climate in the Eastern Mediterranean through the Holocene inferred from Turkish Stalagmites"; Orland et al., "Climate deterioration in the Eastern Mediterranean as revealed by ion microprobe analysis of a speleothem that grew from 2.2 to 0.9 ka in Soreq Cave, Israel"; Cheng et al., "The climate variability in northern Levant over the past 20,000 years"; Flohr et al., "Late Holocene droughts in the Fertile Crescent recorded in a speleothem from northern Iraq"; Bini et al., "Hydrological changes during the Roman Climatic Optimum in northern Tuscany (Central Italy) as evidenced by speleothem records and archaeological data"; Regattieri et al., "Lateglacial to Holocene trace element record (Ba, Mg, Sr) from Corchia Cave (Apuan Alps, central Italy): paleoenvironmental implications"; Sinha et al. "Role of climate in the rise and fall of the Neo-Assyrian Empire".
22   Flohr et al., "Late Holocene droughts in the Fertile Crescent recorded in a speleothem from northern Iraq".
23   E.g., Schilman et al., "Global climate instability reflected by eastern Mediterranean marine records during the late Holocene"; Lacey et al., "A high-resolution Late Glacial to Holocene record of environmental change in the Mediterranean from Lake Ohrid (Macedonia/Albania)"; Jones et al., "A high-resolution late Holocene lake isotope record from Turkey and links to North Atlantic and monsoon climate"; Sharifi et al., "Abrupt climate variability since the last deglaciation based on a high-resolution, multi-proxy peat record from NW Iran: The hand that rocked the Cradle of Civilization?"; Koutsodendris et al., "Climate variability in SE Europe since 1450 AD based on a varved sediment record from Etoliko Lagoon (Western Greece)"; Katrantsiotis et al., "Eastern Mediterranean hydroclimate reconstruction over the last 3600 years based on sedimentary *n*-alkanes,

ostracods, diatoms, pollen) and non-biogenic materials (e.g., quartz, clays, carbonates). The biogenic component includes the remains of planktic (near-surface-dwelling) and benthic (bottom-dwelling) organisms, which provide a record of climate-related changes in water temperature and salinity, dissolved oxygen in deep water, nutrient or trace element concentrations, etc. Marine sediments also contain biomarkers (organic molecules derived from terrestrial or marine organisms[24]), which can be useful proxies of palaeo-oceanographic conditions or of palaeo-environmental conditions on the adjacent continents. The nature and abundance of terrigenous material is often used as a proxy for hydroclimatic variations on the continents as terrestrial input is linked to vegetation and soil humidity. Furthermore, the input of terrestrial matter is also dependent on the intensity and direction of winds or other modes of sediment transport to or within ocean basins, such as fluvial erosion, ice-rafting, or turbidity currents.[25]

Mediterranean lakes record past changes in climate and water balance via a range of proxy indicators preserved in their sediments. A fundamental distinction can be made between open (in- and outflow of water) and closed lakes (no outflow of water). Most lakes in the drier regions of the Mediterranean lose their water through evaporation and may become hydrologically closed, making their waters saline.[26] At times of negative water balance, the area of a closed lake shrinks, water levels fall, and salinity increases, while the opposite occurs at times of positive water balance. Lake records are of great value primarily in reconstructing fluctuations in climate over multi-decadal and longer timescales.[27] A few hydroclimatic reconstructions from marine and lake sediment with various temporal resolutions are available for the Balkans and central and the eastern Mediterranean.[28] A variety of proxies can be used for

---

their carbon and hydrogen isotope composition and XRF data from the Gialova Lagoon, SW Greece".

24 E.g. Bozyiğit et al., "Middle-late Holocene climate and hydrologic changes in the Gulf of Saros (NE Aegean Sea)" and references therein.
25 Bradley, "Paleoclimatology: Reconstructing Climates of the Quaternary".
26 Roberts, Reed, "Lakes, Wetlands, and Holocene Environmental Change".
27 Fritz, "Deciphering climatic history from lake sediments".
28 E.g., Frogley et al., "Historical biogeography and Late Quaternary environmental change of Lake Pamvotis, Ioannina (North-western Greece): evidence from ostracods"; Roberts et al., "The tempo of Holocene climatic change in the eastern Mediterranean region: new high-resolution crater-lake sediment data from central Turkey"; Schilman et al., "Global climate instability reflected by eastern Mediterranean marine records during the late Holocene"; Stevens et al., "Proposed changes in seasonality of climate during the Lateglacial and Holocene at Lake Zeribar, Iran"; Wick et al., "Evidence of Lateglacial and Holocene climatic change and human impact in eastern Anatolia: high-resolution pollen,

reconstructing hydroclimate, such as oxygen isotopes, pollen, and concentrations of certain trace elements (e.g., titanium in lake sediments as an indicator for aridity).

Tree-ring records are an additional important source of annually resolved information about past climate. They are widespread, well replicated, and can be calibrated against overlapping instrumental records to produce annually resolved reconstructions of past climate variability. However, it is important to note that most tree-ring proxy records reflect seasonal/sub-annual rather than annual climate variability. For moisture-sensitive trees, the climate response can vary across regions. In the Mediterranean, winter, spring, and total annual precipitation (over the October–September hydrological year) usually dominate over moisture variability and therefore tree-ring formation. Luterbacher and colleagues[29] provide a map with the location and climate sensitivity of the approximately 900 tree-ring chronologies of more than 600 years old within the greater Mediterranean region. In the eastern Mediterranean, absolute chronologies of *Quercus* sp. and *Juniperus* sp. from the Aegean-Anatolia region

charcoal, isotopic and geochemical records from the laminated sediments of Lake Van, Turkey"; Jones et al., "A high-resolution late Holocene lake isotope record from Turkey and links to North Atlantic and monsoon climate"; Eastwood et al., "Holocene climate change in the eastern Mediterranean region: a comparison of stable isotope and pollen data from Lake Gölhisar, southwest Turkey"; Jones et al., "Human impact on the hydroenvironment of Lake Parishan, SW Iran, through the late-Holocene"; Kuzucuoğlu at al., "Mid- to late-Holocene climate change in central Turkey: the Tecer Lake record"; Woodbridge, Roberts, "Late Holocene climate of the Eastern Mediterranean inferred from diatom analysis of annually-laminated lake sediments"; Ülgen et al., "Climatic and environmental evolution of Lake Iznik (NW Turkey) over the last ~4700 years"; Magny et al., "Contrasting patterns of precipitation seasonality during the Holocene in the south- and north-central Mediterranean"; Zanchetta et al., "Multiproxy record for the last 4500 years from Lake Shkodra (Albania/Montenegro)"; Francke et al., "A Late Glacial to Holocene record of environmental change from Lake Dojran (Macedonia, Greece)"; Dean et al., "Eastern Mediterranean hydroclimate over the late glacial and Holocene, reconstructed from the sediments of Nar Lake, central Turkey, using stable isotopes and carbonate mineralogy"; Lacey et al., "A high-resolution Late Glacial to Holocene record of environmental change in the Mediterranean from Lake Ohrid (Macedonia/Albania)"; Sharifi et al., "Abrupt climate variability since the last deglaciation based on a high-resolution, multi-proxy peat record from NW Iran: The hand that rocked the Cradle of Civilization?"; Ocakoğlu et al., "A 2800-year multi-proxy sedimentary record of climate change from Lake Çubuk (Göynük, Bolu, NW Anatolia)"; Danladi, Akçer-Ön, "Solar forcing and climate variability during the past millennium as recorded in a high altitude lake: Lake Salda (SW Anatolia)"; Fig. 5; Table 1.

29 Luterbacher et al., "A Review of 2000 Years of Paleoclimatic Evidence in the Mediterranean".

cover the last millennium.[30] Anatolia and Cyprus have yielded large population sample series of *Pinus nigra* covering more than half of the past millennium. Similar data on *Juniperus phoenicia* and *Cedrus libani* exist for the Levant.[31] The *Old World Drought Atlas* provides a new tree-ring-based reconstruction of the summer season (June, July, August [JJA]) self-calibrating Palmer Drought Severity Index (scPDSI).[32] The OWDA consists of 106 tree-ring chronologies to reconstruct scPDSI at 5,414 0.5° grid points over the European Mediterranean domain (27°N–71°N, 12°W–45°E). The locations of the tree-ring chronologies in the Mediterranean part of the OWDA are shown in the original publication[33] along with the approximate start dates of the various records. Recently, Konter and colleagues[34] and Klippel and colleagues[35] presented the longest Mediterranean June–July drought reconstruction (SPI) back to AD 730, which is based on a network of high-elevation tree-ring (*Pinus heldreichii*) sites from Mount Smolikas in the Pindus Mountains (northwestern Greece). Esper and colleagues presented millennium-length June–July precipitation reconstructions back to AD 729.[36] Based on tree material from the same area, Klippel and colleagues[37] produced the currently longest reconstruction of late summer (August–September) temperature in the Mediterranean covering more than 1,250 years.

5 Documentary and Textual Evidence

Apart from natural proxies, there is also the potential to reconstruct palaeoclimate in the Mediterranean using the wealth of textual evidence dating back to

---

30 See: Heinrich et al., "Winter-to-spring temperature dynamics in Turkey derived from tree rings since AD 1125"; Cook et al., "Old World megadroughts and pluvials during the Common Era"; Cook, Anchukaitis et al., "Spatiotemporal drought variability in the Mediterranean over the last 900 years".
31 Cook et al., "Old World megadroughts and pluvials during the Common Era"; Cook, Anchukaitis et al., "Spatiotemporal drought variability in the Mediterranean over the last 900 years".
32 Cook et al., "Old World megadroughts and pluvials during the Common Era".
33 Cook, Anchukaitis et al., "Spatiotemporal drought variability in the Mediterranean over the last 900 years"; Cook et al., "Old World megadroughts and pluvials during the Common Era".
34 Konter et al., "Meet Adonis, Europe's oldest dendrochronologically dated tree".
35 Klippel et al., "A 1286-year hydro-climate reconstruction for the Balkan Peninsula".
36 Esper et al., "Pre-instrumental summer precipitation variability in northwestern Greece from a high-elevation *Pinus heldreichii* network".
37 Klippel et al., "A 1200+ year reconstruction of temperature extremes for the northeastern Mediterranean region".

the Byzantine and Late Roman periods.[38] (The main sources of documentary evidence are shown in Fig. 1.5.) The identification of historical extreme hydrological events – including extended flood and drought periods – is important, as these extremes are main stressors for societies and ecosystems. Descriptive textual proxy data are usually discontinuous and heterogeneous. Furthermore, various sociocultural and general climatic conditions and parameters may affect the perception of the observers, who may add bias through their inclusion or exclusion of climatological information in the texts.[39] Testimonies range from direct observations of climatic or environmental phenomena to indirect evidence for climate such as famine, plague, taxation records, harvest dates, etc. – which are especially suggestive when they are not entirely local. Camuffo and Enzi[40] documented in detail the history of the Tiber floods in Rome over the past 2,400 years. They compiled the written evidence and produce a temporally high-resolution flood series and discuss the limitations and inhomogeneities in the conditions that influence the hydrological and catchment system. The Tiber has a unimodal distribution, with the highest flow in November to December; thus, this long flood series mainly reflects early-winter conditions over Central Italy.

Palaeoclimatic evidence covering the Byzantine time remained largely unexplored for palaeoclimate research until the early 2000s. Telelis[41] presented a catalogue of textual palaeoclimate evidence derived from a variety of Byzantine sources, together with a detailed discussion of the methodological aspects involved in using those data in a climatic context. The main advantages of these data are their temporal resolution, their disentanglement of the temperature and precipitation, their coverage of all months of the year,

---

38 Haldon et al., " The Climate and Environment of Byzantine Anatolia: Integrating Science, History and Archaeology"; Izdebski et al., "The environmental, archaeological and historical evidence for regional climatic changes and their societal impacts in the Eastern Mediterranean in Late Antiquity"; Xoplaki et al., "The Medieval Climate Anomaly and Byzantium: A Review of the Evidence on Climatic Fluctuations, Economic Performance and Societal Change"; Xoplaki et al., "Hydrological changes in Late Antiquity: spatio-temporal characteristics and socioeconomic impacts in the Eastern Mediterranean".

39 E.g., Camuffo, Enzi, "The analysis of two bi-millennial series: Tiber and Po river floods"; Telelis, Μετεωρολογικά φαινόμενα και κλίμα στο Βυζάντιο; Telelis, "Climatic Fluctuations in the Eastern Mediterranean and the Middle East AD 300–1500 from Byzantine Documentary and Proxy Physical Paleoclimatic Evidence – A Comparison".

40 Camuffo, Enzi, "The analysis of two bi-millennial series: Tiber and Po river floods".

41 Telelis, Μετεωρολογικά φαινόμενα και κλίμα στο Βυζάντιο; Telelis, "Climatic Fluctuations in the Eastern Mediterranean and the Middle East AD 300–1500 from Byzantine Documentary and Proxy Physical Paleoclimatic Evidence – A Comparison". See also now Telelis, "Byzantine Textual Sources".

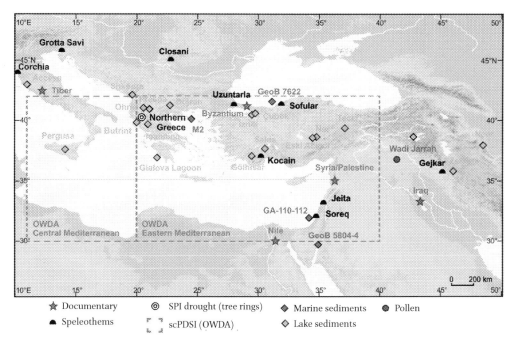

FIGURE 1.5 Natural and documentary records resolving hydroclimate or temperature across the central and eastern Mediterranean, divided by proxy type that cover the full or a large part of the Byzantine period. Basic information on each proxy is presented in Table 1.1

and their high sensitivity to anomalies and natural hazards. Xoplaki and colleagues[42] presented 50-year bins of wet/dry and warm/cool conditions for the Byzantine period (AD 800 to 1300) along with natural proxies. Repapis and colleagues[43] studied monastery and historical records that resolve snow cover and/or freezing of lakes in northern Greece to derive severe winters for the period AD 1200–1900. Building on the work of Telelis, Preiser-Kapeller[44] combined written evidence for extreme events and other climatic phenomena with proxy data for the 10th to 12th and 13th to 14th centuries, highlighting the specific dynamics for the Byzantine regions during the periods generally characterized as the "Medieval Climate Anomaly" or the "Little Ice Age".

42 Xoplaki et al., "The Medieval Climate Anomaly and Byzantium: A Review of the Evidence on Climatic Fluctuations, Economic Performance and Societal Change".
43 Repapis et al., "A note on the frequency of occurrence of severe winters as evidenced in monastery and historical records from Greece during the period 1200–1900 A.D.".
44 Preiser-Kapeller, "A Collapse of the Eastern Mediterranean?"; Preiser-Kapeller/Mitsiou, "The Little Ice Age and Byzantium"; Preiser-Kapeller, Der Lange Sommer und die Kleine Eiszeit.

TABLE 1.1   Proxy records and reconstructions of past climate conditions available for the Byzantine lands

Archive	Proxy	Interpretation	Location	Latitude (N)	Longitude (E)	Resolution	Citation
documentary	flood frequency	hydro-climate	Tiber river (Italy)	41.73	12.23	non-annual	Camuffo and Enzi 1994
documentary	textual evidence precipitation	hydro-climate	Constantinople	41.01	28.95	sub-annual	Telelis, 2004, 2008; Xoplaki et al. 2016
documentary	textual evidence precipitation	hydro-climate	Bagdad (Iraq)	33.33	44.38	sub-annual	Vogt et al. 2011, 2016a,2016b; Schönbein et al. 2016
documentary	textual evidence precipitation	hydro-climate	Syria/Palestine	33.5	36.3	sub-annual	Vogt et al. 2011, 2016a,2016b
documentary	Nile floods	hydro-climate	Nile (Rhoda)	30.03	31.23	annual	Kondrashov et al. 2005
lake sediment	Ti	hydro-climate	Lake Neor (Iran)	37.95	48.55	non-annual	Sharifi et al. 2015
lake sediment	PC1 XRF	hydro-climate	Gialova Lagoon	36.96	21.67	non-annual	Katrantsiotis et al. 2018
lake sediment	$\delta^{18}O$	hydro-climate	Lake Zeribar (Iran)	35.53	46.13	non-annual	Stevens et al. 2001
lake sediment	$\delta^{18}O$	hydro-climate	Lake Eski Acigöl	38.55	34.53	non-annual	Roberts et al. 2011
lake sediment	Aragonite	hydro-climate	Lake Tecer (Turkey)	39.43	37.08	non-annual	Kuzucuoglu et al. 2011
lake sediment	$\delta^{18}O$	hydro-climate	Lago di Pergusa (Sicily)	37.52	14.18	non-annual	Sadori et al. 2016
lake sediment	$\delta^{18}O$	hydro-climate	Shkodra (Albania/Montenegro)	42.17	19.32	sub-annual	Zanchetta et al. 2012
lake sediment	Ti/Ca	hydro-climate	Butrint (Albania)	39.78	20.01	annual	Morellon et al. 2016
lake sediment	$\delta^{18}O$	hydro-climate	Lake Ohrid (Macedonia/Albania)	41.07	20.72	non-annual	Lacey et al. 2015
lake sediment	$\delta^{18}O$	hydro-climate	Lake Prespa (Albania/Greece/North Macedonia)	40.9	21.03	non-annual	Leng et al. 2013
lake sediment	K?	hydro-climate	Lake Dojran (North Macedonia/Greece)	41.2	22.73	non-annual	Francke et al. 2013

TABLE 1.1 Proxy records and reconstructions of past climate conditions (*cont.*)

Archive	Proxy	Interpretation	Location	Latitude (N)	Longitude (E)	Resolution	Citation
lake sediment	δ¹⁸O	hydro-climate	Nar Gölü (Turkey)	38.34	34.46	non-annual	Jones et al. 2006; Dean et al. 2015
lake sediment	Ca?	hydro-climate	Lake Salda (Turkey)	37.55	29.68	non-annual	Danladi and Akçer-Ön 2018
lake sediment	Lake level anomalies	hydro-climate	Lake Accesa (Italy)	43	11	non-annual	Magny et al. 2012
lake sediment	δ¹⁸O and Mg/Ca	hydro-climate	Van (Turkey)	38.62	42.87	non-annual	Wick et al. 2003
lake sediment	δ¹⁸O	hydro-climate	Lake Ioannina (Greece)	39.68	20.83	non-annual	Frogley et al. 2001
lake sediment	δ¹⁸O	hydro-climate	Lake Gölhisar (Turkey)	37.13	29.06	non-annual	Eastwood et al. 2006
lake sediment	δ¹⁸O	hydro-climate	Lake Çubuk (Turkey)	40.48	29.83	non-annual	Ocakoğlu et al. 2016
lake sediment	δ¹⁸O	hydro-climate	Lake İznik	40.43	29.52	non-annual	Ülgen et al. 2012
marine sediment	Clay layer	hydro-climate	GeoB 7622	41.53	31.17	non-annual	Lamy et al. 2006
marine sediment	Terrigenous sand acc. Rate	hydro-climate	GeoB 5804-4	29.5	34.85	non-annual	Lamy et al. 2006
marine sediment	δ¹⁸O	hydro-climate	GA-110-112	31.93	34.37	non-annual	Schilman et al. 2001
Pollen	Shrub-Steppe	hydro-climate	Wadi Jarrah (Syria)	36.83	41.37	non-annual	Kaniewski et al. 2012
speleothem	δ¹⁸O	hydro-climate	Corchia cave (Italy)	43.98	10.22	non-annual	Zanchetta et al. 2007
speleothem	δ¹⁸O	temperature	Grotta Savi (Italian Alps)	45.82	13.89	non-annual	Frisia et al. 2005
speleothem	δ¹³C	hydro-climate	Sofular cave (Turkey)	41.42	31.93	non-annual	Fleitmann et al. 2009
speleothem	δ¹⁸O	hydro-climate	Soreq cave (Israel)	31.45	35.02	non-annual	Bar-Matthews et al. 2003; Orland et al. 2009
speleothem	δ¹³C	hydro-climate	Jeita cave (Lebanon)	33.95	35.65	non-annual	Cheng et al. 2015
speleothem	δ¹³C	hydro-climate	Uzuntarla Cave (Turkey)	41.58	27.65	non-annual	Göktürk, 2011
speleothem	δ¹³C	hydro-climate	Kocain cave (Turkey)	37.23	30.7	non-annual	Jacobson et al. 2021

TABLE 1.1 Proxy records and reconstructions of past climate conditions (cont.)

Archive	Proxy	Interpretation	Location	Latitude (N)	Longitude (E)	Resolution	Citation
speleothem	Mg and $\delta^{18}O$	hydro-climate	Geykar (Iraq)	35.8	45.15	sub-annual	Flohr et al. 2017
speleothem	Mg/Ca	hydro-climate	Closani Cave (Romania)	45.1	22.8	annual	Warken et al. 2018
tree rings	$\delta^{13}C$	temperature	SW-Turkey	36.6	30.01	annual	Heinrich et al. 2014
tree rings	scPDSI	hydro-climate	Central Mediterranean (OWDA)	30–42.5	10–20	annual	Cook et al. 2015; Cook et al. 2016
tree rings	scPDSI	hydro-climate	Eastern Mediterranean (OWDA)	30–42.5	20–40	annual	Cook et al. 2015; Cook et al. 2016
tree rings	scPDSI	hydro-climate	Northern Greece	40.08	20.92	annual	Klippel et al. 2018

There is limited climate information available from the Middle East and northern African countries based on documentary evidence. A notable exception is the work of Vogt and colleagues[45] and Schönbein and colleagues[46] that make innovative use of Arabic sources to reconstruct past climate in the Middle East as far back as AD 800. They present preliminary results based on a survey of around 50 medieval Arabic historiographical literature sources. The geographical coverage includes Iraq (with Bagdad as its centre), northern Egypt, Syria, and Palestine (with Damascus as its centre), as well as the Hejaz and Yemen. Between the 9th and 15th centuries, the spatial focus of the reports moves from the Abbasid centres of power and science in Iraq to the Ayyubid centres in Syria and Palestine and finally to Fatimid and Mamluk Egypt, reflecting the political and cultural changes in the area. Raphael[47] and

---

45 Vogt et al., "Assessing the Medieval Climate Anomaly in the Middle East: The potential of Arabic documentary sources"; Vogt et al., "From Data to Climatological Indices – The Case of the Grotzfeld Data Set"; Vogt et al., "The Grotzfeld Data Set – Coded Environmental, Climatological and Societal data for the Near and Middle East from AD 801 to 1821".
46 Schönbein et al., "The chronicle of Ibn Tawq – over 7000 climate and environmental records from Damascus, Syria, AD 1481 to 1501".
47 Raphael, *Climate and political climate: environmental disasters in the Medieval Levant*.

Widell[48] present the frequency of years with extreme weather events in the areas of Syria, Palestine, and Northern Iraq as documented in written sources, covering the period AD 1100–1230 and including an analysis of the impact of and reactions to droughts and famines in the Crusader States and neighbouring Muslim polities.

A record from northeastern Africa includes the flood levels of the Nile River. The streamflow of the Nile is a good indicator of climate variations, because it provides an integral measure of the precipitation over the source regions, if other conditions remain unchanged. The Nile flood maxima from the Blue Nile are mostly fed by the monsoonal rains in Ethiopia associated with the northward shift of the Intertropical Convergence Zone (ITCZ); the Nile flood minima originate in tropical East Africa. Shorter-term, interannual fluctuations in the high-level record do also reflect variations in the White Nile contributions. The accumulated precipitation of several preceding seasons affects the level of Lakes Victoria and Albert, both being the sources of the White Nile. Pharaonic and medieval Egypt depended solely on winter agriculture and hence on the summer floods. Several authors compiled the annual maxima and minima of the water level recorded at nilometers (in a general sense, an instrument that measures the height of the Nile waters during its periodical flood) in the Cairo area (in particular at Rodah Island) from AD 622 to 1922.[49]

6   Temperature Conditions during Byzantine Times: An Overview

While hydroclimate proxies are relatively numerous and display regionally specific variability, temperature proxies are rare and mostly reflect summer conditions, which are generally more homogeneous across space. Therefore, in the final section of this chapter, we discuss in more detail the (few) available temperature reconstructions for the medieval Eastern Mediterranean.

A 2,150-year-long, summer mean temperature reconstruction for Europe and the Mediterranean was developed by Luterbacher and colleagues.[50] Nine annually resolved tree-ring width and density records, as well as documentary records from Central Europe (covering the past 500 years), were used in a Bayesian hierarchical modelling (BHM) framework. In Figure 1.6, we use the

---

48   Widell, "Historical Evidence for Climate Instability and Environmental Catastrophes in Northern Syria and the Jazira: The Chronicle of Michael the Syrian".
49   Kondrashov et al., "Oscillatory modes of extended Nile River records (A.D. 622–1922)" and references therein.
50   Luterbacher et al., "European summer temperatures since Roman times".

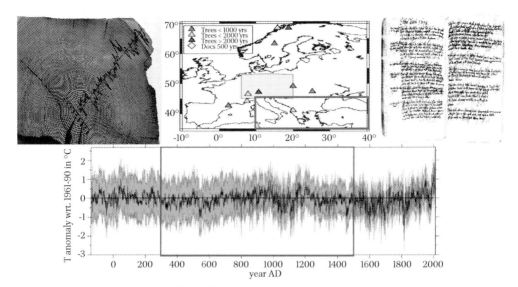

FIGURE 1.6 Tree ring proxies together with documentary evidence (Upper panels left and right) and spatial distribution of proxy records used in the 2150 years summer temperature reconstructions for the central and eastern Mediterranean. (Lower panel) Bayesian Hierarchical Modelling based summer temperature anomalies (with respect to the 1961–1990 climatology), averaged over the red box and the 95% confidence intervals (blue shading) covering the period 137 BC–2003 AD. The blue box denotes the period from 300–1500 AD

same data and method as in Luterbacher et al.,[51] but include two additional tree-ring records from Slovakia and Albania, which correlate significantly with central and southeastern Mediterranean summer temperatures. We then recalculated the temperature reconstructions for the central and eastern Mediterranean. It should be noted that due to the limited tree-ring proxy information available from the Mediterranean region, the reconstruction for the Byzantine period almost entirely depends on tree-ring information from outside the region, and, consequently, caution is required when using these results. The temperature reconstruction shows that the summer temperatures between the early 4th century and the mid-8th century AD were generally lower than today, with the exception of the end of the 7th century. The coolest phase is found in the first half of the 6th century with more than 1 °C lower summer temperatures (compared with 1961–90), recently termed the "Late Antique Little Ice Age" (LALIA).[52] The lower temperatures were most likely

---

51   Luterbacher et al., "European summer temperatures since Roman times".
52   Büntgen et al., "Cooling and societal change during the Late Antique Little Ice Age from 536 to around 660 AD"; Newfield, "The Climate Downturn of 536–50".

caused by three strong tropical volcanic eruptions in AD 536, 540 and 547 and lower solar activity. From AD 800 to AD c.1000, the central to eastern European regions experienced warmer summer conditions compared to today. Between the 11th century and mid-12th century, summers were again much cooler and more variable. There was a strong warming period until the end of the 12th century followed by an abrupt cooling at the beginning of the 13th century AD. The three centuries from AD 1200 to 1500 were rather cool relative to the averaged central and eastern Mediterranean summer temperatures (Fig. 1.6), which is in agreement with the historical sources from and around Constantinople. The lowest reconstructed summer temperatures fell in the mid-15th century and were likely related to the strong tropical volcanic activity taking place at that time.

The spatial mean reconstruction presented in Figure 1.6 does not allow a regionalization within the central and eastern Mediterranean land regions. Palaeoclimatic information that resolves land or sea surface temperatures from central and eastern Mediterranean is currently scarce. Heinrich and colleagues[53] developed a statistically, annually resolved January-to-May temperature for southwestern Turkey based on $\delta^{13}C$ in tree rings of *Juniperus excels*. Their temperature reconstruction exhibits multi-decadal variability with temperatures mostly above current conditions for the period from 1125 to 1510.[54] Xoplaki et al.[55] (their Fig. 9) presented a data collection by Telelis[56] covering the period from AD 850 to 1300, but most of the historical accounts of weather conditions correspond to extreme climatic conditions, whereas "normal" or "mild" conditions are barely mentioned. The imperial capital of Constantinople and adjacent areas were most frequently covered in textual Byzantine sources. Reports of cold or extremely cold months/seasons are most frequently mentioned and appear to cluster during the periods AD 901–950, AD 1051–1100, and AD 1251–1300. Reports of very warm events are rarely reported and only appear in the second half of the 9th and 10th centuries AD. A speleothem $\delta^{18}O$ record from Grotta Savi (SE Alps)[57] indicates a temperature drop around

---

53   Heinrich et al., "Winter-to-spring temperature dynamics in Turkey derived from tree rings since AD 1125".

54   Heinrich et al. "Winter-to-spring temperature dynamics in Turkey derived from tree rings since AD 1125".

55   Xoplaki et al., "The Medieval Climate Anomaly and Byzantium: A Review of the Evidence on Climatic Fluctuations, Economic Performance and Societal Change".

56   Telelis, *Μετεωρολογικά φαινόμενα και κλίμα στο Βυζάντιο*; Telelis, "Climatic Fluctuations in the Eastern Mediterranean and the Middle East AD 300–1500 from Byzantine Documentary and Proxy Physical Paleoclimatic Evidence – A Comparison".

57   Frisia et al., "Climate variability in the SE Alps of Italy over the past 17 000 years reconstructed from stalagmite records".

AD 500–700, followed by an increase until approximately AD 1000. Gogou and colleagues[58] present a decadal to multi-decadal sea surface temperature (SST) reconstruction covering the past 1,500 years from the North Aegean, using alkenone palaeothermometry and a plethora of organic geochemical, micropalaeontological, and pollen proxy indices obtained from the marine multi-core M2. The M2 reconstruction shows generally cooler annual sea surface temperatures (SSTs) from AD 500–1350 (compared to the period AD 1855–1955), with the lowest SSTs occurring between AD 700 and 850. A positive trend in SST starts at the end of the 11th century and reaches its highest values towards the end of the 16th century. From the mid-14th to the mid-15th century, the reconstructed SST values are higher compared to the previous centuries. The differences in the temperature pattern during the Byzantine period across the Mediterranean might be related to climatic conditions, which smooth out smaller-scale variations and proxies resolving different seasonalities.[59] Further, regional and seasonal biases in the natural proxies, the change of density of historical information across the centuries, larger uncertainties back in time due to proxies being fewer and more unequally distributed, dating uncertainties, and differences in reconstruction methods might be responsible for the different temperature patterns.

Figures 1.7 and 1.8 present the spatial correlations between detrended instrumental winter temperatures close to Constantinople (as the centre of cultural production and hence composition of historical sources during the Byzantine times) with the surrounding Mediterranean areas for annually resolved data covering the past 60 years (Fig. 1.7) and for 10-year averaged data covering the past 110 years (Fig. 1.8). Both figures show a homogeneous, high positive correlation pattern, with highest values around the location itself (Constantinople) and a slow decrease further away from the centre of the Byzantine Empire. This pattern suggests that warm or cold conditions around Constantinople were homogeneously distributed across the central and eastern Mediterranean. Lower positive correlations, still significant, can be found over the Balkans, Italy, and northern Africa. The explained variance (correlation squared) in the latter regions is around 25 to 30 per cent. In palaeoclimatology, it is assumed that the modern relationships (identified in instrumental

---

58   Gogou et al., "Climate variability and socio-environmental changes in the northern Aegean (NE Mediterranean) during the last 1500 years".
59   Luterbacher et al., "A Review of 2000 Years of Paleoclimatic Evidence in the Mediterranean"; Xoplaki et al., "The Medieval Climate Anomaly and Byzantium: A Review of the Evidence on Climatic Fluctuations, Economic Performance and Societal Change"; Labuhn et al., "Climatic changes and their impacts in the Mediterranean during the first millennium AD".

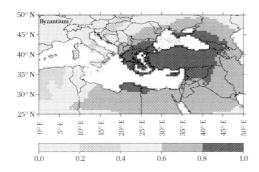

FIGURE 1.7
Spatial Spearman correlation between detrended winter temperature around Constantinople and other areas across the central and eastern Mediterranean for the period 1951–2010. All correlations higher then approximately 0.2 are statistically significant at the 5% level

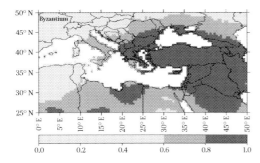

FIGURE 1.8
As Figure 1.7 but for decadal means covering the period 1901–2010. All correlations higher then approximately 0.6 are statistically significant at the 5% level

data) remained constant through times for which we can only use proxy information (i.e., the principles of uniformitarianism and stationarity are applied). In other words, instrumental evidence averaged over a specific season or over a decade is associated with a similar spatial pattern in the present times and in the pre-instrumental period. The homogeneity in the past – for which we have only proxy data – will be smaller compared to the instrumental data (such as those used to produce Figures 1.7 and 1.8) because a proxy does not resolve the full range of temperature variations (i.e., it is not a thermometer; it does not measure temperature) as well as that it includes various uncertainties associated with the proxy (see above). Thus, the significant areas might also be slightly smaller than as shown in Figures 1.7 and 1.8.

7   Conclusions

Our current understanding of hydrological and thermal variability during Byzantine times and the identification of larger-scale patterns is hampered by the scarcity, density, and seasonal bias of proxy climate records, as well as the proxy sensitivity and the existence of contradictory data and – last but not least – of dating uncertainties for specific proxies. This restricts the comparison between different archives and limits the efforts to disentangle the effects of climate forcing. In order to fully comprehend palaeoclimate variability in Byzantine times, it is thus necessary to build bridges between disciplines such as archaeology, history, palaeo-environmental science, and climate modelling in order to transcend disciplinary boundaries and examine the climate history of the eastern Mediterranean basin within a comparative context. This approach has been very successfully addressed by the Princeton Climate Change and History Research Initiative over the last few years and some national and international initiatives, programmes and projects and will continue over the next years, hopefully substantially updating the overview presented in this chapter.[60]

Acknowledgements

Elena Xoplaki acknowledges support by the Academy of Athens and the Greek "National Research Network on Climate Change and its Impact" (200/937) and the German Federal Ministry of Education and Research (BMBF) projects NUKLEUS (01LR2002F) and ClimXtreme/CROP (01LP1903C).

Bibliography

Bar-Matthews, M., Ayalon, A., Gilmour, M.A., Matthews, A., Hawkesworth, C.J., "Sea-land oxygen isotopic relationships from planktonic foraminifera and speleothems in the Eastern Mediterranean region and their implication for paleorainfall during interglacial intervals", *Geochimica et Cosmochimica Acta* 67 (2003), pp. 3181–99.

Bini, M. et al., "Hydrological changes during the Roman Climatic Optimum in northern Tuscany (Central Italy) as evidenced by speleothem records and archaeological data", *Journal of Quaternary Science* 35 (2020), pp. 791–802.

Bozyiğit, C. et al., "Middle-late Holocene climate and hydrologic changes in the Gulf of Saros (NE Aegean Sea)", *Marine Geology*, 443 (2022), 106688, https://doi.org/10.1016/j.margeo.2021.106688.

Bradley, R.S., *Paleoclimatology: Reconstructing Climates of the Quaternary. (3rd edition)*, San Diego, (2014).

Büntgen, U. et al., "Cooling and societal change during the Late Antique Little Ice Age from 536 to around 660 AD", *Nature Geoscience* 9, no. 3 (2016), pp. 231–36.

---

60 Haldon et al., "The Climate and Environment of Byzantine Anatolia: Integrating Science, History and Archaeology".

Camuffo, D., Enzi, S., "The analysis of two bi-millennial series: Tiber and Po river floods", in: P.D. Jones, R.S. Bradley, J. Jouzel (eds.), *Climatic Variations and Forcing Mechanisms of the Last 2000 Years*, Berlin 1996, pp. 433–50.

Cheng, H., et al., "The climate variability in northern Levant over the past 20,000 years", *Geophysical Research Letters* 42 (2015), pp. 8641–50.

Cook, B.I., Anchukaitis, K.J., Touchan, R., Meko, D.M., Cook, E.R., "Spatiotemporal drought variability in the Mediterranean over the last 900 years", *Journal of Geophysical Research: Atmospheres*, 121 (2016), pp. 2060–74.

Cook, E.R., et al., "Old World megadroughts and pluvials during the Common Era", *Science Advances* 1, no. 10 (2015), e1500561.

Danladi, I.B., Akçer-Ön, S., "Solar forcing and climate variability during the past millennium as recorded in a high altitude lake: Lake Salda (SW Anatolia)", *Quaternary International* 486 (2018), pp. 185–98.

Dean, J.R. et al., "Eastern Mediterranean hydroclimate over the late glacial and Holocene, reconstructed from the sediments of Nar Lake, central Turkey, using stable isotopes and carbonate mineralogy", *Quaternary Science Reviews* 124 (2015), pp. 162–74.

Eastwood, W.J., Leng, M.J., Roberts, N., Davis, B., "Holocene climate change in the eastern Mediterranean region: a comparison of stable isotope and pollen data from Lake Gölhisar, southwest Turkey", *Journal Quaternary Science* 22 (2007), pp. 327–41.

Esper, J., Konter, O., Klippel, L., Krusic, P.J., Büntgen, U., "Pre-instrumental summer precipitation variability in northwestern Greece from a high-elevation *Pinus heldreichii* network", *International Journal of Climatology* 41 (2021), pp. 2828–39.

Finné, M. et al., "Speleothem evidence for late Holocene climate variability and floods in Southern Greece", *Quaternary Research* 81 (2014), pp. 213–27.

Finné, M., Woodbridge, J., Labuhn, I., Roberts, N.C., "Holocene hydro-climatic variability in the Mediterranean: A synthetic multi-proxy reconstruction", *The Holocene* 29 (2019), pp. 847–63.

Fleitmann, D. et al., "Holocene ITCZ and Indian monsoon dynamics recorded in stalagmites from Oman and Yemen (Socotra)", *Quaternary Science Reviews* 26 (2007), pp. 170–88.

Fleitmann, D. et al., "Timing and climatic impact of Greenland interstadials recorded in stalagmites from northern Turkey", *Geophysical Research Letters* 36 no. 19 (2009), L19707.

Flohr, P. et al., "Late Holocene droughts in the Fertile Crescent recorded in a speleothem from northern Iraq", *Geophysical Research Letters* 44 (2017), pp. 1528–36.

Francke, A. et al., "A Late Glacial to Holocene record of environmental change from Lake Dojran (Macedonia, Greece)", *Climate of the Past* 9 (2013), pp. 481–98.

Frisia, S., Borsato, A., Spötl, C., Villa, I.M., Cucci, F., "Climate variability in the SE Alps of Italy over the past 17 000 years reconstructed from stalagmite records", *Boreas* 34 (2005), pp. 445–55.

Fritz, S.C., "Deciphering climatic history from lake sediments", *Journal of Paleolimnology* 39 (2008), pp. 5–16.

Frogley, M.R., Griffiths, H.I., Heaton, T.H.E., "Historical biogeography and Late Quaternary environmental change of Lake Pamvotis, Ioannina (North-western Greece): evidence from ostracods", *Journal of Biogeography* 28 (2001), pp. 745–56.

Gogou, A. et al., "Climate variability and socio-environmental changes in the northern Aegean (NE Mediterranean) during the last 1500 years", *Quaternary Science Reviews* 136 (2016), pp. 209–28.

Göktürk, O.M., "Climate in the Eastern Mediterranean through the Holocene inferred from Turkish Stalagmites" (PhD thesis), University of Bern (2011).

Göktürk, O.M., Fleitmann, D., Badertscher, S., Cheng, H., Edwards, R.L., Tüysüz, O., "Climate on the southern Black Sea coast during the Holocene: implications from the Sofular Cave record", *Quaternary Science Reviews* 30 (2011), pp. 2433–45.

Haldon, J. et al., "The Climate and Environment of Byzantine Anatolia: Integrating Science, History and Archaeology", *Journal of Interdisciplinary History* 45 (2014), pp. 113–61.

Harris, I., Osborn, T.J., Jones, P. et al. Version 4 of the CRU TS monthly high-resolution gridded multivariate climate dataset. Sci Data 7, 109 (2020). https://doi.org/10.1038/s41597-020-0453-3.

Heinrich, I., Touchan, R., Liñán, I.D., Vos, H., Helle, G., "Winter-to-spring temperature dynamics in Turkey derived from tree rings since AD 1125", *Climate Dynamics* 41 (2013), pp. 1685–1701.

Ingram, M.J., Underhill, D.J., Farmer, G., "The use of documentary sources for the study of past climates", in T.M.L. Wigley, M.J. Ingram, G. Farmer (eds.), *Climate and History*, Cambridge (1981), pp. 180–213.

Izdebski, A., Pickett, J., Roberts, N., Waliszewski, T., "The environmental, archaeological and historical evidence for regional climatic changes and their societal impacts in the Eastern Mediterranean in Late Antiquity", *Quaternary Science Reviews* 136 (2016), pp. 189–208.

Jacobson, M.J., Flohr, P., Gascoigne, A., Leng, M.J., Sadekov, A., Cheng, H., et al. (2021). Heterogenous late Holocene climate in the Eastern Mediterranean – The Kocain Cave record from SW Turkey. Geophysical Research Letters, 48, e2021GL094733. https://doi.org/10.1029/2021GL094733.

Jones, M.D. et al., "Human impact on the hydroenvironment of Lake Parishan, SW Iran, through the late-Holocene", *Holocene* 25 (2015), pp. 1651–61.

Jones, M.D. et al., "20,000 years of societal vulnerability and adaptation to climate change in southwest Asia", *WIREs Water* 6 (2019), e1330, https://doi.org/10.1002/wat2.1330.

Jones, M.D., Roberts, N., Leng, M.J., Türkeş, M., "A high-resolution late Holocene lake isotope record from Turkey and links to North Atlantic and monsoon climate", *Geology* 34 (2006), pp. 361–64.

Kaniewski, D., Van Campo, E., Weiss, H., "Drought is a recurring challenge in the Middle East", *Proceedings of the National Academy of Sciences of the United States of America* 109 (2012), pp. 3862–67.

Katrantsiotis, C. et al., "Eastern Mediterranean hydroclimate reconstruction over the last 3600 years based on sedimentary *n*-alkanes, their carbon and hydrogen isotope composition and XRF data from the Gialova Lagoon, SW Greece", *Quaternary Science Reviews* 194 (2018), pp. 77–93.

Klippel, L. et al., "A 1286-year hydro-climate reconstruction for the Balkan Peninsula", *Boreas* 47 (2018), pp. 1218–29.

Klippel, L. et al., "A 1200+ year reconstruction of temperature extremes for the northeastern Mediterranean region", *International Journal of Climatology* 39 (2019), pp. 2336–50.

Kondrashov, D., Feliks, Y., Ghil, M., "Oscillatory modes of extended Nile River records (A.D. 622–1922)", *Geophysical Research Letters* 32 (2005), L10702.

Konter, O., Krusic, P.J., Trouet, V., Esper, J., "Meet Adonis, Europe's oldest dendrochronologically dated tree", *Dendrochronologia* 42 (2017), p. 12.

Koutsodendris, A. et al., "Climate variability in SE Europe since 1450 AD based on a varved sediment record from Etoliko Lagoon (Western Greece)", *Quaternary Science Reviews* 159 (2017), pp. 63–76.

Kuzucuoğlu, C., Dörfler, W., Kunesch, S., Goupille, F., "Mid- to late-Holocene climate change in central Turkey: the Tecer Lake record", *Holocene* 21 (2011), pp. 173–88.

Labuhn, I., Finné, M., Izdebski, A., Roberts, N., Woodbridge, J., "Climatic changes and their impacts in the Mediterranean during the first millennium AD", in A. Izdebski, M. Mulryan (eds), *Environment and Society in the Long Late Antiquity*, Leiden 2019, pp. 65–88.

Lacey, J.H., Francke, A., Leng, M.J., Vane, C.H., Wagner, B., "A high-resolution Late Glacial to Holocene record of environmental change in the Mediterranean from Lake Ohrid (Macedonia/Albania)", *International Journal of Earth Sciences* 104 (2015), pp. 1623–38.

Lamy, F., Arz, H.W., Bond, G.C., Bahr, A., Pätzold, J., "Multicentennial-scale hydrological changes in the Black Sea and northern Red Sea during the Holocene and the Arctic/North Atlantic Oscillation", *Paleoceanography and Paleoclimatology* 21 (2006), PA1008.

Luterbacher, J., 48 coauthors, "Mediterranean climate variability over the last centuries: A review", in: P. Lionello, P. Malanotte-Rizzoli, R. Boscolo (eds.), *The Mediterranean Climate: an overview of the main characteristics and issues*, Amsterdam 2006, pp. 27–148.

Luterbacher, J. et al., "A Review of 2000 Years of Paleoclimatic Evidence in the Mediterranean", in P. Lionello at al. (eds.), *The climate of the Mediterranean region: from the past to the future*, Amsterdam 2012, pp. 87–185.

Luterbacher, J. et al., "European summer temperatures since Roman times", *Environmental Research Letters* 11 (2016), 024001.

Magny, M. et al., "Contrasting patterns of precipitation seasonality during the Holocene in the south- and north-central Mediterranean", *Journal of Quaternary Science* 27 (2012), pp. 290–96.

Masi, A., Francke, A., Pepe, C., Thienemann, M., Wagner, B., Sadori, L., "Vegetation history and paleoclimate at Lake Dojran (FYROM/Greece) during the Late Glacial and Holocene", *Climate of the Past* 14 (2018), pp. 351–67.

National Research Council of the National Academies of the USA (NRC), *Surface Temperature Reconstructions for the Last 2,000 Years*, Washington, DC. 2006, https://doi.org/10.17226/11676.

Newfield, T.P., "The Climate Downturn of 536–50", in: S. White, C. Pfister, F. Mauelshagen (eds.), *The Palgrave Handbook of Climate History*, London (2018), pp. 447–93.

Noone, S. et al., "Progress towards a holistic land and marine surface meteorological database and a call for additional contributions", *Geoscience Data Journal* 2020, https://doi.org/10.1002/gdj3.109.

Ocakoğlu, F. et al., "A 2800-year multi-proxy sedimentary record of climate change from Lake Çubuk (Göynük, Bolu, NW Anatolia)" *Holocene* 26 (2016), pp. 205–21.

Orland, I.J. et al., "Climate deterioration in the Eastern Mediterranean as revealed by ion microprobe analysis of a speleothem that grew from 2.2 to 0.9 ka in Soreq Cave, Israel", *Quaternary Research* 71 (2009), pp. 27–35.

Overpeck, J., Whitlock, C., Huntley, B. et al., "Terrestrial Biosphere Dynamics in the Climate System: Past and Future", in K.D. Alverson, R. Bradley, T.F. Pedersen (eds.), *Paleoclimate, Global Change and the Future*, Berlin 2003, pp. 81–103.

Preiser-Kapeller, J., "A Collapse of the Eastern Mediterranean? New results and theories on the interplay between climate and societies in Byzantium and the Near East, ca. 1000–1200 AD", *Jahrbuch der Österreichischen Byzantinistik* 65 (2015), 195–242.

Preiser-Kapeller, J., *Der Lange Sommer und die Kleine Eiszeit. Klima, Pandemien und der Wandel der Alten Welt von 500 bis 1500 n. Chr.*, Vienna 2021.

Preiser-Kapeller, J./Mitsiou, E., "The Little Ice Age and Byzantium within the Eastern Mediterranean, ca. 1200–1350: An Essay on Old Debates and New Scenarios", in M. Bauch/G.J. Schenk (eds.), *The Crisis of the 14th Century. Teleconnections between Environmental and Societal Change?*, Berlin 2020, pp. 190–220.

Raphael, K., *Climate and political climate: environmental disasters in the Medieval Levant*, (Brill's Series in the History of the Environment, 3), Leiden 2013.

Regattieri, E., Zanchetta, G., Drysdale, R.N. et al., "Lateglacial to Holocene trace element record (Ba, Mg, Sr) from Corchia Cave (Apuan Alps, central Italy): paleoenvironmental implications", *Journal of Quaternary Science* 29 (2014), pp. 381–92.

Repapis, C.C., Schuurmans, C.J.E., Zerefos, C.S., Ziomas, J., "A note on the frequency of occurrence of severe winters as evidenced in monastery and historical records from

Greece during the period 1200–1900 A.D.", Theoretical and Applied Climatology 39 (1989), pp. 213–17.

Roberts, N., Reed, J.M., "Lakes, Wetlands, and Holocene Environmental Change", in: J. Woodward (ed.), *The Physical Geography of the Mediterranean*, Oxford 2009, pp. 255–86.

Roberts, N. et al., "The tempo of Holocene climatic change in the eastern Mediterranean region: new high-resolution crater-lake sediment data from central Turkey", *Holocene* 11 (2001), pp. 721–36.

Sadori, L. et al., "Climate, Environment and Society in Southern Italy during the Last 2000 Years. A Review of the Environmental, Historical and Archaeological Evidence", *Quaternary Science Reviews* 136: Special Issue: Mediterranean Holocene Climate, Environment and Human Societies (2016), pp. 173–88.

Schilman, B., Bar-Matthews, M., Almogi-Labin, A., Luz, B., "Global climate instability reflected by eastern Mediterranean marine records during the late Holocene", *Palaeogeography, Palaeoclimatololgy, Palaeoecology* 176 (2001), pp. 157–76.

Schönbein, J. et al., "The chronicle of Ibn Tawq – over 7000 climate and environmental records from Damascus, Syria, AD 1481 to 1501", in R. Glaser, M. Kahle, R. Hologa (eds.), *tambora.org data series vol. II*, 2016, pp. 1–558, http://dx.doi.org/10.6094/tambora.org/2016/c157/serie.pdf.

Sharifi, A. et al., "Abrupt climate variability since the last deglaciation based on a high-resolution, multi-proxy peat record from NW Iran: The hand that rocked the Cradle of Civilization?", *Quaternary Science Review* 123 (2015), pp. 215–30.

Sinha, A. et al., "Role of climate in the rise and fall of the Neo-Assyrian Empire", *Science Advances* 5 (2019), eaax6656, https://doi.org/10.1126/sciadv.aax6656.

Stevens, L.R. et al., "Proposed changes in seasonality of climate during the Lateglacial and Holocene at Lake Zeribar, Iran", *Holocene* 11 (2001), pp. 747–55.

Telelis, I.G., *Μετεωρολογικά φαινόμενα και κλίμα στο Βυζάντιο*, Athens 2004.

Telelis, I.G., "Climatic Fluctuations in the Eastern Mediterranean and the Middle East AD 300–1500 from Byzantine Documentary and Proxy Physical Paleoclimatic Evidence – A Comparison", *Jahrbuch der Öesterreichischen Byzantinistik* 58 (2008), pp. 167–208.

Telelis, I., "Byzantine Textual Sources for Climatic and Environmental Developments", *Byzantine Symmeikta* 32 (2022), pp. 17–41.

Ülgen, U.B., Franz, S.O., Biltekin, D. et al., "Climatic and environmental evolution of Lake Iznik (NW Turkey) over the last ~4700 years", *Quaternary International* 274 (2012), pp. 88–101.

Vogt, S. et al., "Assessing the Medieval Climate Anomaly in the Middle East: The potential of Arabic documentary sources", *PAGES Magazine* 19 (2011), pp. 28–29, https://doi.org/10.22498/pages.19.1.28.

Vogt, S., Glaser, R., Schliermann, E. et al., "From Data to Climatological Indices – The Case of the Grotzfeld Data Set", in: R. Glaser, M. Kahle, R. Hologa (eds.), *tambora.org data series vol. 1*, (2016) pp. 1–7, https://doi.org/10.6094/tambora.org/2016/c156/article.pdf.

Vogt, S. et al., "The Grotzfeld Data Set – Coded Environmental, Climatological and Societal data for the Near and Middle East from AD 801 to 1821", in R. Glaser, M. Kahle, R. Hologa (eds.), *tambora.org data series vol. 1*, (2016), pp. 1–650, http://dx.doi.org/10.6094/tambora.org/2016/c156/serie.pdf.

Warken, S.F. et al., "Reconstruction of late Holocene autumn/winter precipitation variability in SW Romania from a high-resolution speleothem trace element record", *Earth and Planetary Science Letters* 499 (2018), pp. 122–33.

Wick, L., Lemcke, G., Sturm, M., "Evidence of Lateglacial and Holocene climatic change and human impact in eastern Anatolia: high-resolution pollen, charcoal, isotopic and geochemical records from the laminated sediments of Lake Van, Turkey", *Holocene* 13 (2003), pp. 665–75.

Widell, M., "Historical Evidence for Climate Instability and Environmental Catastrophes in Northern Syria and the Jazira: The Chronicle of Michael the Syrian", *Environment and History* 13 (2007), pp. 47–70.

Woodbridge, J., Roberts, N., "Late Holocene climate of the Eastern Mediterranean inferred from diatom analysis of annually-laminated lake sediments", *Quaternary Science Reviews* 30 (2011), pp. 3381–92.

Xoplaki, E., et al., "The Medieval Climate Anomaly and Byzantium: A Review of the Evidence on Climatic Fluctuations, Economic Performance and Societal Change", *Quaternary Science Reviews* 136 (2016), pp. 229–52.

Xoplaki, E., et al., "Modelling Climate and Societal Resilience in the Eastern Mediterranean in the Last Millennium", *Human Ecology* 46 (2018), pp. 363–79.

Xoplaki, E., et al., "Wet season Mediterranean precipitation variability: influence of large-scale dynamics and trends", *Climate Dynamics* 23 (2004), pp. 63–78.

Xoplaki, E., et al., "Hydrological changes in Late Antiquity: spatio-temporal characteristics and socioeconomic impacts in the Eastern Mediterranean", in: P. Erdkamp, J.G. Manning (eds.), *Climate Change and Ancient Societies in Europe and the Near East*. Palgrave Studies in Ancient Economies. Palgrave Macmillan, Cham. https://doi.org/10.1007/978-3-030-81103-7_18 (2021).

Zanchetta, G. et al., "Multiproxy record for the last 4500 years from Lake Shkodra (Albania/Montenegro)", *Journal of Quaternary Science* 27 (2012), pp. 780–89.

Zanchetta, G. et al., "The So-called '4.2 event' in the central Mediterranean and its climatic teleconnections", *Alpine and Mediterranean Quaternary* 29 (2016), 5–17.

CHAPTER 2

Palynology and Historical Research

Adam Izdebski

1   Why Should Palynology Be of Interest to Historians?

Palynology is the study of pollen and spores dispersed by plants in the process of reproduction. Although in the context of this book palynology appears as one of the methods for studying environmental history, the discipline of palynology does not in fact concentrate on the past alone. Many palynologists study modern pollen; they want to understand, for instance, how different allergens spread outside of the areas where the pollen-producing plants actually live, and how they affect human health. However, a number of palynologists dealing with stratigraphy, historical geology, and palaeontology focus on the past and study fossil pollen preserved in a variety of natural archives, such as lakes, lagoons, peat bogs or archaeological sites. They study the history of vegetation of the area that surrounds a given natural archive by establishing the geographical distribution of many plant groups that, over time, were present in the area. Both research approaches, whether interested in the present or the past, are based on a detailed understanding of plant biology and ecology, as well as the complex technical skills involved in distinguishing between pollen grains of different sizes and shapes and attributing them to particular plant taxa, be they species, genera, or families.

The result of the palynologist's work is the creation of what historians, scientists, and archaeologists often call "pollen evidence". It comes in the form of qualitative information (on the presence or absence of key taxa) and quantitative data (i.e. finds of pollen grains of these taxa that inform us about changes in local and regional plant landscape across time). This chapter sets out to explain where the pollen evidence comes from and how historians (and archaeologists) can use it for the purpose of their own research. It is meant as an introduction to palynology for humanities scholars – historians and archaeologists in particular.[1] The chapter is divided in three parts. The first describes the process by which scientists obtain samples of fossil pollen and produce the raw data. The second part presents different methods of interpreting pollen

---

1   More scientifically minded introductions include: Eastwood, *General Issues in the Study of Medieval Logistics*; Gaillard, *Pollen Methods and Studies: Archaeological Applications*.

data in the context of historical analyses. The final part discusses major interpretative problems associated with using pollen data for the study of the past. In this way, this chapter hopes to prepare a historian of Byzantium, or indeed any other period, to engage critically either with pollen data itself or with historical and scientific studies that base their conclusions on such evidence.

It is important to incorporate palynological evidence into the study of history for two reasons. Firstly, it expands our source base for understanding any period of history of interest to us. As environmental historians have demonstrated over the course of the last half a century, landscape reflects the course of human history in very complex and subtle ways.[2] In ecological terms, wherever there are humans, they are part of a larger social ecosystem that involves the environment – and human social, political, economic and cultural structures are part of this ecosystem and contribute to its shape.[3] This means that studying the landscape can also give us a better idea of the social phenomena that were at work in creating and maintaining it, as if we were looking at a negative to get an idea of how the original photographed object actually looked. To put it briefly: pollen data offer historical evidence that can no longer be disregarded and can be used to address important historical questions for which there would otherwise continue to be no convincing answer.

There is also a second reason why the study of history would benefit from engaging with palynology. Pollen evidence comes from the "historical archives" of nature itself: it is the voice from nature's own past that nature's own mechanisms have preserved. In studying it, we are listening to the voice of actors of history – plants and landscapes – to whom we would otherwise be deaf. In this respect, incorporating palynology into our historical narratives is not dissimilar to doing oral history or any other type of "subaltern" studies: it is giving voice to the voiceless in our traditional historical narratives. In fact, it means not only giving voice to nature itself, but also to those social groups who were in close contact with nature – such as Byzantine peasants – but who were disregarded by the written sources produced by the elites. Pollen evidence, therefore, makes it possible to decentre, both socially and geographically, our narratives of the past.

---

2 A classic work on this topic: Cronon, *Changes in the Land*.
3 Crumley, *Historical Ecology*; Balée, *The Research Program of Historical Ecology*.

2   Where Does Pollen Evidence Come From?

The male apparatus of flowers produces pollen grain to transfer genetic material to the female reproductive structure and allow for plant reproduction. Pollination, the dispersal of pollen grain, is mainly entrusted to wind. To increase the success of the pollen spreading, it is produced in large quantities, making it ubiquitous on the earth. Each grain is constituted by various substances and layers, the external one being made of sporopollenin, the most chemically inert of all biological polymers. Sporopollenin can be degraded only by strong oxidation and, for this reason, pollen is preserved even for thousands of years. Usually, when it falls on a peat bog or a lake it becomes part of a humid environment that offers the anaerobic conditions necessary for preservation. All manner of materials and items end up in lakes or peat bogs, like dust, pollen, seeds, shell, insects, and sediment, and so is deposited at the bottom of the water body. Debris from rivers and edges are the main source of sediment and its quantity and composition may change as climatic conditions and vegetation vary. The quantity of sediment accumulated is not constant every year. On the contrary, it may vary consistently over time depending on local geochemical and physical conditions. Nonetheless, the accumulation rises year by year, building up thick layers of what scientists regard as "natural archives". This conglomerate of organic and inorganic matter contains information about the environmental conditions – including the plant landscape – at the time of sediment formation, that is in a specific year, a decade or a few decades in the past. These sediments become an invaluable source of data for a range of scientific disciplines, including palaeoclimatology, geology, and palynology.

All the pollen grains produced by plants in a given place and at a given time are often collectively referred to as a "life assemblage". No life assemblage is ever preserved in its entirety and without disturbance, so the composition of pollen grains actually present in the sediments is recognized to be a different phenomenon, and is referred to as the "death assemblage". This is what palynologists are able to study, and the problems associated with reconstructing a life assemblage and a living landscape that existed at a certain moment in the past on the basis of a measured death assemblage preserved until today are discussed in the final part of this chapter.

Sediments containing fossil pollen are usually obtained through coring in order to maintain the chronological succession of layers. A long, narrow core of lake or peat sediments is retrieved with the help of specialized equipment (and often using rafts, if the core is located in the middle of a lake or lagoon), put into a plastic tube and taken to a laboratory, where it is sampled. Samples

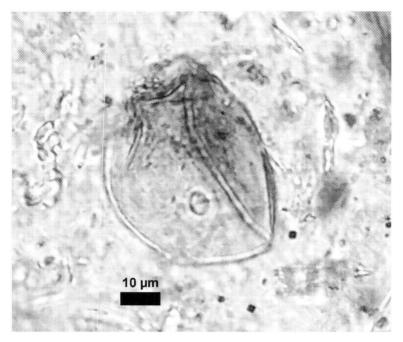
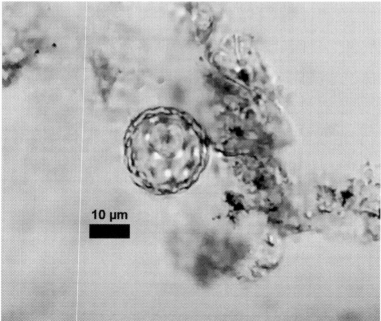

FIGURE 2.1A–B Microscope photographs of pollen grains of wheat (*Triticum/Avena*) and amaranth (*Amaranthaceae*)
COURTESY OF DR. ALESSIA MASI

can be taken at different physical intervals through the core, depending on the sedimentation rate and research strategy of a given project; usually, the entire core would be sampled at equal intervals and additional sampling would be done for intervals of interest (i.e those thought to belong to a given moment in time, or showing interesting changes in sediment composition). Samples of sediment are then processed in a laboratory to extract pollen from the sediment, and the end-result of this process is the preparation of microscope samples with pollen grains from each core sample. These pollen grains are then identified, based on their morphological characteristics (size, shape, characteristic physical features, etc.), to a specific plant species, genus or family. The level of taxonomic attribution – whether a palynologist can be sure she or he is seeing pollen of a specific plant or rather a whole type of plants – depends on how characteristic the pollen grain is: in some cases, the shapes of pollen grains are so unique that a species attribution is possible (as would be the case for a number of forest trees); in other cases, interspecies differences are impossible to detect and attribution remains rather general (as with the majority of grasses). As a result, in palynology, one speaks of "plant taxa" (sing. "taxon") rather than plant species, since the plant/vegetation categories the discipline uses belong to different levels of the taxonomic hierarchy.

Many grains must be counted for each sample if the analysis is to be representative. Usually, the counting ranges between 300 and 1000 grains, and the number of grains counted depends on how much time a palynologist can devote to a given core (and what level of analysis one wants to achieve) and on how well the pollen grains in the sediments are preserved. Several factors influence the quantity of grains in sediment, i.e. the pollen preservation, like the type of sediment, the taphonomic process, the deposition time, the atmospheric conditions during pollination, the chemical treatment applied in the laboratory, etc. All these different aspects are taken into consideration by palynologists to establish the best (target) count for each sequence. The aim is to achieve a fairly large variety of plant taxa representative for each sample. At times, this could mean counting several hundreds of grains, especially if the sample were dominated by a single plant taxon, such as lake-edge vegetation or pine (a tree that produces huge amounts of pollen). In such a situation, increasing the number of pollen grains that are identified and counted increases the quality of the data with the inclusion of rare taxa (the more plants that are included, the more detailed can be the interpretation). In other cases, a palynologist might be unable to count more than 300 grains, when pollen preservation in the sediment would not be good (and there are lakes – including in Greece and Turkey – where sediments have very low pollen preservation, too low for any meaningful pollen analysis to be undertaken). As a result, palynologists speak of a "counting strategy" (as much as there is also a "sampling strategy"!), which takes into account the desired information density and sensitivity of the final data and constitutes the approach to solving the problems inherent to the sediment core being studied. In this context, it is important to remember that pollen analysis is a complex and time-consuming process: processing a single sediment core may take several months for one experienced person working full-time. This means that sampling and counting strategies must strike a balance between the always limited resources that are available and the research goals of the project that involves pollen analysis.

Parallel to counting pollen grains, an investigator needs to establish a chronology of the core. Initially, all we know is that depth is parallel to time, that is, those samples that are lower in our sediment core should be older than those higher up, closer to the top of the core. However, in some cases – for instance, in tectonically active areas – even that is not certain, as there could occur post-depositional changes to the sediment (including as a result of human activity). For a pollen dataset, in order to become meaningful and comparable to other data, each sample has to be assigned a calendar age. This could be done in two ways, either by counting distinguishable sediment layers year by year down the core starting in the present (that is, moving back in time) or by taking radiocarbon dates for a few samples of organic matter recovered from the core and estimating the age of all the other samples. The first situation is the best we can dream of, as it provides very accurate and specific dating, but such a clear deposition is quite rare. In the Balkans and Anatolia, there are only three lakes (Nar and Van in Turkey, Butrint in Albania) that have annually-laminated sediments, so – technically speaking – they could be provided with a robust varve chronology (based on distinguishable and countable annual sediment layers known as "varves"). Such lakes are prevalent in other parts of Europe, such as in northeastern Poland. As a result, radiocarbon dating and age-depth modelling are the dominant methods of providing core samples with estimates of calendar age.

Typically, the process of establishing a chronology for a core involves two steps: radiocarbon dating and mathematical modelling. Radiocarbon dating or, rather, the measurement of radioactive carbon isotopes in a given sample, is a standard method used in archaeology and the natural sciences, so there is no need to discuss its technicalities in this introduction. To put it briefly, it is based on the fact that radiocarbon isotopes decay over time. Their amount is constant in living organisms because they are constantly consumed with food, but, upon death, that resupply ends but isotopes continue to decay. By comparing the amount of stable carbon isotopes against the products of decay of the radioactive carbon, we can reconstruct when a given organism actually ceased to obtain new radioactive carbon; that is, when it died. What matters in the context of palynology, is that radiocarbon dates are always approximate, and they involve two types of uncertainties.

First of all, there is always a measurement error, as with every laboratory measurement, and even though this error is now often less than 50 years, it still exists. This means that a date always comes as a range, usually reported as one standard deviation from the mean (e.g., ±50).

Secondly, the amount of radioactive carbon in the atmosphere (and consequently in plants, animals, and humans) is not stable. Instead, it fluctuates over time depending on variations in solar activity, and, as a result, the theoretical date based on laboratory measurements (including measurement error) – and provided by a laboratory as the end result – needs to be calibrated into actual calendar years. Calibration curves, available separately for the two hemispheres, northern and southern, and for the seas (as radioactive carbon "behaves" differently in marine environments), are mainly based on dendrochronology. Dendrochronology is an independent technique for dating tree rings. Comparing dendro-dates with radiocarbon ones makes it possible to estimate the variation in solar activity over time (and, consequently, in the isotopic composition of the air) and thus enables us to calibrate (to "correct") raw radiocarbon dates, based on laboratory measurements. The calibrated date (the "real" one) can deviate from the radiocarbon one by tens or hundreds of years and, for some periods (for instance, the Roman times), calibration can actually extend the time window attributed to a sample that is being dated. Raw and calibrated radiocarbon dates should be distinguished in a publication, and thus, conventionally, "C14 BP" or "BP" would be used for giving uncalibrated dates (raw results of laboratory measurements), whereas "cal BP" would be used for a calibrated date (BP meaning "before present", that is before AD 1950; radiocarbon dating was first developed in the 1950s; the same "C14/cal" convention would apply to dates given in AD/BC or CE/BCE years).

It is never possible nor rational (given the uncertainties inherent to this method) to ^{14}C-date all the samples from a given core. Rather, on the basis of a number of radiocarbon dates and a number of other dates available for the core (tephra layers reflecting known volcanic eruptions; approximate date for the core top; coin and artefact finds; etc.) an investigator develops a mathematical model that approximates the (changing) relationship between depth and time in a given core. Such a model takes into account the uncertainties involved in laboratory measurement and calibration, and hence one obtains age estimates, again with confidence intervals, rather than precise dates (even if the result comes in the form of single years, i.e. best-age estimates provided with confidence intervals, e.g. 587 ± 49 cal BP). It is the confidence intervals

TABLE 2.1   Dates used for the calculation of Lake Abant age-depth model

ID	^{14}C age (raw laboratory age)	cal year BP (age in calendar years, when known)	Confidence intervals (±)	Depth within the sediment core in cm
Surface (assumed)		−20	50	0
GrN-18627	880		60	196
GrN-18628	2920		60	475
GrN-18629	3880		60	595
GrN-18630	9880		110	961
GrN-12794	10320		90	996

(which define the range in which the real date is present with at least 95 per cent certainty) that an historian should consider in historical interpretation: whether the probable date for a given vegetation change overlaps, precedes, etc., some other historical phenomena of interest. It should be borne in mind that there is no way of determining where exactly within the confidence interval the true date would actually fall (in other words, what were the few years, decade or more, when living plants around a site produced the pollen grains that a palynologist counted). Moreover, it should be also borne in mind that, within the same core, chronological reliability can differ between samples, especially when the number of radiocarbon dates is relatively small. Samples "closer" to radiocarbon dates would have more reliable dating and smaller confidence intervals, while those more distant (in depth, hence, also in time) will have dates that involve more uncertainty.

Figure 2.2 presents an age-depth model for a lake in northwestern Turkey, known as Abant Gölü.[4] It is based on four radiocarbon dates that the original Dutch–Turkish team obtained in the 1980s (expressed in raw ^{14}C years) and on an assumed date for the top (surface) of the core (expressed in calendar years) (see Table 2.1). Each of the five dates used for age-depth modelling is provided with confidence intervals: either resulting from the potential error of laboratory measurement (in the case of radiocarbon dates), or from the uncertainty about the quality of the very top part of the core and lake sediments (in this

---

4   For more details on this lake, see: Izdebski, *The Changing Landscapes of Byzantine Northern Anatolia*; Izdebski, *A Rural Economy in Transition*, 186–90; original publication of this lake's C14 dates and pollen data: Bottema, Woldring, Aytuğ, *Late Quaternary Vegetation History of Northern Turkey*.

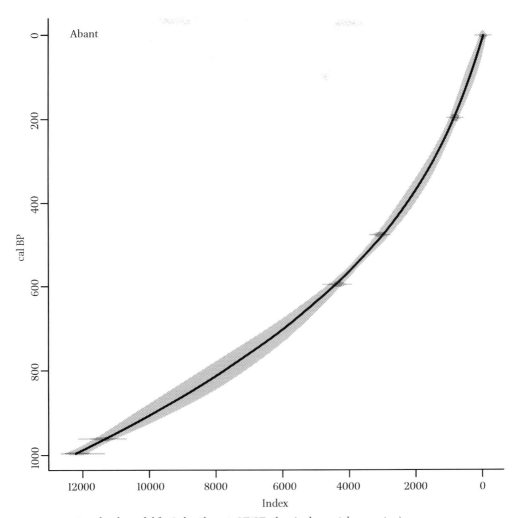

FIGURE 2.2 Age-depth model for Lake Abant in NW Turkey (polynomial regression)

case, there was no way of establishing with certainty whether the top layer of the sediments were deposited right before the core was taken from the lake). A computer software, Clam, developed by Martin Blaauw, was used to model the (changing) relation between core depth and time (expressed in calendar years BP) in this lake.[5] Given the location and the number of dates, the selected method was a polynomial regression, but there are a variety of approaches that could be applied, ranging from linear functions (in particular when just two dates are available) to Bayesian statistics. Dark blue points on the diagram

---

5   Blaauw, *Methods and Code for 'Classical' Age-Modelling of Radiocarbon Sequences.*

represent the four radiocarbon dates with their confidence intervals (thicker for the immediate interval of one standard deviation, with 67 per cent probability that the actual calendar date falls within this range); the same applies to the light blue point, which is the assumed date for the core top (surface). The black line connecting all five points represents the best age estimates for each core depth, centimetre after centimetre. The grey area on either side of this line represents the confidence intervals, which get broader as we move away from the specified radiocarbon dates. Thanks to the age-depth model, which already takes into account the relevant calibration curve, we are able to provide age estimates, with confidence intervals, for all samples from the core, whatever their depth may be. In this way, we transpose the relative chronology of the core, based on depth, into calendar years that enable us to make comparisons with other sites and historical events and processes. In the case of this lake, we are in a relatively good situation, as the sediment accumulation rate seems to have changed gradually over time and we do have a radiocarbon date for the medieval period to make our age estimates for the last two millennia, which are those of interest to byzantinists. This is not always the case, and all factors that have any bearing on a site's chronology should be taken into account and weighted when integrating that site's pollen data into our historical narratives. Fortunately, new techniques, such as Accelerator Mass Spectrometry (AMS), make it possible to reduce the uncertainty involved in the dating, and newer data are often more reliable in this respect than older data. Moreover, calibration curves are constantly being updated, and the same raw radiocarbon dates will often, when calibrated with new curves, translate into different calendar ages. Altogether, this means that old data often benefit from recalibration and remodelling, and in the future the reliability of dating should continue to improve.

The final step in processing a sediment core and producing pollen data, once pollen grains from all samples are counted and calendar ages for all samples are estimated, is the transformation of the pollen counts into proportional values. Among the possible mathematical treatments of the data, the most common are percentage, concentration, and influx (the normalization of data according to sedimentation rate). A percentage is obtained by dividing the pollen count available for each plant in a sample by the total number of pollen grains that were counted in the sample (the so-called pollen sum). The resulting values are the pollen data that scientists, archaeologists, and historians actually interpret. Importantly, pollen sums do not necessarily contain all the pollen grains counted in a sample. Sometimes investigators exclude some taxa (e.g., lake-edge vegetation or grasses) in order to get a more realistic idea of how the proportions of other plants in the wider landscape changed over time. An example of pollen data from Lake Abant is shown in Table 2.1.

TABLE 2.2 Exemplary pollen data from Lake Abant, NW Turkey. Only the percentages of selected plants are reported

Depth (cm)	cal years BP (best estimate)	Pollen sum	Walnut %	Pine %	Oak %	Grasses %	Chestnut %	Olive %	Vine %
270	1279	777	0.26	30.37	7.08	3.47	0.13	0.13	0.13
290	1411	617	1.13	19.29	14.75	12.32	0.00	0.16	0.32
310	1549	810	0.25	26.54	5.19	5.80	0.00	0.00	0.00
330	1695	661	0.00	72.92	1.82	0.91	0.45	0.30	0.00

Usually, a pollen dataset consists of tens of different plants. Most can provide information on the environment. The first data are provided by the AP/NAP curve in which the Arboreal Plant percentage is shown against the Non-Arboreal Plant percentage. High forest cover, in a very general interpretation, is usually related to high humidity and low human impact. The presence or absence of key taxa in a time period is very informative. For instance, cultivation is evident from the presence of cereals correlated with large tracts of deforested areas. Arboreal cultivation, too, can be clearly visible in the high presence of the pollen of cultivated trees such as chestnut, olive, or walnut. Finally, the presence of some plants and non-pollen palynomorphs can provide information on pasturelands. Figure 2.3 presents a simplified pollen profile of a Mediterranean site, with all the different indicators and groups of pollen taxa.

Pollen data can be accessed by historians in different ways. First of all, one should always consult the original publication of the data (usually in the form of a clearly structured journal article), where all the information on the site location, geology, hydrology, modern local climate and vegetation, sediment formation, dating, etc. are presented. Such a publication always presents the data in the form of a standard pollen diagram, which makes it possible to interpret changes in local or regional vegetation cover over time. An overview and discussion of the pollen evidence available for the Byzantine world can be found in recent works on Byzantine environmental history written by the author of this chapter.[6] If more detailed information is necessary and one wishes to access the pollen data themselves for the purpose of a more detailed or comparative study, palynologists very often upload them to the European

---

6 Izdebski, *A Rural Economy in Transition*; Izdebski, Koloch, Słoczyński, *Exploring Byzantine and Ottoman Economic History with the Use of Palynological Data: A Quantitative Approach*.

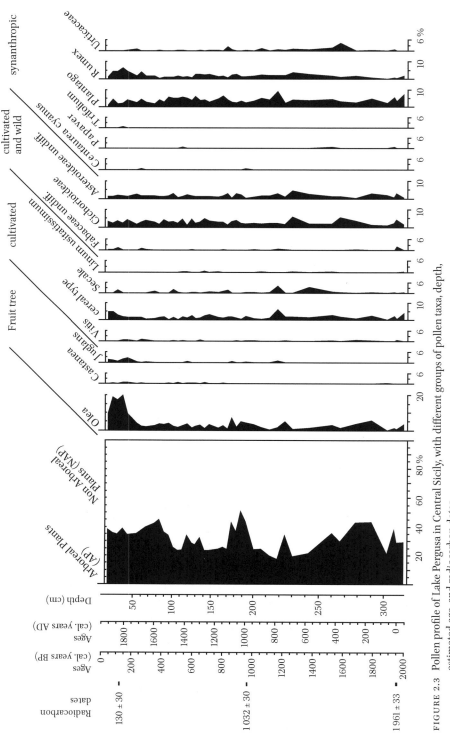

FIGURE 2.3 Pollen profile of Lake Pergusa in Central Sicily, with different groups of pollen taxa, depth, estimated age, and radiocarbon dates
COURTESY OF DR. ALESSIA MASI. DATA PUBLISHED IN SADORI ET AL. 2016

Pollen Database (http://europeanpollendatabase.net/index.php) or Pangaea (https://pangaea.de/).[7] Otherwise, one should contact the original investigator.

3   How to Use Pollen Evidence in Historical Research

Now that we know how the data are obtained, it is worth asking how they can actually be integrated into the historical narrative, along with other sources and types of evidence. In terms of the pollen data themselves, there are at least three ways. First, one can focus on a single site and analyse its vegetation history in the context of our historical and archaeological knowledge of relevant periods. Second, one can study simultaneously and compare a number of sites from the same area, taking into account any potential chronological issues. Analysis of the spatial patterns that emerge from the data can help us to reconstruct not only ecological and economic processes, but also some aspects of social and political change, or even military activity. Third, one can apply mathematical methods to the data in order to establish trends common to a larger number of sites, which allows for a wider-reaching generalization. Such regional trends of vegetation change can then be compared with other sources of information about the society and economy in the past, with the view of achieving an even more profound understanding of socio-economic developments and environmental change. All of these approaches have been applied to Byzantine contexts in recent years, and all three will be discussed in the following part of this chapter.

The most famous of single-site studies is probably the pioneering article by John Haldon about Lake Nar, published in 2007 in a *Festschrift* for Johannes Koder.[8] This ground-breaking study used unique pollen data from Lake Nar in Cappadocia – provided with robust annual dates, based on varve counting – to interpret the social and economic consequences of the Arab raiding in early medieval Anatolia. Haldon demonstrated that the descriptions of the damage wrought by the Arabs in the eastern parts of Byzantine Anatolia are confirmed by what we learn about the landscape of Cappadocia from the Lake Nar data. The overlap between these two types of evidence is almost ideal: the area around this small lake became desolate, with no significant signs of agriculture, in precisely the decade for which the first major Arab raiding is recorded in the textual sources. Thus, Lake Nar was crucial in making byzantinists aware

---

7   Fyfe et al., *The European Pollen Database*.
8   Haldon, *Cappadocia Will Be Given over to Ruin and Become a Desert*; full pollen data for this site were published a year later: England et al., *Historical Landscape Change in Cappadocia*.

of the potential of the pollen evidence and paved the way for future applications of these data to the study of Byzantium.

Unsurprisingly, therefore, other examples of such single-site studies abound in the Byzantine context. It will suffice to cite just three, all of which show the potential of pollen evidence in supplementing the historical knowledge derived from the more "traditional" historical and archaeological sources. Moving westwards, Lake Bafa near Miletus, investigated by a German team in the 1990s, has recently been re-studied in the context of new corings and the Byzantine Miletus excavations. The pollen data from Lake Bafa turned out to show some degree of continuity in land use and agriculture in the hinterlands of Miletus from Late Antiquity to the tenth–eleventh century, thus surviving the Invasion Period and pointing to a substantial degree of continuity, otherwise undocumented. However, in the Middle Byzantine times, already before the coming of the Turks, there occurred a transition to pastoralism, while the most intensive phase of olive cultivation occurred in the fourteenth century.[9]

Another example of pollen data that corrected our narrative of regional socio-economic change comes from Southern Italy. Lago Alimini Piccolo, located in the hinterlands of Otranto, yielded results that showed a remarkable recovery of agriculture in this part of Italy as early as the eighth century: less than two hundred years after the devastating Gothic wars of the mid-sixth century. Already in this period, pollen data show nascent olive cultivation that would later become the main focus of agricultural and economic activity in the region, known as the Salento. If we were to rely on the written sources alone, we would only notice a thriving agrarian economy in this part of Italy some two hundred years later.[10] Another Italian lake, Lago di Pergusa in central Sicily, actually tells a different, equally surprising story (Figure 2.3). Here, large-scale cereal farming that had developed in the fourth and fifth century AD in the context of the re-structuring and expansion of the Central Mediterranean grain trade after the foundation of Constantinople persisted well into the eighth century. Again, other types of evidence (for instance, wax seals and in particular numismatic evidence from the island) provide evidence for the economic life on Sicily in the early medieval period, but none is able to demonstrate the degree of continuity that was characteristic for its agriculture in this period. Altogether, in this case, pollen data help to explain the continuing importance of Sicily for the Eastern Roman state, as well as its

---

9   Izdebski, *The Environmental History of the Hinterland in Late Antiquity and after – the 'status quaestionis' in 2020*.
10 Arthur, Fiorentino, Grasso, *Roads to Recovery*.

political and economic decline – partly related to a climatic change (long-term desiccation) – that paved the way for the Islamic conquest.[11]

In all of these cases, information we obtain from the pollen evidence that comes from a specific location and presents its microhistory adds to an already complex historical puzzle comprising different types of evidence. As is always the case when a new piece of the evidentiary puzzle turns up, it is necessary to adjust the existing historical narratives and reassess our visions of the past. When new information is introduced into the historical debate *en masse*, the overall effect on our understanding of the past can be even stronger. This is made possible when a number of sites that offer pollen evidence are analysed at the same time with the view of reconstructing more general patterns of environmental, agricultural, economic, and, ultimately, social changes. This approach has been applied in particular to Byzantine Anatolia, where pollen evidence is available in larger quantities for three important regions: Bithynia, the northeast, and the southwest (especially Lycia and Pisidia). These data were first analysed by the author of this chapter, and further studies elaborated on this interpretation, demonstrating the potential that pollen evidence has to change our vision of Byzantine history.[12]

Figure 2.4 shows the location of sites – lakes and peat bogs – that provide pollen data for Anatolia in the medieval period. The colour of each circle represents the pattern according to which agriculture in this area changed during the transition from Late Antiquity into the early medieval period. In general, there were three dominant models of change: (1) continuation of mixed and relatively intensive agriculture that included cultivation of cereals, olives, vines, and nuts in different proportions, as well as animal herding – shown here in green; (2) transition into an agricultural regime predominantly focused on cereal cultivation, often supplanted by animal herding – shown in yellow; (3) disappearance of indicators of agriculture from the pollen record, interpreted as abandonment of the area – shown in black. As the map shows, each of the colours clusters in a different part of Anatolia. Black – abandoned areas – dominate in the southeast, the main theatre of war between the Eastern Roman Empire and the Islamic Caliphate; this part of Anatolia was constantly raided by the Arabs for several decades, from the late seventh century onwards. Green concentrates either in the secluded and safe areas of Pisidia and Eastern

---

11   Sadori et al., *Climate, Environment and Society in Southern Italy during the Last 2000 Years. A Review of the Environmental, Historical and Archaeological Evidence.*
12   Izdebski, *A Rural Economy in Transition*; Haldon et al., *The Climate and Environment of Byzantine Anatolia*; Haldon, *The Empire That Would Not Die*; another example of such regional-scale analysis can be found in: Preiser-Kapeller, *A Collapse of the Eastern Mediterranean?*

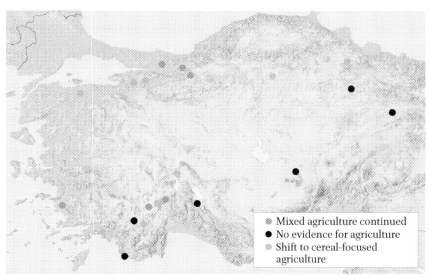

FIGURE 2.4 Pollen sites in Anatolia that provide information on the course of the late antique – early medieval transition in agriculture
Note: Based on Map 9 from Izdebski, *A Rural Economy in Transition*

Bithynia (in the proximity of Constantinople, which would have been an important and easily available market for agriculture produce other than grain and animals). Finally, yellow is the dominant colour, which suggest that, overall, the economy of early medieval Byzantine Anatolia on one hand adjusted to the unsafe conditions of constant war with the Arabs and, on the other, transitioned into an agricultural regime focused on grain production and animal herding – both products being necessary for the army and relatively easy to transport. As John Haldon has recently argued, it is very probable that this shift was encouraged by the state and is recognizable in the taxation system adopted by the Eastern Roman government in the early medieval period.

Any attempt at a more detailed analysis of the scale and timing of regional vegetation change, i.e. one that moves beyond the rather qualitative and cautious analysis of regional patterns described above, requires the development of new mathematical tools that are well-tuned to the specific problems inherent to pollen data. Palynologists themselves have been trying to apply quantitative modelling to their data for more than a decade, with very interesting results.[13] Recently, the results of one such project were interpreted in an historical context and demonstrated that there is a surprisingly close overlap between the spatial distribution of predominantly open landscapes

---

13   Hellman et al., *The REVEALS Model, a New Tool to Estimate Past Regional Plant Abundance from Pollen Data in Large Lakes*.

(dominated by agriculture and pastoral activities) in Europe at the beginning of the Common Era and the territorial extent of the Roman Empire.[14]

In the Byzantine context, a team from Warsaw applied new analytical methods developed with the help of econometrics to the pollen evidence from the Balkans and Anatolia.[15] The result was a reconstruction of trends of vegetation change, featuring very many plant taxa, for seven regions of the Byzantine and Ottoman world. The great advantage of this method is that it makes it possible to compare the scales and chronologies of vegetation change between different regions, and to make relatively easy comparisons with other types of evidence, such as numismatic data or settlement numbers.[16] Figure 2.5 shows such trends in cereals for four major regions of the Byzantine world: two in Greece and two in Western Anatolia. Values on the Y axes show how the share of cereal pollen in the overall pollen sum in this region changed over time (please note: in order to facilitate the comparison between the regions, two Y axes are used). This can be interpreted as the relative importance and spatial scale of cereal cultivation in each region, approximating the area within each region that was taken up by cereal fields. A quick glance at the diagram shows that every region experienced two peaks of cereal farming during the Byzantine era. The first usually falls within broadly understood Late Antiquity, while the second started during the Middle Byzantine period. However, despite all four regions thus sharing a similar trajectory of growth and contraction in cereal farming, the timings of these two peaks are different in each case. In Late Antiquity, both Macedonia and Pisidia experienced a decline in cereal farming after the middle of the fifth century. In both cases, this can be related to economic transformations or security conditions specific to each of these regions. In Greece and Bithynia, an expansion of cereal cultivation only became visible in the fifth century, and in Greece this trend continued well into the early medieval period, reversing only after AD 700. Again, these regional developments, while they can be interpreted as regional responses to more general incentives for agricultural and economic growth, also reveal that local conditions largely determined the scale, timing, and nature of these responses. The same can be said about the Middle Byzantine cycle of growth: it occurs earliest in Pisidia, where it also ends very quickly: this can be interpreted in the context both of the region's relative security and economic significance for the Eastern Roman state in the early Middle Ages and of its relatively early experiencing

---

14 Woodbridge, Roberts, Fyfe, *Vegetation and Land-Use Change in Northern Europe during Late Antiquity*.
15 The method itself first was developed in a Central European context: Izdebski et al., *On the Use of Palynological Data in Economic History*.
16 Such comparisons were undertaken on a significant scale in: Xoplaki et al., *The Medieval Climate Anomaly and Byzantium*.

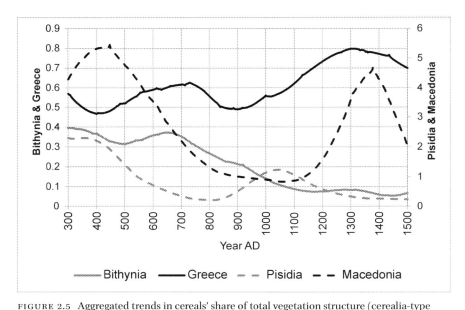

FIGURE 2.5 Aggregated trends in cereals' share of total vegetation structure (cerealia-type pollen, in %) in four major regions of the Byznatine world. Note that different regions' values are shown on different vertical axes
Note: Based on: Izdebski, Koloch, Słoczyński, *Exploring Byzantine and Ottoman Economic History with the Use of Palynological Data: A Quantitative Approach.*

the consequences of the coming of the Turks to Anatolia. Interestingly, in the case of Greece and of Macedonia (where it is even more visible), the expansion of cereal farming halts in the middle of the fourteenth century, which may be related to the outbreak of the Black Death in the Aegean. It is also worth looking at the differences in the scale of change between regions. For instance, in some, the levels of cereal cultivation achieved in the later-medieval period roughly equalled those attained in Late Antiquity (which is the case for Macedonia), while in others they were notably different: in Greece they were higher, in Pisidia and Bithynia they were lower. (In fact, in Bithynia the Middle Byzantine cycle of expansion in cereal farming is visible in a temporary cessation of the early-medieval declining trend rather than in a notable increase in cereal pollen.)

4 What Challenges Are Involved in Using Pollen Evidence in Historical Research?

Despite pollen data having so many different uses for addressing historical questions, their interpretation is far from straightforward. This final section of this chapter will discuss various biases and problems one must bear in mind when making use of pollen data in historical research.

4.1   Issues of Chronology

Since the chronologies of the pollen data are based on radiocarbon dates (except for the unique cases of varve chronologies), they always involve a large degree of probabilistic reasoning, which an historian should be aware of and be able to engage in proficiently.[17] In the context of historical research, this means considering dating uncertainties: changes that we see in the pollen record of individual sites are almost never dated with an annual or even decadal precision. On the contrary, we are only able to determine a specific period ranging from a few decades to more than a century during which a specific change in local vegetation occurred. Such age ranges, however, can then be matched with known natural or historical events, such as climatic changes (often also dated very imprecisely) or wars. Nevertheless, such chronological comparisons will always remain probabilistic (which can be said of much of the traditional historical and archaeological research, even if the uncertainties have different root causes). In the case of more quantitative methods of analysis and interpretations, they develop their own methods for handling chronological uncertainties, which can largely be reduced. We also need to consider the fact that the pollen curve consists of a series of "pictures of the past". There could be some events (changes in vegetation cover) that our curve should register but that, as a result of sedimentation processes or even sampling strategy, is not evident in the pollen analysis because it is located in the middle between two such "pictures". This problem can be overcome only by high-resolution analysis (with a very "dense" sampling strategy).

4.2   Spatial Representativeness

Throughout this chapter, the words "local" and "regional" have been used in different contexts, intentionally avoiding the question of the actual spatial representativeness of the pollen data. This issue is very complex and deserves a separate discussion. Pollen data from a specific site may represent conditions more locally (within a radius of just a few kilometres) or an entire region (tens of kilometres) and in fact usually represent both at the same time. This depends on a number of factors that must be interpreted individually for each pollen site. First, one should consider the size of the sedimentation basin. A large lake would "catch" more of the regional "pollen rain" and thus reflect more regional than local conditions. A small lake or a peat bog would usually

---

17   Many pollen sites, especially older ones, have not been radiocarbon-dated at all – these should not be used in historical interpretations. See Blaauw, *Out of Tune*.

record mostly local conditions. Second, local topography also matters: high mountain chains may separate even a fairly large lake from relatively proximate areas, to give just one of many possible examples of topography influencing the composition of the pollen assemblage that actually gets deposited in a given archive. Third, of equal importance are the winds prevailing over an area during the pollination season. Finally, while considering all of these factors, one has to take into account differences in pollination behaviour and pollen morphology between the plants themselves. Some plants, such as pine, produce pollen that is carried by wind over huge distances (tens or even hundreds of kilometres). Other plants produce pollen that is dispersed very locally (vine or cereals), while many others fall somewhere in between. Altogether, this means that most often a single pollen dataset would record both local and regional pollen signals.

4.3   *Detectable and Undetectable Plants*

Not all plants produce significant quantities of pollen that can be identified by scientists. This is the case with most cultivated trees except for walnut, grapevine, olive and chestnut, all four of which are relatively easy for palynologists to detect. However, even if orchards with other fruit trees were strongly present within a given landscape, we are unable to see that, as most fruit trees belong to the Rosaceae family. Within this family, the pollens of different species are so similar to each other that we cannot tell if we are dealing with a specific fruit tree or some other, non-cultivated species – and this is one of the largest families, with hundreds of species. Some other important cultivars, such as various vegetables and pulses, or millet, cause the same problem: they produce pollen that is not different enough from the pollen of other plants from the same family or genus. In some cases, the abundances of that pollen are so high that they cannot represent a natural assemblage, but in general we are unable to tell whether the pollen that a palynologist counted in a sample actually came from a cultivated plant or a wild species that lived somewhere in an open or semi-open landscape. Nevertheless, pollen data are able to show us changes in major Mediterranean cultivars (cereals, vine, olive, and nuts) as well as in forest species and open landscape vegetation. What is more, there are so-called secondary anthropogenic indicators (also known as "synanthropic plants") – that is, plants that, despite not being cultivated by humans, actually thrive in manmade or man-disturbed ecosystems. These are, for instance, pasture components resistant to grazing, or common weeds of cereal fields. These plant taxa have been identified in Mediterranean contexts and they can greatly help in interpreting the course of vegetation change as it is seen in the pollen record.[18]

4.4 *Equifinality*

Pollen data are a powerful tool for reconstructing how vegetation and a landscape changed over time. However, on their own, they are unable to tell us much more than that. Plant ecosystems are sensitive to many different factors, ranging from variations in local climate, through the spread of plant disease and parasite species, to animal and human activity (be it agriculture or war destruction). This problem is called "equifinality", as different causes could have led to the same end result – that is, the same change in the local vegetation structure.[19] In historical interpretations, therefore, this data becomes meaningful only when accompanied by other types of sources that make it possible to hypothesize the reasons for a given vegetation change. Just as with other historical and archaeological sources, when read in isolation, pollen data would remain problematic and difficult to interpret. When integrated more holistically with all the other information about the past that we have, however, they offer a powerful way of increasing our understanding of the past.

Acknowledgements

This chapter is based on research funded by the National Science Centre, Poland through the Centre's postdoctoral fellowships scheme (DEC-2012/04/S/HS3/00226) and the Ministry of Science and Higher Education, Poland (National Programme for the Development of the Humanities, 2016–2019). The author would also like to thank Dr. Alessia Masi (Sapienza Università di Roma) for a critical reading of the initial manuscript and for providing some of the illustrations for this chapter.

---

18 Behre, *The Interpretation of Anthropogenic Indicators in Pollen Diagrams*; Bottema, Woldring, *Anthropogenic Indicators in the Pollen Record of the Eastern Mediterranean*; Brun, *Anthropogenic Indicators in Pollen Diagrams in Eastern France*; Rattighieri et al., *Anthropogenic Pollen Indicators (API) from Archaeological Sites as Local Evidence of Human-Induced Environments in the Italian Peninsula*; Mercuri et al., *Olea, Juglans and Castanea*.

19 Bunting and Middleton, *Equifinality and Uncertainty in the Interpretation of Pollen Data*.

Bibliography

Arthur, P., Fiorentino, G., Grasso, A.M. "Roads to Recovery: An Investigation of Early Medieval Agrarian Strategies in Byzantine Italy in and around the Eighth Century", *Antiquity* 86, no. 332 (2012), pp. 444–55.

Balée, W. "The Research Program of Historical Ecology", *Annual Review of Anthropology* 35 (2006), pp. 75–98, https://doi.org/10.1146/annurev.anthro.35.081705.123231.

Behre, K.-E. "The Interpretation of Anthropogenic Indicators in Pollen Diagrams", *Pollen et Spores* 23, no. 2 (1981), pp. 225–45.

Blaauw, M. "Methods and Code for 'Classical' Age-modelling of Radiocarbon Sequences", *Quaternary Geochronology* 5, no. 5 (2010), pp. 512–18, https://doi.org/10.1016/j.quageo.2010.01.002.

Blaauw, M. "Out of Tune: The Dangers of Aligning Proxy Archives", *Quaternary Science Reviews* 36, no. 12 (2010), pp. 38–49, corrected proofs, https://doi.org/10.1016/j.quascirev.2010.11.012.

Bottema, S., Woldring, H. "Anthropogenic Indicators in the Pollen Record of the Eastern Mediterranean", in S. Bottema, G. Entjes-Nieborg, W. van Zeist (eds.), *Man's Role in the Shaping of the Eastern Mediterranean Landscape*, Rotterdam 1990, pp. 231–64.

Bottema, S., Woldring, H., Aytuğ, B. "Late Quaternary Vegetation History of Northern Turkey", *Palaeohistoria* 35/36 (1993/1994), pp. 13–72.

Brun, C. "Anthropogenic Indicators in Pollen Diagrams in Eastern France: A Critical Review", *Vegetation History and Archaeobotany* 20, no. 2 (2011), pp. 135–42, https://doi.org/10.1007/s00334-010-0277-8.

Bunting, M.J., Middleton, R. "Equifinality and Uncertainty in the Interpretation of Pollen Data: The Multiple Scenario Approach to Reconstruction of Past Vegetation Mosaics", *The Holocene* 19, no. 5 (2009), pp. 799–803, https://doi.org/10.1177/0959683609105304.

Cronon, W., *Changes in the Land: Indians, Colonists, and the Ecology of New England*, New York 1983.

Crumley, C.L., *Historical Ecology: Cultural Knowledge and Changing Landscapes*, Santa Fe 1994.

Eastwood, W.J. "Palaeoecology and Eastern Mediterranean Landscapes: Theory and Practice", in J.F. Haldon (ed.), *General Issues in the Study of Medieval Logistics: Sources, Problems and Methodologies*, History of Warfare vol. 36, Leiden 2006, pp. 119–58.

England, A., Eastwood, W.J., Roberts, N., Turner, R., Haldon, J. "Historical Landscape Change in Cappadocia (Central Turkey): A Palaeoecological Investigation of Annually-Laminated Sediments from Nar Lake", *The Holocene* 18, no. 8 (2008), pp. 1229–45.

Fyfe, R., de Beaulieu, J.-L., Binney, H.A., Bradshaw, R., Brewer, S., Le Flao, A., Finsinger, W., et al. "The European Pollen Database: Past Efforts and Current Activities", *Vegetation History and Archaeobotany* 18, no. 5 (2009), pp. 417–24, https://doi.org/10.1007/s00334-009-0215-9.

Gaillard, M.-J. "Pollen Methods and Studies: Archaeological Applications", in S. Elias (ed.), *Encyclopedia of Quaternary Science*, Oxford 2007, pp. 2570–95.

Haldon, J. "'Cappadocia Will Be Given over to Ruin and Become a Desert'. Environmental Evidence for Historically-Attested Events in the 7th–10th Centuries", in Koder, J., Belke, K. (eds.), *Byzantina Mediterranea: Festschrift für Johannes Koder zum 65. Geburtstag*, Wien 2007, pp. 215–30.

Haldon, J. *The Empire That Would Not Die: The Paradox of Eastern Roman Survival, 640–740*, Cambridge, Mass. 2016, http://bibdata.princeton.edu/bibliographic/9674734.

Haldon, J., Roberts, N., Izdebski, A., Fleitmann, D., McCormick, M., Cassis, M., Doonan, O., et al. "The Climate and Environment of Byzantine Anatolia: Integrating Science, History and Archaeology", *Journal of Interdisciplinary History* 45, no. 2 (2014), pp. 113–61.

Hellman, S., Gaillard, M.-J., Broström, A., Sugita, S. "The REVEALS Model, a New Tool to Estimate Past Regional Plant Abundance from Pollen Data in Large Lakes: Validation in Southern Sweden", *Journal of Quaternary Science* 23, no. 1 (2008), pp. 21–42 https://doi.org/10.1002/jqs.1126.

Izdebski, A. *A Rural Economy in Transition. Asia Minor from Late Antiquity into the Early Middle Ages*, (Journal of Juristic Papyrology Supplement Series, 18), Warsaw 2013.

Izdebski, A. "The Changing Landscapes of Byzantine Northern Anatolia", *Archaeologica Bulgarica* 16 no. 1 (2012), pp. 47–66.

Izdebski A., "The Environmental History of the Hinterland in Late Antiquity and after – the ›status quaestionis‹ in 2020", *Archäologischer Anzeiger*, no. 1 (2020), pp. 248–251.

Izdebski, A., Koloch, G., Słoczyński, T. "Exploring Byzantine and Ottoman Economic History with the Use of Palynological Data: A Quantitative Approach", *Jahrbuch der Österreichischen Byzantinistik* 65 (2015), pp. 67–110.

Izdebski, A., Koloch, G., Słoczyński, T., Tycner, M. "On the Use of Palynological Data in Economic History: New Methods and an Application to Agricultural Output in Central Europe, 0–2000 AD", *Explorations in Economic History* 59 (2016), pp. 17–39.

Mercuri, A.M., Bandini Mazzanti, M., Florenzano, A., Montecchi, M.C., Rattighieri, E. "Olea, Juglans and Castanea: The OJC Group as Pollen Evidence of the Development of Human-Induced Environments in the Italian Peninsula", *Quaternary International* 303: *The transition from natural to anthropogenic-dominated environmental change in Italy and the surrounding regions since the Neolithic* (2013), pp. 24–42, https://doi.org/10.1016/j.quaint.2013.01.005.

Preiser-Kapeller, J. "A Collapse of the Eastern Mediterranean? New Results and Theories on the Interplay between Climate and Societies in Byzantium and the Near

East, ca. 1000–1200 AD". *Jahrbuch der Österreichischen Byzantinistik* 65 (2015), pp. 195–242.

Rattighieri, E., Montecchi, M.C., Florenzano, A., Mercuri, A.M., Bandini Mazzanti, M., Torri, P. "Anthropogenic Pollen Indicators (API) from Archaeological Sites as Local Evidence of Human-Induced Environments in the Italian Peninsula", *Annali Di Botanica* 3 (2013), pp. 143–53.

Sadori, L., Giraudi, C., Masi, A., Magny, M., Ortu, E., Zanchetta, G., Izdebski, A. "Climate, Environment and Society in Southern Italy during the Last 2000 Years. A Review of the Environmental, Historical and Archaeological Evidence", *Quaternary Science Reviews*, 136: *Special Issue: Mediterranean Holocene Climate, Environment and Human Societies* (2016), pp. 173–88, https://doi.org/10.1016/j.quascirev.2015.09.020.

Woodbridge, J., Roberts, N., Fyfe, R. "Vegetation and Land-Use Change in Northern Europe during Late Antiquity: A Regional-Scale Pollen-Based Reconstruction", in A. Izdebski, M. Mulryan (eds.), *Environment and Society in the Long Late Antiquity*, Leiden 2019, pp. 105–18.

Xoplaki, E., Fleitmann, D., Luterbacher, J., Wagner, S., Haldon, J.F., Zorita, E., Telelis, I., Toreti, A., Izdebski. A. "The Medieval Climate Anomaly and Byzantium: A Review of the Evidence on Climatic Fluctuations, Economic Performance and Societal Change", *Quaternary Science Reviews* 136: *Special Issue: Mediterranean Holocene Climate, Environment and Human Societies* (2016), pp. 229–52, https://doi.org/10.1016/j.quascirev.2015.10.004.

CHAPTER 3

The Byzantine "Ecosystem": Evidence from the Bioarchaeological Record

Chryssi Bourbou

1 Humans and the Environment: A Millennia-Long Affair

Modern populations often complain about environmental degradation due to unsuitable practices of development that led to increases in toxic hazards and severe air pollution, linking these environmental changes to illnesses. In 2016, the World Health Organization published the most comprehensive and systematic report on the environmental causes of disease and how various diseases are influenced by environmental factors in current societies.[1]

The "ecosystem" refers to the compound and interdependent relationship that exists between humans and their natural and cultural environment. Humans have demonstrated their ability to adapt to their environment using cultural mechanisms (i.e., medical practices), and to deal with illness and potential disability through physiological and genetic adjustments to changes at the individual and population level, respectively. Since the plasticity of the human skeleton permits continuous adaptation to natural or cultural changes, it can serve as a repository that potentially displays the various roles held by an individual during his or life and the physical responses to disease. Thus, for the reconstruction of health and disease patterns and the complex interaction between humans and the environment in the past, the contribution of bioarchaeology is essential.[2]

The basic first step in every study of human skeletal remains is their macroscopic analysis, which includes estimation of age and determination of sex, as well as recording of the observed pathological conditions (paleopathology). This first step is usually accompanied by imaging methods, such as plain radiology – still the most popular method for identifying lesions

---

1 Prüss-Ustün et al., "Preventing Disease".
2 Bioarchaeology is the study of human skeletal remains contextualized within the available archaeological and/or historical evidence, see Larsen, "Bioarchaeology", p. 3; Buikstra, "Preface", pp. xvii–xx. Throughout this chapter the term "bioarchaeology" is referring to the study of human remains only.

that are not visible macroscopically. Nevertheless, an increase in the use of Computed Tomography (CT) is currently noted where "slices" of bones offer a more detail view of pathological conditions or biomechanical changes.³ In the last decades, bioarchaeological studies have benefited from the development of new tools of investigation. These new methods – being principally destructive in nature – can be divided into: a) ancient pathogen DNA analysis (molecular analysis for, e.g., the diagnosis of diseases affecting only the soft tissues or the identification of the specific organism causing a disease),⁴ b) histological analysis (analysis of the microstructure of sections of bones and teeth using different types of microscopy, thus allowing more specific diagnosis of a disease),⁵ and c) the application of stable isotope analysis (analysis of chemical constituents in bones and teeth, such as strontium and oxygen for detecting mobility patterns, and, more widely used, carbon and nitrogen for investigating dietary patterns).⁶

In particular, the development and etiology of pathological conditions may be the result of a number of interlacing factors, both intrinsic (i.e., the immune system, age and sex of the individual) and extrinsic (i.e., subsistence, diet, population density, levels of hygiene, geographical location, and climate). Where people live, what they eat or what they do for a living all affect their acquisition of diseases. For example, the type of settlement (i.e., rural or urban), geographic location (e.g., marshy areas, tropical environments), and climatic conditions (especially weather extremes) influence the disease load on a population. Furthermore, effective sewage, clean water supplies, and disposal of domestic waste in conjunction with personal hygiene (i.e., cleaning of the body, clothes, household, and food) affect the sanitary levels at which a population lives.

Various bioarchaeological studies elucidate the impact of environment on human health and disease, as well as the development of specific cultural and physiological mechanisms to adapt to it. It has been suggested that environmental toxicity (high levels of arsenic) has, in association with beliefs about the spiritual world, contributed to the development of the sophisticated artificial mummification system applied by the Chinchoro group on the north coast of Chile.⁷ Arsenic is a severely toxic element causing various maternal – fetal

---

3   See for example, Wanek et al., "Fundamentals".
4   See for example, Nieves-Colón and Stone "Ancient DNA analysis"; Bramanti, "The Use of DNA Analysis".
5   See for example, Schultz, "Paleohistopathology".
6   See for example, Katzenberg, "The Ecological Approach"; Katzenberg and Waters-Rist, "Stable Isotope Analysis".
7   Arriaza, "Arseniasis"; Standen et al., "Chinchorro Mortuary Practices", pp. 69–71.

health complications (i.e., still and premature births, spontaneous abortions). It is thus plausible that the mortuary practice of mummification, especially of non-adult individuals, may have developed as an emotional response to the loss for the diseased offspring and as a symbolic way to ensure the continuity of the group. Lewis has compared four medieval and post-medieval non-adult populations in England in order to assess the effects of environmental conditions – urbanization and later industrialization – to child health.[8] The observed non-adult mortality and disease patterns indicated that environmental conditions have, together with other factors (e.g., urban employment, socio-economic status, weaning and general infant feeding practices), contributed to the differences seen in rural, urban, and industrial settings, but that it was industrialization that had the greatest impact.

Generally, tropical regions are affected more severely by infectious diseases than temperate ones, owing to both biological and environmental factors such as high levels of biodiversity in hosts, vectors, and pathogens.[9] However, infectious diseases are not a "privilege" of tropical environments; in the case of leprosy in Scandinavia, geographic latitude must have played a role, as it appeared to be more common in the south than in northern parts.[10] Furthermore, and rather surprisingly, by the late Middle Ages leprosy declined first in densely populated areas and then in rural communities, possibly indicating that the measures taken immediately (i.e., segregation and institutionalization of affected individuals in towns) had contributed to directly breaking the pathogen chain. Similarly, the link between marshy areas and malaria, specifically *Plasmodium vivax*, provides another example of how climatic conditions, general topography, and geology have played a significant role in the development of the condition. Although malaria does not result in unambiguous skeletal lesions, it results in hemolytic anemia, which can contribute to the development of skeletal lesions known as cribra orbitalia (see below).[11] Gowland and Western have used Geographical Information Systems (GIS) for a spatial analysis of the prevalence of cribra orbitalia in 46 sites (5802 individuals) from Anglo-Saxon England (AD 410–1050), taking in account geographical variables, historically recorded distribution patterns of indigenous malaria, and the habitat of its mosquito vector *Anopheles atroparvus*.[12] Their study demonstrated that individuals living in low-lying regions exhibited higher levels of cribra

8   Lewis, "Impact of Industrialization".
9   Sattenspiel, "Tropical Environments".
10 Boldsen "Leprosy in Medieval Denmark".
11 For an overview on current work on malaria in archaeological populations, see Bourbou, "Health and Disease at the Marshes".
12 Gowland and Western, "Morbidity in the Marshes".

orbitalia than those in non-marshy sites, thus suggesting that *P. vivax* malaria, in conjunction with other comorbidities, are likely to be responsible for the pattern observed.

The examples presented above highlight the complex web of factors that may affect adaptation to a continuously changing environment and predisposition to disease. However, two key points in bioarchaeological studies should be taken under consideration when reconstructing past health and disease patterns. First, those skeletons with lesions may not represent the vulnerable and "unhealthy" individuals, but rather the "healthy" ones – those who survived the acute stage of the disease to then develop bone lesions.[13] Second, that most bone changes as a response to disease are chronic and well healed when observed in the skeletal remains, or that many soft tissue diseases do not affect the skeleton. It is only through an interdisciplinary approach and the overall consideration of environmental and cultural specifics that will enable us to better understand health and disease patterns in the past.

This chapter aims to explore the contribution of bioarchaeology to the investigation of the impact of environmental conditions on human health through the study of specific pathological conditions (i.e., metabolic and hematopoietic conditions, infectious diseases, and trauma) and dietary patterns. Due to the constraints of its length, it should be noted that the main focus is on Greek Byzantine populations (6th–12th centuries AD) and primarily the adult segment of the population; reference will also be made to work in other parts of the Byzantine world that is relevant to our discussion.

2 *Homo Byzantinus* and His Environment

Natural phenomena of extreme or catastrophic character, subsistence crises, pests, and epidemics, are constantly reported in the Byzantine texts. Adverse climatic phenomena (primarily droughts), outbreaks of epidemics – there being no better example than the famous Justinian plague – endemic diseases (i.e., smallpox and malaria), and pests (especially locusts) have formed a stable repertoire where the crisis was in many cases eventually managed by the intervention of a holy man (see also Maguire, Telelis, Mordechai, Eastwood, and Haldon in this volume).[14] Mass graves or unconventional methods of burial (e.g., the use of quicklime in burial contexts has been often interpreted as

---

13   Wood et al., "The Osteological Paradox".
14   See for example, Stathakopoulos, "Reconstructing the Climate"; Stathakopoulos, "Famine and Pestilence"; Stathakopoulos, "Death in the Countryside".

indicating victims of epidemics) are not a frequent find; it seems that the archaeological record remains relatively silent and rarely verifies the disastrous effects of the attested phenomena (see also Tsiamis, Meier in this volume). However, bioarchaeological studies of Byzantine populations are rather patiently putting together fragments of daily encounters with the environment in an attempt to reconstruct possible influences and interactions in a *longue durée*.

Although documentary evidence and artistic representations also depict the bounty of Byzantine nature, this somehow idealistic image of peaceful landscapes and blossomed gardens was definitely not the case of, for example, the Byzantine site of Phaeno, i.e., modern-day Khirbet Fayan in southwestern Jordan. During the Roman and Byzantine era (4th–6th centuries AD), Phaeno was a major copper mining site. The effects of these extensive mining operations have had various environmental consequences, including elevated lead and copper levels in the soil. The study of a small human skeletal collection of 45 individuals recovered from the southern cemetery of the site has revealed interesting information on their origins and disease patterns,[15] as well their level of exposure to the toxic environment produced by mining operations. Copper and lead levels chemical analysis of 35 skeletons demonstrated high concentrations of these elements in almost all individuals, while some of them had notably elevated concentrations, in comparison to a reference sample with "normal" levels of these elements.[16] As such, individuals exposed to these heavy metals likely suffered health consequences from living and performing various activities in the mining camp.

We do not often get such complementary studies of how a specific environmental setting has influenced the living conditions and health patterns of the population, and we only now come to understand the strong association between the environment and Byzantine man. The Early Byzantine period, for example, is characterized as a turbulent era marked by dramatic historical, social, economic, and environmental changes (e.g., invasions, earthquakes, social upheavals). Current bioarchaeological studies have demonstrated that these changes most probably influenced the development of pathological conditions associated with a deficient or poor diet – at least for some individuals.[17]

---

15   Perry et al., "Condemned to *metallum*?".
16   Grattan et al., "Death More Desirable than Life"; González-Reimers et al., "Bone Cadmium and Lead".
17   Bourbou, "Health and Disease".

3 A Healthy and Balanced Diet. Or Maybe Not?

Eating is a fundamental human need and various factors influence dietary choices. The environmental context plays an important role in determining adaptive strategies to access food resources, while socioeconomic and technological factors may also regulate dietary habits by imposing and/or restricting access to particular foodstuff.

Much of our knowledge on Byzantine diet is derived from documentary sources, primarily referring to the sociopolitical and religious elite. Reconstructing Byzantine dietary patterns is a complex task, as it must take into account economic changes, cultural practices, differential access to products based on social discrimination, availability or seasonality of foods, and awareness of the quality and importance of a specific regimen – to name but a few of the factors playing an important role.[18] Our best option is, thus, to apply a multi-disciplinary approach.[19] Researchers today can bring together evidence from different data sets: analysis of fauna, flora, and human remains, with emphasis on specific diseases that could potentially shed more light on the type and adequacy of diet at individual or population level, and isotopic analysis (see also Baron, Izdebski in this volume). Although still few fauna and flora assemblages from Byzantine sites are studied, the analysis of human skeletal remains is far much promising.[20] Despite the promises and pitfalls inherent to each type of information, the great advantage of combining different types of evidence is that they can complement each other.

For many decades now, stable isotope analysis has been widely used at a regional and temporal level to study dietary patterns in past populations, serving as an invaluable addition to archaeological and documentary data by identifying foods that were eaten and defining their relative amounts in the diet.[21] The isotopic analysis of 142 adult humans from eight Byzantine sites (6th–15th centuries AD) throughout Greece suggest that a general "Byzantine

---

18 For an overview, see Bourbou, "Health and Disease", pp. 127–30.
19 Bourbou, "The Biocultural Model Applied".
20 For analysis of faunal remains, see for example, Nobis, "Zur antiken Wild-und Hausterfauna Kretas"; Mylona, "'Etudes zooarchaeologiques"; Mylona, "Τα οστά ζώων"; Mylona, "Fish-Eating in Greece"; for analysis of environmental remains, see for example, van Zeist et al., "Diet and Vegetation"; Sarpaki, "Archaeobotanical Material"; Rabinowitz et al., "Daily Life"; for analysis of human skeletal remains, see for example, Rife, "Isthmia"; and references in Bourbou, "The People", pp. 31–9; Bourbou, "Health and Disease", p. 4, note. 28.
21 An extended presentation on the application of stable isotope analysis for the reconstruction of dietary patterns in archaeological populations is beyond the scope of this chapter; the reader is directed to, for example, Katzenberg, "The Ecological Approach"; Eriksson, "Stable Isotope Analysis of Humans".

diet" existed, despite the large geographical and chronological span of the sites.[22] The isotopic data indicated that the base of the diet was primarily C_3 staples, such as wheat and barley, as already attested in the written sources, and although some millet use was likely, a significant dependence on C_4 grain was not isotopically attested.[23] Millet was broadly considered a grain of lesser quality,[24] and a probable crop failure of the grains primarily in use might have forced the two northern populations where the presence of millet was identified to turn to alternative, albeit inferior, food resources. Documentary and zooarchaeological evidence suggested that the Byzantines highly praised meat and marine food, but their actual consumption has been a controversial issue, as it was thought to be influenced by a number of factors, such as seasonality, price, and fasting rules. However, all eight sites have isotopic results that suggest substantial consumption of meat and/or dairy products. Similarly, the isotopic patterning seen in several groups and the presence of a few individuals with values unambiguously indicating marine resource use suggest that some Greek Byzantine populations consumed significant amounts of marine protein. These results are also very interesting when seen in the cultural context of attitudes towards food, as it seems possible that one factor in the increased consumption of marine resources in the Byzantine era may have been dietary restrictions imposed by the Orthodox Church. Since a number of isotopic studies on medieval Western populations have demonstrated the increasing importance of fish to the diet over time, implicating the impact of fasting regulations and advances in fishing techniques; this is an issue that deserves further investigation.[25]

The isotopic data in conjunction with the observed pathological conditions provide us with a better overview of the interaction between environmental conditions and the adequacy and quality of the foods consumed. The quality of food (i.e., sweetening agents, hard plant tissues, or coarsely ground flour) must have affected the development of dental pathologies in Byzantine populations. The palaeopathological record includes many reports of dental disease and particularly the prevalence of calculus and carious lesions as a reflection of dietary changes. *Dental calculus* (Fig. 3.1) is mineralized bacterial plaque and

---

22 Bourbou et al., "Reconstructing the Diets".
23 A similar predominately C_3 terrestrial based diet is also isotopically documented for Late Antique to Early Byzantine sites in the western Mediterranean, see Fuller et al., "Investigation of diachronic" for S'Hort des Limoners (Ibiza), and Garcia et al., "Régime et societé" for Can Reinés (Mallorca); see also Fuller et al., "Isotopic Reconstruction" for the middle Byzantine site of Sagalassos in southwestern Turkey.
24 Teall, "The Grain Supply", p. 99.
25 Bourbou et al., "Reconstructing the Diets", p. 578.

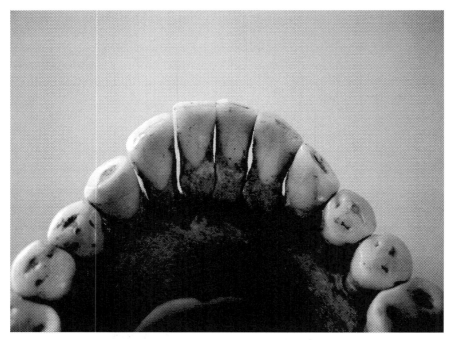

FIGURE 3.1 Alikianos, skeleton 040. Massive concentration of calculus on the mandibular teeth

its formation has been repeatedly attributed to protein consumption.[26] *Carious lesions* are characterized by the local demineralization of dental hard tissues by organic acids produced by bacterial fermentation of dietary carbohydrates.[27] A high prevalence of caries has been broadly linked to consumption of plants, while other foodstuffs are considered as cariostatic (e.g., seafood).[28] The study of eight Greek Byzantine sites has demonstrated that calculus affected 369 teeth (or 11.2 per cent), and carious lesions affected 168 teeth (or 5.1 per cent) of the 3,273 permanent teeth examined. The consumption of considerable amounts of animal protein as evidenced by the isotopic data described above can be suspected to have contributed to the high prevalence of calculus in the sample. Similarly, the isotopic data show a significant input of cariostatic foodstuffs (marine protein) that may have offered some protection against the development of caries, alongside clear evidence of a strong dependence on C_3 plants. It should be noted, though, that although diet plays an important role

26   Lucaks, "Dental Pathology".
27   Idem; Lucaks, "The Caries Corrector Factor".
28   Lieverse, "Diet and Aetiology".

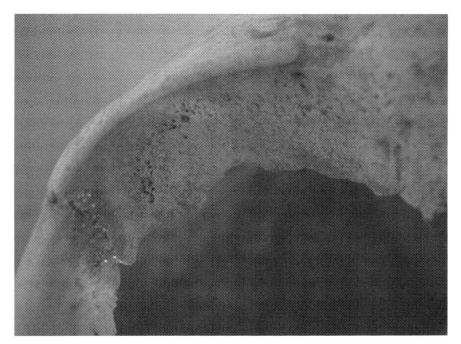

FIGURE 3.2 Alikianos, skeleton 057. Detail of cribra orbitalia

in the formation of caries and calculus, the mechanisms controlling their prevalence are more complex, and diet should be considered as one of a number of possible causative factors.[29]

Evidence of hematopoietic diseases in the presence of *cribra orbitalia* (porous lesions on the orbital roof), and *porotic hyperostosis* (porous lesions on the cranial vault), both resulting from marrow hyperplasia, are often observed in Byzantine populations (Fig. 3.2).[30] Angel's hypothesis that cribra orbitalia and porotic hyperostosis reflect thalassemia genotypes as a response to endemic malaria has strongly influenced the interpretation of these lesions.[31] This argument persisted for Greek Byzantine populations, despite most recorded cases of porotic lesions having failed to provide convincing evidence

---

29 See for example, Lukacs, "Oral Health", pp. 568–71.
30 "Cribra orbitalia" and "porotic hyperostosis" should be viewed as descriptive rather than diagnostic terms.
31 See for example, Angel, "Porotic Hyperostosis, Anemias, Malarias"; Angel, "Anemias of Antiquity"; on anemias, see Ortner, "Identification of Pathological Conditions", pp. 363–70; on thalassemia, see Lewis, "Thalassaemia".

of genetic anemias.[32] Although both cribra orbitalia and porotic hyperostosis became almost synonymous with iron-deficiency anemia in the bioarchaeological literature, Walker and colleagues have argued that iron-deficiency anemia does not provide a reasonable physiological explanation for the marrow hypertrophy that produces porotic hyperostosis and cribra orbitalia, suggesting, instead, that a vitamin B_{12}-deficient diet is much more likely to be the key nutritional component in a set of various interacting variables.[33] Vitamin B_{12} is found in foods that come from animals, including fish and shellfish, meat (especially liver), poultry, eggs, milk, and milk products.[34] Although meat and fish seem to have been consumed, as evidenced by the isotopic data, in the set of various interacting variables (parasite load, infections), a protein-deficient diet can be suspected for at least some of the individuals exhibiting these lesions.[35]

Metabolic disorders occur as a result of the complex interactions between human physiology, culture, and diet. The identification of metabolic disorders in paleopathology is rather problematic, and the criteria for a secure diagnosis have been only recently established.[36]

During the last years, more cases of *scurvy* have entered the paleopathological record owing to years of fruitful research for establishing adequate criteria for the diagnosis of the condition in dry bones.[37] Scurvy is caused by a dietary deficiency in vitamin C (ascorbic acid), a vitamin that has a number of roles in the body and can be found in numerous vegetables and fresh fruits; small amounts are also present in milk, organ meat, and fish.[38] Access to foods containing ascorbic acid is associated with a number of factors, such as climate, seasonality, environmental stress and impoverished conditions, natural or man-made disasters, changes in subsistence patterns, and culturally derived

---

32 See for example, Mallegni, "Analisi dei resti scheletrici", p. 386. Up-to-date ancient DNA analysis of prehistoric Greek populations tentatively suggests that a significant relation exists between the prevalence of the lesions and the ecological settings, such as extreme environments, see Stravopodi et al., "Porotic Hyperostosis in Neolithic Greece".
33 Walker et al., "The Causes". See also for example, McIlvaine, "Implications"; Rivera and Mirazón Lahr "New evidence".
34 WHO, "Vitamin B_{12}", pp. 279–80.
35 See also Rife, "Isthmia", pp. 410–13.
36 Brickley/Ives/Mays, "The Bioarchaeology of Metabolic Bone Disease".
37 See also the special issue on the paleopathology of scurvy published in 2014 in the *International Journal of Paleopathology*, honouring the pioneer work on the subject by the late professor Donald J. Ortner.
38 WHO, "Scurvy and Its Prevention"; Brickley and Ives, "The Bioarchaeology of Metabolic Bone Disease", pp. 41–74; Jacob and Sotoudech, "Vitamin C".

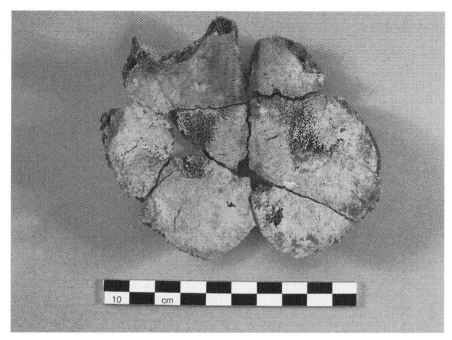

FIGURE 3.3 Alikianos, skeleton 011. Manifestation of scorbutic lesions in the form of dense hypervascularity on the endocranial of the frontal bone (a mixture of active and healed bone plaques, suggestive of a reaction to chronic hemorrhage)

behaviors – to name but a few.[39] In particular, for Byzantine populations, restricted access to fresh food due to natural disasters such as earthquakes and impoverished environmental conditions were proposed for a number of scorbutic cases.[40]

However, based on four additional juvenile cases reported for the middle Byzantine cemetery (10th–11th centuries AD) at Alikianos in western Crete (Fig. 3.3) and isotopic data, it has been suggested that the development of childhood scurvy during the Byzantine era can be also associated with the onset of weaning,[41] as metabolic conditions are often argued to coincide with

---

39 Crandall, "Scurvy in the Greater American Southwest"; Mays, "The Palaeopathology of Scurvy in Europe"; Buckley et al., "Scurvy in a Tropical Paradise?".
40 Bourbou, "The People"; Garvie-Lok, "Weaning Pains"; Stark and Garvie-Lok, "Juvenile Scurvy in the Valley of Stymphalos".
41 Bourbou, "Evidence of Childhood Scurvy"; Bourbou et al., "Nursing Mothers and Feeding Bottles", Bourbou "The Greatest of Treasures".

this critical period in a child's life.[42] The chemical analysis of 61 non-adult human samples from eight Byzantine (6th–15th centuries AD) sites from Greece have shown that weaning was complete by the fourth year, a pattern consistent with the documentary evidence of the era.[43] Byzantine physicians of the 4th to the 7th centuries AD suggested that a child may be brought up on milk until the age of two years and afterwards its diet may be changed to cereal food.[44] In the broadly agricultural and pastoral economy of Byzantine Crete, cereal grains, and especially wheat and barley lacking in vitamin C, would have formed the basis of a daily diet. Thus, weaning practices, and in particular, the introduction of solid, cereal-based supplementary foodstuff, must have played a significant role in putting these infants at risk for scurvy. For example, a study of 174 non-adult individuals from six sites in Crete during the Byzantine period (7th–12th centuries AD), showed that hematopoietic disorders such as cribra orbitalia and porotic hyperostosis tend to develop after the age of three to four years.[45] This time interval, as has been indicated by the relevant isotopic data, coincides with the critical onset of weaning.

A possible case of *adult vitamin D deficiency (osteomalacia)* is observed for a young male (18–25 years old) from the early Byzantine site of Sourtara.[46] The condition has been rarely diagnosed prior to the establishment of sufficient recording criteria.[47] Evidence of vitamin D deficiency in archaeological populations tells much about the interaction between environment, diet, and health; for example, the work by Mensforth, and Brickley et al. has argued for the presence of the condition in urban societies influenced by industrial living and increased atmospheric pollution.[48] Vitamin D – which is rather a pro-hormone than a traditional vitamin – plays a significant role in many bodily functions. Natural foods containing vitamin D include eggs, liver, and oily fish such as salmon, tuna, and mackerel. Unless a rare hereditary or other condition is present, vitamin D deficiency is primarily caused by a prolonged lack of exposure to sunlight and/or deficiency of foodstuffs containing vitamin D; for example, diets low in calcium and often high in phytate from cereal grain can enhance

---

42 See for example, Katzenberg et al., "Weaning and Infant Mortality"; Herring et al., "Investigating the Weaning Process"; Katzenberg, "The Ecological Approach", p. 105.
43 Bourbou et al., "Nursing Mothers and Feeding Bottles".
44 Heiberg, "Paulus Aeginita"; Raeder, "Oribasii collectionum"; Olivieri, "Aetii Amideni libri".
45 Bourbou, "Health and Disease", pp. 113–22.
46 Bourbou, "To Live and Die", pp. 227, 232–3.
47 For diagnostic criteria, see Brickley, Ives and Mays, "The Bioarchaeology of Metabolic Bone Disease"; and the special issue published in 2018 in the *International Journal of Paleopathology*, on Vitamin D deficiency in bioarchaeology and beyond.
48 Mensforth, "Vitamin D Deficiency"; Brickley et al., "An Investigation".

vitamin D deficiency.[49] It is not, thus, surprising that the condition was present in a largely agricultural community in northern Greece, whose dependence on C_3, as well as C_4 staples, was also attested by the isotopic analysis.

4   The Environment as a Reservoir of Pathogens

Already in the late 1960s, Grmek[50] introduced the term "pathocenosis" in analogy to the term "biocenosis" that refers to the coexistence and interaction of all living organisms within a specific setting, thus proposing a temporal and regional approach for understanding the dynamics of infectious conditions. More than any other category of disease, infections offer the researcher a deeper insight into the interplay of disease, diet, ecology, social structure, settlement pattern, plant and animal domestication, sanitation levels, immunological resistance, and physiological stress.

Animals and humans have been sharing a long and complex relationship, making the former a significant reservoir for human disease. Thus, considering human and animal diseases against an environmental background provides a broader perspective to the study of disease in the past. The onset of animal domestication, although it brought many advantages to humans, also brought many changes to patterns of human health and disease.[51] A case study in the Southern Levant has demonstrated that, for example, animals domesticated for longer period share more disease with humans than do others with shorter histories of domestication.[52] *Zoonoses* include any disease or infection that is naturally transmissible from vertebrate animals to humans; they may be bacterial, viral, or parasitic, or may involve unconventional agents. It is argued that 58 per cent of human pathogens are zoonotic; in other words, humans share pathogens with a wide range of animals.[53] Although few zoonotic diseases have been recorded for Byzantine populations, those observed give us is a direct link to the environmental and general living conditions of the past.

Actinomycosis is a disease of humans and cattle that may be systemic or localized, and is caused by the bacterium *Actinomyces israelii*. Its reservoir is endogenous to the human oral cavity.[54] A possible case of actinomycosis was recorded for a young male of around 25 years old from the early Byzantine

49 Brickley, Ives and Mays "The Bioarchaeology of Metabolic Bone Disease".
50 Grmek, "Préliminaire", p. 1476.
51 Brothwell, "On Zoonoses"; Upex and Dobney, "More than Just Mad Cows".
52 Horwitz and Smith, "The Contribution of Animal Domestication".
53 Woolhouse and Gowtage-Sequeria, "Host Range and Emerging".
54 Aufderheide and Rodríguez-Martin, "Human Paleopathology", p. 193.

site of Eleutherna.⁵⁵ *Brucella spp.* bacteria contain three species pathogenic to domestic animals and, through them, to humans. *Brucellosis*, a chronic infection of the lungs and other organs, is usually acquired through ingestion of contaminated meat or dairy products, or regular contact with infected animals.⁵⁶ The osteological and molecular analysis of two individual from Butrint in southwest Albania (10th–13th centuries AD) verified the identification of the condition.⁵⁷ Past Mediterranean diets included the consumption of meat and dairy products, but their processing or preservation did not always follow specific health regulations, and the consumption of contaminated products must have been common.⁵⁸ Consumption, thus, of contaminated milk may not have been uncommon, as *Brucella melitensis* primarily affects goats in the Mediterranean area.⁵⁹ Furthermore, the presence of both conditions suggests that people used to live in close contact with their livestock, which facilitated the transmission of diseases from animals to humans in a generally unsanitary environment.

Tuberculosis results from respiratory or gastrointestinal infection by bacterial members of the *Mycobacterium tuberculosis* complex. The condition in humans is usually caused by *M. tuberculosis* or *M. bovis* and is transmitted by infected droplets or ingestion of contaminated meat or dairy products.⁶⁰ Before effective treatment, which did not arrive until the 1940s and 50s, people in the past probably had little to resort to besides herbal remedies to sooth their symptoms; however, neither the efficacy of treatment nor access to it can be established. Clearly, tuberculosis is a disease with multifactorial etiology, and numerous variables must have contributed to its appearance, but socio-economic status, overcrowded living conditions, high population density, and contact with infected animals must have been of major significance for contracting the disease in the past. The most common site of skeletal involvement is the spinal column, although other parts can be affected (e.g., the skull, flat bones, and bones of the limbs), while in the last decade special attention has been given to lesions on the visceral surfaces of the ribs.⁶¹

---

55   Bourbou, "Health and Disease", p. 74.
56   Ortner, "Identification of Pathological Conditions", pp. 215–21; Pappas et al., "The New Global Map of Human Brucellosis".
57   Mutolo et al., "Identification of Brucellosis".
58   Even today, countries such as Greece and Albania present the highest rates of brucellosis infection in Europe, Pappas et al., "The New Global Map of Human Brucellosis".
59   Ortner, "Identification of Pathological Conditions", p. 216.
60   For a thorough discussion on this reemerging condition, see Roberts/Buikstra, "The Bioarchaeology of Tuberculosis".
61   See for example, Santos/Roberts, "Anatomy of a Serial Killer"; Matos/Santos, "On the Trail of Pulmonary Tuberculosis"; Nicklisch et al., "Rib Lesions".

Rib lesions are still considered a debatable characteristic in the diagnosis of tuberculosis, since other conditions, i.e., pneumonia, chronic bronchitis, and neoplastic conditions, may also produce these lesions. In addition, molecular analysis has significantly enhanced our ability to reach a secure diagnosis.[62] Rib lesions have been identified in a 35-year-old male from early Byzantine Messene and have been subject to molecular analysis for possible identification of tuberculous strains, as part of a larger project on the *"Biomolecular archaeology of tuberculosis in Britain and Europe"*.[63] Although the first set of results is negative, the samples will be further analyzed using a different extraction protocol.[64] It will be of great interest to see if the results are positive, since this would be the very first diagnosed tuberculous case in Byzantine populations and will tell much about the environmental and other constraints that people during the era dealt with.

Osteomyelitis has been sporadically reported for Byzantine populations, i.e., from early Byzantine Messene (a female, 25 years old), and middle Byzantine Filotas (a male, 45 years old).[65] Osteomyelitis is an inflammation of the bone (osteitis) and the bone marrow (myelitis) caused by pus-producing agents (e.g., bacteria, fungi, viruses), with *Staphylococcus aureus* being the causative organism in close to 90 per cent of cases.[66] The absence of evidence of fracture, injury, or surgery indicates that both cases demonstrated a hematogenous osteomyelitis – that is, an infection reaching the skeleton by the hematogenous route from an infected locus. It is possible that the close association between poor diet, lack of or inadequate medical treatment, and generally unhealthy sanitary conditions resulted in the condition becoming chronic and contributed to the deterioration of the health status of these individuals and, consequently, to their death. In pre-antibiotic eras, it would have been difficult to fight the acquired symptoms, like high fever, pain, and restricted mobility. It should be also noted that the skeleton from Messene demonstrated porotic hyperostosis, reinforcing the hypothesis of the close association between infection and malnutrition (see above).

---

62   See for example, Zink et al., "Molecular History of Tuberculosis"; Müller et al., "Biomolecular Identification"; Mays et al., "Investigating the Link".
63   For full details of all participants, see https://www.dur.ac.uk/archaeology/research/projects/all/?mode=project&id=353.
64   C. Roberts, pers. comm. 2015.
65   Bourbou, "Are We What We Eat", pp. 221–2. A case of osteomyelitis in a 3- to 4-year-old child has been recorded for Sourtara, Bourbou, "To Live and Die", pp. 229–30, 233. Most possibly the infectious agents reached the non-adult skeleton via a fracture on the tibial shaft.
66   Ortner, "Identification of Pathological Conditions", p. 181.

In 2013, the *International Journal of Paleopathology* devoted a complete issue on the importance of research into ancient parasites. Among the biological fields linked to archaeology, *paleoparasitology* provides a remarkable contribution for investigating interactions between past societies and their environments, especially since some of these interactions resulted in disease. Paleoparasitology is the study of ancient parasites through microscopy (at their development stage, e.g., eggs) or the application of biomolecular methods (e.g., detection of ancient DNA or proteins produced by the parasite when alive). Such studies greatly contribute to the understanding of past human health and diet, paleoenvironmental conditions, human and animal migrations, trade, and exchange.[67]

Such up-to-date innovative techniques have not yet been applied to Greek Byzantine populations. For the medieval period in the Mediterranean area, only one publication refers to the analysis of a Frankish castle latrine in Cyprus (AD 1200).[68] The study has revealed the presence of the eggs of roundworm and whipworm. Both species are associated with poor sanitation, and thus the results of the study give a unique insight into the hygiene conditions of the Franks a few years after their arrival in Cyprus. However, a pilot paleoparasitological study of soil samples has been conducted by the author and Dr. P. Mitchell at the University of Cambridge.[69] These soil samples were gathered from the pelvic area of nine adult skeletons, together with control samples from the areas of the cranium and the feet, during the excavation of the middle Byzantine cemetery at Alikianos. The soil samples were tested for the cysts of three parasitic protozoa that cause dysentery, namely *Entamoeba histolytica*, *Giardia duodenalis*, and *Cryptosporidium parvum*, and worms such as *Ascaris lumbricoides*. Only one out of the nine samples subject to paleoparasitological analysis was positive for the roundworm *Ascaris lumbricoides*, with one decorticated fertile egg being identified. It is the most common parasitic worm in humans, responsible for the disease *ascariasis*, resulting in stunted growth in children, while the effects in adults are less significant. However, a heavy worm load will still predispose the individual to malnutrition, anemia, and even death from starvation in times of crop failure and famine.[70] The parasite spreads via the fecal – oral route; eggs in contaminated feces can be accidentally consumed (e.g., due to ineffective hand washing, use of human faces as

---

67 Dittmar et al., "The Study of Parasites"; Reinhard and Araújo "Synthesizing Parasitology with Archaeology".
68 Anastasiou and Mitchell, "Human Intestinal Parasites from a Latrine".
69 Mitchell et al., "Intestinal Parasite Analysis".
70 Ngui et al., "Association Between".

crop fertilizer), or drunk (e.g., contaminated water by fecal waste from cesspools or other sanitation structures).[71] As only one out of nine individuals was positive, it is very preliminary to draw any conclusions. It is possible that the actual prevalence of the parasite in the community could have been higher, if non-adults had been tested, since these feco – oral intestinal parasites are more common in children than in adults.[72]

5 Encounters with the Environment

The *International Classification of Disease* defines injury as being caused by acute exposure to physical agents, and classifies it as intentional and unintentional.[73] However, in the paleopathological record, there is little agreement about the definition of trauma, its classification and consequently its recording, usually embracing the disease process and not the wider involvement of emotional and environmental events.[74] Trauma analysis on a population level has provided insight into interaction with fellow humans and the environment, e.g., ecological decline,[75] hazardous occupations,[76] or subsistence change.[77] One of the commonest types of skeletal trauma is *fracture*, which broadly describes any traumatic event that results in partial or complete discontinuity of a bone.

Patterns of fractured bones can be typical of accidents, thus deepening our perspective on how hazardous physical activities were in the past, or they may be the result of inter-personal violence, evidenced by fractured facial and cranial areas and by wounds inflicted by various weapons.[78] The study of Byzantine populations in Crete demonstrated that absolute frequency rate is 3.5 per cent or 43 fractured bones of the 1,199 examined. The majority of these fractures were primarily the consequence of falls caused by the individual's own clumsiness or accidental injuries during the performance of everyday activities.[79] For example, Colles fractures are frequently reported and are almost always

---

71 Ziegelbauer et al., "Effect of Sanitation".
72 Ngui et al., "Association Between".
73 Peden et al., "The Injury Chart Book", pp. 2–6.
74 See Lovell, "Trauma Analysis"; Judd and Redfern, "Trauma".
75 Walker, "Cranial Injuries"; Torres-Ruff and Junquiera, "Interpersonal Violence".
76 Djuric et al., "Fractures"; Van de Merwe et al., "Trauma and Amputations".
77 Dommet and Tayles, "Adult Fracture Patterns".
78 For a review on the bioarchaeology of violence, see Martin and Harrod, "Bioarchaeological Contributions".
79 Bourbou, "Health and Disease", pp. 77–91; Rife, "Isthmia", pp. 429–36.

due to a fall onto an outstretched hand.[80] On the other hand, cases of fractures that presented complications (e.g., infection, bone deformity, traumatic arthritis, joint fusion) were also frequently attested. Most likely, poor access to medical treatment and inadequate immobilization of the afflicted bone during the healing phase resulted in such complications. Similarly, evidence of multiple fractures exist and are unlikely to represent constant physical abuse, since they did not present different stages of healing, and are thus suggestive of an exceptionally dangerous lifestyle or a hazardous occupation.[81] It should be noted, though, that the impact of each fracture must have played a significant role in the performance of daily activities, and especially for individuals involved in manual labor. A farmer, for example, would have been less successful in performing many farming activities due to pain, weakness, and reduced range of motion.

6 The Tales Skeletons Tell: Giving Voice to Those Long Silenced

All these different lines of investigation applied to the study of human bones can reveal aspects of life in the past, shedding light on the deep connections between history, environment, human biology, and disease. Years of bioarchaeological research from across the world and among different cultures enable us to identify patterns of biological outcomes, human – environment relationships, and socio-economic changes.

The environmental impact on health has played a significant role in both past and modern societies. Humans have considerably changed their lifestyle and have adapted to new environments: from constantly mobile hunter – gatherers to settled agriculturalists and, later, workers in industrialized towns. Bioarchaeological studies of Byzantine populations have greatly contributed to the better understanding of the challenges faced by everyday people: broadly agricultural and pastoral communities had access to various food products but also experienced failing crops, relied upon inadequate diets that led to dietary deficiencies, and lived in settled communities, which enhanced the pathogen load including of diseases spread to humans from their animals. As already stated above, we have a long way to walk to fully understand the influence that the environment had upon health and disease during the Byzantine period. Emphasis must be placed on shared and combined research; Byzantine historians and bioarchaeologists should develop a close collaboration working

---

80 Mays, "A Paleopathological Study of Colles' Fracture".
81 Bourbou, "Health and Disease", pp. 78–83, 89.

side-by-side in order that the two disciplines do not continue to follow different trajectories. Furthermore, the widely applied stable isotope analysis now needs a focus on linking evidence of disease with diet and mobility: poor diet can put health at risk, resulting in weaker immune systems and greater susceptibility to disease, and mobility can facilitate the transmission and spread of disease. Many pieces of the puzzle are still missing, but the accelerating interest in the study of Byzantine populations can only make us optimistic about future advances in the numerous questions we want to answer.

Bibliography

Primary Sources

Paulus Aeginita, *Corpus Medicorum Graecorum*, ed. J. Heiberg, 2 vols., Leipzig 1921 and 1924.

Aetii Amideni libri medicinales I–IV (Corpus Medicorum Graecorum), ed. A. Olivieri, Leipzig, 1935.

Aetii Amideni libri medicinales V–VIII (Corpus Medicorum Graecorum), ed. A. Olivieri, Berlin 1950.

Oribasii collectionum medicarum reliquiae, 5 vols (Corpus Medicorum Graecorum), ed. J. Raeder, Leipzig 1928–33.

Secondary Literature

Anastasiou, E./Mitchell, P.D., "Human Intestinal Parasites from a Latrine in the 12th Century Frankish Castle of Saranda Kolones in Cyprus", *International Journal of Paleopathology* 3 (2013), 218–223.

Angel, J.L., "Porotic Hyperostosis, Anemias, Malarias and Marshes in the Prehistoric Mediterranean", *Science* 153 (1966), 760–63.

Angel, J.L., "Anemias of Antiquity: Eastern Mediterranean", in E. Cockburn/A. Cockburn (eds.), *Porotic Hyperostosis: An Enquiry* (Paleopathology Association Monograph 2), Detroit 1977, pp. 1–5.

Arriaza, B.T., "Arseniasis as an Environmental Hypothetical Explanation for the Origin of the Oldest Artificial Mummification Practice in the World", *Chungara Revista de Antropologia Chilena* 37 (2005), 255–260.

Aufderheide, A./Rodríguez-Martín, C., *The Cambridge Encyclopedia of Human Paleopathology*, Cambridge 1998.

Boldsen, J.L., "Leprosy in Medieval Denmark: Osteological and Epidemiological Analyses", *Anthropologischer Anzeiger* 67 (2009), 407–425.

Bourbou, C., *The People of Early Byzantine Eleutherna and Messene (6th–7th Centuries A.D.): A Bioarchaeological Approach*, Athens 2004.

Bourbou, C., *Health and Disease in Byzantine Crete (7th–12th Centuries AD)*, Surrey 2010.

Bourbou, C., "To Live and Die in a Turbulent Era. Bioarchaeological Analysis of the Early Byzantine (6th–7th centuries AD) Population from Sourtara Galaniou Kozanis (Northern Greece)", *Dumbarton Oaks Papers* 63 (2011), 221–234.

Bourbou, C., "Evidence of Childhood Scurvy in a Middle Byzantine Greek Population from Crete, Greece (11th–12th centuries AD)", *International Journal of Paleopathology* 5 (2014), 86–94.

Bourbou, C., "Health and Disease at the Marshes: Deciphering the Human-environment Interaction at Roman Aventicum, Switzerland (1st–3rd c. AD)", in: G. Robbins Schug (ed.), Routledge Handbook of the Bioarchaeology of Environmental Change, London and New York 2020 pp. 141–155.

Bourbou, C., "The Biocultural Model Applied: Synthetic Research on Greek Byzantine Diet (7th–15th c. AD)", in S.Y. Waksman, (ed.) Multidisciplinary Approaches to Food and Foodways in the Medieval Eastern Mediterranean. Lyon 2020, pp. 355–362.

Bourbou, C., "'The greatest of treasures': Advances in the Bioarchaeology of Byzantine-Children", in: L.A. Beaumont/ M., Dillon/ N. Harrington (ed.), *Children in Antiquity. Perspectives and Experiences of Childhood in the Ancient Mediterranean*, London and New York 2021, pp. 594–607.

Bourbou, C./Fuller, B.T./Garvie-Lok, S.J./Richards, M.P., "Reconstructing the Diets of Greek Byzantine Populations (6th–15th centuries AD) Using Carbon and Nitrogen Stable Isotope Ratios", *American Journal of Physical Anthropology* 146 (2011), 569–81.

Bourbou, C./Fuller, B.T./ Garvie-Lok, S.J./ Richards, M.P., "Nursing Mothers and Feeding Bottles: Reconstructing Breastfeeding and Weaning Patterns in Greek Byzantine populations (6th–15th centuries AD) Using Carbon and Nitrogen Stable Isotope Ratios", *Journal of Archaeological Science* 40 (2013), 3903–3913.

Bramanti, B., "The Use of DNA Analysis in the Archaeology of Death and Burial", in S. Tarlow/L. Nilsson Stutz (eds.), *The Oxford Handbook of the Archaeology of Death*, Oxford 2013, pp. 99–122.

Brickley, M.B. / Mays, S. (ed.), "Vitamin D Deficiency in Bioarchaeology and Beyond: The Study of Rickets and Osteomalacia in the Past", *International Journal of Paleopathology* 23 (2018).

Brickley, M./Ives, R./Mays, S., *The Bioarchaeology of Metabolic Bone Disease*, London 2020.

Brothwell, D.R., "On Zoonoses and Their Relevance to Paleopathology", in D.J. Ortner/ A.C. Aufderheide (eds.), *Human Paleopathology. Current Syntheses and Future Options*, Washington 1991, pp. 18–22.

Buckley, H.R./ Kinaston, R. /Halcrow, S.E. /Foster, A. /Spriggs, M./Bedford, S., "Scurvy in a Tropical Paradise? Evaluating the Possibility of Infant and Adult Vitamin C Deficiency in the Lapita Skeletal Sample of Teouma, Vanuatu, Pacific Islands", *International Journal of Paleopathology* 5 (2014), 72–85.

Buikstra, J.E., "Preface", in J.E. Buikstra/L.A. Beck (eds.), *Bioarchaeology: The Contextual Analysis of Human Remains*, Amsterdam 2006, pp. xvii–xx.

Crandall, J.J., "Scurvy in the Greater American Southwest: Modeling Micronutrition and Biosocial Processes in Contexts of Resource Stress", *International Journal of Paleopathology* 5 (2014), 46–54.

Dittmar, K./Araújo, A./Reinhard, K., "The Study of Parasites Through Time: Archaeoparasitology and Paleoparasitology", in A.L. Grauer (ed.), *A Companion to Paleopathology*, Chichester 2012, pp. 170–190.

Djurić, M.P./Roberts, C.A./Rakočević, Z.B./Djonić, D.D./Lešić, A.R., "Fractures in Late Medieval Skeletal Populations from Serbia", *American Journal of Physical Anthropology* 130 (2006), 167–178.

Domett, K.C./Tayles, N., "Adult Fracture Patterns in Prehistoric Thailand", *International Journal of Paleopathology* 16 (2006), 185–199.

Fuller, B.T./Márquez-Grant, N./Richards, M.P., "Investigation of Diachronic Dietary Patterns on the Islands of Ibiza and Formentera, Spain: Evidence from Carbon and Nitrogen Stable Isotope Ratio Analysis", *American Journal of Physical Anthropology* 143 (2010), 512–522.

Fuller, B.T./De Cupere, B./Marinova, E./Van Neer, W./Waelkens, M./Richards, M.P., "Isotopic Reconstruction of Human Diet and Animal Husbandry Practices During the Classical-Hellenistic, Imperial, and Byzantine Periods at Sagalassos, Turkey", *American Journal of Physical Anthropology* 149 (2012), 157–171.

Garcia, E./Subirá, M.E./Richards, M.P., "Régime et societé d'après l'analyse des isotopes stables: l'exemple de la population de 'Can Reinés' (Mallorca, Espagne, 600 ap. J.C.)", *Anthropos* 7 (2004), 171–176.

Garvie-Lok, S.J., "Weaning Pains: Assessing Juvenile Scurvy in a Late Roman Greek Population", Paper presented at the 109th Annual Meeting of the Archaeological Institute of America, Chicago, IL., 2008.

González-Reimers, E./Velasco-Vásquez, J./Arnay-de-la-Rosa, M./Aleberto-Barrosos, V./Gilando-Martín, L./Santolaria-Fernández, F., "Bone Cadmium and Lead in Prehistoric Inhabitants and Domestic Animals from Gran Canaria", *The Science of the Total Environment* 310 (2003), 97–103.

Gowland, R.L./Western, A.G., "Morbidity in the Marshes: Using Spatial Epidemiology to Investigate Skeletal Evidence for Malaria in Anglo-Saxon England (AD 410–1050)", *American Journal of Physical Antropology* 147 (2012), 301–111.

Grattan, J.P./Huxley, S.N./Karaki, L./Toland, H./Gilbertson, D.D./Pyatt, A.J./Saad, Z., "Death More Desirable than Life? The Human Skeletal Record and Toxicological Implications of Ancient Copper Mining and Smelting in Wadi Fayan, South West Jordan", *Toxicology and Industrial Health* 18 (2002), 297–307.

Grmek, M.D., "Préliminaire d' une etude historique des maladies", *Annales, Economies, Scociétés, Civilisations* 24 (1969), 1437–1483.

Herring, D.A./Saunders, S.R./Katzenberg, M.A., "Investigating the Weaning Process in Past Populations", *American Journal of Physical Anthropology* 105 (1998), 425–439.

Horwitz, L.K./ Smith, P., "The Contribution of Animal Domestication to the Spread of Zoonoses: A Case Study from the Southern Levant", *Anthropozoologica* 31 (2000), 77–84.

Jacob, R.A./Sotoudech, G., "Vitamin C Function and Status in Chronic Disease", *Nutrition in Clinical Care* 5 (2002), 66–74.

Judd, M.A./Redfern, R., "Trauma", in A.L. Grauer (ed.), *A Companion to Paleopathology*, Chichester 2012, pp. 359–379.

Katzenberg, M.A., "The Ecological Approach: Understanding Past Diet and the Relationship Between Diet and Disease", in A.L. Grauer (ed.), *A Companion to Paleopathology*, Chichester 2012, pp. 97–113.

Katzenberg, M.A./Herring, D.A./Saunders, S.R., "Weaning and Infant Mortality: Evaluating the Skeletal Evidence", *Yearbook of Physical Anthropology* 39 (1996), 177–99.

Katzenberg, M.A./Waters-Rist, A.L. "Stable Isotope Analysis: A Tool for Studying Past Diet, Demography and Life History", in M.A. Katzenberg, A.L. Grauer (ed.), *Biological Anthropology of the Human Skeleton*, Hoboken, New Jersey, 2019, pp. 467–504.

Larsen, C.S., *Bioarchaeology: Interpreting Behavior from the Human Skeleton*, Cambridge 1997.

Lewis, M.E., "Impact of Industrialization: Comparative Study of Child Health in Four Sites from Medieval and Post Medieval England (A.D. 850–1859)", *American Journal of Physical Anthropology* 119 (2002), 211–223.

Lewis, M.E., "Thalassaemia: Its Diagnosis and Interpretation in Past Skeletal Populations", *International Journal of Osteoarchaeology* 22 (2012), 685–93.

Lieverse, A.R., "Diet and Aetiology of Dental Calculus," *International Journal of Osteoarchaeology* 9 (1999), 219–232.

Lovell, N.C., "Trauma Analysis in Paleopathology", *Yearbook of Physical Anthropology* 40 (1997), 139–170.

Lukacs, J.R., "Dental Palaeopathology: Methods for Reconstructing Dietary Patterns", in M.Y. İşcan/K.A.R. Kennedy (eds.), *Reconstruction of Life from the Skeleton*, New York 1989, pp. 261–86.

Lukacs, J.R., "Oral Health in Past Populations: Context, Concepts and Controversies", in A.L. Grauer (ed.), *A Companion to Paleopathology*, Chichester 2012, pp. 553–581.

Mallegni, F., "Analisi dei resti scheletrici umani", in A. Di Vita (ed.), *Gortina I*, Monografie della Scuola Archeologica di Atene e delle Missioni Italiane in Oriente III, Rome 1988, pp. 339–401.

McIlvaine, B.K., "Implications of Reappraising the Iron Deficiency Anemia hypothesis", *International Journal of Osteoarchaeology* 25 (2015), 997–1000.

Matos, V./Santos, A.L., "On the Trail of Pulmonary Tuberculosis Based on Rib Lesions: Results from the Human Identified Skeletal Collection from the Museu Bocage (Lisbon, Portugal)", *American Journal of Physical Anthropology* 130 (2006), 190–200.

Mays, S.A., "A Paleopathological Study of Colles' Fracture", *International Journal of Osteoarchaeology* 16 (2006), 415–28.

Mays, S., "The Palaeopathology of Scurvy in Europe", *International Journal of Paleopathology* 5 (2014), 55–62.

Mays, S./Fysh, E./Taylor, G.M., "Investigation of the Link Between Visceral Surface Rib Lesions and Tuberculosis in a Medieval Skeletal Series from England Using Ancient DNA", *American Journal of Physical Anthropology* 119 (2002), 27–36.

Mitchell, P.D./Hwang, C./Anastasiou, E., "Intestinal Parasite Analysis of Sediments from 11th–12th Century Burials at Zoodochos Pigi, Alikianos, Crete". Unpublished Report, Department of Archaeology and Anthropology, University of Cambridge, 2012.

Müller, R./Roberts, C.A./Brown, T.A., "Biomolecular Identification of Ancient Mycobacterium tuberculosis Complex DNA in Human Remains from Britain and Continental Europe", *American Journal of Physical Anthropology* 153 (2014), 178–189.

Mutolo, M.J./Jenny, L.L./Buszek, A.R./Fenton, T.W./Foran, D.R., "Osteological and Molecular Identification of Brucellosis in Ancient Butrint, Albania", *American Journal of Physical Anthropology* 147 (2012), 254–263.

Mylona, D., "Etudes zooarchaeologiques", in E. Greco/Th. Kalpaxis/A. Schnapp/D. Vivieers, *Travaux menés en collaboration avec l'Ecole française en 1996, Bulletin de Correspondance Hellénique* 121 (1997), 809–824.

Mylona, D., "Τα οστά ζώων από το Βυζαντινό σπίτι στην Αγία Άννα, Πυργί", in Th. Kalpaxis (ed.), Ελεύθερνα. Τομέας ΙΙ. 3, Βυζαντινό σπίτι στην Αγία Άννα, Rethymno 2008, pp. 335–348.

Mylona, D., *Fish-Eating in Greece from the Fifth Century B.C. to the Seventh Century A.D. A Story of Impoverished Fishermen or Luxurious Fish Banquets?*, (BAR International Series 1754), Oxford 2008.

Ngui, R./Lim, Y.A. /Chong Kin, L./Sek Chuen, C./Jaffar, S., "Association Between Anaemia, Iron Deficiency Anaemia, Neglected Parasitic Infections and Socioeconomic Factors in Rural Children of West Malaysia", *PLoS Neglected Tropical Diseases* 6 (2012), e1550. doi:10.1371/journal.pntd.0001550.

Nicklisch, N./Maixner, F./Ganslmeier, R./Friederich, S./Dresely, V./Meller, H./Zink, A./Alt, K.W., "Rib Lesions in Skeletons From Early Neolithic Sites in Central Germany: On the Trail of Tuberculosis at the Onset of Agriculture", *American Journal of Physical Anthropology* 149 (2012), 391–404.

Nieves-Colón, M.A./ Stone, A.C. "Ancient DNA Analysis of Archaeological Remains", in M.A. Katzenberg, A.L. Grauer (ed.), *Biological Anthropology of the Human Skeleton*, Hoboken, New Jersey, 2019, pp. 515–544.

Nobis, G., "Zur antiken Wild-und Hausterfauna Kretas-nach Studien an Tierresten aus den archaologischen Grabungen Poros bei Iraklion und Eleutherna bei Arkadi", *Tier und Museum* 3/4 (1993), 109–20.

Ortner, D.J., *Identification of Pathological Conditions in Human Skeletal Remains*, San Diego 2003.

Pappas, G./Papadimitriou, P./Akritidis, N./Christou, L./Tsianos, E.V., "The New Global Map of Human Brucellosis", *The Lancet Infectious Diseases* 6 (2006), 91–99.

Peden, M./McGee, K./Sharma, G., *The Injury Chart Book: A Graphical Overview of the Global Burden of Injuries*, Geneva 2002.

Perry, M.A./Coleman, D.S./Dettman, D.L./Gratta, J./al-Shiyab, A.H., "Condemned to Metallum? The Origin and Role of 4th–6th Century A.D. Phaeno Mining Camp Residents Using Multiple Chemical Techniques", *Journal of Archaeological Science* 38 (2011), 558–569.

Prüss-Ustün, A./Wolf, J./Corvalán, C./Bos, R./Neira, M. *Preventing Disease through Healthy Environments. A Global Assessment of the Burden of Disease from Environmental Risks*, Geneva 2016.

Rabinowitz, A./Sedikova, L./Henneberg, R., "Daily Life in a Provincial Late Byzantine City: Recent Multidisciplinary Research in the South Region of Chersonesos", in F. Daim/J. Drauschke (eds.), *Byzanz – Das Römerreich im Mittelalter* (Monographien des Römisch-Germanischen Zentralmuseums 84, vol. 2, 1), Mainz 2010, pp. 425–478.

Reinhard, K.J./Araújo, A., "Synthesizing Parasitology with Archaeology in Paleopathology", in J. Buikstra/C.A. Roberts (eds.), *The Global History of Paleopathology*, Oxford 2013, pp. 751–764.

Rife, J.L., *Isthmia, Vol. IX. The Roman and Byzantine Graves and Human Remains*. (The American School of Classical Studies), Athens 2012.

Rivera, F./Mirazón Lahr, M., "New Evidence Suggesting a Dissociated Etiology for Cribra Orbitalia and Porotic Hyperostosis", *American Journal of Physical Anthropology* 164 (2017). 76–96.

Roberts, C.A./Buikstra, J.E., *The Bioarchaeology of Tuberculosis: A Global View on a Reemerging Disease*, Gainesville 2003.

Santos, A.L./Ann Roberts, C.A., "Anatomy of a Serial Killer: Differential Diagnosis of Tuberculosis Based on Rib Lesions of Adult Individuals from the Coimbra Identified Skeletal Collection, Portugal", *American Journal of Physical Anthropology* 130 (2006), 38–49.

Sarpaki, A., "Archaeobotanical Material from the Site of Pyrgouthi in the Berbati Valley: The Seeds", in J. Hjolman/A. Penttinen/B. Wells (eds.), *Pyrgouthi: A Rural Site in the Berbati Valley from the Early Iron Age to Late Antiquity*, Stockholm 2005, pp. 313–341.

Sattenspiel, L., "Tropical Environments, Human Activities, and the Transmission of Infectious Diseases", *Yearbook of Physical Anthropology* 43 (2000), 3–31.

Schultz, M.P., "Paleohistopathology of Bone: A New Approach to the Study of Ancient Diseases", *American Journal of Physical Anthropology* 44 (2001), 106–47.

Standen, V.G./Arriaza, B.T./Santoro, C.M., "Chinchorro Mortuary Practices on Infants: Northern Chile Archaic Period (BP 7000–3600)", in J.L. Thomson/M.P. Alfonso-Durruty/J.J. Crandall (eds.), *Tracing Childhood. Bioarchaeological Investigations of Early Lives in Antiquity*, Gainesville 2014, pp. 58–74.

Stark, R.J./Garvie-Lok, S.J., "Juvenile Scurvy in the Valley of Stymphalos, Greece: A Radiographic and Macroscopic Assessment", Paper presented at the 79th Annual Meeting of the American Association of Physical Anthropologists, Albuquerque, NM, 2010.

Stathakopoulos, D., "Reconstructing the Climate of the Byzantine Empire: State of the Problem and Case Studies", in J. Laszlovsky/P. Szabó (eds.), *People and Nature in Historical Perspective*, Budapest 2003, pp. 255–256.

Stathakopoulos, D., *Famine and Pestilence in the Late Roman and Early Byzantine Empire. A Systematic Survey of Subsistence Crises and Epidemics*, Aldershot 2004.

Stathakopoulos, D., "Death in the Countryside: Some Thoughts on the Effects of Famine and Pestilence", *Antiquité Tardive* 20 (2012), 105–114.

Stravopodi, E./Manolis, S.K./Kousoulakos, S./Aleporou, V./Schultz, M.P., "Porotic Hyperostosis in Neolithic Greece: New Evidence and Further Implications", in L. Schepartz, S. Fox/C. Bourbou (eds.), *New Directions in the Skeletal Biology of Greece*, (OWLS vol. 1, Hesperia Supplement vol. 43), Athens 2009, pp. 257–70.

Teall, J.L., "The Grain Supply of the Byzantine Empire", *Dumbarton Oaks Papers* 13 (1959), 87–140.

Torres-Rouff, C./Junqueira, M.A.C., "Interpersonal Violence in Prehistoric San Pedro Do Acatama, Chile: Behavioral Implications of Environmental Stress", *American Journal of Physical Anthropology* 130 (2006), 60–70.

Upex, B./Dobney, K., "More than Just Mad Cows: Exploring Human-Animal Relationships through Animal Paleopathology", in A.L. Grauer, (ed.) *A Companion to Paleopathology*, Chichester 2012, pp. 191–213.

Van de Merwe, A.E./Steyn, M./L'Abbé, E.N. "Trauma and Amputations in 19th Century Miners from Kimberley, South Africa", *International Journal of Osteoarchaeology* 20 (2010), 291–306.

Van Zeist, W./Bottema, S./van der Veen, M., *Diet and Vegetation at Ancient Carthage. The Archaeobotanical Evidence*, Groningen 2001.

Walker, P.L., "Cranial Injuries as Evidence of Violence in Prehistoric Southern California", *American Journal of Physical Anthropology* 80 (1989), 313–323.

Walker, P.L./Bathurst, R.R./Richman, R./Gjerdrum, T./Andrushko, V.A., "The Causes of Porotic Hyperostosis and Cribra Orbitalia: A Reappraisal of the Iron-Deficiency-Anemia Hypothesis", *American Journal of Physical Anthropology* 139 (2009), 109–25.

Wanek, J./Papageorgopoulou, C./Rühli, F., "Fundamentals of Paleoimaging Techniques: Bridging the Gap between Physicists and Paleopathologists", in A.L. Grauer, (ed.), *A Companion to Paleopathology*, Chichester 2012, pp. 324–338.

Wood, J.W./Milner, G.R./Harpending, H.C./Weiss, K.M., "The Osteological Paradox: Problems of Inferring Prehistoric Health from Skeletal Samples", *Current Anthropology* 33 (1992), 343–70.

Woolhouse, M.E./Gowtage-Sequeria, S., "Host Range and Emerging and Reemerging Pathogens", *Emerging Infectious Disease* 11 (2005), 1842–1847.

World Health Organization (WHO), *Scurvy and Its Prevention and Control in Major Emergencies*, Geneva 1999.

World Health Organization (WHO), "Vitamin B_{12}", in *Vitamin and Mineral Requirements in Human Nutrition,* (2nd ed.), Geneva 2004.

Ziegelbauer, K./Speich, B./Mausezahl, D./Bos, R./Keiser, J./Utzinger, J., "Effect of Sanitation on Soil-Transmitted Helminth Infection: Systematic Review and Meta-analysis", *PLoS Medicine* 9 (2012), e1001162. doi:10.1371/journal.pmed.1001162.

Zink, A.R./Molnár, E./Motamedi, N./Pálfy, G./Marcsik, A./Nerlich, A.G., "Molecular History of Tuberculosis from Ancient Mummies and Skeletons", *International Journal of Osteoarchaeology* 17 (2007), 380–391.

CHAPTER 4

Historical Epidemiology of the Medieval Eastern Mediterranean

Costas Tsiamis

1   Introduction

The present study is an alternative approach to recorded epidemics in the Byzantine world of the Eastern Mediterranean with the help of the scientific field of historical epidemiology.[1] Historical studies record the causes leading to an epidemic and may interpret them at historic, social, economic, and ecological levels. In turn, epidemiological studies attempt to reconstruct the possible sequence of events leading to an epidemic outbreak, based on medical, environmental, ecological, social, and geographical information. Historical Epidemiology provides a useful tool of historical interdisciplinary research in the study of the disease, as not merely a biological but also a cultural phenomenon.

One of the main missions of epidemiology is to identify and investigate a health event. The basic epidemiological concept on infectious diseases and epidemics is the "epidemiologic triangle". The triangle consists of an infectious agent (bacteria, viruses, parasites), a susceptible host (humans or animals), and their environment. The environment can be a trigger factor in the cases of epidemics due to a direct or indirect relation. In the case of vector-borne diseases, both agents (microbes) and their associated vectors (insects) are in a close and complex relationship, and they depend on the environment and climatic conditions.[2] Like applied epidemiology in the study of the modern health issues, the field of historical epidemiology attempts to use the knowledge of the environmental sciences as an interdisciplinary tool for studying past epidemic outbreaks. Also, historical epidemiology examines time, place, and the individuals and their complex relations with risk factors. A risk factor is any attribute, characteristic, or exposure of an individual that increases the likelihood of that individual developing a disease or injury.[3]

---

1   The full version of the study presented in this chapter is available in my book: Tsiamis, *Plague in Byzantine Times: A medico-historical study*.
2   Patz, "Climate change and infectious diseases", 2003, pp. 103–11.
3   Centers for Disease Control and Prevention 2012, p. 52.

2   Methodology

The study gathered information on all epidemics that broke out in the Byzantine Empire in the period AD 330–1453 as they were recorded in the primary sources, which were divided into direct and indirect. The evaluation of the reliability of the primary sources was based on critical historical studies. The study focused primarily on plague, given that the vast majority of sources were relevant to this disease. In the process of analysis, epidemics were grouped geographically and chronologically so as to determine epidemic "waves", or aggregations of epidemics, whereas epidemic outbreaks (4th–15th centuries) were all categorized in time series spanning 100 years.

3   Are Old Diseases Identical with Contemporary Ones?

Many researchers often raise the question: "Are the diseases that caused epidemics in the past identical with contemporary ones?" The diagnostic capability of a historical-epidemiological study entails a large element of chance. However, these studies should be based on a gold standard. Similarly, the study at hand is based on the assumption that the described disease entity is the same as today. One might thus claim that we have already started a study with a high degree of subjectivity, but the explanation is simple and is based on the man – microbe – symptom relationship.

Phylogenetically, microorganisms may evolve from a non-pathogen microbe into a highly dangerous and fatal microbe. It is very probable that the microorganisms that struck human populations in the past are not exactly the same as the microorganisms that exist today, but this does not detract from the fact of their relationship as it emerges from molecular studies.[4] On the contrary, over the past millennia, the biological laws that govern the human reaction to pathological phenomena have remained essentially unaltered.[5] The human genome may have undergone numerous mutations over the course of millennia, but these mutations have not changed the way the human body reacts to stimuli from microorganisms. On a molecular level, scientific data point to the direction of a slow human biological evolution rate, despite the large number of mutations.[6,7] According to population genetics theory, we are able to calculate the time it takes for a new, advantageous mutation to increase in

---

4   Green, "Taking 'Pandemic' seriously: making the Black Death Global", pp. 27–62.
5   Grmek, *Les maladies à l'aube de la civilisation occidentale*, pp. 20–27.
6   Eyre-Walker, "Estimating the rate of adaptive molecular evolution", pp. 2097–108.
7   Reed, "Mutation, selection and the future of human evolution", pp. 479–84.

TABLE 4.1 Comparison between the symptoms of the three Plague Pandemics

First Pandemic (541) *Bubonic plague*	Third Pandemic (1894) *Bubonic plague*
– Fever	– Fever
– Chills	– Chills
– Pain in inguinal and arm region	– Pain in inguinal and arm region
– Swollen inguinal and arm lymph nodes	– Swollen inguinal and arm lymph nodes
– Headache	– Headache
– Nausea and vomiting	– Nausea and vomiting
– High mortality	– High mortality
Second Pandemic (1347) *Pneumonic plague*	**Third Pandemic (1894)** *Pneumonic plague*
– Cough	– Cough
– Haemoptysis and vomiting	– Haemoptysis and vomiting
– Necrotic skin ulcers	– Necrotic skin ulcers
– Death in 2–3 days	– Death in 2–3 days

frequency; we expect that the population of the strongest among mutants will rise in frequency (from 0.5 per cent to 99.5 per cent) within the next 423 generations, or within the next 10,000 years.[8]

Simply put, this could translate into the defense mechanisms of the human body having remained unchanged, from the time they were created until today. Consequently, people in the 6th or 20th century and before the discovery of antibiotics and vaccines would essentially become ill with the same symptoms and pass away in an identical manner. For thousands of years, the microbes that cause a disease also led to the same chain reaction in the human body's defense systems, namely through the activation and participation of the same organs (bone marrow, blood, thymus, lymph nodes, spleen), the same cellular elements (B- and T-lymphocytes, Mononuclear macrophages, Natural killer cells, etc.), and the same cellular mediators (interleukins, interferons, tumor necrosis factor).

The classic signs and symptoms of inflammation (redness, heat, pain, swelling, loss of function) and general systemic signs and symptoms (such as fever, chills, myalgias, headache and anorexia), are the consequences of the general

---

8 Ibid 4.

human responses to infections.[9] Thus, as microbes' patterns change, so too the dynamics of an epidemic change. But, at the same time, the disease that they diachronically cause in humans has the same symptoms, which may only change in frequency. A brief comparison between the symptoms of plague in the 6th, 14th and 19th centuries is the ideal answer to the question that rightfully arises (Table 4.1).

4 Natural Environment and Epidemics

The famous phrase "a butterfly flapping its wings over the Amazon rainforest may cause rainfall in China" is a literary interpretation of Edward Lorenz' chaos theory. The phenomenon of the sensitive dependence of a system on initial conditions is, to a certain degree, applicable to epidemics. An infinitesimal variation in the flow of events leads, after the lapse of sufficient time, to the history of the system evolving in a fundamentally different manner than it would have if the variation had never occurred. Similarly, in the case of epidemics – which naturally entail a multitude of unpredictable factors – a tiny change or unexpected past event may lead to unforeseen epidemiological surprises in the course of time.

It is a common assumption that infectious diseases, from antiquity until World War II and the discovery of antibiotics, had been the main cause of death among human populations. In general terms, we may classify infectious diseases into two main categories, according to their mode of transmission: on the one hand are those diseases that spread directly from person to person (through direct contact or droplet exposure); on the other hand, there are diseases that spread in an indirect manner, using a non-biological physical vehicle (soil or water) or an intervening vector organism (insects). Moreover, infectious diseases can be classified according to their natural reservoir, either as anthroponoses (human reservoirs) or zoonoses (animal reservoirs).[10]

The factors that make up the epidemiological model of an infectious disease are timeless. Seasonal cycles of infectious diseases have been variously attributed to changes in atmospheric conditions, the prevalence or virulence of the pathogen or the behavior of the host.[11] The dynamic relationship between humans and epidemics is affected by numerous ecological factors. These

9   Opal, "Host responses to infection", pp. 31–52.
10 Patz, "Climate change and infectious diseases", pp. 103–09.
11 Dowell, "Seasonal variation in host susceptibility and cycles of certain infectious diseases", pp. 369–74.

factors have remained essentially the same for centuries, whereas they relate to both the direct effects of the environment (climate change, natural disasters) and the indirect impact of human intervention in the ecosystem (river diversions, drainages, environmental pollution, etc.). Climate may shape the course of an outbreak indirectly via its influence on vegetation and agroecosystems. An indirect result could be the migration of humans and animals and the dissemination of pathogens or reduction of herd immunity against pathogens due to malnutrition or inappropriate living conditions.[12]

There is no reason why we should not believe that environmental changes in the past impacted the evolution of an infectious disease in a similar manner as they do nowadays. Furthermore, the debate on climate change in the northern hemisphere during the Middle Ages is a widespread one. It is possible that the period extending from the 9th to (perhaps) the mid-13th centuries AD, which is broadly known as the "Medieval Warm Period", was associated with warmer conditions compared with the conditions over most of the next five centuries.[13] In addition, hundreds of meteorological and climatic anomalies that had implications for people's daily lives, for agriculture and for livestock farming have been recorded in the Eastern Mediterranean at the time of the Byzantine Empire.[14,15,16] Given that infectious diseases are a multivariate phenomenon, it should be taken for granted that climatic disturbances and their implications affected the endemicity of particular infectious diseases as well. Vector-borne diseases in humans could have been heavily affected by climate changes. As far as we know, temperature, precipitation, humidity, and other climatic factors all have an effect on the reproduction, growth, behavior, and population dynamics of the arthropod vectors of mortal infectious diseases.[17] In any case, how can temperature change affect a microorganism? Every microorganism has a distinct optimum growth temperature, which secures maximum growth and reproduction rates. Most microorganisms grow at temperatures that are also tolerable for humans. Nevertheless, certain bacteria survive at temperatures so extreme that they would not allow the survival of other organisms. Microorganisms are classified into three basic groups, according to their optimum temperature: psychrophiles, mesophiles, and thermophiles. Most

---

12 Luterbacher, "Past pandemics and climate variability across the Mediterranean", 5:46.
13 Hughes, "Was there a Medieval Warm Period", pp. 109–42.
14 Telelis, *Meteorological Phenomena and Climate in Byzantium*, pp. 341, 375, 403–52, 456, 480, 497–500, 518, 512, 528, 533, 537, 541–43, 625–26, 646, 654, 742–50.
15 Koder, "Climatic change in the fifth and sixth centuries?", pp. 270–85.
16 Preiser-Kapeller, "A complex systems approach to the evolutionary dynamics of human history", pp. 1–46.
17 Gage, "Climate and vectorborne Diseases", pp. 436–50.

bacteria only grow within a limited temperature range, where the discrepancy between maximum and minimum temperature is up to 30 °C. Mesophiles are the most common type of microbes, their optimum growth temperature ranging from 25 to 40 °C.[18] The microorganisms that have adapted to living parasitically in animal organisms usually develop an optimum growth temperature similar to that of their host, although they are capable of adapting to new conditions as part of their natural evolution. It is commonly acknowledged, however, that the range of temperatures ultimately defines the expression of the genes that codify the microbial functions. *Yersinia pestis*, the bacterium that causes plague, is a typical example of this. The bacterium features a large "arsenal" of agents that invade the cells of the host. Some of them are the capsular antigen fraction I, the antigens V and W, and a set of secreted proteins called "Yops" (*Yersinia* outer proteins). The genes that codify the synthesis of these agents are thermo-dependent and become active at temperatures ≥ 23 °C, but mainly at 37 °C.[19,20]

5 In Anticipation of an Epidemic: Endemic and Enzootic Diseases as Risk Factors

Given the inadequate resources that would offer us reliable demographic data on the cities of the Byzantine Empire, we cannot be sure as to the actual rates of expansion and mortality of a disease. Thus, we are driven to investigate how infectious diseases changed and progressed in this period. Concerning the Middle Ages then, another question emerges as to a possible change in the European population's susceptibility to infectious diseases. The term "herd immunity" was coined to specify the resistance of a population against a specific infectious disease, which is defined as the proportion of resistant individuals within a population. The epidemiological behavior of a particular infectious disease in a given population is largely influenced by this resistance. After all, we know that, as time goes by, the level of immunity declines (although at varying rates), with the composition of the population varying accordingly due to constant population shifts, with the addition of new individuals and the deaths of others.[21,22]

---

18   Engelkirk, *Burton's Microbiology for the Health Sciences*, pp. 121–23.
19   Zhou, "Molecular and physiological insights into plague transmission, virulence and etiology", pp. 273–84.
20   Straley, "Virulence genes regulated at the transcriptional level", pp. 445–54.
21   John, "Herd Immunity; a rough guide", pp. 911–16.
22   Fine, "Herd immunity and herd effect: new insights", pp. 1–6.

Human populations moving from one place to another has been a diachronic phenomenon from antiquity to the present day. Based on the experience with migration (war, economic, and ecologic refugees) to date, we may distinguish between different types of migration: voluntary vs. forced, temporary vs. permanent, and long- vs. short-distance.[23,24] In this context, the distant migrations and permanent establishments of Germanic and Hunnic tribes (4th–5th centuries AD) must have had an impact on the collective immunity of Western Europe and endemic areas of infectious diseases. Moreover, such massive movements of human populations, along with their domesticated animals, must have had a catalytic impact on the enzooty of the respective areas involved.

The Byzantine cities went through various urban development stages, from early times to the end of the Empire, with urbanization always constituting a serious risk factor for the emergence of an epidemic.[25] The evolution of residential networks in the Byzantine cities, as they grew out throughout the centuries, reveals the contribution of urbanization to the emergence of those factors able to trigger an epidemic. It should be taken for granted that the anarchically structured settlements, which were suffocating in the narrow confines of the walls, their population being disproportionally high with respect to their actual size, in combination with the urbanization of major cities, allowed for the development of risk factors for an epidemic. Despite its advanced cultural level relative to other medieval kingdoms, we would better consider the general level of Byzantine public health to have not differed greatly from that of modern countries in the developing world. Various models have been developed with regard to the situation and general conditions in a medieval town, all of which put forward the neuralgic role of enzootic disease of domestic animals or rodents, in both the outbreak of an urban-type epidemic and the long-term preservation of the endemic character of a disease.[26]

We should point out, of course, that every time a microorganism invades a new area, there have to be the appropriate environmental conditions and suitable hosts in order for the microorganism to survive and for the area to become endemic. The relative importance of the various factors appears likely to be modified greatly by complex interactions of atmospheric conditions, and

23 Joppke, "International migrations, Geography, Politics and Culture in Europe and beyond", pp. 11–13.
24 Prothero, "Disease and mobility", pp. 259–67.
25 Saradi, "The Byzantine Cities (8th–15th centuries): Old Approaches and New Directions", pp. 25–46.
26 Keeling, "Bubonic plague: a metapopulation model of a zoonosis", pp. 2219–30.

by species and strain differences in the genetic constitution of particular pathogenic organisms.[27]

The environment is one of the factors of the epidemiologic triangle (host – agent – environment). The environmental parameters (such as water resources, climate, etc.) often influence and determine the spread of infectious diseases and epidemics. Changes is temperature and rainfall rate can also influence the patterns of transmission of waterborne infections and infections that spread via transmitters. The number of vectors can also be influenced by climate changes. "Weather" and "climate" are two terms that actually represent two aspects of the same spectrum. Weather is defined as the state of the atmosphere at a given point in time and climate is the average weather condition of the atmosphere and the surface of the earth and seas. Also, climate is described by a number of elements such as temperature, wind, humidity, soil moisture, sea surface temperature, and sea ice concentration and thickness.[28]

6   The Spectrum of Infectious Diseases in the Byzantine Empire

Byzantine sources explore only one aspect of infectious diseases of the era, whose range must have been rather broad: the vast majority of sources refer to the great scourge of the time, namely plague. Of course, more diseases are also included in these sources, for which a diagnosis is either directly or indirectly proposed, such as smallpox, severe infections of the digestive system, and malaria. In the first centuries of the Byzantine Empire, we find references to a series of epidemics for which, unfortunately, the clinical picture remains completely ambiguous and the underlying disease indeterminate. Unexplained epidemics have been recorded in this period, i.e. in Syria, Cilicia and Antioch in 333, in Thebes of Egypt in 346, in Amida of Asia Minor in 359, in Ablada in 360, in Phbow and Thebes of Egypt in 360–61, on the Byzantine – Persian border in 361–63, in Illyricum in 378–79, in Northern Greece in 383, in Antioch in 384–85, in Peloponnese in 396, in Palestine and Cappadocia in 406, in Asia Minor and Syria in 429 and, finally, the epidemic wave of 451–54 (or 453–57) that struck Palestine and Asia Minor (Galatia Cappadocia, Cilicia). Moreover, Constantinople was affected by a series of unspecified epidemics between 445 and 447.[29,30]

---

27   Hyslop, "Observations on the survival of pathogens", pp. 195–205.
28   Patz, "Climate change and infectious diseases", pp. 103–09.
29   Stathacopoulos, *Famine and pestilence in the Late Roman and early Byzantine Empire*, pp. 91–99, 113–24, 179, 182, 185, 189–202, 197, 205–06, 209–210, 216–17, 221, 235–36, 238, 249.
30   Ibid 10.

An interesting source of information is based on the reports of Byzantine emperors' deaths, which reveal details on infectious diseases like dysentery and malaria.[31] Dysentery is a bacterial disease of the lower digestive system and is caused by a broad range of microorganisms. The sources do not provide information about the exact type of dysentery, of course, but a heavy diarrheal disease is bacillary dysentery (or Shigellosis), which is caused by bacteria belonging to the genus *Shigella*.

The reports on the deaths of emperors Marcian (450–57) and Zeno (476–91) may approximate the disease, but they offer no information as to whether their deaths were associated with a local outbreak.[32] Another form of diarrheal phenomenon is typhoid fever caused by *Salmonella typhi*. The cases of Palestine and central Asia Minor (451–54) might be proven to have constituted an epidemic of typhoid fever.[33]

It should nevertheless be noted that several of the epidemics reported at these times concerning dysentery are rather associated with poor hygiene accompanying military campaigns and sieges. The modern data support a statistical association of typhoid fever to temperature fluctuations and rainfall. Also, rainfall anomalies due to the climatic changes may play a role in the transmission of enteric pathogens.[34]

As far as malaria is concerned, it has been known since ancient times that the Mediterranean suffered from this disease. In Greece, malaria was a major public health issue until its final eradication in 1974. From the era of the Hippocratic collection until the medico-geographic treatises of travelers during the 19th century, the data support the disease being a burden upon the region.[35] However, the fragmented Byzantine sources do not support a diagnosis; neither do they identify endemic areas. Specific cases resembling malaria include the deaths of emperors Constantius II (336–61) and Andronikos III Palaiologos (1328–41).[36,37] Assuming that malaria was the cause of death of the two emperors, available sources gave no information of epidemiological or geographical interest and cannot be associated with the location of the primary infection.

31   Lascaratos, *Diseases of Byzantine Emperors*, pp. 20–24, 56–64, 72–82, 570–601.
32   Ioannis Malalas, *Chronographia*, ed. L. Dindorf, pp. 376, 391.
33   Ibid 24.
34   Ibid 24, Dewan, "Typhoid fever and its association with environmental factors in Dhaka Metropolitan area of Bangladesh: A Spatial and Time-Series Approach", pp. e1998, Gault, "Rainfall anomalies and typhoid fever in Blantyre, Malawi", pp. e122.
35   Jones, *Malaria and Greek History*, pp. 61–73; Sallares, *Malaria and Rome*; Newfield, "Malaria and malaria-like disease".
36   Nikephoros Gregoras, *Historia Byzantina*, ed. Schopen, pp. 797–98.
37   Ammianus Marcellinus, *Rerum gestarum libri qui supersunt*, ed. Heinemann, pp. 170–73.

In any case, the interaction between the temperature and the biological cycle of the mosquitoes is well established. Temperature fluctuations appear to affect the development of larvae, the survival of mosquitoes, egg-laying time and increases in egg numbers.[38] These parameters are of great importance in endemic areas around the world.

The connection between the seasonality of smallpox and meteorological variables is very much under debate. According to one theory, albeit one now questioned, the introduction of camels to Africa 3500 to 4500 years ago may have coincided with considerable climate changes and contributed to the evolution of a progenitor of the Variola virus. This progenitor virus may have been able to infect a wide range of hosts and was presumably maintained in rodent populations before they encountered camels, which were a new species in Africa.[39] That theory, however, was rooted in attempts to use modern sequencing data to date the origins of the Variola virus. Since its publication, a number of ancient Variola virus genomes have been recovered from human remains.[40] Of these genomes, those closely related to the Variola virus as we know it have been recovered from early modern remains (17th, 18th and 19th centuries), while others that are genetically quite distinct and which possibly caused a disease that was clinically and epidemiologically unlike smallpox have been identified in people who died in Northern Europe in the first millennium AD. Together, the modern sequences and these premodern genomes now suggest that a Variola virus that caused smallpox as we would recognize it emerged in – or more likely after – the late antique period, but sometime before early modernity.[41]

It is possible, but far from proven given the current palaeogenetics of Variola, that smallpox periodically broke out in the Eastern Mediterranean. One possible example is the epidemic of 496 in Edessa, which lasted until 502.[42] Later, the narrative of Michael Psellos about the death of his daughter, Styliane (11th century), and Theodoros Prodromos' description of the clinical picture of his disease (12th century) suggest that smallpox epidemics – or outbreaks caused

---

38   Paaijmansa, "Influence of climate on malaria transmission depends on daily temperature variation", pp. 15135–39; Ezeakacha, "The role of temperature in affecting carry-over effects and larval competition in the globally invasive mosquito *Aedes albopictus*", pp. 12:123.
39   Babkin, "The Origin of the Variola Virus", pp. 1100–12; McDonald, "The Antonine Crisis".
40   Duggan et al., "17th Century Variola Virus Reveals the Recent History of Smallpox"; Ferrari et al., "Variola virus genome sequenced from an eighteenth-century museum specimen"; Mühlemann et al., "Diverse variola virus (smallpox) strains were widespread in northern Europe in the Viking Age".
41   Newfield et al., "Smallpox's antiquity in doubt".
42   Babkin, "The Origin of the Variola Virus", p. 24.

by something similar but ancestral to the Variola virus (the one that caused smallpox) – affected Constantinople and was possibly endemic there.[43,44,45]

7 The First Plague Pandemic (Plague of Justinian)

As already mentioned, the vast majority of Byzantine sources address the two pandemics of plague, namely the Justinian Plague and the Black Death. The pathogen responsible for plague is *Yersinia pestis*, which circulates in animal reservoirs and especially between rodents through fleas. Bubonic plague, which is the most common form of the disease, is the result of a bite from a flea. After an incubation period of two to six days, an individual becomes suddenly ill, the symptoms including headaches, chills, fever, malaise, and pain in the lymph nodes (inguinal, armpit, neck).[46] Modern studies have revealed a relationship between plague and rainfall, according to which the risk of plague increases during dry periods of rainfall below 10 mm.[47] A plague outbreak is the result of complex interactions between the life cycle of its vectors and their geographical distribution, which are influenced by climate variables. The climate can influence plague both directly and indirectly and involves the infectious agent, the transmitter, and the host. Parameters such as drought, rainfall, and relative humidity directly affect the growth and survival of fleas and their populations.[48] The Byzantine sources suggest the existence of drought seasons in the Eastern Mediterranean and the Middle East. The period AD 500–750 is characterized by drought in Thrace (Constantinople), Asia Minor, Egypt, Palestine, Syria, and Mesopotamia.[49]

The disease appeared in the Mediterranean port of Pelusium in Egypt in AD 541, and spread from there to all provinces of the Eastern Roman (Byzantine) Empire.[50] The first time the disease appeared in Constantinople was in 542, whereas the last incident of the first pandemic of bubonic plague in Byzantium dates back to the period AD 748–50/51, in the Arab-dominated regions of Syria

---

43   Lascaratos, "Two cases of smallpox in Byzantium", pp. 792–95.
44   Michael Psellos, *Pselli Miscelanea*, ed. Sathas, pp. 62–87.
45   Theodoros Prodromos, *Epistolae*, ed. Migne, pp. 1239–59.
46   Poland, "Diagnosis and clinical manifestations", pp. 43–50.
47   Stenseth, "Plague dynamics are driven by climate variation", pp. 13110–15; Pham, "Correlates of environmental factors and human plague: An ecological study in Vietnam", pp. 1634–41.
48   Krasnov, "Development rates of two Xenopsylla flea species in relation to air temperature and humidity", pp. 249–58; Krasnov, "Annual cycles of four flea species in the central Negev desert", pp. 266–76.
49   Telelis, *Meteorological Phenomena and Climate in Byzantium*, pp. 850–64.
50   Procopius Caesariensis, *Opera Omnia, De Bellis*, eds. Haury, Wirth, pp. 249–59.

and Mesopotamia.[51,52] Some researchers have even suggested that the frequency of epidemics among urban, suburban and rural areas of the Empire was different, considering the high rates of commercial traffic.[53,54]

Some sources suggest that the course of the first pandemic in Europe can be grouped into 15 waves.[55] On the other hand, modern approaches to the Byzantine epidemics suggest that epidemic waves appeared approximately every 11.6 years.[56] Moreover, the major urban centers of the Empire apparently experienced plague epidemics every 10–15 years.[57] For instance, out of the ten outbreaks that struck Constantinople, six can be traced back to the period extending from the 6th to the 8th centuries, appearing at intervals of 11–17 years, thus raising the average rate to 14.2 years.[58] Seemingly, the ten outbreaks of Constantinople confirm the notion of capital cities as always being more susceptible and exposed to epidemic diseases, given their involvement in extensive trade activities.[59] Interestingly, as far as the epidemics of Antioch are concerned, Evagrios notes that the disease appeared in cycles of fifteen years.[60]

The overall recording of epidemics displays an interesting geographical orientation of the disease, as the regions of Syria (19 outbreaks) and Mesopotamia (13) suffer most from the epidemics, followed by Constantinople with its surroundings (10), Egypt (8), Palestine (7), Asia Minor (7) and Balkan Peninsula (4). The distribution of epidemics per century and per region indicates an interesting fluctuation between Syria and Minor Asia (6th c.), Syria-Mesopotamia-Palestine (7th c.) and Syria-Mesopotamia-Egypt (8th c.). Based on recorded epidemics of the 6th to 8th centuries, increasing trends in epidemic outbreaks are observed in Syria, Mesopotamia, Palestine and Egypt (Table 4.2). Moreover, an increasing trend of plague outbreaks was evident in Constantinople during the 6th century.

The first "epidemic wave" to have struck the Empire dates to the period 541–46 and affected the following Byzantine provinces: Egypt-Palestine (541), Syria-Constantinople (542), Asia Minor (542–43), and Mesopotamia (545–546).

---

51 Zuqnin, *Chronicle,* ed. Harak, pp. 184–89.
52 Morony, "The first bubonic plague pandemic according to Syriac sources", pp. 59–86.
53 Ibid 24.
54 Biraben, "La peste dans le Haut Moyen Age", pp. 1484–510.
55 Ibid 39.
56 Ibid 24.
57 Biraben, "Rapport: La peste du vi^e Siècle dans l'empire byzantine", pp. 121–25.
58 Ibid 24.
59 Duncan, "The impact of the Antonine Plague", pp. 108–36.
60 Evagrios, *Historia Ecclesiastica,* eds. Bidez, Parmentier, pp. 177–79.

HISTORICAL EPIDEMIOLOGY OF THE MEDIEVAL EASTERN MEDITERRANEAN 121

TABLE 4.2   Chronological intervals of epidemic aggregations (AD 541–750/51)

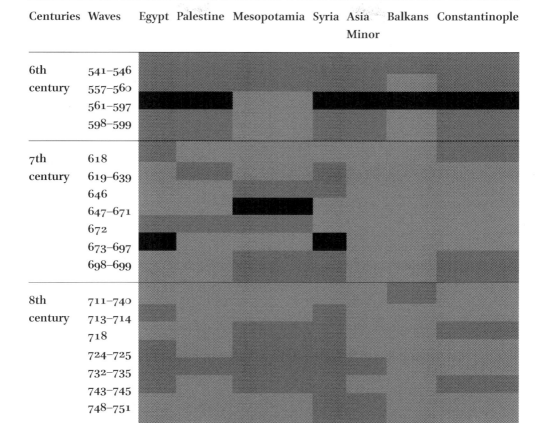

Based on this example, the "first wave" lasted five years, during which a number of epidemics occurred in six different regions. An issue that ought to be clarified is the frequently used terms "waves" or "epidemic waves". The term "wave" was first used at the end of 19th century to define seasonal influenza outbreaks (autumn, winter, and spring waves) after the influenza pandemic of 1889 in Asia.[61] The term "wave" it is considered common and elementary for understanding between different scientific fields. But, in Epidemiology, the term "wave" is related to the way an epidemic affects a region during a period

---

61   Morens, "Understanding influenza backward", pp. 679–80.

of time. In Epidemiology, the "wave" is not a group (or cluster) of a number of epidemics in a region through the years; rather, it is the number of (re)appearances of an epidemic in a region during a period of time, e.g., the number of appearances of the epidemic of SARS-CoV-2 in a country during the period 2019–22. But, if a country had declared the end of the epidemic in 2020, the potential re-appearance of the disease in 2022 would be a case of a new (second) epidemic. In this example, we cannot state that "the disease struck this country in two waves (2019–20 and 2022)". Instead, from the epidemiological point of view, we must define how many waves the epidemic had during the period 2019–20 (the first epidemic) and how many waves it had in 2022 (the second epidemic). Thus, referring to series of discrete epidemics or outbreaks as "waves of epidemics" or "waves of outbreaks" constitutes a problematic use of language. Instead, we could speak of "aggregations of epidemics" within a spatio-temporal frame. We believe that this term is preferable because it enhances the spatio-temporal differences in the emergence of a disease, and it causes no confusion to the reader, as well as being epidemiologically unambiguous.[62]

Approximately ten years after that last outbreak in Mesopotamia, i.e., in 557, a second aggregation of epidemics occurred in the same province, from which it followed an almost reverse course: Mesopotamia (557), Constantinople (558), Syria (558) and Asia Minor (560). Constantinople, Asia Minor, Syria, and the Balkans again experienced nine local epidemic outbreaks in the period 561–97. This endemic period of 38 years was followed by a third aggregation, which started in 598 during an Arab invasion of the Empire. Therefrom, the epidemic spread to Asia Minor and Constantinople, as well as to Syria one year later. A fourth aggregation of epidemics started in Egypt in 618, also affecting Constantinople.

The outbreak of 626 in Palestine marked the fifth aggregation of epidemics. In 634 and 639, both Palestine and Syria were affected by plague, whereas a sixth aggregation occurred in Syria and Mesopotamia in 646, followed by a long period extending from 647 to 671 when epidemic outbreaks were reported in Mesopotamia.

Apparently, the seventh aggregation of epidemics started in Egypt in 672, to then spread to Palestine and Mesopotamia in the same year. Sporadic outbreaks ensued in Egypt and Syria over a long period stretching from 673 to 697. An eighth aggregation of epidemics was responsible for the epidemic of Constantinople in 698, and it seems to be associated with the following year's epidemics in Syria and Mesopotamia. The ninth aggregation occurred over a

---

62 Tsiamis, *Plague in Byzantine Times: A medico-historical study*, pp. 128–30.

period of two years (704–06) and once more affected Syria and Mesopotamia. There seems to be a connection between the epidemics of Crete and the tenth aggregation, although it is rather difficult to chronologically isolate them (sometime between 711 and 740). An eleventh aggregation struck Syria and Egypt in the years 713–14, whereas the twelfth coincides with the Arab siege of Constantinople in 718.

Egypt was affected by a thirteenth aggregation of epidemics in 724, which was probably linked to the outbreaks in Syria and Mesopotamia in 725. The fourteenth aggregation once more struck the region of the Middle East, as it started from Syria or Egypt in 732 and moved on to Palestine and Mesopotamia in 735. Between 743 and 745, Egypt witnessed a fifteenth aggregation that gradually spread to Syria and Mesopotamia, as well as to Italy and Constantinople by sea. The pandemic of the Byzantine world ended with the sixteenth aggregation of 748–50 in Syria and Mesopotamia.

To conclude, we need to mention that the catastrophic impact of the first plague pandemic is debated and the historical, genetic, environmental, and archaeological evidence for this pandemic has recently been reevaluated.[63] Several scholars argue that the scale and broader implications of the demographic disaster are overestimated, because of the tendency of modern historiography to use the highest mortality rates of the second plague pandemic (in particular of its first wave in Europe, the Black Death) as reference for the first pandemic, for the lack of reliable quantitative data on mortality levels. Also, it has been argued that high mortality described by late antique literary sources for the major urban centers was not the rule, but the exception.[64]

8 Epidemics in Byzantium and the Eastern Mediterranean (750–1346)

As it became apparent, during the Plague of Justinian, plague overshadowed all other disease entities, whose failure to be mentioned does not imply that they also disappeared. Twenty-seven epidemic outbreaks have been recorded for the period 750–1346 in various geographic regions and cities of the Byzantine

---

63 Sarris, "New approaches to the plague of Justinian", pp. 315–46; Mordechai, "Rejecting Catastrophe: The Case of the Justinianic Plague", pp. 3–50.

64 Mordechai et al., "The Justinian Plague: An inconsequential pandemic?", pp. 25546–54. For an outline of the opposing view, see Sarris, "New approaches to the Plague of Justinian". A growing list of relevant publications on the First Plague Pandemic can be found in the appendix to the regularly updated online-bibliography of M. Green et al., https://drive.google.com/file/d/1xoD_dwyAwp9xi9sMCW5UvpGfEVH5J2ZA/view.

Empire, but especially among former territories of the Empire now held by the Arabs and, subsequently, by the Seljuks. Unfortunately, no clinical picture exists for these instances and, therefore, it has not been possible to identify them either as plague or as any other disease. There is only one case (Constantinople, 1038) that has been reported as an epidemic of angina, i.e., an acute streptococcal or sometimes staphylococcal infection of the deep tissues of the mouth and adjoining parts of the neck.

More specifically, epidemic outbreaks have been reported in Syria (761), Asia Minor (814), Mesopotamia and Egypt (Baghdad and Cairo, 940), Baghdad (945), Egypt (982, 1006, 1007, 1008), Thrace (1035 or 1051), Constantinople (1038), Baghdad (1047), Mesopotamia / Persia / Syria / Egypt (1056–57), Egypt (1059), Baghdad (1063 & 1064), two epidemics in Cairo (1200), Alexandria / Cairo / Jerusalem / Aleppo (1296) and Babylon (1316). The epidemics of Egypt (1006–08), Mesopotamia / Persia / Syria / Egypt (1056–57), the epidemics of Baghdad (1063–64) and Cairo (1200), and the outbreaks of 1296 in Alexandria, Cairo, Jerusalem, and Aleppo, albeit undiagnosed, give the impression of serious infectious diseases.

The only element of these epidemics that we are able to examine is the geographical area of their appearance and their possible relation to meteorological and climate changes. Our sources indicate that the epidemics are mainly related to the southeast Mediterranean and the Middle East, thus suggesting an area that reminds us of the geographical location of the First Pandemic of plague, although the disease cannot be identified. It is interesting, however, that extreme weather phenomena of drought preceding the outbreak are mentioned in our sources, in seven distinct cases: Syria (761 & 842), Asia Minor (814), Egypt (940), Thrace (1035), and Baghdad (945 & 1047). In addition, our sources reveal that five epidemics in Egypt (982, 1006, 1007, 1008 & 1059) were accompanied by abnormal fluctuations in the level of the Nile, which were unusual for that time and are obviously linked to similar climate anomalies in the areas where the springs of the Nile are located, in Central and Eastern Africa.[65]

9 The Second Plague Pandemic (Black Death) in Byzantium (1347–1453)

The re-emergence of plague in (late medieval) Europe has been the subject of many theories. Modern research attempts to provide answers by taking into account the combination of historical, geographical, and molecular (ancient

---

65   Ibid 10.

DNA) studies of the microbe. The Mongol conquest and the unification of the tribes of Eurasia resulted in the restoration of commercial relations across this vast continent, bringing Central Asia in frequent contact with Europe and the Mediterranean. This transformation is considered instrumental in the movement of *Yersinia pestis* to the West and the passing of plague to immunologically virgin populations in Europe. A recent study of ancient *Yersinia pestis* DNA recovered from the teeth of plague victims buried in a Nestorian (Syriac) cemetery from Issyk Kul in Kyrgyzstan demonstrated – through comparisons with *Yersinia pestis* DNA recovered from European Black Death victims – that the local plague epidemic of 1338–39 was the initial event of the second plague pandemic and its geographical origin.[66]

According to the narrative of De Mussi, the The Black Death originated in the Crimea during the siege of the Genoese colony of Caffa by the Mongols, in 1346:[67] the disease struck the camp of the Mongols, who catapulted the corpses of those who had died by plague into the city when they realized that they were unable to conquer it. The validity of De Mussi's narrative has been debated extensively at both levels of microbiology and epidemiology, i.e., whether the *Yersinia pestis* bacterium can maintain its infectivity and result in the disease after having remained in a dead host or on surfaces in environmental conditions. Studies have so far revealed that *Yersinia pestis* is able to survive for up to 72 hours on surfaces of objects, and for at least 24 days in polluted soil.[68,69] On the other hand, historical research has demonstrated that De Mussi was never an eyewitness of the Mongol siege of Caffa and that his narrative about the catapulting of corpses should be regarded as legend.[70] Nevertheless, from the Crimea, the disease spread like lightning to Constantinople in 1347, with death affecting all ages and social strata, according to historians, deposed emperor Kantakouzenos and the historian Nikephoros Gregoras.[71,72] The symptoms of the disease are described in detail by Kantakouzenos: lung infection, intense chest pains, hemoptysis and intense thirst, lethargy, and ultimately death. This description has led many researchers to believe that Kantakouzenos refers to the pulmonary form of the disease.[73]

---

66   Green, "The Four Black Deaths", pp. 1601–31; Tsiamis, *Plague in Byzantine Times: A medico-historical study*, pp. 158–65; Spyrou et al., "The source of the Black Death".
67   Wheelis, "Biological Warfare at the 1346 Siege of Caffa", pp. 971–75.
68   Rose, "Survival of *Yersinia pestis* on environmental surfaces", pp. 2166–71.
69   Eisen, "Persistence of *Yersinia pestis* in soil", pp. 941–43.
70   Barker, "Laying the Corpses to Rest".
71   Ioannis Kantakouzenos, *Historia Libri IV*, ed. Schopen, pp. 391–411, 426.
72   Nikephoros Gregoras, *Historia Byzantina*, ed. Schopen, pp. 488–89.
73   Miller, "The plague in John VI Cantacuzenus and Thucydides", pp. 385–95.

Beyond Constantinople, by 1347, plague had spread to the islands of the Aegean Sea and Crete, to Thessaloniki and Trebizond, as well as to the Venetian naval bases of Methone and Korone in the Peloponnese.[74,75,76,77] By the following year (1348), the disease had spread to Rhodes – the latest possession of the Order of the Knights of Saint John – as well as to the Venetian ports of Cyprus and the inner Peloponnese in southern Greece.[78]

The epidemic outbreaks in the leftovers of the former Byzantine Empire and the Eastern Mediterranean, during the 14th and 15th century, can be grouped into nine major aggregations of epidemics and eleven individual outbreaks. Based on the geographical distribution of the epidemics for the period 1346–1453, the following cases can be distinguished: Constantinople, along with the surrounding areas of Thrace, were struck 14 times (1347, 1361–64, 1379–80, 1386, 1391, 1397, 1403, 1409–10, 1421–22, 1431, 1435, 1438, 1441, 1448); the Peloponnese was struck 12 times (1347–48, 1362–63, 1375, 1381–82, 1390–91, 1397–1402, 1410–13, 1418, 1422, 1431, 1441, 1448); Crete and Cyprus experienced six outbreaks each: 1347, 1362–65, 1375, 1388–89, 1408–11, 1418–19 and 1348, 1393, 1409–11, 1419–20, 1422, 1438, respectively; similarly, the Ionian Islands were affected by five epidemic outbreaks (1400, 1410–13, 1416, 1420, 1450) and the Aegean Islands by another four outbreaks (1347–48, 1362, 1408, 1445). As far as the mainland of Greece is concerned, various towns, cities and regions were struck by epidemics, in 1347, 1368, 1372, 1374–75, 1378, 1388, 1423, 1426 and 1448. Lastly, the Empire of Trebizond was affected four times, in 1347, 1362–63 and 1435.

The Empire was struck by a first aggregation of epidemics in 1347–48, with Constantinople, Euboea, Crete, Lemnos, Thessaloniki, Trebizond, Methone, Korone, the inner part of the Byzantine Peloponnese, Rhodes, and Cyprus being at the epicenter. For the next 12 years, no reports of plague epidemics exist, whereas subsequent reports refer to the period of the second epidemic aggregation, namely 1361–65. That second aggregation affected the same regions (more or less) as had the first: Constantinople was struck in 1361, followed by subsequent outbreaks in Edirne, Trebizond, Lemnos, Crete, Cyprus, and the Peloponnese, along with mainland Asia Minor.

Apparently, the third aggregation began in Thessaloniki in 1372, to then spread to Epirus, the Peloponnese, and Crete until 1376. According to available sources, the fourth aggregation occurred within the period 1378–82 and struck the monasteries of Mount Athos, as well as the city of Galata, including

---

74 Ibid 55.
75 Ibid 54.
76 Kostis, *During the times of plague. Perspectives for the communities of the Greek peninsula*, pp. 30–48.
77 Thiriet, *Régestes des délibérations du Sénat de Venise concernant la Romani*, pp. 63–64.
78 Loenertz, *Démétrius Cydonès correspondance*, pp. 122, 145–49, 278.

the Genoese colony of Pera in Constantinople, and the Peloponnese. The fifth aggregation started in 1386, and by 1391 it had struck Constantinople, Athens, the Peloponnese, and Crete.

Once more, Constantinople was affected by a sixth epidemic aggregation (1397–1402), which was limited to the Venetian possessions in the Aegean and Ionian Seas. Probably the deadliest aggregation was the seventh (1408–13), which affected mainly the islands and the capital city. The areas under Venetian possession were bound to be affected the most, as it seems that naval bases infected one another, which was the case in Cyprus, Crete, Korone, Methone, and Corfu. Similarly damaging, the eighth aggregation occurred between 1417 and 1423 and struck Constantinople, the largest part of the Greek mainland and, once more, the Venetian areas. The ninth and last major aggregation until the fall of Byzantium occurred in 1435 in Constantinople, and from there the epidemic reached Trebizond in Asia Minor.[79] Since the 1430s until the fall of Constantinople in 1453, a series of outbreaks occurred in: Patras and Constantinople in 1431, Nicosia and the outskirts of Constantinople in 1438, Peran and the Peloponnese in 1441, and Thrace in 1448. Moreover, the same period witnessed another two (of a total 11) epidemic outbreaks, namely in the islands of Chios (1445) and Corfu (1450).

The city that experienced by far the most epidemic outbreaks – ten in total – is Constantinople, as often as every 11.1 years on average. In addition, the Venetian possessions in the Eastern Mediterranean and the Greek islands were struck by the deadly disease 23 times. The particular maritime geography of Greece, which gradually came to correspond to the size of the shrinking Byzantine Empire, combined with the organized military and commercial maritime networks of the Aegean Sea, contributed to the spread of plague.[80]

In essence, this spreading of the disease was further facilitated by the fact that the Aegean is an "enclosed sea" with numerous ports separated by short distances. After all, the maritime network that led to Constantinople passed through the Aegean (Venice / Ragusa / Corfu / Methone / Korone / Cerigo / Negroponte / Thessaloniki / Lemnos / Constantinople), forming standard routes. Another typical route for the armadas of Venice to reach the Middle East was through Venice / Ragusa / Corfu / Methone / Korone / Candia / Famagusta.[81,82] Thus, plague travelled by sea at the speed of galleons, which means that there were particular cases when, due to the short distance among

---

79 Tsiamis, *Plague in Byzantine Times: A medico-historical study*, pp. 168–73.
80 Tsiamis, *Plague in Byzantine Times: A medico-historical study*, pp. 168–69.
81 Koder, "Maritime trade and the food supply of Constantinople in the Middle Ages", pp. 109–24.
82 Lane, *Venice: A maritime Republic*, pp. 66–85.

the ports of the Aegean and the Ionian Seas, the duration of a journey to the Byzantine, Venetian, Genoese, or Ottoman territories was shorter than the incubation period of plague. Two rather typical examples are the Venetian military bases in the Peloponnese, in Methone and Korone, which in all four epidemic outbreaks that struck them were affected simultaneously.

Concerning the Islamic world, Black Death appeared during the first epidemic aggregation and struck Alexandria (1347), Tivrik, Ascalon, Acre, Jerusalem, Sidon, Damascus, Homs, and Aleppo (1348), Antioch, Mecca, Mosul, and Baghdad (1349), and Cairo (1430).[83,84,85]

A notable fluctuation is evident in the overall duration of the various epidemic aggregations in the Eastern Mediterranean. More specifically, the average duration of epidemic aggregations in the 14th century is estimated at 2.3 years, in contrast to the average of 4.2 years in the 15th century.

A documented relationship between the fluctuation of drought and the Byzantine plague epidemics cannot be established. However, a possible correlation could be presented with the help of Palmer Drought Severity Index (PDSI) using the model of the *Old World Drought Atlas* (OWDA).[86] The distinct periods of mostly summer drought mainly occurred during the 1360s, 1420s, and 1430s. Despite the lack of more comprehensive data that could contribute to establishing a strong link, it seems that some epidemics temporally coincide with the periods of intense negative PDSI values. More specifically, the epidemics of 1361–1365 and 1417–1423 appear to concur with extreme negative PDSI values (dry seasons).[87]

Finally, we mention that the current pandemic of the virus SARS-CoV-2 was the trigger factor for the comparison between the modern and the old pandemics, mainly the pandemics of plague and 1918 Spanish Flu pandemic. It seems that the collective fears, social behaviors and emotional reactions were, are and will remain, a human characteristic despite modern medical knowledge.[88] Last but not least, while there is ongoing debate as to the extent of the demographic and socio-political catastrophe caused by the Justinianic

---

83 Varlik, *Disease and Empire: A history of plague epidemics in the early Modern Ottoman Empire (1453–1600)*, pp. 22–49.
84 Gottfried, *The Black Death*, pp. 38–41.
85 Borsch, "Plague Depopulation and Irrigation decay in Medieval Egypt", pp. 125–56.
86 Cook, "Old World megadroughts and pluvial during the Common Era", pp. 1–9.
87 Tsiamis, *Plague in Byzantine Times: A medico-historical study*, pp. 178–81. A growing list of relevant publications on the Second Plague Pandemic can be found in the regularly updated online bibliography of M. Green et al. https://drive.google.com/file/d/1x0D_dwy Awp9xi9sMCW5UvpGfEVH5J2ZA/view (accessed 14.02.2023).
88 Varlık, "Rethinking the history of plague in the time of COVID-19", pp. 285–93; Tsiamis, "From Justinian Plague to Covid-19: a Timeless Story?", pp. 17–21.

Plague, the research, including environmental data, is quite clear in suggesting disastrous demographic and economic consequences of the Black Death for the Byzantine Empire, the collapse of the cultivated landscapes in Greece being among the most significant for all of Europe.[89]

10 Conclusions

Apparently, a number of different reasons contributed to the spread of pathogenic agents throughout the Byzantine world: from the lack of scientific knowledge on the nature of infectious diseases or extreme climate and meteorological changes, to the turbulent periods of wars, intense human migration, or the existence and operation of an extensive and organized maritime network.

What catches our attention is the fact that the eastern Mediterranean basin was a particularly pathogenic region. The sources provide information – either directly or indirectly – on infectious diseases like malaria, smallpox, dysentery, and, of course, plague. The lack of sources on other diseases, however, does not preclude their existence. Until the appearance of Black Death, the references to various infectious diseases among available sources primarily concern the Mediterranean coastline and the mainland of the Middle East. It seems that this situation persisted and was further aggravated during the Justinianic Plague. Of course, contemporary sources focused almost entirely on the new disease, whereas the epidemic aggregations described above reveal that the Middle East was a much more pathogenic region than the Balkans.

As far as plague is concerned, we cannot exclude the possibility that enzootic and endemic foci developed in particular provinces of the Byzantine Empire, and that these gave rise to epidemics under the influence of ideal environmental and climate conditions. Plague can spread either rapidly and over long distances with humans moving from one place to another, or more slowly and locally through rodents.[90] The epidemic of Egypt in 672, which appeared after a disease-free period that lasted 54 years, is indicative of the dynamics of modern epidemics. Other examples of the sort include the epidemic outbreak in the region of Oran (Algeria) in 2003, where no cases of plague had been reported to the World Health Organization (WHO) in the last

---

89 Izdebski et al., "Exploring Byzantine and Ottoman economic history with the use of palynological data"; Izdebski et al., "Palaeoecological data indicates land-use changes across Europe linked to spatial heterogeneity in mortality during the Black Death pandemic".
90 Sallares, "Ecology, Evolution and Epidemiology of Plague", pp. 231–89.

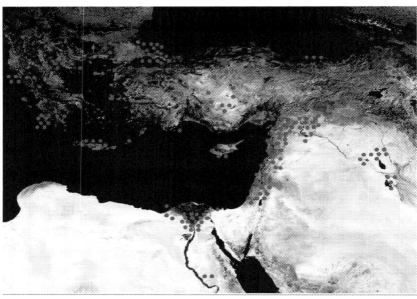

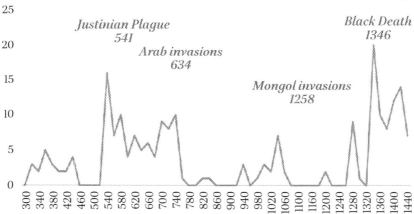

FIGURE 4.1 Geographical distribution of epidemic outbreaks from AD 300 to 1453
(plague, dysentery, diphtheria, smallpox, unknown microbial origin)
Note: Red dots correspond to known cities or extended areas, which do not
necessarily equal the exact geographical location of an epidemic

50 years.[91] Phenomena like these may be explained by the sudden invasion of infected animals and activation of natural foci which have remained inactive for a long time for environmental reasons.[92] The disease can be sustained for

91   Bitam, "Zoonotic focus of Plague, Algeria", pp. 1975–77.
92   Berterat, "Plague Reappearance in Algeria after 50 years", pp. 1459–62.

decades due to the enzootic behavior of rodent populations.[93] An interesting epidemiological model demonstrates that bubonic plague can be sustained for approximately 100 years in an enzootic area that hosts a population of 60,000 rodents, which was a typical number for a medieval town.

The geographical spread of plague reveals the continuous presence of the disease in Syria – particularly in the province of Syria – from which it spread to neighboring Mesopotamia and Palestine. Indeed, the disease seems to have been recycled among these three provinces, with Egypt being also affected on several occasions.

The existence of diseases in the southeast Mediterranean continued in the interim period between the two pandemics of plague. Egypt, Palestine, and Mesopotamia kept struggling with unspecified epidemics in the period 750–1346 whose duration and spread nevertheless point to serious diseases. Of particular interest is the fact that this situation was completely reversed during the presence of the Black Death. In the Greek space, which coincides with the areas of the late Byzantine Empire, the Frankish states, and possessions of Venice and Genoa, the number of epidemics was overwhelmingly higher compared to the Middle East. This can be partly explained by the constant movements and frequent conflicts in the Greek region (Fig. 4.1).

Acknowledgements

I would like to acknowledge Dr. Johannes Preiser-Kapeller and Dr. Adam Izdebski for their kind invitation to contribute to this volume. Also, special thanks to Dr. Ioannis Telelis and Dr. Dionysios Stathakopoulos for our long-term collaboration and their advice.

Bibliography

Primary Sources

Ammianus Marcellinus, *Ammiani Marcellini, Rerum gestarum libri qui supersunt*, ed. W. Heinemann, London 1982–86.

Evagrios, *Historia Ecclesiastica*, ed. J. Bidez, L. Parmentier, A.M. Hakkert, Amsterdam 1964, pp. 177–79.

Ioannis Kantakouzenos, *Historia Libri IV*, ed. L. Schopen, *Corpus Scriptorum Historiae Byzantinae*, Bonnae 1828–32.

---

93   Dennis, "Plague", pp. 402–11.

Ioannis Malalas, *Chronographia*, ed. L. Dindorf, *Corpus Scriptorum Historiae Byzantinae*, Bonnae 1831.

Michael Psellos, *Pselli Miscelanea*, ed. C. Sathas, *Bibliotheca Graeca*, Paris 1876.

Nikephoros Gregoras, *Historia Byzantina*, eds. L. Schopen/J. Bekker, *Corpus Scriptorum Historiae Byzantinae* Ed. Weber, Bonne 1829–32.

Procopius Caesariensis, *Opera Omnia, De Bellis. Libri I–II*, eds. J. Haury/G. Wirth, Leipzig 1905.

Theodoros Prodromos, *Epistolae*, ed. J. Migne, *Patrologia Graeca*, Paris 1864.

Zuqnīn, *Chronicle of Zuqnīn A.D. 488–775*, ed. A. Harak, Toronto 1999.

Secondary Literature

Achtman, M. et al, "Yersinia pestis: the cause of plague is a recently emerged clone of Yersinia pseudotuberculosis", *Proceedings of the National Academy of Science* 96 (1999), 14043–48.

Babkin, I./Babkina, I., "The Origin of the Variola Virus", *Viruses* 7 (2015), 1100–1112.

Barker, H., "Laying the Corpses to Rest: Grain, Embargoes, and Yersinia pestis in the Black Sea, 1346–48", Speculum 96 (2021), 97–126.

Bertherat, E. et al, "Plague Reappearance in Algeria after 50 years, 2003", *Emerging Infectious Diseases* 13 (2007), 1459–62.

Biraben, J./Le Goff, J., "La peste dans le Haut Moyen Age", *Annales ESC* 24.8 (1969), 1484–510.

Bitam, I., et al, "Zoonotic focus of Plague, Algeria", *Emerging Infectious Diseases* 12 (2006),1975–77.

Beutler, E., *Topics in Hematology: Hemolytic anemia in disorders of red cell metabolism*, New York 1978.

Biraben, J-N., "Rapport: La peste du VIe Siècle dans l'empire byzantine", in J. Le Fort/ C. Morrisson/J.P. Sodini (eds.), *Hommes et richesses dans l'empire Byzantin. IVe– VIIe siècles.* Paris 1989, pp. 121–25.

Borsch, S., "Plague Depopulation and Irrigation decay in Medieval Egypt", *The Medieval World* 1 (2014), 125–56.

Burrows, T./Farrell, J./Gillet, W., "The catalase activities of *Pasterela pestis* and other bacteria", *British Journal of Experimental Pathology* 45 (1964), 579–88.

Centers for Disease Control and Prevention, *Principles of Epidemiology in Public Health Practice An Introduction to Applied Epidemiology and Biostatistics.* Atlanta 2012.

Conrad, L., "Epidemic disease in Central Syria in the late sixth century. Some new insights from the verse of Hassān ibn Thābit", *Byzantine and Modern Greek Studies* 18 (1994), 12–58.

Cook, E., et al., "Old World megadroughts and pluvial during the Common Era", *Science Advances* 10 (2015), 1–9.

Dennis, D., "Plague", in G. Strickland, (ed.), *Hunter's Tropical Medicine and Emerging Infectious Diseases*, Philadelphia 2000, pp. 402–11.

Dewan, A., "Typhoid fever and its association with environmental factors in the Dhaka Metropolitan area of Bangladesh: a spatial and time-series approach", PloS Neglected Tropical Diseases 1 (2013), e1998.

Dowell, S., "Seasonal variation in host susceptibility and cycles of certain infectious diseases", *Emerging Infectious Diseases* 7 (2001), 369–74.

Duncan-Jones, R., "The impact of the Antonine Plague", *Journal of Roman Archaeology* 9 (1996), 108–36.

Dennis, D., "Plague", in G. Strickland, (ed.), *Hunter's Tropical Medicine and Emerging Infectious Diseases,* Philadelphia 2000, pp. 402–11.

Duggan, A. et al., "17th Century Variola Virus Reveals the Recent History of Smallpox", *Current Biology* 26 (2016) 3407–3412.

Eisen, R./Petersen, J./Higgins, C./Wong, D., "Persistence of *Yersinia pestis* in soil under natural conditions", *Emerging Infectious Diseases* 14 (2008), 941–43.

Engelkirk, P., *Burton's Microbiology for the Health Sciences*, Philadelphia 2011, pp. 121–23.

Eyre-Walker, A./Keightley, P.D., "Estimating the rate of adaptive molecular evolution in the presence of slightly deleterious mutations and population size change", *Molecular Biology and Evolution* 26 (2009), 2097–108.

Ezeakacha, N./Yee, D., "The role of temperature in affecting carry-over effects and larval competition in the globally invasive mosquito *Aedes albopictus*", *Parasites Vectors* 1(2009), 123.

Feodorova, V./Devdariani, Z., "The interaction of *Yersinia pestis* with erythrocytes", *Journal of Medical Microbiology* 51 (2002),150–58.

Ferrari, G. et al., "Variola virus genome sequenced from an eighteenth-century museum specimen supports the recent origin of smallpox", *Philosophical Transactions of the Royal Society B* 375 (2020) 20190572.

Fine, P./Eames, K./Heymann, D.L., "Herd Immunity; a rough guide", *Clinical Infectious Diseases* 52 (2011), 911–16.

Gage, K./Burkot, T./Eisen, R./Hayes, E., "Climate and vectorborne Diseases", *American Journal of Preventive Medicine* 35 (2008), 436–50.

Gauld, J., et al., "Rainfall anomalies and typhoid fever in Blantyre, Malawi", *Epidemiology and Infection* 150 (2022), e122.

Gottfried, R.S., *The Black Death*, London 1983.

Green, M.H., "Taking "Pandemic" seriously: making the Black Death Global", *The Medieval World* 1 (2014), 27–62.

Green, M.H., "The Four Black Deaths", *The American Historical Review* 5 (2020), 1601–1631.

Grmek, M., *Les maladies à l'aube de la civilisation occidentale*, Paris 1983.

Hassan, F.A., "Extreme Nile floods and famines in Medieval Egypt (AD 930–1500) and their climatic implications", Quaternary International 173–174 (2007), 101–12.

Hughes, M./Diaz, H., "Was there a "Medieval Warm Period", and if so, where and when?", *Climatic Change* 26 (1994), 109–42.

Hyslop, N.S., "Observations on the survival of pathogens in water and air at ambient temperatures and relative humidity", in M. Loutit/J. Miles, *Microbial Ecology*, Berlin 1978, pp. 195–205.

Izdebski A., et al. "Palaeoecological data indicates land-use changes across Europe linked to spatial heterogeneity in mortality during the Black Death pandemic", *Nature Ecology and Evolution* 6 (2022) 297–306.

John, T.J./Samuel, R., "Herd immunity and herd effect: new insights", *European Journal of Epidemiology* 16 (2000), 1–6.

Jones, W.H., *Malaria and Greek History*, Manchester 1909.

Joppke, C./Leboutte, R., "International migrations, Geography, Politics and Culture in Europe and beyond", in R. Leboutte (ed.) *Migrations and Migrant in Historical Perspective*, vol. 12. (Institute Universitaire Européen, Collection Europe Plurielle), Brussels 1997, pp. 11–13.

Keeling, M./Gilligan, C., "Bubonic plague: a metapopulation model of a zoonosis", *Proceedings of Royal Society* (London) 267 (2000), 2219–30.

Koder, J., "Maritime trade and the food supply of Constantinople in the Middle Ages", in R. Macrides (ed.) *Travel in the Byzantine World*, Aldershot 2002, pp. 109–24.

Koder, J., "Climatic change in the fifth and sixth centuries?", in P. Allen/E. Jeffreys (eds.), *The sixth century, end or beginning?*, Brisbane 1996, pp. 270–85.

Kostis, K., *During the times of plague. Perspectives for the communities of the Greek peninsula, 14th–19th century*, Heraklion 1995.

Krasnov, B., et al., "Development rates of two Xenopsylla flea species in relation to air temperature and humidity", *Medical and Veterinary Entomology* 15 (2001), 249–258.

Krasnov, B., et al., "Annual cycles of four flea species in the central Negev desert", *Medical and Veterinary Entomology* 16 (2002), 266–276.

Lane, F., *Venice: A maritime Republic*, Baltimore 1973.

Lascaratos, J., *Diseases of Byzantine Emperors*, Corfu 1995.

Lascaratos, J./Tsiamis, C., "Two cases of smallpox in Byzantium", *International Journal of Dermatology* 41 (2002), 792–95.

Loenertz, R., *Démétrius Cydonès correspondance*, Vatican 1956, pp. 122, 145–49, 278.

Luterbacher, J./Newfield, T./Xoplaki, E./Nowatzki, E., et al., "Past pandemics and climate variability across the Mediterranean", *Euro-Mediterranean Journal for Environmental Integration* 5 (2020):46.

McDonald, B.T., "The Antonine Crisis: Climate Change as a Trigger for Epidemiological and Economic Turmoil", in P. Edrkamp et al. (ed.) *Climate Change and Ancient Societies in Europe and the Near East. Diversity in Collapse and Resilience*, London 2021, pp. Ch. 13.

Miller, T., "The plague in John VI Cantacuzenus and Thucydides", *Greek, Roman and Byzantine Studies* 17 (1976), 385–95.

Mordechai, L./Eisenberg, M., "Rejecting Catastrophe: The Case of the Justinianic Plague", *Past & Present* 1(2019), 3–50.

Mordechai, L., et al., "The Justinianic Plague: An inconsequential pandemic?", *Proceedings of the National Academy of Sciences of the United States of America* 116 (2019), 25546–25554.

Morens, D./Taubenberger, J., "Understanding influenza backward", *Journal of the American Medical Association* 302 (2009), 679–680.

Morony, M., "For whom does the writer write? The first bubonic plague pandemic according to Syriac sources", in L. Little (ed.) *Plague and the End of Antiquity. The Pandemic 541–750*, New York 2007, pp. 59–86.

Mühlemann, B. et al., "Diverse variola virus (smallpox) strains were widespread in northern Europe in the Viking Age", *Science* 369 (2020) eaaw8977.

Newfield, T., "Malaria and malaria-like disease in the early Middle Ages", *Early Medieval Europe* 25/3 (2017), 251–300.

Newfield, T. et al., "Smallpox's antiquity in doubt", *Journal of Roman Archaeology* (2022) 10.1017/S1047759422000290.

Ochman, H./Lawrence, J./Groisman, E., "Lateral gene transfer and the nature of bacterial innovation", *Nature* 405 (2000), 299–304.

Opal, S.M./Keusch, G.T., "Host responses to infection", in J. Cohen/W. Powderly (eds.) *Infectious Diseases*, Philadelphia 2004, pp. 31–52.

Paaijmansa, K./Blanforda, S./Bellb, A./Blanfordc, J, et al. "Influence of climate on malaria transmission depends on daily temperature variation". *Proceedings of the National Academy of Sciences of the United States of America* 34 (2010), 15135–15139.

Paradis, S. et al, "Phylogeny of the Enterobacteriaceae on genes encoding elongation factor Tu and F-ATP-beta unit", *International Journal of Systematic Evolutionary Microbiology* 55 (2005), 2013–25.

Patz, J.A. et al, "Climate change and infectious diseases", in A.J. McMichael (ed.) *Climate change and human health: risks and responses*, Geneva 2003, pp. 103–09.

Perry, R./Fetherson, J., "*Yersinia pestis*-Etiologic Agent of Plague", *Clinical Microbiology Reviews* 10 (1997), 35–66.

Pham, H., et al., "Correlates of environmental factors and human plague: An ecological study in Vietnam", *International Journal of Epidemiology* 38 (2009), 1634–1641.

Poland, J.D./Dennis, D.T., "Diagnosis and clinical manifestations", in D. Dennis/K. Gage/ N. Gratz/J. Poland/E. Tikhomirov (eds.), *Plague Manual: Epidemiology, Distribution, Surveillance and Control*, Geneva 1999, pp. 43–50.

Preiser-Kapeller, J., "A complex systems approach to the evolutionary dynamics of human history: the case of the Late Medieval World crisis", Working Paper EMSCR 2012 (Symposium B)/1–46.

Prothero, R.M., "Disease and mobility: a neglected factor in epidemiology", *International Journal of Epidemiology* 6 (1977), 259–267.

Reed, F.A./Aquardo, C.F., "Mutation, selection and the future of human evolution", *Trends in Genetics* 22 (2006), 479–484.

Rose, L./Donlan, R./Banerjee, S./Arduino, M., "Survival of *Yersinia pestis* on environmental surfaces", *Applied and Environmental Microbiology* 269 (2003), 2166–71.

Sallares, R., *Malaria and Rome: A History of Malaria in Ancient Italy*, Cambridge 2002.

Sallares, R., "Ecology, Evolution and Epidemiology of Plague", in L. Little (ed.) *Plague and the End of Antiquity. The Pandemic 541–750*, New York 2007, pp. 231–89.

Spyrou, M.A. et al, "Ancient pathogen genomics as an emerging tool for infectious disease research",. *Nature Reviews Genetics* 20 (2019), 323–40.

Sarris, P., "New approaches to the Plague of Justinian". *Past and Present* 254 (2022), 315–346.

Spyrou, M.A. et al., "The source of the Black Death in fourteenth-century central Eurasia", Nature 606 (2022), 718–24.

Stathakopoulos, D., *Famine and pestilence in the Late Roman and early Byzantine Empire: A systematic survey of subsistence crises and epidemics* (Birmingham Byzantine and Ottoman Monographs, 9), Aldershot 2004.

Stenseth, N., et al., "Plague dynamics are driven by climate variation", *Proceedings of the National Academy of Science of the United States of America* 103 (2006), 13110–13115.

Saradi, H.G., "The Byzantine Cities (8th–15th centuries): Old Approaches and New Directions", in T. Kiousopoulou (ed.), *The Byzantine Cities (8th–15th centuries)* Rethymno 2012, pp. 25–46.

Straley, S.C./Bowmer, W.S., "Virulence genes regulated at the transcriptional level by Ca^{2+} in *Yersinia pestis* include structural genes for outer membrane proteins", *Infection and immunity* 51 (1986), 445–54.

Telelis, J., *Meteorological Phenomena and Climate in Byzantium. Approach of sources' information and empirical concerning climatic fluctuations in Eastern Mediterranean and the Middle East (A.D. 300–1500)*, Athens 2004.

Thiriet, F., *Régestes des délibérations du Sénat de Venise concernant la Romanie.* Vol. 1 (1329–1399). Paris 1958, pp. 63–64.

Tsiamis, C,. "From Justinian Plague to Covid-19: a Timeless Story?", in R. Rittegerold (ed) *13 Perspectives on the pandemic-Thinking in a state of exception*, Berlin 2020, pp. 17–21.

Tsiamis, C., *Plague in Byzantine Times, a medico-historical study*, Berlin/Boston 2022.

Varlik, N., *Disease and Empire: A history of plague epidemics in the early Modern Ottoman Empire (1453–1600)*, Chicago 2008.

Varlık, N., "Rethinking the history of plague in the time of COVID-19", *Centaurus* 62 (2020), 285–293.

Valentine, D., "The units of experimental taxonomy", *Acta Biotheoretica* 9 (1949), 75–88.

Wheelis, M., "Biological Warfare at the 1346 Siege of Caffa", *Emerging Infectious Diseases* 8 (2002), 971–75.

Zhou, D./Han, Y./Yang, R., "Molecular and physiological insights into plague transmission, virulence and etiology", *Microbes and Infection* 8 (2006), 273–84.

CHAPTER 5

Animals and the Byzantine Environment: Zooarchaeological Approaches

Henriette Baron

1   Introduction

This chapter is dedicated to the roles animals played in Byzantine environmental history and how zooarchaeology – the study of animal remains from archaeological excavations – can contribute to our understanding of them.

In AD 395, when the Roman Empire was divided in two, the Eastern Roman Empire inherited a Mediterranean landscape that had been intensively cultivated and modified for centuries. The Byzantines had impressive agricultural and scientific knowledge at their disposal, and no radical change had taken place that might have made it necessary to reinvent the way the land was used. Byzantine environmental history spans about a millennium and a huge area. This realm consisted not only of cities, harbours, and cultured land but also in some regions vast, in other regions smaller areas of uncultivated hinterland, which was often mountainous and sometimes inhospitable and which extended beyond the zones of the citizens' primary activity. There were deserts, steppes, thick forests, sparsely vegetated mountain slopes, and many other types of habitat.[1] Animals, domestic as well as wild, were a vital and formative part of these Byzantine ecosystems. These ecosystems cannot be understood without knowledge of the interaction between animals and the environment, which can be obtained and acted upon only with regard to relatively small areas: At the local level, or at most that of a specific region. Byzantine environmental history has to take into account the patchiness, the pointillism – in short, the multitude – of micro-ecologies[2] within the area and the roles the respective animals played in them.

The diversity of animals the Byzantine Empire harboured, especially in its early period when it extended along the margins of three continents, is immeasurable. Though only a few species played an economic role and even fewer were domesticated, they nevertheless played a major role in Byzantine

1   Geyer, "Landscape".
2   Horden/Purcell, *Corrupting Sea*.

daily life and accordingly also in the zooarchaeology of this era.[3] The use of domestic animals as working animals, for food, and as providers of raw materials for many crafts was common, as was the exploitation of wild animal populations through fishery, fowling, etc. All these activities had environmental effects and left behind a trail of evidence. These traces can be found in a wide variety of materials. Among the textual sources to mention animals are economic lists, romances, letters, and homilies. Animals are depicted in manuscripts, mosaics and small finds, and are woven into the narratives and imagery of their era. Perhaps the largest quantity of evidence can be discovered in the remains of the animals themselves: their bodies provided raw material for all kinds of objects (from snail-tinted parchment to ivory thrones), and their mortal remains are found in large quantities in the course of excavations. These finds of animal bones that were not worked upon in order to produce artefacts form the subject of this paper. In order to establish links between these finds and environmental aspects, an awareness of the nature of faunal materials from archaeological sites and their role in human–animal interactions must be brought to bear on their examination.

2   The Nature of Faunal Materials

After pottery, animal bones usually constitute the second-most common group of finds uncovered in archaeological excavations. In the course of an excavation, animal bones are usually collected by hand. The animal bones recovered in this way are, in most cases, remains of meals, of butchery, and sometimes of preserved food. Hence, the bulk stems from livestock – sheep, goats, cattle, and pigs – and some domestic fowl. Artisan waste and discarded carcasses are found markedly less often. These deposits also include animals that were not used for their meat, like equids, camels, dogs, and cats. The remains of domestic mammals constitute the main basis of zooarchaeological analyses. They provide only indirect environmental evidence: in most cases, the bone materials consist of ordinary refuse and thus the spectra of domestic animals shed light on general consumption patterns and allow for some deductions concerning animal husbandry practices, their environmental constraints and potential ecological effects.

---

3   For an in-depth overview, including detailed species lists, see Kroll, *Tiere*; Kroll, "Animals"; for an elaboration of Byzantine human–animal interactions and their environmental implications, see Baron, "Human-Animal Interactions".

Small quantities of bones of game animals are found as well. Bones of exploited wild birds and fish appear in lower quantities, as they are easily overlooked due to their size, being more prone to fragmentation and best recovered by means of sieving. Furthermore, they are more difficult to identify because species diversity is higher in these animal groups than reference collections can usually account for. The excavated remains of fish, game, and fowl give evidence of how wild animal populations were harvested. Based on the known habitat needs of the species found, environmental circumstances and activity areas can be reconstructed to some degree.

Only in a few isolated cases does a very diligent excavation technique, which includes large-scale sieving and the time-consuming identification of small vertebrates and/or molluscs, yield evidence of the wildlife that inhabited the site without having been introduced by human agency. The settlement wildlife offers first-hand environmental evidence. These on-site analyses shine spotlights on commensal and synanthropic species and colonizations of settlement habitats. Even though no economic use was made of them, these species were elements of the eco-systems and of material cycles linked to many everyday activities of the population. More than that, the commensals in particular had effects on food security, health, and even demographics – without the ubiquitous rats, for instance, the Justinianic plague would not have been as epidemic as it was. However, analyses that deal with these animals are extremely rare. While archaeology focuses on traces of human actions in the past, off-site analyses of wild biocoenoses that might complement this picture of urban wildlife do not exist.

To sum up: beyond the anthropogenic factors and deposition circumstances that influence the recovered spectra, a certain bias in the spectra of identified species and skeletal elements can be expected due to the applied excavation and identification techniques. Despite these limitations, zooarchaeology complements the sources of classical Byzantine studies because the bone spectra, being a by-product of daily life, convey a picture not distorted by intentional behaviour.

3   Linking Humans, Animals, and the Environment

Depending on the character of the excavated site, the recovered animal remains can give evidence of various human–animal interactions, but their informative potential concerning aspects of environmental history is not easy to unlock. It is linked to other components of the respective eco-systems (flora, soils, hydrology, climate, weather, human demography, and others) as well as daily life, of which we have only little or too general a knowledge.

As the environment was in constant flux through a multitude of factors and agents, environmental history needs a theoretical grounding. It helps to disentangle different elements that played a role and to better understand for which processes of human–environmental interaction it is able to account. In addition, it makes it easier to unravel how the human society and the environment were interwoven and influenced each other.

For modern cases, the European Environment Agency has developed a simple framework of environmental indicators which reflect relations between the environmental system and the human system, the so-called DPSIR-model.[4] DPSIR stands for Drivers, Pressures, States, Impacts, and Responses. The driving forces D are deeply rooted in the respective societies. They include social, demographic, or economic developments which are linked to patterns of production and consumption. The actions that accompany these production and consumption patterns exert pressures P on the environments. These pressures need not necessarily be negative, but, in any case, their impact changes the state S of the environment. These changes can be manifested in altered biological, physical, or chemical conditions. This new state of the environment has an impact I on the societies, for instance regarding the availability of resources. The societies respond R by adapting to the new conditions. These responses again create new drivers and pressures, and a new cycle begins.

This model illustrates that environmental history is only understood in its interrelated dynamics, in actions and changes, and it is clear that they in turn can only be understood on a local to regional scale. The cultural-historical perspective that Byzantine Studies, including zooarchaeology, usually adopt has contributed to a well-known picture of potential driving forces D. These also cannot be generalized – given the vast extent and duration of the empire, they too have regional (and temporal) features. We know little about the pressures P they exerted. With regard to zooarchaeology, drivers and pressures can best be disentangled by interpreting those economic branches that were practised intensively and on a large scale, i.e. animal husbandry and fishing. However, the findings nevertheless remain fragmentary without evidence from other disciplines. The states S of past environmental elements can barely be grasped by means of zooarchaeology, because the faunal materials usually reflect primarily human agency. For this reason, urban wildlife is best suited to the reconstruction of states because it represents local environmental elements not deliberately selected by people. Knowing with whom the people shared

---

4 Smeets/Weterings, "Environmental Indicators".

their homes and towns makes it possible to understand the impacts *I* of this cohabitation and to disentangle potential responses *R*. Other wildlife gives only limited evidence of states, as it was subject to human selection. These animals can be seen as proxies for local environments, and an intensified exploitation of wild resources is often regarded as a response to a crisis.

An overview of economically used species encountered in animal bone materials from Byzantine archaeological excavations has already been published.[5] It is not the aim of this chapter to repeat its results in detail. Instead, the potential of zooarchaeological investigations for environmental research questions shall be brought into focus, as shall its approaches and limitations. This is important because only a holistic approach that includes not only the different actors (including animals), but also the interdependencies arising from their interaction, allows us to unravel the web of environmental history. For this, it is not only necessary to understand how activities involving humans and animals were dependent on environmental conditions, but also the extent to which groups of animals can be used for specific research questions of environmental history. In this way, sampling strategies and requirements for scientific processing can be planned in advance of excavations, or zooarchaeological findings can be embedded in studies of other disciplines.

4 The State of Research

Although zooarchaeology has a tradition reaching back into the 19th century, it still is not a standard component of archaeological fieldwork, particularly not in the Mediterranean.[6] Accordingly, research in the field of Byzantine zooarchaeology is still fragmentary. A few larger studies and a greater share of smaller reports nevertheless add up to a preliminary outline of Byzantine animal use, which no doubt will become incrementally more complete over time.

For the early Byzantine period, when the empire spanned from the Bosporus to the Nile, from Italy to Asia Minor, comparably many bone reports have been published. Among a majority of short reports or examinations with specialized

---

5 Kroll, *Tiere*; Kroll, "Animals". General statements concerning the appearance and distribution of animal species in Byzantine faunal materials in this chapter are based on the literature survey published in these works.

6 Øystein LaBianca had to vindicate the scientific analyses for the Hesban project in the 1970s, LaBianca/Driesch, *Hesban*, p. xxiii. Although they nowadays form integral parts of research projects more often than some decades ago, in many cases unawareness of their potential remains.

foci and research questions (e.g. specific fish bone studies),[7] some deep and broad studies exist, partly based on large amounts of material, which in some cases only touch the Byzantine period marginally. Important early Byzantine sites for which comparably detailed analyses of animal bone materials were performed include Nicopolis ad Istrum on the lower Danube, Sagalassos in Asia Minor, the Tell Hesban project, or Berenike on the Egyptian Red Sea coast.[8] These give an idea of the potential of zooarchaeological research for the study of local Byzantine economies, animal husbandry strategies, and the reconstruction and exploitation of local land- and seascapes. While research into the late Byzantine period is in its infancy,[9] the middle Byzantine period has been satisfactorily examined only for the Dobruja region of the lower Danube, where a few small-scale studies of military and civil sites exist.[10] Hence, the focus of this chapter lies on the early Byzantine period.

As already mentioned, it makes no sense to study the huge area of the Byzantine Empire, especially in its early period, as a single entity. Firstly, the eco-geographical conditions are too diverse, and secondly, the respective historical situations in different parts of the empire have to be taken into account when an interpretation of bone spectra is attempted. Particularly when interpreting animal husbandry patterns, not merely eco-geographical, but also political and economic reasons must be considered, because they can strongly affect herd management strategies (ch. 5). Undoubtedly, ecological conditions can vary greatly even within small zones. These specific environmental situations are reflected to some degree in the animal bone spectra. Although a detailed discussion would go beyond the scope of this chapter,[11] general notions of possible eco-geographical restraints can be detected quite clearly for larger regions with pronounced differences in climate and vegetation. For this reason, the early Byzantine Empire can be divided into seven regions: 1) southern Italy, 2) the western Balkan region with the Peloponnese and Crete, 3) the region on the lower Danube, 4) Asia Minor, 5) Syria and Palestine, 6) Egypt, and 7) north Africa.

---

7   E.g., Van Neer/Depraetere, "Pickled Fish".
8   Poulter, *Nicopolis*; De Cupere, *Sagalassos*; Driesch/Boessneck, "Hesban"; Sidebotham/Wendrich, *Berenike*.
9   A starting point: Pluskowski/Seetah/Hamilton-Dyer, "Stari Bar".
10 E.g., Stanc/Bejenaru, "Oltina".
11 They are discussed in Kroll, *Tiere*.

5   Animal Husbandry: Feeding Them to Feed Us

The main group of domestic mammals kept for meat provision were sheep, goats, cattle, and pigs; for transportation purposes (apart from oxen which hauled the heavy-duty carts) horses, donkeys, and their hybrids were bred; in arid parts of the empire they were joined by dromedaries. Chickens, pigeons, and geese were bred for meat, eggs, dung, and partially for feathers and down. Dogs were kept for a variety of purposes at home and in the fields, while cats were assigned to keeping pests under control. The Byzantines decided which animals to breed, what to feed them, and how to make use of the products gained during the lifetime of the animals. These were, above all, wool and milk in the case of the small ruminants, and labour in the case of the large ungulates. In the end, they chose when to cull them in order to exploit the raw materials they provided in death. These decisions had to be made in awareness of local environmental capacities. Large parts of lands comprising the empire are mountainous, hot, and sparsely vegetated, especially beyond the coastal range benefitting from the favourable Mediterranean climate. Precipitation and fresh water are scarce.[12] Within the boundaries imposed by the landscapes, Byzantine animal husbandry had to adapt to local and regional demand. By finding out what animals were kept, it can be deduced what was feasible in the region and what was perceived as impracticable. The limits thus established offer insights into the local environments in the respective periods.

Still, authentic reconstructions cannot be expected, because in most cases crucial components remain unknown. The reconstruction of animal exploitation strategies is closely linked to our knowledge of landscapes, vegetation, and arable farming. Tillage and animal husbandry are highly interdependent: livestock could be pastured in cultivated areas, where it provided manure for the fields as well as drawing the plough. It is unclear, however, to what extent the cultivated areas fed the Byzantine herds, because the scale of seasonal transhumant pasturing in the hinterland on the one hand and of grazing on cultivable land close to the settlements on the other is unknown.[13] Furthermore, fallow land can only be used for pasture when ample water is available. In dry farming regions where there was neither sufficient precipitation nor irrigation, fallow land had to be kept free of vegetation in order to preserve the hydrologic

---

12   Geyer, "Landscape".
13   Concerning transhumant pastoralism, which seems to have experienced a revival in the middle Byzantine period, Lefort, "The Rural Economy", p. 265. The so-called Farmer's Law, a *corpus juris* presumably compiled prior to the 10th c. in Anatolia, gives evidence of paid herdsmen who pastured animals by day in the vicinity of settlements, using fallow land, groves, and forests, Ashburner, "Farmer's Law"; Humphreys, *Laws of the Isaurian Era*.

balance. In this case, it could not be used for pasture. Hence, the question of animal pasturing strategies can only be answered after gathering more information on Byzantine climatic conditions, field systems, locally cultivated crops, and applied irrigation techniques.

The rural activities, but also the materials the animals introduced into their ecosystem, influenced the environment and could in some cases lead to changes (e.g. degradation through overgrazing) to which their keepers had to adapt. After all, the climate and soils were unfavourable in wide parts of the empire, and it may be assumed that the resilience of some landscapes was rather low.[14] The idea of finding evidence for pressure, i.e. an overstraining of environmental resources as a result of intensive livestock farming, is intriguing. However, zooarchaeological means of proving such effects are limited, and it is often a more likely – or at best probable – explanation for single phenomena than a cast-iron fact.[15] In some cases, results derived from zooarchaeological investigations can support palynological evidence for vegetational changes or geological indications, for instance erosion.[16] Future research will certainly place a stronger focus on an interdisciplinary reconstruction of such instances of interdependence between land-use and landscape changes.

For the following overview, the percentages of the meat-providing animals – sheep and goat (these two species are difficult to identify osteologically and are thus presented as one), cattle, and pig – are analysed by region and compared to the Roman period in order to establish whether the Byzantines adhered to traditional animal husbandry patterns or whether they adapted them to subsequent developments (Fig. 5.1).[17] The composition of the flocks of cattle, sheep, and goats, as well as pigs, as can be deduced from bone material, gives an approximate idea of local animal husbandry practices. Of course, eco-geographical restraints are not the only determining factor. In an advanced market economy like the Byzantine, recovered food debris does not necessarily reflect the composition of the herds, especially not in urban contexts, from which most faunal materials originate. The presence of particular bones

---

14   Geyer, "Landscape", p. 43.
15   In the case of Eléftherna on Crete, Günther Nobis assumed that the decline of pig farming detectable for the early Byzantine period, which is accompanied by decreasing withers heights of the pigs, was due to an opening of the landscapes and a decline of oaks. An increasing number of hare bones in this period is seen as another indication for this theory; Nobis, "Eléftherna", pp. 415–18.
16   As in the case of Sagalassos in SW Turkey. By means of intricate interdisciplinary research, including surveys of the hinterland, a shift from an intensive agriculture towards pastoralism is detectable for the second half of the 3rd c.: Kaptijn et al., "Sagalassos", pp. 88–90.
17   The results for the Roman Period according to King, "Diet".

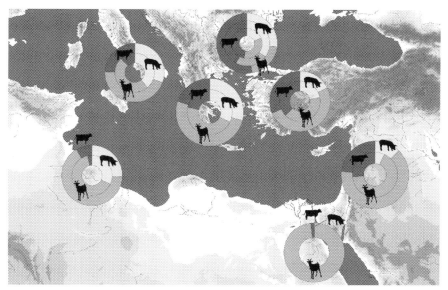

FIGURE 5.1 Arithmetical mean of the main domestic mammal percentages (sheep/goat, cattle, and pig) in the regions of the Empire in comparison to Anthony King's results for the Roman Period (King, "Diet"). Inner circle: Roman, outer circle: Byzantine. Lower Danube region: inner circle: Roman, medium circle: Early Byzantine, outer circle: Middle Byzantine. For Egypt, only the Byzantine percentage is depicted
SOURCE: AUTHOR

may reflect culinary preferences and food distribution systems unknown to us today. Nevertheless, the overall picture of a larger region gives an indication of what staples were regionally available in the respective area, because meat and livestock were not usually commodities that would have been transported over long distances.

Two aspects build the basis for environmental considerations concerning animal husbandry strategies. On the one hand, it has been hypothesized that keeping of all four main domestic mammal species was desirable because of the different benefits the species provided. The small ruminants gave wool and milk, cattle were used for labour, and pork was the meat best suited for preservation by means of salting. The second aspect is the different demands of these species for pasture and water. On a small scale, all these animals can be kept anywhere, except in decidedly arid environments like deserts. Among them, sheep and goats are the most undemanding. The hardy and lively goat, in particular, even feeds on hard-leaved vegetation and does not mind climbing and stretching in order to find food, making it even more frugal than the sheep. As sheep usually appear more often in Byzantine bone materials than goats, a prevalence of the latter is often seen as indicating unfavourable vegetation near a site.[18] Intensive rearing of cattle, however, requires ample vegetation and copious amounts of fresh water. It is clear that, in the area under consideration, these circumstances apply in the lush Danube plains, but sporadically at best beyond them. Conditions favourable to intensive pig husbandry are primarily woodland areas with evergreen oak trees (including parts of the coastal ranges affected by the Mediterranean climate) or in floodplain forests.

In the research area, sheep and goat breeding were already predominant in Roman times. In the western regions, i.e., north Africa, southern Italy, and Greece, livestock husbandry centred on small ruminants, followed by pigs, with cattle ranging third, while in the eastern regions, i.e., Asia Minor and the Levant, sheep and goat were the main domestic species, followed by cattle, with the pig ranking third.[19] This order did not change during the transition to Byzantine times, although shares appear to vary.[20] Already in Roman times, the region on the lower Danube presented an exception to these two patterns as extensive cattle breeding had been practised since the Iron Age. According to Anthony King's results, small ruminants ranked second in Roman times, while pig husbandry played only a minor role. In the early Byzantine period, slight changes can be observed.[21] Cattle were still the main livestock on the Danube, but pig breeding became economically more important. This trend recedes somewhat towards the middle Byzantine period, when cattle breeding played an even bigger role than in Roman times. In the case of this climatically favoured region, these changes can safely be attributed to strategic considerations, not to environmental factors. In Late Antiquity, this area was under almost constant attack by peoples from the north, and the archaeologically detectable militarization of the region[22] is a plausible explanation for these economic changes. As salted pork was part of army provisions under the *annona* system[23] because it could be stored for a comparably long time, the increasing share of pigs hints strongly at a locally organized provisioning system. While minor variations in proportion can be disregarded due to the heterogeneity of the sites included and the rather poor amount of data available,

---

18   For instance at Tell Hesban, where the goat shares increase in the post-Byzantine periods, Driesch/Boessneck, "Hesban", p. 72. Generally, on the appearance of sheep and goat: Kroll, *Tiere*, pp. 157–61.
19   King, "Diet".
20   Kroll, *Tiere*, pp. 149–51.
21   King, "Diet", p. 182; Kroll, *Tiere*, pp. 57–60.
22   See for instance Poulter, *Nicopolis*.
23   Kolias, "Verpflegung".

apart from the Danubian case, two more pronounced alterations to the Roman scheme can be detected. Firstly, more cattle were kept in southern Italy, mainly at the expense of pigs, but the shares of small ruminants decrease there, too. At the same time, the bone materials of this area display a notable heterogeneity in species percentages. What is more, this cannot simply be attributed to particular environmental reasons because the natural preconditions for the respective sites, partly situated close to each other, should not have differed that strongly. Like the Danube area, southern Italy suffered from severe military conflicts with the Vandals and Goths in Late Antiquity, and it was not only the attacks at home, but also the campaigns abroad that led to increasing instability in the Italian hinterland.[24] This triggered a rural exodus into the cities on the one hand and a reorganization towards self-sufficiency of the remaining rural population on the other. Secondly, we encounter increasing shares of small ruminants in Asia Minor, while the percentages of the other two species show a marginal decline. With the exception of the pigs, whose shares are generally low, livestock husbandry was based mostly on small ruminants. Only in some places can a strong emphasis on cattle be detected, notably in Limyra and Sagalassos. As the environmental conditions in these regions do not favour cattle husbandry, the high shares of this species in the bone materials hint as to activities that required such laborious cattle keeping – e.g., upscale dietary preferences, or agricultural and transportation functions.[25] The area, including the western coast of the Balkans, the Peloponnese, and Crete, displays a remarkable continuity in animal husbandry practices. This region was only marginally affected by the migrations and conflicts of the early Byzantine period, and especially the Peloponnese and Crete display unimpaired settlement patterns up to the 7th century.[26] The classical Hellenistic livestock pattern relying strongly on small ruminants and to a lesser extent on pigs and cattle is maintained. This pattern also persists in north Africa. Here, cattle play an even smaller role because, especially in Libya, neither pasture nor fresh water were available in sufficient quantities. Furthermore, cattle were dispensable, because dromedaries could take over most of the labour duties that were elsewhere shouldered by the bovids.

For Byzantine Syria and Palestine, the mean shares of the main domestic species do not differ from the respective Roman percentages, and the high standard deviations detected are comparable to those calculated by Anthony

24   Arthur, "Italian Landscapes".
25   Forstenpointner/Gaggl, "Limyra", p. 424; De Cupere, *Sagalassos*, p. 141.
26   On the Peloponnese, see Hjohlman/Penttinen/Wells, *Pyrgouthi*, p. 127.

King for the Roman period.[27] In this region, the environmental circumstances of the sites included in this study are extremely variable, ranging from the floodplain forests along the Euphrates and Jordan rivers, via the lush slopes of the Carmel mountains and the adjoining coastal area influenced by the mild Mediterranean climate, to the deserts around the Dead Sea. Accordingly, the bone materials of this area tell of a diversity of animal husbandry strategies adjusted in each case to the respective eco-geographical situation.[28] Generally, small ruminants prevail. Large proportions of pig bones were found in the bone materials from Zeugma on the Euphrates and from the port of Caesarea. Apparently, the floodplains of the Euphrates and the coastal area around Caesarea with its Mediterranean climate permitted a certain degree of pig keeping. In the case of Tell Hesban, which is located on the Jordan, not far from the eastern shore of the Dead Sea, the share of pig bones is smaller. These bones may originate from animals pastured along the green riverbanks of the Jordan, but might also be relics of salted pork that people travelling between the Mediterranean and the Red Sea brought with them – the desert forts of En Boqeq and Upper Zohar, located in the Negev, where pigs were almost impossible to keep, show similar shares. The animal bone spectra of these Negev forts demonstrate an idiosyncrasy that can also be attributed to the arid environment: an exceedingly high share of chicken bones.[29] This animal is generally apt to substitute other protein sources in difficult environmental situations, because it can be kept anywhere, demands little, and gives a lot.

The isolated material from the Egyptian Red Sea port Berenike[30] also exhibits a livestock composition largely dictated by environmental conditions. Here, keeping pigs was absolutely not feasible, and, had cattle not been imported from the fertile Nile valley,[31] of these four species only sheep and goats would be in evidence. In contrast to the Negev, chickens played no noteworthy role in the diet. This certainly can be attributed to the Red Sea's inexhaustible abundance of fish.

In general, the bulk of zooarchaeological bone finds forms a picture of environmental stability: possible climatic or vegetational changes in the early Byzantine period did not have a conspicuous impact on animal husbandry strategies.

27 A comparison of these arithmetical parameters for the Roman (according to King, "Diet") and Byzantine periods is given in Kroll, "Animals", p. 96, Table 1.
28 An overview of the animal bone shares is given in Kroll, *Tiere*, pp. 101–6.
29 Lernau, "En Boqeq"; Croft, "Upper Zohar".
30 Among other reports: Van Neer/Lentacker, "Faunal Remains".
31 Van Neer/Lentacker, "Faunal Remains", p. 348.

6 Wild Animals as Ecological Proxies

Due to their specific demands concerning food, shelter, and water, most wild living vertebrates that inhabited the Byzantine territory implicitly give information about the biospheres in the vicinity of the archaeological sites. While some species are very fastidious in their demands and are hence strong ecological indicators, other species can adapt to a variety of conditions and are likely to be met in all parts of the Empire, from the desert to the forest. The biotopes in the research area can be very roughly subdivided into water bodies of different kinds, forests, culture steppes, and arid regions, and comparisons can be made based on the bone finds to establish the extent to which eco-systems were exploited.

Bones of game and wildfowl mostly appear only in small percentages, which can usually be ascribed to infrequent hunting trips, activities in the hinterland, or occasional purchases from the rural population. There is no evidence that game played an appreciable role in the everyday Byzantine diet and economy. Venison could not be traded over long distances without spoiling. In the case of winged game, the birds would often have been trapped alive, but they too would surely not have travelled far. Accordingly, the game and wildfowl species spectra primarily give evidence for eco-systems in nearby activity zones.

Since the economy was based on agriculture, the surroundings of villages and towns consisted largely of areas suitable for the cultivation of crops. These cultivated habitats showed varied vegetation covers, subdivided into open and semi-open areas, with trees, shrubland, fields, and grassland with their respective faunas, which occasionally ended up in the bone materials (Figs. 5.2 and 5.3).[32] By far the most important bird family among them are the Phasianidae. This is mostly due to the esteem in which red-legged partridges of the genus *Alectoris* were held, these accounting for nearly three quarters of this family's bone finds. These birds had already been favoured by the Romans. In the Byzantine Empire, the chukar partridge *Alectoris chukar*, which populates Asia Minor and the Near East, appears particularly often in the bone materials of these regions, sometimes in large quantities.[33] In areas where animals were difficult to breed and meat was scarce, fowling was a means to tackle shortages.[34] Furthermore, the animals were not too difficult to trap

---

32   For the actual find spots of the birds and the complete species spectrum of this ecological group, see Kroll, *Tiere*, pp. 259–60 and pp. 186–9.

33   At Sagalassos it was the main fowling target after the 5th c., De Cupere, *Sagalassos*, pp. 20–32.

34   In the arid regions of Palestine, fowling was pursued to such a degree that it became economically relevant, e.g., at Upper Zohar, Croft, "Upper Zohar", pp. 87–93.

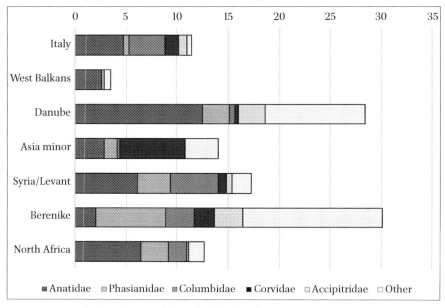

FIGURE 5.2 Arithmetical mean of identified bird family percentages in faunal materials from different regions, with the exception of the domestic chicken
SOURCE: AUTHOR

when caged decoys were used.[35] The second-best represented family of birds are the corvids (family Corvidae), which are very intelligent and ecologically extremely adaptable, but often live in farmlands and towns, feeding on the crops. From a variety of Byzantine sites, remains of the common raven *Corvus corax*, jackdaw *Corvus monedula*, European magpie *Pica pica*, as well as the rook *Corvus frugilegus* and carrion crow *Corvus corone* have been recorded. It is unclear whether these animals were killed because they were regarded as agricultural pests, or whether they were ever eaten, kept as pets, or just died of natural causes in the cities and settlements. Among the mammals, the clearest indicators for open landscapes are the hares *Lepus* sp. Their bones appear consistently in nearly all Byzantine bone assemblages throughout the empire – a clear indicator of occasional small game hunting. In north Africa and the eastern Balkans, hare bones constitute nearly half the game in evidence, and in Asia Minor they also achieve considerable shares. Deer finds appear frequently, too. Roe deer *Capreolus capreolus* and fallow deer *Dama dama* prefer the fringes of forests verging on cultivated areas. Roe deer bones appear in most faunal materials of southern Italy, the west coast of the Balkans between

---

35   For Byzantine depictions of chukar fowling and a caged chukar, see Kroll, *Tiere*, pp. 109–10.

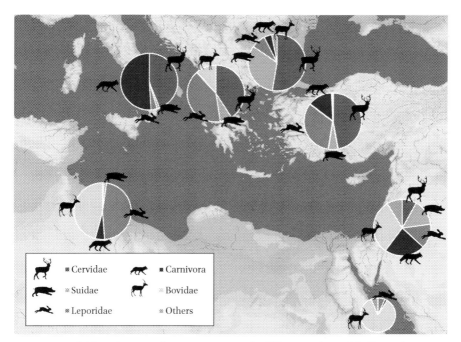

FIGURE 5.3 Arithmetic mean of game percentages in different regions of the Byzantine Empire. In the north, a high share of deer; in the south, more bovids
SOURCE: AUTHOR

the Dalmatian coast and Greece, and the lower Danube region. Sporadic finds stem from Constantinople, Asia Minor, and the Euphrates region. Byzantine fallow deer finds originate from the same regions, but are decidedly rarer.

To what extent woodland existed in the Byzantine Empire is still being debated.[36] Birds typical of wooded areas rarely appear in the bone assemblages.[37] The only comparably high the occurrence is that of pigeons or doves (family Columbidae) and of birds of prey of the family Accipitridae, both comprising species with a preference for woodland habitats. Among the doves detected in Byzantine materials, this preference is shared by the stock dove *Columba oenas* and the wood dove *Columba palumbus*. These animals appear occasionally throughout the empire and their sporadic occurrence could be seen to indicate only limited areas of woodland. On the other hand, it must be taken into account that fowling is more difficult in tree-covered areas than in regions with low vegetation. The game finds, however, hint

36   Dunn, "Woodland".
37   Kroll, *Tiere*, pp. 189–91, 260.

more strongly at an exploitation of wooded areas. Red deer *Cervus elaphus* finds are distributed across the whole area, but are most strongly in evidence in the northern Mediterranean region between Italy and the lower Danube. However, the incidence of this family may be distorted by the significance of antlers as raw material: antler fragments often constitute a considerable part of the deer finds. On the Danube, other woodland game species appear steadily and partially in substantial numbers. The wild boar *Sus scrofa* was mainly hunted in the forests of the lower Danube. Westwards and in the areas to the southeast of this region, bones of wild boars are very rarely detectable; at Tell Hesban, however, they were numerous. Given the arid region where the city was located, it must be assumed that the animals roamed the floodplain forests of the Jordan. Furthermore, some finds were identified at Carthage.[38] This distribution is congruent with the modern range of the animal. On the lower Danube, not only deer and wild boar were hunted, but also the beaver *Castor fiber*, partly in high proportions.[39] The presence of this animal clearly points to hunting in floodplain forests and waters, as the beaver needs both fresh water and large amounts of wood for food and for its lodges. The bird spectra show a great variety of species caught or shot on the coasts and riverbanks. In the light of the location of most Byzantine settlements and towns in close proximity either to the sea or to a river, it is not surprising that fowling activities often resulted in a high percentage of waterfowl. This applies particularly to the northeastern and eastern Mediterranean, between the Dalmatian coast and the lower Danube, as well as to Asia Minor, Syria, and Palestine.[40] Some of these birds were killed in their breeding areas; others were shot or trapped during their seasonal migrations. The larger part of waterfowl belongs to members of the Anatidae family, meaning ducks, geese, and swans. Among this family, the ducks are best represented. A distinctly smaller part of the bones was identified as belonging to geese, and swans appear only sporadically. Among the rails Rallidae, the Eurasian coot *Fulica atra* is most frequent. Other waterfowl species include, for instance, pelicans (the great white pelican *Pelecanus onocratulus* and Dalmatian pelican *Pelecanus crispus*), hunted on the Danube and in Asia Minor, the common crane *Grus grus* and the great cormorant *Phalacrocorax carbo*, as well as herons.

In the southern territories of the early Byzantine Empire, the fauna had adapted to sparse vegetation and minimal supply of freshwater. Certainly, these wild animals benefitted to an even stronger degree from the presence of

---

38 Driesch/Boessneck, "Hesban", pp. 85–93; Nobis, "Karthago", pp. 586–8.
39 Kroll, *Tiere*, pp. 197, 258.
40 For the find spots, see Kroll, *Tiere*, pp. 183–6, 258–9.

humans than their kin in more temperate climates, because the irrigated fields and groves, wells and cisterns provided them with easy access to food and drink. At the same time, they were attractive prey for the Byzantines, because in these surroundings meat from domestic animals was scarce. Accordingly, in these areas a conspicuously wide variety of game is in evidence. In Palestine, Egypt, and north Africa, the bovid family, including the wild forms and relatives of sheep, goat, and cattle, as well as antelopes and gazelles, played a role comparable to that of the cervids in the northern Mediterranean.[41] In the three areas, members of this family represent the largest proportion of identified game. In the eastern and southern Mediterranean, mainly gazelles were hunted. These frugal animals inhabit the deserts of these regions and were discovered in the area between Syria and Carthage, appearing in slightly higher numbers in the Dead Sea zone. Where determinable to species level, the Palestine gazelles were identified as mountain gazelles *Gazella gazella*. The dorcas gazelle *Gazella dorcas* represents the largest share of game shot at Berenike on the Red Sea. It was also detected in Libya.[42] Other inhabitants of the south Mediterranean deserts that appear as scattered finds are the oryx *Oryx leucoryx*, the hartebeest *Alcelaphus buselaphus*, the barbary sheep *Ammotragus lervia,* and the ibex *Capra ibex*. Birds that dwell in these sparsely vegetated areas appeared solely in the areas between the Dead Sea, Egypt and Carthage, and it is only at the Red Sea Port of Berenike that they represent most of the sporadic finds of winged game.[43] The most common member of this ecological group is the sand partridge *Ammoperdix heyi*, which was detected in the bone materials primarily stemming from desert sites. Bones of the ostrich *Struthio camelus* are scarce, recorded only for Carthage and Leptiminus. Fragments of its eggshells were excavated at En Boqeq, Carthage and Berenice/Benghazi.[44]

7   Fish Stocks

Although the Mediterranean Sea, or at least its eastern basin, undoubtedly was the heart of the empire, there were also other large bodies of waters: the Black

---

41   Kroll, *Tiere*, pp. 195–7, 257.
42   For Berenike, see e.g. Van Neer/Lentacker, "Faunal remains", p. 340 Table 20.2 and p. 345 Table 20.5; another example: Van der Veen/Grant/Barker, "Romano-Libyan Agriculture", p. 242 Table 8.6.
43   Kroll, *Tiere*, pp. 191, 261.
44   Nobis, "Karthago", p. 615 Table 18; Schwartz, "Fauna", p. 249 Table 7; Burke, "Animal bones", p. 444; Lernau, "En Boqeq", pp. 158–60; Reese, "Faunal remains", pp. 139–40; Barker, "Berenice".

Sea, the Danube, as well as, in the early Byzantine period, the Red Sea and the Nile. The evidence found there permits some preliminary general zooarchaeological insights into Byzantine fisheries.[45] The animal bone reports testify to a local exploitation of fish populations, in the case of the three inland seas mainly of coastal areas. Environmentally, the fish finds are of particular interest concerning the development of the fish populations in different periods. However, the state of research does not yet allow for this issue to be addressed comprehensively.

The fish spectra evidenced for sites located by the aforementioned waters correspond well with modern catches in the respective regions and show neither unexpected deviations, nor signs of populations under stress. The two large rivers, the Danube and the Nile, harboured a fauna that sufficed to feed the people living along their shores and beyond, so that no regular imports of saltwater fish were necessary. On the Danube, in most cases the fish bone materials comprise primarily cyprinids (family Cyprinidae), among which the carp *Cyprinus carpio* usually strongly prevails. Concerning the faunal history of this animal, the early Byzantine period is of special interest, because these centuries link two crucial phases of carp domestication: The Roman period, when carp were kept in ponds for pleasure but not bred systematically, and the High Middle Ages, when the actual domestication process is assumed to have commenced.[46] In the early Middle Ages, the carp spread northwestwards and was then reportedly bred in the western monasteries. Thereby, the monks intended to secure a steady supply of food suitable for lent and other fast days. Unfortunately, research on carp domestication concentrates on central Europe and a possible domestication in the animal's heartland has yet to be discussed. However, it is known that Byzantine monasteries, for instance on Mount Athos, operated vivaria profitably in the middle and late Byzantine periods.[47]

Aquaculture is one approach to reaching a degree of independence from natural catch fluctuations. Fishermen will not always be able to return to the harbour with a bountiful catch – this does not necessarily point to populations under stress. With one exception, fish populations in the area under investigation seem to have sufficed for local populations, at least until around the year 1000. It is assumed that until that point human agency had led only to minor changes in aquatic environments between the Mediterranean and central Europe. From then on, however, alluvial deposits as a result of deforestation, the damming of mill streams, and a strong nutrient influx in urban areas led to

---

45   Kroll, *Tiere*, pp. 200–219.
46   Hoffmann, "culture of common carp".
47   Dagron, "Poissons", p. 59.

aquatic modifications in central Europe.[48] Very little is known about these processes in the Mediterranean environment of the Byzantine Empire. However, the legislation of Leo VI concerning fixed-net fishery off Constantinople waterside property and the regulation of the capital's fish market point to fish shortages and an increasing need for more sustainable fishery practices.[49] Future research will certainly pay more attention to such changes in the composition of fish spectra, the size of the individual fish, and local extinctions. The impact that the discovery of caviar as a delicacy in the middle Byzantine period had on the sturgeon populations, for instance, is also widely unclear.[50]

The only exception, one area where fish was seemingly not available in abundance and where measures had to be taken to ensure at least a basic supply of this important food item, is the Levant (Fig. 5.4). Due to its hydrological conditions, the Levantine Sea has for most of its existence offered a poor supply of fish.[51] Although Mediterranean mullet, sea bream, grouper, and drum (families Mugilidae, Sparidae, Serranidae and Sciaenidae, among other, rarer families) were caught, faunal materials in this region also comprise comparably high shares of freshwater fish, primarily of the genera *Tilapia* and *Clarias*.[52] Fresh water, however, was scarce, too. In fact, only the Sea of Galilee, the Jordan, and the Euphrates harboured populations that could be fished on a large scale. It seems, however, that yields were still insufficient. As the area was a trade hub between the Mediterranean and the whole Near East in its wider sense, transportation networks were utilized to import preserved fish from adjacent regions with better stocks.[53] Hence, forts in the Negev as well as other Levantine sites sometimes show high shares of Red Sea species like parrotfish, but also some Nilotic fish. Scattered archaeological evidence from Coptic monasteries on the Nile indicates that the monks were employed in local fishery and in the processing – and supposedly also the trade – of Nilotic fish.[54] Apart from the imports, some archaeological features in the Levant point to a perpetuation of the Roman technique of keeping fish in basins,[55] another means of ensuring sufficient supplies.

---

48 Hoffmann, "culture of common carp", p. 61.
49 Maniatis, "Fish market".
50 Bartosiewicz/Bonsall/Şişu, "Sturgeon fishing"; Jacoby, "Caviar".
51 Van Neer et al., "trade connections", p. 136. This changed after the Suez Canal was opened in 1869. Since then, many Red Sea fish species have invaded the Mediterranean, many of which are now commercially important for local fisheries.
52 Kroll, *Tiere*, pp. 98–100, 217.
53 Van Neer et al., "trade connections", p. 109.
54 Van Neer/Depraetere, "Pickled Fish".
55 Mango, "Fishing in the desert".

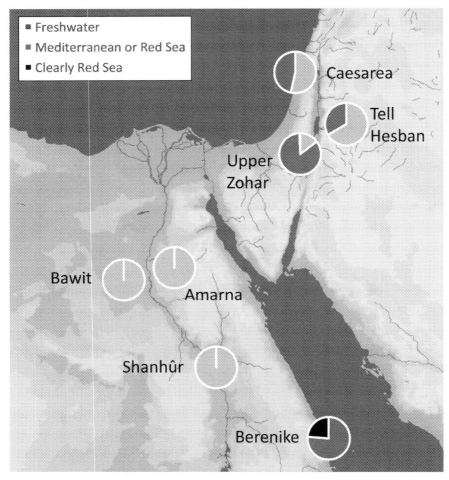

FIGURE 5.4   Attribution of fish families found in Byzantine faunal materials to different water bodies. On the Nile, a purely Nilotic fauna; in Berenike, a Red Sea fauna with some families that occur also in the Mediterranean; and, in the Levant, a mixed fauna of freshwater and marine origin
SOURCE: AUTHOR

8   Urban Ecology

The zooarchaeology of "useless" fauna, i.e. animals that were not exploited economically, is rarely studied. For the Byzantine Empire, there are a few promising examples that highlight the biodiversity of urban ecosystems. Given that the study of urban ecology and urban wildlife is rather a new branch of the study of modern cities, there is no proper framework yet that would help to interpret the fauna detected in the late antique sites. A number of observations, however, may be presented, based on some faunal materials from various areas of the early Byzantine Empire with different environments: the Upper Zohar fort in the Negev desert, and the cities of Nicopolis ad Istrum on the lower Danube and, currently, Caričin Grad in southern Serbia. Due to intensive sieving, these sites provided evidence for small vertebrates – first of all rodents, but also other small mammals, as well as reptiles, amphibians, and birds.

The small mammal spectra are usually dominated by commensal species, first and foremost the black rat. Rats are extremely hardy and can adapt to many inconveniences. The mass distribution of the black rat had taken place in the Roman period by means of human traffic, and they had successfully filled ecological niches in towns. In Byzantine strata, they are found regularly. In Nicopolis ad Istrum, the first rat finds stem from strata dating to the first decades after the town was founded in AD 108.[56] The rats' strong dependence on shelter, food, and water, ideally provided by humans, make them an indicator of occupation phases. For the Upper Zohar desert fort it was suggested that ratless strata which contained remains of the lesser mole-rat *Spalax leucodon* and fat sand rat *Psammomys obesus* date from after the fortification was abandoned.[57] In Caričin Grad, rat finds dominate the small mammal fauna of dwelling quarters, accompanied by smaller percentages of other murids and only few bones from non-murid species (Fig. 5.5). In this 6th-century city, spatial differences in the small mammal spectra can be attributed to the activity ranges of animals as well as human activity, though the recorded differences are strongly biased by the circumstances of deposition. In particular, accumulations of small mammals identified by raptor pellets must be taken into account.[58] An example for such a pellet fauna was found in the Acropolis towers of Caričin Grad. One tower yielded a particularly large accumulation of small mammal remains deriving from a diverse spectrum of open-country species like voles and moles, which appear only rarely in other sieve samples of the city. A large number of raptor species, among them owls and hawks, was also identified at Caričin Grad. In combination with archaeobotanical results and high-resolution archaeological analyses regarding formation processes, these findings help reconstruct vital parts of urban human ecosystems, which were the home and living environment for many people in the Byzantine world.

---

56   Parfitt, "Small mammals", p. 210.
57   Croft, "Upper Zohar", p. 93.
58   See, e.g., Forstenpointner et al., "Archäozoologie", p. 233. For first results from Caričin Grad, see Schreg et al., "Wirtschaftliche Ressourcen", p. 16.

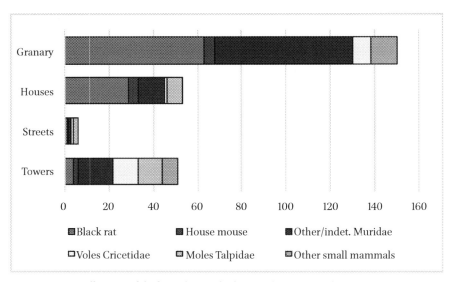

FIGURE 5.5 Small mammal finds on the North Plateau of Caričin Grad. Formative processes and human activity massively influence the spectra of wild urban vertebrates
HENRIETTE BARON

Bibliography

Arthur, P., "From Vicus to Village: Italian Landscapes, AD 400–1000", in: N. Christie (ed.), *Landscapes of Change. Rural Evolutions in Late Antiquity and the Early Middle Ages*, Aldershot 2004, pp. 103–34.

Ashburner, W., "The Farmer's Law", *Journal of Hellenic Studies* 32, 1912, 87–95.

Barker, G., "Economic Life at Berenice: The Animal and Fish Bones, Marine Mollusca and Plant Remains", in: J. Lloyd (ed.), *Excavations at Sidi Khrebish, Benghazi (Berenice)*, vol. 2, (Libya Antiqua Supplem. 5), Tripoli 1979, pp. 1–49.

Baron, H., "An approach to Byzantine Environmental History: Human-Animal Interactions", in: H. Baron/F. Daim (eds), *A Most Plesant Scene and an Inexhaustible Resource, Steps Towards a Byzantine Environmental History*, Byzanz zwischen Orient und Okzident 6, Mainz 2017, pp. 171–98.

Bartosiewicz, L./Bonsall, C./Şişu, V., "Sturgeon fishing in the Middle and Lower Danube region'", in: C. Bonsall/V. Boronean/I. Radovanovi (eds.), *The Iron Gates in Prehistory: new perspectives*, (British Archaeological Reports, International Series 1893), Oxford 2008, pp. 39–54.

Burke, A., "Animal Bones", in: L.M. Stirling/D.J. Mattingly/N. Ben Lazreg (eds.), *Leptiminus (Lamta). Report 2. The East Baths, Cemeteries, Kilns, Venus Mosaic, Site Museum and Other Studies*, (Journal of Roman Archaeology Suppl. Ser. 41), Portsmouth 2001, pp. 442–56.

Croft, P., "Bird and Small Mammalian Remains from Upper Zohar", in: R.P. Harper (ed.), *Upper Zohar. An Early Byzantine Fort in Palaestina Tertia. Final Report of Excavations in 1985–1986*, Oxford 1995, pp. 87–96.

Dagron, G., "Poissons, pêcheurs et poissonniers de Constantinople", in: C. Mango/ G. Dagron (eds.), *Constantinople and its Hinterland*, (Papers from the Twenty-seventh Spring Symposium of Byzantine Studies, Oxford, April 1993), Aldershot 1993, pp. 57–73.

De Cupere, B., *Animals at Ancient Sagalassos: Evidence of the Bone Remains* (Studies in Eastern Mediterranean Archaeology 4), Turnhout 2001.

Driesch, A. von den/Boessneck, J., "Final Report on the Zooarchaeological Investigation of Animal Bone Finds from Tell Hesban, Jordan", in: LaBianca/Driesch, *Hesban*, pp. 67–108.

Dunn, A., "The exploitation of *woodland* and *scrubland* in the Byzantine world", *Byzantine and Modern Greek Studies* 16, 1992, pp. 235–98.

Forstenpointner, G./ Gaggl, G., "Archäozoologische Untersuchungen an Tierresten aus Limyra", *Jahreshefte des Österreichischen Archäologischen Institutes* 66, 1997, pp. 419–26.

Forstenpointner, G./Galik, A./Weissengruber, G./Zohmann, St., "Archäozoologie", in: Steskal, M./La Torre, M. (eds), *Das Vediusgymnasium in Ephesos. Archäologie und Baubefund*, Vienna 2008, pp. 211–34.

Geyer, B., "Physical Factors in the Evolution of the Landscape and Land Use". In: Laiou, *Economic History*, vol. 1, pp. 31–45.

Hjohlman, J./Penttinen, A./Wells, A. (eds.), *Pyrgouthi: A Rural Site in the Berbati Valley from the Early Iron Age to Late Antiquity*, (Skrifter Svenska Institutet i Athen 4° 52), Athen 2005.

Hoffmann, R.C., "Environmental change and the culture of common carp in medieval Europe", *Guelph Ichtyology Revue* 3, 1995, pp. 57–85.

Horden, P./Purcell, N., *The Corrupting Sea. A Study of Mediterranean History*, Malden 2000.

Humphreys, M., *The Laws of the Isaurian Era, The Ecloga and its Appendices, Translated with an introduction and commentary by Mike Humphreys*, Translated Texts for Byzantinists 3, Liverpool 2017.

Jacoby, D., "Caviar Trading in Byzantium", in: R. Shukurov (ed.), *Mare et Litora* (Festschrift für Sergei Karpov), Moscow 2009, pp. 349–64.

Kaptijn, E./Poblome, J./Vanhaverbeke, H./Bakker, J./Waelkens, M., "Societal changes in the Hellenistic, Roman and Early Byzantine periods. Results from the Sagalassos Territorial Archaeological Survey 2008 (southwest Turkey)", *Anatolian Studies* 63, 2013, pp. 75–95.

King, A.C., "Diet in the Roman World. A Regional inter-site comparison of the mammal bones", *Journal of Roman Archaeology* 12, 1999, pp. 168–202.

Kolias, T., "Eßgewohnheiten und Verpflegung im byzantinischen Heer", in: W. Hörandner/J. Koder/O. Kresten/E. Trapp (eds.), ΒΥΖΑΝΤΙΟΣ (Festschrift für Herbert Hunger zum 70. Geburtstag. Dargebracht von Schülern und Mitarbeitern), Vienna 1984, pp. 193–202.

Kroll, H., *Tiere im Byzantinischen Reich. Archäozoologische Forschungen im Überblick*, (Monographien des Römisch-Germanischen Zentralmuseums 87), Mainz 2010.

Kroll, H., "Animals in the Byzantine Empire. An overview of the archaeozoological evidence", *Archaeologia medievale* 39, 2012, pp. 93–121.

LaBianca, Ø.S./A. von den Driesch (eds.), *Faunal Remains: Taphonomical and Zooarchaeological Studies of the Animal Remains from Tell Hesban and Vicinity*, (Hesban 13), Berrien Springs 1995.

Laiou, A.E. (ed.), *The Economic History of Byzantium. From the Seventh through the Fifteenth Century*, 3 vols., Dumbarton Oaks 2002.

Lefort, J., "The Rural Economy, Seventh-Twelfth Centuries", in: Laiou, *Economic History*, vol. 1, pp. 231–310.

Lernau, H., "Geflügel- und Fischknochen aus En Boqeq", in: M. Fischer/O. Tal (eds.), *Excavations in an Oasis on the Dead Sea II. The Officina, an Early Roman Building on the Dead Sea Shore*, Mainz 2000, pp. 149–80.

Mango, M., "Fishing in the Desert", *Palaeoslavica* 10, 2002, 1, pp. 323–30.

Maniatis, G.C., "The Organizational Setup and Functioning of the Fish Market in Tenth-Century Constantinople", Dumbarton Oaks Papers 54, 2000, pp. 13–42.

Nobis, G., "Studien an Tierresten aus den archäologischen Grabungen Poros bei Iraklion und Eléftherna bei Arkhadi – ein Beitrag zur antiken Wild- und Haustierfauna Kretas", in: P. Anreiter/L. Bartosziewicz/E. Jerem/W. Meid (eds.): *Man and the Animal World. Studies in Archaeozoology, Archaeology, Anthropology and Palaeolinguistics in memoriam Sándor Bökönyi*, Budapest 1998, pp. 409–34.

Nobis, G., "Die Tierreste von Karthago", in: F. Rakob (ed.), *Die Deutschen Ausgrabungen in Karthago 3*, Mainz 1999, pp. 574–631.

Parfitt, S.A., "The Small Mammals", in; Poulter, *Nicopolis*, pp. 198–223.

Pluskowski, A./Seetah, K., "The Animal Bones from the 2004 Excavations at Stari Bar, Montenegro. (With a report on fish by Sheila Hamilton-Dyer)", in: S. Gelichi (ed.), *The Archaeology of an Abandoned Town. The 2005 Project in Stari Bar*, Florence 2006, pp. 97–111.

Poulter, A.G. (ed.), *Nicopolis ad Istrum, A late Roman and Early Byzantine City. The Finds and the Biological Remains*, Oxford 2007.

Reese, D.S., "Faunal Remains (Osteological and Marine Forms) 1975–76", in: J. Humphrey (ed.), *Excavations at Carthage 1976. Conducted by the University of Michigan*, vol. 3, Ann Arbor 1977, pp. 131–65.

Schreg, R./Birk, J./Fiedler, S./Kroll, H./Marković, N./Reuter, A.E./Röhl, C./Steinborn, M., "Wirtschaftliche Ressourcen und soziales Kapital, Gründung und Unterhalt der

Stadt Iustiniana Prima", *Mitteilungen der Deutschen Gesellschaft für die Archäologie des Mittelalters und der Neuzeit* 29, 2016, pp. 9–20.

Schwartz, J.H., "The (Primarily) Mammalian Fauna", in: H.R. Hurst (ed.), *Excavations at Carthage: The British Mission. Vol. 1, pt. 1: The Avenue du Président Habib Bourguiba, Salammbo. The Site and Finds Other Than Pottery*, Sheffield 1984, pp. 229–56.

Sidebotham, S.E./Wendrich, W.Z. (eds.), *Berenike 1996: Report of the Excavations at Berenike (Egyptian Red Sea Coast) and the Survey of the Eastern Desert*, Leiden 1998.

Smeets, E./Weterings, R., "Environmental Indicators: Typology and Overview", *European Environment Agency, Technical Report 25*, Copenhagen 1999.

Stanc, S./Bejenaru, L., "Exploatarea faunei de către locuitorii aşezării de la Oltina (Constanţa)." *Arheologia Moldovei. Editura Academiei Romane Iaşi* XXVIII, 2005, 313–24.

Van der Veen, M./Grant, A./Barker, G., "Romano-Libyan Agriculture: Crops and Animals", in: G. Barker (ed.), *Farming the Desert: The UNESCO Libyan Valleys Archaeological Survey*, vol. 1, Paris 1996, pp. 227–63.

Van Neer, W./Depraetere, D., "Pickled fish from the Egyptian Nile: osteological evidence from a Byzantine (Coptic) context at Shanhûr", *Revue de Paléobiologie*, Dec. 2005, Vol. Spec. 10, 159–70.

Van Neer, W./Lentacker, A., "The Faunal Remains", in: Sidebotham/Wendrich, *Berenike*, pp. 337–55.

Van Neer, W./Lernau, O./Friedman, R./Mumford, G./Poblome, J./Waelkens, M., "Fish remains from archaeological sites as indicators of former trade connections in the Eastern Mediterranean", *Paléorient* 30/1, 2004, 101–48.

CHAPTER 6

Historical Seismology

Lee Mordechai

Earthquakes feature regularly in 21st-century news. The immense casualties and damage associated with major seismic events such as those in the Indian Ocean (2004), Haiti (2010), Japan (2011) and Nepal (2015), alongside their prolonged coverage and documentation, have attracted Western public and scholarly attention. Scholars and experts in different fields all agree that as the world's wealth, population, and population density grow, the severity of the impact of earthquakes and other natural disasters on human societies will likely increase.[1] As a result, future events could be even more destructive. Historical seismology, the study of past seismic events (earthquakes and tsunamis), is important in this context for understanding an area's seismicity by determining the frequency and magnitude of its past seismic events. This avenue of research is also relevant for historical studies since it illuminates some of the environmental events past societies faced.

The eastern Mediterranean and Asia Minor in particular have long been recognized as seismically active.[2] Historical and epigraphic sources frequently report destructive premodern seismic events. There is written evidence for several hundred earthquakes in the entire Mediterranean area until AD 1500, most of which are concentrated in Asia Minor, the Levant and the Aegean.[3] The ubiquity of the phenomenon in the region has led premodern contemporaries to theorize about the causes of these seismic events.[4] Modern scholars reading the catastrophic descriptions in the primary sources have sometimes ascribed destruction, decline, and even collapse of whole societies to such events.[5]

---

1 Matthewman 2015, 4.
2 This is the result of tectonic plate movement by (1) the Arabian plate, moving north from Arabia and Syria; (2) the Anatolian plate, moving west and southwest against the Eurasian plate in the Balkans; (3) the African plate, moving north from Egypt and the Mediterranean. The theory of tectonic plates was suggested in the early 20th century but became accepted only in the 1950s and 1960s.
3 (See Guidoboni and Comastri 2005) The latest catalog refers to 2,000 earthquakes in the Mediterranean and Middle East over the past two thousand years, (N. Ambraseys 2009, 13).
4 Explanations have shifted between natural and divine means. (Guidoboni and Ebel 2009, 147–94 for the development of the scientific understanding of earthquakes since antiquity.)
5 See the survey of the discourse about collapse at (Middleton 2012; Haldon et al. 2020; also Nur and Burgess 2008).

Over the past few decades, however, the consensus in disaster studies has shifted away from the view that natural disasters afflict passive societies.[6] Current models ascribe more agency to the human societies that experience such events. Societies can mitigate *hazards* such as earthquakes, which become *disasters* only if they fail to do so.[7] Disasters, in this sense, highlight a society's strengths and weaknesses.[8] Contemporary evidence indicates that societies can significantly influence the outcome of a natural hazard. A comparison between the 2010 earthquakes that hit Port-au-Prince, Haiti and Christchurch, New Zealand demonstrates the differential effects of similar events. Both were of comparable magnitude and hit nearby population centers. The former was perhaps the second deadliest earthquake of the 21st century so far, causing between 100,000 and 300,000 casualties in Haiti, a country in the 145th place of the UN's Human Development Index (2010).[9] The country was still struggling to recover more than a decade after the event.[10] In New Zealand, located in the 3rd place of the same index, the Christchurch earthquake had a certain economic cost but caused only injuries. Commentators have explained the vastly different outcome by a series of variables that included construction materials, emergency services and infrastructure.[11] Recent scholarship has shown how social capital, in particular, is a key variable in determining the effects of a disaster on a society or community.[12] Much historical scholarship, however, has not caught up yet with these broader developments and still follows the obsolete model that assumes natural hazards would result in catastrophic damage.

As natural hazards, earthquakes are perceptible movements of the earth's surface.[13] They occur as a result of vibrations (seismic waves) that radiate from a sudden fracturing in the earth's crust. Most earthquakes happen near the boundaries of tectonic plates and can occur at different depths below

---

6   Wisner et al. 2004; Smith 2013, 1–22.
7   The Emergency Database run by the Centre for research on the Epidemiology of Disasters defines disasters post-1900 as events that conform to at least one of the following: (1) 10 or more people dead; (2) 100 or more people affected; (3) The declaration of a state of emergency; (4) a call for international assistance. See (Centre for research on the Epidemiology of Disasters 2022). The database includes all such events since 1900.
8   Fritz in Knowles 2011, 209.
9   UNDP (United Nations Development Programme) 2010, 148–50.
10 Sael, Savard, and Clormeus n.d.
11 Bilham 2010; Matthewman 2015, 27; also Kahn 2005.
12 Aldrich 2012, 15.
13 For a more detailed description of earthquakes see Guidoboni and Ebel 2009, 11–26; also N. Ambraseys 2009, 1–59.

ground.[14] The epicenter is the point directly above the fracture, where the shaking is most violent. Earthquakes are often measured on the logarithmic Moment Magnitude Scale (MMS).[15] Earthquakes under 3.0 are often imperceptible and cause no damage. Earthquakes above 7.0 can wreak havoc in large areas. Earthquake duration and frequency are closely correlated with their intensity.[16]

Earthquakes also have a significant social component since they are complex events that affect human societies in different stages. The brief tremors that cause the collapse of buildings are only the primary effect of an earthquake. Secondary and tertiary effects take place over the next days to months. Some, such as fires, are triggered directly by the shaking. Others are part of an entangled cascade of causes and effects. These could include crises of varying severity such as food shortages due to the destruction of food stocks or epidemics due to the deteriorated sanitary conditions and destroyed infrastructure. Serious events stimulate population movement and general societal unrest that can ripple across a region. Throughout this model, local environmental conditions (e.g. temperature, crop yield) interact with societal characteristics (e.g. social cohesion, central coordination of relief efforts) to create different outcomes. As a result, a high intensity earthquake does not necessarily imply a high number of casualties and vice versa.

Although premodern earthquakes sometimes strained local societies, surviving primary sources often refer only to central government involvement due to their nature. Central governments tended to react by providing temporary tax reliefs to afflicted areas, but would sometimes also send funds, manpower or supplies to augment local efforts. They tended to focus their resources on the most conspicuous buildings in cities such as major churches, or defensive structures such as city walls.[17] Governors and local representatives of the central government such as bishops were responsible for executing these plans. In antiquity and Late Antiquity there are more references to the seemingly independent actions of local elites, who tended to be local benefactors that repaired or rebuilt a certain building or small area. Their activity is often commemorated on inscriptions. There are also a few cases in antiquity in which

---

14   Shallow earthquakes are closer to the surface and cause more damage.
15   Thus, the amplitude of the seismic waves triggered by a 5.0 earthquake is ten times as much as those triggered by a 4.0 earthquake.
16   There are far more small earthquakes than big ones. For example, there will be about 10 times more 4.0 earthquakes than 5.0 earthquakes around the world in a given time period. Smaller earthquakes will be much shorter (a few seconds) than bigger ones (up to a few minutes of shaking).
17   Mordechai and Pickett 2018.

foreign rulers provided assistance to afflicted communities as well for propaganda purposes.[18] In this context, it seems clear that local non-elites bore the brunt of reconstruction efforts using their own means.

All in all, response efforts were inherently local, as structural limitations on communication and movement severely hindered any attempts of the imperial center to centrally manage the disaster. This in turn required decentralizing authority to local representatives and likely sanctioning their decisions retroactively. Rebuilding was not the only response communities chose, and in some cases settlements were abandoned.[19] There is no clear evidence that past societies adapted their building practices to better prepare for future earthquakes, a phenomenon that appears also in modern comparative data from rural inhabitant interviews.[20]

1 Historical Seismology: The Sources

Earthquakes are unique among natural hazards as relatively frequent short-term cataclysmic events (SCEs) that appear in the three main types of sources: historical-textual, archaeological and natural (see Fig. 6.1). These are not always independent.[21] Synthesizing all sources offers the greatest potential to learn about past seismic events and how societies reacted to them. However, the critical analysis of this multivariate source base requires an uncommon skillset that is best addressed in collaborative work. The absence of such a skillset has contributed to the circular reasoning that is frequent in the field.[22]

Historical sources – literary and epigraphic for the Byzantine period – have traditionally been the foundation of attempts to understand discrete historical seismic events. As such, they form the backbone of earthquake catalogs.[23]

---

18 For a famous example, see the case of Rhodes in the 3rd century BC in (Berthold 2009, 92–93).

19 This response pattern continued into the 20th century. It seems that smaller settlements were abandoned more often than larger ones. Their inhabitants could found a new settlement a few hundred meters away or move elsewhere. (Guidoboni and Ebel 2009, 364–66; N. Ambraseys 2009, 40ff for photos demonstrating the extent of damage involved.)

20 See for instance N. Ambraseys 2009, 15.

21 Agnon 2014, 202.

22 (Rucker and Niemi 2010) The circular reasoning often takes the form of an archaeologist interpreting a destruction layer as evidence for an earthquake, then using an earthquake catalog to assign a date to the destruction. This is written into the historical narrative by historians, whose research is used by future archaeologists as evidence for the earthquake, and vice versa.

23 For a detailed discussion of historical sources, (Guidoboni and Ebel 2009, 39–146).

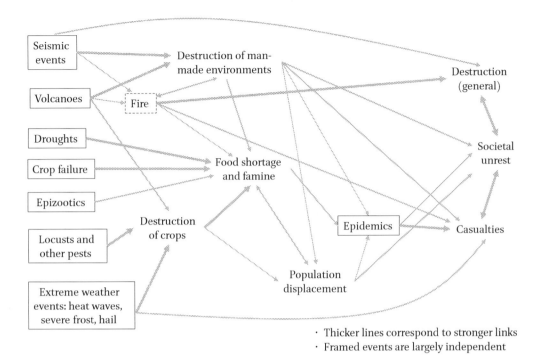

FIGURE 6.1   SCEs and their effects

Many earthquakes appear in traditional historical writings such as chronicles, but additional events have been identified through inscriptions, letters, archival material, poetry, and even liturgical references. Historical sources are the most direct in the information they provide, and they often note a seismic event that occurred at a given time and place. These are sometimes rough estimates, but it is not uncommon for sources to refer to specific locations (cities or provinces) and times (sometimes as precise as the hour in which the event occurred). The sources sometimes add information about the resulting damage and numbers of casualties. On a few occasions, direct or secondhand eyewitness reports survive.

Developments in critical historical research have called almost all of these details into question. Closer examination of the transmission between surviving texts has revealed that many sources depend on others and therefore add little value to the original accounts. Manuscript studies have revealed the instability of numbers, for instance, when a manuscript is copied. Reports can be undated or misdated by the source, causing one event to appear as two distinct earthquakes among contemporary sources, a problem known as duplication. Sources (or modern scholars) can also amalgamate earthquakes – that is, mistakenly interpret several smaller earthquakes as a single large event. Earlier earthquake descriptions can be copied to describe later events.[24] Even eyewitness reports have been called into question, as premodern authors often employ earthquakes as a literary tool that allows them to make broader claims about their society. Different literary traditions and genres, therefore, use earthquakes in distinct ways. Some, such as the medieval Armenian tradition, emphasize divine wrath, while Greco-Roman inscriptions tend to glorify a local elite or ruler who donated funds for rebuilding efforts. The terms each tradition uses are different, as are the adjectives they employ to describe an event's magnitude and effects.[25] The coverage of historical sources is partial as well. More central locations to authors, such as Constantinople or Antioch, are far better covered than peripheral areas such as northern Anatolia or post-classical Greece despite the high seismic activity in these regions. The reports about the extent of damage, the buildings destroyed and the financed rebuilding are all heavily influenced by an author's agenda. Notably, even today, local information regarding earthquake damage is "more often than not grossly exaggerated".[26] As we will see below, these issues plague earthquake catalogs.

Archaeology has been used to support historical findings.[27] Archaeology, in this regard, consists in excavating a certain site even though any findings about earthquakes tend to be incidental to the main purpose of the excavations. Compared to the historical evidence, which describes a region or a city, archaeology is often much narrower in scope, focusing on buildings and streets within a city. The result is a down-to-earth account of what happened at a specific point, including destruction layers, fires, and even post-disaster rebuilding. A recent archaeological study of a *tell* in northern Israel, for instance, demonstrated evidence for no fewer than five seismically induced slips[28] in structure walls built over the last three thousand years.[29] Technology is playing a growing role in this field. For example, LiDAR (Light detection and ranging) scanning can now identify minute changes in tilting that past earthquakes caused.[30]

Archaeological evidence brings in another set of issues. Central to this is the problem of *equifinality*, namely that a large number of causes have the same

---

24   For instance in (Guidoboni and Ebel 2009, 248–50).
25   For examples, (Guidoboni and Ebel 2009, 338–41).
26   N. Ambraseys 2009, 16.
27   N.N. Ambraseys 2006; Guidoboni and Ebel 2009, 418–72; Manuel Sintubin 2011.
28   Slips are defined as the movement on both sides of a fault line, displacing one side in relation to the other.
29   Ellenblum et al. 2015.
30   Yerli et al. 2010.

observed effect in the archaeological record. A collapsed building might be a result of a specific known earthquake, but it could also be the result of a different earthquake, an enemy raid, a storm, or dilapidation. Although there are ways to mitigate this problem, for instance by comparing destruction levels in several buildings and dating them with coins or other objects, this is not always possible.[31] Archaeologists are therefore forced to depend on historical sources and studies, but this can quickly lead to circular reasoning.[32] Archaeologists might ascribe destruction to an earthquake historians describe as big, and their results would be adopted by another generation of historians as independent evidence for the earthquake's magnitude. Excavations are also far more expensive and slow than historical research. Their results can remain unpublished for an indefinite period after their conclusion.[33] Since the second half of the 20th century, large-scale archaeology has become rare, partially since urban growth has prevented careful archaeological excavations in most major Byzantine-era urban centers such as Constantinople/Istanbul, Thessaloniki and Antioch/Antakya.[34] Contemporary excavations often take place in smaller centers, for which there is less textual evidence.

Natural sources are the most recent addition to the study of historical earthquakes. Several methodologies have been suggested to uncover past seismic events. Geomorphological studies can reveal changes in the landscape. Faulting, the surface fracture in the ground, is associated with powerful and shallow earthquakes.[35] Other geological processes such as uplift can also be identified *in situ*. In the AD 365 earthquake in the eastern Mediterranean, for instance, such surveys have found evidence for an uplift of up to 9–10 meters by marks of marine fossils above the water level.[36] Tsunami-inducing earthquakes can be identified by shell deposits found inland, or by underwater debris levels,

---

31 N. Ambraseys 2009, 36–37.
32 Rucker and Niemi 2010.
33 For example, Kletter and De-Groot pointed out in 2001 that 86 percent of seasons of excavations in the Holy Land (i.e. Israel) between 1980 and 1989 remained unpublished, see (Kletter and De-Groot 2001, 77). In the excavations in Beirut, hailed at the time as "the largest urban dig ever known", the vast majority of over 200 excavated sites were never published or published very briefly, see (Mordechai 2020, 208–11).
34 When excavations do take place in these centers they are generally classified as rescue archeology in which archaeologists attempt to rescue the information in the site as quickly as possible.
35 N. Ambraseys 2009, 26–27 listed 78 cases of actual or inferred faulting before 1900 (based on historical sources) and 72 cases after 1900.
36 Stiros 2010; see also Elias et al. 2007.

such as those caused by an earthquake around Caesarea Maritima, deposited by wave movement.[37]

Other scientific approaches can further illuminate questions relating to historical earthquakes, although their application to answer such questions is not yet widespread. Several studies have shown that speleothems (stalagmites and stalactites) can record past earthquakes.[38] Strong earthquakes would cause them to break, while weaker events can change their growth angle. By analyzing speleothems, scientists can date these changes or breakages to an annual level of precision.[39] Since speleothems develop in caves in karst landscapes, common in Anatolia, this approach could have potential for future studies. Some scholars have identified earthquake traces in short-term changes in local agriculture as reflected in pollen data.[40] A recent study has creatively used pollen in dust recovered from under amphorae in a workshop destroyed by an earthquake to date the destruction.[41] Scholars have also found evidence for past earthquakes in tree-ring data, although this seems to affect only trees that are very close to the fault zone and is more useful for more recent earthquakes in areas without a long written historical tradition.[42] Many of these scientific methods have been developed for other purposes and have only recently been used to glean information about historical earthquakes. They all require specialized technical knowledge, are costly to produce and their results depend heavily on statistics and therefore often include error margins.

A recent development with potential to contribute to the studies of past seismic events is earthquake modeling tools. These are digital models that receive a few variables as input, such as location and intensity, and return estimates of the resulting ground movements in different areas, as well as rough estimates for casualties and destruction. The models take into consideration many other variables "under the hood" such as population density, local building practices, soil composition, a country's effectiveness in mobilizing its resources, and even the time of day (night earthquakes cause more casualties since more people are in buildings). These models are implemented to analyze contemporary events and determine government and NGO response to

---

37 Dey and Goodman-Tchernov 2010; Goodman-Tchernov et al. 2009.
38 See for example (Lacave, Koller and Egozcue 2004; Panno et al. 2009; for an example from the region: Akgöz and Eren 2015).
39 This process requires removing them, a process scientists are reluctant to do *en masse*.
40 Leroy et al. 2010.
41 Langgut et al. 2016.
42 Bekker 2010; Stoffel et al. 2010.

immediate emergencies, but future research might use them to examine the effects of premodern seismic events.[43]

2 Earthquake Catalogs

Historical earthquake catalogs aggregate the results of historical earthquake research and make it accessible to the broader scholarly audience.[44] The Eastern Mediterranean is one of the best-documented regions and therefore several dozen publications have compiled lists of relevant earthquakes.[45] There are also a few dozen tsunami catalogs.[46] These catalogs, which have been published since the 15th century, often define their coverage through a combination of spatial and chronological criteria and vary greatly in their quality.[47] Some might be unreferenced tables of events that might include a harmonized chronological window, the estimated earthquake epicenter, other affected areas and an estimate of the earthquake's intensity. Others could include critical discussions of specific events together with the relevant historical source material and modern bibliographies. Online publishing has made some of these catalogs even more accessible. Current aggregations of catalogs cover the entire world over centuries.[48]

These catalogs, however, have several inherent issues which are easy to overlook when using their polished results. First and foremost, as discussed above, the original data is neither well-organized nor precise. The large number of events and the variety of sources used means that less editorial attention is given to each particular event. The brief and vague mentions of earthquakes in the sources or the discrepancies between sources are the cause of much confusion, sometimes causing editors to amalgamate different earthquakes as a single event, or to mistakenly duplicate a single event in multiple entries.

---

43 The USGS n.d. reports the results of their current model (closed access) on their website; offers open access tools GEM Foundation 2019; other institutions have developed additional tools, e.g. Geoscience Australia 2014.
44 Although there is a trend promoting a more qualitative approach, Manuel Sintubin 2011.
45 See the survey in (N. Ambraseys 2009, 4–7, the latest critical comprehensive catalog for the Mediterranean region). Other accessible catalogs are (Guidoboni 1994; Guidoboni and Comastri 2005; Guidoboni et al. 2019).
46 Maramai, Brizuela and Graziani 2014 also online; the new version is Maramai, Graziani, and Brizuela 2019; see also National Geophysical Data Center 2022; N. Ambraseys 2009, 58–59 is more critical.
47 For a survey of past cataloging practices, see Guidoboni and Ebel 2009, 26–35.
48 Albini et al. 2013.

Moreover, especially in older catalogs, the criteria that led the editors to accept certain events and reject others are not adequately explained.[49] Since a significant number of earthquakes that appear in the sources probably never happened, editorial selection processes can greatly influence the eventual shape of the catalog. Recent catalogs have begun to rectify this by also listing earthquakes that they believe did not exist.[50] Unfortunately, since all recent earthquake catalogs are based on previous catalogs, they sometimes duplicate their erroneous findings or include earthquakes that had been omitted correctly.

Even critical catalogs often differ in their estimates of a seismic event's specific time and place. Perhaps the most disputed statistic, however, is the estimated intensity of the event. To estimate earthquakes without the use of instruments, in modern or historical times, scholars have proposed over 60 different intensity scales that convey the effects of an earthquake on structures, objects and on the ground on an I–XII scale. These results can then be converted back to the MMS scale. Unfortunately, most of these scales – often used interchangeably and by non-experts – have been devised for 20th-century European constructions. As such, even medium-sized intensities of VII or VIII could cause almost complete destruction in the historical Near East, where buildings were much more vulnerable than in modern developed countries.[51] As a result of these shortcomings, the most recent critical catalog has not included intensity estimates in its analysis.[52] This, in turn, limits the usefulness of the catalog by making it more difficult to compare earthquakes.

These catalog limitations are often glossed over when compiling digital catalogs, which offer the significant advantage of quick and easy visualization of past events based on selected criteria. However, by displaying similar data (e.g. all earthquakes around the Mediterranean, AD 500–1000) from different databases and overlaying them on the same map, it is immediately clear that the agreement between datasets is much lower than one would hope.

At the current state of research, catalogs are useful as compilations of primary source references that could and should be traced back and examined critically. Their analysis often suggests the main issues concerning a specific event. Some include primary source translations which are also helpful for non-specialists. As such, they offer a quick and easy starting point for any

---

49   Zohar, Salamon, and Rubin 2016 have suggested a concrete method to assess the reliability of an earthquake report in catalogs.
50   See for example N. Ambraseys 2009.
51   Intensity scales have multiple other problems, see N. Ambraseys 2009, 52–55.
52   N. Ambraseys 2009; notably, the accompanying parametric catalog (online only) does include a partial list of about 600 earthquakes with intensity estimates.

investigation of past seismic events, as long as users remember their limitations, but should not be accepted as authoritative on any given earthquake.

3 Case Studies

The lack of detailed evidence for most historical earthquakes requires a certain amount of extrapolation between case studies from premodern and modern times to assess an earthquake's effect. In-depth studies of premodern events are fewer and concentrate around major disasters. The historical sources attest to a marked increase in seismic events in the Eastern Mediterranean during Late Antiquity. A major earthquake in AD 365 caused a tsunami that affected much of the eastern Mediterranean.[53] This was part of a series of up to eight strong earthquakes that occurred over less than a decade in the region.[54] The earthquake of AD 551 wreaked havoc on several cities in the Byzantine Levant.[55] Another massive earthquake in AD 749 caused much destruction in northern Palestine,[56] although Ambraseys has argued that this was an amalgamation of three different earthquakes.[57] In both the mid-6th and the mid-8th century events there is evidence for coincidental change in settlement patterns in these regions.

Over the past several decades, scholars have posited a causal connection between earthquakes and a general or specific notion of decline of the cities they affected. This catastrophist argument is often based on a combination of circular reasoning, a positivist reading of the destruction the sources describe, and the retrospective observation of the collapse of the Roman political system in the Levant during the 7th-century Persian and Arab invasions and conquests.[58] While some of these seismic events undoubtedly placed severe strains on local social structures, the automatic attribution of destruction and urban decline to an earthquake is an easy but often imprecise explanation.

---

53 (Shaw et al. 2008; Guidoboni and Ebel 2009, 404–13). On this event see also the recent (Stiros 2020).
54 Guidoboni and Ebel 2009, 316; Russell 1980; the interval is AD 358–363; more broadly Pirazzoli, Laborel and Stiros 1996.
55 Mordechai 2020.
56 Marco et al. 2003; Wechsler et al. 2009; Dey, Goodman-Tchernov, and Sharvit 2014; Liebeschuetz 2015, 268–69, 274 is more hesitant.
57 N.N. Ambraseys 2005; the earthquakes are dated to AD 746, 749/50 and 757.
58 (Malalas 2000, 419–24; Downey 1961, 525, 559 for Antioch; Waelkens et al. 2000; Manuel Sintubin et al. 2003 for Sagalassos; Altunel et al. 2003, 150 for Knidos; Jacobs 2009, 213 for Hierapolis; Darawcheh et al. 2000 for Beirut and its environs; Russell 1985 for a broader survey). (Liebeschuetz 2015, 267 is more hesitant.)

A closer examination of the available evidence can suggest alternative explanations or more nuanced interpretations. Antioch, which experienced at least five major earthquakes over the 6th century, is a case in point. Despite repeated references to its destruction in both primary and secondary sources, multiple sources refer to the survival of the city's population, major buildings and cultural life.[59]

Other longitudinal case studies that examine a given region are rare. Raphael has surveyed environmental disasters in the Levant during the Crusades, combining a regional interval of high seismicity with other short-term cataclysmic events such as droughts and famines, and political change.[60] Recent work has been done on sites overlapping with Byzantium's sphere of influence in Sicily,[61] L'Aquila,[62] Malta[63] and the Crimea.[64] Longitudinal surveys of other regions are still needed. Constantinople has the best documentation throughout the Byzantine period, with dozens of reported earthquakes. Nikaea and Nikomedia have been affected by major earthquakes in the 4th and 5th centuries, which may have stimulated their decline as urban centers. Salamis (Cyprus) suffered three earthquakes over the 4th century, while the archaeological excavations in it might better illuminate local responses to these earthquakes. Closer investigation of these case studies – and others – would contribute to our understanding of the broader phenomenon of seismic events and their effects on premodern societies.

Bibliography

Agnon, Amotz. 2014. "Pre-Instrumental Earthquakes Along the Dead Sea Rift." In *Dead Sea Transform Fault System: Reviews*, edited by Zvi Garfunkel, Zvi Ben-Avraham, and Elisa Kagan, 207–61. Modern Approaches in Solid Earth Sciences 6. Springer Netherlands. https://doi.org/10.1007/978-94-017-8872-4_8.

Akgöz, Murat, and Muhsin Eren. 2015. "Traces of Earthquakes in the Caves: Sakarlak Ponor and Kepez Cave, Mersin, (Southern Turkey)." *Journal of Cave and Karst Studies* 77 (1): 63–74.

Albini, P., R.M.W. Musson, A.A. Gomez Capera, M. Locati, A. Rovida, M. Stucchi, and D. Viganò. 2013. *Global Historical Earthquake Archive and Catalogue (1000–1903)*, GEM

---

59 Mordechai 2018; for a more nuanced study of a single earthquake, see 2020.
60 Raphael 2013.
61 Bottari 2016.
62 Guidoboni et al. 2012.
63 Main et al. 2022.
64 Nikonov 2016.

Technical Report 2013-01 V1.0.0. Pavia: GEM Foundation. https://www.globalquake model.org/media/publication/GEGD-Historical-Earthquake-Archive-Catalogue-20 1301-V01.pdf.

Aldrich, Daniel P. 2012. *Building Resilience: Social Capital in Post-Disaster Recovery*. Chicago: University of Chicago Press.

Altunel, Erhan, Iain S. Stewart, Aykut Barka, and Luigi Piccardi. 2003. "Earthquake Faulting in Ancient Cnidus, SW Turkey." *Turkish Journal of Earth Sciences* 12: 137–51.

Ambraseys, N.N. 2005. "The Seismic Activity in Syria and Palestine during the Middle of the 8th Century; an Amalgamation of Historical Earthquakes." *Journal of Seismology* 9 (1): 115–25. https://doi.org/10.1007/s10950-005-7743-2.

Ambraseys, N.N. 2006. "Earthquakes and Archaeology." *Journal of Archaeological Science* 33 (7): 1008–16. https://doi.org/10.1016/j.jas.2005.11.006.

Ambraseys, Nicholas. 2009. *Earthquakes in the Mediterranean and Middle East: A Multidisciplinary Study of Seismicity up to 1900*. Cambridge: Cambridge University Press.

Bekker, Matthew F. 2010. "Tree Rings and Earthquakes." In *Tree Rings and Natural Hazards*, edited by Markus Stoffel, Michelle Bollschweiler, David R. Butler, and Brian H. Luckman, 391–97. Advances in Global Change Research 41. Dordrecht and New York: Springer. https://doi.org/10.1007/978-90-481-8736-2_36.

Berthold, Richard M. 2009. *Rhodes in the Hellenistic Age*. Cornell University Press.

Bilham, Roger. 2010. "Lessons from the Haiti Earthquake." *Nature* 463 (7283): 878–79. https://doi.org/10.1038/463878a.

Bottari, Carla. 2016. "Archaeoseismology in Sicily: Past Earthquakes and Effects on Ancient Society." In *Earthquakes and Their Impact on Society*, edited by Sebastiano D'Amico, 491–504. Springer Natural Hazards. New York: Springer International Publishing. https://doi.org/10.1007/978-3-319-21753-6_20.

Centre for research on the Epidemiology of Disasters. 2022. "The International Disaster Database | Frequently Asked Questions." 2022. https://www.emdat.be/frequently-asked-questions.

Darawcheh, Ryad, Mohamed Reda Sbeinati, Claudio Margottini, and Salvatore Paolini. 2000. "The 9 July 551 AD Beirut Earthquake, Eastern Mediterranean Region." *Journal of Earthquake Engineering* 4 (4): 403–14.

Dey, Hendrik, and Beverly Goodman-Tchernov. 2010. "Tsunamis and the Port of Caesarea Maritima over the Longue Durée: A Geoarchaeological Perspective." *Journal of Roman Archaeology* 23: 265–84.

Dey, Hendrik, Beverly Goodman-Tchernov, and Jacob Sharvit. 2014. "Archaeological Evidence for the Tsunami of January 18, A.D. 749: A Chapter in the History of Early Islamic Qâysariyah (Caesarea Maritima)." *Journal of Roman Archaeology* 27 (January): 357–73. https://doi.org/10.1017/S1047759414001287.

Downey, Glanville. 1961. *A History of Antioch in Syria: From Seleucus to the Arab Conquest*. Princeton: Princeton University Press.

Elias, Ata, Paul Tapponnier, Satish C. Singh, Geoffrey C.P. King, Anne Briais, Mathieu Daëron, Helene Carton, et al. 2007. "Active Thrusting Offshore Mount Lebanon: Source of the Tsunamigenic A.D. 551 Beirut-Tripoli Earthquake." *Geology* 35 (8): 755–58.

Ellenblum, Ronnie, Shmuel Marco, Robert Kool, Uri Davidovitch, Roi Porat, and Amotz Agnon. 2015. "Archaeological Record of Earthquake Ruptures in Tell Ateret, the Dead Sea Fault." *Tectonics* 34 (10): 2105–17. https://doi.org/10.1002/2014TC003815.

GEM Foundation. 2019. "GEM – Global Earthquake Model." 2019. https://www.globalquakemodel.org/.

Geoscience Australia. 2014. "How Do We Model Earthquake?" May 15, 2014. http://www.ga.gov.au/scientific-topics/hazards/earthquake/capabilties/modelling/.

Goodman-Tchernov, Beverly N., Hendrik W. Dey, Eduard G. Reinhardt, Floyd McCoy, and Yossi Mart. 2009. "Tsunami Waves Generated by the Santorini Eruption Reached Eastern Mediterranean Shores." *Geology* 37 (10): 943–46. https://doi.org/10.1130/G25704A.1.

Guidoboni, Emanuela. 1994. *Catalogue of Ancient Earthquakes in the Mediterranean Area Up to the 10th Century.* Rome: Istituto Nazionale di Geofisica.

Guidoboni, Emanuela, and Alberto Comastri. 2005. *Catalogue of Earthquakes and Tsunamis in the Mediterranean Area from the 11th to the 15th Century.* Rome: Istituto Nazionale di Geofisica e Vulcanologia.

Guidoboni, Emanuela, Alberto Comastri, Dante Mariotti, Cecilia Ciuccarelli, and Maria Giovanna Bianchi. 2012. "Ancient and Medieval Earthquakes in the Area of L'Aquila (Northwestern Abruzzo, Central Italy), A.D. 1–1500: A Critical Revision of the Historical and Archaeological Data." *Bulletin of the Seismological Society of America* 102 (4): 1600–1617. https://doi.org/10.1785/0120110173.

Guidoboni, Emanuela, and John E. Ebel. 2009. *Earthquakes and Tsunamis in the Past: A Guide to Techniques in Historical Seismology.* Cambridge: Cambridge University Press.

Guidoboni, Emanuela, Graziano Ferrari, Gabriele Tarabusi, Giulia Sgattoni, Alberto Comastri, Dante Mariotti, Cecilia Ciuccarelli, Maria Giovanna Bianchi, and Gianluca Valensise. 2019. "CFTI5Med, the New Release of the Catalogue of Strong Earthquakes in Italy and in the Mediterranean Area." *Scientific Data* 6 (1): 80. https://doi.org/10.1038/s41597-019-0091-9.

Haldon, John, Arlen F. Chase, Warren Eastwood, Martin Medina-Elizalde, Adam Izdebski, Francis Ludlow, Guy Middleton, Lee Mordechai, Jason Nesbitt, and B.L. Turner. 2020. "Demystifying Collapse: Climate, environment, and social agency in pre-modern societies." *Millennium* 17 (1):1–33. https://doi.org/10.1515/mill-2020-0002.

Jacobs, Ine. 2009. "'Encroachment' in the Eastern Mediterranean between the Fourth and the Seventh Century AD." *Ancient Society* 39 (January): 203–44.

Kahn, Matthew E. 2005. "The Death Toll from Natural Disasters: The Role of Income, Geography, and Institutions." *The Review of Economics and Statistics*, 271–84.

Kletter, Raz, and Alon De-Groot. 2001. "Excavating to Excess?: The Last Decade of Archaeology in Israel and Its Implications." *Journal of Mediterranean Archaeology* 14 (1): 76–85.

Knowles, Scott Gabriel. 2011. *The Disaster Experts: Mastering Risk in Modern America*. Philadelphia: University of Pennsylvania Press.

Lacave, C., M.G. Koller, and J.J. Egozcue. 2004. "What Can Be Concluded about Seismic History from Broken and Unbroken Speleothems?" *Journal of Earthquake Engineering* 08 (03): 431–55. https://doi.org/10.1142/S1363246904001493.

Langgut, Dafna, Eli Yannai, Itamar Taxel, Amotz Agnon, and Shmuel Marco. 2016. "Resolving a Historical Earthquake Date at Tel Yavneh (Central Israel) Using Pollen Seasonality." *Palynology* 40 (2): 145–59. https://doi.org/10.1080/01916122.2015.1035405.

Leroy, S. a. G., S. Marco, R. Bookman, and C.S. Miller. 2010. "Impact of Earthquakes on Agriculture during the Roman–Byzantine Period from Pollen Records of the Dead Sea Laminated Sediment." *Quaternary Research* 73 (2): 191–200.

Liebeschuetz, J.H.W.F. 2015. *East and West in Late Antiquity: Invasion, Settlement, Ethnogenesis and Conflicts of Religion*. Leiden: Brill.

Main, Geoff, Ritienne Gauci, John A. Schembri, and David K. Chester. 2022. "A Multi-Hazard Historical Catalogue for the City-Island-State of Malta (Central Mediterranean)." *Natural Hazards*, June. https://doi.org/10.1007/s11069-022-05403-x.

Malalas, Ioannes. 2000. *Chronographia* (*Published as Ioannis Malalae Chronographia*). Edited by Johannes Thurn. Corpus Fontium Historiae Byzantinae 35. Berlin and New York: De Gruyter.

Maramai, Alessandra, Beatriz Brizuela, and Laura Graziani. 2014. "The Euro-Mediterranean Tsunami Catalogue." *Annals of Geophysics* 57 (4): S0435.

Maramai, Alessandra, Laura Graziani, and Beatriz Brizuela. 2019. "Euro-Mediterranean Tsunami Catalogue (EMTC), Version 2.0." Text/csv,application/vnd.openxmlformats-officedocument.spreadsheetml.sheet,application/pdf,application/x-zipped-shp. Istituto Nazionale di Geofisica e Vulcanologia (INGV). https://doi.org/10.13127/TSUNAMI/EMTC.2.0.

Marco, Shmuel, Moshe Hartal, Nissim Hazan, Lilach Lev, and Mordechai Stein. 2003. "Archaeology, History, and Geology of the A.D. 749 Earthquake, Dead Sea Transform." *Geology* 31 (8): 665–68. https://doi.org/10.1130/G19516.1.

Matthewman, Steve. 2015. *Disasters, Risks and Revelation: Making Sense of Our Times*. Houndmills, UK: Springer.

Middleton, Guy D. 2012. "Nothing Lasts Forever: Environmental Discourses on the Collapse of Past Societies." *Journal of Archaeological Research* 20 (3): 257–307. https://doi.org/10.1007/s10814-011-9054-1.

Mordechai, Lee. 2018. "Antioch in the Sixth Century: Resilience or Vulnerability?" *Late Antique Archaeology* 12: 25–41.

Mordechai, Lee. 2020. "Berytus and the Aftermath of the 551 Earthquake." *Late Antiquity – Studies in Source Criticism* 17–18: 197–241.

Mordechai, Lee, and Jordan Pickett. 2018. "Earthquakes as the Quintessential SCE: Methodology and Societal Resilience." *Human Ecology* 46 (3): 335–48. https://doi.org/10.1007/s10745-018-9985-y.

National Geophysical Data Center. 2022. "Global Historical Tsunami Database." NOAA National Centers for Environmental Information. https://doi.org/10.7289/V5PN93H7.

Nikonov, A.A. 2016. "Ancient Destructive Earthquakes in Chersonesus Taurica and Their Importance for a Long-Term Seismic Hazard Assessment of the Southwestern Crimea Region." *Seismic Instruments* 52 (2): 164–94. https://doi.org/10.3103/S0747923916020067.

Nur, Amos, and Dawn Burgess. 2008. *Apocalypse: Earthquakes, Archaeology, and the Wrath of God*. Princeton: Princeton University Press.

Panno, Samuel V., Craig C. Lundstrom, Keith C. Hackley, Brandon B. Curry, Bruce W. Fouke, and Zaofeng Zhang. 2009. "Major Earthquakes Recorded by Speleothems in Midwestern U.S. Caves." *Bulletin of the Seismological Society of America* 99 (4): 2147–54. https://doi.org/10.1785/0120080261.

Pirazzoli, P.A., J. Laborel, and S.C. Stiros. 1996. "Earthquake Clustering in the Eastern Mediterranean during Historical Times." *Journal of Geophysical Research: Solid Earth* 101 (B3): 6083–97. https://doi.org/10.1029/95JB00914.

Raphael, Sarah Kate. 2013. *Climate and Political Climate: Environmental Disasters in the Medieval Levant*. Leiden: Brill.

Rucker, John D., and Tina M. Niemi. 2010. "Historical Earthquake Catalogues and Archaeological Data: Achieving Synthesis without Circular Reasoning." In *Ancient Earthquakes*, edited by M. Sintubin, 97–106. Boulder: Geological Society of America.

Russell, Kenneth W. 1980. "The Earthquake of May 19, A.D. 363." *Bulletin of the American Schools of Oriental Research* 238: 47–64. https://doi.org/10.2307/1356515.

Russell, Kenneth W. 1985. "The Earthquake Chronology of Palestine and Northwest Arabia from the 2nd Through the Mid-8th Century A.D." *Bulletin of the American Schools of Oriental Research* 260: 37–59. https://doi.org/10.2307/1356863.

Sael, Emmanuel, Jean-François Savard, and Joseph Jr Clormeus. n.d. "A Decade after the Earthquake, Haiti Still Struggles to Recover." The Conversation. Accessed July 4, 2022. http://theconversation.com/a-decade-after-the-earthquake-haiti-still-struggles-to-recover-129670.

Shaw, B., N.N. Ambraseys, P.C. England, M.A. Floyd, G.J. Gorman, T.F.G. Higham, J.A. Jackson, J.-M. Nocquet, C.C. Pain, and M.D. Piggott. 2008. "Eastern Mediterranean Tectonics and Tsunami Hazard Inferred from the AD 365 Earthquake." *Nature Geoscience* 1 (4): 268–76. https://doi.org/10.1038/ngeo151.

Sintubin, Manuel. 2011. "Archaeoseismology: Past, Present and Future." *Quaternary International*, Earthquake Archaeology and Paleoseismology, 242 (1): 4–10. https://doi.org/10.1016/j.quaint.2011.03.056.

Sintubin, Manuel, Philippe Muchez, Dominique Similox-Tohon, Griet Verhaert, Etienne Paulissen, and Marc Waelkens. 2003. "Seismic Catastrophes at the Ancient City of Sagalassos (SW Turkey) and Their Implications for Seismotectonics in the Burdur–Isparta Area." *Geological Journal* 38 (3–4): 359–74. https://doi.org/10.1002/gj.960.

Smith, Keith. 2013. *Environmental Hazards: Assessing Risk and Reducing Disaster*. New York: Routledge.

Stiros, Stathis C. 2010. "The 8.5+ Magnitude, AD 365 Earthquake in Crete: Coastal Uplift, Topography Changes, Archaeological and Historical Signature." *Quaternary International*, Landscape Evolution and Geoarchaeology, 216 (1–2): 54–63. https://doi.org/10.1016/j.quaint.2009.05.005.

Stiros, Stathis C. 2020. "Was Alexandria (Egypt) Destroyed in A.D. 365? A Famous Historical Tsunami Revisited." *Seismological Research Letters* 91 (5): 2662–73. https://doi.org/10.1785/0220200045.

Stoffel, Markus, Michelle Bollschweiler, David R. Butler, and Brian H. Luckman. 2010. *Tree Rings and Natural Hazards: A State-of-Art*. Dordrecht: Springer.

UNDP (United Nations Development Programme). 2010. *Human Development Report 2010: 20th Anniversary Edition. The Real Wealth of Nations: Pathways to Human Development*. New York: Palgrave Macmillan.

USGS. n.d. "OnePAGER Information." Accessed January 1, 2017. https://earthquake.usgs.gov/data/pager/onepager.php.

Waelkens, Marc, Manuel Sintubin, Philippe Muchez, and Etienne Paulissen. 2000. "Archaeological, Geomorphological and Geological Evidence for a Major Earthquake at Sagalassos (SW Turkey) around the Middle of the Seventh Century AD." *Geological Society, London, Special Publications* 171 (1): 373–83. https://doi.org/10.1144/GSL.SP.2000.171.01.27.

Wechsler, Neta, Oded Katz, Yehoshua Dray, Ilana Gonen, and Shmuel Marco. 2009. "Estimating Location and Size of Historical Earthquake by Combining Archaeology and Geology in Umm-El-Qanatir, Dead Sea Transform." *Natural Hazards* 50 (1): 27–43. http://dx.doi.org/10.1007/s11069-008-9315-6.

Wisner, Ben, Piers M. Blaikie, Piers Blaikie, Terry Cannon, and Ian Davis. 2004. *At Risk: Natural Hazards, People's Vulnerability and Disasters*. Psychology Press.

Yerli, Barış, Johan ten Veen, Manuel Sintubin, Volkan Karabacak, C. Çağlar Yalçıner, and Erhan Altunel. 2010. "Assessment of Seismically Induced Damage Using LIDAR: The Ancient City of Pınara (SW Turkey) as a Case Study." In *Ancient Earthquakes*, edited by Manuel Sintubin, 157–70. Boulder: Geological Society of America.

Zohar, Motti, Amos Salamon, and Rehav Rubin. 2016. "Reappraised List of Historical Earthquakes That Affected Israel and Its Close Surroundings." *Journal of Seismology* 20 (3): 971–85.

PART 2

Case Studies: Environmental History at Work

CHAPTER 7

The Byzantines and Nature in the Christian Worldview

Henry Maguire

1   Written Sources and the State of Research

This chapter is concerned not with the natural environment in which the Byzantines lived, but rather with their attitudes toward nature and its place in the Christian worldview. At the date of writing, there has been relatively little research on this topic. The few publications that exist have tended to concentrate on the field of patristics, examining the attitudes of the Greek Church Fathers toward terrestrial creation,[1] or on rhetorical and secular literature, especially the genre of ekphrasis and the medieval romances.[2] There are also several recent publications on the topic of gardens in Byzantium, which represent attempts by the Byzantines to tame nature and to order it for their enjoyment and delectation.[3]

In the early Byzantine period, from the fourth to the seventh centuries, the principal written sources describing the natural environment from a Christian perspective are the sermons and commentaries on the *Hexaemeron*, or the first six days of the world.[4] These writings attempted to take the whole of creation, which hitherto had been in the purview of pagan cults, and to inscribe it into the Christian faith. The texts typically consist of a more or less systematic listing of natural phenomena, including animals and plants. Sometimes the individual elements of creation are allegorized, as in the case of the vine; at other times they are simply described as wonders of God's handiwork. The most

---

1 Wallace-Hadrill, *The Greek Patristic View of Nature*; Attfield, "Christian Attitudes to Nature"; for a recent exploration of the theology of nature in Byzantium, see Della Dora, *Landscape, Nature, and the Sacred in Byzantium*.
2 Maguire, *Art and Eloquence in Byzantium*, pp. 42–52; M.-L. Dolezal/M. Mavroudi, "Theodore Hyrtakenos' *Description of the Garden of St. Anna* and the Ekphrasis of Gardens"; Maguire, *Nectar and Illusion*, pp. 48–77; K. Demoen, "A Homeric Garden in Tenth-Century Constantinople"; I. Nilsson, "Nature controlled by Artistry".
3 Littlewood, Maguire, and Wolschke-Bulmahn, *Byzantine Garden Culture*; Bodin and Hedlund, *Byzantine Gardens and Beyond*.
4 Maguire, *Earth and Ocean*, pp. 17–20, 31–3, 41–4.

important and influential of these texts was the *Hexaemeron* of the fourth-century church father Basil the Great.[5] Later *Hexaemera* include the verse composition by the seventh-century author George of Pisidia,[6] and the highly allegorized version attributed spuriously to the seventh-century writer Anastasios of Sinai.[7] Another important text that should be mentioned here is the *Second Theological Oration* delivered in Constantinople by the Church Father Gregory of Nazianzus in the year 380, which contains a general celebration of nature through which the magnificence of God is revealed; like the *Hexaemera*, the text catalogues all of earthly creation, describing each of its divisions in turn.[8] In the medieval period of Byzantium from the eighth century onwards, the tradition of *Hexaemeron* writing declined, although creation continued to be described in the World Chronicles, such as the twelfth-century *Biblos chronike* by Michael Glykas, where the first six days of creation received an extended treatment.[9]

Another major category of Byzantine writing that was often concerned with descriptions of the natural environment was the rhetorical genre of ekphrasis. In the handbook composed by the ancient rhetor Hermogenes, ekphrasis was defined as the description of "persons, deeds, times, places, seasons, and many other things."[10] Many ekphraseis described works of art which themselves portrayed the natural world; thus these literary works provide us with a response to nature at one remove. Ekphraseis could either be relatively long, encompassing the whole of creation, as in the case of the description of Creation that opens the verse chronicle written by Constantine Manasses in the mid-twelfth century,[11] or relatively short, as in the case of the bravura descriptions of peacocks that authors of *Hexaemera* liked to insert into their sermons.[12] An ekphrasis could also be devoted to a landscape, such as the evocative account of the countryside around the Kosmosoteira Monastery at Pherrai in Thrace contained in the monastery's *typikon* drawn up by Isaac Comnenus in 1152.[13] We also find ekphraseis of nature adorning secular works,

---

5   Basil the Great, *Hexaemeron*, ed. Giet.
6   George of Pisidia, *Hexaemeron*, Patrologia Graeca 92, cols. 1425–1578.
7   *Hexaemeron*, Patrologia Graeca 89, cols. 851–1077.
8   Gregory of Nazianzus, *Homilia XXVIII* (*Second Theological Oration*), ed. Gallay/Jourjon, pp. 100–74.
9   Michael Glykas, *Biblos chronike*, ed. Bekker, pp. 3–160.
10 Hermogenes, *Progymnasmata*, 10, ed. Rabe, p. 22.
11 Constantine Manasses, *Synopsis chronike*, lines 27–285, ed. Lampsidis, pp. 6–19. For a discussion of this ekphrasis, see Nilsson, "Narrating Images", pp. 129–36, 140–46.
12 Maguire, *Nectar and Illusion*, pp. 52–3.
13 Isaac Comnenus, *Typikon of the Kosmosoteira Monastery*, ed. Petit, p. 57, trans. N. Ševčenko, in Thomas/Hero, *Byzantine Monastic Foundation Documents*, vol. 2, p. 833.

most notably the extended descriptions of gardens that are to be found in medieval Romances.[14]

2 The Opposition to Pagan Nature Worship

In the early Byzantine period, Christians had to frame their responses to the natural environment in opposition to the pagan cults of nature which formerly had held sway. As an example of a cult that proved problematic, we may take the annual festival of the rising of the Nile, which continued into the fifth century, long after the official establishment of Christianity.[15] The cult is illustrated by a splendid floor mosaic that has been discovered in the city of Sepphoris in Galilee.[16] The mosaic adorned a large room in an important building of uncertain function. It seems to have been some kind of public structure, and not a private house, for it lacks the usual appurtenances of a grand private dwelling, such as a dining room or a bath. The date of the building is as uncertain as its purpose, but the most likely date is the one suggested by the excavators, that is, around the turn of the fourth and the fifth centuries. At the top of the mosaic, at the centre, there is a Nilometer, which marks the level of the flood. A putto is carving the letters Iota Zeta onto the Nilometer, to indicate the number of 17 cubits, the optimum level for the rising of the river, which was called the *semeion*. *Semeion* was also the name given to the festival celebrating the event. When the flood had reached the right level, the news was spread through the land of Egypt to allow the flood-gates to be opened to irrigate the fields. The spreading of the good news was personified by the figure of Semasia, who is depicted on the mosaic as a young woman riding at a gallop towards the city of Alexandria, which is identified by an inscription and by its flaming lighthouse. The letters Iota Zeta appear again beside Semasia, indicating the joyful purpose of her ride. The season of the *semeion* was accompanied by a general festival, which included processions featuring garlanded statues of the Nile. At the top of the panel, in the top right corner, the personified river appears reclining on the back of a hippopotamus, and in the top left corner Egypt is shown, with her right elbow resting on a basket full of fruit and holding a cornucopia in her left hand. Beside Egypt are the flocks in their fields, while the river itself, with its usual aquatic plants and birds, flows below. All of this is

---

14 I. Nilsson, "Nature controlled by Artistry".
15 Hermann, "Der Nil und die Christen".
16 Weiss/Talgam, "The Nile Festival Building"; Talgam, *Mosaics of Faith*, pp. 355–63, figs. 441–9.

accompanied by an inscription in the upper border, which enjoins the viewer to "Use in good fortune."

In Egypt, the Nile's rising, so richly portrayed by this mosaic, was encouraged by hymns that addressed the river as a pagan deity, invoking his abundance. For example, a hymn dating to around the year 300 describes the blessings brought by the swollen Nile, before concluding with an invocation to the immortal powers of the river.[17] It is not surprising that the cult of the Nile caused the Christian authorities considerable unease, yet they found it difficult to eradicate. Toward the end of the fourth century, the pagan orator Libanius taunted the Christians on account of their acquiescence in the Nile festivities because of their worries about the food supply,[18] while a papyrus from Oxyrhynchus informs us that the Nile Festival was being celebrated as late as 424. Another papyrus, of the sixth century, hails the river as "the most sacred Nile, the festival with its sacred rites of abundance".[19]

Reacting to the continuing strength of the cult of the Nile, Christian orators developed an opposition between the waters of the Nile, which they characterized as corrupt and corrupting, and those of the baptismal font, which gave birth to eternal life. This idea is already contained in the treatise on the Errors of Pagan Religions by Firmicus Maternus, composed in the mid-fourth century. According to Firmicus: "The inhabitants of Egypt adore water, implore water, and venerate water in the superstitious routine of their offerings." He then proceeds to link the Nile with the unsavory cult of Osiris – whose body had been dismembered and dispersed along the banks of the river, and whose companion was the dog-headed Anubis. "In vain do you suppose," says Firmicus, addressing the Egyptians, "that this water can bring you any advantage. But there exists another water by which men are renewed and reborn. This water of fire, which you scorn, is ennobled by the majesty of the venerable spirit."[20] As late as the eighth century we find this theme repeated by Andrew of Crete, in his encomium of St. Patapios, who was born in Egypt. Andrew of Crete was brought up in Palestine, and may well have visited Egypt. In the course of his address, Andrew described the saint's native land; this description of the protagonist's fatherland was a necessary part of any panegyric, Christian or pagan. But instead of praising the saint's physical birth-place, as was customary, Andrew of Crete condemned it by elaborating the old contrast between the

---

17 Cribiore, "A Hymn to the Nile".
18 Libanius, *Oratio XXX*, 35.
19 Weiss/Talgam, "The Nile Festival Building", p. 70.
20 Firmicus Maternus, *De errore profanarum religionum*, 2.1–5, ed. Turcan, pp. 77–9.

two waters, the water of Egypt, where the saint had been born, and the water of the baptismal font, where he had been spiritually reborn:

> Egypt is the generator of darkness and gloom, while the font is the mother of immaterial light. One [Egypt] is the nurse of misfortunes, while the other [the font] is the orchestrator of righteous acts. One is the guide to death, the other the leader to eternal life; one is the manufacturer of the earthly passions, the other the teacher of the passionless way of life. This one is the place of grief, that one the treasury of joy, this the shady abode of evil, that the brilliant abode of virtue.[21]

It was not only the Nile that drew the ire of Christian writers; other water cults were equally condemned. For example, the first Mystagogical Catechesis, attributed either to the fourth-century Bishop Cyril of Jerusalem or to his successor, John, condemned the lighting of lamps and incense to springs and rivers, and the practice of having recourse to them for the cure of bodily diseases.[22] The official opposition to the pagan cults of water had a direct effect on works of art, as can be seen most strikingly in a pavement in the baths of a Roman house at El Haouria in Tunisia.[23] Here there was a floor mosaic that originally depicted a frontal mask of Ocean. Although the mosaic has been deliberately damaged, we can reconstruct its original appearance with reference to other mosaics of the same subject that have survived intact, such as a late-fourth or early-fifth-century floor at Ain-Témouchent, near Sétif in Algeria.[24] In the latter mosaic, the head of Ocean has long flowing hair and beard together with claws growing out of his forehead. The eyes of Ocean are large and staring, a feature that gave the image its power, for the inscription below the mosaic calls on the steely gaze of the mask to destroy the hearts of the envious. In the house at El Haouria there had been a similar mask. However, at some time after its completion, the face of Ocean was carefully picked out, leaving behind just his curved beard and the claws that had projected from his hair. Only the figures that had surrounded the mask in the four corners of its frame, erotes and hippocamps, were allowed to remain, presumably because whoever destroyed the central mask believed these marginal motifs to be harmless. In this example of iconoclasm, we can see clearly the unease provoked by a nature deity in a house that had become Christian.

---

21 Andrew of Crete, *In S. Patapium*, Patrologia Graeca, 97, col. 1217.
22 *Mystagogica catechesis*, 1.8, Patrologia Graeca 33, col. 1072B.
23 Poinssot, "Mosaïques d'El-Haouria", pp. 189–95, fig. 3.
24 Dunbabin, *Mosaics of Roman North Africa*, pp. 151–2, pl. 143.

3 The Absorption of Nature into the Christian Worldview

From Christian opposition to the veneration of water, we will turn to the conversion of the waters that had been pagan, and to their incorporation into Christian art. Even while some Christian writers, such as Andrew of Crete, continued the antithetical rhetoric that set the veneration of rivers in opposition to salvation through the font, there was another view that recognized the benefits brought by the terrestrial waters, but attributed these benefits to the power of God, rather than to the created elements themselves. In some sixth-century texts from Egypt, for example, we begin to find the Nile treated as a subject, rather than as a rival of Christ. The poet Dioscorus of Aphrodito, in an epithalamium delivered at a wedding, attached the power of the river to Christ, in order to convey a blessing upon the bride and groom: "Easily protecting … the Nile with his many children, may god grant a superlative marriage free from the accursed envy of others."[25] A sixth-century papyrus from Antinoe in Egypt preserves a hymn addressed to the Nile that begins in a manner similar to the pagan invocations, but ends with an appeal to the Christian deity. For the most part, the poem contains nothing that is explicitly Christian; only at its conclusion do we find a prayer to Christ, the true source of the river's power.[26] The supplicant appears to call upon the river as Christ's agent, almost as if he were making an appeal to a saint.

The theme of the subjection of the waters to the command of Christ is well illustrated by the mosaic that survives in the dome of the baptistery attached to the Arian Cathedral in Ravenna, which dates to the late fifth or early sixth century (fig. 7.1).[27] On the right of the image in the central medallion, John baptizes Christ, who stands unclothed in the water, beneath the dove of the Holy Spirit. On the left is the personification of the river, who is portrayed in the same way as pagan river gods, with a cloth draping the lower half of the body, long flowing strands of beard and hair, and the attribute of an upturned vase signifying the source of the water.[28] But here, at Ravenna, the personification of the Jordan has an additional attribute, for a pair of red claws sprouts from the top of his head. As we have seen above, the claws are usually associated with depictions of Ocean in ancient art. The attribute of the claws extends the meaning of the personification of the Jordan river to include all

---

25 Mac Coull, *Dioscorus of Aphrodito*, pp. 111–12.
26 Manfredi, "Inno cristiano al Nilo", p. 56.
27 Deichmann, *Frühchristliche Bauten und Mosaiken*, pls. 251–4; Deichmann, *Geschichte und Monumente*, pp. 209–12; Deichmann, *Kommentar*, part 1, pp. 254–5.
28 On the personification of the Jordan, see Jensen, *Living Water*, pp. 117–23, 134–6.

FIGURE 7.1
Ravenna, Arian Baptistery, dome mosaic: Baptism of Christ in the river Jordan
PHOTO: HENRY MAGUIRE

of the terrestrial waters. In the mosaic at Ravenna, the figure of Jordan/Ocean raises his left hand to acknowledge his master, the true God, Christ. The mosaic can be related to a sermon on the Baptism delivered by St. Peter Chrysologus, who was Archbishop of Ravenna during the second quarter of the fifth century. In his homily, Peter Chrysologus quoted the following passage from the 28th Psalm:

> The voice of the Lord is over the waters;
> the glory of God thunders,
> the Lord over many waters ....
> The lord sits enthroned over the flood;
> The Lords sits enthroned as king for ever.
> May the Lord give strength to his people!
> May the Lord bless his people with peace!

Commenting on this passage, Peter associated the triumphant words of the psalm with the Baptism of Christ. "Today," he said, "the Lord is over the waters. And he is rightly said to be over the waters, and not under the waters, because

FIGURE 7.2 Thessaloniki, Hosios David, apse mosaic: Christ in Glory with river deity below
PHOTO: HIRMER FOTOARCHIV

Christ in his Baptism does not serve, but commands the waters." The homilist then proceeded to ask how it was that the Jordan did not flee at the presence of the Trinity during the Baptism of Christ, as it had formerly fled, or drawn back, to allow the passage of the Ark of the Covenant, in the time of Joshua. The reason, he said, is that the river had been changed. In Peter's words: "the one that has submitted to reverence begins not to be in fear."[29]

In this sermon, therefore, an Early Christian preacher in Ravenna described the submission and conversion of water, the most fundamental element of terrestrial nature. The same concept was expressed visually in the mosaic that survives in the dome of the baptistery of the Arian Cathedral.

Another mosaic that may be of the same period as the Arian Baptistery, or possibly slightly later, and that portrays a similar idea, is the composition in the apse of the church of Hosios David in Thessaloniki (fig. 7.2).[30] In this case

---

29 Peter Chrysologus, *Sermo CLX*, Patrologia Latina 52, cols. 621–62.
30 Spieser, "Remarques complémentaires sur la mosaïque de Osios David", pp. 295–306; Bakirtzis/Kourkoutidou-Nikolaidou/Mavropoulou Tsioumi, *Mosaics of Thessaloniki*, pp. 182–95.

a splendid vision of Christ enthroned in his glory fills the vault. Christ sits on a rainbow in an aureole of light, held up by the four winged symbols of the evangelists. This theophany is flanked by two unidentified personages with haloes, one sitting in apparent thought on the right, the other lifting his hands up in a gesture that may convey his awe as he witnesses the vision. The identity of these two men is uncertain. They are usually said to be either prophets, apostles or evangelists; in the later Middle Ages they were identified as Ezekiel and Habakkuk. The feet of the Lord rest on a hill from which issue the four rivers of Paradise, which then turn into a fish-filled stream flowing along the bottom of the mosaic. In the lower border of the mosaic there is an inscription, the start of which associates the water with the water of life: "A life-giving source, accepting and nourishing the souls of the faithful [is] this most venerable house." Barely visible in the life-bringing stream, just to the left of the Christ's feet, a shadowy form appears. This is the conquered, or converted, figure of the old pagan god, who is delineated in a white grisaille against the blue background of the water. The deity emerges from the stream, with the nude torso, long hair and flowing beard of the pagan river gods. He lifts up both arms, spreading his palms in amazed acknowledgement of the heavenly apparition above him, deferring to Christ as his master. In spite of his hirsute and uncouth appearance, the god of the waters makes the same gesture as the Christian holy man standing on the shore at the left. Here, therefore, in the very fountain of life, the converted ghost of the pagan past joins in acclamation of the Christian vision.

The Christian rehabilitation of the river cults was helped by the identification of the four rivers of paradise with the four principal rivers of the terrestrial world, which were believed to have their origin in the Fountain in Paradise. Many people thought that the Tigris, the Euphrates, the Nile and a fourth river, often identified with the Ganges or the Danube, all had their source in the terrestrial paradise, which was thought to be located in the east, beyond the great ocean that surrounded the inhabited world.[31] Thus in the early Byzantine period, mortals enjoyed a direct connection with Paradise, provided by the water flowing in these four great rivers. The early-sixth-century poet Avitus wrote that the Phison, which he identified with the Ganges in India, steals the wealth of Paradise and conveys it to our place of banishment.[32] This linking of the four rivers with Paradise allowed a fusion of their spiritual and their physical values; they gave life to souls at the same time as they gave life to fields and crops. Accordingly, in some early Christian baptisteries the four rivers were

---

31   Maguire, *Earth and Ocean*, pp. 17–28.
32   Avitus, *Poematum de mosaicae historicae gestis*, Patrologia Latina 59, col. 330.

portrayed in the pavement surrounding the font. For example, in the floor mosaics of a fifth-century baptistery excavated at Ohrid, they are shown with identifying inscriptions in the form of masks with water streaming from their mouths.[33] Between the masks are depictions of paradisal fountains flanked by birds and deer.

4   Hesitations Concerning Portrayals of Nature

The four rivers, therefore, were accepted into churches, because their origin was in the gem-encrusted spring of Paradise. But the fact remained that they had been the focus of pagan cults before the triumph of Christianity, and this stain could never completely be erased. The problem was especially acute in the case of the Nile, for this river, above all other waters, was associated not only with bounty, but also with the rites and idolatry that had tried to ensure its annual flood. The sixth-century poet Romanos, in his hymn on the Holy Innocents, said that when Christ arrived at the Land of Egypt and of the fruitful Nile, he overthrew there all of their idols.[34] Consequently, the Christians were careful about how they represented the Nile and other rivers in their churches. For the most part, in churches, artists avoided personifying one of the rivers of Paradise on its own, without the company of the other three rivers to act as chaperons. The fear was that an isolated half-naked human form might encourage idolatry by tempting viewers to venerate the created rather than the creator. The only exception to the rule that personified rivers did not appear singly in churches is the case of the Jordan in portrayals of the Baptism of Christ. But here, as we have seen, the personification of the river is very clearly placed subordinate to Christ's power, and under his command as his creation.

In one of his letters, Sidonius Apollinaris, a fifth-century bishop of Clermont in Gaul, praised the bath house of a villa because its walls were bare concrete instead of being adorned with pagan myths and "the nude beauty of painted figures".[35] A similar sentiment is found in a sixth-century encomium addressed to Marcian, the bishop of Gaza, by the orator Choricius. In his ekphrasis of the now lost church of St. Stephen in that city, which the bishop had been instrumental in building, Choricius described the motifs shown in the aisles of the basilica, which portrayed the animals and plants associated with the

---

33 Bitrakova-Grozdanova, *Monuments paléochrétiens de la région d'Ohrid*, 55–65, pl. 4.
34 Romanos, *Holy Innocents*, strophe 15, ed. Grosdidier de Matons, vol. 2, p. 222.
35 Sidonius Apollinaris, *Epistulae*, 2.2.5–7, ed. Loyen.

river Nile. The river, he said with approval, was "nowhere portrayed in the way painters portray rivers". In other words, the Nile was not represented by a personification. Instead, said Choricius, the Nile was "suggested by means of distinctive currents and symbols, as well as by the meadows along its banks" where "various kinds of birds that often wash in that river's streams dwell in the meadows".[36] In St. Stephen at Gaza, then, as in many surviving early Byzantine churches, the Nile was evoked only by means of its typical flora or fauna. The beautiful pavements depicting water birds and lotus plants in the transepts of the church of the Multiplying of the Loaves and Fishes at Tabgha in Israel, which date to the second half of the fifth century, illustrate the kind of motifs that Choricius was describing.[37] Similar scenes from the Nile can be found on the sixth-century pavement of the church of St. John the Baptist at Gerasa, where the river is also evoked through depictions of its cities, such as Alexandria.[38]

When we find the Nile personified in human form in churches, it only appears alongside the other three rivers of Paradise, who make the Christian import of the image manifest. An interesting example survives in Greece, in the nave mosaic of the basilica of Thyrsos at Tegea in the Peloponnese, which probably was set in the late fifth century.[39] Here we see a map-like composition, representing the earth and the surrounding ocean. The ocean is represented by the border around the mosaic, which portrays sea creatures in octagons. The earth is evoked by personifications of the twelve months, depicted in bust form in the central panel of the mosaic, each holding its seasonal attributes. For example, August carries a pumpkin and an egg plant. In the four corners of the central panel we find personifications of the four rivers of Paradise, identified as Gehon, or the Nile, and Phison, nearest to the sanctuary, and Tigris and Euphrates, nearest to the entrance.

A somewhat similar composition can be found in the mosaic that covers the floor of the Chapel of the Martyr Theodore adjoining the atrium of the cathedral church at Madaba, in Jordan.[40] An inscription dates the completion of the chapel and its mosaic to the year 562. In this pavement the central panel is made up of a geometrical interlace that forms circles, lozenges and octagons enclosing a variety of subjects, including birds, fishes, baskets of fruit and farm workers; scenes of pastoralism and hunting fill the borders. All of these

---

36   Choricius, *Laudatio Marciani II*, 50–51, ed. Foerster/Richsteig.
37   Talgam, *Mosaics of Faith*, p. 110.
38   Kraeling, *Gerasa*, pp. 324–9, 480, pls. 66–70.
39   Orlandos, "Palaiochristianika kai byzantina mnemeia Tegeas-Nykliou", pp. 27–43, figs. 6–12, pl. A.
40   Piccirillo, *Mosaics of Jordan*, p. 117, figs. 110–15.

FIGURE 7.3 Umm al-Rasas, Church of St. Stephen, nave pavement, detail: iconoclastic erasures
PHOTO: HENRY MAGUIRE

motifs were evocative of terrestrial bounty. As at Tegea, personifications of the four rivers were portrayed at the corners of the rectangular composition, again being labeled by inscriptions as Geon, Phison, Euphrates and Tigris. These floors, therefore, portrayed the inhabited earth, represented by its creatures and its fruits, and watered at its four corners by the Rivers of Paradise.

The pavement of the Chapel of the Martyr Theodore was one of the mosaics that were damaged in the course of the eighth century, when the floors of a number of churches in Palestine suffered iconoclastic interventions, as can be seen in figure 7.3, a detail of the nave pavement in the church of St. Stephen at Umm al-Rasas in Jordan.[41] In the case of the Chapel of the Martyr Theodore, it may be noted that the erasures were targeted especially at the human figures in the central panel, in particular the personifications of the rivers of Paradise. The iconoclasts permitted most of the depictions of animals to remain, and for the most part they also left alone the images of hunters and pastoralists in the borders. The reasons for the iconoclasm in the floor mosaics of Palestine are complex and debated. It is generally agreed that the destruction was carried out by the Christians themselves, for in many cases it was done carefully and expertly. The motivation often has been attributed to pressure from the

41   Piccirillo/Alliata, *Umm al-Rasas/Mayfa'ah*, vol. 1, pp. 134–40.

Arabs, the new rulers of the region. As Muslims, the Arab authorities did not allow representations of living creatures in their own places of worship. But it is more likely that the primary impetus for iconoclasm in the churches came from the Christians themselves, and from their long-lasting concerns about the appropriateness of nature imagery in their places of worship.[42]

It may be noted that in the Chapel of the Martyr Theodore, the human figures were excised in such a way that the inscriptions identifying them were preserved. In other words, the iconoclasts destroyed the images, but not the concepts. After the erasures, the congregation was left with aniconic representations of the four rivers – with the octagons that contained just their names. A similar kind of aniconic representation of the waters of the world, its seas and its rivers, existed already in the sixth century, in the great church of Hagia Sophia in Constantinople, at the heart of the Byzantine empire. The floor of Hagia Sophia was not paved with colorful figured mosaics, like the churches that we have seen, but by large slabs of Proconnesian marble, which was considered a more costly form of pavement. However, for the Byzantines the marble floor of the church represented more than luxury, it was also associated with the element of water.[43] In a well-known passage, the courtier Paul the Silentiary, in a poem recited in honor of the reconstruction of the church in 563, compared the ambo of Hagia Sophia to an island rising amidst the white-capped billows of the sea.[44] This poetic description of the slabs of white Proconnesian marble, with their veins of blue, had a significance that went beyond the rhetoric of a literary metaphor. It was also an expression of the idea that the church evoked not only the luminosity of divine light, but also the spiritual and material bounty of the terrestrial world created by God. Paul the Silentiary says explicitly that the book-matched marbles on the walls of the church resemble the art of painting, and he sees in their veins landscape features such as meadows, green hills and rushing flower-banked steams, as well as fields of ripe corn, the shade of thick forests, skipping flocks of sheep, and vines with flourishing tendrils.[45]

Another water reference that is contained within the pavement of Hagia Sophia is the insertion of four bands of green marble that cross the Proconnesian floor at irregular intervals, and that were later used to mark stopping places for various liturgical processions.[46] As we discover from the *Narratio de Sancta Sophia*, a legendary account of the construction of Hagia Sophia, by the eighth

---

42　Maguire, *Nectar and Illusion*, pp. 35–47; Reynolds, "Rethinking Palestinian Iconoclasm".
43　Barry, "Walking on Water".
44　Paul the Silentiary, *Descriptio ambonis*, lines 224–39, ed. Friedländer.
45　Paul the Silentiary, *Descriptio S. Sophiae*, lines 286–95, 618, ed. Friedländer.
46　Majeska, "Notes on the Archaeology of St. Sophia".

or the ninth century these bands were referred to as the four rivers that flow out of Paradise, and it is quite possible that they had this name from the beginning. The same text also reported that visitors to the church marveled at the floor "because it appeared like the sea or the flowing waters of a river, thanks to the great variety of its marble".[47] In this way, the interior of Hagia Sophia contrived to be iconic and aniconic at the same time, and thus avoided the problem of the pagan connotations of images drawn from the natural world.

5   Reaction to Environmental Change

There are some striking exceptions to the picture that has been painted above, of relative discretion and restraint with regard to the portrayal of water personifications in church buildings. These exceptions all come from the floor mosaics of churches in Jordan, and they all concern personifications of the sea. The most blatant example is a well-preserved mosaic in the nave of the church of the Apostles at Madaba, which is dated by an inscription to 578–9.[48] Here we see a colorful carpet of parrots, flowers and fruits, in the center of which is a large medallion containing a half-naked woman rising from fish-filled waves (fig. 7.4). She is labeled as *Thalassa*, or the sea. The pagan resonances of this image are hardly counteracted by the encircling inscription, which is an invocation on behalf of the donors, reading: "O Lord God, who has made the heavens and the earth, give life to Anastasius, to Thomas and Theodora …"

A recently discovered church at Petra provides another Jordanian example of the personification of the sea.[49] Here the nave, the sanctuary, and the central apse were covered with an expensive opus sectile pavement of purple sandstone and imported marble, but the two side aisles were carpeted in the mid-sixth century with tessellated mosaics. The pavement of the south aisle portrayed creatures of sea, land and air, together with personifications of the ocean, the earth, the four seasons and wisdom. Ocean was depicted as a half-nude man with claws growing out of his head, holding a ship in his left hand and a rudder in his right, and planting his left foot upon a dolphin. Other portrayals of the sea in human form have been found in the churches of Jordan. For example, in the church of Bishop Sergius at Umm al-Rasas, dated to 587 or 588, there were two prominent personifications at either end of the floor mosaic in the nave – the one at the western end, in front of the entrance, was

47   *Narratio de S. Sophia*, 26, ed. Preger, pp. 102–3.
48   Piccirillo, *Madaba*, pp. 190–92.
49   Talgam, *Mosaics of Faith*, 210, fig. 300.

FIGURE 7.4 Madaba, Church of the Apostles, nave pavement, detail: personification of the sea
PHOTO: HENRY MAGUIRE

labeled Ge, or Earth, while the one occupying the more important location, at the eastern end of the nave adjacent to the sanctuary, was labeled Abyssos, or the abyss.[50]

50   Talgam, *Mosaics of Faith*, 210, figs. 301–2.

In churches, these personifications of the sea appear almost exclusively in the floor mosaics of Jordan,[51] although, as we have seen, in other parts of the ancient Roman world Ocean was commonly portrayed in private houses. Even in secular contexts, however, the portraits of Ocean could be troubling, as we saw in the case of the erased mosaic in the villa at El Haouria in Tunisia. Why, then, do we find these bold evocations of Ocean in human form in the churches of Jordan? And why are these marine images so far from the sea? It is tempting to link the personifications with the situation of Jordan at the edge of the desert, and with the climatic conditions that prevailed there during the sixth and the seventh centuries AD. There is considerable evidence that the region of modern-day Jordan and Israel underwent an increasingly dry period between AD c.500 and c.800, which would have made the inhabitants of this region especially interested in the provision of water.[52] The clearest demonstration that the climate changed during this period is the dramatic drop in the level of the Dead Sea, which serves as a catchment basin for the rain that falls on the land surrounding it, including Jordan. The level of the water in the Dead Sea at various periods in history has been plotted through the radiocarbon dating of organic sediments along its shores. From these sediments it is evident that the lake reached its highest level in the late Roman period, AD c.400, and then began a precipitous decline between the sixth and eighth centuries. In the salt caves on the shore, examinations of the flood-related width of passages and of the deposition of driftwood tend to confirm a drier climate during this time, as do analyses of pollen samples from cores taken from the sea bed.[53]

We may have a confirmation of the drying up of the Dead Sea during this period in one of the floor mosaics of Jordan, the famous map that covered the floor of the so-called Church of the Map in Madaba.[54] As can be seen in standard maps of the Dead Sea, those produced up until the 1950s, the sea has two basins, an elongated north basin and a shorter south one; the two basins are joined by a narrow channel. The north basin is very deep – around 400 meters, but the south basin is shallow – it had a depth of around six meters in the 1950s. The channel between the northern basin and the southern basin is actually a sill. When the water level in the northern basin is high, it spills

51 Hachlili, *Ancient Mosaic Pavements*, p. 180.
52 Telelis, "Climatic fluctuations", p. 186.
53 Frumkin/Magaritz/Carmi/Zak, "The Holocene Climatic Record of the Salt Caves of Mount Sedom, Israel"; Heim/Nowaczyk/Negendank/Leroy/Ben-Avraham, "Near East Desertification: Evidence from the Dead Sea"; Enzel/Bookman/Sharon/Gvirtzman/Dayan/Ziv/Stein, "Late Holocene Climates of the Near East Deduced from Dead Sea Level Variations"; Bookman/Enzel/Agnon/Stein, "Late Holocene Lake Levels of the Dead Sea".
54 Piccirillo, *The Madaba Map Centenary*.

THE BYZANTINES AND NATURE   197

over into the southern basin, which becomes part of the sea. When the water level is low, the southern basin dries up. The mosaic map in Madaba probably dates to the second half of the sixth century, or perhaps to the early seventh. It depicts Palestine and northern Egypt with geographical features such as seas, rivers, mountains and cities, with Jerusalem prominently shown. Significantly, the map only depicts the northern basin of the Dead Sea, with the river Jordan entering it from the north; we do not see the south basin or the channel that connects the two bodies of water. This may indicate that at the time that the map was made the southern basin was dry.[55] Thus we have evidence from church floors that may confirm the conclusions of scientists, that the sixth century was a period of decreasing rainfall. Since the decline in the levels of the Dead Sea was precipitous, to have lived during this period of increasing drought must indeed have been a frightening experience for those on the edge of the desert, whose livelihood depended on rain. It is no wonder that the Christians of the region wished to invoke the powers of water in their churches in the most explicit manner possible. As we have seen, their boldness eventually provoked a vehement iconoclastic reaction, which rejected the blatancy of such images as pagan.

6   Virtue and the Productivity of the Land

After the iconclasms of the eighth century, it was no longer possible for the Byzantines to appeal to semi-pagan personifications drawn from nature in the face of environmental challenges and changes. In the medieval worldview, natural events such as droughts were produced by God, and therefore the best defense against them was not to evoke the cultic practices of the pagan past, but rather to win the favor of God through piety and virtue. This attitude is exemplified by a remarkable group of medieval Byzantine caskets, which can be dated to the tenth and eleventh centuries. These small wooden boxes were used to keep valuables such as coins or jewels, and they were richly decorated with carved plaques of ivory and bone. The carvings portray the story of Adam and Eve, their creation, their temptation and fall, their expulsion from Paradise, and their subsequent grief and labor.[56] Two of the boxes accompany these scenes with depictions of the personification of wealth. For example, a casket now in the Landesmuseum at Darmstadt begins its telling

---

55   Amiran, "The Madaba Mosaic Map as a Climate Indicator".
56   Goldschmidt/Weitzmann, *Die Byzantinischen Elfenbeinskulpturen*, vol. 1, pp. 48–55, nos. 67–93, pls. 47–55.

FIGURE 7.5 Darmstadt, Landesmuseum, ivory box: personification of
wealth with Adam and Eve laboring and grieving
PHOTO: GIRAUDON/ART RESOURCE, NEW YORK

of the Genesis story on the back of the box, with carvings portraying Adam and Eve in Paradise, their temptation and fall, and God accusing Adam in the garden. The left end of the box shows an angel expelling the guilty couple from Paradise. The plaques on the front of the box portray them sitting and weeping with their hands held against their heads and, afterwards, Adam laboring at tilling the earth, reaping his harvest, and carrying it home (fig. 7.5, above and center). The right end of the box is decorated with three plaques, two flanking the original lock plate and one beneath it (fig. 7.5, below). The carvings on each side of the lock show Adam and Eve working together in a forge, with Eve pumping a pair of bellows, and Adam working at an anvil. On the plaque beneath the lock, a man is shown seated and holding a bag full of coins. He is identified by an inscription as Ο ΠΛΟΥΤΟΣ, or the personification of wealth.[57] Another casket, now in the Hermitage Museum at St. Petersburg, presents a similar group of scenes, except that here the personification of wealth, on the left end of the box, is flanked by the weeping figures of Adam and Eve.[58]

This association of agricultural labor, its resulting wealth, and the laments of Adam and Eve can be explained with reference to Byzantine commentaries on the Book of Genesis, which explained that wealth can only be gained as a consequence of an individual's grief and penance for his or her sins. Of special relevance was Genesis 3:17, which gives God's words to Adam after the Fall: "Because you hearkened unto the voice of your wife, and you ate from the tree from which I enjoined you not to eat, cursed will be the earth in all your labors." In his commentary on this verse, the sixth-century author Procopius of Gaza referred to the misfortunes suffered by farmers and explained that God, having made the fruits, did not bless, but cursed them, for he knew of the forthcoming sin of man and so kept the possibility of punishing man through the fruits of the earth. When men were sinning, the fruits would dry up, but when they were atoning for their misdeeds through their remorse, the fruits would be abundant.[59] In the Byzantine view, therefore, there was a kind of equation, in which grief and penance were balanced by the possibility of plenty. We can see, then, that the message of the tenth- and eleventh-century ivory boxes was profoundly different from that of the early Byzantine floor mosaics. The early pavements appealed to nature personifications as an assurance of plenty, making use of an imagery that was pagan in its derivation, and only thinly Christianized. In the later carvings, agricultural plenty was assured only through a Christian's mindfulness of the Christian God and through his or her penance for sin.

Bibliography

Primary Sources

Andrew of Crete, *In S. Patapium*, Patrologia Graeca 97, cols. 1205–1222.
Avitus, *Poematum de mosaicae historicae gestis*, Patrologia Latina 59.

---

57 Goldschmidt/Weitzmann, *Die Byzantinischen Elfenbeinskulpturen*, vol. 1, p. 50, no. 69, pl. 50.
58 Goldschmidt/Weitzmann, *Die Byzantinischen Elfenbeinskulpturen*, vol. 1, pp. 49–50, no. 68, pls. 48–9.
59 Procopius of Gaza, *Commentarii in Genesim*, 3.17, Patrologia Graeca 87, 1, col. 213.

Basil the Great, *Hexaemeron*, ed. S. Giet, *Basile de Césarée, Homélies sur l'Hexaéméron* (Sources chrétiennes, 26), Paris 1949.

Choricius, *Laudatio Marciani II*, ed. R. Foerster, E. Richsteig, *Choricii Gazaei opera*, Leipzig 1929.

Constantine Manasses, *Synopsis chronike*, ed. O Lampsidis, *Constantini Manassis Breviarium chronicum*, Athens 1996.

Firmicus Maternus, *De errore profanarum religionum*, ed. R. Turcan, *L'erreur des religions païennes/Firmicus Maternus*, Paris 1982.

George of Pisidia, *Hexaemeron*, Patrologia Graeca 92, cols. 1425–1578.

Gregory of Nazianzus, *Homilia XXVIII (Second Theological Oration)*, ed. P. Gallay/ M. Jourjon, *Grégoire de Nazianze, Discours 27–31 (Discours théologiques)* (Sources chrétiennes, 250), Paris 1978.

Hermogenes, *Progymnasmata*, ed. H. Rabe, *Hermogenes, opera*, Leipzig 1913.

Isaac Comnenus, *Typikon of the Kosmosoteira Monastery*, ed. L. Petit, "Typikon du monastère de la Kosmosoteira près d'Aenos (1152)", *Izvestiia Russkago Archeologicheskago Instituta v Konstantinople* 13 (1908), 17–75.

Libanius, *Oratio XXX*, ed. A.F. Norman, *Libanius, Selected Works*, vol. 2, Cambridge MA. 1977.

Michael Glykas, *Biblos chronike*, ed. I. Bekker, *Michaelis Glycae annales* (Corpus scriptorum historiae byzantinae), Bonn 1836.

Narratio de S. Sophia, ed. Th. Preger, *Scriptores originum Constantinopolitanarum*, vol. 1, Leipzig 1901.

Paul the Silentiary, *Descriptio S. Sophiae* and *Descriptio ambonis*, ed. P. Friedländer, *Johannes von Gaza und Paulus Silentiarius*, Leipzig-Berlin 1912, pp. 227–65.

Peter Chrysologus, *Sermo CLX*, Patrologia Latina 52, cols. 621–62.

Procopius of Gaza, *Commentarii in Genesim*, Patrologia Graeca 87, 1.

Romanos, *Hymns*, ed. J. Grosdidier de Matons, *Romanos le Mélode. Hymnes* (Sources chrétiennes), 5 vols., Paris 1964–81.

Sidonius Apollinaris, *Epistulae*, ed. A. Loyen, Paris 1960–1970.

Secondary Literature

Amiran, D.H.K., "The Madaba Mosaic Map as a Climate Indicator for the Sixth Century", *Israel Exploration Journal* 47, 1–2 (1997), 97–99.

Attfield, R., "Christian Attitudes to Nature", *Journal of the History of Ideas* 44 (1983), 369–86.

Bakirtzis, Ch./E. Kourkoutidou-Nikolaidou/Ch. Mavropoulou-Tsioumi, *Mosaics of Thessaloniki, 4th–14th Century*, Athens 2012.

Barry, F., "Walking on Water: Cosmic Floors in Antiquity and the Middle Ages", *Art Bulletin* 89 (2007), 627–56.

Bitrakova-Grozdanova, V., *Monuments paléochrétiens de la région d'Ohrid*, Ohrid 1975.

Bodin, H./Hedlund, R. (eds.), *Byzantine Gardens and Beyond*, Uppsala 2013.

Bookman, R./Enzel, Y./Agnon, A./Stein, M., "Late Holocene Lake Levels of the Dead Sea", *Geological Society of America Bulletin* 116, 5–6 (2004), 555–71.

Cribiore, R., "A Hymn to the Nile", *Zeitschrift für Papyrologie und Epigraphik* 106 (1995), 97–106.

Deichmann, F.W., *Frühchristliche Bauten und Mosaiken von Ravenna*, Baden-Baden 1958.

Deichmann, F.W., *Ravenna, Hauptstadt des spätantiken Abendlandes*, vol. 1, *Geschichte und Monumente*, vol. 2, *Kommentar*, parts 1–3, Wiesbaden 1969–89.

Della Dora, V. *Landscape, Nature, and the Sacred in Byzantium*, Cambridge 2016.

Demoen, K., "A Homeric Garden in Tenth-Century Constantinople", in H. Bodin/ R. Hedlund (eds.), *Byzantine Gardens and Beyond*, Uppsala 2013, 114–27.

Dolezal, M.-L./M. Mavroudi, "Theodore Hyrtakenos' *Description of the Garden of St. Anna* and the Ekphrasis of Gardens", in A. Littlewood/H. Maguire/J. Wolschke-Bulmahn (eds.), *Byzantine Garden Culture*, Washington D.C. 2002, pp. 105–58.

Dunbabin, K.M.D., *The Mosaics of Roman North Africa*, Oxford 1978.

Enzel, Y./R. Bookman/D. Sharon/H. Gvirtzman/U. Dayan/B. Ziv/M. Stein, "Late Holocene Climates of the Near East Deduced from Dead Sea Level Variations and Modern Regional Winter Rainfall", *Quaternary Research* 60 (2003), 263–73.

Frumkin, A./M. Magaritz/I. Carmi/I. Zak, "The Holocene Climatic Record of the Salt Caves of Mount Sedom, Israel", *The Holocene* 1,3 (1991), 191–200.

Goldschmidt, A./Weitzmann, K., *Die Byzantinischen Elfenbeinskulpturen des X.–XIII. Jahrhunderts*, 2 vols., Berlin 1930–34.

Hachlili, R., *Ancient Mosaic Pavements*, Leiden 2009.

Heim, C./N.R. Nowaczyk/J.F.W. Negendank/S.A.G. Leroy/Z. Ben-Avraham, "Near East Desertification: Evidence from the Dead Sea", *Naturwissenschaften* 84 (1997), 398–401.

Hermann, A., "Der Nil und die Christen", *Jahrbuch für Antike und Christentum* 2 (1959), 30–69.

Jensen, R.M., *Living Water: Images, Symbols, and Settings of Early Christian Baptism*, Leiden 2011.

Kraeling, C.H., *Gerasa, City of the Decapolis*, New Haven 1938.

Littlewood, A./ Maguire, H./Wolschke-Bulmahn, J. (eds.), *Byzantine Garden Culture*, Washington D.C. 2002.

Mac Coull, L.S.B., *Dioscorus of Aphrodito: his Work and his World*, Berkeley 1988.

Maguire, H., *Art and Eloquence in Byzantium*, Princeton 1981.

Maguire, H., *Earth and Ocean: the Terrestrial World in Early Byzantine Art* (Monographs on the Fine Arts Sponsored by the College Art Association of America 43), University Park 1987.

Maguire, H., *Nectar and Illusion, Nature in Byzantine Art and Literature*, New York 2012.

Majeska, G.P., "Notes on the Archaeology of St. Sophia at Constantinople: the Green Marble Bands on the Floor", *Dumbarton Oaks Papers* 32 (1978), 299–308.

Manfredi, M., "Inno cristiano al Nilo", in P.J. Parsons/J.R. Rea (eds.), *Papyri Greek and Egyptian Edited by Various Hands in Honour of Eric Gardner Turner*, London 1981, pp. 49–69.

Nilsson, I., "Narrating Images in Byzantine Literature: the Ekphraseis of Konstantinos Manasses", *Jahrbuch der Österreichischen Byzantinistik* 55 (2005), 121–46.

Nilsson, I., "Nature Controlled by Artistry: the Poetics of the Literary Garden in Byzantium", in H. Bodin/ R. Hedlund (eds.), *Byzantine Gardens and Beyond*, Uppsala 2013, pp. 14–29.

Orlandos, A.K., "Palaiochristianika kai byzantina mnemeia Tegeas-Nykliou", *Archeion ton Byzantinon Mnemeion tes Hellados* 12 (1973), 12–81.

Piccirillo, M., *Madaba, le chiese e i mosaici*, Milan 1989.

Piccirillo, M., *The Mosaics of Jordan*, Amman 1993.

Piccirillo, M./Alliata, E., *Umm al-Rasas/Mayfa'ah*, vol. 1, *Gli scavi del complesso di Santo Stefano*, Jeruslem 1994.

Piccirillo, M./Alliata, E. (eds.), *The Madaba Map Centenary, 1897–1997: Travelling through the Byzantine Umayyad Period, Proceedings of the International Conference Held in Amman, 7–9 April, 1997*, Jerusalem 1999.

Poinssot, L., "Mosaïques d'El-Haouria", *Revue Africaine* 76 (1935), 183–206.

Reynolds, D. "Rethinking Palestinian Iconoclasm", *Dumbarton Oaks Papers* 71 (2017), 1–64.

Spieser, J.-M., "Remarques complémentaires sur la mosaïque de Osios David", *Hetaireia Makedonikon Spoudon, Makenonike Bibliotheke* 82 (1995), 295–306.

Talgam, R., *Mosaics of Faith: Floors of Pagans, Jews, Samaritans, Christians, and Muslims in the Holy Land*, Jerusalem 2014.

Telelis, I.G., "Climatic Fluctuations in the Eastern Mediterranean and the Middle East AD 300–1500 from Byzantine Documentary and Proxy Physical Paleoclimatic Evidence – a Comparison", *Jahrbuch der Österreichischen Byzantinistik* 58 (2008), 167–207.

Thomas, J./Hero, A.C., *Byzantine Monastic Foundation Documents*, 5 vols., Washington D.C. 2000.

Wallace-Hadrill, D.S., *The Greek Patristic View of Nature*, New York, 1968.

Weiss, Z./Talgam, R., "The Nile Festival Building and its Mosaics: Mythological Representations in Early Byzantine Sepphoris", in J.H. Humphrey (ed.), *The Roman and Byzantine Near East*, vol. 3, Portsmouth RI 2002, pp. 55–90.

CHAPTER 8

Water and the Urban Environment of Constantinople and Thessaloniki

James Crow

1   Introduction

This chapter is concerned with water and the urban environment of Constantinople, with reference to other Byzantine cities and especially, the second-city of the empire, Thessaloniki. Although the late antique origins of the Constantinopolitan system are considered, the primary focus is on the period from the 6th century onwards. The urban planner and historian Peter Hall, in his study of the contrasting hydraulic infrastructures of ancient Rome and 19th-century Paris and London, prefaced his case studies with the following:

> The essential disorder of cities has at least two main origins. First, great cites are big cities, and bigness implies complexity. Villages get their water from wells or small streams, small towns from small rivers that happen to flow through them; they dispose of their wastes into the soil or into those same watercourses, without much bother. But big cities need much more water than that, more water than can ever be supplied by local sources: so they must impound their rivers to build huge upstream storage reservoirs, or bring water from distant river basins, or both. And then if they are not to be racked with epidemics, they must channel their wastes for long distances downstream, to distant purification plants well out of contamination's way.[1]

By the mid-6th century AD there is little question that Constantinople was the largest city in the Roman world, comparable only with great urban centres in China and perhaps Mesoamerica. In size, it outstripped its rivals around the shores of the Mediterranean: Alexandria, Carthage, Antioch and old Rome.

Constructing a new water supply system for a city with the ambitions to be the New Rome was a great challenge, but only one of a number of massive new urban infrastructure projects which, for the most part, were largely

---

1   Hall, *Cities in Civilization*, p. 612.

completed between 330 and 450. Little is known of either the urban or extra mural landscapes of the pre-Constantinian city of Byzantium. What is clear is that the new undertaking required a massive investment in earth moving, evidenced by the terraces recorded across the city, many of which came to be associated with the location of later Byzantine cisterns. The sculpted hills provided a setting for the colonnaded streets and piazzas which emerged over the first century of the city's expansion and, with them, the new town houses and insula blocks, together with the great civic buildings, baths, harbours and palaces which are recorded in the early 5th century *Notitia Urbis* of *c.*425, our best single source for the topography and infrastructures of the city. The new dwellings on the higher ground set out towards the Constantinian and then Theodosian walls, enclosing an urban area which by the early 5th century was totalling an area of 7.9 sq. km.

The land and sea walls defined the urban environment of the city, beyond which were suburban estates, farms and forests. Extending westwards into Thrace and bounded by the Black Sea, the north part of this region remains quite densely forested despite the predations of recent developments such as the new airport to the northwest of Istanbul and the link roads for the two most recent Bosporus bridges. These forested Strandja hills continue west towards the modern border with Bulgaria and were the catchments for the new water supply systems surveyed and constructed in the 4th and 5th centuries.

In addition, this region will also have provided an important resource of wood for building and for fuel, as they still do today. In the southern half, the peninsula bordering the Sea of Marmara the land is lower and open, more suitable for cultivation and settlement, studded with farms and settlements.[2] Because of a lack of archaeological field surveys in advance of rapid urban developments over the past half century, what cannot be demonstrated with any certainty is how far this region may have expanded during the life of the Byzantine city in response to increasing and changing demands for agricultural production, as is demonstrable in the hinterland of Rome.[3]

How do we define an urban environment? This paper is primarily concerned with a key element: water, but in this context the environment will be considered under the headings of the four traditional elements: earth, air, fire and water. *Earth* to represent the surface landscape together with geology and geomorphology some aspects of which has been briefly noted. Here it is important to identify the availability of construction materials for the new

[2] Crow and Turner, "Silivri and the Thracian hinterland".
[3] Thomas and Wilson, "Water Supply".

WATER & URBAN ENVIRONMENT OF CONSTANTINOPLE & THESSALONIKI 205

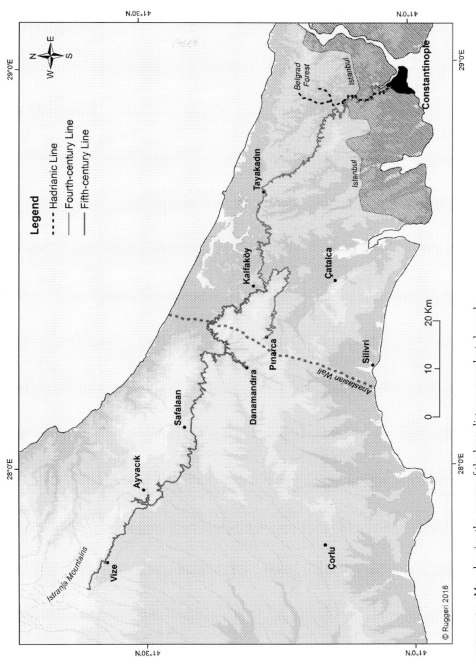

FIGURE 8.1 Map showing the course of the long-distance aqueduct channels
DRAWN BY FRANCESCA RUGGERI

city, stone quarries, and especially clay resources required for the massive brick making enterprises needed for construction, and also as a pozzalanic to create high-quality hydraulic mortars – the pink brick-encrusted mortars which bond so much of Byzantium's walls and vaults.[4] The question of cultivation and water and will be addressed later.

Air represents weather and climate. The recent decade has witnessed an expansion of academic enterprise dedicated to the climate history of the classical and early medieval world. Recent scholarship has been able to document long-term changes in climate, including the definition of the Late Antique Little Ice Age. Unlike marginal rural settlements, which were especially susceptible to capricious weather and natural disasters, it might be expected that a great city drawing on the resources of empire could mitigate these external vagaries. But a great accumulation of population could be equally sensitive to drought and other deficiencies, especially apparent as we shall see in relation to water provision and consumption. The third element, *Fire*, was an important source of energy and illumination, but the heading also acts as a surrogate for a range of urban hazards, including the widespread city fires which are attested throughout the city's history up to the 20th century.[5] Then there were also other natural catastrophes, seismic and climatic – earthquakes which shook down the walls and domes of the city, or the two freak storms in the 10th and 11th centuries which filled the Theodosian harbour with 25 shipwrecks and an Ottoman period tsunami which inundated the southern part of the peninsula.[6]

A key agent of many of these hazards was the final element: *Water*. According to Procopius in his account of Justinian's *Buildings*, water defined the city.[7] But the waters he celebrates were those salt-water seas that surrounded the peninsula. Marine trade ensured the city was fed from Egypt until the capture of Alexandria by the Sasanians in 619, and finally lost to the followers of Mohammed in 640. Deprived of that source, new resources came from other Byzantine territories – first from Sicily in the 7th and 8th centuries, and later from the Aegean coastlands and the Black Sea.[8] But the seas around the city and in the Black Sea did not only facilitate trade and communication across an increasingly maritime focused empire, they could be harvested for rich shoals

---

4   Snyder, "Building the Longest Water Supply".
5   While the reliance on timber buildings offered some protection during earthquakes, they exposed the city to the constant threat of fire, often ignited as a form of protest. See for example, Madden, "Fires of the Fourth Crusade"; Mansell, *Constantinople*, pp. 224–5.
6   Perinçek et al., "Geoarchaeology of the excavation site"; Bony et al., "A high energy deposit".
7   See now the discussion in Pickett, "Water and Empire".
8   Haldon, *The empire that would not die*, Figs. 6.2, 6.4.

of fish throughout the year. Although many modern observers dwell on the potential for urban cultivation within the Theodosian circuit, these fish stocks from the Marmara and the Black Seas were an exceptional resource for protein for the common people as well as emperors, marking out Constantinople's resources above many other coastal cities. Furthermore, the available fish were much more plentiful than the more meagre and variable fish reserves of the Mediterranean itself.[9]

Procopius' paean to the city's marine setting conceals one of Constantinople's critical deficits as a new urban centre with an expanding population: a deficit of abundant drinking water.[10] Unlike Rome, the new city has neither the resources of a major river, nor access to groundwater through ample local springs and wells, nor major springs within close proximity. It would appear that immediate local resources were adequate for the Greek colony of Byzantium. But the Roman city had greater demands and, according to later texts, Hadrian constructed an aqueduct, although no trace survives in the city itself.[11] This aqueduct was sourced a short distance from the city in the valley of the Alibey Dere (Hydrales river) and from sources in the Forest of Belgrade, later redeveloped as the major source for the Ottoman aqueducts constructed in the 16th century.[12] But for Constantine's new city these sources were insufficient and within seven years of his death, his son, Constantius II, commissioned surveyors to identify new water sources for the growing city. A city, which the orator Themistius claimed now became "truly a city and no longer a mere sketch" and was like a beautiful woman bedecked with jewels but thirstier "than those who are dressed in rags".[13] Thus began the story of what has been termed *"The Longest Roman Water Supply Line"*,[14] one of the greatest achievements of Roman infrastructure engineering which was to remain an enduring resource for the city of Constantinople for the next eight centuries.

This chapter is primarily concerned to outline the latest research on the long-distance water supply of Constantinople, both the transmission of the water from its distant sources and the latest assessment of the distribution of water within the city. In turn, this new evidence is able to inform our understanding of water consumption and usage as well as wider issues of settlement history over the long course of the Byzantine city's life.

---

9   Dagron, "Poisson, pêcheurs et poissoniers"; Hordern / Purcell, *The Corrupting Sea*.
10 Mango, *Le développement urbain*.
11 Crow et al., *Water Supply*, pp. 10–14.
12 Gilles, *Itinéraires*, pp. 116–17.
13 Them. *Orat* XI, 151a–152b quoted in Crow et al., *Water Supply*, p. 224.
14 Çeçen, *The Longest Roman*.

2   The Source of Water

Constantius' surveyors faced a daunting task that would challenge modern engineers.[15] They identified two main group of springs, the first on the valley of the Karaman Dere, a river which flows north into Terkos Lake and the Black Sea (Fig. 8.1). These springs around Danamandıra, were supplemented by at least one other, and provided a single long-distance channel to the city. A second source was located to the east where three springs are known close to the village of Pınarca, on the east side of the north – south ridge occupied by the early-6th century Anastasian Wall. These channels follow the southern flank of the main Strandja ridge and eventually join the main line near Dağyenice, having passed through one long tunnel.[16]

The water channels are set into the hillsides and sinuously flow with the contours to allow gravity to pull the water towards its goal. Following a new study of the topography as part of the recent "Engineering the Water supply of Byzantine Constantinople Project",[17] the total length of this 4th-century line, constructed between c.345 and 373 has been recently recalculated at a total of 246 km: 205 km to Danamandıra, plus 41 km for the line from Pınarca[18] – nearly twice as long as any previous known Roman aqueduct. From Dağyenice, the channel passed through another long tunnel and then followed the valley of the Alibey Dere towards the Golden Horn; few traces are known in this sector closer towards the city. Crucially, this long-distance line from Thrace was able to enter the city close to the Edirne Kapı at an elevation of 63–64 m above sea level, which is over 30 m in elevation above the estimated Hadrianic line. The high-level waters flowed on across the Aqueduct of Valens, the Bozdoğan Kemer, a 971-m-long bridge between the fourth and the third hills leading towards the Forum of Theosodius at Bayezit, where a great nymphaeum was constructed shortly after the completion of the aqueduct. By bringing this higher-level line, the emperors were able to provide water for those new, elevated areas of the city, beyond the boundary of Byzantium's walls and out towards the new parts of the city bounded by the wall of Constantine.

---

15   Snyder, "Building the Longest"; and Snyder et al., "Agent-Based Modelling", for an analysis of the construction process of the Thracian system.
16   Crow et al., *Water Supply*, pp. 52–3, 75–80, maps 5, 6, 7.
17   Project funded by Leverhulme Research Trust, grant agreement, RPG-2013-410, combined engineers and archaeologists from the University of Edinburgh and Northumbria University: Martin Crapper, James Crow, Francesca Ruggeri, Simon Smith, Riley Snyder, and Kate West.
18   Ruggeri et al., "GIS based assessment".

The next phase of the long-distance line is less well documented. However, a 6th-century author Hysechios's mythic account of the city records that the inhabitants of the city drew water from a nymph named Byzye, also the name of a Thracian city, modern Vize.[19] But if there are limited texts, the archaeological remains attest to a massive programme of rebuilding and extension of the earlier line, over 160 km from the city. In many places the new works are associated with broader channels and larger more robust bridges. The line itself was extended westwards to capture springs beyond Vize at Pazarli and at Ergene, with other possible sources near Binkılıç. The two systems ran in parallel after the new bridge at Ballıgerme, initially over 10 m difference in height, but gradually coming together towards the city. The new extension was 180 km in length, giving a total length of 426 km, excluding the channels of the Hadrianic line which seems to have been restored at about the same time.[20] The date of the new construction remains uncertain; it is possible the repairs were required after an earthquake in Thrace in 394 and certainly a number of earlier bridges were rebuilt in a much more monumental manner, notably at Kurşunlugerme, Talas, Büyükgerme, Keçigerme and Kumarlidere.[21] The city itself grew westwards with the new Theodosian Land walls completed by c.415. Only shortly afterwards, the first of the three great open-air reservoirs of Aetius was completed in 421. Although there is no explicit evidence, it is difficult not to associate the completion of this new reservoir with the arrival of the new long-distance water.[22]

Outside of the city, further works are attested throughout the 6th century, with perhaps two main phases of construction, one of which is associated with the only dateable inscription in situ from the entire line – the work of construction directed by Longinus, a former prefect of the city, dated after 542. These

19 Hesychius 9, quoted in Crow et al., *Water Supply*, pp. 227–8.
20 The estimates are based on the recent study by Ruggeri et al., "A GIS based assessment", See the works described at the Kovuk Kemer, Çeçen, *Sinan's Water Supply*, pp. 169–73; comparison of the structures in the Belgrat Forest with the great 5th-century bridges in Thrace suggests that the late Roman works closer to the city were on an equally massive scale, but almost completely refurbished by later Byzantine and more especially Ottoman works.
21 Crow, "Blessing and Security", p. 170, n. 46; see also Crow, "The Wonderful Works".
22 To the three open reservoirs in the outer zone may be added the remains of a large open cistern north of the Mese at Babiâlı Caddesi, identified with the cistern of Philoxenus and the *cisterna Theodosiana*, the latter is noted in the *Notitia Urbis*, therefore dating before c.425; see, Bardill, "Palace of Lausus", 69–75, 83, Fig. 2. The most secure dating evidence from the new bridges derives from the elaborate decoration of the bridge at Kurşunlugerme, which suggests the works may have been completed by the mid-5th century at the latest, see Crow, "Blessing or Security?", pp. 165–7.

works are situated in an arc between Luka Dere and Karatepe. And may reflect several episodes of seismic damage, some of which may be associated with an earthquake known to have affected the nearby Anastasian Wall before the attack by the Kutrigurs in 559.[23]

The most significant disruption to the city's water supply occurred during the great siege of 626 when the Avars are known to have cut the long-distance supply, an inevitable fate given the great length of the system. However, it is important to note that there is no evidence to suggest that the Hadrianic line was affected, and it is only the long-distance line of Valens that was restored by Constantine V. This work drew in workers from across the Aegean lands, Thrace and Anatolia and is one of the certain indicators of the great revival in imperial fortunes during the late-8th century. Further maintenance and restorations continued over the next two centuries and at the great bridge at Ballıgerme restoration characteristic of middle-Byzantine construction may be associated with an inscription of Basil II and Constantine VIII after 1000.[24] Especially important for this text is that it demonstrates repairs and continuing usage of the extended aqueduct line flowing from Vize.

Before considering the water usage and distribution within the city, it is important to assess the impact of this great enterprise of the landscape and communities of Thrace. The catchments and tunnels have been noted but, for the most part, the waters were sourced and flowed through forested regions – a remote environment which protected the security of the system from attackers. Water capture of springs and other sources for transport to Constantinople may have disadvantaged some rural communities, but not on the scale described for instance in the more densely populated rural and urban environments of Campagna by the Aqua Augusta.[25] The only city on the route to Bizye (modern Vize) was probably located at too high an elevation above the sources at Pazarli so probably did not suffer and will have relied on alternative springs as a well as a nearby river. As the waters flowed closer to Constantinople's immediate hinterland, the aqueduct channels presented an opportunity for private landowners. Throughout the history of Roman laws about water usage, there was a concern for the abuse of public water for private means. A number of imperial edicts dating from the 4th and into the early 6th centuries show how the state struggled to control unlicensed tapping of the water sources for mills,

---

23 Crow, "Water and late antique Constantinople", pp. 129–32; Crow, Hydraulic Infrastructure and Use, pp. 77–8.
24 Crow et al., *Water Supply*, pp. 91–2, 238.
25 See the study of the Aqua Augusta and its ecologies by Keenan-Jones, "Large-scale water management".

irrigation and other domestic uses. In turn, this presents an important insight on irrigation, an aspect of late antique and Byzantine land management on which most contemporary sources are silent.[26] Earlier legislation for Rome was applied to Constantinople and landowners on the line of the channels were exempted from specific burdens but were required to keep the conduits clear and to ensure the line of the aqueduct was kept free from tree roots 15 feet to the right and left of the channel itself.[27] For this and later 4th-century laws, the terminology is in Latin, but later in the 5th and 6th centuries we observe the emergence of Greek words, often used uniquely in this context. Thus, in one law of Zeno there is reference to public springs in Constantinople originally public but made private, although here we can be fairly sure that the concern is for sources outside the city, although without explicitly noting they were for the city's usage.[28]

A subsequent rescript of Zeno, addressed to Spontius,[29] presents more intriguing aspects of the water supply system.[30] The rescript opens by forbidding those of rank from tampering with either the *fontes publicos* (public springs) as noted in the previous rescript or the *munuscularios aquaeductus*, both of which flow into the public aqueducts. In this case we are certainly concerned with the process of water capture and delivery outside the city, since we are looking at waters supplying the public system. Earlier 4th-century rescripts from Rome mention the conduits and main aqueduct channels as *formae meatus*.[31] However, *munusculus* literally translates as a gift, and could in this context define the lesser channels fed by subsidiary springs contributing to the main line, a feature we observed during fieldwork in a number of places along

---

26 For a recent discussion of this legislation see Biavaschi et al., "Dalla scrittura su tabulae"; and Bruun, "Roman Emperors".
27 C.Th. 15.2.1, C.Just 11.43.1, the law was originally addressed to the *consularis aquarum* in Rome in AD 330.
28 In this context, *publici fontes* is better understood as springs rather than fountains, C.Just 11.43.9, addressed to Sporacius.
29 The names are corrupt and Sporacius is probably cognate with Spontius.
30 C.Just. 43.8.10, see the translation in Frier et al., *Codex of Justinian*, 2722–3; this translation and others of the *Codex Justinianus* are to be preferred to those quoted in Crow et al., *Water Supply*.
31 C.Just. 43.1.1; 43.1.3; Frier et al., *Codex of Justinian*, 2716–17; see Biavaschi, "Della Scrittura" 111 translates the term as "piccolo canali". A law of 389 addressed to Albinus Prefect of the city of Rome differentiates between *formae* and *matrices* and the *aquaeductus* itself, C.Just. 11.43.3, Jaillette/ Reduzzi Merola, "L' eau à usage", 231, describe the *matrices* as conduits. Since the law also mentions reservoirs (*castella*), this is likely to be an urban context in Rome, but how the elements represented a hierarchy of water distribution is not clear, unless the *matrices* are better understood as points of distribution.

the main aqueduct channel and which may be defined as a dendritic system.³² In the next section of Zeno's rescript concerned with water theft, the term *munusculus* is employed as a synonym for the Greek term *paragogia* (παραγώγια), here to be also understood as side channels from the main channel (*publica aquaeductus*).³³ Further addressing concern for the security of the main channel, the rescript continues by defining the penalties of confiscation of property for which public water was channelled off, here listed as suburban properties, estates, water mills, baths and gardens. While, as we will observe, for the city itself agriculture was not exclusively extra-mural, the list presents a range of farming activities, including horticulture, requiring additional water and irrigation outside the city. The locations are unknown, but presumably the main offenders were situated close to the two main water supplies for the city, the long-distance aqueduct of Valens and the waters of the Aqueduct of Hadrian from the Forest of Belgrade. These would have properties to the west and northwest of the city, along the Alibey Dere (Hydrales) and north towards Kemerburgaz, although the Roman water sources are neither specified nor located. The rescript concludes by noting the staff of *aquarii* and *aquarum custodies*, water guards, translated into Greek as *hydrophylakes*, intended to maintain and protect the city's supplies.³⁴

Surprisingly, irrigation is rarely mentioned in later Byzantine texts.³⁵ Although the main body of Roman laws including water rights was codified under Theodosius and Justinian, in the early medieval *Farmers Law* there are only two brief mentions of water, both in the context of mills. Yet the late antique law codes reveal how there was a demand for water by landowners and farmers, which was a problem for water managers apparent since the time of Frontinus in Rome.³⁶

3   Water in the City

Before considering the main issues of delivery, distribution and consumption of water by the urban population, it is worth continuing the theme of

---

32   Crow et al., *Water Supply*, p. 61.
33   Frier, *Codex of Justinian*, 2722–3 translates *paragogia* as service-pipes; Biavaschi, "Della Scrittura" 111, does not discuss this rare term.
34   For the maintenance of the system see Crow, "Ruling the waters".
35   The Farmer's Law notes water in the context of mills, Humphreys, *Laws*, pp. 138–9; for a fragmentary inscription recording repairs to an aqueduct channel from Phrygia dating from the 7th–8th century see Tabbernee, and Lampe, *Pepouza*, p. 117; I am grateful to Jordan Pickett for this reference.
36   Bruun, "Roman Emperors".

water for agriculture and horticulture within the city, since this has become the focus of a number of recent studies concerned with urban ecology. In particular, a Swedish collective project called *The Urban Mind*, and a subsequent study by Barthel and Isendahl, have focused on the potential urban resilience of Constantinople. They argue that this derived from its green/blue infrastructure,[37] a combination based in part on the lines of water channels and water storage, but also on the extensive areas of intra-mural cultivation available, especially in the green zone between the Constantinian and Theodosian Walls. Many of these ideas derive from an influential paper by Koder published more than 20 years ago on "Fresh vegetables for the capital".[38] As we have already noted, the city's marine environment provided a rich harvest of fish, and it could be argued that, as a populous medieval city, its population had wider access to protein, especially marine, than elsewhere, although this proposition requires further consideration.[39]

There is no question that the zone between the two land walls was only partly built up.[40] However, any discussion of this theme needs to recognize that the density of market gardens, orchards, cemeteries, monasteries, palaces and other dwellings will have changed over time responding to the fluctuating patterns of the city's demography over the 1000 years after the construction of the outer land walls in 415.[41] To take two instances in the mid-8th century. During Constantine V's siege to recapture the city from Artabasdus in 743, Theophanes reports on the shortages in the city and the attempts of the defenders to acquire grain from outside the city. On this occasion the green zone clearly could not contribute enough. Three years later, at the final iteration of the Justinianic plague in 746, the chronicle reported that "When all the urban and suburban cemeteries had been filled up as well as empty cisterns and ditches, and many vineyards had been dug up and even the orchards within the old walls (of Constantine) to make room for the burial of human bodies."[42] While this latter description of vineyards and orchards within the city certainly supports the concept of extensive intra-mural horticulture, the

---

37 See papers in Sinclair et al., *The Urban Mind*; Berthl/Isendahl, "Urban gardens", with no intentional pun concerning the city's circus factions.
38 Koder, "Fresh vegetables".
39 See Zuckerman, "On a bountiful harvest", p. 749, which proposes that the role of bread in the Byzantine diet has been overestimated.
40 226 hect. in area based on a recent estimate by Kate Ward; see discussion in Dark/Özgümüş, *Constantinople*, pp. 98–103.
41 See Varinlioğlu, "Urban monasteries", for a more nuanced and diachronic attempt to model the distribution of monasteries and their estates in the city, and in particular the "green zone".
42 Theophanes, *Chron.* AD 6235; 6238; Mango and Scott, *Chronicle of Theophanes*, pp. 580–81; 585–6.

example of the siege reveals the city's continuing vulnerability during long periods without external food supplies. The reference to dry cisterns may indicate those areas in the city above the Hadrianic water channel, which remained the city's only main water supply until the restoration of the Valens Aqueduct in 766.[43] However, there is no question that extensive parts of the city were given over to gardens and cultivation, a continuing feature of the Ottoman city.[44] What may be questioned is how far urban cultivation will have been on a scale to significantly impact the water demand in the city, certainly in comparison to the real problems of water theft for irrigation outside of the city as demonstrated by the late antique law codes.

One of the main themes of the recent research project "Engineering the Water Supply of Constantinople"[45] has focused on the demand for and distribution of water within the Byzantine city using as sources the city's topography, the network of cisterns and our current knowledge of water channels, combined with new estimates of available water flow and demand. Preliminary results have been able to challenge some of the conclusions from the previous studies. In particular, our 2008 monograph suggested that the line of the Hadrianic aqueduct passed along the flanks of the hills overlooking the Golden Horn to be able to access the Yerebatan Saray (Basilica cistern), and the baths and palaces at the east end of the peninsula.[46] However, careful GIS analysis by Kate Ward has been able to demonstrate that the Byzantine low level system sourced from the Belgrade Forest is more likely to have taken a similar line to that later adopted by the Ottoman channels from the Kırkçeşme springs (Fig. 8.2). From a taksim or distribution centre at Tezgâhçılar Kubbesi, situated on the north side of the Valens Aqueduct, the Ottoman system followed a line around the south side of the peninsula, although a more northern branch could have continued above the shoreline of the Golden Horn as far as the northwest flanks of the second hill.[47] The main south branch will have been able to reach all the main consumers at the east end of the peninsula, the Great Palace, the Zeuxippus Baths, the Basilica Cistern and the cistern in the Sphendone of the Hippodrome.[48] The new analysis makes fewer changes to the suggested line of the high level system which flowed across the Aqueduct

---

43 Theophanes, *Chron.* AD 6258; Mango and Scott, *Chronicle of Theophanes*, p. 608; Magdalino stresses the importance of this action in the revival of the fortunes of the city, Magdalino, "Culture of Water", p. 132.
44 See Aktaş, "The change analysis".
45 See note 16.
46 Crow et al., *Water Supply*, Fig. 2.2.
47 Ward et al., "Water-supply infrastructure", pp. 180–85, Fig. 4.
48 Ward et al., "Water-supply infrastructure", Fig. 7.

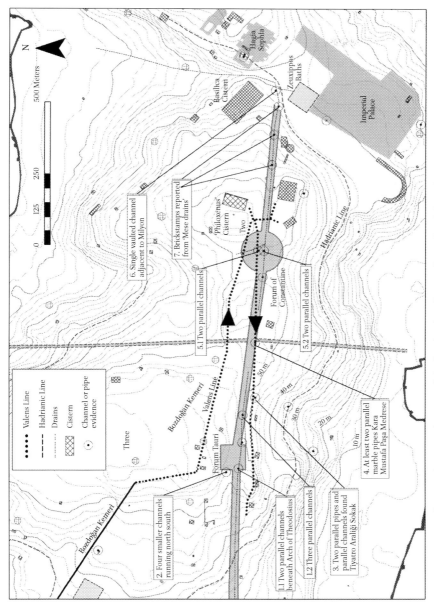

FIGURE 8.2 Map showing the revised course of the low-level Hadrianic channel and the Valens channel
DRAWN BY KATE WARD (WARD ET AL. "WATER SUPPLY INFRASTRUCTURE", FIG. 4)

of Valens. There is a discussion of possible channels to the west of the bridge as well as a discussion of the evidence for stone channels known from below the line of the Mese. The study concludes that the main high level line was situated to the north and parallel to the Mese and, importantly, is able to document the location of the channels and drains between the Forum of Constantine and the Forum Tauri.[49]

In addition to documenting the known channels and modelling the main distribution lines, the new project has been able to reassess the concordance of cisterns from within the city. Bardill's previous desk-based assessment listed a total of 159 cisterns on the historic peninsula.[50] A further study by Kerim Altuğ was able document 158 entries in part based on the archives of the Istanbul City Council. Through comparison of the two lists, it has been possible to identify 211 unique examples, including some examples documented from the 19th and early 20th centuries[51] (Fig. 8.3). In size they vary from the massive open reservoirs located in the intermural zone to very small cisterns providing water for individual dwellings.[52] Although the smallest may have benefited from rainwater collection, the vast majority represent a network of water supply and distribution ranging in scale across the city. Current studies are investigating how water will have been allocated. The new location map of cisterns closely reflects previous studies,[53] with the preponderance of cisterns occupying the higher ground in a band north side of the Valens line, but with clusters around the Column of Marcian and more marked towards the Forum Taurii, and then more or less uniformly across the east end of the peninsula. What we have not yet considered is the effect of later urban developments on either the identification or the destruction of cisterns and how this has influenced their known distributions.

Historically, cisterns are known to have been constructed in the city from the 4th century onwards. However, the appearance of large reservoirs and covered cisterns is better documented from the 5th and 6th centuries.[54] The open reservoirs within the walls were all constructed in the 5th century, and it is difficult not to associate their construction with the additional water supply from the extension of the Valens Aqueduct to Bizye. How they functioned and contributed to the water supply as whole remains obscure. The discovery

49   Ward et al., "Water-supply infrastructure", pp. 1185–90, Fig. 7.
50   Bardill, in Crow et al., *Water Supply*, pp. 143–55.
51   Ward et al., "Byzantine cisterns", see also Altuğ, "Planlama İlkeleri ve Yapım", with coloured illustrations and plans of many of the city's cisterns.
52   Ward et al., "Byzantine cisterns", Fig. 3; Ward et al., "Water supply", Fig. 9.
53   Compare Crow et al., "Water Supply", Maps 12–15; Ward et al., "Byzantine Cisterns", Fig. 2.
54   Crow et al., *Water Supply*, p. 128; Crow, "Still waters run deep".

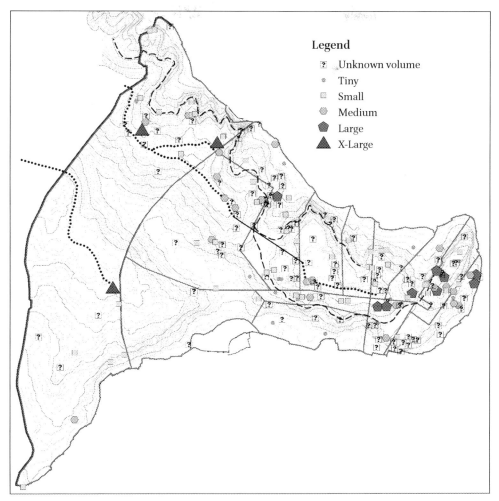

FIGURE 8.3   Map showing the distribution of 210 Byzantine period cisterns in Constantinople, the line of the two main channels and the approximate boundaries of the city's regions
DRAWN BY KATE WARD (SEE WARD ET AL. "BYZANTINE CISTERNS", FIG. 1)

of a chamber beside the cistern of Asper in the grounds of the Yavuz Sultan Selim Camii may provide a clue as to how water was extracted and dispersed from this great reservoir, but investigation and publication remain limited.[55] The reign of Anastasius possibly saw the beginning of the construction of very large, covered cisterns in the heart of the city with the Binbirdirek, although

---

55   Sav, "Yavuz Sultan Selim", p. 10; we are most grateful to Dr. Kerim Altuğ for drawing our attention to this structure.

the chronology of this cistern is insecure.[56] This is the deepest of the large urban cisterns and reflects the need to create a vast storage space in what was a crowded urban region allowing for a limited footprint. Also associated with Anastasius was the creation of the Cold Cistern in the Spendone of the Hippodrome. The Cold Cistern is the earliest example of inserting a cistern into an existing large building.[57] Soon after came the largest of the covered cisterns, the Yerebatan Saray, the Basilica Cistern constructed by Justinian.[58] In addition, from the Chronicon Pascale we learn that after the Nika riot in 532 the emperor constructed a cistern as well as granaries and bakeries within the palace "in case of popular crises".[59] Clearly these large water infrastructure projects were responding to the needs of the city and were not mere vanity programmes like the nymphea and baths of earlier Roman cities.[60]

Recent stable oxygen and carbon isotope analysis of carbonate (sinter) deposits from the long-distance water channels has concluded that the annual pattern of supply varied according to local circumstances. The study found that the isotopic analysis from the karstic springs which sourced the Pinarca and Danamandira (4th century) channels reflect seasonal variations in discharge, whilst the results from the sinter analysis from the more distant springs at Pazarli and Ergene show a consistent annual flow and less seasonal range, reflecting evenly distributed rainfall across the year.[61] These findings derive from samples representing the last 27 years of the aqueducts' activity in the later twelfth century, indicative of a longstanding regime of channel maintenance. An alternative approach using macrophysical climate modelling formed part of the studies by Ruggeri and Crapper, who conclude that contemporary weather and flow data for the Thracian springs were appropriate proxies for the past conditions.[62] Overall, these findings question the significance of climatic change on past water resources as the determining factor in the evolving pattern of urban water storage and distribution. In turn, they would challenge reductionist views of climate historians such as Michael McCormick and colleagues, who proposed that the construction of the Basilica cistern

56 Also of similar date was the cistern in Divânı Ali Sokağı, Bardill, *Brickstamps*, pp. 129–30; located between the Forum of Constantine and the Forum Taurii, see Crow et al., *Water Supply*, p. 151, Map 15, F7/1.
57 Forchheimer and Strzygowski, *Byzantinischen Wasserbehälter*, pp. 104–5.
58 Crow et al., *Water Supply*, pp. 17–19.
59 Chronicon Paschale, 629; Whitby and Whitby, *Chronicon Paschale*, p. 127.
60 For an attempt to describe the nymphaea of Constantinople see Stephenson and Hedlund, "Monumental Waterworks".
61 Sürmelihindi et al., "Carbonates from the ancient world's longest aqueduct", pp. 645–9.
62 Ruggeri, Engineering the Byzantine water Supply, pp. 130–46; Crapper, "The Valens Aqueduct", pp. 431–5.

was a specific response to certain climate events in the late-5th century.[63] As a recent study of paleo-climate in Southwest Turkey has concluded, "Considering the heterogeneity of climate and the multitude of impacts on records, palaeoclimatic interpretations are complex and care must be taken, especially when they are utilized for discussions of societal impacts".[64] In practice, we need to consider a wider range hazards; the threat of catastrophic seismic episodes has been noted[65] and it can be suggested that the concentration of water storage in the most densely occupied east end of the peninsula may be a response to increasing security threats in the Balkans affecting the city's hinterland. Certainly it corresponds with Anastasius' decision to construct a new barrier wall only 74 km west of the Land Walls of the city, which protected part of the water supply network at Danamadın and Pinarca but left exposed much of the outer line to Bizye.[66] Any such concerns about the security of the long-distance aqueducts were confirmed at the time of the Avar siege of 626 when, later reports indicate, the Valens system was cut and not restored until 767. The restoration of the long-distance system by Constantine v has already been noted and is recognized as a turning point in the fortunes of the city.[67]

A continuing feature of the new cisterns was their insertion into pre-existing elite buildings. This is apparent in the great cistern which occupies a late antique rotunda below the new palace of Romanus Lecapenus at the Myrelaion and also the new cisterns inserted into the large hall north of the Palace of Antiochus, and west of the hippodrome.[68] But this was not simply an age of reuse. The literary sources for water usage and patronage remain elusive and enigmatic, although water continues as a theme of elite literature and learning: *paideia*.[69] But one of the most important new cisterns of the middle-Byzantine period was the cistern constructed as part of the church complex at Küçükyalı, formerly interpreted as the Palace of Bryas, but now convincingly associated with the monastery of Satyros founded by the Patriarch Ignatios between 867 and 877. Located close to the east coast of the Sea of Marmara, the monastery survives as a rectangular platform of 70 by 51 m above the level coastal plain.

---

63   McCormick et al., "Climate Change", 197–8, n. 22.
64   Jacobson et al., "Heterogenous Late Holocene Climate", p. 9.
65   See n. 567; a recent survey of the city's defences stresses the threat of earthquakes to the fabric of the walls, McGeer, "Defence of Constantinople", p. 124.
66   Crow, "Recent Research".
67   See note 24.
68   Müller-Wiener, *Bildlexikon*, Figs. 272, 273; Niewöhner, "Rotunda", Fig. 2; note that on the accession of Romanus Lecapenus the Myrelaion became a monastery; for the cisterns west of the Hippodrome, and the Palace of Antiochus, later the church of St. Euphemia, see Müller-Wiener, *Bildlexikon*, Fig. 109, C, D; Fig. 269.
69   Magdalino, "The culture of water".

A small, intricately designed church is located at the east end of the platform, with an open atrium to the west. Below was an extensive cistern which partly mirrors the plan of the church to the east but was supported by a vaulted roof based on piers, now lost, to the west. There is a well preserved channel to the east, below the church, with a settling tank before the entrance to the cistern. The complex of cistern and church and other structures is now among the best documented middle-Byzantine structures in the city and its suburbs. It is estimated that the cistern could have contained a total volume of water of 3000 m^3.[70] Water storage and management was clearly a major concern of the builders from the outset, and the quantity of water will have exceeded the needs of a monastic community. We can suggest therefore that the water was distributed to the surrounding communities for either domestic or agricultural reasons. More significantly, it provided the monastery with a resource it could control.

None of the known *typika* from monasteries in Constantinople refer to water usage or rights. However, from Thessaloniki, there is very clear evidence for the management and control of the city's water resources by the main monasteries, a role that continued into the Ottoman period. A recent study from Thessaloniki has been able to document the Byzantine water network and the role of the urban monasteries, and especially the monastery of Vlatadon, which was able to store and distribute water from a branch of the aqueduct from the Choriatis springs 22 kms outside the city.[71] However in contrast with the Constatinopolitan examples the middle Byzantine period cisterns associated with monasteries at Thessaloniki such as Vlatadon (II/Δ7) have a limited capacity of 430 m^3 and at Agioi Apostoloi (IV/Δ4), which had a capacity of 800 m^3. At the same time, older buildings around the city were utilized for water storage, including the monumental vestibule of the Octagon at the Galerian complex (II/Δ37), with a capacity of 1250 m^3, and the Cryptoporticus of the Ancient Forum (III/Δ21), with a capacity of 4500–5000 m^3.

From Constantinople, a number of cisterns are associated with known monastic churches including the Studios and the Chora Monasteries. One of the most important surviving middle-Byzantine monasteries is the Pantokrator (Zeyrek Camii), and a significant cluster of cisterns are known in its vicinity.[72] Below the ecclesiastical complex and close to Attatürk Bulevard is the cistern

---

70   Ricci, "Rediscovery of the Patriarchal Monastery".
71   Gala-Georgila, Δρόμοι του νερού, esp. cisterns of Vlatadon, pp. 102–3; pp. 236–8; Map 4, cisterns 5, 6, 7 are all quite small in volume; see also, Manoledakis, Water supply of Roman Thessaloniki.
72   Crow et al., *Water Supply*, pp. 148–9, Map 14; for the chronological relationship of the Studios basilica and cistern see Crow, "Still Waters Run Deep", pp. 119–20.

of Unkapanı. It was constructed into the hillside with scalloped buttresses facing the road. There is no independent dating evidence, and there is nothing such as brick stamps or specific types of capitals to suggest an early date. Given the example of the complexity of the construction and design at Küçükyalı from the late-9th century, it seems reasonable to consider that the Unkapani cistern with a maximum internal capacity of 3500 m³ was constructed in the same time as the Comnenian monastery and was regulated in a similar manner to the monasteries in Thessaloniki.[73]

It is important to recognize that archaeological evidence within Constantinople and elsewhere attests to the maintenance and continuing development of Byzantine hydraulic technologies. A recently surveyed 11th-century monastery from Pamphylia provides significant evidence for a water tower intended to balance pressure for a water channel leading into the monastery,[74] and similar features are also attested in Thessaloniki. These towers were later known as *suterazı* and were widely used by the Ottomans, but how far there was technology transfer from the Byzantines to early Ottoman engineers remains to be investigated.[75] A feature of the very large reservoirs was the need to control the volume and pressure of outflow. At the Fildamı Reservoir outside of the city and north of the Hebdomen Palace, a chamber was added which could more effectively control the outflow and hence reduce friction and erosion to the outflowing water channels. It is suggested that the Fildamı most likely dates at the end of the 6th century or later, but, more significantly, the water tower in question was constructed in a very different construction method and is likely to be later still in date.[76] Within another reservoir in the city, the Aetios Reservoir, a circular structure was constructed in the northwest corner; it is different structurally from the Fildamı, and its function is unclear. However, it probably served to manage the outflow, or to aerate the waters. The reservoir was the earliest of the large open reservoirs outside the Constantinian Wall, but the form of construction of the tower is clearly middle-Byzantine in date. Aeration was a recognized problem in maintaining water quality as is apparent from the openings and windows in many of the larger covered cisterns, including the Unkapanı noted above. As a precious indication of the widespread awareness

---

73 Forchheimer/ Strzygowski, *Byzantinischen Wasserbehälter*, pp. 70–71; Crow et al., *Water Supply*, Map 14, E5/2, Fig. 5.1, the only comparable buttresses are from the Fildamı, but the cistern is open and not vaulted.
74 Tiryaki, "Kisleçukuru Manastırı", pp. 455–6, Fig. 14.
75 For the early Ottoman water supply of the Topkapı Palace, see the recent study of a newly identified manuscript description, Neçipioğlu, "Virtual Archaeology"; see now Crow "The City Thirsts".
76 Crow et al., *Water Supply*, p. 19, n. 53; pp. 132–7.

of advanced water technology in the Byzantine world, the evidence from structural observations is rarely if ever reflected in literary texts, although the discussion of "Besieging a City" in Leo VI's *Taktika* included the detailed advice on the importance of aeration and how to keep water fresh in stored containers.[77]

A great city like Constantinople needed to retain the lessons of the past and also to be able to adapt and, if possible, innovate. Such attributes are not immediately apparent in many aspects of Byzantine society and culture. Yet, as Constantinople regained its confidence in the later 8th century, a key symbol of its potential was the restoration of the long-distance water supply. As Peter Hall's quotation asserts, this demand to restore the earlier infrastructure was a response to an emerging greater urban complexity. Formerly, the distribution of water and its specific delivery was an imperial privilege,[78] but by analogy with the evidence from Thessaloniki and the recent study from Küçükyalı it seems reasonable to propose that many of Constantinople's urban monasteries came to take on a role as distribution centres across the city, although imperial patronage continued into the 11th century with a major restructuring under the Comnenoi. More water-based features (cisterns, baths, conduits, drains) survive from the Byzantine city than any other category of monuments, and this extensive inventory asserts how Constantinople not only retained the skills of old Roman hydraulic engineers, but were able to devise new systems, a legacy adopted by the Ottomans after 1453.

Bibliography

Primary Sources

Codex Justinianus, recognovit P. Krüger, Berolini 1877; *Codex Justinianus*, Frier, B.W. (ed.) *The Codex of Justinian: a new annotated translation, with parallel Latin and Greek text based on a translation by Justice Fred H. Blume*, Cambridge 2016.

Leo VI, Taktika, *The Taktika of Leo VI, text, transl. and commentary* by G.T. Dennis (CFHB 49), Washington DC 2014, revised edition.

Pierrre Gilles, *Itinéraires byzantines, introduction, traduction du latin et notes* J-P. Grélois, CNRS Centre de Recherche d'historie et civilization de Byzance, Monographies 28, Paris 2007.

---

[77] Leo, *Taktika*, 15, 63–4, including the advice that water keeps better in large containers.
[78] Crow, "Water and Late Antique Constantinople", pp. 125–7.

Theophanis *Chronographia*, recognovit C. de Boor, Lipsiae 1883–1885, [reprinted. Hildesheim – New York 1980]; Mango, C. and Scott, R. *The Chronicle of Theophanes Confessor: Byzantine and near eastern history AD 284–813* Oxford 1997.

Secondary Sources

Aktaş, N.K., "The change analysis of the green spaces of the Historic Peninsula", in S.J. Kluiving/ E.B. Guttmann-Bond (eds.), *Landscape Archaeology between Art and Science From a Multi- to an Interdisciplinary Approach*, Amsterdam 2012 pp. 81–96.

Altuğ. K., "Planlama İlkeleri ve Yapım Teknikleri Açısından, Tarihi Yarımada'daki Bizans Dönemi Sarnıçları"(Notes on planning and construction techniques of Byzantine cisterns in the historical peninsula of Istanbul), *Restorasyon/Konservasyon* 15 (2012), pp. 3–22.

Barthel, S. and Isendahl, C., "Urban gardens, agriculture, and water management: Sources of resilience for long-term food security in cities", *Ecological Economics* 86 (2013), 224–234.

Bardill, J. "The Palace of Lausus and nearby monuments in Constantinople: a topographical study", *American Journal of Archaeology* 101 (1997), pp. 67–95.

Bardill, J. *Brickstamps of Constantinople*, Oxford 2004.

Biavaschi, P., "Dalla scrittura su tabulae alla scrittura sulla pelle: il valore del documento scritto nelle costituzioni del titolo De aquaeductu del Codice Teodosiano", in G. Bassanelli Sommariva/S. Tarozzi/P. Biavaschi, *Ravenna capitale: permanenze del mondo giuridico romano in Occidente nei secoli V–VIII: instrumenta, civitates, collegia, studium iuris* Santarcangelo di Romagna 2014, pp. 95–118.

Bony, G., Marriner, N., Morhange, C., Kaniewski, D., and Perinçek, D., "A high-energy deposit in the Byzantine harbour of Yenikapı, Istanbul (Turkey)", *Quaternary International* 266 (2012), pp. 117–130.

Bruun, C., "Roman emperors and legislation on public water use in the Roman Empire: clarification and problems", *Water History* 4,1 (2012), pp. 11–34.

Caglar, E., Gorgülü, M., and Kuscu, O., "Dental Caries and Tooth Wear in a Byzantine Paediatric Population (7th to 10th Centuries AD) from Yenikapı-Constantinople, Istanbul", *Caries Research* 50 (4) (2016), pp. 394–399.

Çeçen, K., *The longest Roman water supply line*, Istanbul 1996.

Çeçen, K., *Sinan's Water Supply System in Istanbul*, Istanbul 1996.

Crow, J. "Water and Late Antique Constantinople: 'It would be abominable for the inhabitants of this Beautiful City to be compelled to purchase water'", L. Grig/ G. Kelly, (eds.) *Two Romes: From Rome to Constantinople*, New York 2012, pp. 116–135.

Crow, J. "Ruling the waters: managing the water supply of Constantinople", *Water History* 4, 1 (2012), pp. 35–56.

Crow, J. "Blessing or Security? Understanding the Christian Symbols of a Monumental Aqueduct Bridge in The Hinterland of Late Antique Constantinople", in I. Garipzanov/C. Goodson,/H. Maguire (eds.), *Graphic Signs of Power and Faith in Late Antiquity and The Early Middle Ages: Essays on Early Graphicacy*, Turnhout 2017, pp. 147–174.

Crow, J., "Still waters run deep': cisterns and the hydraulic infrastructure of Constantinople and Alexandria", in L'eau dans la ville tardo-antique, *Antiquité Tardive* 28, (2020), pp. 113–127.

Crow, J. "Recent research on the Anastasian Wall in Thrace and late antique linear barriers around the Black Sea", in Hodgson, N./Bidwell, P./Schachtmann. J. (eds.), *Roman Frontier Studies 2009*, Oxford 2017, pp. 131–138.

Crow, J., Bardill, J., and Bayliss, R., *The Water Supply of Byzantine Constantinople*, JRS Monographs 11, London 2008.

Crow, J., and Turner, S., "Silivri and the Thracian hinterland of Istanbul: an historic landscape", *Anatolian Studies* 59 (2009), pp. 167–81.

Dagron, G. "Poisson, pêcheurs et poissoniers de Constantinople", in C. Mango / G. Dagron (eds.), Constantinople and Its Hinterland: papers from the twenty-seventh Spring Symposium of Byzantine Studies, Oxford, April 1993, Aldershot 1995, pp. 57–76.

Dark, K., and Özgümüş, F., *Constantinople, Archaeology of a Byzantine Megalopolis*, Oxford 2013.

Forchheimer, P. and Strzygowski, J., *Die Byzantinischen Wasserbehälter von Konstantinopel* Byzantinische Denkmäler 2, Vienna 1893.

Γκαλά-Γεωργιλά, Ἐ., Δρόμοι του νερού και οργάνωση του χώρου στη Θεσσαλονίκη κατά τη Μέση και ύστερη Βυζαντινή περίοδο, Θεσσαλονίκη 2015, 2 vols.

Haldon, J.F., *The Empire that would not die, the paradox of the East Roman survival, 640–740*, Harvard 2016.

Hordern, P. and Purcell, P. *The Corrupting Sea, a study of Mediterranean history*, Oxford 2000.

Humphreys, M., *The Laws of the Isaurian Era, The Ecloga and its Appendices*, Translated Texts for Byzantinists, Liverpool 2017.

Jacobson, M.J., Flohr, P., Gascoigne, A., Leng, M.J., Sadekov, A., Cheng, H., et al. "Heterogenous late Holocene climate in the Eastern Mediterranean – The Kocain Cave record from SW Turkey", *Geophysical Research Letters*, 48 (2021), e2021GL094733, https://doi.org/10.1029/2021GL094733.

Jaillette, P./F. Reduzzi Merola, "L' eau à usage agricole dans la législation romaine de l'époque tardive: du Code Théodosien au Code Justinien" in E. Hermon, E. *Vers une gestion integree de l'eau dans l'empire romain*. Rome 2008, pp. 229–242.

Keenan-Jones, D., "Large-scale water management projects in Roman central-southern Italy", in W.V. Harris, (ed.) *The Ancient Mediterranean Environment Between Science and History*, Columbia Studies in the Classical Tradition, 39 (2013), pp. 233–256.

Koder, J., "Fresh vegetables for the capital", in C. Mango/G. Dagron (eds.), *Constantinople and Its Hinterland: papers from the twenty-seventh Spring Symposium of Byzantine Studies, Oxford, April 1993* Aldershot 1995, pp. 49–56.

Madden, T.F., "The Fires of the Fourth Crusade in Constantinople, 1203–1204: A Damage Assessment," *Byzantinische Zeitschrift*, 84/85 (1991/1992), 72–85.

McCormick, M. et al. "Climate change during and after the Roman Empire: reconstructing the past from scientific and historical evidence", *Journal of Interdisciplinary History* 43 (2012), pp. 169–220.

McGeer, E., "The defence of Constantinople", in *Cambridge Companion to Constantinople*, (ed.) S. Bassett, Cambridge 2022, pp. 117–134.

Magdalino, P. "The culture of water in the Macedonian renaissance", in Shilling and Stephenson, *Fountains*, pp. 130–144.

Mango, C., "The water supply of Constantinople", in C. Mango and G. Dagron (eds.), *Constantinople and Its Hinterland: papers from the twenty-seventh Spring Symposium of Byzantine Studies, Oxford, April 1993* (Aldershot, 1995), pp. 9–18.

Mango, C., *Le développement urbain de Constantinople (IVe–VIIe siècles)*. 3rd ed. Paris 2004.

Manolodakis, M., "The water supply of Roman Thessaloniki", in Aristodemou, G. et al. *Great Water Works in Roman Greece, Aqueducts and monumental fountain structures, function and context*, Oxford 2018, pp. 50–68.

Mansell, P., *Constantinople, City of a World's Desire, 1453–1924*, London. 1995.

Müller-Wiener, W., *Bildlexikon zur Topographie Istanbuls*, Tübingen 1977.

Necipioglu, G., "'Virtual Archaeology' in Light of a new document on the Topkapı Palace's waterworks and earliest buildings, circa 1509", *Muqarnas*, 30, 2013, pp. 315–350.

Niewöhner, P., "The rotunda at the Myrelaion in Constantinople: pilaster capitals, mosaics and brick stamps", in Ödekan, A. et al (eds.). *The Byzantine court source of power and culture*, Istanbul 2013, pp. 25–36.

Perinçek, D., "Geoarchaeology of the excavation site for the last 8000 years and traces of natural catastrophes in the geological profile", in U. Kocabaş (ed.) *Proceedings of the 1st Symposium on the Marmaray Salvage excavations, 5th to 6th May, 2008*, Istanbul 2010, pp. 191–217.

Pickett, J. "Water and Empire in the *De aedificiis* of Procopius", *Dumbarton Oaks Papers* 71 (2017), pp. 95–125.

Ricci, A. "Rediscovery of the Patriarchal Monastery of Satyros (Küçükyalı, Istanbul): Architecture, Archaeology and Hagiography", Bizantinistica Rivista di Studi Bizantini e Slavi 2nd Ser. 19, (2018), pp. 247–276.

Ruggeri, F., *Engineering the Byzantine Water Supply of Constantinople: mapping, hydrology and hydraulics* (PhD thesis University of Edinburgh) Edinburgh 2018.

Ruggeri, F., Crapper, M., Snyder, J.R., and Crow, J. "A GIS based assessment of the Byzantine water supply system of Constantinople", *Water Science and Technology: Water Supply* 17.6 (2017), 1534–1543.

Sav, M., "Yavuz Sultan Selim Camii Çevresi veya Istanbul'un Beşinci Tepesinin Arkeolojik Topografyası", *Restorasyon*, 1 (2010), pp. 4–13.

Shilling, B., & Stephenson, P. (eds.), *Fountains and Water Culture in Byzantium*, Cambridge 2016.

Sinclair, P., Gullög, N., Herschend, F. and Isendahl, C., *The Urban mind, Cultural and Environmental Dynamics*, Studies in Global Archaeology 15, Uppsala, 2010.

Stephenson, P. and Hedlund, R. "Monumental waterworks in late antique Constantinople", in Shilling/Stephenson, *Fountains*, pp. 36–54.

Snyder, J.R., "Building the longest water supply system: Large-scale construction in Constantinople's hinterland", *İstanbul Araştirmalari Yilliği / Annual of İstanbul Studies*, 5 (2016), pp. 1–19.

Sümelihindi, G., Passchier, C., Crow, J., Spotl, C., Mertz-Kraus, R., "Carbonate in the longest aqueduct of the ancient world: a witness of Byzantine water management and maintenance," *Geoarchaeology: an international journal*, 36 (3) (2021), pp. 643–659.

Snyder, J.R., Dilaver, O, Stephenson, L.C., Mackie, J., and Smith, S.D., "Agent-based modelling and construction – reconstructing antiquity's largest infrastructure project" *Construction Management and Economics*, 2017 DOI:10.1080/01446193.2017.1403639.

Thomas, R., and Wilson, A. "Water Supply for Roman Farms in Latium and South Etruria." *Papers of the British School at Rome*, 62 (1994), pp. 139–196.

Tiryaki, A., "Kisleçukru Manastiri: Antalya'da on ikinçi yüzila ait bizans manastiri", in A. Ödekan, et al. (eds.), *Change in the Byzantine World in the Twelfth and Thirteenth Centuries. Proceedings of the First International Sevgi Gönül Byzantine Studies Symposium*, Istanbul 2010, pp. 447–457.

Tabbernee, W. and Lampe, P., *Pepouza and Tymion. The Discovery and Archaeological Exploration of a Lost Ancient City and an Imperial Estate*, Berlin 2008.

Ward, K., *An engineering exploration of the water supply system of Constantinople*, PhD University of Edinburgh 201s8.

Ward, K., Crow, J. and Crapper, M., "Water-supply infrastructure of Byzantine Constantinople", *Journal of Roman Archaeology*, 30 (2107), pp. 175–195.

Ward, K., Crapper, M., Altuğ, K., and Crow, J., "The Byzantine cisterns of Constantinople", *Water Science and Technology: Water Supply* 17.6 (2017), pp. 1499–1505.

Varinlioğlu, G. "Urban monasteries in Constantinople and Thessaloniki: Distribution Patterns in Time and Urban Topography", J. Emerick/D. Deliyannis (eds), *Archaeology and Architecture: Studies in Honor of Cecil L. Striker*, Mainz 2005, pp. 187–198.

Zuckerman, C. "On a bountiful harvest at Antioch of Pisidia (with special regard to the Byzantine *modios* and the Mediterranean diet)," in Delouis, O. et al., *Le saint, le moine et le paysan, Mélanges d'histroire byzantine offerts à Michel Kaplan*, Paris, 2016, pp. 731–751.

CHAPTER 9

Continuities and Discontinuities in the Agriculture of the Levant in the Late Antique and Early Islamic Period

Michael J. Decker

1   Introduction

Throughout much of the Levant and Mesopotamia, Late Antiquity (the 4th through 7th centuries AD) was a time of demographic and economic expansion. In both Byzantium and the Sasanian Empire, there were areas that witnessed large-scale regional intensification of agriculture and areas where agrarian communities became more deeply linked to exchange networks. In the eastern Mediterranean, the movement of the seat of government from Rome to various eastern cities and then, finally, Constantinople and the increasing weakness of state structures in the western Mediterranean from the 3rd century onwards led gradually to eastern domination of overseas trade and with it the supply of many luxury and staple agricultural commodities. In supplying this demand, eastern Romans expanded production of the items of agricultural trade. Alongside this Levantine dominance of long-distance exchange, numerous environmental and social conditions created a positive environment for intensive agriculture over large swathes of the Levant from the 4th to the 5th centuries AD (see Fig. 9.1).

2   Climate Trends in the Levant

Historians and others interested in past environments often look for sudden changes as well as more gradual shifts in the environment that could have triggered a crisis or, conversely, abetted economic expansion, political stability, or other similar beneficial conditions. In the broad chronological scope under investigation here, two significant climatic boundaries bracket the period under discussion. On the one hand, the centuries-long warming trend, the "Roman climatic optimum", came to an end around AD 400. Already by the mid-3rd century in certain regions, the climate was apparently less stable

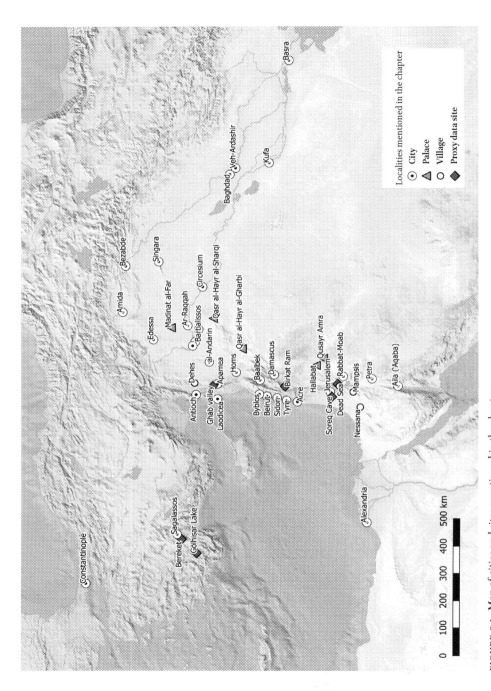

FIGURE 9.1 Map of cities and sites mentioned in the chapter
DRAWN BY JOHANNES PREISER-KAPELLER

and trending cooler.[1] On the other hand, the cooler conditions that prevailed throughout Late Antiquity may have been due to reduced periodic solar activity, sharp episodes of volcanic activity, or some combination of these. The prominent advance of glaciers worldwide in the 6th century indicates an important episode of global cooling followed by a general rise in temperatures as early as the 8th century in some regions. This multi-century warming trend was fully underway by the end of the Early Islamic era (AD c.1000) and apparently had begun centuries earlier in the southern Levant.[2]

It should be stressed that the Levant has been dominated by the Mediterranean climate regime over the past 6,500 years. Of course, the region has experienced both long-term and short-term disruptions within the dominant regime; these alterations are slight when viewed in geological time, but in human terms they could be quite historically significant. The Roman and Byzantine eras were marked by climatic instability with an overall trend toward desiccation, but the precise timing of the long-term drying and role of short-term abrupt episodes in rendering the environment requires additional study. Evidence from the Soreq Cave in the Judean Hills of Israel indicates a marked decrease in the level of precipitation from AD c.100–700.[3] Dead Sea levels peaked c.300–350 and declined sharply thereafter, falling to a low point in AD c.700.[4] Recent research in Israel provides additional resolution to the rather unclear picture. From AD 100 to 450, rainfall fell from an estimated 570 mm to 280 mm; the decades close to the years 100 and 400 witnessed appreciable drops in moisture.[5] Since we are reliant upon analysis of geological proxy data, the fine-grained annual sequences and near-certain indicators of short-term changes are not really satisfactory for historians interested in interpreting events recorded in texts, but these high-quality data do lend themselves to a fairly clear long-term picture.

Analysis of sediments from Lake Gölhisar and the Bereket Basin in southwest Turkey, by contrast, indicate an increase in environmental moisture during the late Roman to early Byzantine eras until AD c.700. In southwestern Anatolia it appears that the early Roman era was comparatively dry and warm from

---

1 McCormick et al., "Climate Change", p. 75. All dates, unless otherwise stated, are AD.
2 Glacial advance in 6th and early 7th century: Wanner et al., "Mid-late Holocene Climate Change".
3 Bar-Matthews/Ayalon, "Speleotherms".
4 Enzel et al., "Late Holocene Climates of the Near East"; Bookman, "Late Holocene Lake Levels", p. 566; Whitehead et al., "Modelling Dead Sea Levels", p. 148, Fig. 3.
5 Orland et al., "Climate Deterioration", p. 34.

AD 130 to 450, followed by wetter conditions from AD 450 to 650.[6] In central and western and central Anatolia, proxy data indicate a drier phase c.300–560 followed by a period of elevated moisture until AD c.730, when Anatolia and most of the eastern Mediterranean experienced increased climatic aridity.[7] During the wetter phase of Late Antiquity in central and western Anatolia (AD c.560–730) it is nonetheless likely that the Levantine coast from around Antioch to Palestine remained drier, as winter moisture-bearing cyclonic lows were funneled over Anatolia and remained at latitudes well north of most of Syria and Palestine. These drier conditions prevailed in the Levant through the 11th century AD.[8]

Vegetation records help to fill out the picture. Over the 7th and 8th centuries, a period of reforestation began in the environs of Sagalassos in southwestern Asia Minor; it has prevailed until the present and likewise over most of Asia Minor, implying a decrease in arable farming.[9] From the Ghab valley in northern Syria, pollen records indicate increasing pine (*Pinus*) pollen at the end of Late Antiquity; pine is a pioneer species that colonizes abandoned orchards or former tilled spaces and generally indicates a lack of intensive farming activity.[10] In the Golan, core samples from Lake Birkat Ram record a sharp decline in olive pollen around the 680s, with Roman-Byzantine levels only attained once more in the Mamluk era (16th century).[11] The decrease in olive pollen, one of the prime indicators of human activity in the regional landscape, and coincidental rise of other forms of arboreal pollen suggests a decline in farming in the Golan after the Muslim Conquests. Further south, the Dead Sea has been demonstrated to have been quite sensitive to regional environmental change, especially that from the Judaean Hills; thus, data collected there offer the opportunity to reconstruct the past environment of southern Syria-Palestine. A decline in farming at the end of Late Antiquity is evidenced by lowered proportions of olive (*Olea europaea*) pollen, which fell at the end

6   Kaniewski et al., "A High-Resolution Late Holocene Landscape Ecological History", p. 2213. On Anatolia see now: Haldon et al., "The Climate and Environment of Byzantine Anatolia".
7   Lake Gölhisar: Eastwood et al., "Holocene Climate Change in the Eastern Mediterranean": Anatolia: Haldon et al. "The Climate and Environment of Byzantine Anatolia"; Levantine precipitation: Finné et al., "Speleotherm Evidence for Late Holocene Climate Variability", p. 3167; Fig. 6; p. 3168.
8   Enzel et al., "Late Holocene Climates of the Near East", p. 268.
9   Sagalassos: Vermoere, et al., "Pollen Sequences from the City of Sagalassos", p. 170; for the regional pollen picture of northern Anatolia see Izdebski, "The Changing Landscapes of Byzantine Anatolia".
10 Yasuda/Kitagawa/Nakagawa, "The Earliest Record of Major Anthropogenic Deforestation", p. 135.
11 Schwab et al., "Holocene Paleoecology of the Golan Heights", p. 1730.

of Late Antiquity as early as AD 500 or as late as the mid-7th century. The drop in olive pollen coincides with lower water levels in the Dead Sea; the latter values are a clear indicator of drought conditions. Throughout the early medieval period, olive pollen values remained low and pine forests expanded, probably in response to increased aridity accompanied by the abandonment of orchards and fields in marginal areas.[12] More recent studies offer a somewhat different view, such as speleothem-derived oxygen and carbon isotope data from northern Iraq, which indicate a long-term environmental aridification beginning AD c.950.[13] Additional correctives or countervailing data for the late-antique Levant also recently has been analyzed and hypothesizes drier conditions prevailing in the Levant earlier than Iraq, beginning AD c.670.[14]

Two points need to be stressed: first, there is a great deal of new research in this area, and continuing interdisciplinary discussion is quite healthy; second, regional studies are crucial, since it is clear that contemporary environmental conditions in one area could be quite different from one another. In studies such as that by Xoplaki et al., there is considerable sophistication both in the climatic reconstructions from an ever-expanding database which, compared to those studies done twenty or even ten years ago, is richer in both quality and quantity – and in terms of historiographical nuance. In the case of the high-medieval period in Anatolia by Xoplaki et al., Haldon stresses that the apogee of Byzantine economic prosperity occurred against a backdrop of deteriorating environmental conditions; such studies are clearly needed to answer what are evidently interesting but ultimately counterproductive deterministic studies.[15]

Still in debate is the sway over agrarian life and economy of the Levant held by various historically attested catastrophes; among these calamities are sudden climate change, earthquake damage, Malthusian subsistence crises caused by various agents, and the Justinianic Plague. Claudine Dauphin and others have argued that in the 6th century the citizens of the empire suffered such a series of grave manmade and natural disasters that tested – and ultimately broke – their collective resilience.[16] The event in the catalog of terrors with the most potential to affect life in the Levant was the visitation of the

---

12 Baruch, "The Late Holocene Vegetational History"; Neumann et al. "Palynology, Sedimentology and Palaeoecology" pp. 1491–92; Neumann et al. "Vegetation History", p. 762; Leroy, "Pollen Analysis of Core DS7-1SC", pp. 312–13; Ackermann, "Palaeoenvironment and anthropogenic activity", pp. 237–38.
13 Flohr et al., "Late Holocene droughts in the Fertile Crescent".
14 Izedbski et al., "The environmental, archaeological, and historical evidence".
15 Xoplaki et al., "The medieval climate anomaly and Byzantium"; Harper, *The Fate of Rome*.
16 Dauphine, *La Palestine byzantine: peuplement et populations*.

bubonic plague beginning in AD 541–42 with six subsequent visitations upon the empire prior to AD 750.[17] Those who view the effects of the plague as devastating and wide-ranging believe it was instrumental in urban and rural decline long prior to the arrival of the Muslim armies.[18] Whether caused by warfare or environmental change, those who view the 6th century as a watershed believe that villages in the marginal areas declined sometime in the 7th century. To some, the drastic tapering of civic and church construction attested by trends in the epigraphic record is perhaps telling of this decline, while surges in the number of epitaphs could be linked to high mortality events like the plague.[19] After AD 600, the general waning of the Greek epigraphic habit both deprives us of precious data and introduces another layer of problems, including the question of the meaning of this shift as an indicator of cultural and social transformation. Likewise contested is whether the chronology and extent of the vivacity of the hundreds of Limestone Massif villages of northern Syria was precarious: the only excavated village site, Dehes, has been subjected to starkly conflicting interpretations.[20] In such a fragile system with numerous tensions, slight climatic changes could have rendered this area forlorn, as could labor shortages, poor strategies of crop choices, crop failure caused by pests or disease, animal and human deaths from zoonotic disease, or any of a number of deleterious events.

3 Ein Gedi: Victim of Natural or Manmade Disaster?

The remains of Ein Gedi (or En Gedi) lie one km from the present western shoreline of the Dead Sea, approximately 50 km southeast of Jerusalem. The village was occupied by Jews from the 1st century AD through the end of the 7th century, followed by a hiatus until its reoccupation in the 13th century. Ein Gedi covered approximately 40 hectares during its Roman peak just prior to the Bar Kochba Revolt (AD 132–35), when the village suffered at the hands of the Romans, who confiscated the territory and incorporated it into an imperial estate. According to Eusebius, who wrote AD *c.*324, Ein Gedi was a "very large

---

17 Stathakopoulos, *Famine and Pestilence*, p. 31.
18 Kennedy, "From *Polis* to *Madina*".
19 Di Segni, "Epigraphic evidence for building", p. 164; Di Segni noted that the drop in building inscriptions *may* have been related to plague, but we await further study; on this issue, see now Benovitz, 2014.
20 Best exemplified by the work of Tchalenko, *Villages antiques* and Kennedy, "From *Polis* to *Madina*"; Sodini et al., "Déhès"; disputed by Magness, "The archaeology of the Early Islamic settlement", pp. 196–208.

Jewish village" and the latest excavator to work on the site, Hirschfeld, estimated that the Byzantine era (from the 4th to 7th centuries AD) population numbered 1,000 people or more. Hirschfeld viewed the Byzantine-era occupation as another population peak for the settlement.[21] During its late-antique floruit, the village possessed not only numerous houses and agricultural installations and processing facilities, but also retail establishments, a bathhouse, and a synagogue, as well as a watermill. Ein Gedi was an economically vibrant place whose inhabitants earned a living through trading products from the Dead Sea, such as bitumen and tar and other products unique to the area. Balsam (probably extracted from *Commiphora gileadensis*), a precious aromatic and medicinal plant, was especially important. The specialized cultivation and extraction of balsam products generated considerable cash and allowed those living at Ein Gedi to import most of the foodstuffs and other materials they needed to live.

Evidence of the effects of ancient climate change are certainly visible at Ein Gedi. Of ten springs active in the Byzantine era, only four are flowing today. Flow from the major Ein Gedi spring, whence the region derives its name, formerly drove a Byzantine watermill. Charcoal in the floor plaster of this installation yielded a ^{14}C date of AD 530–680.[22] Traces of abandoned terracing along the higher elevations in the village hinterlands attest irrigation from now-vanished springs. This fragile environment suffered several earthquakes during Late Antiquity. From the 4th through 7th centuries, nine earthquakes whose epicenters were located within 1,000 km of the Dead Sea are known. Of these, five magnitude 7 or higher quakes (AD 363, 419, 502, 551, and 749) had their epicenters within 150 km of the Dead Sea; these seismic events thus were likely to have caused substantial damage to the region. The massive quakes of AD 363 and 749, known from both geological indicators and texts, involved rupture along of the Dead Sea Fault between the Dead Sea and the Sea of Galilee with a high potential for disaster.[23] Seismic waves from any number of these locally significant tremors may have adversely affected the groundwater table and diminished or even stopped the flow of several springs, though this question awaits full consideration.[24] It is believed that the fate of the Byzantine village of Ein Gedi was sealed by an attack by Bedouins in the 7th century; the latest coin finds are from the reign of Maurice (580–602) and there are signs of a widespread destruction layer attributable to burning. Nonetheless, it is

---

21   Eusebius, *Onom.* §86; Hirschfeld, "Ein-Gedi", p. 328.
22   Hadas, "Ein Gedi Water Mills", p. 77.
23   Girdler, "The Dead Sea transform fault system", pp. 239–40.
24   Liu/Roeloffs/Zheng, "Seismically induced water level fluctuations".

highly probable that environmental circumstances, namely droughty conditions and seismicity, played a role in the decline of the balsam production on which the settlement primarily depended.

The abandonment of Ein Gedi testifies to discontinuity reflected more broadly in the regional landscapes of the early medieval Middle East. Among the several features of late-antique agriculture in the Levant that the village typifies are specialization, intensive production based on significant labor and capital input, and access to markets and networks of long-distance exchange. It also represents another broader feature – the exploitation of niche resources, especially in marginal areas. At the end of Late Antiquity, there was a major reorientation of the economy of the Levant, which now looked increasingly inwards or eastwards toward inland Syria, the lands of the new caliphate in Mesopotamia, or even further east to India and southeast Asia. Thence came a flood of new commodities in quantities that greatly exceeded those imported from the east of the Byzantine era. Ein Gedi might have been re-founded and balsam again been produced there, were it not for the surge of plentiful south- and southeast-Asian aromatics that crowded Levantine and Arabian products out of the marketplace and from elite cultural space in the new Arab empire.[25] If the Levant and the Arabian Peninsula suffered alongside one another in a decline in precipitation throughout Late Antiquity, the dislocation of traditional forms of agriculture, including the production of the Arabian incense plants like *Commiphora gileadensis*, must be taken as a serious possibility. In addition, the longer-term drying of the environment may have been a primary cause of the abandonment of Ein Gedi, as declining aquifers led to the vanishing of spring waters. This would have been a rather slow process normally, but other environmental shocks, such as earthquakes, could have played a role. In the Negev Highlands, the human and environmental conditions permitting a considerable growth in agriculture faded sometime in the 8th century, which fact may also indicate a decline in precipitation and groundwater resources.[26] Before one decry a return to Huntingtonian scholarship and environmental determinism, I stress that our knowledge of the past environment of the Levant, while enlarged considerably and fairly refined over the past two decades, remains open to further study. In any case, environmental conditions should be considered equally alongside anthropogenic agency in attempts to understand some of the changes that occurred from the 6th to 8th centuries AD.

---

25 Zohar, "Trends in the use of perfumes and incense".
26 On settlement in the marginal reaches of southern Palestine see Avni, *Nomads, farmers, and town-dwellers*.

4   Population Disruption and Late-Antique Agriculture

Hirschfeld's interpretation of the abandonment of Ein Gedi in the face of attack serves to illustrate tension within archaeology and history over the period of transition: what, if any, was the role of violence in the abandonment of farmed landscapes? Even if the late-antique desertion of Ein Gedi was not solely due to human violence, the presumed attack probably played a major role in its demise. How do we assess the consequences of warfare, including the direct costs such as death and disease, but also indirect actions, such as the flight of elites whose wealth was formerly invested in farming? In what regions was there dislocation among the upper (ruling) classes and to what extent might have their removal affected things like intensive farming and the long-distance exchange of commodities? Could the disruption of elites have undercut some of the long-distance networks that in part helped to foster prosperity over a sizeable portion of the Byzantine East of the 4th through 6th centuries and if so, to what degree? What, too, of the possible effects on agricultural labor caused by the widespread dislocation of poorer laborers who fled or were made captive during the decades of warfare, especially around the time of the Sasanian invasion and withdrawal from the Levant from AD 611 to 628?

We are relatively poorly informed of the status of Syrian and Egyptian elites during the Arab Conquest period from the 630s AD up to the fall of Alexandria in November of AD 641 and even later when the still-unsettled political situation included raids by the Byzantine fleet and the transfer of populations from the coastlands to more secure inland regions. Well-known is the episode recorded in the *vita* of John the Almsgiver (§6), when the latter succored refugees fleeing the Persian advance. Inhabitants and clergy from all the cities of Syria were said to have arrived in a press upon Alexandria and, while we must allow for the usual exaggeration, there is some other evidence from elsewhere that there was a considerable flow of refugees around the Mediterranean linked with the Byzantine–Persian Wars of Heraclius. Another famous instance of flight was the retreat of Maximus Confessor from his monastery in Asia Minor to Carthage. The reigns of Tiberius (AD 574–82) and Maurice witnessed the large-scale capture or deportation and settlement within Byzantium of Persians, one raid in Arzanene netting many captives who were settled in Cyprus.[27] In AD 602 the emperor ordered the settlement of 30,000 Armenian families in the Balkans.[28] For their part, from the 4th century and later, the Sasanians made numerous deportations amounting to many thousands uprooted and resettled beyond

---

27   Whitby, *The emperor Maurice*, p. 269.
28   Michael the Syrian x.21, vol. II, pp. 363–64; Sebeos ch. 20.

Roman boundaries. Shapur II (AD 309–79) led away captive the inhabitants of Singara and Ziata and at least 9,000 from Bezabde (modern Cirzre) along with numerous others who were established in Kuzestan and elsewhere in the empire.[29] More Romans were taken captive in AD 395 by the Huns and sold to the Persians, who settled thousands of them in Veh-Ardashir (Seleukia in Iraq). During the wars with Anatasius and his successors, the effects of large-scale captive-taking, as at Amida, where as many as 80,000 were taken, were apparently locally pronounced. Similar episodes in AD 501–02 at Edessa, Antioch in AD 540, and in AD 573 with as many as 92,000 (elsewhere said to number 292,000) from Apamea and northern Syria. During the last confrontation between the Sasanians and Byzantines, Khusrow II (AD 590–628) sent captives from Mesopotamia, Syria, Palestine, and Phoenicia.[30] In AD 609 the Sasanians sacked Edessa and sent the survivors to Sistan and Khorasan on the northeastern marches of the empire. There is, however, no easy way to tally these population transfers in the overall balance sheets of either state. But it does seem that skilled laborers, which would have included those who were knowledgeable in technical aspects of intensive farming, such as irrigation works, potters, and others upon whom this kind of agriculture was dependent, were subject to deportation in large numbers. The Persians exempted the old and infirm and interviewed captives so as to select skilled laborers for forced transference east. One would like to link at least a portion of the development of late Sasanian royal centers and their territories, such as the region of the Diyala with this influx of immigrant skilled and agrarian labor.[31] If this hypothesis is correct, the loss to Byzantium was acute and the benefit to the Sasanians quite substantial.

Following the end of the war in AD c.628, there was a great movement of refugees across the frontiers. This included not only Byzantine captives returning home but also Sasanian captives in the hands of the Byzantines.[32] Some Persian communities in the Levant did not return home; during the early years of Muslim advances into the region, some of these settlers are attested at Baalbek in Phoenice, where they lived alongside communities of "Greeks" and Arabs. In the first decades of the caliphate, Mu'awiya ordered the re-settlement of Persians from Antioch, Homs, and Baalbek to Tyre, Acre, and other coastal cities. Soon after, the caliph ordered the resettling of Persian cavalry from Kufa and Basra along with Persian families from Baalbek and Homs

---

29 See Perry "Deportations" for what follows.
30 Theophanes *Chron.* ed de Boor, 1.293–5.
31 On the Diyala, see Adams, *Land behind Baghdad*.
32 Sebeos, trans. Thomson, p. 39.

to Antioch.³³ These movements attest that open land was available to support such groups who scarcely could have relied on the *diwan* for their subsistence. These Umayyad population transferals await a full study, but they likely were prompted by some combination of several factors, including the availability of land abandoned in the decades prior due to warfare or environmental hazards, including earthquakes and plague. The emplacement of colonists may well have enhanced the diffusion of certain crops and techniques into the former lands of the Byzantine Levant.

Likewise, immigration into the empire, especially into the provinces of Arabia and Palestine from Arabia may have been important in the transference or revival of certain technological aspects. This is especially true in marginal areas where one should envision multiple introductions of technologies that came into and fell out of use in certain regions. In any case, while we cannot be certain of the direction of diffusion(s) of the *qanat* from its origins in ancient Persia through the Roman Empire as far south as the Egyptian oases, an Arabian route cannot be discounted. It seems that the widespread utilization of qanat technology along the desert margins was certainly a pre-Islamic phenomenon, as recent work from Israel, Jordan, and Syria indicate, though we lack the means to pinpoint these technological transfers with precision.³⁴ Arabic-speaking cultivators were certainly involved in some of the unique and impressive farming regimes at places like Petra and Nessana, as indicated by onomastic evidence in the papyri. Their presence in places like Androna (al-Andarin) in Syria may support the view of Issar and others that northward migration by tribes into the empire was due primarily to increasing pressures on water resources in Late Antiquity.³⁵ Certainly historical evidence supports the view that there were important population movements by tribes into the Roman periphery in Late Antiquity, and the archaeological evidence supports the use of sophisticated hydraulic and cropping methods among segments of the population of pre-Islamic Arabia.³⁶ As discussed in more detail below, at present it seems that the first widespread technological transfers in hydraulic management long predated the Muslim conquests, though we cannot firmly date precisely where, or when many technologies were first used or exactly how they were diffused, nor rule out multiple later re-introductions.

33 Baladhuri, *Futuh* ed. trans. Hitti, p. 180.
34 Avner, "Ancient water management in the Southern Negv"; Decker, *Tilling the Hateful Earth*; Abudanh, "Innovation or Technology Immigration".
35 Issar, "Climate change in the Levant"; Kedar, "The Arab Conquests and agriculture": these ideas are of course not new: Huntington, *Palestine and its Transformation*.
36 Hoyland, *Arabia and the Arabs*, pp. 231–32.

Around AD 500, the southwest monsoon that delivered most of the moisture to South Arabia weakened, perhaps due to a southward shift of the ITCZ (Intertropical Convergence Zone, where the trade winds meet around the solar equator). This climatic shift was part of an era of environmental flux between otherwise long-term settled patterns.[37] The gradual destruction and abandonment of the Marib Dam after cycles of repair and deterioration in the 5th and 6th centuries may have been due to short-term extreme climate events that were part of the collective memory of the inhabitants of Arabia (e.g., the catastrophic flood remembered in Qurʿan *Sura* 34 as the primary catalyst for the end of the hydraulic society at Marib). Inscriptions record efforts to repair the dam, and medieval historians recalled that flooding led to failures of significant portions of the system.[38] Presumably the eight-millennium-long era of relative dryness was punctuated by cycles of drought and very short-term heavy rainfall events. Episodes of violent rains and associated flooding broke portions of the Marib dam system and led to major repair efforts in AD 449, 450, and 542. The flood of AD *c*.570 occurred during a time of social and political instability and the dam was not repaired. There was no Islamic-era revival of the Marib Dam and its accompanying irrigated croplands. Though portions of the ancient system functioned in a limited capacity via small discreet water-harvesting and water-lifting systems, these could not water even half of the irrigated surface area of the dam at its peak.[39] Many of the people reliant on such systems in South Arabia were apparently among those who migrated into the Roman and Persian empires at the end of antiquity, though once more the net effect is poorly understood. Did these newcomers bring or renew knowledge of qanat technologies and floodwater farming to areas such as the central Syrian edge of the imperial frontier or the new small cities of the Negev? On balance it seems that episodic settlement by sizeable groups of Arabic-speaking farmers, perhaps beginning around the time of the absorption of the Nabataean kingdom, had a marked influence on the semi-arid landscapes of the Levant. These relative latecomers from North Arabia made marked progress in marginal regions, where land was both plentiful and their experience in irrigation allowed new lands to be exploited.

Perhaps of more importance to the landscape history of the region were the effects of the Arab conquest upon the elite population of Syria. Did some

---

37   Wündsch et al., "ENSO and monsoon variability"; Böll et al., "Late Holocene primary productivity".
38   Glasser, "Der Damm von Mārib".
39   Brunner, "Die Erforschung der antiken Oase von Marib"; Brunner, "The Great Dam and the Sabean oasis of Maʿrib", pp. 176–77.

combination of the flight of major landowners or outright seizure of lands by the new Muslim government lead to any marked reconfiguration in agricultural production? From the Hellenistic period (323–31 BC) agriculture over most of the Levant had changed only by degrees. The movements of large numbers of people and tremendous reorganization of political boundaries at the advent of the Hellenistic era was in some senses homologous to conditions prevailing at the end of Late Antiquity wherein the Persian and Arab Conquests broke down Roman and Sasanian political authority over the Near East. But the retreat of elites, whose fortunes were built mostly from control of land and labor, is notoriously difficult to detect and little studied. In the Persian Empire, where the triumph of Arab-led armies was bloody and total and the resistance of most elite families generally quite fierce, these were mostly annihilated.[40] The massive influx of Arab settlers in places like Kufa and Basra led to the occupation of former Sasanian elite estates fairly quickly after the first battles of the first half of the 7th century. In Syria, the story of the family John of Damascus (d. AD 749) is well known and perhaps broadly indicative of at least groups of elites who remained more or less in place. John's grandfather, Mansur was the governor of Damascus and a key figure in the handover of the city to the Muslims and who served the caliph Muʿawiya (AD 661–80) in a high administrative capacity.[41] Much of the Ghassanid confederacy remained in Syria and many were prominent under the Umayyads. There are other instances, though, when we can detect considerable attrition among the ranks of elites in both the Levant and Egypt. Some fled, such as the alleged 30,000 members of the ruling elites who left by sea from Alexandria at the time of the Arab conquest, and Banaji thinks it notable that none of the great estate families of the Byzantine period appears in the 7th-century papyri.[42] In Syria, the Byzantines ("Greeks") of Byblos, Beirut and Sidon, among others, were expelled when the cities fell. The elites of Tripoli were evacuated by the Byzantine fleet; this probably represented the flight of the most prominent landowners and officials but not the bulk of the Greek-speaking population. In northern Syria, the population around Barbalissos and Kasirin (Dibsi Faraj?) are said to have left the area and settled in Byzantine territory or elsewhere in Mesopotamia. In AD 718, the Byzantine fleet captured and plundered Lattakia (Roman and Byzantine Laodicea) and carried off its population.[43] Such episodes show that there were fairly frequent local disruptions that affected considerable numbers of people,

40 Banaji, "Late antique Legacies".
41 Sahas, "John of Damascus on Islam", p. 26.
42 Ibn ʿAbd al-Hakam, *Futuh Misr*, ed. Torrey, 82, 1; Banaji, "Late antique Legacies", p. 167.
43 Baladhuri, trans. Hitti, pp. 194, 204.

probably in the low thousands for the larger incidents. Again, the aggregate effect of these human-caused deaths and movements is unknown, but by the early Umayyad era there was certainly land available to be assigned to garrisons and administrators.

Along the desert margins of Syria-Palestine, where Byzantine-era expansion was pronounced, there appears broad continuity of a high level of exploitation through the end of the Umayyad era. Elsewhere, I have argued that a combination of Arabic-speaking migrants, demographic expansion inside Byzantium, and favorable market and environmental knowledge allowed significant encroachment into the semi-desert spaces along the frontiers of the Roman world from the 4th to 7th centuries. On balance it seems that many of these places continued into at least the 8th century. In southern Jordan, for example, the churches and monasteries survived long enough to suffer at the hands of iconoclasts under the Umayyads. One of the earliest views of continuity in settlement and administrative practices comes from Nessana (Nitzana, Israel) in Palestine, where a Roman and Byzantine city had flourished throughout Late Antiquity. There, early Umayyad officials levied considerable charges on the community, as evidenced in *P. Ness.* 58, which attests that the impressive sum of 37.5 solidi was paid as tax to the governor Meslem (Maslama). As is well known, Byzantine Nessana, though a village, boasted public spaces, impressive ecclesiastical structures, and a fairly diverse and vibrant local economy in the 5th–8th centuries.

Despite evidence for warmer, drier conditions over Palestine III (Palaestina Tertia or Palaestina Salutaris), settlements seemingly expanded (or at least remained stable). These settlements relied mainly upon irrigated agriculture of one sort or another. "New" urban settlements, which were large villages rather than *poleis* like Mampsis in the Negev or Areopolis (Rabbat-Moab) in Palestine III, survived beyond the conquests. Petra, once thought to have entered terminal decline following the tremendous earthquake of 363 also apparently continued to thrive at least through the 6th century, and probably beyond. At the moment, the balance of evidence from this region indicates there was no serious decay in either the size or number of sites in southern Syria immediately before or after the conquests, either due to climatic conditions or potential disruptions from the Sasanian or Arab invasions.[44] Avni, for example, has investigated sites from the Negev and these seem also to have flourished at least through the 8th century. Aila ('Aqaba), a major maritime outlet for the products of the Negev, such as dates and wine, remained prominent in the Umayyad period and was rebuilt astride a regular grid and equipped

---

44   Petra: Browning, *Petra*; the evidence for continuity grows: see Caldwell, "Beyond the rock".

with an impressive set of walls in the model of Byzantine urbanism. The case of Palestine III provides another instance of continuity of late-antique extension of the arable landscape, expanding settlement, production geared toward the market, and intensively farmed specialist crops.[45]

Expansion of agriculture also proceeded elsewhere in the Levant, especially in inland regions. One of the consequences of the rise of the caliphate was that, for the first time in more than 800 years, the Euphrates did not form the edge of competing states. Though over much of its course the Euphrates has cut deep into its channel and is pent up by relatively high stone banks, the middle courses that formed the boundary between Byzantium and Persia had potential for irrigation that could not be developed on a large scale due to friction between the two empires. This situation certainly changed under the later Umayyads and early 'Abbasids, who restored ancient derelict systems, some of them belonging to the Bronze Age, and developed others as they embarked on schemes of agricultural improvement and development.

The investment on the marginal or undeveloped land by those at the pinnacle of the elite raises a number of interesting questions, especially regarding the availability of land that seems to have been scarce just a few generations removed from the first great grabs of the conquests. It likely tells also of the continuation of many of the same crops and forms of intensive farming practiced in the region far before the conquests and the recovery of the urban markets of Mesopotamia. The caliph Hisham b. Abd al-Malik (AD 724–43) is credited with ordering sweeping irrigation projects in the region of the former Byzantine–Sasanian frontier; prior to the conquest, this region was irrigated by smaller-scale and localized canal networks. The former Byzantine *limes* on the Middle Euphrates lay beyond the 200 mm isohyet in which dry farming of cereals (mostly barley) was possible; irrigation was therefore an absolute necessity. Near ancient Barbalissos (Maskanah), Hisham's brother, Maslama b. 'Abd al-Malik (d. AD c.729), ordered the excavation and channeling of the Bet Balish canal; waters from this installation irrigated the region of the palace and estate known as Hisn Maslama (Madinat al-Far).[46] The riparian landscape from Maskanah to Ar-Raqqah was developed especially under the later Umayyads. Formerly the frontier fortress city of Callinicum near the confluence of the Balikh and Euphrates, Ar-Raqqa was recognized for its strategic value close to the restive anti-regime elements in Iraq and also possessed of abundant abandoned or otherwise unclaimed potential farmland on which peasants could be

---

45 Avni, *Nomads, farmers, and town-dwellers*; Avni, *The Byzantine-Islamic transition in Palestine*, p. 19; Whitcomb, "The misr of Ayla".

46 Madinat al-Far as the possible Hisn Maslama: Haas, "Madinat al-Far/Hisn Maslama".

settled and cash-generating estate agriculture established. Around Ar-Raqqa, Hisham ordered the construction of two major canal networks, the Hani and al-Mari, each of which watered an eponymous royal estate that must have been of great size. The excavation of new canals, the renovation of derelict ancient systems, or some combination of the two resulted in a considerable growth in the agricultural capacity of the region and vast revenues. Finally, in the region of ancient Circesium (Al-Busayrah) at the confluence of the Khabur and Euphrates, Hisham's engineers built the Zaytunah canal.[47] The Zuqnin Chronicle emphasizes the verdancy of the spaces made possible by these large-scale irrigation works; the parks, fields and farms of the large Umayyad estates were "adorned with plants of all kinds".[48] Maslama also invested in the marshlands of southern Iraq, which the Umayyads were busy in draining, as their Sasanian predecessors had. According to Baladhuri (d. AD 892), when al-Walid balked at the estimate of three million dirhams required to repair breaches in the dykes in the marshlands of the Tigris-Euphrates, Maslama offered to pay for the repair costs if he could keep the lands that were thereby reclaimed.[49] It was also an area where many lands were intensively farmed and where jockeying for control of the best arable was heated; one of the keys to the downfall of the caliph 'Uthman (AD 632–34) was his offer to the elites of Madina to trade lands in South Arabia for lucrative parcels in the rich lands of Mesopotamia, where massive Umayyad investment in agricultural and urbanism apparently had reversed whatever decline had occurred there under the later Sasanians. Umayyad estates in Mesopotamia were vast and intensively cultivated. The portions of the al-Muhallaban estate of the Omani Muhallab family, confiscated by the Marwanids and returned to them by the first 'Abbasid caliph Abul al-'Abbas al-Saffah (AD 749–54) yielded the astounding sum of 4,000 dinars (solidi) per day![50] Banaji has drawn a vivid picture of the teeming economic activity of Iraq in the late-Umayyad period, where tax receipts under the Umayyads and early 'Abbasids amounted to something like ten million dinars – and this massive sum excluded receipts from Khuzistan.[51] It seems that the rich fertile lands of the Sawad benefited especially from renewed efforts at reclaiming marshland where the hot climate, long growing season, and abundance of water favored the spread of cash crops one most associated with early Islamic agriculture such as rice and saffron.[52] Iraq faced its share of

47 EI^2 "Rakka"; Zaytunah: Yaqut III, p. 163; on the *Wasit al-Raqqa* see Yaqut V, pp. 451–52.
48 *Chronicle of Zuqnin*, trans. Harrak, pp. 160–61.
49 Baladhuri, trans. Hitti, p. 456.
50 Hinds, *An early Islamic family from Oman*, p. 84; Banaji, "Late antique Legacies", p. 171.
51 Banaji, "Late antique Legacies".
52 Morony, "Landholding and Social Change"; Dūrī, *Arabische Wirtschaftsgeshichte*.

disturbances and rebellion and therefore witnessed military activity, of course. But whatever damage Iraq incurred from war and environmental degradation (whether natural or human-caused), it seems the trajectory of Umayyad and early 'Abbasid farming was generally upwards.

Unlike the vast reclamation projects found in Mesopotamia, but equally intriguing, is another curious feature of Umayyad agriculture are the so-called Desert Castles, a string of residences garlanded on the edge of the North Arabian Desert like a string of pearls. At places like Qasr al-Hayr al-Sharqi, Qasr al-Hayr al-Gharbi, Hallabat and Qusayr Amra, various Umayyad princes built palatial complexes and irrigation works.[53] Though scholars have puzzled over the nature of these places for generations, their domestic and agricultural infrastructure makes it clear that describing them as fortified farms is not wholly appropriate. Most are in the midst of poor soils with little hope for much of a return on crops without significant nutrient input, either through manuring or some other method. It is doubtful that the qanats and saqiyas of the Desert Castles were primarily intended to serve an agricultural function; a domestic one for drinking and bathing seems likely to be their primary use. At most of these sites, the qanats and territories they watered do not today appear sufficiently extensive to support large-scale agriculture. But it is not unrealistic to see enclosed gardens, intensively worked and carefully managed in the fashion that people of Arabia and the Levant had for centuries, as centerpieces in these complexes. The image of paradise captured in the splendid mosaics of the Great Mosque of Damascus was reflected in these intimate desert parks that also echoed the great lush game and pleasure *paradeisoi* of Byzantium and Persia. For the space dedicated to edibles, priority was no doubt given to succulents and fresh fruits to adorn the tables of the elites during periodic visits to these isolated spots. The Desert Castle enclosures and other royal garden spaces were probably among the earliest experimental gardens in the Islamic world. In these precincts, exotic plants could have been propagated and thereby acclimated to new environments. Rarer plants (sugar cane) were likely grown for pleasure rather than profit in places like the enclosure at Qasr al-Hayr al-Sharqi, which lies on the desert route from Damascus to the Euphrates and not far from Rusafa.[54] Lest we find the idea fanciful, one need look no further than the royal botanical gardens and intensive agriculture as practiced in Umayyad Spain for later parallels or the early 'Abbasid translations from Greek by Qusta ibn Luqa (d. 912/13) into Arabic of numerous Greek and Syriac

---

53 Genequand, "Some thoughts on Qasr al-Hayr al-Gharbi".
54 Genequand, "From 'desert castles' to medieval town", p. 353.

technical treatises, including at least one surviving agronomic work.[55] Interest in such literature was acute and its translation fits well within the overall picture of the world of early Islam: confident, vast, and expansive.

5   Crops and Techniques

Crops and techniques certainly diffused westwards and northwards through lands under the caliphate. The claims made by most historians about the pace and depth of change, and even the technologies and crops involved, are greatly exaggerated. While Andrew Watson brought deserved attention to the contributions of agriculturists of medieval Islam a wide and much-deserved audience, the assertions of him and others like Donald Hill and Thomas Glick ignored the considerable evidence for ancient achievements in the areas of plant and animal husbandry, as well as in the mechanical sciences as they related to agriculture. These scholars also tend to focus on a slender portion of the Mediterranean world as well, being focused almost exclusively on the Iberian Peninsula. While Toufic Fahd has provided an edition and commentary on the vast *Kitab al-filaha al-nabatiyya* attributed to Ibn Wahshiyya (10th century), there has been comparatively little work done on agriculture in the eastern lands of Islam.[56] Space and time do not permit their full articulation herein, but in exploring continuity and change in Levantine agriculture after antiquity, some of the main pillars of the so-called "Green Revolution" may be explored.

Those who advocate the Islamic "Green Revolution" insist that a surge in the use and spread of irrigation technology during the first centuries of Islam underpinned a massive expansion of the farmed area into former wastelands and an intensification of cultivation, and that it aided the introduction of new crops, mostly of tropical origin, into the Mediterranean and surrounding regions. However, hydraulic technologies that were believed to have been diffused so rapidly were already in widespread use over much of the Roman Empire. Devices such as the saqiya, *shaduf,* and qanat had long been in use within Byzantine territory prior to the arrival of Islam. Part of the problem in tracing the spread and depth of the dissemination of these technologies is the nature of the materials used in their construction. In places where wood

---

55   Bolens, "Engrais et protection de la fertilité"; Bolens, "La revolution agricole andalouse"; Bolens, "La greffe et les metamorphoses"; Bolens "Riquezas de la tierra andaluza"; Lagardè, "Cépages, raisin et vin en al-Andalus".
56   Fahd, "Materiaux pour l'histoire de l'agriculture en Irak".

was rare – Egypt for example – Wilson presciently has argued that saqiya pots (qadus jars) in clay have allowed us to recover a clear picture of their ubiquity, but in areas where wood was more plentiful and where wooden compartments or buckets were favored, the archaeological evidence tends to be scarce.[57] If the late-antique Levant is any indication of the prevalence of the saqiya (and by extension similar contemporary lifting technologies) then these devices were depended upon heavily from Syria through Egypt. While specific evidence from the Maghreb and Iberia are lacking at this time, we have to await either further archaeological discoveries or textual evidence before we make a full assessment of the technological milieu across the years of Byzantine–Umayyad rule. However, given the close relationship between Iberia and North Africa prior to and after the Umayyad conquests, it scarcely seems believable that these regions did not share in these technological innovations. Indeed, Butzer indicates that foundational elements of Iberian agriculture were Roman, and Shaw has noted that many of the key features of irrigation in North Africa pre-dated the arrival of the Romans. Certainly the Berber and Carthaginian communities were experts at managing their environment and practiced forms of intensive agriculture for centuries before the Roman and Islamic conquests.

Nor does there appear to be in the Umayyad and early ʿAbbasid periods, at least, a broad shift in the cropping regime. Barley continued to be a major staple in the dry-farmed and irrigated environments of the Jazira and Iraq, just as it had been when those regions were governed by the Byzantines and Sasanians.[58] The crop was well adapted and a safe choice for cultivators there, as its durability in the archaeological record attests. Crops that were more recent introductions, but which nonetheless had been part of the diet in parts of Persia and the Levant since the Hellenistic period at the latest, continued to be grown in those regions to which they were well-suited. Rice was widely known in the Roman Empire and was not likely to be an Arab introduction into most of the former lands of the empire.[59]

As I have explained elsewhere, the changes engendered by the arrival of Islamic rule did not necessarily imprint themselves in the countryside. In many regions, the basic mix of staple crops known to many as the Mediterranean triad of grain, wine, and olive oil, were already in place by the Bronze Age at the latest. Over much of the Levant, Muslim taboos on wine rendered the latter a socially risky commodity that may well have rendered one vulnerable to discrimination and persecution at the hands of Muslim elites, however rare such

---

57   Wilson, "Classical water technology in the early Islamic world".
58   Decker, "Settlement and agriculture in the Levant, 6th–8th centuries".
59   Decker, "Plants and progress".

persecutions may have been. In Egypt, for example, the explosive growth of wine production that accompanied the Christianization of the countryside in parallel with significant pressures on cereal-producing flooded fields and the continued spread of Hellenistic or Near Eastern irrigation technology like the saqiya, led to significant changes in cropping strategies, labor, and investment. Egypt trailed Palestine in realizing the potential for selling wine abroad – by the time it was poised to do so, conditions of the 7th and 8th centuries no longer favored the long-distance exchange of wine. Instead, during the Early Islamic period, Egypt apparently absorbed large quantities of the beverage internally and exported small quantities to Palestine and perhaps communities around the Red Sea.[60]

Both significant continuity and equally considerable change are evident through the first centuries of the Arab dominion of the Levant. In the broadest sense, agriculture remained relatively stable. Regional difference is readily apparent in continued expansion in some marginal regions but abandonment in others (the post-Umayyad Golan and Negev). An exploration of these acute regional changes will offer a more complete picture of this pivotal period in the history of humans and their environment.

Bibliography

Abudanh, F. and S. Twaissi, "Innovation or Technology Immigration? The Qanat Systems in the Regions of Udhruh and Ma'an in Southern Jordan." *Bulletin of the American Schools of Oriental Research*, (2010), pp. 67–87.

Adams, R.McC., *Land Behind Baghdad: A History of Settlement on the Diyala Plains* (Chicago 1965).

Avner, U., "Acient Water Management in the Southern Negev", *ARAM* 13–14 (2001–2002) pp. 403–21.

Avni, G., *Nomads, Farmers, and Town-Dwellers: Pastoralist-Sedentist Interaction in the Negev Highlands, Sixth–Eighth Centuries CE* (Jerusalem, 1996).

Avni, G., *The Byzantine-Islamic Transition in Palestine: An Archaeological Approach* (Oxford, 2014).

Banaji, J., "Late Antique Legacies and Muslim Economic Expansion", in J.F. Haldon (ed.), *Money, Power and Politics in Early Islamic Syria a Review of Current Debates* (Burlington, VT) pp. 165–76.

Baruch, U., "The Late Holocene Vegetational History of Lake Kinneret (Sea of Galilee), Israel", *Paléorient*, (1986), pp. 37–48.

---

60 Decker, forthcoming.

Benovitz, N., "The Justinianic Plague: Evidence from the Dated Greek Epitaphs of Byzantine Palestine and Arabia." *Journal of Roman Archaeology* 27 (2014), 487–98.

Bolens, L., "Engrais et protection de la fertilité dans l'agronomie Hispano-Arabe xie–xiie siècles", *Études rurales* 46 (1972), pp. 34–60.

Bolens, L., "La greffe et les métamorphoses du jardin Andalou au Moyen Age (Xi^e–Xii^e Siècles)." *Études rurales* (1977), pp. 93–106.

Bolens, L., "La révolution agricole Andalouse du xie siècle." *Studia Islamica* 47 (1978), pp. 121–41.

Bolens, L., "Riquezas de la tierra Andaluza y primacía del aceite de oliva en la sociedad y la civilización de Al-Andalus (Siglos x–xvi)", *Agricultura y sociedad* 80–81 (1996), pp. 181–216.

Böll, A. *et al.*, "Late Holocene Primary Productivity and Sea Surface Temperature Variations in the Northeastern Arabian Sea: Implications for Winter Monsoon Variability", *Paleoceanography* 29, no. 8 (2014): pp. 778–94.

Bookman, R., Y. Enzel, A. Agnon and M. Stein, "Late Holocene Lake Levels of the Dead Sea", *Geological Society of America Bulletin* 116, no. 5–6 (2004), pp. 555–71.

Brunner, U., "The Great Dam and the Sabean Oasis of Ma'rib", *Irrigation and Drainage Systems* 14, no. 3 (2000), pp. 167–82.

Brunner, U., *Die Erforschung Der Antiken Oase Von Marib Mit Hilfe Geomorphologischer Untersuchungsmethoden* (Mainz 1983).

Caldwell, R.C. and T. Gagos, "Beyond the Rock: Petra in the Sixth Century C.E. in the light of the Papyri," in T.E. Levy, P.M. Daviau, R.W. Younker and M. Sha'er (eds.), *Crossing Jordan: North American Contributions to the Archaeology of Jordan* (London 2007), pp. 425–33.

Dauphine, Cl., *La Palestine byzantineL peuplement et populations* (Oxford 1998).

Decker, M.J., "Plants and Progress: Rethinking the Islamic Agricultural Revolution." *Journal of World History* 20, no. 2 (2009), pp. 187–206.

Decker, M.J., *Tilling the Hateful Earth: Agricultural Production and Trade in the Late Antique East* (Oxford 2009).

Decker, M.J., "Settlement and Agriculture in the Levant, 6th–8th Centuries." In A. Borrut (ed.), *Le Proche-Orient De Justinien Aux Abassides: Peuplement et dynamiques spatiales : Actes Du Colloque "Continuités De L'occupation Entre Les Périodes Byzantine Et Abbasside Au Proche-Orient, Vii^e–Ix^e Siècles," Paris, 18–20 Octobre 2007* (Turnhout, Belgium 2011) pp. 1–6.

Decker, M.J., "Egypt in the Wine Trade of Late Antiquity and the Early Middle Ages." (forthcoming).

Di Segni, L., "Epigraphic Documentation on Building in the Provinces of Palaestina and Arabia, 4th–7th C." in J.H. Humphrey (ed.), *The Roman and Byzantine near East, Volume 2* (Ann Arbor MI 1999) pp. 149–78.

Dūrī, ʿA., *Arabische Wirtschaftsgeschichte*. Translated by Jürgen Jacobi. Zurich and Munich, 1979.

Eastwood, W.J., M.J. Leng, N. Roberts and B. Davis, "Holocene Climate Change in the Eastern Mediterranean Region: A Comparison of Stable Isotope and Pollen Data from Lake Gölhisar, Southwest Turkey", *Journal of Quaternary Science* 22, no. 4 (2007), pp. 327–41.

Enzel, Y., et al., "Late Holocene Climates of the near East Deduced from Dead Sea Level Variations and Modern Regional Winter Rainfall", *Quaternary Research* 60, no. 3 (2003) pp. 263–73.

Fahd, T., "Materiaux pour l'histoire de L'agriculture en Irak: Al-Filāḥa n-Nabaṭiyya" *Handbuch der Orientalistik* I.VI.1, (1952), pp. 276–377.

Finné, M., et al., "Speleothem Evidence for Late Holocene Climate Variability and Floods in Southern Greece", *Quaternary Research* (2014), pp. 213–27.

Floh, P. et al., "Late Holocene droughts in the Fertile Crescent recorded in a speleothem from northern Iraq," *Geophysical Research Letters* 44, no. 3 (2017), pp. 1528–1536.

Genequand, D., "From 'Desert Castle' to Medieval Town: Qasr Al-Hayr Al-Sharqi (Syria)", *Antiquity* 79, no. 304 (2005), pp. 350–61.

Genequand, D., "Some Thoughts on Qasr Al-Hayr Al-Gharbi, Its Dam, Its Monastery and the Ghassanids." *Levant* 38, no. 1 (2006) pp. 63–84.

Girdler, R.W., "The Dead Sea Transform Fault System", *Tectonophysics* 180, no. 1 (1990), pp. 1–13.

Harper, K., *The Fate of Rome: Climate, Disease, and the End of an Empire* (Princeton 2017).

Haase, Cl.-P., "Madinat Al-Far/Hisn Maslama-First Archaeological Soundings at the Site and the History of an Umayyad Domain in Abbasid Times." In M. Bakhit and R. Schick (eds.), *Bilad al-Sham During the Abbasid Period. Proceedings of the Fifth International Conference on the History of Bilad al-Sham* (Amman 1991) pp. 206–25.

Hadas, G., "Ein Gedi Water Mills", *Bulletin of the Anglo-Israel Archaeological Society* 19–20, (2001–2002), pp. 71–97.

Haldon, J. et al., "The Climate and Environment of Byzantine Anatolia: Integrating Science, History, and Archaeology", *Journal of Interdisciplinary History* 45, no. 2 (2014) pp. 113–61.

Hinds, M., *An Early Islamic Family from Oman: Al-ʾAwtabī's Account of the Muhallabids*. Translated by Martin Hinds (Manchester 1991).

Hirschfeld, Y., "En-Gedi: 'A Very Large Village of Jews'", *Liber Annuus* 55, no. 1 (2005) pp. 327–54.

Hoyland, R.G., *Arabia and the Arabs: From the Bronze Age to the Coming of Islam* (London 2001).

Huntington, E., *Palestine and Its Transformation* (Boston 1911).

Issar, A.S., *Climate Changes During the Holocene and Their Impact on Hydrological Systems* (Cambridge 2003).

Izdebski, A., "The Changing Landscapes of Byzantine Northern Anatolia", *Archaeologia Bulgarica* 16, no. 1 (2012) pp. 47–66.

Izdebski, A., *et al.* "The environmental, archaeological and historical evidence for regional climatic changes and their societal impacts in the Eastern Mediterranean in Late Antiquity," *Quaternary Science Reviews* 136 (2016) pp. 189–208.

Kaniewski, D. *et al.*, "The Medieval Climate Anomaly and the Little Ice Age in Coastal Syria Inferred from Pollen-Derived Palaeoclimatic Patterns", *Global and Planetary Change* 78, no. 3 (2011) pp. 178–87.

Kedar, B.Z., "The Arab Conquests and Agriculture: A Seventh-Century Apocalypse, Satellite Imagery, and Palynology", *Asian and African Studies* 19 (1985) pp. 1–15.

Kennedy, H., "From Polis to Madina: Urban Change in Late Antique and Early Islamic Syria." *Past & Present*, no. 106 (1985) pp. 3–27.

Lagardère, V. "Cépages, raisin et vin en Al-Andalus (x^e–xve siècle)", *Médiévales* 16, no. 33 (1997) pp. 81–90.

Leroy, S., "Pollen Analysis of Core Ds7-1sc (Dead Sea) Showing Intertwined Effects of Climatic Change and Human Activities in the Late Holocene", *Journal of Archaeological Science* 37, no. 2 (2010) pp. 306–16.

Liu, L.-B., E. Roeloffs and X.-Y. Zheng, "Seismically Induced Water Level Fluctuations in the Wali Well, Beijing, China", *Journal of Geophysical Research: Solid Earth (1978–2012)* 94, no. B7 (1989) pp. 9453–62.

Magness, J., *The Archaeology of the Early Islamic Settlement in Palestine* (Winona Lake, IN 2003).

McCormick, M., "Climate Change During and After the Roman Empire: Reconstructing the Past from Scientific and Historical Evidence", *Journal of Interdisciplinary History* 43 (2012) pp. 169–220.

Morony, M., "Landholding and Social Change: Lower Al-'Irāq in the Early Islamic Period." In T. Khalidi (ed.) *Land Tenure and Social Transformation in the Middle East* (Beirut 1984) pp. 209–22.

Neumann, F.H., E.J. Kagan, S.A.G. Leroy and U. Baruch, "Vegetation History and Climate Fluctuations on a Transect Along the Dead Sea West Shore and Their Impact on Past Societies over the Last 3500 Years." *Journal of Arid Environments* 74, no. 7 (2010) pp. 756–64.

Neumann, F.H., E.J. Kagan, M.J. Schwab and M. Stein, "Palynology, Sedimentology and Palaeoecology of the Late Holocene Dead Sea", *Quaternary Science Reviews* 26, no. 11 (2007) pp. 1476–98.

Orland, I.J., M. Bar-Matthews, N.T. Kita, A. Ayalon, A. Matthews and J.W. Valley, "Climate Deterioration in the Eastern Mediterranean as Revealed by Ion Microprobe Analysis of a Speleothem That Grew from 2.2 to 0.9 ka in Soreq Cave, Israel", *Quaternary Research* 71, no. 1 (2009) pp. 27–35.

Perry, J.R., A.S. Shahbazi, E. Kettenhofen, "Deportations" *Encyclopaedia Iranica* http://www.iranicaonline.org/articles/deportations (accessed January 4 2015).

Sahas, D.J., *John of Damascus on Islam: The "Heresy of the Ishmaelites"* (Leiden 1972).

Schwab, M.J., F. Neumann, T. Litt, J.F.W. Negendank and M. Stein, "Holocene Palaeoecology of the Golan Heights (near East): Investigation of Lacustrine Sediments from Birkat Ram Crater Lake." *Quaternary Science Reviews* 23, no. 16 (2004) pp. 1723–31.

Sodini, J.-P. *et al.*, "Déhès (Syrie du Nord), Campagnes I–III (1976–1978): Recherches sur l'habitat rural", *Syria* 57 (1980) pp. 1–103.

Stathakopoulos, D.Ch., *Famine and Pestilence in the Late Roman and Early Byzantine Empire: A Systematic Survey of Subsistence Crises and Epidemics* (Aldershot, Hants, England 2004).

Tchalenko, G., *Villages Antiques de la Syrie du Nord: Le Massif du Bélus à L'époque Romaine*. 3 vols. (Paris 1953–58).

Vermoere, M. *et al.*, "Pollen Sequences from the City of Sagalassos (Pisidia, Southwest Turkey)." *Anatolian Studies* 53 (2003) pp. 161–73.

Whitby, M., *The Emperor Maurice and His Historian: Theophylact Simocatta on Persian and Balkan Warfare* (Oxford 1988).

Whitcomb, D., "The *Misr* of Ayla: Settlement at Al-'Aqaba in the Early Islamic Period." In G.R.D. King and A. Cameron (eds.) *The Byzantine and Early Islamic Near East, II: Land Use and Settlement Patterns* (Princeton, N.J. 1994) pp. 155–70.

Wündsch, M. *et al.*, "ENSO and Monsoon variability during the Past 1.5 kyr as reflected in sediments from Lake Kalimpaa, Central Sulawesi (Indonesia)", *Holocene* 24, no. 12 (2014) pp. 1743–56.

Xoplaki, E., *et al.* "The Medieval Climate Anomaly and Byzantium: A review of the evidence on climatic fluctuations, economic performance and societal change", *Quaternary Science Reviews* 136 (2016) pp. 229–52.

Yasuda, Y., H. Kitagawa and T. Nakagawa, "The Earliest Record of Major Anthropogenic Deforestation in the Ghab Valley, Northwest Syria: A Palynological Study", *Quaternary International* 73–74 (2000) pp. 127–36.

Zohar, A. and E. Lev, "Trends in the Use of Perfumes and Incense in the near East after the Muslim Conquests", *Journal of the Royal Asiatic Society (Third Series)* 23,1 (2013) pp. 11–30.

CHAPTER 10

Sagalassos and Its Environs during Late Roman and Byzantine Times

Johan Bakker, Eva Kaptijn, Peter Talloen, Ralf Vandam and Jeroen Poblome

Introduction

Sagalassos is an archaeological site in the southwestern Taurus Mountains, Turkey (Fig. 10.1). The region in which Sagalassos is located has been frequented since Middle Palaeolithic times,[1] while the earliest archaeological traces of the presence of an organized community at the site date to the (later) 5th century BC.[2] The polis saw its heydays during later Hellenistic and Roman Imperial times, which was reflected in the surrounding landscape by an increase in fire activity, erosion of the hillsides and agricultural practices.[3] The site remained permanently occupied until AD c.1200,[4] while the surrounding rural landscape can be assumed to have been continuously inhabited until the present.

Since 1986, the Sagalassos Archaeological Research Project has been involved in studying, surveying and excavating the ancient city. From the outset, the project aimed at an interdisciplinary approach, documenting all aspects of the environment and daily life in antiquity[5] and therefore started to include an array of natural sciences, including geography, geology, palaeozoology, archaeobotany, palynology, and archaeometry. The combined efforts of all specialties involved provide valuable information not only on how the town itself developed over time, but also its relationship with the surrounding rural landscape, and the interrelatedness of man and environment.

---

1 Vandam et al., "On the Margins", pp. 323–5; Daems and Poblome, "Pottery of Late Achaemenid Sagalassos".
2 Talloen and Poblome, "Control excavations on and around the Upper Agora", p. 114.
3 Kaniewski et al., "Long term effects of human impact", p. 1994; Six et al., "Late Holocene sediment characteristics and sediment accumulation", p. 206.
4 Vionis et al., "Ceramic continuity and daily life", pp. 203–4; Poblome et al., "Sagalassos", pp. 308–11.
5 Waelkens et al., "Man and environment", p. 697; Poblome (Ed.), *Exempli Gratia*.

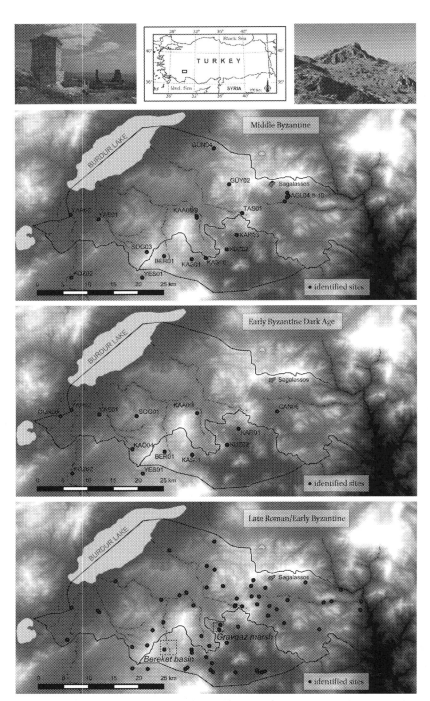

FIGURE 10.1 Settlement patterns in the territory of ancient Sagalassos (black line: territory boundary, inner line is Hellenistic border, outer line is Roman imperial border)

Until recently, the focus of these research efforts lay mostly with the Roman Imperial and Early Byzantine periods, with a special focus on the Beyşehir Occupation Phase (BO Phase). This period, distinguished in palynological records as a characteristic increase in human impact, and first observed in palynological records from the Beyşehir basin (Southwest Turkey),[6] occurred roughly between 3000 and 1300 years before present. These dates are generalizations however, as its chronology can vary quite significantly between sites, even among relatively well-dated records or records located at a relatively small distance from one another, as evidenced by the research presented in this chapter.[7]

From an archaeo-environmental standpoint, the period following the BO Phase is far less understood. In recent years, more attention is being paid to other forms of society beside the hierarchical, urbanized community of the Roman period.[8] Chronologically, this includes a focus on earlier and later centuries.[9] Within this new research focus of the project, key moments of change in the nature–society nexus play a crucial role. The period encompassing the end of the Roman age and the Byzantine period is of particular interest, as it covers a series of important shifts in habitation pattern and land use, as well as several notable shifts in environmental conditions. This chapter combines the current understanding of the archaeology, palynology and other relevant disciplines to provide an overview of the identified changes in land use, vegetation, and environment in the study area of Sagalassos, from the 3rd until the 13th centuries AD.[10]

---

6   Eastwood et al., "Palaeoecological and Archaeological Evidence", p. 70.
7   E.g. Bottema and Woldring, "Anthropogenic indicators"; Bottema et al., "Palynological investigations"; Eastwood et al., "Palaeoecological and archaelogical evidence"; van Zeist et al., "Late Quaternary Vegetation and climate". See Roberts, "Revisiting the Beyşehir Occupation Phase" for a recent detailed overview.
8   E.g. Poblome, "Shifting societal complexity".
9   Bakker, *Late Holocene vegetation dynamics*; Vandam, "Everybody needs good neighbours".
10 The time span discussed here encompasses the most important changes in the archaeological record as well as in the environment. While the Late Roman period is generally considered to start in AD 300, the entire 3rd century is included as changes in environment are already visible then. Similarly, the 13th century AD is included. Although activity at the city of Sagalassos is currently thought to end around c.1200, the wet conditions of the Medieval Climatic Anomaly continue until the mid-13th century AD. The different types of information combined in this article sometimes result in a different periodization (based on historical event, archaeological data and environmental changes). An overview is given in Table 10.1.

1 Changing Habitation Patterns and City-Countryside Relations from the 3rd to the 13th Century AD

In the territory of Sagalassos, the Late Roman/Early Byzantine period (AD 300–650) is characterized by a high settlement density. Throughout the entire territory, settlements have been found ranging from farms, hamlets to farms and (large) villages (Fig. 10.1).[11] Press weights (Fig. 10.2h) and grinding stones have been found at several locations and, together with the presence of settlements, show that the countryside surrounding Sagalassos was intensively cultivated. The occurrence over the entire territory of Sagalassos Red Slip Ware sherds, produced at Sagalassos, and the presence in the city of agricultural products from the territory show the close connection between the city and its hinterland in this period.[12]

The central position Sagalassos occupied during the Roman period seems to have weakened during the Byzantine Dark Ages (mid-7th to 9th century AD). Not only had Sagalassos itself started to de-urbanize from the middle of the 6th century,[13] but in most parts of the territory the number of identified rural settlements is significantly lower than for the previous period (see Fig. 10.1). An exception is formed by the area southeast of Sagalassos. A recent intensive survey has identified several villages, and settlement density even increases during the Byzantine Dark Ages (see below).[14] Several potential causes may have contributed to this decentralization and loss of complexity of the society. From AD 541/2 onward, the Justinianic plague reappeared several times, from 640 onward Arab incursions reached inland Anatolia, there was a decline in long-distance trade, and Sagalassos and its territory were hit by a severe earthquake around the middle of the 7th century AD.[15] Additionally, there is a dis-

---

11 Vanhaverbeke, "The evolution of the settlement pattern"; Waelkens et al., "The 1994 and 1995 surveys"; Waelkens et al., "The 1996 and 1997 surveys". This pattern has been corroborated in the intensive surveys: Vanhaverbeke et al., "The 2008 and 2009 survey seasons"; Kaptijn et al., "Inhabiting the Burdur Plain"; Kaptijn et al., "Societal changes in the Bereket valley"; Vandam et al., "The 2012 archaeological survey"; Vandam et al., "Living on the margins".
12 Poblome and Degeest, "The archaeological evidence: ceramics", p. 140; e.g. Vanhaverbeke et al., "Urban-rural integration".
13 Vionis et al., "The hidden material culture of the Dark Ages", p. 149.
14 Vandam et al., "Living on the margins".
15 The earthquake was dated using radiocarbon dated pellets (540–620, 95.4 per cent) from owls inhabiting a (partly) abandoned bath building prior to the earthquake; coins dating to the later part of the reign of Heraclius (630–641) have been found in several locations underneath the earthquake debris, which indicate a later date for the earthquake. De Cupere et al., "Eagle owl (Bubo bubo) pellets from Roman Sagalassos", p. 4.

tinction in the potential recovery rate of Byzantine Dark Ages sites and those of the preceding period. The former are generally smaller (with the exception of the area southeast of Sagalassos) and lack significant structural remains, and are hence less obtrusive. None of these phenomena can conclusively be held responsible for the attested societal shift, but they may all have contributed to some extent. The possible influence of climatic change upon settlement patterns will be discussed later in this chapter. While there is no complete break between the Late Roman/Early Byzantine period and the Byzantine Dark Ages, and several aspects of society and material culture continue, a gradual social transformation seems to have occurred away from an intensively exploited countryside focussed on a provincial urban centre towards a more village-oriented society. This transition is accompanied by reduced archaeological visibility, which possibly makes the distinction between the two periods appear larger than it was in reality.

At Sagalassos, indications of loss of complexity are already present in the second half of the 6th century; few new building activities were initiated, artisanal and commercial units on the Lower and Upper Agora and along the colonnaded street were one by one deserted, but never completely, and activity did continue to some degree.[16] At the moment of the earthquake, Sagalassos was not the characteristic ancient urban centre it had previously been. But the earthquake did not mean the end of Sagalassos as a centre. Continued occupation is clearly attested by the clearance of debris, e.g. the clean-up of the interior of the Bouleuterion Basilica and the drums of fallen columns which were pushed to the side of the colonnaded street.[17] However, occupation continued in different ways. During the 7th century, a fortification wall with towers was constructed, closing off one of the main roads in the city and enclosing a now inhabited promontory in front of the ancient city around the ruins of the sanctuary of Antoninus Pius. This fortified settlement might have functioned as a *kastron*.[18] Research also indicates that cattle is kept closer to the polluted urban centre of the city, and no longer appears to originate from elsewhere in the territory.[19] While Sagalassos was reduced in size and importance, the present evidence suggest that it continued to fulfil certain regional functions.

---

16 Waelkens et al., "The Late Antique to Early Byzantine City", pp. 231–5; Jacobs, "From Early Byzantium to the Middle Ages".
17 Poblome et al., "Sagalassos", pp. 304–305; Jacobs, "From Early Byzantium to the Middle Ages".
18 Poblome et al., "Sagalassos".
19 Fuller et al., "Isotopic reconstruction of human diet", pp. 163–4, Vanhaverbeke et al., "Urban-rural integration", pp. 80–1.

Its functioning as a *kastron* was further sustained by the continued presence of a bishop.[20]

In the countryside, regional differences occur: the direct vicinity of Sagalassos shows a very different settlement than more remote parts of the territory. Unfortunately, it is impossible to date the rural settlements very precisely, as they have only been surveyed, not excavated. In the wider territory we observe that, into the second half of the 6th century, the number of settlements remained high, while only a smaller portion could be dated to the Byzantine Dark Ages a century later (see Fig. 10.1). While there are clear differences between the Late Roman/Early Byzantine period and the Byzantine Dark Ages, i.e. in the settlement pattern and the character of Sagalassos, there is also a lot of continuity. The settlements of the Byzantine Dark Ages had almost exclusively been large village settlements during the Roman Imperial period (see Table 10.2). While the isolated farms, hamlets and farmstead sites disappeared, the collected pottery shows that the larger villages continued to be inhabited during the Byzantine Dark Ages. Only four new sites originated in this period in the more remote areas of the territory. Two of these are simple pottery concentrations in caves, probably left by shepherds who occasionally took shelter there, and one is a small site along the Düğer river in the middle of agricultural land – a location that resembles Roman settlement preference. The newly founded site of Soğanlı – Ilyas Tepesi (SOG01) is markedly different. This single period site is located on the highest spot in the middle of the badlands to the east of Lake Burdur (see Fig. 10.1).[21] The wide vicinity is unsuitable for crop cultivation, and the only reason to occupy this inaccessible remote location seem to be the wide views. The choice for this location is the only indication that times might not have been entirely peaceful, and that overview and possibly seclusion were desirable at times.

While the location of this site and the fortified promontory at Sagalassos could suggest the presence of a threat,[22] the majority of the rural villages show little or no signs suggesting a concern for security. Several Arab inland expeditions have been recorded in the region of Pisidia,[23] but small rural villages in remote inland valleys like those in the territory of Sagalassos do not seem to have been substantially affected.

20 Mitchell, "The settlement of Pisidia", p. 150; Poblome, "Shifting societal complexity", p. 6; Poblome et al., "Sagalassos", p. 306.
21 Waelkens et al., "The 1996 and 1997 surveys", p. 129.
22 Fortifications can also be erected to claim status, express ownership, inspire awe, etc., and do not necessarily have a defensive role.
23 Although none have been recorded in our research area. Belke and Mersich, *Tabula Imperii Byzantini* 7, p. 86.

In the direct vicinity of Sagalassos, the settlement data from the Dereköy Highlands in particular (8 km to the southeast of the former), but also from recent discoveries immediately south of the city,[24] illustrate the presence of a considerable Byzantine population in the countryside close to Sagalassos, with a clear continuation of the Late Antique settlement pattern. The recently conducted intensive survey in the Dereköy Highlands revealed remains of a large number of sites, ranging from isolated farms, churches, (agricultural) villages, and even a secondary settlement, i.e. Düldül Yüzü.[25] Not only did many settlements continue from Late Antiquity into the Byzantine Dark Ages but also several new sites were founded. The only difference that can be observed in the surveyed find scatters between the Late Antique and Byzantine Dark Ages in the Dereköy Highlands is that the last period displays denser artefact clusters and hence potentially more nucleation, which might correlate with the "concern for security" idea, although other scenarios could be considered, including productive specialization. Thus, the picture that emerges from areas close to Sagalassos stands in contrast to the other regions of intensive survey located at greater distances, where Byzantine remains were much scarcer. Perhaps the proximity of Sagalassos and its changing role explains the different settlement patterns. Furthermore, recent similar findings from elsewhere in Anatolia could indicate that the Byzantine Dark Ages were less "dark" than previously assumed.[26]

The concern for security is clearly visible in the Middle Byzantine settlement pattern (early 10th to mid-13th century AD). While most of the larger Roman villages continue into the Middle Byzantine period, the settlements numbers dropped significantly in the vicinity of Sagalassos and a set of new sites appeared on steep mountain tops throughout the territory (see Fig. 10.1, Fig. 10.2d). The less steep slopes of these tops were closed off by defensive walls. These walls were, however, not necessarily built by Middle Byzantine people, as these sites were also occupied during the Archaic/Achaemenid (c.750–333 BC) or Hellenistic period (333–25 BC) and the remains of such constructions are unfortunately difficult to date. The size of the walled area of these sites varies, but except for the site (YAS01) that continued from the Roman period and was most likely a small fort or watchtower, and the re-occupied mid-Hellenistic fort

---

24   Vandam et al., "Living on the margins"; Talloen et al., "A Byzantine church discovered in the village of Ağlasun".
25   Vandam et al., "Living on the margins"; Vandam et al., "Düldïl Yüzü"; Vandam et al. "Highlands and lowlands".
26   Roberts et al., "Not the end of the world".

TABLE 10.2 Byzantine sites in the territory of Sagalassos (Sites continuing from a previous period are indicated in grey.)

Early Byzantine Dark Age	Middle Byzantine
Village in valley	
KAS01	KAS01
YAR02	YAR02
KUZ01	KUZ01
BER01	BER01
KOZ02	KOZ02
YES01	YES01
KAÖ04	AGL08–10
DÜG06	
SOG01	
Hilltop settlement with fortification walls	
YAS01	YAS01
	TAS01
	KAS06
	GÜY02
	SOG03
	KAR03 (?)
	KAA08 (?)
Cave site	
KAA09	KAA09
KAR01	GÜN04 (?)
?	
CAN06 (?)	

above Sagalassos, all encompass several hectares.[27] The fact that no Middle Byzantine villages have been found in the valleys near these hilltop settlements can be explained by the fact that most of the territory was only covered by

---

27 Waelkens et al. "the 1994 and 1995 surveys"; idem "the 1996 and 1997 surveys"; Talloen et al. "Investigating the defences of Sagalassos".

non-intensive survey, while the intensively surveyed areas are located in different parts of the territory. The small artefact scatters of which Byzantine Dark Age and Middle Byzantine sites often consist, are less easily detected than the Roman period sites that usually contain more conspicuous remains such as monumental architecture or press weights (Fig. 10.2e–g vs 10.2h,i).

At Sagalassos, more evidence is available from the Middle Byzantine period. The fortified promontory or *kastron* continued to be occupied until c.1200.[28] In the former city, there was also some occupation and building activity including a cemetery, some burials of which were radiocarbon dated between the early 11th and the late 13th century AD.[29] During the 12th century, a fort was constructed on top of Alexander's hill, a steep hill southwest of the *kastron*, but this was violently destroyed shortly afterwards, somewhere between the middle of the 12th and the early 13th century.[30] During the first half of the 13th century, organized occupation at the site seems to have ended.[31] DNA analysis of skeletal material from Sagalassos and the modern population of the nearby village of Ağlasun suggests that a large decrease in population (c.90 per cent) only occurred around the time that Sagalassos was abandoned and not earlier, e.g. after the 7th-century earthquake or the Justinian Plague.[32]

In the valley below Sagalassos, near the agricultural fields, a village of considerable size had emerged somewhere during the Middle Byzantine period. In times of need, the *kastron* at Sagalassos might have acted as a refuge for the people living nearby. This site continued into the Seljuk, Beylik, and Ottoman periods.[33] During the 13th century, a Seljuk-style hamam and kervansaray were erected in the modern town of Ağlasun.[34]

Unfortunately, almost nothing is known on the Seljuk settlement pattern. This is most likely because the local pottery is poorly known, as no excavations have documented this period. The same applied to the Byzantine Dark Age and Middle Byzantine periods before 2000 when no such material had been excavated yet. The absence of Seljuk sites should therefore not be taken as an absence of habitation.

---

28 Waelkens, "Report on the 2003 excavation", pp. 427–8; Waelkens, "Report on the 2004 excavation", pp. 277–8; Poblome et al., "Sagalassos".
29 Waelkens, "Report on the 2006 and 2007 excavation", p. 444; Ottoni et al., "Mitochondrial analysis", p. 572; Cleymans and Talloen, "Protection in life and death".
30 Vionis et al., "A middle–Late Byzantine pottery assemblage", pp. 424–31.
31 Poblome et al., "Sagalassos".
32 Ottoni et al., "Mitochondrial analysis".
33 Vionis, "Medieval and Post-Medieval Ceramic Study 2009".
34 Vanhaverbeke et al., "A Selçuk hamam at Ağlasun".

FIGURE 10.2 a. Sagalassos seen from its southern entrance, b. the Bereket basin, c. Gravgaz marsh, d. fortified hilltop settlement KAA08, e./g. pattern burnished sherd (Early Byzantine Dark Age), f. Middle Byzantine pottery, h. press weight (Roman), i. monumental (funerary) architecture (Roman)

2 Environmental Change from the 3rd to the 13th Century AD

When the research of the Sagalassos Project spread out into the countryside, palaeo-environmental studies initially focussed on the whole of the Holocene period.[35] More recent research efforts have focussed specifically on the post-BO Phase period, combining pollen, non-pollen palynomorph (fungi, algae, etc.), charcoal data, and sedimentological research from two wetlands: the Gravgaz marsh and the Bereket Basin (see Fig. 10.1, 10.2b,c).[36]

One of the main research objectives was to attempt to distinguish between climatic and anthropogenically driven vegetation change, and to disentangle the interrelatedness between man, climate, and vegetation. Meeting such goals is a tricky business. Often, there is a tendency towards determinism, a researcher being all too ready to link this or that change in vegetation patterns to climate change, or all too readily dismissing any influence of the natural world, and instead explaining every observation in terms of politics and war. A further complication comes in the form of the reliability of dating techniques. While radiocarbon dating techniques have become ever more trustworthy, the resulting age ranges are still too imprecise to be used for a direct comparison with historical or archaeological data.[37]

At Sagalassos, the recent palaeo-environmental research is supported by a high-resolution chronology based on a large number of radiocarbon dates for both the Gravgaz marsh and the Bereket basin. Additionally, the pottery production centre excavated at Sagalassos has provided an exceptional chronological framework that allowed precise dating of assemblages within the city which could be typologically extrapolated to sites in the territory.[38] A critical re-assessment of older records in light of the newly collected data further helped corroborate the data that these most recent research efforts brought to light. Recent palynological research attempted to use a number of multivariate statistical analyses to distinguish between human- and climate-driven vegetation change. Although such an approach is not without its risks and uncertainties,[39] the resulting "climatic" pollen signals are corroborated by non-pollen palynomorph and sedimentological analyses. These perhaps only

---

35 E.g. Vermoere et al., "Palynological evidence for late Holocene human occupation", pp. 580–83; Kaniewski et al., "A high-resolution Late Holocene landscape ecological history", pp. 2211–16; Six et al., "Late Holocene sediment characteristics"; Dusar et al., "Sensitivity of the Eastern Mediterranean geomorphic system".

36 E.g. Bakker et al., "Numerically-derived evidence for late Holocene climate change", pp. 433–6.

37 Huntley, "Reconstructing palaeoclimates from biological proxies", pp. 10–11.

38 Poblome, *Sagalassos Red Slip Ware*.

39 Izdebski et al., "The environmental, archaeological and historical evidence", pp. 198–200.

indicate local environmental conditions, but could as well be indicative of larger-scale changes if they occur simultaneously at multiple sites. An independently collected set of tree-ring data also showed remarkable similarities in both the radiocarbon-based chronological framework as well as the succession of climatic changes indicated by statistical analyses performed on the palynological record.[40] As such, the results of the statistical analyses can be used to illustrate how the local vegetation responded to both changes in environmental conditions as well as human impact observed in other sources. An overview of the observed changes in climate, landscape use, habitation patterns within the territory of Sagalassos, and changes in the structure of the city itself, are indicated in Table 10.1.[41]

2.1 Late Roman and Early Byzantine Period (AD 300–650)

Signs of intensive crop cultivation, characteristic of the BO Phase (cereal, grape, olive, chestnut, walnut, and manna ash), started to decline from the second half of the 3rd century AD onwards in both records. At Bereket, all markers for the BO Phase seem to disappear completely by AD c.300–350. At Gravgaz, crop cultivation decreased notably, retaining a diminished presence until disappearing completely during the mid-7th century AD. This early decrease/disappearance of human impact is in stark contrast with estimates given by other palynological and archaeological records from the wider region, which place the decline in human activity roughly between the mid-6th and mid-7th centuries, although estimates vary strongly from site to site.[42] Especially between AD 300 and the mid-7th century AD, the Eastern Mediterranean displays an intensification of agriculture.[43] Similarly, as described in part 1, the archaeological records of Sagalassos and its territory indicate a continued high population density (Fig. 10.1).

Sedimentological and regional pollen records from the territory of Sagalassos indicate that the period from the late 3rd to the mid-7th century was relatively moist. At present, this moist period is tentatively linked to the Roman Warm

---

40 Touchan et al., "May–June precipitation reconstruction", pp. 199–201.
41 The pollen and sediment records, and the pollen-derived moisture availability curve are discussed in detail in Bakker et al., "Climate, people, fire and vegetation", pp. 74–9.
42 E.g. Eastwood et al., "Palaeoecological and archaeological evidence", p. 70. For an illustrated overview of the start and end dates of the various climatic periods from selected locations in the Middle East, see Bakker et al., "Climate, people, fire and vegetation", p. 60.
43 E.g. Izdebski, "Why did agriculture flourish in the late Antique east?", pp. 295–8; Roberts et al., "Not the end of the world".

TABLE 10.1 An overview of the main changes in vegetation, climate, and settlement patterns, placed along a temporal axis. The "Historical periods" column displays only the historical periods recorded in the territory of Sagalassos, and the start- and end-dates relevant to this particular region. These may differ from more general start- and end-dates applied to the Byzantine empire as a whole

Age (yr AD)	Vegetation	Climatic periods	Historical periods	Settlement patterns
1000	Decline of human impact. Establishment of pine forest. High moisture availability	MCA (Medieval Climate Anomaly)	Late Byzantine and Seljuk period	No data available concerning Late Byzantine Settlement patterns
	Resurgence in Agriculture. Increased moisture availability.		Mid Byzantine period	New mountaintop sites appear, showing a strong focus on security and self-reliance. Unclear whether these sites are actual villages or places of refuge. Sagalassos continued to be occupied until first half of 13th Century, while a large village developed in the valley below.
	Decreased moisture availability. BO Phase ends in Gravgaz. Switch to pastoralism in both basins.	DACP (Dark Ages Cold Period)	Byzantine Dark Ages	Apparent strong decrease in number of settlements. Continued de-urbanization at Sagalassos. Smaller hamlets and villages disappear, while larger villages continue to exist.
500	Increase in moisture availability. Decrease in agriculture in Gravgaz marsh. End of BO Phase in Bereket basin.	RWP (Roman Warm Period)	Early Byzantine period	Demographic decline, increased self-reliance of villages, lack of new building activities at Sagalassos
0	Extensive arboriculture and crop cultivation in Gravgaz and Bereket.		Late Roman Period	High Settlement density throughout entire territory, ranging from farms, hamlets, villa's to large villages. Countryside extensively cultivated

Period (RWP).[44] The exact start and end dates of this climatic period, characterized in the Eastern Mediterranean and Middle East by warm and moist conditions, perhaps unsurprisingly, varies quite drastically from one climatic record to the other, nor was it uniformly warm and wet everywhere it occurred. However, a general pattern of wet and warm climatic conditions during the Late Roman and Early Byzantine periods continues to prevail in the Eastern Mediterranean.[45]

Why agricultural activity diminishes so strongly and early in the two records from the territory of Sagalassos remains unknown. Currently it is hypothesized that the prevailing environmental conditions made the basins too moist for crop cultivation. Most arable land on the hillslopes surrounding Gravgaz marsh, the Bereket basin, and the wider territory in general, is considered to have eroded away during the height of the Beyşehir Occupation Phase,[46] leaving little room for agriculture in between at Gravgaz and even less at Bereket. An increase in wetlands from the 3rd century onwards has also been found in the Ağlasun Çay valley, at the foot of Sagalassos.[47] The occurrence of a relatively short but intense dry period between AD c.350 and 470 observed in various palaeoclimatic proxies[48] is not observed in the sedimentological and palynological records collected within the territory of Sagalassos. The opposite seems to be the case here. As archaeological evidence suggests, if this period of drought did occur within the region, Sagalassos itself does not seem to have suffered very much from its effects.

While not to be ignored, the possibility of a link between changing attitudes towards land use and the decrease in agricultural practices indicated by the pollen records is considered less likely. As described in part one of this chapter, the town of Sagalassos appears to become somewhat more self-reliant and less

---

44 See Bakker et al., "Climate, people, fire and vegetation", pp. 73–4, for a detailed discussion on this matter.

45 E.g. Bookman (Ken-Tor) et al., "Late Holocene lake levels", p. 569; Leroy, "Pollen analysis of core DS7-1SC", pp. 312–13; Sorrel et al., "Climate variability in the Aral Sea basin", pp. 365–7; England et al., "Historical landscape change", p. 1240; Sorell et al., "Climate variability in the Aral Sea basin", p. 368; Haldon et al., "The climate and environment of Byzantine Anatolia", pp. 123–5.

46 Dusar, *Late Holocene sediment dynamics*, pp. 132–4. Van Loo et al., "Human induced soil erosion", show how storage of soils in the valley bottoms compensated the loss of land suitable for crop cultivation on surrounding mountain slopes. But the local environmental conditions at these valley floors must still be suitable for cultivation as well.

47 Vermoere, "Holocene vegetation history in the territory of Sagalassos"; Fuller et al., "Isotopic reconstruction of human diet and animal husbandry practices".

48 A detailed overview of this and other periods of climatic change from the Late Roman until the Mid Byzantine periods, see: Izdebski et al., "The environmental, archaeological and historical evidence", pp. 192–8.

complex in Late Antiquity, and this change might occur in the wider territory, but this should not necessarily be seen as a decrease in prosperity, but rather a community adapting to a changing political and societal context as the number of settlements in the wider territory remains high.[49]

2.2 The Byzantine Dark Ages (AD 650–867)

The pollen record shows how the last traces of crop cultivation disappeared around the mid-7th century AD. The last remnants of deciduous oak woodlands, once a major component of the vegetation throughout the region, disappeared too. Sedimentological data indicates a drastic shift towards drier local environmental conditions during the mid-7th (Bereket) and the 8th century AD (Gravgaz) and lasting into the mid-10th century. Both the pollen record and records of macroscopic plant remains reflect this shift. Dry, open steppe vegetation became more important, replacing a more wet open landscape at Bereket. This vegetation change was quickly followed by an increased importance of pine in the palynological record. It must be noted, however, that pine pollen can travel over long distances. High pine pollen percentages can therefore be representative of either the presence of pine forests in the vicinity of a sample site, or an exposed and open site devoid of most or all trees.[50] Intervals of high sedimentation rates at Bereket imply that, at least there, the latter was the case.

The disappearance of crop cultivation and increase in open steppe vegetation seem to imply a shift in agricultural practices towards pastoralism, rather than a disappearance of human activity in the region. This is in accordance with the perhaps generally decreased, but otherwise continued human presence attested by the archaeological survey and excavation results. Recent findings show how the component of sheep and goat meat increased in importance during Early/Middle Byzantine times at Sagalassos, further indicating a shift in agricultural practices from crop cultivation towards pastoralism.[51]

An important question remains whether the observed switch in agricultural practices is a result of the local population adapting to a more unstable political situation, opting for a more mobile means of sustenance, whether they were forced to change their habits as a result of drier environmental conditions, or a combination of factors. Previously, the observed environmental shift, from

---

49   Poblome et al., "Sagalassos".
50   An analysis of a number of modern pollen samples revealed that pine pollen percentages reach 70 per cent or higher in samples either from within pine forests, or exposed locations with 15 per cent or less forest coverage within a 1000 m radius. See Bakker, *Late Holocene Vegetation Dynamics*.
51   De Cupere et al., "Subsistence economy and land use strategies", p. 9, Fig. 5; Fuller et al., "Isotopic reconstruction of human diet", p. 162; Vanhaverbeke et al., "Urban-rural integration", pp. 80–81.

relatively wet conditions to distinctly dry conditions at Sagalassos was linked with the start of the Dark Ages Cold Period (DACP). The DACP was identified as a period of drier and colder climatic conditions in the Eastern Mediterranean and considered to have started around the mid-7th century AD.[52] A link between the disappearance of the last remnants of cereal cultivation – a crop sensitive to small variations in rain and snowfall – and a deteriorating climate is easily made. Additionally, the disappearance of signs of olive cultivation from the pollen records of Sagalassos is usually attributed to climatic deterioration. Within the territory of Sagalassos, the palynological and archaeological records attest to the cultivation and processing of olive prior to the mid-7th century AD at altitudes presently too cold for olive cultivation.[53]

However, recent research results from Anatolia and the Levant suggest some reluctance is needed when linking changes in climate and land use. While changes in land-use and settlement patterns are visible in many parts of the Eastern Mediterranean from AD c.640 onward, evidence of a shift towards drier climatic conditions only become apparent a century or so later in a number of independent climatic proxies (give or take several decades depending on the location of a climatic proxy and the study that cites a particular palaeoclimatic record). Furthermore, changes in temperature and precipitation are not as closely linked as previously thought, casting doubt on the idea of a cold and dry DACP.[54]

What remains is that the onset of relatively dry conditions at Bereket and Gravgaz does coincide with a shift in land use and at both locations is dated to the mid-7th century. Perhaps dry conditions did occur earlier in the territory of Sagalassos compared to the general estimated date of the mid-8th century AD. This date is after all a generalized estimate based upon multiple environmental records of various natures, from various parts of the Eastern Mediterranean, with varying start- and end-dates. In this light, it is advisable that sufficient attention be given to the impact of the local or regional topography on the timing and nature of environmental change.

All things considered, it is dangerous to try and seek one single main cause for the observed changes in habitation, land use, and vegetation. But in light of recent findings, the notion that political and societal developments brought forth the need for a change in settlement patterns and land use, rather than

---

52   Neumann et al., "Palynology, Sedimentology, and palaeoecology", pp. 1492–3.
53   Vermoere et al., "Modern and ancient olive stands", p. 221.
54   For recent entries in the discussion whether climate did or did not play a role in changing land use, see e.g. Izdebski et al., "The environmental, archaeological and historical evidence", p. 205; Roberts et al., "Not the end of the world", p. 12. An overview of several major climatic proxies showing the start- and end-dates of major dry and wet trends is provided in Bakker et al., "Climate, people, fire and vegetation", p. 60.

climate change, is the most elegant. Changes in the natural environment could have helped dictate the course this process should take, whenever, wherever, and however this occurred.

It is interesting to observe how the BO Phase ends at two different dates, centuries apart, within two different locations within the same relatively small area. It is already clear that the end of the BO Phase is not a single phenomenon caused by a single factor during one time period,[55] but the situation in the territory of Sagalassos illustrates how important local conditions, be they anthropogenic or environmental, could have been.

2.3 Middle Byzantine and Seljuk Periods (AD 867–1243)

The mid-10th to the late 13th century AD, a period roughly coinciding with the Middle Byzantine and Seljuk periods, is characterized by a limited process of deforestation and resurgence in agriculture. Signs of crop cultivation remain limited. Signs of cereal cultivation are present but only at a very low level. Cultivation may have taken place, but only on a much smaller scale compared to the BO Phase. There are no indications of arboriculture. The focus of human activity remained on pastoralism. The pollen records from the territory of Sagalassos are the first originating from southwestern Turkey to display this (limited) return to crop cultivation and deforestation. Yet, the same process is observed in other regions of Anatolia, such as the pollen record from Nar Lake.[56]

In both cases, the observed vegetation change coincides with a social, military, and economic revival observed throughout the Byzantine Empire. While the seeds of this Byzantine Golden Age were sown as early as the 8th/9th century AD, its effects only became noticeable in the Byzantine countryside from the 10th century onward.[57] The rather small scale at which agriculture returned during the Mid-Byzantine period at Sagalassos and Nar Lake could be a result of the political and military instability which continued throughout this period of resurgence[58] and which is also reflected in the settlement pattern within the territory of Sagalassos and its apparent preoccupation

---

55 Izdebski, "A rural economy in transition"; Haldon et al., "The climate and environment of Byzantine Anatolia", pp. 142–3.

56 England et al., "Historical landscape change"; Eastwood et al., "Integrating Palaeoecological and Archaeo-Historical records", p. 58.

57 Haldon, "Cappadocia will be given over to ruin and become a desert", p. 222; Vionis et al., "Ceramic continuity and daily life", p. 197.

58 For a general overview of the political developments that affected the countryside during this period, we refer to Gregory, *A history of Byzantium*. A more detailed discussion of how these developments affected the territory of Sagalassos in particular may be found in Bakker et al., "Climate, people, fire and vegetation" and Bakker, *Late Holocene vegetation dynamics*.

with security. Crops such as cereals, which can be harvested yearly, and flocks of goat and sheep, which can quickly be moved to safer locations, would be more attractive means of income than cultivated trees, which need years before reaching maturity and starting to deliver produce.[59] The possibility to cultivate crops is limited in the vicinity of the fortified mountain top sites that characterize the Middle Byzantine period at Sagalassos, further indicating a continued heavy reliance on animal products and the relative insignificance of cereal cultivation in the pollen records. Palynological evidence indicates that anthropogenic activity around Gravgaz and Bereket stopped abruptly during the mid-12th century AD, the landscape becoming increasingly dominated by pine. A similar phenomenon was observed at Nar Lake, indicating that this phenomenon was not limited to the territory of Sagalassos.

The mid-10th-century resurgence in agriculture coincides not only with societal change. Sedimentological and palynological data indicate how environmental conditions within the valleys of Sagalassos became relatively moist until the mid-12th century, after which a drastic shift to dry conditions occurred. This pattern is mirrored in tree-ring records from the Antalya and Mersin Districts, indicating we are dealing with more than just local environmental change.[60] Previously, this change in environmental conditions was tentatively linked to the onset of the so-called Medieval Climate Anomaly (MCA) from circa the 11th century AD onward (with the usual variation in the exact start and end dates from record to record). As with the end of the BO Phase and the DACP, one must be careful when linking local or regional climate data to large-scale climatic periods such as the DACP or the MCA, the timing and impact of such periods varying from place to place. Recent publications have indicated how the climate deteriorated during the 10th century AD.[61] Other records indicate that the climate improved during the same period and deteriorated later, during the 11th or 12th century AD, more in line with the timing of the environmental change encountered at Sagalassos.[62]

59   Eastwood et al., "Integrating Palaeoecological and Archaeo-Historical records", p. 58.
60   Touchan et al., "May–June precipitation reconstruction", pp. 199–201.
61   E.g. Preiser-Kapeller, "A collapse of the Eastern Mediterranean"; Xoplaki et al., "The Medieval Climate Anomaly and Byzantium".
62   Bakker et al., "Climate, people, fire and vegetation", pp. 73–4. Preiser-Kapeller, "A collapse of the Eastern Mediterranean", proposes that the period from AD 950 to 1030 was an especially dry period, citing climatic reconstruction in the Aral Sea among other proxies. Simultaneously, other climatic proxies such as Lake Van and Nar Lake indicate a wetter climate from AD c.900 to 1000 onward. See e.g. Wick et al., "Evidence of Lateglacial and Holocene climatic change and human impact in eastern Anatolia"; Jones et al., "A high-resolution late Holocene lake isotope from Turkey"; Haldon et al., "The climate and environment of Byzantine Anatolia", pp. 144–45.

Archaeological, historical, and palaeo-environmental records indicate that this deterioration, whenever it is said to have occurred, seems to have taken the form of increased climatic instability and short periods of extremely poor conditions, rather than a general continuous trend. Even if the sediment and pollen records are not of a sufficient resolution to properly record such short-term events, this does not explain why the nearby tree-ring records only show a climatic deterioration from the 12th century onward. It is more likely that environmental conditions simply deteriorated from the 12th century onwards, the observed starting date still falling comfortably within the range of dates available in other records. The mid-10th century AD increase in moisture availability in the territory of Sagalassos and beyond would have been beneficial for the increased agricultural needs of the re-emerging Byzantine Empire, but the local populace clearly only made limited use of the opportunities that the climate presented.

The final complete disappearance of human impact until well after the end of the Middle Ages coincides with an extreme decrease in the population, as indicated by the DNA research described earlier in this chapter. As stated in part 1 of this chapter, little is known about the settlement pattern within the territory of Sagalassos for this period and those which follow, but a lack of archaeological findings does not imply there is nothing to find. However, as signs of agriculture, including pastoralism, are absent from the palaeo-environmental record, it is possible that we do see the effects of land abandonment, rather than a change in land use.

What drove the observed societal and vegetation changes at Sagalassos is currently still up for debate. Several recent papers have tried to link the political unrest and decline of the Byzantine Empire to drier and colder climatic conditions.[63] While a climatic deterioration is not clearly observable in the pollen record – pine becoming too dominant – the sediment records from Sagalassos and the nearby tree-ring data do show a climatic deterioration. This occurred sometime after the disappearance of human activity from the pollen record, making a link with climatic change less probable, at least for the territory of Sagalassos. Although the continuing survey effort keeps yielding new data about the settlement pattern of the Byzantine age and later, much more data is needed in order to assess what drove the land abandonment at the end of the Byzantine era at Sagalassos.

---

63   E.g. Preiser-Kapeller, "A collapse of the Eastern Mediterranean", pp. 22–4; Xoplaki et al., "The Medieval Climate Anomaly and Byzantium", p. 21. Preiser-Kapeller does note that it is sometimes unclear how a climatic deterioration is linked with increasing political unrest and notes several instances of political and societal prosperity despite the prevalence of adverse environmental conditions.

In Conclusion

Recent results of the archaeological surveys contest the old idea of a near total collapse of society after AD c.650. While there was certainly a decrease in sites and Sagalassos itself changed in importance and size, more and more sites from this period are being discovered. Currently, it appears that settlement density even increased in some parts of the territory, despite Sagalassos being close to the frontier between Byzantine and Arab controlled territories. The same location on the edge of the Empire limited the impact of the Byzantine Empire's temporary return to strength during the Mid-Byzantine period. Certainly, the notable preoccupation with security seen in the settlement pattern hints at the troubled times Sagalassos faced during the Middle Byzantine period.

The combined archaeological and palaeo-environmental data from Sagalassos show that, at least in this part of the Byzantine Empire, climate change did not play a major role in driving societal change. Shifts in land use, such as the abandonment phase of the mid-12th century AD, predated a switch to dry environmental conditions by decades, if not more than a century. The end of the BO Phase in one pollen record did correspond to a shift towards drier environmental conditions. However, human impact started to decline at the sites of both pollen records much earlier, corresponding with a process of de-urbanization and an increased focus on self-reliance of the villages in the territory of Sagalassos during the Early Byzantine period. Shifts in environmental conditions from wet to dry, or vice versa, did cause vegetation change, but the main periods of reforestation and deforestation are linked to changes in land use.

All in all, the town and territory of Sagalassos sometimes conform to established large-scale trends in land use, settlement patterns, vegetation change, and environmental trends, and sometimes there are notable differences. This illustrates how important it is not to ignore local circumstances, be they cultural, political or natural, when trying to fit research results from a certain location into a bigger framework.

Acknowledgements

The research upon which this chapter is based, was carried out within the Sagalassos Archaeological Research Project of the Katholieke Universiteit Leuven directed by Prof. M. Waelkens and, since 2014, by Prof. J. Poblome and, among others, made possible by a Methusalem grant awarded to Prof. M. Waelkens by the Flemish Ministry for Science Policy. All analytical and interdisciplinary research within the framework of the Sagalassos Project was carried out by the Centre for Archaeological Sciences of the Katholieke Universiteit Leuven. We would like to thank Dr. Adam Izdebski for offering the chance to contribute to the present volume, Prof. Dr. Etienne Paulissen, for providing valuable sedimentological data, adding greatly to the current understanding concerning environmental change in the territory of Sagalassos, Dr. David Kaniewski and Prof. Dr. Gert Verstraeten for their help and support in making the palaeo-ecological research possible, and of course Prof. Dr. Marc Waelkens without whom Sagalassos would never have revealed so many of its secrets.

This research was supported by the Belgian Programme on Interuniversity Poles of Attraction, the Research Fund of the University of Leuven, the Research Foundation Flanders (FWO) and the Flemish Ministry for Science Policy.

Bibliography

Bakker, J., Late Holocene vegetation dynamics in a mountainous environment in the territory of Sagalassos, Southwest Turkey (Unpublished PhD thesis, Katholieke Universiteit Leuven), Leuven 2012.

Bakker, J./D. Kaniewski/G. Verstraeten/V. de Laet/M. Waelkens, "Numerically derived evidence for late-Holocene climate change and its impact on human presence in the southwest Taurus Mountains, Turkey", the Holocene 22(4) (2011), 425–438.

Bakker, J./E. Paulissen/D. Kaniewski/V. De Laet/G. Verstraeten/M. Waelkens, "Climate, people, fire and vegetation: new insights into post-Beyşehir occupation phase vegetation dynamics in the Near East", *Climate of the Past* 9 (2013), 57–87.

Belke, K./R. Mersich, *Tabula Imperii Byzantini 7. Phrygien und Pisidien* (Denkschriften der Österreichische Akademie der Wissenschaften Philosophisch-Historische Klasse), Wien 1990.

Bookman (Ken-Tor), R./Y. Enzel/A. Agnon/M. Stein, "Late Holocene lake levels of the Dead Sea", Geological Society of America Bulletin 116(5/6) (2004), 555–571.

Bottema, S./H. Woldring/B. Aytug, "Palynological investigations on the relation between prehistoric man and vegetation in Turkey: the Beyşehir Occupation Phase" in H. Demiriz/N. Özhatay (eds), *Proceedings of the 5th OPTIMA Meeting*, Istanbul, 1986, pp. 315–328.

Bottema, S./H. Woldring, "Athropogenic indicators in the pollen records of the Eastern Meditteranean", in S. Bottema/G. Entjes-Nieborg/W. Van Zeist (eds), *Man's Role in the Shaping of the Eastern Mediterranean Landscape*, Rotterdam, 1990, pp. 231–264.

Cleymans, S./P. Talloen, "Protection in life and death: Pendant crosses from the cemetery of Apollo Klarios at Sagalassos", *European Journal of Archaeology* (published online DOI: https://doi.org/10.1017/eaa.2017.55).

Daems, D./J. Poblome, "The pottery of late Achaemenid Sagalassos: an overview", *HEROM. Journal on Hellenistic and Roman Material Culture* 6.1 (2017), 49–62.

De Cupere, B./S. Thys/W. Van Neer/A. Ervynck/M. Corremans/M. Waelkens, "Eagle owl (Bubo bubo) pellets from Roman Sagalassos (SW Turkey): distinguishing the prey remains from nest and roost sites", *International Journal of Osteoarchaeology* 19/1 (2009), 1–22.

De Cupere, B./D. Frémondeau/E. Kaptijn/E. Marinova/J. Poblome/R. Vandam/ W. Van Neer, "Subsistence economy and land use strategies in the Burdur province (SW Anatolia) from prehistory to the Byzantine period", *Quaternary International* 436/part B (2017), 4–17.

Dusar, B., *Late Holocene Sediment Dynamics in a Mediterranean Mountain Environment* (Unpublished PhD thesis, Katholieke Universiteit Leuven), Leuven 2011.

Dusar, B./G. Vertraeten/K. D'Haen/J. Bakker/E. Kaptijn/M. Waelkens, "Sensitivity of the Eastern Mediterranean geomorphic system towards environmental change during the Late Holocene: a chronological perspective", *Journal of Quaternary Science* 27/4 (2012), 371–382.

Eastwood, W.J./N. Roberts/H.F. Lamb, "Palaeoecological and archaeological evidence for human occupance in Southwest Turkey: The Beyşehir Occupation Phase", *Anatolian Studies* 48 (1998), 69–86.

Eastwood, W.J./O. Gümüşçü/H. Yiğitbaşıoğlu/J.F. Haldon/A. England, "Integrating Palaeoecological and Archaeo-Historical records: Land use and Landscape change in Cappadocia (central Turkey) since late Antiquity", in T. Vorderstrasse/J. Roodenberg (eds.), *Archaeology of the Countryside in Medieval Anatolia (Pihans 119)*, Leiden 2009, pp. 45–69.

England, A./W.J. Eastwood/C.N. Roberts/R. Turner/J.F. Haldon, "Historical landscape change in Cappadocia (central Turkey): a palaeoecological investigation of annually laminated sediments from Nar lake", *The Holocene* 18/8 (2008), 1229–45.

Fuller, B.T./B. De Cupere/E. Marinova/W. Van Neer/M. Waelkens/M.P. Richards, "Isotopic reconstruction of human diet and animal husbandry practices during the Classical-Hellenistic, imperial, and Byzantine periods at Sagalassos, Turkey", *American Journal of Physical Anthropology* 149/2 (2012), 157–71.

Gregory, T.E., *A History of Byzantium*, Chichester 2010.

Haldon, J.F., "'Cappadocia will be given over to ruin and become a desert'. Environmental evidence for historically-attested events in the 7th–10th centuries", in K. Belke, E. Kislinger, A. Külzer, and M.A. Stassinopoulou (eds.), *Byzantina Mediterranea. Festschrift für Johannes Koder, zum 65 Geburtstag*, Vienna 2007, pp. 215–30.

Haldon, J./N. Roberts/A. Izdebski/D. Fleitmann/M. McCormick/M. Cassis/O. Doonan/ W. Eastwood/H. Elton/S. Ladstätter/S. Manning/J. Newhard/K. Nicoll/I. Telelis/ E. Xoplaki, "The Climate and Environment of Byzantine Anatolia: Integrating Science, History, and Archaeology", *The Journal of Interdisciplinary History* 45/2 (2014), 113–61.

Huntley, B., "Reconstructing palaeoclimates from biological proxies: Some often overlooked sources of uncertainty". Quaternary Science Reviews 31 (2012), 1–16.

Issar, A.S., "Climatic Change and the History of the Middle East", American Scientist 83/4 (1995), 350–55.

Izdebski, "Why did agriculture flourish in the late antique East? The role of climate fluctuations in the development and contraction of agriculture in Asia Minor and the Middle East from the 4th till the 7th c. AD", Millennium 8 (2011), 291–312.

Izdebski, A., A rural economy in transition. Asia Minor from late Antiquity into the Early Middle Ages, Warshaw (2013).

Izdebski, A./G. Koloch/T. Słoczyński, "Exploring Byzantine and Ottoman economic history with the use of palynological data: a quantitative approach", Jahrbuch der Österreichischen Byzantinistik 65 (2015), 67–110.

Izdebski, A./J. Pickett/N. Roberts/T. Waliszewski, "The environmental, archaeological and historical evidence for regional climatic changes and their societal impacts in the Eastern Mediterranean in Late Antiquity", Quaternary Science Reviews 136 (2016), 189–208.

Jacobs, I., "From Early Byzantium to the Middle Ages at Sagalassos", in A. Gnasso/ E.E. Intagliata/T.J. MacMaster/B.N. Morris (eds): The Long Seventh Century. Continuity and Discontinuity in an Age of Transition, Oxford 2015, pp. 163–98.

Jones, M.D./C.N. Roberts/M.J. Leng/M. Türkeş, "A high-resolution late Holocene lake isotope from Turkey and links to North Atlantic and monsoon climate", Geology 34 (2006), 361–4.

Kaniewski, D./E. Paulissen/V. De Laet/K. Dossche/M. Waelkens, "A high-resolution Late Holocene landscape ecological history inferred from an intramontane basin in the Western Taurus Mountains, Turkey", Quaternary Science Reviews 26/17–18 (2007), 2201–18.

Kaniewski, D./V. De Laet/E. Paulissen/M. Waelkens, "Long-term effects of human impact on mountainous ecosystems, western Taurus Mountains, Turkey", Journal of Biogeography 34 (2007), 1975–97.

Kaniewski, D./E. Van Campo/E. Paulissen/H. Weiss/T. Otto/J. Bakker/I. Rossignol/ K. Van Lerberghe, "Medieval coastal Syrian vegetation patterns in the principality of Antioch", The Holocene 21/2 (2011), 251–62.

Kaptijn, E./R. Vandam/J. Poblome/M. Waelkens, "Inhabiting the Plain of Burdur. Results from the 2010 and 2011 Sagalassos Project Survey", News of Archaeology from Anatolia's Mediterrean Areas 10 (2012), 142–7.

Kaptijn, E./J. Poblome/H. Vanhaverbeke/J. Bakker/M. Waelkens, "Societal changes in the Bereket valley in the Hellenistic, Roman and Early Byzantine periods. Results from the Sagalassos Territorial Archaeological Survey 2008 (SW Turkey)", Anatolian Studies 63 (2013), 75–95.

Lambeck, K./M. Anzidei/F. Antonioli/A. Benini/A. Esposito, "Sea level in Roman time in the Central Mediterranean and implications for recent change", *Earth and Planetary Science Letters* 224/3–4 (2004), 563–75.

Leroy, S.A.G., "Pollen analysis of core DS7-1SC (Dead Sea) showing intertwined effects of climatic change and human activities in the Late Holocene", *Journal of Archaeological Science* 37/2 (2010), 306–16.

Mitchell, S., "The settlement of Pisidia in Late Antiquity and the Byzantine Period: Methological problems", in, *Byzanz als Raum. Zu Methoden und Inhalten der historischen Geographie des östlichen Mittelmeerraums*, Wien 2000, pp. 139–52.

Neumann, F.H./E.J. Kagan/M.J. Schwab/M. Stein, "Palynology, sedimentology and palaeoecology of the late Holocene Dead Sea", Quaternary Science Reviews (2007), 1476–98.

Ottoni, C./F.-X. Ricaut/N. Vanderheyden/N. Brucato/M. Waelkens/R. Decorte, "Mitochondrial analysis of a Byzantine population reveals the differential impact of multiple historical events in South Anatolia", *European Journal of Human Genetics* 19 (2011), 571–76.

Ottoni, C./R. Rasteiro/R. Willet/J. Claeys/P. Talloen/K. Van de Vijver/L. Chikhi/ J. Poblome/R. Decorte, "Comparing maternal genetic variation across two millennia reveals the demographic history of an ancient human population in southwest Turkey", *Royal Society Open Science* 3/2 (2016), 1–9.

Poblome, J., *Sagalassos red slip ware: typology and chronology* (Studies in Eastern Mediterranean Archaeology 2), Turnhout 1999.

Poblome, J., "Shifting societal complexity in Byzantine Asia Minor and Dark Age pottery", in N. Poulou-Papadimitriou/E. Nodarou/V. Kilikoglou (eds.), LRCW 4 *Late Roman Coarse Wares, Cooking Wares and Amphorae in the Mediterranean: Archaeology and archaeometry. The Mediterranean: a market without frontiers*, Oxford 2014, pp. 623–42.

Poblome, J./R. Degeest, "The archaeological evidence: ceramics", in H. Vanhaverbeke/ M. Waelkens (eds.), *The chora of Sagalassos. The evolution of the settlement pattern from Prehistoric until recent times*, Turnhout 2003, pp. 138–42.

Poblome, J./P. Talloen/E. Kaptijn, "Sagalassos", in P. Niewoehner (ed.), *The Archaeology of Byzantine Anatolia. From Late Antiquity to the Coming of the Turks*, Oxford 2017, pp. 302–11.

Preiser-Kapeller, J., "A Collapse of the Eastern Mediterranean? New results and theories on the interplay between climate and societies in Byzantium and the Near East, ca. 1000–1200 AD", *Jahrbuch der Österreichischen Byzantinistik* 65/2015 (2016), 195–242.

Roberts, N./M. Cassis/O. Doonan/W. Eastwood/H. Elton/J. Haldon/A. Izdebski/ J. Newhard, "Not the End of the World? Post-Classical Decline and Recovery in Rural Anatolia", *Human Ecology* (2018), 1–18.

Roberts, N., "Revisiting the Beyşehir Occupation Phase: Land-cover change and the rural economy in the Eastern Mediterranean during the first millenium AD", *Late Antique Archaeology* (in press).

Six, S./E. Paulissen/T. Van Tuyne/J. Lambrechts/M. Vermoere/V. De Laet/M. Waelkens, "Late Holocene Sediment characteristics and sediment accumulation in the marsh of Gravgaz: evidence for abrupt environmental changes", in P. Degryse/M. Waelkens (eds.), Sagalassos VI. Geo- and Bioarchaeology at Sagalassos and in its territory, Leuven 2008, pp. 189–210.

Sorrel, P./S.-M. Popescu/S. Klotz, J.-P. Suc/H. Oberhänsli, "Climate variability in the Aral Sea basin (Central Asia) during the late Holocene based on vegetation changes", *Quaternary Research* 67/3 (2007), 357–70.

Talloen, P./M. Albayrak/J. Poblome, "Investigating the defences of Sagalassos: the 2017 excavations on the Akra", *News Bulletin on Archaeology from Mediterranean Anatolia* 16 (in press).

Talloen, P./J. Poblome, "The 2014 and 2015 control excavations on and around the Upper Agora of Sagalassos: The structural remains and general phasing", *Anatolica* 42 (2016), 111–50.

Talloen, P./R., Vandam/M. Broisch/J. Poblome, "A Byzantine church discovered in the village of Ağlasun (Burdur): Some more light on Dark Age Pisidia", *Adalya* 20 (2017), 375–404.

Touchan, R./Ü. Akkemik/M.K. Hughes/N. Erkan, "May–June precipitation reconstruction of southwestern Anatolia, Turkey during the last 900 years from tree rings", *Quaternary Research* 68/2 (2007), 196–202.

Vandam, R./E. Kaptijn/J. Poblome/M. Waelkens, "The 2012 archaeological survey of the Sagalassos Archaeological Survey Project", *News of Archaeology from Anatolia's Mediterranean Areas* 11 (2013), 230–3.

Vandam, R., Everybody needs good neighbours. Exploring Late Prehistoric settlement strategies and socio-economic behaviour in the Burdur Plain, SW Turkey (Unpublished PhD thesis, Katholieke Universiteit Leuven), Leuven 2014.

Vandam, R/P.T. Willett/J. Poblome, "Chapter 15: Living on the margins. First results from the Dereköy Archaeological Survey of the Sagalassos Project in the Western Taurus Mountains", in S.R. Steadman/G. McMahon (eds.), *The Archaeology of Anatolia: Recent Discoveries (2014–2016)*, Vol. II, Cambridge 2017, pp. 321–46.

Vandam, R./E. Kaptijn/P.T. Willett/J. Poblome, "Highlands and lowlands: different landscapes, different archaeologies? A diachronic case-study from the Taurus Mountains (SW Turkey)", in A. Garcia (ed.), *Archaeology of Mountain Landscapes. Interdisciplinary Research Strategies of Agro-Pastoralism in Upland Regions*, Albany accepted.

Vandam, R./P. Talloen/Y. Zenger/J. Poblome, "Düldül Yüzü: The exploration of a secondary center in the territory of Sagalassos", *News Bulletin on Archaeology from Mediterranean Anatolia* 16 (2018/in press).

Vanhaverbeke, H., "The evolution of the settlement pattern", in H. Vanhaverbeke and M. Waelkens (eds.), *The chora of Sagalassos. The evolution of the settlement pattern from Prehistoric until recent times*, Turnhout 2003, pp. 149–326.

Vanhaverbeke, H./Ö. Başağaç/K. Paul/M. Waelkens, "A Selçuk hamam at Ağlasun, Burdur province, Turkey", *Turcica. Revue d'Études Turques* 37 (2005), 309–36.

Vanhaverbeke, H./P. Degryse/B. De Cupere/W. Van Neer/M. Waelkens/P. Muchez, "Urban-rural integration at ancient Sagalassos (SW Turkey). Archaeological, archaeozoological and geochemical evidence", *Archaeofauna* 20 (2011), 73–83.

Vanhaverbeke, H./M. Waelkens/I. Jacobs/M. Lefere/E. Kaptijn/J. Poblome, "The 2008 and 2009 survey season in territory of Sagalassos", in A.N. Toy/C. Keskin (eds.), *XXVIII. Araştırma Sonuçları Toplantısı 24–28 May 2010, Istanbul*, Ankara 2011, pp. 139–53.

Van Loo, M./B. Dusar/G. Verstraeten/H. Renssen/B. Notebaert/K. D'Haen/J. Bakker, "Human induced soil erosion and the implications on crop yield in a small mountainous Mediterranean catchment (SW-Turkey)", *Catena* 149/1 (2017), 491–504.

van Zeist, W./H. Woldring/D. Stapert, "Late Quaternary vegetation and climate of Southwestern Turkey", *Palaeohistoria* 17 (1975), 55–143.

Vermoere, M., *Holocene vegetation history in the territory of Sagalassos (Southwest Turkey). A palynological approach* (Unpublished PhD thesis, Katholieke Universiteit Leuven), Leuven 2011.

Vermoere, M./S. Bottema/L. Vanhecke/M. Waelkens/E. Paulissen/E. Smets, "Palynological evidence for late-Holocene human occupation recorded in two wetlands in SW Turkey", *The Holocene* 12 (5) (2002), 569–84.

Vermoere, M./L. Vanhecke/M. Waelkens/E. Smets, "Modern and ancient olive stands near Sagalassos (south-west Turkey) and reconstruction of the ancient agricultural landscape in two valleys", *Global Ecology & Biogeography* 12/3 (2003), 217–35.

Vionis, A.K., "Medieval and Post-Medieval Ceramic Study 2009: surface survey pottery from Akyamaç", *Web report Sagalassos Porject 2009*, http://www.Sagalassos.be/en/node/1121 (2009).

Vionis, A.K./J. Poblome/B. De Cupere/M. Waelkens, "A middle-Late Byzantine pottery assemblage from Sagalassos. Typo-chronology and sociocultural interpretation", *Hesperia* 79 (2010), 423–64.

Vionis, A.K./J. Poblome/M. Waelkens, "Ceramic continuity and daily life in Medieval Sagalassos, southwest Anatolia (ca. 650–1250 AD)", in T. Vorderstrasse/J.J. Roodenberg (eds.), *Archaeology of the Countryside in Medieval Anatolia*, Leiden 2009, pp. 191–213.

Vionis, A.K./J. Poblome/M. Waelkens, "The hidden material culture of the Dark Ages. Early medieval ceramics at Sagalassos (Turkey): new evidence (ca AD 650–800)", *Antolian Studies* 59 (2009), 146–65.

Waelkens, M., "Report on the 2003 excavation and restoration campaign at Sagalassos", in K. Olşen/H. Dönmez/A. Özme (eds.), XXVI. *Kazı Sonuçları Toplantısı, Konya 24–28 Mayıs 2004*, Ankara 2005, pp. 421–43.

Waelkens, M., "Report on the 2004 excavation and restoration campaign at Sagalassos", in K. Olşen/H. Dönmez/A. Özme (eds.), XXVII. *Kazı Sonuçları Toplantısı, Antalya 30 Mayıs–3 Haziran 2005*, Ankara 2006, pp. 271–86.

Waelkens, M., "Report on the 2006 and 2007 excavation and restoration activities at Tepe Düzen and at Sagalssos", in H. Dönmez/A. Özme (eds.), XXX. *Kazı Sonuçları Toplantısı, 26–30 Mayıs 2008, Ankara*, Ankara 2009, pp. 427–56.

Waelkens, M./E. Paulissen/H. Vanhaverbeke/Ö. Ilhame/B. De Cupere/H.A. Ekinci/P.M. Vermeersch/J. Poblome/R. Degeest, "The 1994 and 1995 surveys in the territory of Sagalassos", in M. Waelkens/J. Poblome (eds.), *Sagalassos IV. Report on the survey and excavation campaigns of 1994 and 1995*, Leuven 1997, pp. 11–102.

Waelkens, M./E. Paulissen/H. Vanhaverbeke/J. Reyniers/J. Poblome/R. Degeest/ W. Viaene/J. Deckers/B. De Cupere/W. Van Neer/H.A. Ekinci/M.O. Erbay, "The 1996 and 1997 surveys in the territory of Sagalassos", in M. Waelkens/L. Loots (eds.), *Sagalassos V. Report on the Survey and Excavation Campaigns of 1996 and 1997*, Leuven 2000, pp. 17–216.

Waelkens, M./E. Paulissen/M. Vermoere/P. Degryse/D. Celis/K. Schroyen/B.D. Cupere/ I. Librecht/K. Nackaerts/H. Vanhaverbeke/W. Viaene/P. Muchez/R. Ottenburgs/ S. Deckers/W. Van Neer/E. Smets/G. Govers/G. Verstraeten/A. Steegen/ K. Cauwenberhs, "Man and environment in the territory of Sagalassos, a classical city in (SW) Turkey", *Quaternary Science Reviews* 18/4–5 (1999), 697–709.

Wick, L./G. Lemcke/M. Sturm, "Evidence of Lateglacial and Holocene climatic change and human impact in eastern Anatolia: high-resolution pollen, charcoal, isotopic and geochemical records from the laminated sediments of Lake Van, Turkey", *Holocene* 13 (2003), 665–675.

Xoplaki, E./D. Fleitmann/J. Luterbacher/S. Wagner/J.F. Haldon/E. Zorita/I. Telelis/ A. Toreti/A. Izdebski, "The Medieval Climate Anomaly and Byzantium: A review of the evidence on climatic fluctuations, economic performance and societal change", *Quaternary Science Reviews* 136 (2016), 229–52.

CHAPTER 11

Euchaïta, Landscape and Climate in the Byzantine Period

Warren Eastwood and John Haldon

1   **State of Research**

Euchaïta, modern Beyözü (and, until the 1960s, Avkat), was a small town in eastern Paphlagonia a little under 50 km west of the ancient city of Amaseia. It owed its prominence in the late Roman and Byzantine periods entirely to the presence there of the cult of St. Theodore Tiro ("the recruit"). There is no written mention in any known text of the place before the late 4th century, but as a cult and pilgrimage centre it attracted visitors from all over the late Roman world. A late 4th-century church dedicated to the saint was destroyed in a Persian attack, probably in the 620s and, according to the 11th-century *Miracula* (a collection originally written in the later 7th century, however), was shortly thereafter rebuilt by the bishop, Eleutherios. Between the 660s and later 9th century, and as a result of the changed strategic geography of the region following upon the early Arab-Islamic conquests, Euchaïta became a military base and may have been the command headquarters of the Armeniakon division. Frequently employed as a place of internal exile because of its relative isolation, its mid-11th-century bishop John Mauropous describes it as located in a barren and inhospitable landscape with few amenities, although during the annual *panēgyris*, or fair, held in the saint's honour, it became for a week or so a bustling and thriving market centre. After the Turkish conquest of Anatolia in the later 11th century, the town fell into obscurity. By the time it appears in an Ottoman tax register of 1530, the settlement had shrunk to a small village of some 29 households, although there is sufficient evidence to show that it has remained continuously occupied until the present day. Never of great economic significance, it nevertheless represents a typical small early-middle Byzantine urban settlement in the central Anatolian region. Until recently there had been no archaeological work undertaken in the area, although that has now changed, and archaeological survey work from 2006–10 traced some important aspects of its evolution.[1]

---

[1] Details of the survey and results can be found online at: www.princeton.edu/avkat. See also Haldon, Elton and Newhard 2015; Haldon 2016; Haldon, Elton and Newhard 2017.

1.1 *Geography, Geomorphology and Climate*

Euchaïta is located on the southern flank of the Avkat Dağı, along the northern edge of the Mecitözü valley. Situated some 220 km ENE of the Turkish capital, Ankara, and about 125 km from the Black Sea coast, it lies on the Anatolian plateau. The valley lies at an altitude of ~800 m and is some 10 km wide and 40 km long. The Efendik River,[2] which rises at the western end of the Kırklar Dağı (peak height 1791 m), runs along the southern side of the valley, which is itself separated by the Kırklar Dağı from the parallel Çorum River valley to the south. Both rivers flow in an easterly direction and feed into the Yeşilırmak. The northern part of the valley is defined by Avkat Dağı to the west and Çakır Dağı to the east, and descends gradually towards Amasya (at 392 m). Along with other similar valleys to the west (such as that running from Sungurlu to Alaca and then on to Zela), the Mecitözü valley serves to link central Anatolia and Cappadocia with the Black Sea at Amisus (modern Samsun) and Sinope (Fig 11.1).

From the point of view of geography and geomorphology, Euchaïta lies in the Black Sea Region of northern Turkey in the transitional area between the Central Anatolia plateau to the south and the North Anatolian (Pontic)/Black Sea Mountains to the north. The northern part of the region is more mountainous and includes many mountain ranges and peaks, including Ilgaz (2587 m), Köroğlu (2044 m), Çal (1732 m), Kavak (1473 m), Alagöz (1558 m) and Köse mountains (1693 m), which are located within and proximal to the North Anatolian Fault Zone (NAFZ) (Fig 11.2). By contrast, the central and southern part of the region is characterized by areas of more intermediate or subdued relief, although this is punctuated by areas of higher relief and major peaks including Urlu (1336 m), Elmalı (1042 m) and Keslik (1414 m) to the west and southwest of Çorum city. The Mecitözü Plain (mean elevation 950 m) lies ~30 km east of Çorum city and is bounded by the Eğerli mountains (1756 m) to the north and the Kırlar (1812 m) and Karadağ (1566 m) mountains to the south. These latter mountain ranges form part of the Kırıkkale-Erbaa Fault Zone (KEFZ). The overall geology exerts a strong structural control on the topography. Pre-Tertiary, Permo-Triassic and Jurassic limestones are hard and generally more resistant to erosion; therefore, they generally form topography of higher relief. In contrast to this, the slightly undulating plains covering a large area of Çorum Province, including the Mecitözü Plain, are composed mainly of much softer and therefore more erodible carbonate rocks of Palaeocene to Early Miocene and Middle Miocene to Pliocene age.

---

2 This is the modern name – on older maps it appears as the Efennik, the Tanözü, or the Mecitözü Çayı.

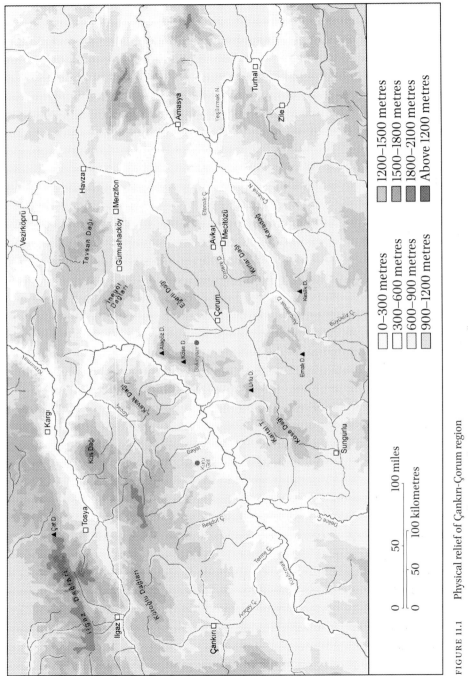

FIGURE 11.1 Physical relief of Çankırı-Çorum region
REDRAWN FROM TÜRKIYE COĞRAFYA ATLASI, D.B.R. DOĞAN-BURDA-RIZZOLI, İSTANBUL 2004

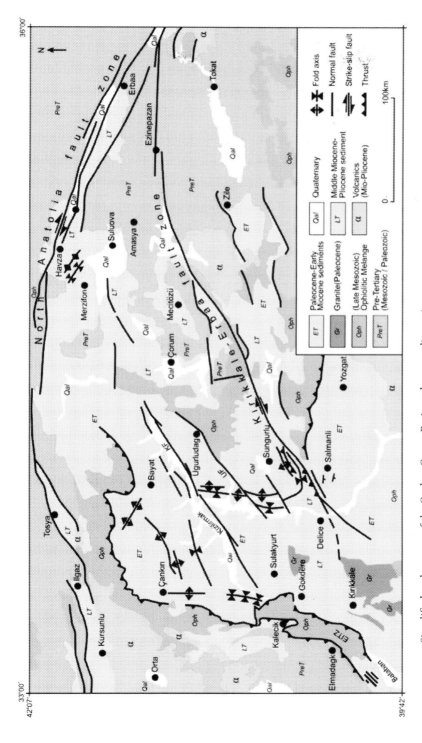

FIGURE 11.2   Simplified geology map of the Çankırı-Çorum Basin and surrounding region
REDRAWN FROM GÖKTEN ET AL. 2013 AND MTA 1:500K GEOLOGICAL MAP

The geology also exerts a strong structural control on the major drainage basins, these being orientated predominantly east–west and controlled to a large extent by the NAFZ and its branches. However, very large rivers such as the Kızılırmak (ancient Halys) and Yeşilırmak (ancient Iris) Rivers not only flow along the NAFZ in places, but have the erosional power to cut diagonally across the region's geography as well. The biggest tributary of the Kızılırmak, the Delice River, flows into the Kızılırmak near Sungurlu and, because of the Delice's course through gypsiferous marls, produces brackish river water. The Kızılırmak is also influenced by gypsiferous geology in the upper reaches of its course in the region of Sivas in addition to other tributaries flowing off gypsiferous geologies, for example the Acıçay ("bitter") River in the region of Çankırı. In addition to these relatively large rivers, there are many smaller rivers and tributaries including the Çekerek (ancient Scylax) and its tributaries the Çorum Çat suyu (Derinçay), Mecitözü Çayı and Büyükoz Rivers, which flow east into the Yeşilırmak. All rivers in Çorum Province have irregular flow regimes: peak flow is during the spring following snow melt and generally higher precipitation, which then decreases to low flow conditions corresponding to the drier summer months (Fig 11.2).

The main soil types of Çorum Province are brown forest soils covering 640,060 hectares with brown soils covering an area of 343,973 hectares. Alluvial valley fill soils are generally found alongside the major rivers and stream courses of the Kızılırmak, Çekerek and Çat Suyu rivers. On the whole, these latter soils are found in landscapes of generally lower relief and are the best soils of the region with generally lower soil erodibility potential (lower K value) compared with the other major soil groups. Much of lowland Çorum province is given over to agricultural production of crops including cereals (81 per cent) comprising wheat and barley, industrial cash crops such as sugar beet and sunflower (3 per cent), legumes (12 per cent) including lentil and chickpea, and root crops (4 per cent), including potato and onion, while orchards and vineyards are also locally important in places. Forestry is an important resource in the more mountainous parts of the region (comprising an area of 28 per cent), while permanent pasture and meadow comprises 34 per cent, crop areas 24 per cent, fallow areas 6 per cent, vegetables, orchards and vineyards 0.3 per cent, while unused and undeveloped but potentially productive land and non-agricultural land comprise 0.3 per cent and 7 per cent respectively.[3]

---

3 Şahin 2006.

The climate of the Çorum region is characteristic of its location between the Anatolian Plateau to the south and the North Anatolian (Pontic) Mountains to the north, and in general is semi-arid with distinct seasonal variations. Summers are usually hot and dry with average summer temperatures in the region of 22.5 °C for Çankırı, 20.1 °C for Çorum and 22.3 °C for Amasya. In contrast, winters can be quite severe with average temperatures of 1.5 °C for Çankırı, 0.8 °C for Çorum and 3.3 °C for Amasya. Precipitation falls largely between December and May, with a distinct May peak characteristic of an inland continental climatic regime.[4] Average annual precipitation amounts range from 408 mm for Çankırı to 424 mm for Çorum and 447 mm for Amasya. Precipitation is the key factor that controls all aspects of the soil-water balance and undoubtedly has the biggest influence on soil processes that affect the viability and variability of field crops and rain-fed (dry farming) agriculture, for both the contemporary and historical periods. Mean monthly precipitation for Çorum increases from 13.9 mm in August (the driest month) to an average of 37.6 mm for the winter months (DJF) to 61.5 mm peak rainfall for May (Figure 11.3).

The timings and amounts of precipitation are critical: a decrease in monthly totals for winter and spring can mean that crops may have a large soil water deficit during the arid summer months. Drought is one of the most damaging and challenging climate-related hazards and although it can be a normal part of the climate cycle it can, in some instances, develop as an extreme event that can have severe impacts upon local crop production and human-environmental systems. Within recent times, low winter rainfall totals for 2000/2001 experienced across the Çorum region of Turkey caused a severe soil water deficit and drought conditions for the summer months and, despite an elevated mean monthly total of the May peak for that year (97.5 mm), resulted in a marked decrease in crop production and concomitant food shortages.[5] It can reasonably be inferred that the high variability of the climate for the Çorum region leading to severe drought conditions is not a recent phenomenon and must have occurred frequently within historical and prehistorical times.

1.2   Modern-Day Vegetation Patterns

The structural and climatic controls outlined above play a dominant role in determining natural vegetation patterns in Turkey. The Euxinian vegetation type of northern Turkey comprises mixed mesic, summer-green *forests* that are

---

4   Sarış et al. 2010.
5   Şahin 2006; Kömüşçü et al. 2004.

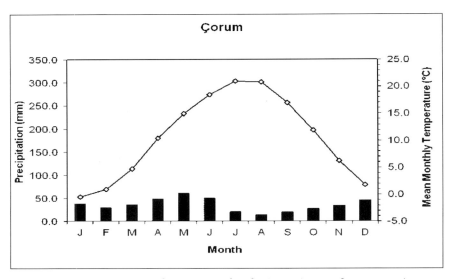

FIGURE 11.3   Precipitation and temperature data for Çorum (average for 1930–2000)

adapted to a humid-temperate climatic regime. These forests comprise mainly broadleaf deciduous trees. At lower elevations the relatively well-watered slopes of the North Anatolian (Pontic) Mountains support coastal forests comprising oaks (*Quercus* spp.) and hornbeam (*Carpinus betulus*) with chestnut (*Castanea saliva*) and other deciduous trees, while at higher elevations beech (*Fagus orientalis*) forests predominate along with sub-Pontic oak forests with conifers.[6] Fir, spruce and pine conifer forests (*Abies nordmanniana, A. bornmuelleriana, Picea orientalis, Pinus sylvestris*) are also found in the mountains of northern Turkey. The Black Pine (*Pinus pallasiana*) has its easternmost occurrence in the Çorum region of northern Turkey and is found in mountainous areas where the mean annual temperature is 7/8–12 °C and the mean annual rainfall is over 400 mm.[7]

At lower elevations and in more southerly parts of the region, where mean annual precipitation is below 400 mm, Pontic woodland formations become increasingly open, and the environment becomes significantly steppic in character and comprises typically those plants that are adapted to colder and drier climatic conditions. This reflects the increasing rain shadow effect that the North Anatolian (Pontic) Mountains exert on floral formations and further penetration into the central parts of inner Anatolia leads to still drier, winter-cold conditions. Today, the lower elevation parts of central Anatolia are

---

6   Kavgaci et al. 2012.
7   Atalay and Efe 2012.

virtually treeless where fields on deep alluvial soils alternate with steppe on the drier hills. There is, however, still much debate with regard to the extent to which the central Anatolian steppe in this region is a result of climatically- or human-induced factors (e.g., in the form of deforestation).[8] Present day Çorum province is therefore located in this transitional area between the sub-humid climatic conditions of the North Anatolian (Pontic) region and the semi-arid conditions of the interior, and the natural vegetation reflects this (mixed broadleaved and needle leaved woodland resistant to cold).[9] The dominant tree is *Quercus pubescens*, subsp. *anatolica* (O. Schwarz), a deciduous oak species with pine (comprising mainly Black Pine, *Pinus pallasiana*) in upland areas receiving higher precipitation (500–900 mm PA). To the south of Çorum, floral formations are mainly steppic comprising grasses and *Astragalus* spp. with *Artemisia* (mugwort/wormwood) and chenopods (Chenopodiaceae or goosefoot) in drier locations.

1.3   Past Vegetation and Palaeoenvironmental Reconstructions

The proxy data for climate and for land-use together with archaeological data from across Anatolia for the period from the 6th to the 11th century indicate a considerable degree of interregional variation, suggesting that shifts in the established patterns of land use across this period depended on specific local factors.[10] It is likely that the plague of Justinian also played a demographic role, however varied its impact by area, population, settlement density and natural environmental factors, such as the dust-veil event of the late 530s. It is generally recognized that cooler and less stable climatic conditions in Anatolia after the 6th century will have rendered some agricultural activities more marginal than before, possibly accounting for the development of a less vulnerable, simpler and safer mode of agrarian economy. Northern Anatolia in particular seems to have been affected by such shifts.[11]

The regionally specific range of crops and other agrarian products typical of the period up to the 6th and early 7th centuries appears to have survived in some areas, such as parts of Bithynia, Paphlagonia, and the central plateau, into the 8th century, regardless of changes in climatic conditions. Elsewhere, however, changes in land-use evident in the palynological data seem to have taken place during periods when the evidence suggests no climatic changes

---

8   Walter 1956; Asouti et al. 2014.
9   Bottema et al. 1993.
10 See Danladi et al. 2023; Jacobson et al. 2022; Dönmez et al. 2021.
11 See Haldon et al. 2014 and Izdebski 2012 for a survey of the key proxy data for these developments; for a broader survey: Izdebski 2013.

were taking place, with the obvious conclusion that human agency played a key role here. Interventions by farmers and herdsmen, for example, in response to market forces, to state fiscal pressure or to hostile military activity, can have significant impacts and are not uncommon. Such factors must certainly have played a role in moulding the patterns of agrarian and pastoral activity in the Avkat survey area.

1.4 Palynology

Once analysed and interpreted, the study of fossilized pollen grains, spores and other micro- and macrofossils recovered from sediments that accumulate in lake basins and other depressions provides the potential to reconstruct vegetation and environmental sequences back through time. Once these sequences have been "accurately" dated, they allow comparisons to be made with archaeological and settlement survey data for investigating human–environment interactions and long-term landscape dynamics. However, the accuracy and hence the reliability of palaeo-environmental or palaeoecological chronologies – particularly those originating from sites in the eastern Mediterranean – can be a problem. This is because many sequences are often based on a limited number of radiocarbon (^{14}C) ages, with interpolation between adjacent ^{14}C ages; this approach produces a constant sediment accumulation rate between dated horizons. However, where a phase of landscape disturbance is highlighted in a palaeoecological dataset, sediment accumulation rates may have varied considerably, thereby significantly affecting the dating and hence duration of recorded clearance phases. Furthermore, the core top is often assumed to date to the present day, which may or may not be valid and thus introduces further uncertainty in any age-depth modelling of the sequence.

The accuracy and precision of the actual ^{14}C age can also be a problem; AMS-derived ages may have a precision that is several times better than standard or bulk ^{14}C radiometric ages, but once calibrated to calendar ages the resulting age range may still be unsuitable for direct comparison with historical and textual data sources at sub-centennial resolution. This in turn can produce problems with the elucidation of possible cause and effect relationships; a problem Baillie (1993) succinctly refers to as the "suck-in and smear" effect. The presence of tephra or volcanic ash layers (tephrochronology) originating from explosive volcanic eruptions (when present in the sediment core or archaeological context and accurately attributed to a particular dated eruption) produce time synchronous marker horizons and therefore have the potential to significantly increase the temporal precision of palaeoecological and archaeological data.

Many earlier studies that have been published for northern Turkey report uncalibrated (e.g. "raw") radiocarbon ages (^{14}C age yr BP) derived from the analysis of bulk samples of sediment submitted for radiocarbon dating. Increasingly, more recent studies report calibrated or conventional radiocarbon ages (Cal yr BP) to facilitate direct comparison with archaeological and historical datasets. In spite of the issues noted above, AMS dating techniques do permit the dating of very minute amounts of sediment, so therefore offers the potential to increase the number of dated horizons within a palaeoecological sequence and thus may improve the chronology for the sites in the Avkat region. The re-investigation of sites in northern Turkey using more advanced AMS dating techniques together with targeted palynology on post BO Phase vegetation changes is required in order to shed more light on the character and nature of environmental changes in this region and to compare with other regions in Turkey. In the ensuing discussion, the original uncalibrated radiocarbon age will be stated along with the calibrated or conventional age; conventional ages were calibrated using the INTCAL04 curve.[12]

Although at the time of writing there are no palaeoenvironmental sequences located within present-day Çorum province, lake sites yielding important palaeoecological and palaeoclimatological data are located to the east of the region (Lâdik, Kaz, Tecer), while a number of small to medium-size freshwater lakes, mainly of tectonic origin, lie along the NAFZ to the west in the region of Bolu (Melen, Abant, Yeniçağa). In addition to these, a short sequence retrieved from a small pool of solution origin located on the Miocene gypsum plateau near Çankırı (Çöl Gölü) has also been subject to a suite of palaeoecological and palaeolimnological techniques.[13] To the south of the Çorum region, two sites in the Cappadocia region of Turkey (Nar Gölü and Eski Acıgöl) provide important palaeoenvironmental data.

Three of these pollen sequences, Abant, Yeniçağa and Lâdik, extend back to the end of the last ice age and the Late Glacial period (between ~15 and ~10 thousand ^{14}C years ago) at which time arboreal or tree pollen (AP) percentage values which indicate total tree cover in northern Anatolia were significantly reduced alongside a much greater expansion of steppic pollen types.[14] Speleothem δ^{18}O data from Sofular Cave near Zonguldak[15] show that this region of Turkey experienced significant climate changes comparable with the Greenland Interstadials recorded in the ice core records of Greenland.

---

12 Reimer et al. 2004.
13 Roberts et al. 2009.
14 Bottema et al. 1993.
15 Fleitmann et al. 2009; Göktürk et al. 2011; 2008.

Importantly, δ13C data also show that northern Turkey was an important region for refugia for forest trees at this time.[16] At the onset of warming during the early Holocene period (from 11.7k Cal yr BP onwards), there was an almost immediate expansion of woodland at Abant, whereas at the other sites (Yeniçağa, Lâdik and Kaz) a slower response of woodland to climatic warming can be inferred, with the maximum extent of woodland not being achieved until around 8k yr BP (6th Millennium BC), this presumably being a response to differential rates of afforestation of arboreal elements spreading out from isolated refugial regions. The early to mid-Holocene in most pollen diagrams from the region is characterized by the establishment of woodland in this region. From late-Holocene times, however, a notable feature in many pollen sequences is the expression of a cultural phase which has close affinities to the Beyşehir Occupation Phase of southwestern Anatolia,[17] characterized by arboriculture (cultivation of fruit and nut) together with cereal farming and pastoral activities.

To a certain extent, the sites of Abant, Yeniçağa, Kaz and Lâdik in northern Turkey record elements of this cultural phase, whereas at other sites (e.g., Küçük Akgöl, Adatepe, Büyük, Demiyurt, Tuzla, Seyfe, Melen and Tatlı) the phase is lacking or is only very weakly expressed.

At Abant (Figure 11.4) this cultural (BO) phase of agriculture began at ~3k yr BP (c.650 BC) with the cultivation of pistachio, sweet chestnut, walnut, olive and vine, cereal growing and pastoralism. The phase ended at ~800 yr BP (AD c.1100) although cereal growing and pastoralism continued, albeit at reduced intensities. At Yeniçağa (Figure 11.5) the BO phase began at ~4.4k yr BP (c.3200 BC), but the main emphasis at this site was cereal cultivation and pastoralism, and the phase ended at ~3.5k yr BP (c.1840 BC). At Kaz (Figure 11.6) the BO phase commenced at ~2.2k yr BP (c.250 BC) with the cultivation of pistachio, sweet chestnut, walnut, olive and vine, cereal growing and pastoralism and ended at ~1350 yr BP (AD c.600), although cereal growing and pastoralism continued. The BO phase at Lâdik (Fig. 11.7) commenced at ~3.5k yr BP (c.1840 BC) with the cultivation of pistachio, sweet chestnut, walnut, olive and vine, cereal growing and pastoralism and ended at ~1250 yr BP (AD c.650), although cereal growing and pastoralism continued during post-BO phase times.

Although the BO phase, as expressed in pollen diagrams from southwest Turkey, also shows a range of dates for its commencement and ending, most of the ages in this region indicate that it began during the later second millennium BC after the volcanic eruption of Santorini[18] and ended during

---

16   Fleitmann et al. 2009.
17   Eastwood et al. 1998; Bottema et al. 1986.
18   Eastwood et al. 1998; Zanchetta et al. 2011.

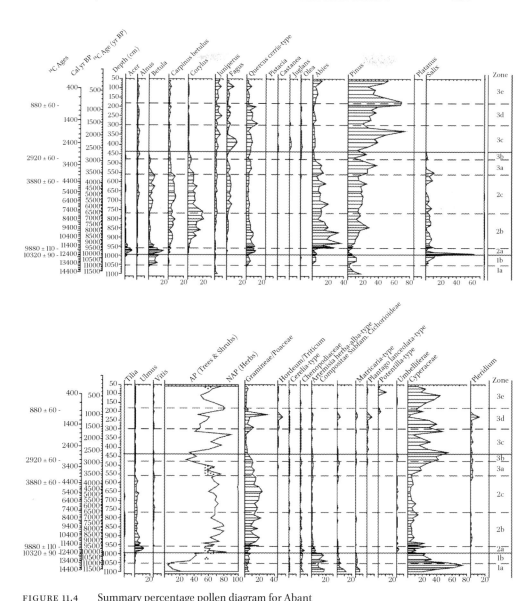

FIGURE 11.4   Summary percentage pollen diagram for Abant
REDRAWN FROM BOTTEMA ET AL. 1993

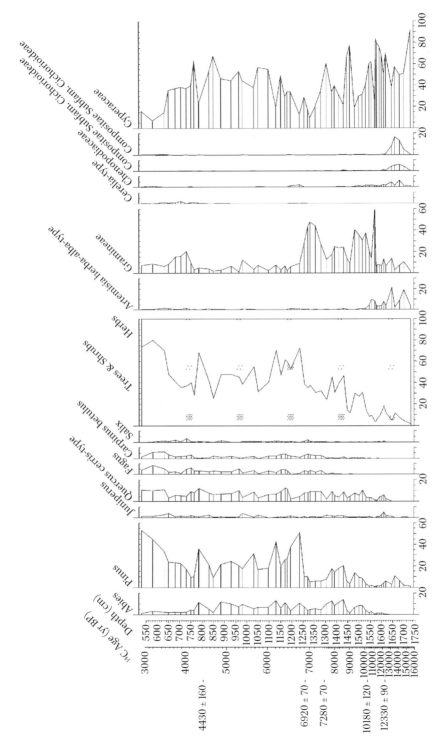

FIGURE 11.5 Summary percentage pollen diagram for Yeniçağa
REDRAWN FROM BOTTEMA ET AL. 1993

EUCHAÏTA, LANDSCAPE AND CLIMATE IN THE BYZANTINE PERIOD 291

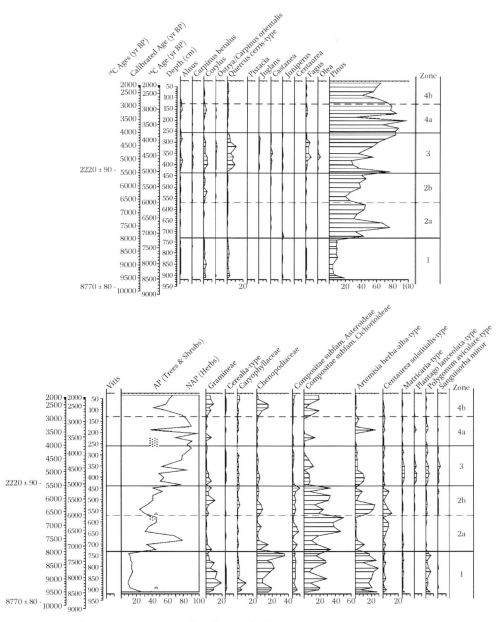

FIGURE 11.6 Summary percentage pollen diagram for Kaz
REDRAWN FROM BOTTEMA ET AL. 1993

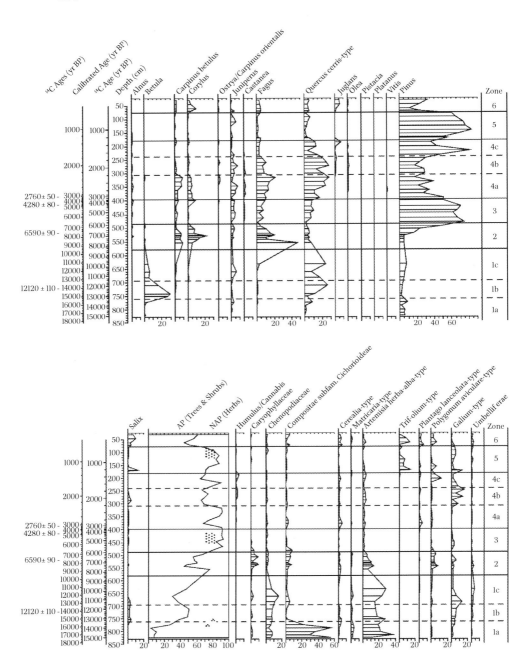

FIGURE 11.7   Summary percentage pollen diagram for Lâdik
REDRAWN FROM BOTTEMA ET AL. 1993

the mid-first millennium AD around the time of the Arab raids and the Arab–Byzantine wars. After this cultural phase ended in southwest Turkey, pollen types indicating cultural activity mostly disappear from the pollen diagrams and there is often a marked and frequently sustained increase in pine pollen. One notable difference between pollen diagrams recording the BO phase in its core region of southwest Turkey and other sites – for example, Gölcük (Sardis) in western Anatolia, Nar Gölü (Cappadocia) and the sites discussed above in northern Turkey – is the record of post BO phase changes. At these sites, there is pollen evidence of agricultural activity continuing well into early medieval and medieval periods. Pollen data for Gölcük (Sardis) suggest that the BO phase came to an end around ~1750 yr BP (AD c.250). Olive, sweet chestnut, walnut and pistachio were still cultivated, although on a lesser scale, between AD 250 and 950. Yet cereal cultivation appears to have increased and pastoralism continued to be well-represented into the medieval period despite the decline in arboriculture. But this is in marked contrast not only to those sites in southwest Turkey, but also to Cappadocia (Lake Nar), and is different again from northern Turkey, where once again cereal production and livestock farming seem to have increased at the expense of arboriculture. The key point is quite simply that the BO Phase has a great deal of heterogeneity and, crucially, we cannot assume that the picture derived for the better-studied southwest applies elsewhere, nor that it can support the sort of historical developments found elsewhere.[19]

Similarly, pollen data for Nar Gölü suggest that, although the typical BO-phase arboricultural elements did not continue after the BO phase ended at AD c.670, coeval with Arab raiding in the region, once the Byzantines had regained control of Cappadocia during the late 9th century AD cereal cultivation and pastoralism were practised by the returning Byzantines and this continued through the Seljuk, Karaman and Ottoman periods, representing a period of more or less unbroken landscape continuity in the region.[20] Pollen data for Abant, Kaz and Lâdik in northern Turkey (the pollen record for Yeniçağa terminates at ~3000 yr BP) also show post BO phase quasi-continuity of agricultural activity in the form of cereal cultivation and pastoralism; these data suggest that there were distinct regional differences in the trajectory of landscape change once the BO cultural phase came to an end, although more detailed work is required to elucidate and tease out important nuances of the nature, character and timings of post BO phase changes in this part of

19 Sullivan 1989. See now Danladi et al. 2023.
20 England et al. 2008; Eastwood et al. 2009.

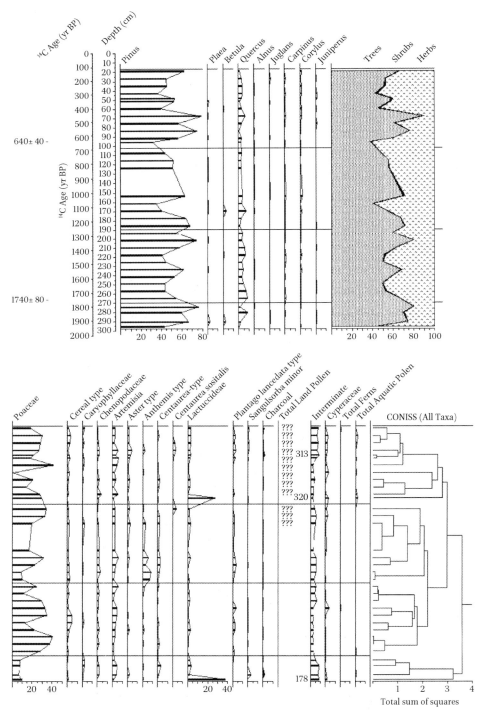

FIGURE 11.8 Summary percentage pollen diagram for Çöl
REDRAWN FROM ROBERTS ET AL. 2009

northern Turkey for comparison with archaeological and historical evidence of land-use change.[21]

The relatively short pollen record from Çöl Gölü located on the Miocene gypsum plateau near Çankırı is the closest pollen sequence to Çorum province and Avkat and covers the last 2,000 years or so and is notable for its absence of a Beyşehir Occupation-type phase (Figure 11.8). According to radiocarbon dating, at the time of the end of the BO Phase elsewhere (6th to 8th centuries AD) there was a slight decline in cereal-type pollen and grazing indicators (e.g. *Plantago lanceolata*) and an increase in pine pollen percentage values, although other cultural indicators are absent or only show a sporadic or trace presence (e.g. walnut; *Juglans*). Pollen data therefore suggest that the gypsum plateau around Çöl Gölü experienced a different land-use history from most other areas of northern Anatolia, and this may be attributable largely to its location in a mostly barren environment devoid of trees. This must have always been a marginalized landscape for agriculture on account of the saline soils (derived from the gypsum regolith) and a lack of potable water – an attribute of its geology; past environmental conditions would not have been dissimilar from the present day. However, the Çöl pollen data also suggest a quasi-continuity of low intensity agricultural activity in the form of cereal cultivation and pastoralism persisting at this site to sub-recent times, as shown at other sites in northern Turkey.[22]

1.5   Other Proxy Data

Alongside pollen data, there are other important proxy techniques or indicators that have the potential to inform on environmental and climatic changes, including magnetic susceptibility, mineralogy and sediment geochemistry analyses. Whereas pollen data from Çöl Gölü are relatively complacent in showing significant land-use changes, Sr-Ca ratio data and mineralogical data, in contrast, can be *tentatively* interpreted in terms of climatic change, and do suggest a marked change to drier climatic conditions at AD 1400 according to the radiocarbon-dated chronology for the site. This climatic shift has been found in other lake sediment records elsewhere in Anatolia and dated to around the start of the European Little Ice Age (LIA); however, in the north-central region of Anatolia, palaeoclimatic data suggest a significant shift to a drier climate, rather than a wetter climate that characterizes the climate of the LIA in Europe. Stable isotopic and carbonate mineralogy data from the highly-resolved and annually-laminated crater lake sequence from Nar Gölü in

---

21   Izdebski 2012.
22   Roberts et al. 2009.

Cappadocia also show a clear switch at this time,[23] and when the Çöl and Nar sequences are plotted on a common timescale,[24] a good overall correspondence is achieved, not only for the period around AD 1400, but for other periods as well. This includes drier climatic conditions recorded at Nar Gölü from the start of the record (300 CE) to AD 530, an earlier shorter-lived phase of drier climatic conditions from AD 750 to 950, and an intervening phase of relatively wetter conditions from AD 530–750.[25] Later phases of notable arid periods recorded at Nar Gölü are centred around AD 1600, 1720, 1790, the 1870s and the 1920s.[26]

Mineralogical and lithological data for the last 6000 years from the lake site of Tecer Gölü located ~40 km south of Sivas[27] show significant changes in climate. The mid-Holocene transition (from the 6th to 3rd millennia BP) is characterized by the alternation of multicentennial wet and dry phases with intense droughts occurring at the end of the 6th, 5th and 4th millennia BP, while the later Holocene (the last two millennia) is characterized by short-lived 50–100-yr dry/wet episodes. In particular, the period 2020–1450 yr BP (70 BC–AD 500) corresponds to the so-called Roman Climatic Optimum (Roman Warm Period)[28] and from AD c.250 to 400 in particular, the data suggest climatic aridity, which closely mirrors the data from Nar Gölü. The record of the transition to the Medieval Climatic Anomaly at Tecer (1450–1130 yr BP; AD 500–820) is characterized by increasingly wetter climatic conditions; again, the data from Tecer Gölü match very closely those from Nar for the same time period (AD 530–750). These trends in humidity can be interpreted as an increase in winter rainfall and a decrease in summer evaporation. The period AD 820–1000 at Tecer is characterized by progressively drier climatic conditions followed by a phase of increased rainfall and cooler temperatures dated AD 1000–1150; again, there is a close correspondence between the two sequences with the Nar sequence indicating drier climatic conditions recorded for the period AD 850–950 and wetter between AD 950–1100 and then

23 Jones et al. 2006.
24 Roberts et al. 2009; Jones et al. 2006.
25 Roberts et al. 2009.
26 Jones et al. 2006.
27 Kuzucuoğlu et al. 2011.
28 A concept that has recently been brought into question, since it assumes that conditions in the western provinces of the empire (the basis for the concept lies in data from the Alps and Scandinavia) prevailed across the Mediterranean more widely. See, e.g., Bini et al. 2020, and discussion in Luterbacher et al. 2021. We retain it for the present simply as a reference point.

EUCHAÏTA, LANDSCAPE AND CLIMATE IN THE BYZANTINE PERIOD

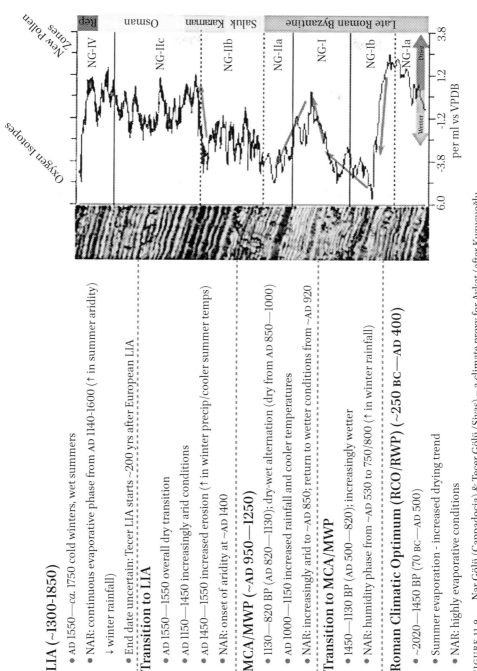

LIA (~1300-1850)
- AD 1550—ca. 1750 cold winters, wet summers
- NAR: continuous evaporative phase from AD 1140-1600 (↑ in summer aridity/ ↓ winter rainfall)
- End date uncertain: Tecer LIA starts ~200 yrs after European LIA

Transition to LIA
- AD 1550—1550 overall dry transition
- AD 1150—1450 increasingly arid conditions
- AD 1450—1550 increased erosion (↑ in winter precip/cooler summer temps)
- NAR: onset of aridity at ~AD 1400

MCA/MWP (~AD 950—1250)
- 1130—820 BP (AD 820—1130); dry-wet alternation (dry from AD 850—1000)
- AD 1000—1150 increased rainfall and cooler temperatures
- NAR: increasingly arid to ~AD 850; return to wetter conditions from ~AD 920

Transition to MCA/MWP
- 1450—1130 BP (AD 500—820); increasingly wetter
- NAR: humidity phase from ~AD 530 to 750/800 (↑ in winter rainfall)

Roman Climatic Optimum (RCO/RWP) (~250 BC—AD 400)
- ~2020—1450 BP (70 BC—AD 500)
- Summer evaporation - increased drying trend
- NAR: highly evaporative conditions

FIGURE 11.9 Nar Gölü (Cappadocia) & Tecer Gölü (Sivas) – a climate proxy for Avkat (after Kuzucuoğlu et al. 2011; Jones et al. 2006; England et al. 2008)

a generally wetter period until AD 1400. The European Little Ice Age is also recorded in the Tecer lake sediment archive. From AD 1150 to 1450, increasing climatic aridity is indicated with a decrease in winter rainfall and an increase in summer temperatures; this corresponding to climatic aridity recorded in the Nar sequence from AD 1400.

From AD c.1400, however, the Tecer and Nar records apparently diverge; at Nar a continued evaporative phase (i.e. drier climatic conditions) is recorded from AD 1400 to 1960, whereas the data from Tecer for the period AD 1450 to 1550 suggest an increase in winter precipitation and possibly cooler summer temperatures. From AD 1550 the Tecer data suggest climatic conditions resembling the LIA in western Europe (cold winters and wet summers). The Tecer sequence ends at AD 1750 and subsequent data are unreliable, due most likely to mixing of sediments. Although there is some mismatch between the Nar and Tecer climatic inferences, particularly for later periods, the records closely resemble each other. As indicated by Figure 11.9, today the sites of Tecer and Nar Gölü are located in the same "inland" climatic regime.[29] The fact that the Nar, Tecer and, to a certain extent, the Çöl climate records resemble each other for much of the historical period lends credence to the suggestion that this inland climatic regime is characteristic of the broader geographic region both spatially and temporally. This "locational correspondence" furthermore allows inferences to be made for the climate history of the Çorum region as well as broader assessments on the coherency of the climate signal for this region through time. It also permits broader inferences on hemispherical controlling mechanisms and processes affecting climate in north-central Turkey.

1.6   Evidence for the Byzantine and Medieval Environment

The situation of Euchaïta was not favourable, and Strabo describes the area, which represented the southerly portion of Phazemonitis bordering on the district called Diakopene, as "in general bare of trees and productive of grain".[30] The 11th-century bishop John Mauropous describes the region around Euchaïta in the following terms:

> the land is very desolate, uninhabited, unpleasant and without trees, vegetation, woods or shade, a total wilderness full of neglect ... It abounds, however, in the production of grain, although this also is achieved with

---

29   As defined by Sarış et al. 2010.
30   Strabo, *Geography*, xii, 3. 38. Phazemon (mod. Merzifon) was renamed Neapolis by Pompey, although its ancient name survived. For Diakopene, which runs along the southern fringe of the Phazemonitis, see xii, 3.39.

much toil, but with regard to wine and oil and next to such products, the land is unfortunate owing to its utter poverty and want ... it lacks fruit and fish and in addition anything that comforts people ... as well as that which is necessary for the enjoyment of a sumptuous table.[31]

This situation matches the topographical and climatic context and is fairly typical of the northern fringes of the Anatolian plateau, although, in the more favourable district around Amaseia, both olive- and vine-cultivation flourished.[32] The picture painted by Mauropous is comparable to that drawn by Leo, the bishop of Synnada, a century earlier, for his city. While located some 350 miles from Euchaïta, this city was located likewise on the fringe of the central Anatolian plateau and, according to Leo, produces neither olive oil nor wine, "because of the high altitude and the short growing season", nor even wheat, producing only barley. Wood is scarce, so the local rural population make dung-cakes (*zarzaka*), which they burn as their main source of heat. In modern Avkat such dung-cakes, known as *tezek*, are still prepared, although employed chiefly outdoors and for heating the çay urn. They remain a common feature of the Anatolian plateau.[33] European travellers from the 16th century noted a similar landscape.[34]

Modern studies of the Byzantine agricultural economy provide a general sketch of Byzantine farming synthesized primarily from the textual sources, dealing with the agricultural cycle and seasons, techniques of arable and pastoral exploitation, and the evidence for the rates of return on seed sown, taking account of regional variation as well as historical evolution in the period from the 6th to the 11th century in particular.[35] Closer to Avakt in time and location, the data generated by the work carried out at Çadır Höyük, near Peyniryemez, some distance to the SSW of Euchaïta, also offers useful information on farming

31 Mauropous, *Letters*, Ep. 64. 55–62 (see also Hendy, *Studies*: 140–41).
32 See the excellent introduction to the basic geography and topography of the Pontus in Bryer and Winfield 1985: 1–7.
33 For a detailed discussion of Leo's comments on *zarzakon* and on the more recent history of *tezek* in Asia Minor, see Robert 1961: 115–34; Vinson 1985: Ep. 43. 7–13; 20–21.
34 Dernschwam and Busbeck, in Babinger 1923: 201f., 206–7; 198 (see Yerasimos 1991: 230–33, at 232). The imperial ambassador Busbeck travelled across Asia Minor to Amaseia on one of his missions in the same years but offers no account of the landscape and merely mentions Çorum in passing, although he does give a short account of the tekke at Elvan Çelebi: see Yerasimos 1991: 239–42, at 241; Busbeck (trans. Forster): 54–6; Anderson 1903: 5–17. For a collection of more recent travelers across the central Anatolian plateau, with similar observations, and whose comments bear also on conditions in and around Avkat/Euchaïta, see Robert 1961: 117–25.
35 Kaplan 1992: esp. 25–87; Lefort 2002.

and land-use.³⁶ But there is virtually no specific data from medieval written sources, and very little from the archaeology, to help in detecting shifts in patterns of production and consumption that may have been the consequence or were at least associated with changes in environmental conditions in the region and more widely.

The proxy data for pre-modern climate discussed above indicate a somewhat wetter climate in much of Anatolia during the 6th and up to the middle of the 8th century, stretching in some areas into the 9th century. The point at which this phase ends varied according to whether we look at the data from the southwest, the Aegean, the centre or the north, as the evidence from sites from these different regions would seem to demonstrate. In contrast, evidence from sites in southwest Anatolia, as well as in the southern Caucasus and the area around L. Van, suggests an earlier onset of aridity, from the middle of the 7th century.³⁷ These data may be limited, but they nevertheless illustrate the variations in the pace and nature of climate change, especially from humid to arid and from warm to cold, across Anatolia. It is complemented by documentary evidence for the period, which hints at the instability that such conditions promoted: a comparatively greater number of severe winters from c.570 into the 740s in the Levant and some parts of Asia Minor, with occasional droughts and aridity-related events.³⁸

As noted above, palynological data suggest some marked regional and sub-regional variations in land use. This evidence, together with archaeological data, shows that land was relatively intensively exploited into the 6th and 7th centuries, with variations according to local conditions, but including marginal land. A fairly densely settled landscape characterized by mixed farming was typical of many areas. From the middle of the 5th century, peaking by the middle and later 7th century, this regime receded. The established pattern is slowly replaced, in some cases by natural vegetation or, more often, by a more limited range of crops. Cereal production and livestock raising come to dominate, viticulture and oleoculture recede and almost vanish from many areas, while evidence of fruticulture is also sparse.

The data suggest that a simplified agrarian economy evolved in many parts of Anatolia from the 6th or 7th century, notably in Cappadocia, in parts of

---

36 See Cassis 2009.
37 Results from analyses of data from several sites across Asia Minor are briefly summarized in Izdebski 2013: conclusions at 201–14; a briefer account: Izdebski 2012; see also Barlas Şimşek and Çağatay 2018 for L. Van.
38 Evidence summarized in tabular form in Telelis 2004 and Stathakopoulos 2004.

southwestern Asia Minor, to a degree in Bithynia and the northwest, and in eastern Paphlagonia.[39] This general picture fits with what is known from the textual and the archaeological evidence about conditions during this period.[40] In contrast, a further shift in the pollen evidence from the later 10th century onwards reflects at several sites an intensification of this simplified regime, an expansion of large-scale pastoral farming and, in some cases, the reappearance in some contexts of vines, olives and fruit. These are features that coincide with the political and economic recovery of the empire in the course of the later 9th and 10th centuries, and also with the end of the arid period that lasts from the 7th/8th century into the 10th/11th century.[41] The fact that northern Anatolia experienced a cooler and wetter regime during the period from the 6th/7th into the 8th/9th centuries is thus important for any appreciation of the regional economy, settlement pattern and politics, and certainly needs to be considered when looking at the history of Euchaïta across this period.[42]

1.7 Oleoculture

Strabo notes the large-scale olive production on the Black Sea coast, whereas for the interior only Phanaroea, a fertile valley northeast of Amasya, was a producer of olives.[43] Olives are not grown today in the Mecitözü Valley and Çorum province does not record the commercial production of olives. Local winters at 800 m are too harsh for the trees to grow. Yet the presence of numerous press weights in many villages in the area, often ornamented with Christian symbols, were described by Anderson, who assumed they were for olive presses.[44] The survey, however, found no evidence for olive crushing, and there is only a single element from a crushing or grinding facility on display in the Çorum Museum. If the press-weights in question were for olives, then they can be explained only by either a change in climate or by the import of olives. Since no crushing elements were located in the Euchaïta area, the importing of olives to be crushed locally seems unlikely, albeit not impossible. An alternative may be that the press weights were employed in wine production, as may have been the case

---

39   For example, Baird 2004.
40   See Cassis et al. 2018; Roberts et al. 2018; Haldon et al. 2014; Brubaker and Haldon 2011: 531–63.
41   Izdebski 2012 and 2013.
42   Haldon 2019. For the broader archaeological and settlement-demographic context see Newhard et al. 2021.
43   Strabo, *Geography*, ii.1.15, xii.3.12; xii, 3.30.
44   Anderson 1903: 14–16; Paton and Myres 1898.

at Amorium and Hadrianopolis,[45] although it is also the case that the archaeological evidence for oil as opposed to wine production is not always clear.[46]

While the proxy data for the wider northern Anatolian regions suggest that olive production had been limited to a few specific areas, what olive cultivation there had been in the region in Late Antiquity and during the early Byzantine period appears to have been badly affected by climatic changes. Thus, the region around Sinop, while known in antiquity as especially favourable for the production of olives (and is described by Strabo in the 1st century BC as densely covered by olive groves), seems to have suffered a dramatic drop in settlement density that corresponds with the 7th century and the cooler and wetter climatic conditions that came to prevail around that time.[47] Since oleoculture is especially sensitive to temperature conditions, it would be sensitive to this climatic shift. Both the documentary evidence and proxy data for climate show that severe winters became increasingly common from the 6th century onward, thus rendering olive trees at or above 1000 m above sea level very vulnerable. The late antique decline in olive cultivation indicated in the palynology and the archaeology is thus likely to have been due to climatic adversity (and the dramatic reduction in rural settlement in the hinterland of Sinop would be explained by, inter alia, the collapse of the olive industry in the region).[48]

The Avkat region today has a low population, and it is likely that this was also the case in earlier periods. The survey of the hinterland of Beyözü suggests that settlement patterns in antiquity were similar to those of the modern era – that is, nucleated settlements with intervening farmsteads. The widespread distribution of ceramics indicates a denser pattern of small settlements, but until the ceramic picture becomes clearer it is impossible to determine whether this changed during the later 6th or 7th century, as seems to have been the case in the Sinop region, for example, and as has been noted for a number of other regions in Anatolia and indeed throughout the late Roman eastern Mediterranean world. The relatively low volume of ceramics and the low volume of imports noted from the surface survey would nevertheless suggest that the picture here was similar. The major shift to wetter conditions that took place in the late 6th century onwards in this region may have benefited

---

45   Lightfoot 2003: 73–4, 78, Pl. v/10; Laflı and Zäh 2008: 711 and text fig. 9.
46   Kassab-Tezgör and Tatlıcan 1998: 438–440; Doonan 2004: 150–51.
47   Doonan 2004. Strabo, *Geography*, ii, 1. 15; xii, 3. 12, implies that this coast of Sinope held a monopoly on Black Sea olive production because of its unique micro-climate. For discussion, see Doonan 2003; Kassab Tezgör, Tatlıcan and Özdaş 1998; Doonan et al. 2014.
48   For further discussion of past changes to olive cultivation in Anatolia, see England et al. 2008; Roberts 1990.

agricultural output, especially in respect of cereal production and possibly livestock. More proxy data are needed for the region, however, before definite conclusions can be reached. If this provisional conclusion is correct, it may well help to explain, in part at least, the relative rise in significance of Euchaïta during the period from the 7th to 10th centuries.

Bibliography

Primary Sources

Forster, E.S. 1968. *The Turkish letters of Ogier Ghiselin de Busbecq, imperial ambassador at Constantinople 1554–1562* (Oxford).

Babinger, F. 1923/1986. *Hans Dernschwam's Tagebuch einer Reise nach Konstantinopel und Kleinasien (1553/55). Nach der Urschrift im Fugger-Archiv herausgegeben und erläutert* (Berlin-Munich).

Karpozilos, A. (ed.) 1990. *The Letters of Ioannes Mauropous Metropolitan of Euchaita* (CFHB 34. Thessalonica).

The Geography of Strabo, transl. H.L. Jones (Loeb Classical Library. London-NY 1928), 8 vols.

Secondary Literature

Anderson, J.G.C. 1903. *Studia Pontica I. A Journey of Exploration in Pontus* (Brussels).

Asouti, E. and C. Kabukcu. 2014. "Holocene semi-arid oak woodlands in the Irano-Anatolian region of Southwest Asia: natural or anthropogenic", *Quaternary Science Reviews* 90: 158–82.

Atalay, I. and R. Efe. 2012. "Ecological attributes and distribution of Anatolian black pine [*Pinus nigra* Arnold. subsp. *pallasiana* Lamb. Holmboe] in Turkey", *Journal of Environmental Biology* 33: 509–19.

Baird, D. 2004. "Settlement expansion on the Konya Plain, Anatolia: 5th–7th centuries A.D.", in Bowden, Lavan and Machado 2004: 219–46.

Barlas Şimşek, F. and M.N. Çağatay. 2018. "Late Holocene high resolution multiproxy climate and environmental records from Lake Van, eastern Turkey", *Quaternary International* 486: 57–72.

Bini, M., Zanchetta, G., Regattieri, E., Isola, I., Drysdale, R.N., Fabiani, F., Genovesi, S. and J.C. Hellstrom. 2020. "Hydrological changes during the Roman Climatic Optimum in northern Tuscany (Central Italy) as evidenced by speleothem records and archaeological data", *Journal of Quaternary Science* 35/6: 791–802 https://doi.org/10.1002/jqs.3224.

Bottema, S., Woldring, H. and B. Aytuğ. 1993. "Late Quaternary vegetation history of northern Turkey", *Palaeohistoria* 35/36: 13–72.

Bottema, S., Woldring, H. and B. Aytuğ. 1986. 'Palynological investigations on the relations between prehistoric man and vegetation in Turkey: the Beyşehir Occupation Phase', *Proceedings of the 5th Optima Congress, September 1986* (Istanbul): 315–28.

Bowden, W., L. Lavan and C. Machado, eds. 2004. *Recent research on the late Antique countryside* (Leiden).

Brubaker, L. and J.F. Haldon. 2011. *Byzantium in the iconoclast era (c. 680–850). A history* (Cambridge).

Bryer, A.A.M. and D. Winfield. 1985. *The Byzantine monuments and topography of the Pontos*, 2 vols. (Washington D.C.).

Cassis, M. 2009. "Çadir Höyük: a rural settlement in Byzantine Anatolia", in Vorderstrasse & Roodenberg 2009: 1–24.

Cassis, M., Doonan, O., Elton, H. and J. Newhard. 2018. "Evaluating archaeological evidence for demographics, abandonment, and recovery in Late Antique and Byzantine Anatolia", in Haldon et al. 2018: 381–398.

Danladi, I.B., Akçer-Ön, S., Litt, T., Bora Ön, Z. and L. Wacker. 2023. "A Late Holocene climate reconstruction from the high-altitude Lake Gölcük sedimentary records, Isparta (SW Anatolia)", *Quaternary Research*: 1–14 https://doi.org/10.1017/qua.2023.26.

Dönmez, E.O., Ocakoğlu, F., Aydın Akbulut, Tunoğlu, C., Gümüş, B.A., Tuncer, A., Görüm, T. and M. Tün. 2021. "Vegetation record of the last three millennia in central Anatolia: archaeological and palaeoclimatic insights from Mogan Lake (Ankara, Turkey)", *Quaternary Science Reviews* 262: 106973 https://doi.org/10.1016/j.quascirev.2021.106973.

Doonan, O.P. et al. 2014. "Sinop bölgesel arkeoloji projesi 2012 saha çalışmaları", *Araştırma Sonuçları Toplantısı* 31 Ankara).

Doonan, O.P. 2004. *Sinop landscapes: exploring connections in a Black Sea hinterland* (Philadelphia).

Doonan, O.P. 2003. "Production in a Pontic landscape: the hinterland of Greek and Roman Sinope", in M. Faudot et al., eds., *Pont-Euxin et commerce: la genèse de la "Route de soie"* (Besançon): 185–98.

Eastwood, W.J., O. Gümüşçü, H. Yiğitbaşioğlu, J.F. Haldon and A. England. 2009, "Integrating palaeoecological and archaeo-historical records: land use and landscape change in Cappadocia (central Turkey) since late Antiquity", in Vorderstrasse and Roodenberg 2009: 45–69.

Eastwood, W.J., Roberts, C.N. and H.F. Lamb, "Palaeoecological and srchaeological evidence for human occupancy in southwest Turkey: the Beyşehir Occupation Phase", *Anatolian Studies* 48 (1998), 69–86.

England, A., Eastwood, W.J., Roberts, C.N., Turner, R. and J.F. Haldon. 2008. "Historical landscape change in Cappadocia (central Turkey): a paleoecological investigation of annually-laminated sediments from Nar Lake", *The Holocene* 18/8: 1229–1245.

Fleitmann, D., et al. 2009. "Timing and climatic impact of Greenland interstadials recorded in stalagmites from northern Turkey", *Geophysical Research Letters* 36: L19707, doi:10.1029/2009GL040050.

Göktürk, O.M., Fleitmann, D., Badertsscher, S., Cheng, H., Edwards, R.L., Leuenberger, M., Fankhauser, A., Tuysuz, O. and J. Kramers. 2011. "Climate on the southern Black Sea coast during the Holocene: implications from the Sofular Cave record", *Quaternary Science Reviews* 30: 2433–45.

Göktürk, O.M., Bozkurt, D., Şen, O.L. and M. Karaca. 2008. "Quality control and homogeneity of Turkish precipitation data", *Hydrological Processes* 22: 3210–18.

Haldon, J.F. 2019. "Some thoughts on climate change, local environment and grain production in Byzantine northern Anatolia", in A. Izdebski and M. Mulryan, eds., *Environment and society in the long Late Antiquity*. Late Antique Archaeology 12 (Leiden): 200–206.

Haldon, J.F. 2016. *A tale of two saints. The martyrdoms and miracles of Sts Theodore 'the recruit' and 'the general'* (Liverpool).

Haldon, J., Rosen, A.M., White, S., Akçer-Ön, S., Allcock, S., Bozkurt, D., Cassis, M., Doonan, O., Eastwood, W.J., Elton, H., Fleitmann, D., Izdebski, A., Laparidou, S., Lüterbacher, J., Mordechai, L., Newhard, J., Pickett, J., Preiser-Kapeller, J., Roberts, N., Sargent, A., Soroush, M., Toreti, A., Wagner, S., Xoplaki, E. and E. Zorita. 2018. *Society and environment in the East Mediterranean ca 300–1800 CE. Resilience, adaptation, transformation.* Special Issue, *Human Ecology* 46/3: 273–398.

Haldon, J.F., Elton, H. and J. Newhard. 2017. "Euchaïta", in Ph. Niewöhner, ed., *The archaeology of Byzantine Anatolia: from Late Antiquity to the coming of the Turks* (Oxford): 375–88.

Haldon, J.F., Elton, H. and J. Newhard. 2015. "Euchaïta", in S. Steadman and G. McMahon, eds., *The archaeology of Anatolia: current work* (Cambridge): 332–55.

Haldon, J.F., Roberts, N., Izdebski, A., Fleitmann, D., McCormick, M., Cassis, M., Doonan, O., Eastwood, W., Elton, H., Ladstätter, S., Manning, S., Newhard, J., Nicoll, K., Telelis, I., and E. Xoplaki. 2014. "The Climate and Environment of Byzantine Anatolia: Integrating Science, History, and Archaeology", *Journal of Interdisciplinary History* 45.2: 113–61.

Hendy, M.F. 1985. *Studies in the Byzantine monetary economy, c.300–1450* (Cambridge).

Izdebski, A. 2013. *A rural economy in transition. Asia Minor from the end of Antiquity into the early middle ages* (Leiden).

Izdebski, A. 2012. "The changing landscapes of Byzantine northern Anatolia", *Archaeologia Bulgarica* 16: 47–66.

Jacobson, M.J., Pickett, J., Gascoigne, J., Elton, H. and D. Fleitmann. 2022. "Settlement, environment, and climate change in SW Anatolia: dynamics of regional variation and the end of Antiquity", *PLoS ONE* 17/6: e0270295. https://doi.org/10.1371/journal.pone.0270295.

Jones, M.D., Roberts, C.N., Leng, M.J., and M. Türkeş. 2006. "A high-resolution late Holocene lake isotope record from Turkey and links to North Atlantic and monsoon climate", *Geology* 34: 361–64.

Kaplan, M. 1992. *Les hommes et la terre à Byzance du VIe au XIe siècle. Propriété et exploitation du sol* (Paris).

Kassab-Tezgör, D. and İ. Tatlıcan. 1998. "Fouilles des ateliers d'amphores à Demirci", *Anatolia Antiqua* 6: 423–42.

Kassab Tezgör, D., Tatlıcan, I., and H. Özdaş. 1998. "Prospection sous-marine près de la coté sinopeénne: Transport d'amphores depuis l'atelier et navigation en Mer Noire", *Anatolia Antiqua* 6: 443–49.

Kavgaci, A., Arslan, M., Bingöl, Ü., Erdoğan, N. and A. Çarni. 2012. "Classification and phytogeographical differentiation of oriental beech forests in Turkey and Bulgaria", *Biologia* 67/3: 461–73.

Kömüşçü, A.Ü., Erkan, A., Turgu, E. and F.K. Sönmez. 2004. "A new insight into drought vulnerability in Turkey using the standard precipitation index", *Journal of Environmental Hydrology* 12/8: 1–17.

Kuzucuoğlu, C., Dörfler, W., Kunesch, S. and F. Goupille. 2011. "Mid-Holocene climate change in central Turkey: the Tecer lake record", *The Holocene* 21/1:173–88.

Laflı, E. and A. Zäh. 2008. "Archäologische Forschungen im Byzantinischen Hadrianupolis in Paphlagonien", *Byzantinische Zeitschrift* 101: 681–713.

Lefort, J. 2002. "The rural economy, seventh-twelfth centuries", in Laiou, A.E. et al. 2002 (ed.), *The Economic History of Byzantium. From the seventh through the fifteenth century* (Washington, D.C.): 231–310.

Lightfoot, C.S. 2003. "Stone screw press weights", in C.S. Lightfoot, ed., *Amorium reports* II: *Research papers and technical reports* (BAR International Series, 1170. Oxford), no. 4.

Luterbacher, J., Newfield, T.P., Xoplaki, E., Nowatzki, E., Luther, N., Zhang, M., and N. Khelifi. 2021. "Past pandemics and climate variability across the Mediterranean", *Euro-Mediterranean Journal for Environmental Integration* 5: 46 https://doi.org/10.1007/s41207-020-00197-5.

Newhard, J., Elton, H. and J. Haldon. 2021. "Assessing continuity and change in the sixth to ninth century landscape of North-Central Anatolia", in C. Roosevelt and J. Haldon., eds., *Değişim Rüzgarları: Anadolu'da Çevre ve Toplum – Winds of Change: Environment and Society in Anatolia. Papers of the 15th International ANAMED Annual Symposium* (Istanbul): 141–157.

Paton, W.R. and Myres, J.L. 1898. "On Some Karian and Hellenic Oil-Presses", *JHS* 18: 209–17.

Reimer, P.J., Baillie, M.G.L., Bard, E. et al. 2004. "IntCal04 terrestrial radiocarbon age Calibration, 0–26 cal kyr BP", *Radiocarbon* 46: 1029–1058.

Robert, L. 1961. "Les kordakia de Nicée, le combustible de Synnade et les poissons-scies. Sur les lettres d'un métropolite de Phrygie au Xe siècle. Philologie et réalités, I", *Journal des Savants*: 97–166.

Roberts, C.N., Eastwood, W.J. and J. Carolan. 2009. "Palaeolimnological investigations in Paphlagonia", in C. Glatz and R. Matthews, eds., *At empire's edge: Project Paphlagonia: regional survey in north-central Turkey* (London): 64–73.

Roberts, C.N. 1990. "Human-Induced Landscape Change in South and South-West Turkey during the Later Holocene", in Bottema, G. Entjes-Nieborg, and W. Van Zeist, eds., *Man's role in the shaping of the eastern Mediterranean landscape* (Rotterdam): 53–67.

Roberts, N., Cassis, M., Doonan, O., Eastwood, W., Elton, H., Haldon, J., Izdebski, A. and J. Newhard. 2018. "Not the end of the world? Post-classical decline and recovery in rural Anatolia", in Haldon et al. 2018: 305–322.

Şahin, K. 2006. "An example of applied agricultural climatology: Çorum Plain and its vicinity", *Kastamonu Eğitim Dergisi* 14/2: 587–98.

Sariş, F., Hannah, D.M. and W.J. Eastwood. 2010. "Spatial variability of precipitation regimes over Turkey", *Hydrological Sciences Journal* 55(2): 234–49. (doi: 10.1080/02626660903546142).

Stathakopoulos, D. 2004. *Famine and Pestilence in the Late Roman and Early Byzantine Empire* (Aldershot).

Sullivan, D.G. 1989. *Human-induced vegetation change in western Turkey: Pollen evidence from central Lydia* (unpublished PhD Thesis. University of California, Berkeley).

Telelis, I.G. 2004. *Μετεωρολογικά Φαινόμενα και κλίμα στο Βυζάντιο*. 2 vols. (Athens).

Vinson, M. 1985. ed. and trans., *The correspondence of Leo metropolitan of Synada and syncellus* (DOT 8. Washington, D.C.).

Vorderstrasse, T. and J. Roodenberg, eds. 2009. *Archaeology of the countryside in medieval Anatolia* (Leiden).

Walter, H. 1956. "Das Problem der zentralanatolischen Steppe", *Flora* 143: 295–326.

Yerasimos, S. 1991. *Les voyageurs dans l'empire ottoman (XIVe–XVIe siècles). Bibliographie, itinéraires et inventaire des lieux habités* (Conseil suprême d'Atatürk pour culture, langue et histoire. Publications de la société turque d'histoire Ser. VII, n. 117. Ankara).

Zanchetta, G., Sulpizio, R., Roberts, C.N., Cioni, R., Eastwood, W.J. and G. Siani. 2011. "Nephrostratigraphy, chronology and climatic events of the Mediterranean basin during the Holocene: An overview", *The Holocene* 21: 33–52.

CHAPTER 12

Ecology, Irrigation and Lordship in the Lake Van Region: A Long-Term View from Urartu to Vaspurakan

Johannes Preiser-Kapeller

1   The Geography and Climate of Historical Armenia

The historical Armenian highlands, which today lie mostly within the borders of Turkey and in smaller part within the Republic of Armenia and in Azerbaijan, are characterized by a landscape fragmented by various mountain ranges and larger alluvial plains around rivers and lakes. These were of central economic importance, but also often show a delicate ecological balance regarding temperatures, precipitation, and evaporation.[1] One central region of historical Armenia was the area around Lake Van (at an altitude of 1719 m above sea level), today in southeastern Turkey (see Fig. 12.1). While one of the largest water bodies in the entire Middle East (at 3740 km^2), the lake's alkaline water (with a pH of 9.8) is unsuitable for any agricultural use. The climate is continental, with cold winters (though, due to the salinity, ice very rarely forms on the lake) and warm, dry summers. Most of the precipitation, which varies between 300 and 400 mm over the year, occurs between October and December and between March and May (see Fig. 12.2). Various mountain ranges fragment the lake's environs into a series of smaller plains, which amount to only 15 per cent of the area around Lake Van. One of the largest of these, to the east of the lake around the ancient and modern city of Van, is characterized by the aforementioned tenuous balance of precipitation, evaporation, and temperature, which provides challenges for rain-fed agriculture without the use of irrigation. Furthermore, due to long snow coverage and cold, fields often could only be planted in May and therefore needed water especially in June and July, when rainfall was usually insufficient. Therefore, until the early 20th century,

---

1 Hewsen, "Van in this World", pp. 13–14; Schweizer, *Untersuchungen zur Physiogeographie*; Stadelbauer, *Studien zur Agrargeographie Transkaukasiens*; Çevik, "The Change of Settlement Patterns", p. 75; Grekyan, "When the gods leave people", pp. 57–58.

ECOLOGY, IRRIGATION AND LORDSHIP IN THE LAKE VAN REGION 309

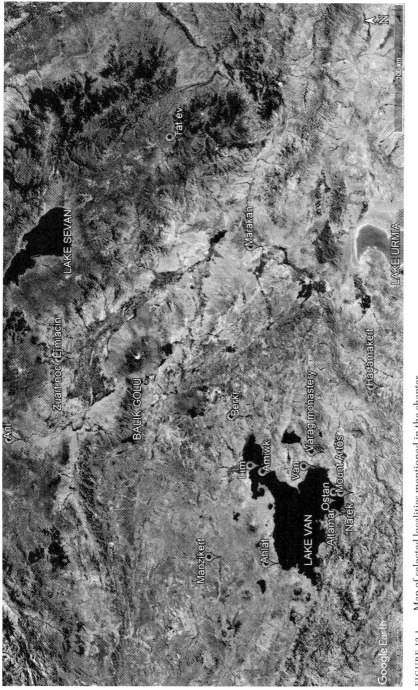

FIGURE 12.1   Map of selected localities mentioned in the chapter
J. PREISER-KAPELLER, OEAW, 2021; BASE MAP: GOOGLEEARTH

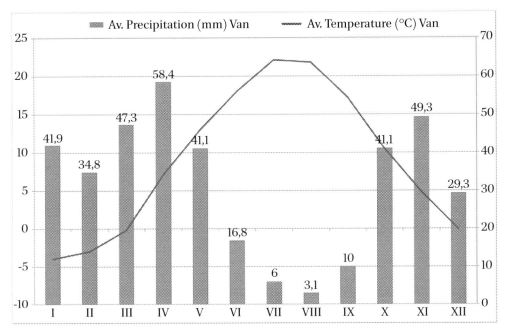

FIGURE 12.2   Diagram of modern-day monthly average temperature (degree Celsius) and precipitation (mm) in the city of Van
J. PREISER-KAPELLER, OEAW, 2021

in many areas, animal husbandry had a much higher share in the activities of the local population than farming.[2]

Due to its specific ecology, however, Lake Van constitutes an important archive of palaeoclimatic and palaeo-environmental conditions in the Near East, which has been used for various studies – the latest PaleoVan-project ranging back to 600,000 years BP ("before present", "the present" being AD 1950). Based on the concentrations of pollen, charcoal, and isotopes, reconstructions of past conditions of temperature and precipitation as well as of land cover and human impact were created. The proxies published so far, however, have a temporal resolution not as fine-grained as historians may wish and allow for a

---

2 Wick/Lemcke/Sturm, "Evidence of Lateglacial and Holocene climatic change", pp. 666–67; Çifçi, *The Socio-Economic Organisation of the Urartian Kingdom*, pp. 20–23, 29–30, 45–50 (on climatic risks for contemporary agriculture in the area); Barlas Şimşek, *Late Holocene high resolution multi-proxy climate and environmental records*, pp. 34–43; Barlas Şimşek/Çağatay, "Late Holocene high resolution multi–proxy climate"; Cukur et al., "Water level changes in Lake Van"; Çevik, "The Change of Settlement Patterns", pp. 75–76. An overview on earlier scholarship on the region of Van from the 19th century onwards, including many drawings and maps from this time, is provided in Cuneo, "Étude sur la topographie", pp. 140–80.

reconstruction of climatic parameters for centuries or half-centuries, but not for decades or years. Furthermore, recent publications stemming from different projects (and different corings in the sediments of Lake Van) provide inconsistent data, with a specific century identified as (on average) warm and humid in one dataset and as cold and arid in another (see below).[3] In the following pages, we will therefore first rely mainly on the written and archaeological evidence for the dynamics of power and irrigation in the Lake Van region, before trying to connect these sources with the proxy data from natural sciences.

2   The Origins of Irrigation Systems in the Lake Van Region in the Time of Urartu

Despite challenging ecological parameters, the Lake Van area became the core region of the first large-scale complex polity in Southern Caucasia between the 9th and 7th century BC. This kingdom of Urartu has been called "a striking anomaly in the history of the region it dominated, which is not noted for political coherence or cultural complexity", since "geographic conditions would appear to militate against any kind of unity in a land where mountain chains intersect in a confused pattern of ridges and volcanic peaks."[4] Özlem Çevik stated that "this hostile environment was not able to prevent the emergence of the Urartian civilization in Lake Van basin during the first millennium BCE."[5]

The rulers of Urartu, however, significantly modified the landscape of their core region. Originally, their newly built capital city of Van-Tušpa and its hinterland were provided with water from local sources, with cisterns and with elaborate installations of the qanat-type; today, still more than 28 km of qanats are active. But to secure the water supply of his growing capital, King Menua of Urartu (who ruled in c.810–785 BC) ordered the construction of a canal that would feed water from one of the biggest springss of the area in the Hoşap Valley over a series of sophisticated constructions with a total length of 54 km to the plain of Van (see Fig. 12.3). The Menua Canal is the most impressive artefact of Urartian irrigation works and is still operational after almost 3000 years.

---

3   Lemcke/Sturm, "δ18O and trace element measurements"; Litt et al., "A 600,000 year long continental pollen record"; Wick/Lemcke/Sturm, "Evidence"; Barlas Şimşek, *Late Holocene high resolution multi-proxy climate and environmental records*, pp. 5–8, 108–13; Barlas Şimşek/Çağatay, "Late Holocene high resolution multi-proxy climate".

4   Sagona/Zimansky, *Ancient Turkey*, pp. 316–47, esp. p. 316 for the citation. On competing models for the emergence of Urartian statehood, see Çifçi, *The Socio-Economic Organisation of the Urartian Kingdom*, pp. 9–13.

5   Çevik, "The Change of Settlement Patterns", p. 74.

FIGURE 12.3   Map of irrigation installations in the region of the city of Van: waves = fountain of a canal; star = artificial lake; triangle = dam
J. PREISER-KAPELLER, OEAW, 2021; BASE MAP: GOOGLEEARTH

The magnitude of this achievement was celebrated by Menua in a series of 14 cuneiform inscriptions, which present the king as a ruler over nature who would transform wasteland into blooming gardens.[6]

As Julia Linke has demonstrated in her study on Urartian kingship, similar motives can be found in documents of contemporary rulers, such as in Assyria; but in Urartian texts, this aspect of royal power was especially prominent.[7] This is confirmed in the inscriptions of one of Menua's successors, King Rusa II, in the 7th century BC (between c.680 and 650 BC). Rusa II founded a new capital to the east of Van-Tušpa, named after himself ("Rusahinili"), with a second citadel of Toprakkale. As Rusa II explained in his inscriptions, he ordered an artificial lake to be constructed with the help of two big dams of 80 and 55 m in length to the east of the city as an additional water reservoir.[8] In one of these texts we read:

> massive quantities of water I dammed here for canals and flows; I decided its name to be Lake Rusa. I directed a canal from here to the city of Rusahinili, and for the land, which was later to be cultivated, but which had previously remained uncultivated.[9]

This lake – the modern day Keşiş Gölü – still exists today (see Fig. 12.3); from there, especially during springtime, water could be conducted to the Van plain.

---

6 Garbrecht, "The Water Supply System"; Belli, "Dams, reservoirs and irrigation channels"; Cuneo, "Étude sur la topographie", pp. 131–33; Çevik, "The Change of Settlement Patterns", 88; Dan, *From the Armenian Highland to Iran*, pp. 58–60; Sagona/Zimansky, *Ancient Turkey*, p. 323; Çifçi, *The Socio-Economic Organisation of the Urartian Kingdom*, pp. 34–37, 187–92; Kaspar/Kaspar, *Das Königreich Urartu*, pp. 14–15, 75–121. On palaeobotanical evidence of Urartian agriculture see also Dönmez/Belli, "Urartian Plant Cultivation". For a geological analysis of the stones used for Urartian buildings in the region and the underlying necessary logistics see Karabaşoğlu/Karaoğlu/Kuvanç, "Petrographic Observations Related to Rocks used in Urartu Settlements". On the development of qanat-irrigation see Rahimi-Laridjani, *Die Entwicklung der Bewässerungslandwirtschaft*, pp. 435–44.

7 Linke, *Das Charisma der Könige*, pp. 227–30; Smith, "Rendering the political aesthetic"; Çifçi, *The Socio-Economic Organisation of the Urartian Kingdom*, p. 211; Grekyan, "When the gods leave people".

8 Belli, "Dams, reservoirs and irrigation channels"; Çevik, "The Change of Settlement Patterns", p. 88; Orhan/Özdemir/Eyduran, "Urartian Water Constructions"; Sagona/Zimansky, *Ancient Turkey*, pp. 329–30; Çifçi, *The Socio-Economic Organisation of the Urartian Kingdom*, pp. 37–38, 192–95; Grekyan, "When the gods leave people", pp. 58–60; Kaspar/Kaspar, *Das Königreich Urartu*, pp. 28–35, 122–43, and 175, 193, 221, 264–65 for other irrigation projects of the kings of Urartu in the Lake Van region as well as in the Araxes valley.

9 Linke, *Das Charisma der Könige*, p. 227; Dan, *From the Armenian Highland to Iran*, pp. 61–62; Çifçi, *The Socio-Economic Organisation of the Urartian Kingdom*, p. 38.

Günter Garbrecht has provided calculations on the capacity of these hydraulic installations: via the Menua-Canal, approximately 45 million cubic metres of water per year could be channelled; considering losses due to evaporation, this amount would suffice to irrigate at least 2000 hectares of land, from which approximately 5000 individuals could be fed. The cannels connected to the lake of King Rusa II would have provided another 20 million cubic metres of water. In total, the two irrigation systems may have doubled the potential population of the city of Van and its environs.[10]

While the Urartian kings at the peak of their power controlled most of the historical Armenian highlands between the Upper Euphrates in the West and the Araxes in the East and were among the most dangerous opponents of the Assyrian Empire to the south, their rule collapsed in the late 7th century BC due to constant pressure from the Assyrians and new invaders from beyond the Caucasus, such as the Cimmerians. Equally, climatic factors have been proposed, especially a change towards more arid conditions in the 7th century.[11] Such a scenario finds partial confirmation in some of the climate reconstructions from Lake Van,[12] as well as in a recent analysis of proxy data indicating a severe drought in neighbouring Northern Mesopotamia during the same period, presumably contributing to the collapse of the Assyrian Empire.[13]

For the following centuries, written information on the region of Van becomes scarce.[14] However, after the region, now under the name of "Armenia", had been integrated into the Persian Empire in c.547 BC, also the Achaemenids and their representatives had some interest in the Lake Van area, as indicated by an inscription of King Xerxes (486–65 BC) near the citadel of Van. As in other provinces of their empire, the Achaemenids may also have taken care of the maintenance of the irrigation system, although we lack written evidence for this.[15]

---

10   Garbrecht, "The Water Supply System"; Garbrecht, "Historische Wasserbauten"; Zimansky, *Ecology and Empire*; Dan, *From the Armenian Highland to Iran*, pp. 59–62; Çevik, "The Change of Settlement Patterns", p. 86; Çifçi, *The Socio-Economic Organisation of the Urartian Kingdom*, pp. 28–34.
11   See especially Grekyan, "When the gods leave people".
12   Lemcke/Sturm, "δ18O and trace element measurements"; Wick/Lemcke/Sturm, "Evidence of Lateglacial and Holocene climatic change".
13   Sinha et al., "Role of climate".
14   Kaspar/Kaspar, *Das Königreich Urartu*, pp. 21–37; Dan, *From the Armenian Highland to Iran*, pp. 4–7; Dusinberre, *Authority and Autonomy in Achaemenid Anatolia*, pp. 18–19.
15   Dan, *From the Armenian Highland to Iran*, pp. 7–20; Kleiss, "Urartäische und achämenidische Wasserbauten"; Dusinberre, *Authority, and Autonomy in Achaemenid Anatolia*, pp. 51–53, 59–60, 181–83.

3 Van, Queen Semiramis, and Ancient Armenia

Only with the emergence of the Armenian kingdom from the 3rd century BC onwards, and especially for the period of the Arsacid dynasty between the 1st and 4th century AD, we receive some information (from later sources) that royal favour returned to the Van area, which also included the erection of new hydraulic installations. This is found in the "History of the House of Arcruni", an Armenian noble family, who ruled over a small princedom to the southeast of Lake Van beginning in the 4th century AD and expanded their control over most of the area in the 9th to 11th centuries AD. Their "History" was written down by one of them, T'ovma Arcruni, in the years around 900 AD. T'ovma's work ended in the year 904 but was later continued by anonymous authors up to the 14th century.[16]

On the building activities of the Armenian kings in Van, we read in T'ovma's history:

> As it pleased him, [the king of Armenia] built a palace of rough rock as a royal autumn residence [in Van], a splendid building, beautifully walled, looking out across the delightful lake to the north. (...) Around the fortress-like palace he encircled the hill with a wall of roughly hewn rocks, fortifying the valley [into] a populous city. Above the gushing spring he also walled in the steep rock with very strong constructions, in order to protect the source of water (...). On the highest hill to the southern side he discovered a lesser fountain, whose water he brought along a canal through the valley.[17]

Tentatively, the passage in T'ovma Arcruni can be connected to a series of dams on the Doni Çayi, which added a southern axis of supply from Lake Rusa to the northern axis from Urartian times and can be dated to the first centuries AD (see Fig. 12.3).[18]

Equally, the wording of the Armenian text shows similarities to the inscriptions of King Rusa II. Those, however, no one was able to read by the time of the Armenian kings or T'ovma Arcruni – and the Kingdom of Urartu did

---

16 T'ovma Arcruni, *History*, ed. Patkanean; trans. Thomson. For further information cf. also Thomson, "Tovma Artsruni: Historian of Vaspurakan"; Thomson, *A Bibliography of Classical Armenian Literature*, pp. 204–05; Thomson, "Supplement", p. 202; Greenwood, "T'ovma Artsruni"; Greenwood, "Historical Tradition, Memory and Law", pp. 27–35 (with some new considerations on the identity of the author).
17 T'ovma Arcruni, *History*, ed. Patkanean I, 8, pp. 52–53; trans. Thomson, pp. 116–17.
18 Garbrecht, "Historische Wasserbauten".

not become part of the historical tradition of Armenia until the 19th century, when the cuneiform texts of Assyria and Urartu were deciphered.[19] In contrast, based on the reading of Classical Greek texts such as Herodotus or Strabo, the impressive irrigation works of the Urartians in early Armenian historiography were attributed to their Assyrian archenemies, especially their legendary Queen Semiramis. Movsēs Xorenacʻi, who claimed to be an author of the 5th century, but whose history was most probably written down in the 8th century,[20] stated on the earlier history of Van:

> Here [at Van] that resolute and lascivious Semiramis, after careful examination, ordered 42,000 skilled workers from Assyria and other lands of the empire and 6000 chosen from her most talented craftsmen (…) to be brought without delay to the desired spot. (…) First, she ordered the canal for the river to be built in hard and massive stone, cemented with mortar and sand, of infinite length and height; it has remained firm, as they, until the present time. (…) She diverted part of the river through the city to serve every necessity and for the irrigation of the parks and flower gardens.[21]

Thus, until today, the Canal of Menua is also known as Semiramis-Canal. Equally, the noble house of the Arcruni tried to trace its origins back to Assyrian kings, especially Sennacherib (705–680 BC) and the legendary Semiramis. The princes and kings of the Arcruni in the 10th century tried to emulate or even to outdo the deeds of these forefathers and -mothers (see below). At the same time, they thereby legitimized their claim on the territories once ruled and cultivated by their presumed ancestors.[22]

4   The Emergence of Vaspurakan between Persian and Arab Domination

The blooming of the ancient Armenian Kingdom of the Arsacids ended in the late 4th century AD after a series of devastating attacks, especially from the

---

19   On the history of the "re-discovery" of Urartu, see Çifçi, *The Socio-Economic Organisation of the Urartian Kingdom*, pp. 3–8; Kaspar/Kaspar, *Das Königreich Urartu*, pp. 39–61.
20   Movsēs Xorenacʻi, *History*, trans. Thomson, pp. 1–10; trans. Mahé/Mahé, pp. 9–24.
21   Movsēs Xorenacʻi, *History*, I, 16, trans. Thomson, pp. 99–101; trans. Mahé/Mahé, pp. 132–33. See also Hewsen, "Van in this World", pp. 15–16; Cuneo, "Étude sur la topographie", pp. 128–29.
22   Dédéyan, "Princes et rois du Vaspurakan", 58; Pogossian, "Locating Religion, Controlling Territory", pp. 207–08; Greenwood, "Historical Tradition, Memory and Law", pp. 35–36.

side of the Persian Great Kings of the Sasanian dynasty, who in AD 368 also conquered the city of Van and deported its population to Persia.[23] Afterwards, and especially after the division of the kingdom of Greater Armenia between the Roman Empire and Persia in AD 387, the Lake Van region came under closer supervision of the Sasanian administration than the rest of the country. This was maybe indicated by the term "Vaspurakan", which according to one interpretation meant "special" or "particular", in the sense of a "special" or "private" domain of the Great Kings and was used for that area from that period onwards. A limiting factor for the administrative grasp of the Sasanian imperial centre on the Lake Van area, however, was the continued power of the traditional Armenian noble houses. In the 4th century AD, not fewer than 14 of them (including the Arcruni) ruled over the 35 districts registered by the 7th century "Armenian Geography" for the province of Vaspurakan (which covered approximately 40,000 km² according to the calculations of Robert H. Hewsen).[24]

In various regions of Anatolia, Caucasia, and the Middle East, from the mid-6th century onwards, constant warfare first between the Roman Empire and the Sasanians and then between Rome and the newly emerging Arab Caliphate (which replaced the Persians as overlords of most of Armenia in the second half of the 7th century) contributed to a decrease in agriculture and population. (The impact of the so-called "Justinianic plague" in Armenia is hard to estimate due to a lack of references in the sources.) Similarly, as for the Byzantine-Arab borderlands, where studies, and especially those based on palynological evidence, have highlighted a decline in land cultivation in areas around proxy sites (such as the Nar Gölü in Cappadocia) from the late 7th century onwards that can be connected to the effects of Arab raids and changes in the survival strategies of the local population,[25] we can identify the turn from the 7th to the 8th century and the 8th century itself as a period of decline of human activity around Lake Van, including in terms of building activity (see Fig. 12.4).[26] This agrees with our information on the impact of frequent rebellions against Arab rule and the reduction in the number of noble houses in

---

23 T'ovma Arcruni, *History*, ed. Patkanean I, 10, pp. 63–64; trans. Thomson, p. 128; Cuneo, "Étude sur la topographie", p. 133; Hewsen, "Van in this World", pp. 17–18.
24 Ananias of Širak, *Armenian Geography*, trans. Hewsen, pp. 63–65; Hewsen, "Van in this World", pp. 17–23 (also on the various interpretations of the term "Vaspurakan"). For a map of Vaspurakan see also Hewsen, *Armenia: A Historical Atlas*, map N° 93.
25 Asa Eger, *The Islamic-Byzantine Frontier*; Haldon et al., "The Climate and Environment of Byzantine Anatolia"; Izdebski, *A Rural Economy in Transition*; Roberts, "Not the End of the World?"; Cassis/Doonan/Elton/Newhard, "Evaluating Archaeological Evidence for Demographics, Abandonment, and Recovery in Late Antique and Byzantine Anatolia".
26 Thierry, *Monuments arméniens*; Thierry, *Armenien im Mittelalter*.

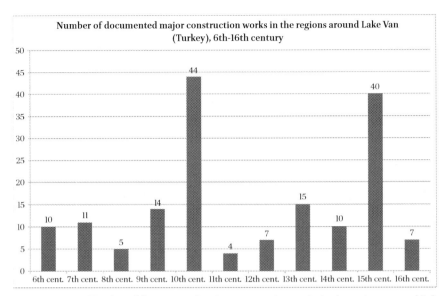

FIGURE 12.4 Number of documented major construction works in the regions around Lake Van (Turkey) between the 6th and 16th centuries
DATA: THIERRY, *MONUMENTS ARMÉNIENS DU VASPURAKAN*; GRAPH: J. PREISER-KAPELLER, OEAW, 2021

Armenia.[27] It also converges with a change in climatic conditions around Lake Van towards cooler conditions in the late 6th century, which can be found in the main proxy datasets, overlapping with the so-called "Late Antique Little Ice Age" identified for larger parts of the Northern Hemisphere for the period AD 536 to 660, and also beyond.[28] For the winter of 698, for instance, the chronicler Samuel of Ani reports that the lake was entirely frozen up, for which very low temperatures were necessary due to the salinity of its water.[29]

5 The Rise of the Arcruni and the Peak of Medieval Settlement and Building Activity

The destruction of Armenian aristocratic rule in various areas allowed for the emergence of new Muslim centres of power, including in core areas such as the

---

27 Cuneo, "Étude sur la topographie", pp. 133–35; Vacca, "Conflict and Community in the Medieval Caucasus".
28 Büntgen et al., "Cooling and societal change".
29 Samuel of Ani, trans. *Patrologia Graeca* 19, p. 696; Telelis, Μετεωρολογικά φαινόμενα, nr. 240.

Araxes valley or around Lake Van. But, equally, various ancient noble houses of Armenia, depending on their strategic position and policies of confrontation or cooperation with Arab power, were able to profit from the disappearance of former competitors, enlarging their dominions.[30] Also the distinguished, but not-too-powerful noble house of Arcruni benefitted from this process and expanded its territories, especially in the 8th to 9th centuries, towards the plains around Lake Van and towards the Araxes (see Fig. 12.1). This development was only stopped for some time by the devastating campaigns of the general Bugha "the Elder", which between AD 851 and 855 marked the last attempt of the Abbasid Caliphate to enforce its control over the various Christian and Muslim potentates in Southern Caucasia and also affected Vaspurakan.[31]

Eventually, however, after the definite weakening of the central power in the Abbasid Caliphate in the late 9th century, the Arcruni princedom would, at the beginning of the 10th century (in 908) and with Muslim consent, even rise to royalty in competition with the earlier established Armenian Kingdom of the Bagratuni dynasty (since AD 884/885) in the north.[32] The establishment of the Arcruni monarchy was accompanied by a process of increasing land development and building activity, as monumental and historiographic evidence confirms and as is paralleled by similar developments in Cappadocia and the Byzantine frontier lands, where the end of continuous Arab raids (and maybe improving climatic conditions) fostered a re-expansion of land cultivation.[33]

Zarui Pogossian, one of the leading scholars on this period, sums up the new economic and religious dynamics thus:

---

30   Marquart, *Südarmenien*, pp. 79*–85*; Dédéyan, "Princes et rois du Vaspurakan", pp. 59–63; Vardanyan, "The Armenian princely system in Vaspurakan"; Pogossian, "Locating Religion, Controlling Territory", pp. 178–79; Vacca, "Conflict and Community in the Medieval Caucasus". On Vaspurakan and the Arcruni in Arabic sources see now Vacca, "Al-Basfurrağān and Banū l-Dayrānī".

31   Marquart, *Südarmenien*, pp. 85*–89*; Vacca, *Non-Muslim Provinces*, pp. 139, 167–68; Vacca, "Conflict and Community in the Medieval Caucasus", pp. 77–79 and 87–89; Preiser-Kapeller, "Complex processes of migration", pp. 308–09. For a map of the expansion of the territories of the Arcruni see Hewsen, *Armenia: A Historical Atlas*, map N° 73.

32   Garsoïan, "The Independent Kingdoms", pp. 146–49, 156–57; Hewsen, "Van in this World", pp. 24–26; Dédéyan, "Princes et rois du Vaspurakan", 63–65; Pogossian, "The Foundation of the Monastery of Sevan", pp. 182–83; Pogossian, "Locating Religion, Controlling Territory", pp. 176–78; Vacca, *Non-Muslim Provinces*, pp. 8–10, 144–45; Mahé, "Préambule"; Pogossian/Vardanyan, "Introduction"; Pogossian, "Relics, Rulers, Patronage", pp. 180–81.

33   Haldon et al., "The Climate"; Izdebski/Koloch/Słoczyński, "Exploring Byzantine and Ottoman economic history"; Cassis/Doonan/Elton/Newhard, "Evaluating Archaeological Evidence for Demographics, Abandonment, and Recovery in Late Antique and Byzantine Anatolia".

By creating new religious spaces or re-enforcing the pre-existing ones, sponsoring monastic foundations in their old or recently acquired territories, in other words by "locating religion", the Armenian princes not only visually marked their domains, publicly and constantly declaring their ownership, but also gave an impetus for the development and use of their resources. The latter aspect was especially important in the context of the expanding economy in the second half of the ninth and the first of the tenth centuries. Moreover, the hostilities between the invigorated Byzantine Empire under the Macedonian dynasty and the disintegrating Abbasid Caliphate caused a shift in international trade routes which now passed through Armenia – a neutral territory between the two antagonistic empires. This had a significant impact on the involvement of Armenia in international trade, with the subsequent growth of economic wealth and the availability of a new type of capital to the hereditary princes. The period also witnessed the development of urban settlements, especially those on trading routes, such as the already important cities of Dvin, Naxčawan (Nakhčiwān) and Partaw, but also new ones such as Ani, Kars, Arcn, as well as Van and Ostan in Vaspurakan. Industries, particularly textile production and other related crafts, the various branches of metallurgy, glass production, and others developed in these cities. The revival of Armenian monastic culture, including numerous princely and royal foundations, cannot be imagined without all these factors.[34]

Focal points of the Acruni's expansion of power and their sponsoring of monumental building (of fortresses, monasteries, and churches) in that period can be found to the east and south of Lake Van, while at the northern and western shores the Arcruni had to share control with a number of Muslim Emirates.[35] The ancestral heartland of the Arcruni was in the province of Ałbag around the city of Hadamakert (now Başkale), which served as residence and then traditional burial place of the family (see Fig. 12.1). Here in the mountains east of Lake Van, the weather conditions were cooler, but the precipitation was a little more reliable, so that no artificial irrigation was necessary. At the same time, the mountainous region was characterized by a relatively favourable strategic position away from the common Arab routes of invasion.[36]

34 Pogossian, "Locating Religion, Controlling Territory", pp. 178–79. See also Garsoïan, "The Independent Kingdoms", pp. 176–84; Pogossian, "The Foundation of the Monastery of Sevan".
35 Pogossian, "Locating Religion, Controlling Territory", pp. 175–76.
36 Thierry, *Monuments arméniens*, pp. 42, 465–78; Dédéyan, "Princes et rois du Vaspurakan", pp. 57–58.

A relatively early acquisition of the Arcruni was the province of Čuaš with the city of Marakan in the northeast of Vaspurakan (see Fig. 12.1). Despite its position at the periphery of the Arcruni realm, it served as winter quarters of the princes and their retinue due to its relatively mild conditions, as we learn from T'ovma Arcruni.[37] In addition, it was situated near the valley of the Araxes River, the centre of settlement, commerce, and political power in Armenia's north. Also, the first King of Vaspurakan, Gagik Arcruni (AD 904/908–943),[38] despite his preference for the twin residences of Ostan andAłtamar at Lake Van (see below), often spent time there and erected both a hunting pavilion and a fortress near Marakan on the river Karmir.[39]

The beginnings of this period of prosperity in the country after the turmoil of the preceding decades are attributed by T'ovma Arcruni already to Gagik's father prince Grigor-Derenik (c.857–87), who:

> strengthened by the power of Christ, became glorious and renowned throughout the whole land of Armenia; and the country had respite from the confusions that had befallen it. The country began to experience a renewal, the churches to shine with ornamentation and splendid rituals; those scattered rushed back to their own places to build, plant, and forget the pains and afflictions they had endured.[40]

Especially Grigor-Derenik and Gagik Arcruni were also active in the ancient city of Van and its citadel, whose strategic position allowed access to regional and trans-regional trade routes. Van became one of the royal residences and was decorated with several new churches, whose dedication connected the place to Jerusalem and the cult of the Holy Cross, which was promoted by the Arcruni at other places also.[41] Among these was the nearby monastery on Mount Varag, which hosted a widely known relic fragment of the "true" holy cross, whose veneration, together with the building of new churches and

---

37 T'ovma Arcruni, *History*, ed. Patkanean III, 20, p. 225; trans. Thomson, p. 289. Marquart, *Südarmenien*, pp. 205–06.
38 PmbZ N° 22052.
39 T'ovma Arcruni, *History*, ed. Patkanean, III 14, 20 and 29, pp. 204–05, 225–27 and 253–54; trans. Thomson, pp. 268, 289–90 and 316–17. Vacca, "Al-Basfurraǧān and Banū l-Dayrānī", pp. 83–85. Thierry, *Monuments arméniens*, pp. 479–98.
40 T'ovma Arcruni, *History*, ed. Patkanean III, 14, pp. 204–05; trans. Thomson, p. 268.
41 Berkian, *Armenischer Wehrbau*, pp. 155–56; Hewsen, "Van in this World", pp. 26–28; Pogossian, "Locating Religion, Controlling Territory", pp. 186–87, 208–11; Vacca, "Al-Basfurraǧān and Banū l-Dayrānī", pp. 94–95; Pogossian, "Relics, Rulers, Patronage", p. 128. On topography and routes in Southern Caucasia, see also Fabian, "Moving in the Mountains".

donations by the Arcruni, added to the "sacralization" of these newly gained territories. Furthermore, the control over Varag allowed access to important water sources for some of the installations leading towards Van since the Urartian period, as well as rich pasturages in the area (see Fig. 12.3).[42] In addition, Tʿovma Arcruni mentions the installation of further canals by Gagik Arcruni from Mount Varag (the 3200-m-high Erek Dağı) to the west into the plain of Van.[43]

One can find in the valley of Engusner Çayi the dam of Faruk Bendi, which is dated to the late 1st millennium AD and thus could have been part of the building activity of the Arcruni (see Fig. 12.3). With a height of 12 metres and a length of 40 metres, Faruk Bendi competes with the installations of the kings of Urartu – or rather of Queen Semiramis, to whom medieval Armenian tradition now attributed these constructions (see above). She is mentioned as the royal role model who had to be outdone; for this purpose, however, adding another dam to "her" system at Van would not do.[44]

Before Gagik would finally excel Semiramis with his new capital on the island of Ałtamar (see below), the Arcruni princes had established another place of residence in the city of Ostan (today Gevaş, in the regional tradition blessed by another relic of the holy cross) on the southeastern shore of Lake Van (see Fig. 12.5). One of the region's advantages, which is evident both in contemporary sources and from the analysis of modern climate data, was the more reliable supply of water through both more regular rainfall and water storage by Mount Artos (today Çadır Dağı) in the south (see Fig. 12.5).[45] The same sources also mention a valuable fishing ground in the area.[46]

---

42 Pogossian, "Locating Religion, Controlling Territory", pp. 185–93, 212–13; Pogossian, "Relics, Rulers, Patronage", pp. 126–28, and with a detailed discussion of the (inventions) of tradition of this monastery and its relic starting in the 7th century on the following pages; Çevik, "The Change of Settlement Patterns", p. 85. Among the monastic centres in the Kingdom of Vaspurakan were also the convents on the island of Lim in Lake Van, of Hogeacʿvankʿ and of Narek (founded during the reign of Gagik Arcruni), see Thierry, *Monuments arméniens du Vaspurakan*, pp. 177–88, 327–30, 452–58; Hewsen, "Van in this World".

43 Tʿovma Arcruni, *History*, ed. Patkanean III 29, pp. 252–53; trans. Thomson, pp. 315–16. See also Dédéyan, "Princes et rois du Vaspurakan", pp. 65–66; Pogossian, "Locating Religion, Controlling Territory", pp. 210–11.

44 Thierry, *Monuments arméniens*, pp. 123–58; Garbrecht, "Historische Wasserbauten", pp. 67–75.

45 Tʿovma Arcruni, *History*, ed. Patkanean IV 6, pp. 290–92; trans. Thomson, pp. 352–54; Thierry, *Monuments arméniens*, pp. 324–26; Hewsen, "Van in this World", pp. 27–28; Pogossian, "Locating Religion, Controlling Territory", pp. 198–204; Pogossian, "Relics, Rulers, Patronage", pp. 181–82.

46 Special species of fish, which can be found until today mainly in the estuaries of the sweet water rivers running into Lake Van, are already mentioned as export product of

ECOLOGY, IRRIGATION AND LORDSHIP IN THE LAKE VAN REGION 323

FIGURE 12.5   Map of the area around the Arcruni residences of Ostan and Altʻamar
J. PREISER-KAPELLER, OEAW, 2021; BASE MAP: GOOGLEEARTH

Off the coast of Ostan, finally, King Gagik Arcruni expanded the settlement on the island of Ałtamar[47] (see Fig. 12.5) as his new residence with a splendid palace, which earned him the highest degree of admiration of the historians of his family, who claim that, thereby, Gagik "surpassed" the wonders of Queen Semiramis.[48] The nowadays only visible remain of Gagik's island capital on Ałtamar and without doubt the most important monument of this period and part of the UNESCO world cultural heritage is the Church of the Holy Cross, erected in the years AD 915 to 921. The prehistory of this building is another example of the "typical" combination of territorial expansion, religious legitimation, and material manifestation of the rule of the Arcruni mentioned above, since the material for the construction of the church was taken from an Arab fortress located a Kotom to the southwest of Lake Van which King Gagik had destroyed.[49]

The church not only became another focal point in the sacred topography of the new kingdom (marked by the various relics and churches of the Holy Cross[50]), but in its spectacular external decoration praised the king's power and ancestry, as well as the abundance of nature and his mastery over it. As art historians have demonstrated, Gagik Arcruni is depicted as "King of Paradise" parallel to Adam, who is represented below him. Gagik sits in the centre of a circular frieze of vine branches, in which various scenes of hunting, animal husbandry, and agriculture are embedded. The king seizes one of the grapes, while holding a cup of wine; Sasanian and contemporary Islamic imagery of royal power is combined with biblical and Christian references (see Fig. 12.6).[51] Equally, the anonymous continuator of T'ovma Arcruni in his

Vaspurakan in Ananias of Širak, *Armenian Geography*, trans. Hewsen, p. 63. For a modern study on fish in Lake Van see Akkuş et al., "The discovery of a microbialite-associated freshwater fish".

47 On the earlier history of the island see Pogossian, "Locating Religion, Controlling Territory", pp. 195–96.

48 T'ovma Arcruni, *History*, ed. Patkanean IV, 7, p. 294; trans. Thomson, p. 356. See also Dédéyan, "Princes et rois du Vaspurakan", 66–68; Thomson, "Armenian Biblical Exegesis", pp. 224–25. On the palace of King Gagik and a possible reconstruction see Kertmenjian, "Reflections on the Architecture".

49 T'ovma Arcruni, *History*, ed. Patkanean IV 8, pp. 297–98; trans. Thomson, pp. 359–60. Cf. also Marquart, *Südarmenien*, pp. 333–34; Jones, *Between Islam and Byzantium*; Thomson, "Armenian Biblical Exegesis", pp. 225–26; Pogossian, "Locating Religion, Controlling Territory", pp. 196–98, writes about "Gagik's Control and Sacralization of Key Locations in Vaspurakan". On the architectonical models for the church see also Donabédian, "Sainte-Croix d'Ałt'amar"; Kazaryan, "The Church of Ałt'amar".

50 Pogossian, "Relics, Rulers, Patronage", pp. 183–84.

51 Der Nersessian, *Aght'amar*; Thierry, *Monuments arméniens*, pp. 271–91; Jones, *Between Islam and Byzantium*; Dorfmann-Lazarev, "Kingship and Hospitality"; Pogossian/

FIGURE 12.6
Depiction of King Gagik Arcruni (904/908–943 CE) on the Church of the Holy Cross on the island of Ałtamar in Lake Van
IMAGE BY ATTALEIV, HTTPS://COMMONS.WIKIMEDIA.ORG/WIKI/FILE:VAN-AKDAM_(7).JPG?USELANG=DE, CREATIVE COMMONS

praise of the king compares Gagik Arcruni with a "sweet-smelling garden, filled with resplendent flowers", with "a verdant plant with golden leaves" and "an ever-flowing source of wisdom". Both in a real and in a metaphorical sense, the king "irrigated" the land with his deeds and his skills.[52]

Yet despite the clear preference of King Gagik for Ałtamar, the kingdom of the Arcruni did not possess one predominant centre, but relied on a polycentric spatial organization, which we have tried to reconstruct in a digital spatial

---

Vardanyan, "Introduction", pp. 8–14; Thomson, "Armenian Biblical Exegesis"; La Porta, "Beyond Image and Text"; Beledian, "L'invention des images"; Donabédian, "Sainte-Croix d'Ałt'amar"; Vardanyan, "Les sujets bibliques"; Grigoryan, "King Gagik Arcruni's Portrait"; Vacca, *Non-Muslim Provinces*, pp. 145–46.

52 T'ovma Arcruni, *History*, ed. Patkanean IV, 11, p. 304; trans. Thomson, p. 367. See also Pogossian, "Locating Religion, Controlling Territory", pp. 218–21.

network models in an earlier publication.[53] This corresponds with the description of a kind of "itinerant kingship" we find in the history of Tʻovma Arcruni; according to his text, the Arcruni would regularly migrate between their traditional power bases and new centres in the regions they had acquired in the 8th to 9th centuries.[54] This itinerancy allowed for a demonstration of presence and power in the various corners of their realm and equally facilitated the supply of the ruler and his retinue from various clusters of agricultural productivity, partly enhanced by the old and new irrigation infrastructure. Similar observations have been made on the earlier Kingdom of Urartu in the same region:

> The administrative system of the Urartian state was divided like its topography. Indeed, this multi-centre system was the result of the long and harsh winters which caused the break down the communications among the sites. This is what Zimansky called a decentralized state, peculiar to Urartu. The storage of the agricultural products in different places also provided an economic advantage to the state by preventing the collapse of the whole economic system during attacks.[55]

These patterns of territorial control and usage would allow for more than a century of Arcruni royal power in a highly unstable geopolitical environment.

6 Power and Irrigation in Ancient and Medieval Southern Caucasia

The interplay between royal power and irrigation in the Lake Van region may bring to mind Karl August Wittfogel's theory of "hydraulic empires", according to which the necessity for the organization and coordination of artificial irrigation demanded the rise of centralized, bureaucratic and "despotic" regimes and favoured their continued existence.[56] As we have seen both on the basis of the written as well as of the monumental evidence, phases of significant irrigation building activities seem to overlap with periods of strong royal power and presence in the region of Van – under the Urartians (9th to 7th century BC), the Arsacids (1st to 3rd century AD) and the Arcruni (9th to 11th century AD) (see

---

53 Preiser-Kapeller, "Small Kingdoms in a Big World".
54 On itinerant kingship in the medieval west in that period, especially in the German Kingdom (as part of the "Holy" Roman Empire) of the Ottonians, cf. Bernhardt, *Itinerant kingship*; Althoff, *Die Ottonen*.
55 Çevik, "The Change of Settlement Patterns", p. 86.
56 Gallagher/McIntosh, "Agriculture and Urbanism"; Blaschke, *Euphrat und Tigris*, pp. 468–70.

Fig. 12.4). But in the centuries between these periods, which account for most of these millennia, these installations were maintained in the absence of central royal power in an often highly fragmented political landscape. The amount of work and energy invested in the maintenance and repair of buildings during these centuries must be assessed at least as highly as the deeds of the kings. As we also learn from recent times, the impact of extreme events such as flood waters could be devastating: the dam of Faruk Bendi, stemming from the medieval period, was partly destroyed in 1987. Another constant threat in the seismically highly active Lake Van regions was that of earthquakes, whose traces (along with those of subsequent repairs) have been identified at various hydraulic installations. Still, they mostly remain operational until today.[57]

Besides verbose praises of royal initiative, however, we lack for the Van region more detailed information on how the workforce was mobilized not only for the building, but especially for the maintenance of these installations – and how the distribution of and access to the precious water was organized or restricted; in other words, who had to contribute to and who profited from these hydraulic infrastructures?

For the medieval period, we find further examples for the investment of the leading elites – both secular and ecclesiastical – of Southern Caucasia into irrigation systems. In the 7th century, Katholikos Nersēs III Šinoł (AD 641–61) had an irrigation canal built for the residence he erected near the famous church of Zuartʻnocʻ; exceeding 6 km in length, it connected the new settlement with the Kʻasal River (see Fig. 12.1). As the contemporary history attributed to Sebēos describes: "He [Nersēs III] brought water, directed [a channel] of the river, and put to cultivation all the rough ground. He planted vines and trees and surrounded his residence with a high wall."[58] A later successor of Nersēs III, Katholikos Yovhannēs Drasxanakertcʻi (in office AD 897/98–924/25)[59] also mentions the (unfree) labour force necessary for this project: "Moreover, he populated the place with a great many serfs in accordance with the standards of the city dwellers and bringing water from the Kʻasal river, he cultivated the sandy and rocky plain, planting orchards and gardens."[60] After the initial initiative of Nersēs III, however, these installations were (partly) maintained also

---

57 Garbrecht, "Wasserbauten"; Selçuk, "Evaluation of the relative tectonic activity"; Albini et al., "In Search of the Predecessors of the 2011 Van (Turkey) Earthquake"; Taskin et al., "The aftermath of 2011 Van earthquakes"; Tosun, "Re-evaluation of Large Dams in Van Inner Basin, Turkey". On the special geology of the region, see also Azizi/Tsuboi, "The Van Microplate".
58 Sebēos, *History*, c. 45, ed. Abgaryan, p. 147; trans. Thomson, p. 112.
59 PmbZ N° 28467.
60 Yovhannēs Drasxanakertcʻi, *History*, c. 19, 48, trans. Maksoudian, p. 104.

during the following eight centuries, when the Katholikoi of Armenia resided elsewhere before they returned to the nearby old centre of Ējmiacin in 1441 (see Fig. 12.1). From then on, the Patriarchs of Armenia added further hydraulic installations up to the time of Katholikos Nersēs V (1843–57), namesake of the first irrigating Katholikos in that area 1200 year before and eponym of the "Nersessian Lake" near the Ējmiacin Monastery.[61]

More information on the restriction of access to the water of such installations in medieval Armenia can be found in the history of the province of Siwnikʿ (to the northeast of Vaspurakan), compiled by the metropolitan bishop of Siwnikʿ, Stepʿannos Ōrbēlean, in AD c.1299. As Tim Greenwood recently analysed, Stepʿannos had access to older charters and inscriptions, starting from the mid-9th century, especially on donations and purchases of land and entire villages by the famous monastery of Tatʿev (see Fig. 12.1), including detailed descriptions of their boundaries, arid and watered lands, pastures, fields, and meadows.[62]

Of special interest is a transaction of the year 932 (and thus contemporaneous to the reign of King Gagik of Vaspurakan) of Bishop Yakob of Siwnikʿ, who "purchased the water of the Çagēçor River, called Vararak, from Lord Pʿilippē, son of Prince Vasak of Siwnikʿ" to cultivate an area near the monastery, where he also erected a chapel with the following inscription:

> I, Yakob, by the grace of God bishop of Siwnikʿ, purchased the Vararak water from the God-kept Lord Pʿilippē, lord of Siwnikʿ for 12,000 drams and a rare gem. With great expense and very great labour, with assistance from On High, I brought water from Mount Çagēçor to irrigate this rose garden and I planted choice grape vines, beautiful vineyards, and gardens full of flowers and fruits (…). Regarding the water, there is no issue [about its use], not from the people of [the neighbouring settlements of] Norik, Xotan, Šnhērik, or Halik, nor from any individual. It may not be diverted into any field or used to irrigate gardens. It may only be used, with a basin, to provide thirsty folk and animals with a drink of water. Now, should anyone dare to divert this water, may that person be cursed by God.[63]

---

61   Cowe, "Ejmiatsin".
62   Greenwood, "A contested jurisdiction: Armenia in late antiquity", pp. 212–16. See also Pogossian, "The Foundation of the Monastery of Sevan", pp. 184–85. On the most probable existence of similar documents for similar acts of donation, foundation, etc. in Vaspurakan see Greenwood, "Historical Tradition, Memory and Law", pp. 41–45. On Tatʿev, see also Berkian, *Armenischer Wehrbau*, pp. 195–98.
63   Stepʿannos Ōrbēlean, *History*, ch. 49, ed. Šahnazareancʿ, p. 133; trans. Bedrosian.

The restrictions on the use of water from the new irrigation canal are equally found in the document issued by the seller of the water rights, prince Pʻilippē, and cited by Stepʻannos Ōrbēlean:

> I and my sons and other relatives renounce [ownership of] that water hereafter, until eternity. The people of Norik, Xotan, Šnhērik, and Halik have no claims whatever, great or small, [on the water] to divert it to their fields and meadows. People and animals may only drink from it, using a basin. Should I or my children deviate from these provisions, or think to divert the water to irrigate fields and meadows or for any other purpose, may we be anathematized by God.[64]

While adjoining landowners and communities were allowed to drink and to water their farm animals from the canal, it was strictly forbidden to divert water to their fields and meadows, which would have comprised a manipulation or damaging of the canal's structure. The same stipulation can be found in a similar document on another irrigation system built for the monastery in AD 1008.[65] These examples from 10th- to 11th-century Siwnikʻ suggest that the building of irrigation systems by princes, bishops, and abbots not only entailed benefits for settlements and agriculture (as equally praised in the inscriptions and texts from the Lake Van region), but also new mechanisms of control over a scarce resource to the possible disadvantage of less-privileged communities in the area.

A model for the administration and maintenance of irrigation structures beyond (or complementary to) princely control is found in the 12th-century collection of Armenian law texts of Mxitʻar Goš, who included regulations from various preceding centuries. There, the distribution of water and work is mostly organized at the level of the village community or a group of neighbouring settlements. Chapter 216 determines: "When a village is built for the first time, the division (bažanumn) of land and water and other such things is not fixed until enough inhabitants have gathered; then let the division be confirmed (...)".[66] The community would also pronounce a judgement in cases of conflict, "if it happens that someone brings water through a channel for some

---

64   Stepʻannos Ōrbēlean, *History*, ch. 49, ed. Šahnazareancʻ, p. 134; trans. Bedrosian. See also Pogossian, "Relics, Rulers, Patronage", pp. 160–62.
65   Stepʻannos Ōrbēlean, *History*, ch. 50, ed. Šahnazareancʻ, p. 137; trans. Bedrosian.
66   Mxitʻar Goš, *Dastanagirkʻ*, trans. Thomson, p. 263.

purpose of for the sake of irrigation, and he finished his task and leaves, and causes damage to his neighbour's vineyard or field or habitation".[67]

If various villages along a canal, maybe together with the urban community in the region, would coordinate their efforts, then so too major installations such as the Menua/Semiramis-Canal could survive in the absence of centralizing royal power, as Paul Halstead has demonstrated for other examples across the Mediterranean.[68] Another illustrative case is the Ferhat Canal at the Lake Balık (Arm. *Gaylatu*, see Fig. 12.1) in the former Armenian district of Kogovit, an area disputed between Vaspurakan and the Bagratuni Kingdom of the North in the 10th century. Also, this canal was erected in the period of Urartu, further used by the Armenians in the Middle Ages (as a text from the 7th century documents) and is operational until today; during these centuries, Kogovit never became a focal point of royal power again as Van did.[69]

We also have illustrative counterexamples from the neighbouring areas of modern-day Azerbaijan, such as today's Mughan steppe at the river Aras (Araxes), which became the target of increased settlement and irrigation activities of the Sasanian imperial regime in the 5th and 6th centuries AD. As recent excavations and surveys document, the scale of these imperial projects was impressive; "in the northern areas of the Aras River, in the Mil Steppe, the Sasanians constructed a canal 120 km in length, which (...) was used not only for irrigation and agriculture, but also as a source of water for the cities along the canal".[70] The largest of these new settlements established on the Mughan Steppe was the site of Ultan Qalası (which, according to C14-dating, was founded in the first half of the 5th century AD), with a citadel of about 33 ha and a total area of more than 70 ha; it was surrounded by a network of canals.[71] In order to build and populate these settlements and their infrastructure, the Sasanian Great Kings also resorted to, for instance, relocating people from other areas of their empire and deporting captives from campaigns into the Roman Empire. The entire settlement system therefore very much depended on "centralized management and centralized authority", identified by Karim Alizadeh (2014) as prerequisites for the "construction and operation of large irrigation systems". Accordingly, these settlements and the irrigation canals fell out of use with the collapse of the Sasanian Empire in the 7th century; surveys did not "encounter any Islamic ceramics at the sites along canals". And "the collapse of the intensive Sasanian irrigation system created a void on

---

67   Mxit'ar Goš, *Dastanagirkʻ*, trans. Thomson, p. 291.
68   Halstead, *Two Oxen Ahead*, pp. 277–81.
69   Belli, "Urartian Dams and Artificial Lakes"; Kuşlu/Üstun, "Water Structures in Anatolia from Past to Present".
70   Alizadeh, "Borderland Projects of Sasanian Empire", p. 98.
71   Alizadeh, "Ultan Qalası".

the steppe, which was eventually filled by pastoral nomadic groups" up to the 20th century, when Moḥammad-Reżā-Šāh Pahlavī (r. 1941–79) tried to imitate his predecessors as Great Kings of Iran by initiating new large-scale irrigation projects in the Mughan Steppe within the framework of the so-called "White Revolution" (Pers. *Enghelāb-e Sefid*).[72]

The Lake Van area and Sasanian Azerbaijan thus both illustrate the significance of centralized state power for the emergence of larger-scale irrigation systems in ancient and medieval Southern Caucasia. However, they also document, it seems, different trajectories of the development and maintenance of such projects in the face of the eclipse of central authorities. Infrastructural maintenance appears to depend on local socio-political structures and regional patterns of land use, in which irrigation infrastructure was used to buffer against environmental stress.

7 Palaeoclimatology, Proxy Data, and Their Challenges

This leaves us with the question of the palaeoclimatic background to these investments in irrigation infrastructures. As already mentioned, phases of significant irrigation building activities overlap with periods of strong royal power in the region of Van – under the Urartians (9th–7th century BC), the Arsacids (2nd–3rd century AD) and the Arcruni (9th–10th century AD). Except for single extreme events such as the freezing of Lake Van in AD 698 (see above), however, we do not get more detailed (much less systematic) meteorological observations from the written evidence. As for many other regions, we therefore may place our hope on the "archives of nature".[73]

A comparison with proxy data based on stable oxygen isotopes from Lake Van and published in 1997 and 2003 by Wick, Lemcke, and Sturm suggests that the early Urartian and Arsacid building activities overlap with transitions to (on average) more humid conditions. Only in the Arcruni period, increasing aridity may have provided additional motivation for the extension of irrigation (see Fig. 12.7).[74] This would concur with the surviving narrative sources, which identify the construction of these installations as manifestations of a

---

72 Alizadeh, "Borderland Projects of Sasanian Empire". For another case study (Qaratəpə) in the region see Wordsworth/Wencel, "The Dramatic Abandonment of a Late-Antique Settlement".
73 Brönnimann/Pfister/White, "Archives of Nature and Archives of Societies"; Preiser-Kapeller, *Der Lange Sommer und die Kleine Eiszeit*, pp. 13–16.
74 Lemcke/Sturm, "δ18O and trace element measurements"; Wick/Lemcke/Sturm, "Evidence of Lateglacial and Holocene climatic change"; McCormick et al., "Climate Change", 180, 184 (Fig. 12.7), pp. 219–20.

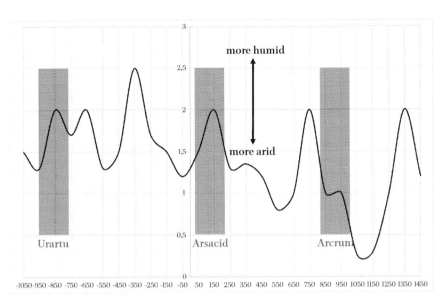

FIGURE 12.7 Reconstruction of average humidity conditions in the Lake Van area based on oxygen isotope data, with periods of increased construction of irrigation infrastructure marked in red
DATA: WICK/LEMCKE/STURM, "EVIDENCE OF LATEGLACIAL AND HOLOCENE CLIMATIC CHANGE"; GRAPH: J. PREISER-KAPELLER, OEAW, 2021

blooming kingship augmenting the agricultural potential of the region, not as symptoms of adaption to crisis.

Different reconstructions of temperature and humidity conditions, however, were published by Barlas Şimşek and Çağatay in 2018 based on another coring project; they stated that their stable oxygen isotope data differs "significantly from those published by" Wick, Lemcke and Sturm. They concede, though, that the oxygen isotope record from their drill core "may not be very reliable for climate reconstruction, perhaps because of detrital carbonate influx at this core site, which is near to the mouth of the Engil River." Nevertheless, Barlas Şimşek and Çağatay provided a chronological reconstruction of temperature and humidity conditions for the last 3500 years based on other proxy evidence, which differs from the earlier one: they identify most of the Urartian centuries between 950 and 650 BC as "cold and dry", which provides a less "beneficial" climatic background to the irrigation projects of this period. Barlas Şimşek's, and Çağatay's reconstruction, however, largely conforms with the one of Wick, Lemcke, and Sturm regarding the Arsacid period between the 1st and 3rd centuries AD. Again, however, they differ when it comes to the "peak" of the rule of the Arcruni, which in Barlas Şimşek's and Çağatay's data is

Time	Temperature	Precipitation	Time	Temperature	Precipitation
-1550	cold	dry	350	cold	dry
-1500	cold	dry	400	cold	dry
-1450	cold	dry	450	cold	dry
-1400	cold	dry	500	warm	humid
-1350	warm	humid	550	warm	humid
-1300	warm	humid	600	cold	dry
-1250	warm	humid	650	cold	dry
-1200	warm	humid	700	cold	dry
-1150	warm	humid	750	cold	dry
-1100	warm	humid	800	cold	dry
-1050	warm	humid	850	cold	dry
-1000	warm	humid	900	warm	humid
-950	cold	dry	950	warm	humid
-900	cold	dry	1000	warm	humid
-850	cold	dry	1050	warm	humid
-800	cold	dry	1100	warm	humid
-750	cold	dry	1150	warm	humid
-700	cold	dry	1200	cold	dry
-650	warm	humid	1250	cold	dry
-600	warm	humid	1300	cold	dry
-550	warm	humid	1350	warm	humid
-500	warm	humid	1400	warm	humid
-450	cold	dry	1450	cold	dry
-400	cold	dry	1500	cold	dry
-350	warm	humid	1550	cold	dry
-300	warm	humid	1600	warm	humid
-250	warm	humid	1650	warm	humid
-200	warm	humid	1700	warm	humid
-150	cold	dry	1750	cold	dry
-100	cold	dry	1800	cold	dry
-50	cold	dry	1850	cold	dry
0	cold	dry	1900	cold	dry
50	cold	dry	1950	cold	dry
100	cold	dry			
150	warm	humid			
200	warm	humid			
250	warm	humid			
300	warm	humid			

FIGURE 12.8 Reconstruction of average humidity and temperature conditions in the Lake Van area, with periods of increased construction of irrigation infrastructure marked in red letters
DATA: BARLAS ŞIMŞEK/ ÇAĞATAY, "LATE HOLOCENE HIGH RESOLUTION MULTI-PROXY CLIMATE AND ENVIRONMENTAL RECORDS"; GRAPH: J. PREISER-KAPELLER, OEAW, 2021

characterized by "warm and humid" conditions from AD 900 onwards, continuing until the end of the 12th century (see Fig. 12.8).[75]

The interpretation of this data is further complicated by its rather coarse-grained temporal resolution; Wick, Lemke, and Sturm, for instance, indicated that the minimum time interval between two of their oxygen isotope samples is 16.7 years and may vary between 16.7 and 83.4 years.[76] Thus, the proxy data may conceal short-term fluctuations in precipitation or even single extreme droughts which may have contributed to the decision-making on these investments in hydraulic infrastructure in the 9th century BC, the first centuries AD or the 10th century AD. Unless further research provides data with a robust, maybe even annual resolution for parts of the sediments as from the Nar Gölü in Cappadocia,[77] for instance, any reconstruction of the interplay between climatic dynamics and the expansion of irrigation installations in the Lake Van region remains rather hypothetical.

8   The "Decline" of Vaspurakan, Byzantine Rule and the "Armenian Paradise" of Van until the 20th Century

The temperature and humidity reconstructions provide conflicting results for the period of "decline" of the Arcruni Kingdom of Vaspurakan in the 11th century, which is characterized as extremely arid in the 2003 data, but as "warm and humid" in the publication from 2018 (see Fig. 12.7 and Fig. 12.8).[78] Regardless of the actual climatic trend (which was less favourable in various regions of the Middle East in the 11th century[79]), historiography and the decrease in number of monumental buildings (see Fig. 12.4) both indicate demographic and/or economic recession.

Written sources mainly identify geopolitical and domestic political factors for the "decline" of Vaspurakan. A combination of increasing danger from Turkmen nomadic groups, who defeated the army of the Arcruni in 1017,

---

75 Barlas Şimşek/Çağatay, "Late Holocene high resolution multi-proxy climate".
76 Lemcke/Sturm, "δ18O and trace element measurements"; Wick/Lemcke/Sturm, "Evidence of Lateglacial and Holocene climatic change".
77 Woodbridge/Roberts, "Late Holocene climate of the Eastern Mediterranean"; Haldon et al., "The Climate and Environment of Byzantine Anatolia".
78 Wick/Lemcke/Sturm, "Evidence of Lateglacial and Holocene climatic change"; Barlas Şimşek/Çağatay, "Late Holocene high resolution multi-proxy climate".
79 Ellenblum, *The Collapse of the Eastern Mediterranean*, but with a critical evaluation in Preiser-Kapeller, "A Collapse of the Eastern Mediterranean". See, equally, the chapter of Preiser-Kapeller in the present volume, also with reference to other Armenian sources on the 11th century.

diplomatic pressure from Byzantium, and internal precariousness of his position motivated King Yovhannēs-Senekʿerim Arcruni[80] in 1022/1023 to hand over Vaspurakan to Emperor Basil II in return for new domains in Cappadocia, into which an exodus of reportedly 14,000 families now took place.[81] Based on calculations by Zimansky,[82] for the maximum extent of cultivated land in the Lake Van region, one could assume a maximum "carrying capacity" for the area of the Kingdom of Vaspurakan of ~250,000 people (on the basis of a minimum of 0.5 ha arable land per head). Even if we assume that the Kingdom reached this number of inhabitants, 14,000 families (maybe 60,000 to 70,000 people) would have represented a significant demographic bleeding. Of course, the figure reported by the continuator of the history of Tʿovma Arcruni can only be used with caution.[83] Matthew of Edessa, writing in the 12th century, provides an impressive, albeit maybe equally exaggerated description of the settlement density and wealth of the kingdom of Vaspurakan and of the exodus of its ruling dynasty:

> In turn Senekʿerim handed over the land of Vaspurakan to the emperor, including seventy-two regional fortresses and four thousand four hundred villages and the monasteries; he did not give up, but kept, one hundred and fifteen monasteries where prayers were said for him. He gave all of this in writing to Basil. (…) After this Basil gave (…) gave Senekʿerim Sebasteia [modern-day Siwas, in Cappadocia[84]] with its innumerable surrounding districts. Senekʿerim, going forth with his whole household and people, came to Sebasteia; and thus Armenia was abandoned by its kings and princes.[85]

Vaspurakan became a military province (a Katepanate) of the Byzantine Empire. As Tim Greenwood recently illustrated based on material for Vaspurakan, but also for the neighbouring region of Tarōn, which had already become

---

80   PmbZ Nº 27008.
81   Seibt, "Die Eingliederung von Vaspurakan"; Garsoïan, "The Byzantine Annexation", pp. 189–90; Cuneo, "Étude sur la topographie", p. 138; Cheynet, "Byzance et le Vaspurakan au xᵉ siècle", for the prehistory of relations between the Byzantine Empire and Vaspurakan, and pp. 61–63 for the annexation. See also Mahé, "La Sainte-Mère-de-Dieu d'Aparankʿ".
82   Zimansky, *Ecology and Empire*, pp. 15–19.
83   Felix, *Byzanz und die islamische Welt*, pp. 137–41; Hewsen, "Van in this World", pp. 28–30; Tʿovma Arcruni, *History*, ed. Patkanean, IV, 12, pp. 307–08, trans. Thomson, pp. 370–71.
84   For a map of the territories allocated to the Arcruni in Cappadocia, see Hewsen, *Armenia: A Historical Atlas*, map Nº 106.
85   Matthew of Edessa, *History* I, 49, trans. Dostourian, pp. 45–46. Hewsen, "Van in this World", pp. 29–30; Greenwood, "Historical Tradition, Memory and Law", pp. 41–42.

part of the empire in 966/967, the impact of the emigration of larger parts of the Armenian elites and other population and of the new regime must have been significant. Byzantium was represented by military and ecclesiastical officials, who also laid claim to now-orphaned possessions. Some estates were also directly integrated into the imperial domain. Furthermore, population from other provinces of the empire such as Bulgaria was deported to Vaspurakan.[86]

The Byzantine Empire, however, was not able to defend the region against the increasing Seljuk advance, especially from the 1040s onwards.[87] Any collapse of defences here would open the core regions of Byzantine Anatolia to invaders, as it did for the Seljuks, who advanced mainly through a corridor north of Lake Van and through the valley of the Araxes-river. Tʿovma Arcruni continuatus reports:

> When news of the kings' [Senekʿerim of Vaspurakan and Gagik II Bagratuni of Ani] departure from Armenia and the Roman control [of that country] reached the camp of the impious, bloodthirsty, ferocious race of Elim, then the ruler of the Elimites [= the Seljuks], who was called Sultan Tullup [Toġrïl], launched a cavalry attack like an eagle swooping on flocks of birds. Reaching the metropolis of Ani [the Bagratuni capital in northern Armenia, annexed by Byzantium in 1045], he besieged it; having captured it, he put [the inhabitants] to the sword.

The Seljuk conquest of Ani took place in 1064, that is after the death of Sultan Toġrïl (in 1063), but the causal chain of events indicated by the author becomes clear.[88] At the same time, the region was very much suitable for the nomadic lifestyle of core elements of the Seljuk retinue. Accordingly, Emperor Romanos IV Diogenes tried to get hold of the cities of Manzikert and Ahlat to the north of Lake Van to regain control over this corridor in summer 1071 (see Fig. 12.1) – with the well-known fatal result, which would also herald the end of Roman rule in Eastern Anatolia and the Caucasus region.[89]

Despite the Byzantine and then Seljuk invasions and following periods of Turkmen, Mongol or, finally, Ottoman rule, Armenian settlement in the region of Van would continue over the following centuries; the irrigation system put in place by the Urartians and expanded by the Arcruni King would continue to

---

86 Greenwood, "Social change in eleventh-century Armenia: the evidence from Tarōn". On deportations of Bulgarian prisoners of war to Vaspurakan see PmbZ N° 21580, 21680.
87 Lebeniotes, *Η πολιτική κατάρρευση*, pp. 145–77; Seibt, "Die Eingliederung von Vaspurakan".
88 Tʿovma Arcruni, *History*, ed. Patkanean, p. 308, trans. Thomson, p. 371.
89 Lebeniotes, *Η πολιτική κατάρρευση*, pp. 145–77; Nicolle, *Manzikert 1071*; Peacock, "Nomadic society".

water the so-called "Garden City" to the east of the ancient and medieval fortress of Van with up to 35,000 inhabitants; its beauty would inspire the Armenian saying "Van in this World, Paradise in the next". Only with World War I and the genocide of 1915 to 1916 would the Armenian history of Van end. Also, several monuments mentioned in this chapter fell victim to destruction.[90]

The Canal of Menua (or Semiramis), however, is still operational today. Recent demographic growth, urbanization and intensification of agriculture, though, threaten to overburden the scarce sweet water streams and wells in the Lake Van area – with Lake Urmia in neighbouring northwestern Iran (see Fig. 12.1), which had contracted to a third of its original extent by 2014, standing as a cautionary tale.[91] The irrigation systems around Van have proved their resilience for almost three millennia now;[92] the coming decades may impose a further endurance test on these infrastructures and the communities that depend on them.

Bibliography

Primary Sources

Ananias of Širak, *Armenian Geography*, trans. R.H. Hewsen, *The Geography of Ananias of Širak (Ašxarhacʻoycʻ). The long and the short Recension*, Wiesbaden 1992.

Matthew of Edessa, *History*, trans. A.E. Dostourian, *Armenia and the Crusades, Tenth to Twelfth Centuries. The Chronicle of Matthew of Edessa*, Lanham 1993.

Movsēs Xorenacʻi, *History*, trans. R.W. Thomson, *Moses Khorenatsʻi, History of the Armenians. Translation and Commentary on the Literary Sources*, Cambridge Mass. 1978.

Movsēs Xorenacʻi, *History*, trans. A. Mahé/J.-P. Mahé, *Histoire de l'Arménie par Moïse de Khorène*, Paris 1993.

Mxitʻar Goš, *Dastanagirkʻ*, trans. R.W. Thomson, *The Lawcode [Datastanagirkʻ] of Mxitʻar Goš*, Amsterdam 2000.

Samuel of Ani, trans. *Patrologia Graeca* 19, Paris 1857, pp. 601–740.

Sebēos, *History*, ed. G.V. Abgaryan, *Patmutʻiwn Sebēosi*, Erevan 1979.

---

[90] Cuneo, "Étude sur la topographie"; Hewsen, "Van in this World", pp. 30–42; Ter Minassian, "The City of Van"; Ferrari, "Van: il Paradiso Perduto degli Armeni"; Kazaryan, "The Church of Ałtʻamar", pp. 351–52. For a map of Van in the early 20th century, see Hewsen, *Armenia: A Historical Atlas*, map N° 197.

[91] Yerli, "An assessment of the urban water footprint"; Sima et al., "Managing Lake Urmia".

[92] For the concept of resilience and its various implications see Curtis, *Coping with Crisis*; Haldon/Rosen, "Society and environment"; Izdebski/Mordechai/White, "The Social Burden of Resilience"; Xoplaki et al., "Modelling Climate and Societal Resilience".

Sebēos, *History*, trans. R.W. Thomson, *The Armenian History attributed to Sebeos*, historical commentary by J. Howard-Johnston, assistance from T. Greenwood, 2 vols., Liverpool 1999.

Stepʻannos Ōrbēlean, *History*, ed. K. Šahnazareancʻ, *Patmutʻiwn nahangin Sisakan*, Paris 1860.

Stepʻannos Ōrbēlean, *History*, trans. R. Bedrosian, *Stepʻanos Orbelian, History of the State of Sisakan*, Long Branch, NJ, 2012 (online: https://archive.org/details/HistoryOfTheStateOfSisakan).

Tʻovma Arcruni, *History*, ed. K. Patkanean, *Tʻovmayi vardapeti Arcrownwoy Patmowtʻiwn tann Arcrowneacʻ*, St. Petersburg 1887 (Reprint Tbilisi 1917).

Tʻovma Arcruni, *History*, trans. R.W. Thomson, *Thomas Artsruni, History of the House of the Artsrunikʻ*, Detroit 1985.

Yohannēs Drasχanakertcʻi, *History*, trans. K.H. Maksoudian, *Yovhannēs Drasxanakertcʻi, History of Armenia*, Atlanta 1987.

Secondary Literature

Akkuş, M., et al., "The discovery of a microbialite-associated freshwater fish in the world's largest saline soda lake, Lake Van (Turkey)", *Zoosystematics and Evolution* 97 (2021), 181–89.

Albini, P., et al., "In Search of the Predecessors of the 2011 Van (Turkey) Earthquake", *Seismological Research Letters* 83/5 (2012), 855–62.

Alizadeh, K., "Ultan Qalas: A Fortified Site in the Sasanian Borderlands (Mughan Steppe, Iranian Azerbaijan)", *Iran* 49 (2011), 55–77.

Alizadeh, K., "Borderland Projects of Sasanian Empire: Intersection of Domestic and Foreign Policies", *Journal of Ancient History* 2/2 (2014), 254–88.

Althoff, G., *Die Ottonen: Königsherrschaft ohne Staat*, Stuttgart 2013.

Asa Eger, A., *The Islamic-Byzantine Frontier. Interaction and Exchange among Muslim and Christian Communities*, London 2015.

Azizi, H./Motohiro, T., "The Van Microplate: A New Microcontinent at the Junction of Iran, Turkey, and Armenia", *Frontiers in Earth Sciences* 8 (2021), 574385, doi: 10.3389/feart.2020.574385.

Barlas Şimşek, F./Çağatay, M.N, "Late Holocene high resolution multi-proxy climate and environmental records from Lake Van, eastern Turkey", *Quaternary International* 486 (2018), 57–72.

Barlas Şimşek, F., *Late Holocene high resolution multi-proxy climate and environmental records from Lake Van, eastern Turkey*, Dissertation, Istanbul Technical University 2015.

Beledian, K., "L'invention des images: une expérience du regard au Vaspurakan", in Z. Pogossian/E. Vardanyan (eds.), *The Church of the Holy Cross ofAłtʻamar. Politics, Art, Spirituality in the Kingdom of Vaspurakan*, Leiden 2019, pp. 253–90.

Belli, O., "Dams, reservoirs and irrigation channels of the Van plain in the period of the Urartian Kingdom", *Anatolian Studies* 49 (1999), 11–26.

Belli, O., "Urartian Dams and Artificial Lakes Recently Discovered in Eastern Anatolia", *Journal of the Institute of Archaeology of Tel Aviv University* 21 (1994), 77–117.

Berkian, A.J., *Armenischer Wehrbau im Mittelalter*, Darmstadt 1976.

Bernhardt, J.W., *Itinerant kingship and royal monasteries in early medieval Germany, 936–1075*, Cambridge 1993.

Blaschke, Th., *Euphrat und Tigris im Alten Orient*, Wiesbaden 2018.

Brönnimann, St./Pfister, Ch./White, S., "Archives of Nature and Archives of Societies", in S. White/Ch. Pfister/F. Mauelshagen (eds.), *The Palgrave Handbook of Climate History*, London 2018, pp. 27–36.

Büntgen, U., et al., "Cooling and societal change during the Late Antique Little Ice Age from 536 to around 660 AD", *Nature Geoscience* 9 (2016), 231–36, https://doi.org/10.1038/ngeo2652.

Cassis, M./Doonan, O./Elton, H./Newhard, J., "Evaluating Archaeological Evidence for Demographics, Abandonment, and Recovery in Late Antique and Byzantine Anatolia", *Human Ecology* 46 (2018), 381–98.

Çevik, Ö., "The Change of Settlement Patterns in Lake Van Basin: Ecological Constraints caused by Highland Landscape", *Altorientalische Forschungen* 32 (2005), 74–96.

Cheynet, Jean-Claude, "Byzance et le Vaspurakan au Xe siècle", in Z. Pogossian/E. Vardanyan (eds.), *The Church of the Holy Cross of Ałt'amar. Politics, Art, Spirituality in the Kingdom of Vaspurakan*, Leiden 2019, pp. 49–66.

Çifçi, A., *The Socio-Economic Organisation of the Urartian Kingdom* (Culture and History of the Ancient Near East 89), Leiden 2017.

Cowe, S.P., "Ejmiatsin", in *Encyclopaedia Iranica* 8/3, pp. 278–81, online: https://iranicaonline.org/articles/ejmiatsin.

Cukur, D., et al., "Water level changes in Lake Van, Turkey, during the past ca. 600 ka: climatic, volcanic and tectonic controls", *Journal of Paleolimnology* 52 (2014), 201–14.

Cuneo, P., "Étude sur la topographie et l'iconographie historique de la ville de Van", in D. Kouymjian (ed.), *Armenian Studies/Etudes Armenienne in Memoriam Haïg Berbérian*, Lisbon 1986, pp. 125–84.

Curtis, D.R., *Coping with Crisis. The Resilience and Vulnerability of Pre-Industrial Settlements*, Farnham 2014.

Dan, R., *From the Armenian Highland to Iran. A Study on the Relations between the Kingdom of Urartu and the Achaemenid Empire* (Serie Orientale Roma 4), Rome 2015.

Dédéyan, G., "Princes et rois du Vaspurakan face à leur Église (VIII–XIe siècles)", *Revue théologique de Kaslik* 3–4 (2009–2010), 57–72.

Der Nersessian, S., *Aght'amar. Church of the Holy Cross*, Cambridge; Mass. 1965.

Donabédian, Patrick, "Sainte-Croix d'Ałt'amar. Sens symbolique, architectural et iconographique de la dédicace", in: Z. Pogossian/E. Vardanyan (eds.), *The Church of the Holy Cross of Aḷtʻamar. Politics, Art, Spirituality in the Kingdom of Vaspurakan*, Leiden 2019, pp. 291–346.

Dönmez, E.O./Belli, O., "Urartian Plant Cultivation at Yoncatepe (Van), Eastern Turkey". *Economic Botany* 61 (3) (2007), 290–98.

Dorfmann-Lazarev, I., "Kingship and Hospitality in the Iconography of the Palatine Church at Aḷtʻamar", *Rivista di Storia e Letteratura Religiosa* 52 (2016), 479–516.

Dusinberre, E.R.M., *Empire, Authority, and Autonomy in Achaemenid Anatolia*, Cambridge 2013.

Ellenblum, R., *The Collapse of the Eastern Mediterranean. Climate Change and the Decline of the East, 950–1072*, Cambridge 2012.

Fabian, L., "Moving in the Mountains: GIS and Mapping the Phenomenology of Travel through the South Caucasus", in W. Anderson/K. Hopper/A. Robinson (eds.), *Landscape Archaeology in Southern Caucasia*, Vienna 2018, pp. 23–35.

Felix, W., *Byzanz und die islamische Welt im früheren 11. Jahrhundert* (Byzantina Vindobonensia 14), Vienna 1981.

Ferrari, A., "Van: il Paradiso Perduto degli Armeni", *Eurasiatica* 4 (2016), 317–35.

Gallagher, D.E./McIntosh, R.J., "Agriculture and Urbanism", in G. Barker/C. Goucher (eds.), *The Cambridge World History, Vol. II: A World with Agriculture, 12,000 BCE–500 CE*, Cambridge 2015, pp. 186–209.

Garbrecht, G., "The Water Supply System at Tuspa (Urartu)", *World Archaeology* 11/3 (1980), 306–12.

Garbrecht, G., "Historische Wasserbauten in Ostanatolien – Königreich Urartu, 9.–7. Jh. v. Chr.", in Ch. Ohlig (ed.), *Wasserbauten im Königreich Urartu und weitere Beiträge zur Hydrotechnik der Antike*, Siegburg 2004, pp. 1–104.

Garsoïan, N., "The Independent Kingdoms of Medieval Armenia", in R.G. Hovannisian (ed.), *The Armenian People from Ancient to Modern Times. Volume I The Dynastic Periods: From Antiquity to the Fourteenth Century*, New York 1997, pp. 143–85.

Garsoïan, N., "The Byzantine Annexation of the Armenian Kingdoms in the Eleventh Century", in R.G. Hovannisian (ed.), *The Armenian People from Ancient to Modern Times. Volume I The Dynastic Periods: From Antiquity to the Fourteenth Century*, New York 1997, pp. 187–98.

Greenwood, T., "Tʻovma Artsruni", in D. Thomas (ed.), *Christian-Muslim Relations 600–1500*, consulted online on 27 February 2018: http://dx.doi.org/10.1163/1877-8054_cmri_COM_24278.

Greenwood, T., "Historical Tradition, Memory and Law in Vaspurakan in the Era of Gagik Arcruni", in Z. Pogossian/E. Vardanyan (eds.), *The Church of the Holy Cross of Aḷtʻamar. Politics, Art, Spirituality in the Kingdom of Vaspurakan*, Leiden 2019, pp. 27–48.

Greenwood, T., "Social change in eleventh-century Armenia: the evidence from Tarōn", in J. Howard-Johnston (ed.), *Social Change in Town and Country in Eleventh-Century Byzantium*, Oxford 2020, pp. 196–219.

Greenwood, T., "A contested jurisdiction: Armenia in late antiquity", in E.W. Sauer (ed.), *Sasanian Persia: Between Rome and the Steppes of Eurasia*, Edinburgh 2017, pp. 199–220.

Grekyan, V., "When the gods leave people (The Climatological Hypothesis of the Collapse of the Urartian State)", in A. Kosyan/Y. Grekyan/A. Bobokhyan (eds.), *The Black & the White. Studies on history, archaeology, mythology and philology in honor of Armen Petrosyan in occasion of his 65th birthday*, Yerewan 2014, pp. 57–94.

Grigoryan, G., "King Gagik Arcruni's Portrait on the Church of Ałtʻamar", in Z. Pogossian/ E. Vardanyan (eds.), *The Church of the Holy Cross of Ałtʻamar. Politics, Art, Spirituality in the Kingdom of Vaspurakan*, Leiden 2019, pp. 416–40.

Haldon, J.F., et al., "The Climate and Environment of Byzantine Anatolia: Integrating Science, History, and Archaeology", *Journal of Interdisciplinary History* 45,2 (2014), 113–61.

Haldon, J.F./Rosen, A., "Society and environment in the East Mediterranean ca 300–1800 CE. Problems of resilience, adaptation and transformation", *Human Ecology* 46 (2018), 275–90.

Halstead, P., *Two Oxen Ahead. Pre-Mechanized Farming in the Mediterranean*, Chichester 2014.

Hewsen, R.H., "Van in this World, Paradise in the next. The historical geography of Van/Vaspurakan", in R.G. Hovannisian (ed.), *Armenian Van/Vaspurakan*, Costa Mesa, CA 2000, pp. 13–42.

Hewsen, R.H., *Armenia: A Historical Atlas*, Chicago 2001.

Izdebski, A., *A Rural Economy in Transition. Asia Minor from Late Antiquity into the Early Middle Ages* (Journal of Juristic Papyrology, Supplement vol. 18), Warsaw 2013.

Izdebski, A./Koloch, G./Słoczyński, T., "Exploring Byzantine and Ottoman economic history with the use of palynological data: a quantitative approach", *Jahrbuch der Österreichischen Byzantinistik* 65 (2015), 67–110.

Izdebski, A./Mordechai, L./White, S., "The Social Burden of Resilience: A Historical Perspective", *Human Ecology* 46 (2018), 291–303.

Jones, L., *Between Islam and Byzantium. Aghtʻamar and the visual Construction of Medieval Armenian Rulership*, Aldershot 2007.

Karabaşoğlu, A./Karaoğlu, Ö./Kuvanç, R., "Petrographic Observations Related to Rocks used in Urartu Settlements (Van Castle, Aşağı and Yukarı Anzaf, Çavuştepe, Ayanis, Toprakkale, Zivistan, Keçikıran, Aliler, Körzüt and Menua Canal Historical Sites) around Van (Eastern Turkey)", *Türkiye Jeoloji Bülteni/Geological Bulletin of Turkey* 64 (2021) 199–222 [in Turkish].

Kaspar, H.-D./Kaspar, E., *Das Königreich Urartu. Geschichte, Forschungsgeschichte, Königsresidenzen*, Norderstedt 2021.

Kazaryan, A., "The Church of Ałtʻamar: a New Image in the Medieval Architecture", in Z. Pogossian/E. Vardanyan (eds.), *The Church of the Holy Cross of Ałtʻamar. Politics, Art, Spirituality in the Kingdom of Vaspurakan*, Leiden 2019, pp. 347–69.

Kertmenjian, D., "Reflections on the Architecture of the Palace Complex on the Island ofAłtʻamar", in Z. Pogossian/E. Vardanyan (eds.), *The Church of the Holy Cross of Ałtʻamar. Politics, Art, Spirituality in the Kingdom of Vaspurakan*, Leiden 2019, pp. 370–79.

Kleiss, W., "Urartäische und achämenidische Wasserbauten", In S. Kroll, et al. (eds.), *Biainili-Urartu. The Proceedings of the Symposium held in Munich 12–14 October 2007*, Peeters 2012, pp. 61–76.

Kuşlu, Y./Üstun, S., "Water Structures in Anatolia from Past to Present", *Journal of Applied Sciences Research* 5(12) (2009), 2109–16.

La Porta, S., "Beyond Image and Text: Armenian Readings of the Old Testament Scenes on the Church at Ałtʻamar", in Z. Pogossian/E. Vardanyan (eds.), *The Church of the Holy Cross of Ałtʻamar. Politics, Art, Spirituality in the Kingdom of Vaspurakan*, Leiden 2019, pp. 242–52.

Lebeniotes, G.A., *Η πολιτική κατάρρευση του Βυζαντίου στην Ανατολή. Το ανατολικό σύνορο και η κεντρική Μικρά Ασία κατά το β' ήμισυ του 11ου αι.*, 2 Vols., Thessalonike 2007.

Lemcke, G./Sturm, M., "δ18O and trace element measurements as proxy for the reconstruction of climate changes at Lake Van (Turkey): Preliminary results", in H.N. Dalfes/G. Kukla/H. Weiss (eds.), *Third Millennium BC Climate Change and Old World Collapse*, Berlin 1997, pp. 653–78.

Linke, J., *Das Charisma der Könige. Zur Konzeption des altorientalischen Königtums im Hinblick auf Urartu*, Wiesbaden 2015.

Litt, Th., et al., "A 600,000 year long continental pollen record from Lake Van, eastern Anatolia (Turkey)", *Quaternary Science Reviews* 104 (2014), 30–41.

Mahé, J.-P., "Préambule", in Z. Pogossian/E. Vardanyan (eds.), *The Church of the Holy Cross of Ałtʻamar. Politics, Art, Spirituality in the Kingdom of Vaspurakan*, Leiden 2019, pp. XVI–XXIII.

Mahé, J.-P., "La Sainte-Mère-de-Dieu d'Aparankʻ: politique, diplomatie et spiritualité (983–995)", in Z. Pogossian/E. Vardanyan (eds.), *The Church of the Holy Cross of Ałtʻamar. Politics, Art, Spirituality in the Kingdom of Vaspurakan*, Leiden 2019, pp. 207–23.

Marquart, J., *Südarmenien und die Tigrisquellen nach griechischen und arabischen Geographen*, Vienna 1930.

McCormick, M., et al., "Climate Change during and after the Roman Empire: Reconstructing the Past from Scientific and Historical Evidence", *Journal of Interdisciplinary History* 43,2 (2012), 169–220.

Nicolle, D., *Manzikert 1071: The breaking of Byzantium*, Oxford 2013.

Orhan, A.H./Özdemir, T./Eyduran, E., "Urartian Water Constructions and Hydraulics", *Journal of Applied Science Research* 2/2 (2006), 346–54.

Peacock, A.C.S., "Nomadic society and the Seljuk campaigns in Caucasia", *Iran and the Caucasus* 9 (2005), 205–30.

PmbZ: Lilie, R.J., et al., *Prosopographie der mittelbyzantinischen Zeit Online*, Berlin 1998–2013, https://doi.org/10.1515/pmbz.

Pogossian, Z., "Locating Religion, Controlling Territory: Conquest and Legitimation in Late Ninth-Century Vaspurakan and its Interreligious Context", in R. Glei/N. Jaspert (eds.), *Locating Religions. Contact, Diversity, and Translocality*, Boston 2017, pp. 173–233.

Pogossian, Z., "The Foundation of the Monastery of Sevan: A Case Study on Monasteries, Economy and Political Power in IX–X Century Armenia", in *Le Valli dei Monaci: Atti del III Convegno Internazionale di Studio "De Re Monastica", Roma–Subiaco, 17–19 maggio, 2010*, Vol. 1, Spoleto 2012, pp. 181–215.

Pogossian, Z./Vardanyan, E., "Introduction", in Z. Pogossian/E. Vardanyan (eds.), *The Church of the Holy Cross of Aŀtʿamar. Politics, Art, Spirituality in the Kingdom of Vaspurakan*, Leiden 2019, pp. 1–26.

Pogossian, Z., "Relics, Rulers, Patronage: the True Cross of Varag and the Church of the Holy Cross on Aŀtʿamar", in Z. Pogossian/E. Vardanyan (eds.), *The Church of the Holy Cross of Aŀtʿamar. Politics, Art, Spirituality in the Kingdom of Vaspurakan*, Leiden 2019, pp. 126–206.

Preiser-Kapeller, J., "A Collapse of the Eastern Mediterranean? New results and theories on the interplay between climate and societies in Byzantium and the Near East, ca. 1000–1200 AD", *Jahrbuch der Österreichischen Byzantinistik* 65 (2015), 195–242.

Preiser-Kapeller, J., "Complex processes of migration: the south Caucasus in the early Islamic Empire (7th–10th century AD)", in H. Mehler et al. (eds.), *Migration und Integration von der Urgeschichte bis zum Mittelalter*, Halle 2017, pp. 295–313.

Preiser-Kapeller, J., "Small Kingdoms in a Big World: Patterns of Power in Early Medieval Southern Armenia", in M.St. Popović/V. Polloczek/B. Koschicek/St. Eichert (eds.), *Power in Landscape. Geographic and Digital Approaches on Historical Research*, Leipzig 2019, pp. 107–19.

Preiser-Kapeller, J., *Der Lange Sommer und die Kleine Eiszeit. Klima, Pandemien und der Wandel der Alten Welt von 500 bis 1500 n. Chr.*, Vienna 2021.

Rahimi-Laridjani, F., *Die Entwicklung der Bewässerungslandwirtschaft im Iran bis in sasanidisch-frühislamische Zeit*, Wiesbaden 1988.

Roberts, N., "Not the End of the World? Post-Classical Decline and Recovery in Rural Anatolia", *Human Ecology* 46 (2018), 305–22.

Sagona, A./Zimansky, P.E., *Ancient Turkey* (Routledge World Archaeology), Abingdon 2009.

Schweizer, G., *Untersuchungen zur Physiogeographie von Ostanatolien und Nordwestiran*, Tübingen 1975.

Seibt, W., "Die Eingliederung von Vaspurakan in das Byzantinische Reich (etwa Anfang 1019 bzw. Anfang 1022)", *Handes Amsorya* 92 (1978), 49–66.

Selçuk, A.S., "Evaluation of the relative tectonic activity in the eastern Lake Van basin, East Turkey", *Geomorphology* 270 (2016), 9–21.

Sima, S., et al., "Managing Lake Urmia, Iran for diverse restoration objectives: Moving beyond a uniform target lake level", *Journal of Hydrology: Regional Studies* 35 (2021) 100812, https://doi.org/10.1016/j.ejrh.2021.100812.

Sinha, A. et al., "Role of climate in the rise and fall of the Neo-Assyrian Empire", *Science Advance* 5/11 (2019), online: https://www.science.org/doi/10.1126/sciadv.aax6656.

Smith, A.T., "Rendering the political aesthetic: Political legitimacy in Urartian representations of the built environment", *Journal of Anthropological Archaeology* 19 (2000), 131–63.

Stadelbauer, J., *Studien zur Agrargeographie Transkaukasiens*, Berlin 1983.

Taskin, B., et al., "The aftermath of 2011 Van earthquakes: evaluation of strong motion, geotechnical and structural issues", *Bulletin of Earthquake Engineering* 11 (2013), 285–312.

Telelis, I.G., *Μετεωρολογικά φαινόμενα και κλίμα στο Βυζάντιο*, 2 vols., Athens 2004.

Ter Minassian, A., "The City of Van at the Turn of the Twentieth Century", in R.G. Hovannisian (ed.), *Armenian Van/Vaspurakan*, Costa Mesa, CA 2000, pp. 171–94.

Thierry, J.M., *Monuments arméniens du Vaspurakan*, Paris 1989.

Thierry, J.M., "Notes de géographie historique sur le Vaspurakan", *Revue des études byzantines* 34 (1976). 159–73.

Thierry, J.M., *Armenien im Mittelalter*, Regensburg 2002.

Thomson, R.W., *A Bibliography of Classical Armenian Literature to 1500 AD* (Corpus Scriptorum Christianorum Orientalium), Turnhout 1995.

Thomson, R.W., "Tovma Artsruni: Historian of Vaspurakan", in R.G. Hovannisian (ed.), *Armenian Van/Vaspurakan*, Costa Mesa CA 2000, pp. 57–72.

Thomson, R.W., "Supplement to 'A Bibliography of Classical Armenian Literature to 1500 AD'. Publications 1993–2005", *Le Muséon* 120 (2007), 163–233.

Thomson, R.W., "Armenian Biblical Exegesis and the Sculptures of the Church on Ałtʻamar", in Z. Pogossian/E. Vardanyan (eds.), *The Church of the Holy Cross of Ałtʻamar. Politics, Art, Spirituality in the Kingdom of Vaspurakan*, Leiden 2019, pp. 224–41.

Tosun, H., "Re-evaluation of Large Dams in Van Inner Basin, Turkey", in *5th World Congress on Civil, Structural, and Environmental Engineering (CSEE'20) Lisbon, Portugal Virtual Conference – October 2020*, Paper No. ICGRE 192, doi: 10.11159/icgre20.192.

Vacca, A.M., *Non-Muslim Provinces under Early Islam. Islamic Rule and Iranian Legitimacy in Armenia and Caucasian Albania*, Cambridge 2017.

Vacca, A.M., "Conflict and Community in the Medieval Caucasus", *Al-ʿUṣūr al-Wusṭā* 25 (2017), 66–112.

Vacca, A.M., "Al-Basfurrağān and Banū l-Dayrānī: Vaspurakan and the Arcrunikʻ in Arabic Sources", in Z. Pogossian/E. Vardanyan (eds.), *The Church of the Holy Cross of Aḷtʻamar. Politics, Art, Spirituality in the Kingdom of Vaspurakan*, Leiden 2019, pp. 67–99.

Vardanyan, E., "Les sujets bibliques de la frise de la vigne dans le décor sculpté de l'église de la Sainte-Croix d'Aḷtʻamar : le cycle d'Isaac", in Z. Pogossian/E. Vardanyan (eds.), *The Church of the Holy Cross of Aḷtʻamar. Politics, Art, Spirituality in the Kingdom of Vaspurakan*, Leiden 2019, pp. 380–415.

Vardanyan, V.M., "The Armenian princely system in Vaspurakan during the struggle of the Armenian people against the Arab Caliphate's dominance (the 8th century)", *Fundamental Armenology* 2 (2015), online: http://www.fundamentalarmenology.am/datas/pdfs/183.pdf.

Wick, L./Lemcke, G./Sturm, M., "Evidence of Lateglacial and Holocene climatic change and human impact in eastern Anatolia: high-resolution pollen, charcoal, isotopic and geochemical records from the laminated sediments of Lake Van, Turkey", *Holocene* 13 (2003), 665–75.

Woodbridge, J./Roberts, N., "Late Holocene climate of the Eastern Mediterranean inferred from diatom analysis of annually-laminated lake sediments", *Quaternary Science Reviews* 30 (2011), 3381–392.

Wordsworth, P.D./Wencel, M.M., "The Dramatic Abandonment of a Late-Antique Settlement in the South Caucasus: The First Archaeological Findings from Qaratəpə, Bərdə Rayon, Azerbaijan", *Journal of Field Archaeology* 43 (2018), 300–14.

Yerli, C., "An assessment of the urban water footprint and blue water scarcity: A case study for Van (Turkey)", *Brazilian Journal of Biology* 82 (2022), e249745, https://doi.org/10.1590/1519-6984.249745.

Xoplaki, E., et al., "Modelling Climate and Societal Resilience in the Eastern Mediterranean in the Last Millennium", *Human Ecology* 46 (2018), 363–79.

Zimansky, P.E., *Ecology and Empire: The Structure of the Urartian State*, Chicago 1985.

CHAPTER 13

Sea of Agency: Islands and Coasts of the Byzantine Aegean in Environmental Perspective

Myrto Veikou

"A Sea of Agency" were, back in 2008, Kostas Kotsakis' words to describe the Neolithic Aegean.[1] As early as the dawn of human civilization, this sea was an important natural feature of the Mediterranean region, possessing several unique characteristics that make it of considerable interest.

First of all, the Aegean Sea has an intricate configuration and could well be considered as a bay within the eastern Mediterranean basin, to which it is connected by the straits to the west and east of Crete. It is connected through the straits of the Dardanelles, the Sea of Marmara, and the Bosporus to the Black Sea, while the island of Crete can be taken as marking its southern boundary.

Yet, this sea is much more than an empty, watery space between Europe, Asia and Africa. Instead, it has been – and still remains – an important communication route east–west and north–south, providing great ease of mutual contact.[2] It contains a great number of islands that are, on one hand, neatly self-defined and isolated biogeographical units[3] and, on the other, parts of a unity, of "a single 'far-flung city' of criss-crossing islands and settlements within networks of communication and of economic and political interdependence".[4] Throughout the entire Aegean shoreline – that is, both the continental shores surrounding the sea and those of the islands – bays, ports, and shelter creeks are abundant. These also facilitated the task of seamen traveling this sea, having made longer voyages possible even at the times when shipbuilding was in its infancy.

Rather than separating the inhabitants scattered around its shores, the Aegean waters have been connecting them, facilitating the movement of goods, people, and ideas and creating ties between disparate communities.[5]

---

1 Kotsakis, "Sea".
2 Horden/Purcell, *Corrupting Sea*, 13; Steel, *Materiality*, 3.
3 Renfrew and Wagstaff, *Island Polity*.
4 Asdrahas, "Archipelago".
5 See Tartaron, *Maritime Networks*, 6–7, 80, 88; Preiser-Kapeller, "Harbours", 12–13, 18–19.

Mainland and insular harbors have functioned as gateways not only for the entrance of people, goods, and knowledge but also of diseases and enemy attacks.[6] So, the entire space of the Aegean has also repeatedly been seen as continuous, and as forming a "dispersed liquid city".[7] The implication is that human agency, active in historical contexts, can overcome the physical barriers imposed by natural features that are usually perceived as determining factors.[8] This has been happening diachronically in the case of the Aegean Sea; for its size, no other maritime area of the Mediterranean has comparable coastline development.[9] In what follows, I will compare data and narratives in an effort to understand the reasons for this remarkability and its specific attributes during the Byzantine period.

1 A 'Complex' Geography (Figs. 13.1 and 13.2)

The Aegean Sea (Greek *Αιγαίο Πέλαγος* or *Αρχιπέλαγος*, Turkish *Eğe Deniz*) is an arm of the Mediterranean Sea, located between the Greek peninsula to the west and Asia Minor to the east (Fig. 13.3). About 380 miles (612 km) long and 186 miles (299 km) wide, it has a total area of some 83,000 square miles (215,000 square km), and its maximum depth of 11,627 feet (3,544 meters) is to be found east of Crete.[10] Its coastline includes abundant bays and gulfs of diverse geomorphological features, which have been in constant use since antiquity. Last but not least, so numerous are the islands of the Aegean that the Greek name *Archipelago* has been applied to the sea. Their vast majority belong to Greece and are arranged into nine administrative groups, from north to south, as outlined below. Of these islands, Euboea, although technically an island, is considered a part of the Greek mainland, being connected to Boeotia by a bridge. The only sizable possessions of Turkey in the Aegean Sea are Imbros and Tenedos (Gökçeada and Bozcaada in Turkish since 1970),[11] in the northeastern part of the Sea, having reverted to Turkey after the 1923 Treaty of Lausanne that concluded the Greek–Turkish war.[12]

---

6 For recent approaches to Roman and medieval harbours see Preiser-Kapeller/Daim, *Harbours*.
7 Romano, *Paese Italia*; Veikou, "Rural Towns".
8 Kotsakis, "Sea", 52.
9 "Aegean Sea".
10 Ibid.
11 Alexandridis, "Identity", 120.
12 On the history of the two islands, which are still ground of European actions protecting Greek–Turkish cohabitation, see Gross, "Gökçeada".

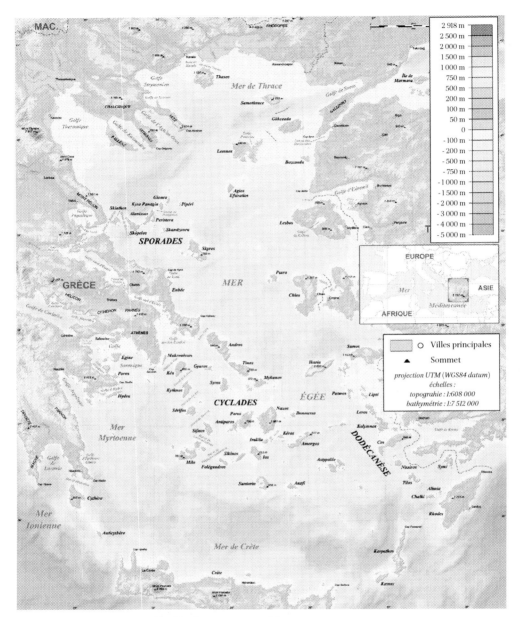

FIGURE 13.1　Topographical and bathymetric map of the Aegean Sea area
COPYRIGHT ERIC GABA (STING – FR:STING) [GFDL (HTTP://WWW.GNU.ORG
/COPYLEFT/FDL.HTML) OR CC BY-SA 4.0-3.0-2.5-2.0-1.0 (HTTPS://CREATIVE
COMMONS.ORG/LICENSES/BY-SA/4.0-3.0-2.5-2.0-1.0)], VIA WIKIMEDIA COMMONS
FROM WIKIMEDIA COMMONS: (HTTPS://COMMONS.WIKIMEDIA.ORG/WIKI/FILE
:AEGEAN_SEA_MAP_BATHYMETRY-FR.JPG)

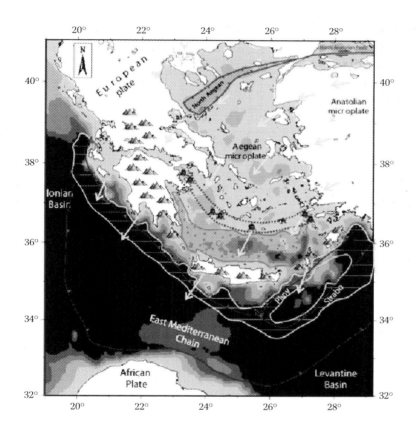

Legend

- ▲ Aegean Volcanic Arc
- ◌ Back-Arc Cretan Basin
- ⛰ Peloponnese-Crete Island Arc
- ◯ Hellenic Trench
- G.P.S. Movements

20 mm/yr

- ◡ Plate Tectonic Boundary
- ⊢⊣ Active Marginal Faults of North Aegean Basin

Bathymetry: 0, -500, -1500, -2500, -3500

FIGURE 13.2 Simplified map of the present-day geodynamic structure of the Hellenic Arc, showing the modern Aegean volcanic arc developed behind the Hellenic trench, the Peloponnese–Crete island arc and the Cretan back-arc basin. Note that the African plate to the south subducts beneath the Eurasian plate to the north along the red lines just to the south of Crete. Yellow arrows indicate the GPS rates (approximately 40 mm/yr) of the Aegean towards the African plate (considered stable). (SOURCE: NOMIKOU ET AL., "VOLCANOES", 124: FIG. 1). COURTESY OF ASS. PROF. PARASKEVI NOMIKOU, DEPARTMENT OF GEOLOGY, UNIVERSITY OF ATHENS, GREECE

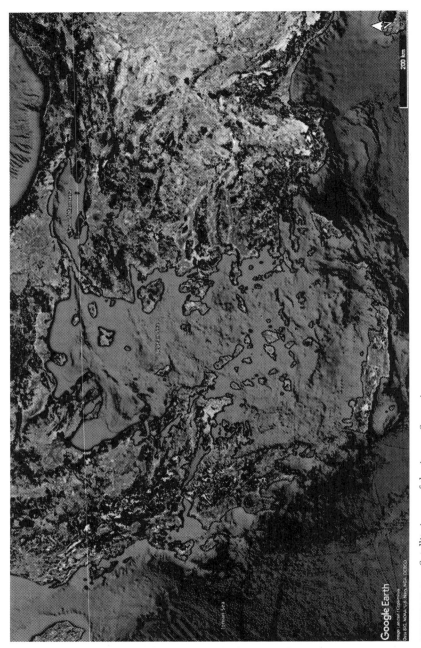

FIGURE 13.3 Satellite image of the Aegean Sea region
COURTESY OF GOOGLE EARTH

The geography of the Aegean area is slightly fragmented; it is formed by smaller maritime regions including island groups and their nearby coastal areas, with different levels of diachronic connectivity. These regions are the following, from north to south (Fig. 13.1).

1. The Greek Thracian and Macedonian coastline with the Thracian-Sea island group, including Thassos, Samothrace, Lemnos, and Agios Efstratios, allows communication with the Balkans and the rest of the Aegean to the south through the Chalkidiki Peninsula including the Cassandra and the Singitic Gulfs, the Strymonian Gulf and the Gulf of Kavala. The Turkish Dardanelles coastal areas (Çanakkale Province) with the islands of Imbros/Gökçeada and Tenedos/Bozcaada allow communication between Thrace (through Saros Gulf), the Bosphorus, the Black Sea and the rest of the Aegean regions.

2. The Greek East Aegean Island group, including Lesvos, Chios, Ikaria, and Samos, has offered communication routes between Greek and Turkish Aegean coasts (through the Gulfs of Edremit, Dikili, Çandarlı, İzmir, Kuşadası) from antiquity to the present day.

3. The Greek Thessalian coastline with the Pagasetic Gulf and the Northern Sporades islands (Skiathos, Skopelos, Allonissos, Peristera, Kyra-Panagia, Gioura, Skantzoura, Skyros, Skyropoula, Sarakino, and their satellite islets) allow communication between the Greek mainland and the East Aegean Island group and Euboea.

4. The Greek Aegean coasts of Boeotia and Attica with the island of Euboea (connected to the mainland by a bridge at Chalkida, documented as early as 1435)[13] with their many satellite and offshore islets, offer several central nodes of communication in the Aegean Sea, diachronically.

5. The coastlines of Attica and the northeastern Peloponnese with the Argolic and Saronic Gulfs and the Saronic Islands (Salamis, Aegina, Poros, Hydra, and Spetses, including many satellite and offshore islets) are a densely populated area diachronically. It has been connected with the Greek mainland and the rest of the Aegean through the Myrtoan Sea, the Cycladic complex, the Gulf of Petalioi and the Southern Gulf of Euboea.

6. The Cyclades, located at the center of the Aegean, are connected with: Attica and Boeotia through the Petalioi Gulf, which connects with the South and North Euboic Sea; the east coastline of the Peloponnese through the Myrtoan Sea; the Dodecannese; and Crete through the Cretan Sea. The Cycladic complex includes Amorgos, Anafi, Andros, Antiparos, Delos, Folegandros, Ios, Kea, Kimolos, Kythnos, Milos, Mykonos, Naxos,

---

13 Telelis, Φαινόμενα, 697.

Paros, Serifos, Sifnos, Sikinos, Syros, Tinos, and Thira or Santoríni, as well as several minor islands like Donousa, Eschati, Gyaros, Irakleia, Koufonisia, Makronisos, and Schoinoussa.

7. The Southern Sporades, including the Dodecanese and the complex of Ikaria, Fournoi, and Samos, offer contacts with the Cyclades and through that with the Greek mainland, with Crete, and with the Eastern coasts of Turkey through the gulfs of Kazıklı, Güllük, Gökova, Hisarönü, Sömbeki, Marmaris, Karaağaç, and Fethiye. The Dodecannese consists of twelve main islands, as its name indicates (Rhodes, Kos, Patmos, Astypalaia, Kalymnos, Karpathos, Kassos, Leros, Nisyros, Symi, Tilos, and Kastellorizo), and of several minor ones such as Agathonisi, Lipsoi, Alimia, Arkoi, Chalki, Farmakonisi, Gyali, Kinaros, Levitha, Marathos, Nimos, Pserimos, Saria, Strongyli, Syrna, and Telendos.

8. The island of Crete with its satellite islets and the islands of Kythira, Antikythira, and Elaphonissos is connected with: the Dodecannese and the Turkish coast to the east; the Cyclades through the Cretan Sea; the southeast coastline of the Peloponnese through the Myrtoan Sea and the Gulfs of Epidauros Limira, Laconia, and Messinia; and the northern coast of Africa through the Southern Cretan and Libyan Seas.[14] The island's main gateways are the gulfs of Mirabellou, Herakleion, Almyros, Souda, and Chania on the north coast, and of Messara on the south coast.

All of these regions and many of these locations seem to have been settled with a higher or lower density from the 4th to the 15th century.[15] Archaeology, geo-archaeology, and the study of textual sources provide evidence for Byzantine agency in the Aegean Sea and its environmental aspects, as will be discussed next. The main discussion issues are, first of all, the ways in which environmental issues affected, disturbed, or modified different human activities and, secondly, the human response with new agencies aiming to control environmental changes or turn them to some advantage or simply to adjust to them.

2 An "Entangled", Unstable Geology

A feature of the Aegean Sea that determines the limits of human agency therein is its geological structure: this determines the islands' physical resources,

---

14 While there are no officially operating lines of maritime communication between Crete and Northern Africa nowadays, the recent inflow of immigrants from Libya to the Cretan southern coasts shows that the historical communication channels between the two continents through this particular island still exist. For references see the Greek Press during the years 2015–17 (e.g. *Iefimerida* 05/09/2017).

15 Külzer, "Υπόβαθρο", passim.

settlement, and economy. The geology of the Aegean Sea is an entanglement of three main features: a) the rocks that make its floor are mainly limestone, which is often greatly altered by: b) volcanic activity within the South Aegean Active Volcanic Arc, and c) subsequent frequent seismic activity originating from the area of the Hellenic or Aegean Arc.

The South Aegean Volcanic Arc is a chain of volcanic islands in the South Aegean Sea formed by plate tectonics as a consequence of the subduction of the African tectonic plate beneath the Eurasian plate (Fig. 13.2).[16] The active portion of the South Aegean Arc comprises a number of dormant and historically active volcanoes, at the islands of Aegina, Methana, Milos, Thira and Kolumbo, Kos, Nisyros, and Yali.[17] Of these, Thira was last active in 1925; its eruption in AD 726 was spectacular: floating pumice was noted by the Byzantine emperor Leo III in Constantinople.[18] The volcanos of Nisyros and Kolumbo are still active.[19] Milos' volcano last exploded in AD 205.[20]

The result of this geological feature on the Aegean subsoil is a mixture of volcanic sediments (such as the richly colored soils in Thira and Milos), of limestone, and of excellent marble (quarried since antiquity and through the Byzantine period in Cape Tainaron, Corinth, Attica, Syros, Naxos, Paros, Tinos, Andros, Dilos, Siphnos, Euboea, Skyros, Thassos, Lesvos, Chios, Rhodes, Aphrodisias, Priene, Teos, Iassos, Mylasa, Herakleia and Latmum, Ephessos, and Sardis)[21] and granite (in Dilos and Troad).[22] Alyki in Thassos was one of the most popular marble quarries in the empire: a rise in sea level after an earthquake in the 7th century submerged some quarries, but production continued at a minor scale until Ottoman times.[23] The special marbles from Eretria and Karystos in Euboea, Thassos, Paros, Naxos, Skyros, and Chios were highly prized and exported in Byzantine times.[24] Milos was famous for its obsidian quarries, and its volcanic tuffs into which catacombs were cut.[25]

Other results of the Aegean geology are the widespread sources of minerals (e.g., Milos and Kimolos produced minerals for medicinal purposes, such as kaolin, bentonite, and sulfur),[26] and also metals (e.g., iron mines existed

---

16   Phytikas/Vougioukalakis, *Arc*.
17   Nomikou et al., "Volcanos".
18   Higgins/Higgins, *Companion*, 195.
19   Ibid., 167–68.
20   Ibid., 184.
21   Higgins/Higgins, *Companion*, passim; Sodini, "Marble", 130–31.
22   Higgins/Higgins, *Companion*, 173.
23   Higgins/Higgins, *Companion*, 121; Sodini, "Marble", 136. On the 7th-century crisis of marble quarrying in the Aegean, see Sodini, "Marble", 135–36.
24   Sodini, "Marble", 131.
25   Higgins/Higgins, *Companion*, 184–86.
26   Ibid., 186.

in Serifos, Sifnos, and Chalkis in Euboea).[27] Thassos and Sifnos, in particular, had mines of iron, silver and gold since antiquity; however, the gold and silver mines in Sifnos were soon exhausted.[28] Hot springs (sometimes of healing sulfurous water) are another result of this geology. In Samothrace, a particularly seismic area that used to be volcanic, has a hot spring on its north coast near Loutra that is said to have medicinal properties and has been frequented since at least Byzantine times.[29] Another one on the south coast of Kos was famous in antiquity for its sulfurous springs used for medicinal purposes.[30] Another spring in Lesvos issues from volcanic rocks.[31] The water of some springs on the south coast of Ikaria reach a temperature of 33–58 °C.[32] Other volcanic, warm springs (14–33 °C) issue underwater just off Yiali Bay, on Yiali, and deposit iron oxides just like the waters at Kameni, Thira, while nearby volcanic Nisyros was celebrated in antiquity for its hot spring.[33] Milos has no other water except for hot springs.[34] Finally, the main product of Limnos since antiquity was Limnian Earth, exported for its medicinal properties.[35]

The Eastern Mediterranean Ridge to the south of Crete, on the other hand, has diachronically been producing important seismic activity with ensuing seismic waves in the area of the Hellenic or Aegean Arc and beyond (Fig. 13.4).[36] Partly due to this activity, the Aegean Sea level in Byzantine times seems to be approximately 1.2 m below its present level.[37] Evidence of earlier sea levels is visible at the shoreline of the western part of Crete: a major, rapid uplift of the island (of up to 10 m) sometime between AD 430 and 580.[38] Although there are no historical records of this event, a major earthquake in AD 551 was known to have caused drastic damage further east. Phalassarna was uplifted by 7 meters. The consequences of this earthquake were, firstly, that the harbor dried out and was relocated far above sea level, and secondly, that the ancient quarries to the south of the town were also relocated far from the shoreline at a different level.[39] During the same event, there was a five-meter uplift of

27 Ibid., passim.
28 Ibid., 118–20, 177.
29 Ibid., 122.
30 Ibid., 158.
31 Ibid., 134.
32 Ibid., 144.
33 Ibid., 161.
34 Ibid., 182, 186.
35 Ibid., 123.
36 Papadopoulos et al., 2014.
37 Higgins/Higgins, *Companion*, 206
38 Ibid., 199.
39 Ibid., 199.

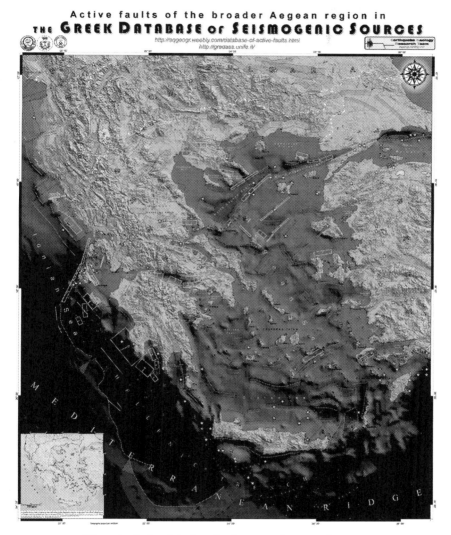

FIGURE 13.4   The active faults of the broader Aegean region on 2018.04.05
(SOURCE: EARTHQUAKE GEOLOGY IN GREECE, GREDASS PROJECT).
COURTESY OF PROF. SPYROS PAVLIDES AND DR. ALEXANDROS
CHATZIPETROS, DEPARTMENT OF GEOLOGY, ARISTOTLE UNIVERSITY OF
THESSALONIKI, GREECE

the coast, from Ayia Roumeli eastwards to Chora Sfakion. In this area, many consequent uplift-related sea levels are visible (5, 10, 20, 40 m);[40] this indicates that this transformation was the outcome of a series of seismic events in the area, rather than of a single incident.[41] Indeed, the coasts of central and eastern Crete appear to have subsided by 1–2 meters since antiquity, with the exception of the southeastern coast.[42]

Earthquakes are certainly quite common in the south of the island of Crete, and one of the most devastating historical ones occurred on July 21st, 365.[43] Geologists today estimate that it occurred underwater and had a magnitude of around 8.6;[44] it caused widespread destruction on Crete as well as in central and southern Greece, northern Africa, Cyprus, Sicily, and Spain.[45] The ensuing tsunami devastated the southern and eastern coasts of the Mediterranean, causing the loss of thousands of lives and hurling ships three kilometers inland according to the sources.[46] Its epicenter was most likely somewhere between Crete and the southwestern coasts of the Peloponnese in the vicinity of the Ionian fault.[47]

Recent geological studies view both aforementioned earthquakes in connection with a clustering of major seismic activity in the Eastern Mediterranean between the 4th and 6th centuries, which may have reflected a reactivation of all major plate boundaries in the region.[48] The devastating earthquake of AD 365 also largely affected the southeastern coasts of the Peloponnese, such as the Epidauros Coast in the Argolid, and Methoni Coast in Messenia.[49] Argolid is a very seismic area on its own, where earthquakes are common roughly every 300 years, and the Gulf of Corinth is susceptible to tsunamis. Two terrible earthquakes in this area are dated to the 6th century, one of which was during the spring of 551: the latter was followed by a tsunami that affected the areas of the Argolic and the Malian gulfs.[50] During all this seismic activity of Late Antiquity, part of the ancient city on the Kranae Island near Gytheio in Laconia was submerged below sea level, thus partly preserving the ruins that were created by the earthquake.[51] Another terrible earthquake affected

40 Ibid., 202.
41 Stiros, "Earthquake".
42 Higgins/Higgins, *Companion*, 199.
43 Ibid., 199.
44 Stiros, "Earthquake".
45 Ammianus Marcellinus, *Res Gestae* XXVI.10.15–19.
46 Papazachos/Dimitriu, "Tsunamis"; Antonopoulos, "Data", 154–56.
47 Antonopoulos, "Data", 155–56; Stiros, "Earthquake".
48 Stiros, "Earthquake", 545.
49 Higgins/Higgins, *Companion*, 199.
50 Ibid., 42; Antonopoulos, "Data", 165.
51 Higgins/Higgins, *Companion*, 55.

Kos in 554, and caused the progressive abandonment of the emporium at Halassarna.[52] It seems that this activity continued in later centuries, judging from the mentions of events in later sources. Apart from the aforementioned eruption of the volcano of Thira in the 8th century, a strong earthquake near Chios was followed by a devastating seismic wave on March 20, 1389,[53] while another earthquake in 1402 induced a tsunami at the western part of the Gulf of Corinth.[54]

Thus, while the volcanic environment offered certain economic benefits, seismic activity can be assumed to have been a frequent experience for the people living around the Aegean during the Byzantine period. Furthermore, it included some very important events with remarkable consequences for human life. The latter can indeed be considered as environmental parameters that caused both severe casualties and modifications or discontinuities of settlement.

3   An "Intensive" Coastal Change

The physical oceanography of the Aegean Sea is controlled mainly by the regional climate, the freshwater discharge from major rivers draining from southeastern Europe, and the seasonal variations in the Black Sea surface water outflow through the Dardanelles Strait. The current outline of the coastline dates back to about 4000 BC, yet it has been subjected to considerable change in the areas around numerous points of freshwater discharge.[55] Many major rivers (catchments of >1000 km^2) from the surrounding areas of the Balkans and Turkey flow into the Aegean Sea, collectively constituting an important source of land-derived organic matter.[56] In these areas, a complexity of phenomena has radically altered the geomorphology of the Mediterranean coasts as compared to their late antique and medieval state.[57] Specifically, these fluvial systems caused geological phenomena that interacted with fluctuations in sea level to produce a long-term process of geomorphological change; some of these phenomena are quite recent and therefore have radically changed the landscape since Byzantine times.[58]

The processes of coastal change can be roughly described as follows. The important fluvial systems in this area are formed by large rivers rising in

52   Ibid., 160.
53   Antonopoulos, "Data", 189–90.
54   Papazachos/Dimitriu, "Tsunamis", 162.
55   "Aegean Sea"
56   Gogou et al., "Climate", 3.
57   Fouache, *Alluvionnement*, 7–32.
58   Fouache, *Alluvionnement*, 11.

the mountainous hinterland of Greece and Asia Minor and discharging into the Aegean Sea. Their flow transports sediments (eroded material), depositing them in riverine and coastal lowlands; these are known as "alluvial deposits". They cause morphological changes to the river basins, while the sedimentation process also produces morphodynamic phenomena in the coastal areas where they are discharged, known as "deltas".[59] A delta is a coastal deposit of sediment extending above and below sea level. It is created at the mouth of a river where that river flows into a large body of water (ocean, sea, lake, another river, etc.) discharging sediments at a faster rate than the seawater is able to absorb.[60] The sedimentary deposit thus causes a gradual seaward progradation of the shoreline. Deltaic morphodynamic phenomena are complex because they constantly "respond" to the continual changes in external conditions. Specifically, the alluvial deposits provoke a gradual transformation of topography that in turn transforms the limit conditions for the liquid dynamic, which afterwards develops in such a way as to further change how sediment is transported and deposited.[61] This happens because the coastline "responds" to the phenomenon of alluvial deposition in a variety of ways depending on: its extent, geological structure, and tectonic context; the type and quantity of deposited sediment; sea level; sea currents; wave mechanisms; and the surrounding land and marine environments.[62] The interaction of these factors alters shoreline progradation, marine transgression, or stability (i.e., it displaces the land in relation to the sea) forming the architecture of the deltas.[63] The coast is a system: its morphodynamics involve a complex mutual co-adjustment of forms and processes.[64]

Geological and geoarchaeological research around major rivers in the mainland of Greece and Asia Minor has shown different physical expressions of such dynamics in lower deltaic and surrounding coastal areas during the Byzantine period.[65] For example, Argolid in the Peloponnese consists of rich alluvial soil but lacks harbors; the only really safe one is Nauplia. A considerable increase in soil erosion is dated to the Byzantine period, around AD 1000. Sediments deposited by the rivers filled in the shallow bay, forcing the shoreline southwards. There have been plenty of marshes in this area up

59 Cowel/Thom, "Morphodynamics", 33.
60 Sutter 1994, 87–88.
61 Cowel/Thom, "Morphodynamics", 33.
62 Carter/Woodroffe, "Coastal Evolution", 8–9.
63 Postma, "Causes", 9.
64 Carter/Woodroffe, "Coastal Evolution", 8–9.
65 For an example of how these changes have periodically been affecting Byzantine settlement, see Veikou, *Epirus*, 28–37.

SEA OF AGENCY 359

FIGURE 13.5   Ephesos deltaic area. J. Preiser-Kapeller, "Harbours and Maritime Networks as Complex Adaptive Systems – a Thematic Introduction", in: J. Preiser-Kapeller & F. Daim (eds.), *Harbours and Maritime Networks as Complex Adaptive Systems*, RGZM Tagungen 23 (Mainz), 6: Fig. 3

until modern times.[66] High sedimentation is also observed in the Malian Gulf, where a period of high sea level is dated to AD c.1100.[67] Other examples of radical coastal transformation are the deltaic areas of Pinios in Thessaly, Xerias in Argolid, Strymon in Macedonia, and Kaystros at Ephessos.[68] Additional information can be drawn from the study of major rivers discharging into the Ionian Sea.[69]

Similar alluvial phenomena take place in the areas of smaller fluvial systems on the islands. For instance, the Early Byzantine settlement at Emborio in Chios lies on alluvial plains; here limestone blocks protected the volcanic rock from sea erosion.[70] In Samos, in the area of Pythagorion, two lagoons are fed by springs of water in the alluvial plain. Remains of the ancient harbor mole lie south of the present breakwater, under 3–4 m of water. Most of this submergence is due to erosion, but the level of some surviving harbor installations indicates that the level of the land has sunk about by about 50 cm over the last 2500 years.[71]

The aforementioned environmental changes have had substantial consequences on both the short- and the long-term history of settlement in the Aegean area. First of all, the unpredictable changes in the balance of water and land in the lower deltaic areas necessitated constant human agency in order to defend public health and economic subsistence; this agency involved undertaking large-scale technical works such as river-channel diversions, marsh-draining, construction of harbor facilities.[72] Secondly, they progressively altered the relief so as to impose the relocation of settlements and harbors, as in the case of Ephesos (Fig. 13.5).

4   A Constructive, Yet Challenging Climate

The Aegean coasts and islands enjoy a mild Mediterranean climate, with recurring windy and wet weather but with relatively high temperatures and year-round sunshine. North winds prevail especially in the summer; from the

---

66   Higgins/Higgins, *Companion*, 45–46.
67   Higgins/Higgins, *Companion*, 82.
68   Fouache, *Alluvionnement*; Dunn, "Strymon"; Gogou et al., "Climate"; Daim/Ladstätter, *Ephesos*, esp. 242–45.
69   See Fouache, *Alluvionnement*; Papageorgiou/Steiros, "Μεταβολή", 239–41; Jing/Rapp, "Coastal evolution"; Veikou, *Epirus*, esp. 27–39.
70   Higgins/Higgins, *Companion*, 138.
71   Higgins/Higgins, *Companion*, 147.
72   See, for example, the case studies of Ephesos and Rogoi in Daim/Ladstätter, *Ephesos*; Veikou, *Epirus*, 477.

end of September to the end of May, during the mild winter season, these winds alternate with southwesterlies.[73] The tides of the Aegean basin seem generally to follow the movements of those in the eastern Mediterranean. The tide of Euripus – a strait lying between continental Greece and the island of Euboea in the Aegean – is, however, extremely important, because it displays a tidal phenomenon of international significance, namely the euripus phenomenon, which is characterized by violent and uncertain currents and has been studied since the time of Aristotle.[74] Aegean currents are generally not smooth, whether considered from the viewpoint of either speed or direction, and they are chiefly influenced by blowing winds.[75] Water temperatures in the Aegean are influenced by the cold-water masses that flow in from the Black Sea in the northeast.[76]

During the Byzantine period, the relevant climatic reconstructions were still imperfect, since systematic and homogeneous research on various types of proxy data is still desirable;[77] Relevant issues are discussed in other parts of this volume.[78] Two recent studies have been specifically concerned with the southwestern and the northern parts of the Aegean and the impact of climatic condition on local economies. The first one has shown an expanding late antique economy in the east of the Peloponnese around the Aegean coast, interrupted by a severe dry episode (c.650–700), and followed by wetter conditions from the 8th century onwards.[79] Thereafter (AD 1000–1200), a very close correspondence between the environmental and archaeological-historical records suggests agropastoral intensification across the Peloponnese and Attica.[80]

The second study has shown that the lands of Macedonia and the Rhodope experienced a major cycle of medieval economic and demographic expansion (culminating in AD 1200–1350).[81] Crucially, the study has provided new evidence on sea surface temperature (SST) variations and paleoceanographic changes over the past 1500 years for the north Aegean Sea (NE Mediterranean). Sea surface temperature reconstructions have been based on multiproxy analyses obtained from the high-resolution (decadal to multidecadal) marine core M2 retrieved from the Athos basin.[82] The period from AD c.700 to 900 is

---

73 "Aegean sea".
74 Aristotle, *Meteorologica*, II 366a.8–12.
75 "Aegean sea".
76 "Aegean sea".
77 Finné, Holmgren, "Variability", 30.
78 See the chapters by Juerg Luterbacher and Elena Xoplaki.
79 Weiberg et al., "Peloponnese", 51.
80 Ibid., 51.
81 Gogou et al., "Climate", 13.
82 Gogou et al., "Climate", 1.

characterized by relatively stable SSTs and a tendency towards higher precipitation and thus increased supply from continental or riverine runoffs. From AD c.1100 to 1300, SSTs were rising. For this period, independent multi-proxy evidence from biomarkers, marine microfossils, and pollen indicates a transition from arid-like conditions towards more humid conditions in the Northern Aegean region. A cooling phase of almost 1.5 °C (for the sea surface temperature) is observed from AD c.1600 to 1700. This seems, however, to in fact have been the starting point of a continuous SST warming trend that continued until the end of the reconstructed period, interrupted by two prominent cooling events at AD 1832 ±15 and AD 1995 ±1, possibly related to the "unknown" volcano eruption of 1809 and the April 1815 Tambora eruption. The last 100 years of instrumental SST data are characterized by rising SSTs, accompanied by enhanced terrigenous inputs. Intensified riverine or continental runoffs after AD c.1450 in the north Aegean record suggest a humidity increase followed by drier conditions; the SST peak at AD c.1600 is related to wet conditions. The researchers showed that the economic growth based on a cultivation of temperature-sensitive crops (i.e., walnut, vine, and olive) co-occurred with stable and warmer temperatures, while its end coincided with a significant episode of cooler temperatures.[83] Periods of agricultural growth in Macedonia coincided with periods of warmer and more stable sea surface temperatures in the Aegean Sea.[84]

As we move our attention to the written sources, they allow us to see the gales, storms, and heavy seas that the Byzantines experienced over the Aegean in much more detail. In general, according to Critoboulos' statement, made in the years 1454–55, sudden storms with huge waves and strong winds are common in the Aegean.[85] To some degree, such narratives seem to reflect realistic intense weather phenomena and everyday events in which seamen were faced with danger and their efforts dealing with bad weather and heavy seas, either successfully or not.[86] In July to August of 533, strong winds from Abydos led a ship to Sigeion; there, they seem to have calmed down and the ship was quickly navigated to Maleas, where the winds calmed down completely.[87] In 541, strong westerly winds and a storm were mentioned near Tristomon, Myra, and in 807 another strong storm occurred at Myra.[88] In 678, there was a fleet wreck due

---

83   Gogou et al., "Climate", 16.
84   Ibid., 1.
85   Critoboulos, *History* 2:4.3: "Ἄφνης δὲ σφοδροῦ καταρραγέντος χειμῶνος καὶ κλύδωνος μετὰ λάβρων ὑετῶν καὶ ἀστραπῶν καὶ βροντῶν καὶ πνευμάτων ἐξαισίων καὶ σκότους τῆς τε θαλάσσης ἀγριουμένης καὶ τρικυμίας ἐγειρούσης μεγάλας, ὥσπερ σύνηθες τῷ Αἰγαίῳ ..."
86   Bazaiou-Barabas, "Θαλάσσιοι δρόμοι".
87   Telelis, *Φαινόμενα*, 220.
88   Ibid., 368–69.

to a storm by Syllaeon near Pergamon,[89] and between December and February of the years 821–23, tempests are mentioned around Northern Asia Minor.[90] A big storm is also mentioned in Rhodes in 619. The area of Lesvos seems to be particularly dangerous for navigators: big storms are recorded in the years 761, 725 and 1454–45; the second one was a terrible thunderstorm while the third one caused the sinking of a fleet.[91]

In other stories, the weather phenomena appear to have been so intense that ships were pushed off course and immobilized in some Aegean island for a long period of time (sometimes months) due to the bad weather conditions. For example, Thomas Magistros narrated in a letter how, during his trip from Thessaloniki to Constantinople, strong winds pushed his ship towards Limnos, where it was impossible to dock; he and the crew were trapped on the ship wandering around the Northern Aegean for days.[92] So common were storms and heavy seas that they are often used as narrative tools for justifying the emergence of holy miraculous events (such as the rescue of navigators by saints, the sinking of enemy ships threatening Constantinople inside the Golder Horn, etc.)[93] Indicatively, in 324 a storm in the northeastern Aegean, near the entrance of the Marmara Sea, sank a fleet;[94] on August 15th, 718, strong winds and a storm destroyed an enemy fleet;[95] and in November 1185, a storm in the Aegean sank a Norman ship near Ellispondos.[96]

Secondly, many incidents of wet conditions and extreme cold weather refer to Aegean coasts and islands. Thick hale is mentioned for the island of Paros, in the Cyclades, on May 12th, 1148.[97] In Crete, a heavy and wet winter occurred in 960/61.[98] Very strong cold weather is mentioned for Kythera and Monemvasia in 921–22 and for Euboea in August 1435.[99]

Under these conditions, the obvious advantage of navigation in the Aegean Sea, reported by John Chrysostom, is the permanent proximity to land. He states that travelling in a harborless sea is a cause of terror to sailors, who find comfort only in the security of a safe harbor as shelter during rough seas.[100] In

89   Ibid., 310–12.
90   Ibid., 382–83.
91   Ibid., 292–93, 329, 340, 705.
92   Karpozilos, "Ταξιδιωτικές περιγραφές", 524–27.
93   See examples in Telelis, Φαινόμενα, 422–23, 475–76, 525, 673.
94   Telelis, Φαινόμενα, 86–7.
95   Ibid., 324–26.
96   Ibid., 621.
97   Ibid., 595–96.
98   Ibid., 463–64.
99   Ibid., 439, 697.
100 John Chrysostom, col. 241: "Εἰς τὸ ἀποστολικὸν ῥητὸν, ς τὸ ἀποστολικόνί ναῦται τοῦτο μάλιστα φιλοῦσι τοῦ πελάγους τὸ μέρος, ὅπερ ἂν λιμέσι πυκνοῖς καὶ νήσοις διειλημμένον ᾖ. Τὸ μὲν

the same case, he also describes how navigation within a sea lined with harbors and coasts provides the possibility of getting to a safe shelter, even if bad weather occurs suddenly.

5 "Complicated" Communications, and a "Diversified" Socio-Economic Life

In 821–23, Theophanes Continuatus characterized the Aegean islands as "miserable islands".[101] These islands, which nowadays constitute one of the most famous tourist destinations globally and derive most of their income from associated economic activities, have otherwise limited natural resources. Although most of the coasts (especially in the deltaic areas of big rivers) and the larger islands (i.e., Lesbos, Chios, Rhodes, and Crete) have fertile, well-cultivated plains, many of the islands and much of the coastline (e.g., Mani in Laconia) are rocky and quite barren, with terraces to conserve the sparse soil and semi-arid cultivations.[102] Fishing and a sometimes quite sophisticated pastoral activity provided additional food alternatives to the limited agricultural products.[103] The agrarian economy in the Aegean mainly consists of practices for diversifying, storing, and redistributing;[104] an example of these practices studied with a historical perspective comes from the islands of Karpathos and Amorgos.[105] The Byzantine agrarian lands on the islands have been outlined by Elisabeth Malamut.[106] Estate structures, economic activity, and monetary values are known through the monastic contexts around the Aegean coasts and islands.[107] It is remarkable that an entire island could be considered an estate, as in the case of the Gymnopelagesio (modern Kyra-Panagia Island in the Northern Sporades) which was sold, together with the monastery built on

γὰρ ἀλίμενον πέλαγος, κἂν γαλήνην ἔχῃ, πολὺν παρέχει τοῖς πλέουσι τὸν τρόμον· ῥένθα δὲ ἂν ὦσιν ὅρμοι, καὶ ἀκταί, καὶ αἰγιαλοὶ πανταχόθεν ἐκτεταμμένοι, μετὰ πολλῆς πλέουσι τῆς ἀσφαλείας. Κἂν γὰρ βραχὺ διεγερθεῖσαν τὴν θάλασσαν ἴδωσι, δι' ὀλίγου τὴν καταφυγὴν ἔχοντες, ταχίστην καὶ εὔκολον τῶν ἐπικειμένων κακῶν ἀπαλλαγὴν εὕρασθαι δύναιντ' ἄν. Διὰ δὴ ταῦτα, οὐχ ὅταν πλησίον λιμένος ἐλαύνωσιν μόνον, ἀλλὰ κἂν πόρρωθεν ὦσι, πολλὴν καὶ ἀπὸ τῆς ὄψεως ταύτης παράκλησιν δέχονται."

101 Theophanes Continuatus II, 20: "ταῖς ταλαιπώροις νήσοις".
102 "Aegean Sea"; Horden/Purcell, *Corrupting Sea*, 178–82.
103 Horden/Purcell, *Corrupting Sea*, 175–76, 190–95, 197–230; Malamut, *Iles*, 988, 433–34.
104 Horden/Purcell, *Corrupting Sea*, 178–82.
105 Halstead/Jones, "Ecology", 1997.
106 Malamut, *Iles*, 411–31.
107 Malamut, *Iles*, 411–25; *Typika*, 135–66, 193–312, 564–605, 782–849; 954–72, 1196–206, 1303–10, 1331–37, 1389–95, 1408–82, 1579–1624; Kondyli, "Lemnos", 2010.

it, to the Lavra Monastery of Mount Athos by the monastery's last two monks for 70 solidi in 993.[108]

The forests also constituted sources of many materials and foods; of the islands, those of the north are generally more wooded than those of the south (except Rhodes).[109] Wetlands also sometimes had specific economic roles by hosting specialized productions (e.g., the water chestnut in Strymon delta), while salt production has been central diachronically (e.g., on Thassos).[110] We know of agricultural products from the coasts and islands that were adequate and good enough to be exported; wine and mastic from Samos and Chios were much-appreciated in the capital.[111] Certain islands, especially those hosting Jewish communities, developed a considerable silk production (e.g., Andros, Chios, Rhodes, Crete).[112] Crete is also mentioned as a leather production center in a 12th-century Greek Jewish letter.[113]

Settlement around the Aegean has diachronically been adjusting to the aforementioned environmental parameters and to their economic implications, as well as to political intentions by the central administration (such as in the case of Byzantine insular naval posts).[114] Naturally, it developed in those areas that provided economic sustainability during the Byzantine period. These areas have been largely outlined by several studies during the last 40 years or so;[115] however, a thorough archaeological mapping of Byzantine occupation in many Aegean islands and islets still remains a desideratum. The constant adjustment of occupation to modifications of regional networks due to environmental or political change has produced an elective, flexible settlement around the Aegean, which has been non-uniform and diachronically unstable.[116]

Communication by sea allowed a set of many more economic and social activities around the coasts and islands of the Byzantine Aegean. However, the latter were based on guidelines and fixed itineraries, which relied on the

---

108 *Actes de Lavra*, 124: No. 10 of year 993 (cf. 129: No. 11 of year 994).
109 "Aegean Sea".
110 Horden/Purcell, *Corrupting Sea*, 195–97.
111 Gerolymatou, Αγορές, 133.
112 Malamut, *Iles*, 165–170, 431; Gerolymatou, Αγορές, 86–88; Holo, *Jewry*, 29, 140, 165.
113 Holo, *Jewry*, 170.
114 Veikou, "Histories", 179–80, n. 56.
115 For literature on recent and older archaeological and historical research on the Aegean islands see, indicatively: Malamut, *Iles*; Koder, *Aigaion Pelagos*; Tsougarakis, *Crete*, 303–49; Vionis, *Crusader* (lit.); Deligiannakis, *Dodecanese* (lit.); Tsigonaki/Sarris, "Dynamics" (lit.); Magdalino et al., "Naxos" (lit.); Bevan/Conolly, *Antikythera*; Sigala, *Chalki.*; Preiser-Kapeller/Kolias/Daim, Seasides.
116 Ibid.; For specific examples see Veikou, "Island"; Gogou et al., "Climate".

seamen's extensive experience and available infrastructure, as manifested by the surviving scattered Byzantine texts.[117] The reason for that was that the combination of geomorphology and climate makes the Aegean Sea one of the most difficult to navigate. As described in international Sailing Guidelines:

> the navigation of the Aegean Sea, though easy, requires constant attention, and a place of shelter should always be kept in view, so that safety may be assured before dark in the event of an approaching gale; the weather may become so thick that among the labyrinth of islands the land may be hardly seen in time to avoid it.[118]

Constantine Porphyrogennitus says of this sea that it has waves that are difficult to navigate, are high and look like mountains.[119] Indeed, the diverse calamities narrated by Byzantine texts present a characteristically Aegean cocktail of hazards: violent squalls and heavy seas that arise at night, forced by high northerly winds and swift, shifting coastal currents, driving ships toward nearly invisible rocks and shoals on a rugged coastline with few opportunities for safe anchorage. Due to these complications, the Byzantines limited their maritime activity within a specific period of the year and tried to avoid extreme climatic phenomena, even if that meant changing their program and itinerary.[120]

Maritime trade was certainly an important activity and a real stimulus for local economies;[121] as seen, for example, through the 5th–7th-century production of amphorae at several coastal and insular sites.[122] However, it involved considerable risk: three horoscopes of sea trips dated to the last quarter of the 5th century reveal people's worries about the fate of the ship and transported merchandise.[123] The specific conditions of the Aegean Sea necessitated the presence of an expert on the ship – someone who knew the wind speed and direction, the locations of reefs and shallow waters and, above all, the distances to the nearest ports and harbors. In many cases, the lack of this knowledge led to shipwrecking.[124] Shipwrecks of different periods have been

---

117 Avramea, "Communications", 77–88.
118 USNOO, *Directions*, 18. For a detailed analysis, see Tartaron, *Maritime Networks*, 90–138.
119 Constantine Porphyrogennetos, *De Thematibus*, ιζ', l. 30: "βαρύπλουν ... καὶ δυσπέρατον καὶ κύματα μακρὰ καὶ ὄρεσιν ἐοικότα προσανεγείρον τοῖς πλέουσιν."
120 Avramea, "Communications", 77–78.
121 Gerolymatou, *Αγορές*, passim; Kokkorou-Alevras et al., "Maritime Connections".
122 Such sites were Paros, Kos, Samos, Chios, Thasos, Crete, the Peloponnese, and the Western and southern fringes of Asia Minor: Pieri, "Exchanges", 31, 32, 35. For case studies, see Diamandi, *Halasarna*; Diamandi, "Paros".
123 *Horoscopes*, 117–33.
124 *Naumachika*, 46: "τήν τε θαλάσσης πεῖραν, ὅπως καταπνεόμενη κυμαίνεται καὶ τοὺς ἀπογείους ἀνέμους καὶ τοὺς ὑφάλους λίθους καὶ τοὺς ἀβαθεῖς τόπους, ὁμοίως δὲ καὶ τὴν παραπλεομένην

discovered along the same routes – and indeed often in the same positions or clusters (e.g. around Rhodes and the Sporades).[125] This is definitely indicative of the degree to which seamen stuck to predetermined routes associated with particular markets.[126] However, it can also be associated with the existence of specific maritime locations that present higher degrees of environmental danger in navigation.[127]

Other important reasons for crossing the Aegean Sea to other coasts were pilgrimage, business, and diplomacy, so commercial ships seem to have often had passengers travelling for these reasons.[128] These passengers were better educated than the seamen and they shared their travel experiences through personal letters, which seem to have been rather common after the 12th century.[129] According to a letter by Synesius of Cyrene, even if a shipwreck was avoided, the captain's competence and experience were also essential factors in the trip's duration, quality, and final destination.[130] Johannes Koder's study of navigation in the Aegean led to similar conclusions: the port of origin of the vessel or its crew were not important, but the type of ship and the competence of the captain and the seamen were factors of great significance.[131] Different durations and conditions are mentioned for the same trips made by different people at approximately the same time of year and in similar weather conditions, and in many cases the passengers reached a destination different from the one intended.[132]

γῆν καὶ τὰς παρακειμένας αὐτῇ νήσους, τοὺς λιμένας, τὰ ἐξ ἑτέρου τούτων εἰς ἕτερα διαστήματα, τὰ χωρία, τὰ ὕδατα· ὅπολλοὶ γὰρ ἀπειρίᾳ τῆς θαλάσσης καὶ τῶν τόπων ἀπώλοντο, καθάπερ καὶ πλεῖστοι τῶν ἄλλων. Χρὴ δὲ οὐ μόνον ἐκείνης τῆς θαλάσσης πεῖραν ἔχειν αὐτούς, ἀλλὰ καὶ τῶν παρακειμένων αὐτῇ χωρίων· ὁπολλάκις γὰρ ἄνεμοι καταπνεύσαντες ἄλλην ἀλλαχοῦ τῶν νηῶν διεσκέδασαν."

125 Avramea, "Communications", 80; McCormick, "Movements", 83, and Fig. 3.11.
126 Avramea, "Communications", 80; McCormick, "Movements".
127 See, e.g., McCormcik, "Movements", 83: Fig. 3.11., and 86: Fig. 3.13. Cf. Tartaron, *Maritime Networks*, 99: Fig. 4.6.
128 Chrysos, "Διπλωματία"; Irmscher, "Προσκυνήματα".
129 Karpozilos, "Ταξιδιωτικές περιγραφές".
130 Synesius Cyrenae, Letter no. 4, l. 1–10: "Λύσαντες ἐν Βενδιδείου πρὸ δείλης ἑῴας, μόλις ὑπὲρ μεσοῦσαν ἡμέραν τὸν Φάριον Μύρμηκα παρηλλάξαμεν, δίς που καὶ τρὶς ἐνσχεθείσης τῆς νεὼς τῷ τοῦ λιμένος ἐδάφει. εὐθὺς μὲν οὖν καὶ τοῦτο πονηρὸς οἰωνὸς ἐδόκει, καὶ σοφὸν ἦν ἀποβῆναι νεὼς ἐκ πρώτης ἀφετηρίας οὐκ εὐτυχοῦς· ἀλλὰ φυγεῖν παρ' ὑμῖν ἔγκλημα δειλίας ᾐσχύνθημεν, καὶ διὰ τοῦτο οὔπως ἔτι ἔσκεν ὑποτρέσαι οὐδ' ἀναδῦναι. ὥστε σᾶν εἴ τι συμβαίη, δι' ὑμᾶς ἀπολούμεθα. καίτοι τί δεινὸν ἦν ὑμᾶς τε γελᾶν καὶ ἡμᾶς ἔξω κινδύνων ἑστάναι".
131 Koder, "Νησιωτική επικοινωνία".
132 Koder "Νησιωτική επικοινωνία"; Karpozilos, "Ταξιδιωτικές περιγραφές", 514–17; Avramea, "Communications", 78–79.

6　A "Busy" Military Sea

The aspiration for domination over the sea was the basis of the power and security of the Byzantine empire.[133] Thus, Liutprand of Cremona recorded that, when he was in Constantinople in 968, after the Byzantine–Arab War, Nicephorus Phokas had boasted that: "Sailing is my only strength. When I want to attack your [the Saracens'] master, I will ruin all his maritime cities and I will burn to ashes all that he possesses at the mouths of rivers."[134] Similarly, the Strategikon by Kekaumenos (11th century) advises the emperor to always care for the maintenance of flourishing naval forces, because "the navy is the glory of Romania".[135] Furthermore, maritime communication was essential for the function of the state and it was associated with financial investment in maritime trade as a central strategy for Byzantium's economic prosperity and growth.[136]

However, medieval technology for protecting ships from rot and shipworm was not particularly effective, and neglect would lead quickly to the material decay of fleets. War fleets also depended on skilled seamen, who could not be produced overnight. The Byzantine Aegean coasts and islands served as areas of provenance of these skilled maritime professionals. Indicatively, in the 7th century, Mardaites are brought to settle the area of the theme of Kephallenia, while in c.1107 Alexios I ordered a fleet to be prepared in the Cyclades and maritime cities in Asia Minor and the Balkans, to be sent to Dyrrachion.[137] Boarding actions and hand-to-hand fighting determined the outcome of most naval battles in the Middle Ages, as we can see in the illustration from the Madrid Skylitzes showing the Byzantine fleet repelling the Rus' attack on Constantinople in 941, and the use of spurs to smash the oars of the Rus' vessels.[138] The very invention of Greek Fire as an efficient weapon to be used in water environments shows the importance of naval battles for the Byzantines. Last but not least, as mentioned in the narration of a military event dated to 645–46, while the Byzantines still had mastery at sea and could attack at will, watch towers and a signaling system were established along the Aegean coasts.[139]

133　A historical discussion of this idea is provided by Ahrweiler, *Mer*.
134　Pryor/Jeffreys, *ΔΡΟΜΩΝ*, 76.
135　Kekaumenos, Strategikon (Λόγος νουθετητικός πρός βασιλέα), 101, l. 33–34: "ὁ γὰρ στόλος ἐστίν ἡ δόξα τῆς ῥωμανίας".
136　Chrysos, "Διπλωματία"; Asdracha, "Επικοινωνία".
137　Veikou, *Epirus*, 43–4; Pryor/Jeffreys, *ΔΡΟΜΩΝ*, 110–11.
138　Chronicle of John Skylitzes, cod. Vitr. 26–2, fol. 130, Madrid National Library.
139　Pryor/Jeffreys, *ΔΡΟΜΩΝ*, 24.

The islands and sea lanes in the Aegean were the essential heartland of the Byzantine Empire, sometimes conceived as an extension of the imperial power in the capital; Prokopios narrated a 6th-century sea-borne invasion of Africa organized from Constantinople as a massive undertaking, with Belisarius conquering the outline of Mediterranean coasts and insular area.[140] The important military role of insular and coastal areas is evident in the formation of the thematic administration at the time of the Arab threat: the Byzantine fleet of Karabisianoi, based on Samos, was the first to be created, probably as a front line of defense after the Byzantine defeat at the Battle of the Masts in 655.[141] It is also evident in the year 727's political involvement by the fleets of Hellas and Cyclades, which proclaimed a certain Kosmas as emperor and sailed to Constantinople to impose him; they were scattered by the imperial fleet using Greek Fire.[142] As a result of the Arab raids in the Aegean, Crete became Arab in c.824–27, and there followed many Byzantine attempts to take it back until 866, then none until the time of Leo VI.[143] In response to Andalusi raids in the second half of the 9th century, the northern Aegean islands were erected into the maritime theme of Aigaion Pelagos and the southern ones into that of Samos.[144]

After Phokas, there was a period of pacification in the Aegean. The last military event was a pillaging of the Cyclades in 1035; then, Muslim incursions into the Aegean ceased entirely and that caused the decline of the maritime themata of Kibyrrhaiotai, Samos, and Aegaion Pelagos.[145] By the ascension of Alexios I Komnenos, the Byzantine navy had virtually disappeared, perhaps due to a lack of enemies.[146] During the 11th century, small squadrons based locally at Kephallenia, Abydos, Samos, Chios, Naupaktos, and other places in support of terrestrial forces and against corsairs became more important.[147]

The loss of control in the Aegean was a serious and recurring threat for the Byzantine Empire. The most notable threat was the Arab fleet that first attacked Rhodes in 667 (and occupied it until 680), Cyprus in 670, and Crete in 672, and sieged Constantinople for seven years from 672, with the Muslim squadrons variously retiring to Kyzikos, Crete, and Rhodes to winter over and

---

140　Pryor/Jeffreys, *ΔΡΟΜΩΝ*, 10–11.
141　Ibid., 25.
142　Ibid., 32.
143　Ibid., 46–47.
144　Ibid., 46–47.
145　Ibid., 86.
146　Ibid., 87.
147　Ibid., 87.

then returning each spring.[148] Crete even became Arab in c.824–27. Its loss fundamentally altered the strategic makeup of the eastern Mediterranean. From a new fortress port at Chandax on the northern coast of the island, the Andalusi raided the Aegean for slaves and booty, exercised some control over the southern Aegean, and periodically occupied some islands: Aigina, Kos, Kythera, and Karpathos, for example. Some others, such as Naxos, were forced to pay tribute, while the Andalusi exercised influence over Rhodes and Cyprus.[149]

There were several recurring events of this kind until 1035 and even later. The Egyptians raided the Byzantine coasts during the second half of the 9th century while the Andalusi raided the Cyclades and mainland, penetrating through the Dardanelles as far as Proikonessos in c.860.[150] In 904, Leo of Tripoli sacked Abydos and Thessaloniki before retiring back to Tripoli via Crete, his fleet laden with booty and prisoners.[151] The Seljuk amir Tzachas constructed a fleet at Smyrna in c.1088 and began to raid across the Aegean and to seize control of its islands.[152] The Venetian fleet sacked Samos, Chios, Lesbos, and Andros in 1125, while Roger II, in 1147, sent his fleet into the Aegean where Thebes and Corinth were plundered.[153]

A peculiar geographical feature of the Aegean Sea made all this warfare based on medieval technology possible in the Aegean: the availability of numerous stop-over possibilities.[154] When the emperor Justinian sent Konstantinianos to Dyrrachion, the latter sailed to Epidauros and then to Salones.[155] The inventory of the expedition of 949 included a portulan and a stadiodromikon, which, if we can believe it, gave the distances from Constantinople to Crete, specifying 14 traverses *en route*.[156] No traverse was given at more than 100 Byzantine milia (~85 English miles) (none more than two days before the prevailing northerly to northeasterly summer winds and at an average speed of 2 knots by Byzantine military ships (dromones).[157] In fact, Byzantine fleets operating against Crete did not traditionally sail direct from Constantinople with all forces aboard but rather made a *rendezvous* with cavalry and other forces on the southwest coast of Asia Minor, leaving only a short passage to Crete.[158] For

148   Ibid., 26.
149   Ibid., 47.
150   Ibid., 47.
151   Ibid., 62.
152   Ibid., 101.
153   Ibid., 106, 111.
154   See e.g. Ginalis, Northern Sporades.
155   Pryor/Jeffreys, $\Delta POM\Omega N$, 14.
156   Ibid., 264 and note 335.
157   Ibid., 264.
158   Ibid., 265.

example, Phygela, one of the harbors of Ephessos, was the normal staging post for the 10th-century assaults on Crete.[159] Conversely, a medieval galley is theoretically capable of crossing the sea in all conditions, though not without limit: during the First Crusade, the Pisan and Venetian fleets with their new ships (galleys) would winter in Rhodes 1099–1100, on their way to the Levant.[160]

The stopovers were not just the closest points of land: they seem to have had special attributes such as fresh water and some sort of harboring facilities. J. Pryor and E. Jeffreys have made the following estimations about the Aegean military stopovers.[161] It must be assumed that the traverses were from mooring to mooring, not merely from landmark to landmark. In support of the first interpretation is the fact that Herakleia, Proikonnesos, Abydos, Tenedos, Mytilene, Chios, and Naxos were indeed moorings for Byzantine squadrons and would have been logical stopovers. However, Ta Peukia/Pefkia, the Fournoi islets, Thera-Therasia, Ta Christiana, Dia, and even Samos had no anchorages for large fleets. Moreover, one major purpose for making stopovers would have been to take on water, but the Phournoi islets, Thera, Ta Christiana, and Dia had little or no water. Ta Christiana is an isolated, waterless uninhabited islet and the Phournoi islets were also uninhabited. Passages without the ability to provision for water were from Samos to Naxos and from Ios to Chandax (both ~125 km).[162]

On the other hand, other environmental features, such as climatic conditions and seismic activity also affected warfare. For example, in the year 718, Theophanes the Confessor wrote that the Muslim fleet retiring through the Aegean after the failed siege of Constantinople in 716–18 was struck by a "fiery shower" that made the sea boil up, and that the ships were then sunk because their pitch was gone.[163] Mango suggested that "though doubtless embellished", the report of boiling waters in the Aegean may well have been connected with unusual volcanic activity that culminated in the eruption of Thera in 726, as also reported by Theophanes.[164] According to Pryor and Jeffreys, this is an obviously improbable story, but the point is that such a melting of the pitch would affect only ships that depended on intra-seam caulking: ships whose planks were connected using mortise-and-tenon joints and a coat of pitch over the whole hull would not be sunk by its melting, at least not straight away.[165]

---

159   Tsougarakis, *Crete*, 63.
160   Pryor/Jeffreys, *ΔΡΟΜΩΝ*, 105, 264.
161   Ibid., 264.
162   Ibid., 264.
163   Theophanes, *Chronographia*, A.M. 6210, 1, 399. Cf. Pryor/Jeffreys, *ΔΡΟΜΩΝ*, 149, note 70.
164   Theophanes, *Chronographia*, A.M. 6210, 550–551: n. 9; cf. A.M. 6218, 559.
165   Pryor, *Geography*, 149–50.

In their opinion, Theophanes' father had held some kind of command in the islands of the Aegean Sea and Theophanes may have had some real knowledge of ships and the sea and an unusual familiarity with Byzantine fleets.[166] His story, then, seems to reflect an age in which ships depended on intra-seam driven caulking for water tightness.

Last but not least, the particular geographical and geomorphological features of the Aegean Sea, i.e. the availability of numerous stop-over possibilities as well as its many rocky islands with large, deep coves (appropriate for hiding ships and booty) made it a fitting environment for the development of another, "guerrilla" type of Muslim maritime warfare or "maritime terrorism": piracy.[167] A common aggressive practice in these waters had existed since prehistory,[168] piracy seems to have revived periodically during the medieval period. It seems to have been practiced by Muslim populations in a non-organized way, from the 9th century and the short-lived Emirate of Crete: numerous Byzantine texts mention "pirate" attacks from the sea by "Saracens" who looted coastal towns and cities; one of them even repented for his acts and stayed in Western Greece becoming a Christian holy man known as "Saint Barbarian" (*Hagios Barbaros*).[169] In the 12th century it is mentioned in relation to the silk trade.[170] In later centuries (15th–18th), it seems to have constituted a flourishing economic activity – often practiced by the insular communities themselves and indirectly encouraged by the Ottoman Empire.[171] It greatly affected settlement and agency especially in this later period, hence the Aegean Sea's characterization as *Archipelagus turbatus*.[172]

7   The Aegean: A Closed-and-Open Mediterranean "Neighborhood"

Determining the causal value – the level of impact – of the complex interactions between climate, environment and society poses a series of difficulties, as shown by recent research.[173] First of all, some environmental or climatic

---

166   Ibid.
167   Koder, "Νησιωτική επικοινωνία", 446; Krantonelli, *Ιστορία της πειρατείας*.
168   Glotz, *Aegean civilization*, 48, 51, 157, 159, 189, 205, 225.
169   Constantine Akropolitis, *Vie de Saint Barbaros*, 409f.; for a discussion of the passage, see Veikou, *Epirus*, 419.
170   Holo, *Jewry*, 158.
171   Krantonelli, *Ιστορία της πειρατείας*, 241; Lock, *Crusades*, 438; Dimitropoulos, "Η πειρατεία στο Αιγαίο".
172   Slot, *Archipelagus turbatus*.
173   Haldon/Rosen, "Society and Environment", 3.

shifts may have more or less significance, depending on the particular historical context and cultural habit; secondly, the specification of this significance by a collaboration among natural scientists, historians, and archaeologists often proves challenging itself, due to methodological and practical differences.[174] On the other hand, Byzantium is a case in which a very diverse and connected sea, the Aegean, formed its heartland throughout its entire history; this was not even a matter of chance but the result of constant perseverance on the part of Byzantine authorities. Thus, in this case, an environmental aspect "charged" with integral historical and cultural value is indeed shown to have been extremely significant for the particular societies and cultures diachronically.

The meaning of having such a sea as the heartland of the Byzantine empire is obviously hard to determine; it requires that a very broad and complex set of questions be asked, and any pursuit of equally broad and complex answers exceeds the narrow limits of this chapter. This work has aimed, first of all, to illustrate several ways in which Byzantine politics, economy, and culture have been essentially concerned with and centered around the Aegean world. Secondly, it argued that this region diachronically formed a closed-and-open "neighborhood" in the Eastern Mediterranean, especially in the Middle Ages when land divided and water unified. This "neighborhood" functioned as a microcosm with its very own life of mobility and contact, which was largely independent of the occasional centers of power and central administration. However, as one of many Mediterranean neighborhoods – and a well-placed one – it also always remained open to contact from all directions. This "closed-and-open" attribute appears more pronounced if one monitors human agency during periods of crisis and uncertainty, when very interesting cultural implications occur. A good example of this is the circulation of foreign coinage along the Aegean coasts during the Late Byzantine period, as recently discussed by Julian Baker.[175] Thirdly, the tenacity of organized, long-distance or regional trade, as well as the recurrence of piracy, designates the enormous economic potential of a maritime "neighborhood" of that size – whether viewed from an entrepreneurial or opportunist perspective. And finally, should one add up the political and military value of a "populated sea" (a combination of waters and lands "inhabited" in fair amounts and at regular intervals) to this economic and cultural microcosm, one is left indeed with an excellent basis for a late-antique and medieval empire – definitely a territory worth struggling to keep.

---

174   Haldon/Rosen, "Society and Environment", 3; Izdebski et al., "Realising consilience"; Von Rüden/Lichtenberger, "Introduction".
175   Baker, "Circulation".

Bibliography

Primary Sources

Actes de Lavra, ed. P. Lemerle, A. Guillou, N. Svoronos & D. Papachryssanthou, *Actes de Lavra Première Partie: Des origines à 1204* (Archives de l'Athos, V), Paris 1970.

Ammianus Marcellinus, *Res Gestae*, ed. & trans. J.C. Rolfe, *The Roman History of Ammianus Marcellinus*, II, Loeb Classical Library, Cambridge, MA: Harvard University Press, 1940.

Aristotle, *Meteorologica*, ed. & trans. H.D.P. Lee, Loeb Classical Library 397, Cambridge, MA: Harvard University Press, 1952.

Constantine Akropolitis, *Vie de Saint Barbaros*, ed. Papadopoulos-Kerameus, « Κωνσταντίνου Ἀκροπολίτη, Λόγος εις τον Ἅγιον Βάρβαρον », *Analekta Ierosolymitikis Stachyologias* 1 (1891), 405–430.

Constantine Porphyrogennitus, *De Thematibus*, ed. A. Pertusi, *Costantino Porfirogenito. De thematibus*. Studi e Testi 160, Vatican City 1952, pp. 59–100.

Critoboulos, *History*, ed. D.R. Reinsch, *Critobuli Imbriotae historiae*, CFHB 22, Berlin 1983.

Horoscopes, ed. G. Dagron/J. Rougé, Trois horoscopes de voyages en mer (5ᵉ siècle après J.-C.), *Révue des Etudes Byzantines* 40 (1982), 117–133.

Kekaumenos, *Strategikon*, ed. B. Wassilievskij/V. Jernstedt, *Cecaumeni Strategicon et incerti scriptoris de officiis regiis libellus*, Petropoli 1965.

Typika, ed. J. Thomas/A. Constantinides Hero/G. Constable, *Byzantine monastic foundation documents: a complete translation of the surviving founders' typika and testaments*, Washington, D.C.: Dumbarton Oaks Research Library and Collection, 2000.

Naumachika, ed. A. Dain, *Naumachica, partim adhuc inedita in unum nunc primum congessit et indice auxit*, Paris 1943.

St. John Chrysostome, ed. J.-P. Migne, *S. Johannes Chrysostomus. Patrologia Graeca* 51, Paris 1862.

Synesius Cerynae, *Epistula*, ed. R. Hercher, *Epistolographi Graeci*, Paris 1873 (reprint Amsterdam 1965) 638–739.

Theophanes The Confessor, Theophanis Chronografia, ed. C. de Boor, 2 vols. (Leipzig 1883). Vol. I trans. C. Mango and R. Scott, The Chronicle of Theophanes Confessor: Byzantine and Near Eastern History AD 284–813, Oxford 1997.

Theophanes Continuatus, ed. I. Bekker, *Theophanes Continuatus, Ioannes Caminiata, Symeon Magister, Georgius Monachus*, CSHB, Bonnae 1838, pp. 3–481.

Secondary Literature

(Editors), "Aegean Sea", *Encyclopaedia Britannica* (June 27, 2016), online at https://www.britannica.com/place/Aegean-Sea (last accessed on 2018-03-28).

Alexandridis, A., "The Identity Issue of the Minorities in Greece and Turkey", in R. Hirschon (ed.), *Crossing the Aegean: An Appraisal of the 1923 Compulsory Population Exchange Between Greece and Turkey*, New York – Oxford 2004, pp. 117–132.

Ahrweiler, H., *Byzance et la Mer*, Paris 1966.
Antonopoulos, J.A., "Data from the investigation of seismic sea-wave events in the Eastern Mediterranean from the birth of Christ to 1980 AD", *Ann. Geophys.* 33 (1980), 141–248.
Asdraha, A., « Η επιλεκτική επικοινωνία: η κινητικότητα του βυζαντινού διοικητικού προσωπικού », in Moschonas (ed.), *Επικοινωνία*, pp. 389–396.
Asdrahas, S., "The Greek archipelago. A far-flung city", in V. Sphyroeras/A. Avramea/S. Asdrahas (eds), *Maps and Map-Makers of the Aegean*, Athens: Olkos 1985, pp. 235–48.
Avramea, A., "Land and Sea Communications, Fourth–Fifteenth Centuries", in A. Laiou (ed.), *The Economic History of Byzantium from the seventh to the fifteenth century* (Dumbarton Oaks Studies XXXIX), Washington D.C. 2002, vol. I, pp. 57–90.
Baker, J., "Circulation of non-Byzantine coins in the two coasts of the Aegean", *Proceedings of the 23rd International Congress of Byzantine Studies 2016*, Belgrade: Serbian National Committee of AIEB, pp. 1394–1399.
Bazaiou-Barabas, Th., « Θαλάσσιοι δρόμοι: δυνατότητες και δυσκολίες της θαλάσσιας επικοινωνίας σε βυζαντινά λόγια κείμενα », in Moschonas (ed.), *Επικοινωνία*, pp. 435–443.
Bescoby, D./J. Barclay/J. Andrews, "Saints and Sinners: a tephrochronology for Late Antique landscape change in Epirus from the eruptive history of Lipari, Aeolian Islands", *Journal of Archaeological Science* 35 (2008) 2574–2579.
Bevan, A./J. Conolly, *Mediterranean Islands, Fragile Communities and Persistent Landscapes. Antikythera in Long-Term Perspective*, Cambridge: Cambridge University Press 2013.
Carter, R.W.G./C.D. Woodroffe (eds), *Coastal Evolution*, Cambridge 1994.
Carter, R.W.G./C.D. Woodroffe, "Coastal Evolution: an Introduction", in Carter/Woodroffe (eds) *Coastal Evolution*, pp. 1–32.
Chrysos, E., « Η βυζαντινή διπλωματία ως μέσο επικοινωνίας », in Moschonas (ed.), *Επικοινωνία*, pp. 399–407.
Mc Cormick, M., "Movements and Markets in the First Millenium. Information, Containers, and Shipwrecks", in Morrisson (ed.), *Trade and Markets*, pp. 51–98.
Cowell, P.J./B.G. Thom, "Morphodynamics of Coastal Evolution", in Carter/Woodroffe (eds) *Coastal Evolution*, pp. 33–86.
Daim, F./S. Ladstätter, *Ephesos in byzantinischer Zeit*, Mainz: RZGM 2011.
Deligiannakis, G., *The Dodecanese "and" the eastern Aegean Islands in Late Antiquity AD 300–700*, Oxford: Oxford University Press 2016.
Diamandi, Ch., *Local Production and Import of Amphoras at Halasarna of Kos Island (5th–7th c.)*, Athens: University of Athens – Saripolos Foundation 2010.
Diamandi, Ch., "The Late Roman Amphora workshops of Paros island in the Aegean Sea – Recent results", *Rei Cretariae Romanae Fautorum Acta* 44 (2016), 691–698.
Dimitropoulos, D., « Η πειρατεία στο Αιγαίο. Όψεις και αντιφάσεις των στερεοτύπων », *Επιστημονικό Συμπόσιο: Μύθοι και ιδεολογήματα στη σύγχρονη Ελλάδα (23–24*

Νοεμβρίου 2005), Athens: Εταιρεία Σπουδών Νεοελληνικού Πολιτισμού και Γενικής Παιδείας 2007, pp. 115–134.

Dunn, A., "From polis to kastron in Southern Macedonia: Amphipolis, Khrysoupolis, and the Strymon Delta", in *Archéologie des espaces agraires méditerranéens au Moyen Âge* (1999), 399–414.

Finné, M./K. Holmgren, "Climate Variability in the Eastern Mediterranean and the Middle East during the Holocene", in P.J.J. Sinclair/G. Nordquist/F. Herschend/C. Isendahl (eds), *The Urban Mind, Cultural and Environmental Dynamics* (African and Comparative Archaeology, Department of Archaeology and Ancient History), Uppsala: Uppsala University 2010, pp. 29–60.

Fouache, E., *L'alluvionnement historique en Grèce Occidentale et au Péloponnèse* (BCH Supplément 35), Paris 1999.

Gerolymatou, M., *Αγορές, έμποροι και εμπόριο στο Βυζάντιο ($9^{ος}/12^{ος}$ αιώνας)*, Athens: E.I.E. 2008.

Ginalis, A., The Northern Sporades from Late Antiquity to the end of the medieval times. An important junction of the Aegean trading routes, Graeco-Arabica 11 (2011) 279–294.

Glotz, G., *The Aegean civilization*, London-New York: Routledge 2011.

Gogou, A./M. Triantaphyllou/E. Xoplaki/A. Izdebski/C. Parinos/M. Dimiza/I. Bouloubassi/J. Luterbacher/K. Kouli/B. Martrat/A. Toreti/D. Fleitmann/G. Rousakis/H. Kaberi/M. Athanasiou/V. Lykousis, "Climate variability and socio-environmental changes in the northern Aegean (NE Mediterranean) during the last 1500 years", *Quaternary Science Reviews* xxx (2016) 1–20.

Gross, A., "Gökçeada (Imbros) and Bozcaada (Tenedos): preserving the bicultural character of the two Turkish islands as a model for co-operation between Turkey and Greece in the interest of the people concerned", *Report for the Committee on Legal Affairs and Human Rights, Parliamentary Assembly of the Council of Europe, 6 June 2008*, http://assembly.coe.int/nw/xml/XRef/Xref-XML2HTML-en.asp?fileid=12011&lang=en (last accessed 2018.04.05).

Haldon, J./A. Rosen, "Society and Environment in the East Mediterranean ca 300–1800 CE. Problems of Resilience, Adaptation and Transformation. Introductory Essay", *Human Ecology* 14/03/2018, online at https://doi.org/10.1007/s10745-018-9972-3 (last accessed 2018.04.05).

Halstead, P./G. Jones, "Agrarian Ecology in the Greek Islands: Time Stress, Scale and Risk", in P.N. Kardulias/M.T. Shutes (eds), *Aegean strategies: studies of culture and environment on the European fringe*, Lanham, Md.: Rowman & Littlefield, 1997, pp. 271–293.

Higgins, M.D./R.A. Higgins, *A Geological companion to Greece and the Aegean*, London: Duckworth Publishers 1996.

Holo, J., Byzantine Jewry in the Mediterranean Economy, Cambridge University Press 2009.
Horden, P./N. Purcell, The *Corrupting Sea: A Study of Mediterranean History*, Oxford: Blackwell 2000.
Höghammar K./B. Alroth/A. Lindhagen (eds), *Ancient Ports. The Geography of Connections* (Boreas 34), Uppsala 2016.
Iefimerida, 05/09/2017, « Κρήτη: 103 μετανάστες εντοπίστηκαν σε ξύλινο σκάφος στα ανατολικά του νησιού », http://www.iefimerida.gr/news/360155/kriti-103-metanastes-entopistikan-se-xylino-skafos-sta-anatolika-toy-nisioy (last accessed on 2018-04-05).
Irmscher, J., « Βυζαντινά προσκυνήματα », in N.G. Moschonas (ed.), *Η επικοινωνία στο Βυζάντιο*, Athens: Κέντρο Βυζαντινών Ερευνών / Ε.Ι.Ε. 1993, pp. 347–350.
Izdebski, A./K. Holmgren/E. Weiberg/S.R. Stocker/U. Büntgen/A. Florenzano/ A. Gogou/S.A.G. Leroy/J. Luterbacher/B. Martrat/A. Masi/A.M. Mercuri/P. Montagna/ L. Sadori/A. Schneider/M.-A. Sicre/M. Triantaphyllou/E. Xoplaki, "Realising consilience: How better communication between archaeologists, historians and natural scientists can transform the study of past climate change in the Mediterranean", *Quaternary Science Reviews* 136 (2016) 5–22.
Jing, Z./G.R. Rapp, "The coastal evolution of the Ambracian embayment and its relationship to archaeological settings", in J. Wiseman/K. Zachos (eds), *Landscape archaeology in Southern Epirus, Greece*, I (Hesperia Supplement 32), Princeton NJ 2003, pp. 157–198.
Kardulias, P.N./M.T. Shutes (eds), *Aegean strategies: studies of culture and environment on the European fringe*, Lanham, Md.: Rowman & Littlefield, 1997.
Karpozilos, A., « Ταξιδιωτικές περιγραφές και εντυπώσεις σε επιστολογραφικά κείμενα », in Moschonas (ed.), *Επικοινωνία*, pp. 511–541.
Koder, J., (unter Mitarbeit von P. Soustal und A. Koder), *Aigaion Pelagos* (Die nördliche Ägäis) (Tabula Imperii Byzantini 10), Vienna: Verlag der Österreichischen Akademie der Wissenschaften 1988.
Koder, J., « Νησιωτική επικοινωνία στο Αιγαίο κατά τον όψιμο μεσαίωνα », in Moschonas (ed.), *Επικοινωνία*, pp. 445–455.
Kokkorou-Alevras, G./D. Grigoropoulos/Ch. Diamanti/M. Koutsoumpou, "Maritime Connections of Halasarna on Cos from Prehistory to Late Antiquity: A View Based on the Pottery and Other Finds", in Höghammar/Alroth/Lindhagen (eds), *Ancient Ports*, pp. 167–200.
Kondyli, F., "Tracing Monastic Economic Interests and Their Impact on the Rural Landscape of Late Byzantine Lemnos", *Dumbarton Oaks Papers* 64 (2010), 129–150.
Kotsakis, K., "A Sea of Agency: Crete in the Context of the Earliest Neolithic in Greece", in Isaakidou, V./P. Tomkins (eds), *Escaping the Labyrinth. The Cretan Neolithic in Context*. Oxford 2008, pp. 52–75.

Krantonelli, A., Ιστορία της πειρατείας στους πρώτους χρόνους της τουρκοκρατίας 1390–1538, Athens 1985.
Külzer, A., « Το γεωγραφικό υπόβαθρο του Βυζαντίου », in T. Loungis (ed.), Βυζάντιο. Ιστορία και πολιτισμός (Byzantium. History and Culture), II, Athens: Erodotos 2014, pp. 1–32.
Lock, P., The Routledge Companion to the Crusades. London: Routledge 2006.
Magdalino, P./D. Chatzilazarou/Ch. Diamanti/D. Hill/H. Roland/K. Ødegård/J. Crow/ S. Turner/M.Z. Sigala/A.K. Vionis/E. Tzavella, "Round Table: Byzantine Naxos in the Light of Recent Research", Proceedings of the 23rd International Congress of Byzantine Studies 2016. Belgrade: Serbian National Committee of AIEB, pp. 308–337.
Malamut, E., Les Iles de l'Empire byzantine, Paris 1988.
Morrisson, C. (ed.), Trade and Markets in Byzantium (Dumbarton Oaks Byzantine Symposia and Colloquia), Washington D.C. 2012.
Moschonas, N.G. (ed.), Η επικοινωνία στο Βυζάντιο, Athens: Κέντρο Βυζαντινών Ερευνών / E.I.E. 1993.
Nomikou, P./D. Papanikolaou/M. Alexandri/D. Sakellariou/G. Rousakis, « Submarine volcanoes along the Aegean volcanic arc », Tectonophysics 597–598 (2013), 123–146.
Papadopoulos, G.A./E. Gràcia/R. Urgeles/V. Sallares/P.M. De Martini/D. Pantosti/ M. González/A.C. Yalciner/J. Mascle/D. Sakellariou/A. Salamon/S. Tinti/ V. Karastathis/A. Fokaefs/A. Camerlenghi/T. Novikova/A. Papageorgiou, "Historical and pre-historical tsunamis in the Mediterranean and its connected seas: Geological signatures, generation mechanisms and coastal impacts", Marine Geology 354 (2014) 81–109.
Papageorgiou, S./S. Steiros, « Μεταβολή παλαιοαναγλύφου, σεισμική δραστηριότητα και αρχαιολογική έρευνα στη βορειοδυτική Ελλάδα », Πρακτικά Α΄ Αρχαιολογικού και Ιστορικού Συνεδρίου Αιτωλοακαρνανίας (Αγρίνιο 21–23 Οκτωβρίου 1988), Agrinio 1991, pp. 233–241.
Papazachos, B.C./P.P. Dimitriu, "Tsunamis in and Near Greece and their Relation to the Earthquake Focal Mechanisms", Natural Hazards 4 (1991), 161–170.
Phytikas, M./G.E. Vougioukalakis, The South Aegean Active Volcanic Arc: Present Knowledge and Future Perspectives, Elsevier 2005.
Pieri, D., "Regional and Interregional Exchanges in the Eastern Mediterranean during the Early Byzantine period. The Evidence of the Amphorae", in Morrisson (ed.), Trade and Markets, pp. 27–50.
Postma, G., "Causes of architectural variation in deltas", in M.N. Oti/G. Postma (eds), Geology of Deltas, Rotterdam 1995, pp. 3–16.
Preiser-Kapeller, J., "Harbours and Maritime Networks as Complex Adaptive Systems – a Thematic Introduction", in Preiser-Kapeller/Daim (eds), Harbours, pp. 1–23.
Preiser-Kapeller, J./F. Daim (eds), Harbours and Maritime Networks as Complex Adaptive Systems (RGZM Tagungen 23), Mainz 2015.

Preiser-Kapeller, J./ T.G. Kolias/ F. Daim (eds), Seasides of Byzantium – Harbours and Anchorages of a Mediterranean Empire, Byzanz zwischen Orient und Okzident Bd. 21, Mainz: Verlag des Römisch-Germanischen Zentralmuseums 2021.

Pryor, J.H., *Geography, Technology, and War Studies in the Maritime History of the Mediterranean, 649–1571*, Cambridge: Cambridge University Press 1988.

Pryor, J.H./E.M. Jeffreys, *The Age of the ΔΡΟΜΩΝ* (The Medieval Mediterranean 62), Leiden-Boston: Brill NV 2006.

Renfrew, C./M. Wagstaff, *An Island Polity*, Cambridge: Cambridge University Press 1982.

Romano, R., *Paese Italia. Venti Secoli di Identità*, Rome: Donzelli 1994.

von Rüden, C./A. Lichtenberger, "Introduction", in A. Lichtenberger/C. von Rüden (eds), *Multiple Mediterranean Realities. Spaces, Resources and Connectivities*, Padeborn: Ferdinand Schöningh 2015, pp. 1–14.

Sigala, M., *Η Χάλκη από την παλαιοχριστιανική εποχή μέχρι και το τέλος της περιόδου της Ιπποτοκρατίας (4ος–1523μΧ.): μνημεία, αρχιτεκτονική, τοπογραφία, κοινωνία*, Athens 2011 (online at https://culture.academia.edu/MariaSigala, last accessed on 2018-04-19).

Slot, B.J., *Archipelagus turbatus. Les Cyclades entre colonisation latine et occupation ottomane c. 1500–1718*, 1, Istanbul 1982.

Sodini, J.-P., "Marble and Stoneworking in Byzantium, Seventh–Fifteenth Centuries", in A. Laiou (ed.), *The Economic History of Byzantium from the seventh to the fifteenth century* (Dumbarton Oaks Studies XXXIX), Washington D.C. 2002, I, pp. 129–146.

Steel, L., *Materiality and Consumption in the Bronze Age Mediterranean*, New York – London 2013.

Stiros, S.C., "The 8.5+ magnitude, AD 365 earthquake in Crete: Coastal uplift, topography changes, archaeological and historical signature", *Quaternary International 216 (1–2) (2010), 54–63*.

Sutter, J.R., "Deltaic coasts", in R.W.G. Carter/C.D. Woodroffe, *Coastal evolution*, Cambridge 1994, pp. 87–120.

Tartaron, T., *Maritime Networks in the Mycenaean World*, Cambridge: Cambridge University Press 2013.

Telelis, I., *Μετεωρολογικά Φαινόμενα και Κλίμα στο Βυζάντιο* (Ἀκαδημία Ἀθηνῶν – Κέντρον Ἐρεύνης τῆς Ἑλληνικῆς καὶ Λατινικῆς Γραμματείας, Πονήματα αρ. 5), Athens 2004.

Telelis, I., "The great climatic risks of the past: The drought described by Byzantine sources (4th–6th cent. A.D.)", *Proceedings of SEP Pollution Meeting in Padova, Italy*, 29. 3.–2. 4. 1992, pp. 289–301.

Tsigonaki, Ch./A. Sarris, "Recapturing the Dynamics of the Early Byzantine Settlements in Crete: Old Problems – New Interpretations through an Interdisciplinary Approach", *Proceedings of the 3rd International Landscape Archaeology Conference 2014, Rome, 17th–20th of September 2014*, Amsterdam, online at DOI 10.5463/lac.2014.5 (last accessed on 2018.04.05).

Tsougarakis, D., *Byzantine Crete from the 5th century to the Venetian Conquest*, Athens 1988.

USNOO (U.S. Naval Oceanographic Office), *Sailing Directions (Enroute) for the Eastern Mediterranean (H.O. Pub. No. 132)*. Washington, DC: United States Government Printing Office 1971.

Veikou, M., "'Rural Towns' and 'In-between Spaces'. Settlement Patterns in Byzantine Epirus (7th–11th centuries) in an Interdisciplinary Approach", *Archeologia Medievale* 36 (2009), 43–54.

Veikou, M., "Byzantine Histories, Settlement Stories: Kastra, 'Isles of Refuge', and 'Unspecified Settlements' as In-between or Third Spaces", in T. Kioussopoulou (ed.), *Byzantine Cities, 8th–15th centuries*, Rethymno: University of Crete 2012, pp. 159–206.

Veikou, M., *Byzantine Epirus: A topography of transformation. Settlements from the 7th to the 12th centuries* (The Medieval Mediterranean 95), Leiden – New York: Brill NV 2012.

Veikou, M., "One Island, three Capitals. Insularity and the Successive Relocations of the Capital of Cyprus from Late Antiquity to the Middle Ages", in Rogge S./M. Grünbart (eds) *Cyprus in Medieval Times. A place of Cultural Encounter*, Münster: Waxmann 2015, pp. 357–387.

Vionis, A., *Crusader, Ottoman, and Early Modern Aegean Archaeology: Built Environment and Domestic Material Culture in the Medieval and Post-Medieval Cyclades, Greece (13th–20th Centuries AD)*, Leiden 2008.

Weiberg, E./I. Unkel/K. Kouli/K. Holmgren/P. Avramidis/A. Bonnier/F. Dibble/M. Finné/A. Izdebski/C. Katrantsiotis/S.R. Stocker/M. Andwinge/K. Baika/M. Boyd/C. Heymann, "The socio-environmental history of the Peloponnese during the Holocene: Towards an integrated understanding of the past", *Quaternary Science Reviews* 136 (2016) 40–65.

CHAPTER 14

"The Other Age of Justinian": Environment, Extreme Events, and the Transformation of the Mediterranean, 5th–7th Century

Mischa Meier

1 Two Ages of Justinian

The year 534: impressive victories over barbarian bands; an "eternal" peace negotiated with the Persians (AD 532); the successful suppression of the *Nika* Revolt in Constantinople (532); the initiation of promising discussions with opponents of the Chalcedonian creed (532/33); the completion of the massive codification and reorganization of Roman law in an extremely short time (528–34); and now the frightening Kingdom of the Vandals in Northern Africa, the existence of which had gnawed at Roman pride for a century, swept away at a stroke (533/34). God himself, as it may have seemed to contemporaries, had given his special blessing to the reign of Emperor Justinian (527–65). And the emperor was aware of the grace conferred on him: *laeta saecula*[1] were in the offing; a new, happy "Age of Justinian" had finally brought a phase of decline and misgovernment to an end. The unexpected victory over the Vandals gave the emperor a spectacular opportunity to celebrate the dawn of this new era, which was founded on an optimistic prognosis for the future. Evoking the ancient traditions of the Republican triumph and, by association, the Secular Games – and thus indirectly also Augustus, the founder of the monarchy and a model for all Roman rulers – Justinian staged a memorable spectacle: Belisarius, the victorious general in the Vandalic War and consul designate for the following year, was permitted to walk from his urban home to the hippodrome accompanied by the joyous masses. There, he presented the war booty and prisoners to the astonished spectators, including the unfortunate last King of the Vandals, Gelimer, who was demonstratively stripped of his purple mantle. The general then humbly prostrated himself before the emperor's loge and paid homage to the actual author of the victory and the ruler of the Oecumene: Emperor

---

1 Justinian, *C. Tanta 6b*, ed. Mommsen/Krueger.

Justinian.² What the contemporary writer Procopius (mis)understood as the base humiliation of Belisarius may in fact have been a daring attempt, on the one hand, to honor his achievements and to prepare him for further tasks as a loyal follower and, on the other, to direct the focus of the entire ceremony onto the emperor as the source of all the beneficial developments of recent years: the new age would bear his name alone. As Procopius and others correctly perceived, this well-staged spectacle exploited a subtle cluster of associations that referred back especially to the triumphs of the Roman Republic and Early Empire. Belisarius' procession through Constantinople corresponded to the ritual "that the Romans call a triumph" (ὃν δὴ θρίαμβον καλοῦσι 'Ρωμαῖοι)³ – as Procopius states, although he subsequently indicates significant differences from these ancient Roman celebrations, differences that he believed reflected the emperor's self-aggrandizement. In spite of all that, though: "It seemed as if an ancient custom were being revived after a long time" (καὶ τι τῶν οὐκ εἰωθότων ἀνανεοῦσθαι τῷ χρόνῳ ἔδοξε).⁴

Not for nothing have modern scholars considered the triumph of 534 a perfect example of the "classicism" of the early Justinianic period, that is, of the striking tendency to draw on established Roman historical paradigms, to defend innovations as measures intended to restore past conditions, and indeed to evoke the ancient Roman past as a reference and argument in political discourse – patterns of thinking and acting from which not least the concept of *renovatio imperii* would gradually emerge in subsequent years.

The year 559: the Hunnic Kutrigurs had breached the "Long Walls", a defensive wall between the Black Sea and the Sea of Marmara about 65 km west of Constantinople. Panic ran rampant in the capital, and only a daring maneuver by the aged general Belisarius warded off the immediate threat.⁵ Fearing further attacks, Emperor Justinian took an extraordinary measure: he left Constantinople in order personally to supervise the repair work on the walls in Selymbria (modern Silivri). He returned to the capital in the early morning of August 11, 559. The description of an *adventus* in the *Book of Ceremonies* of Constantine VII Porphyrogenitus, apparently taken from an official record, must be referring to this event. The route Justinian chose for his entrance into the city – probably on account of an earthquake in 557 – was unusual: the

---

2 Proc. *BV* 2.9; cf. Iord. *Get.* 171, ed. Mommsen. On Justinian's triumph over the Vandals, see McCormick, *Eternal Victory*, pp. 125–28; Meier, *Zeitalter*, pp. 150–80 (including the link to Justinian's conception of a new age); Leppin, *Justinian*, p. 156f.; Börm, "Justinians Triumph".
3 Proc. *BV* 2.9.3.
4 Proc. *BV* 2.9.16.
5 Agath. 5.11–25, ed. Keydell; Vict. Tunn. ad ann. 560, ed. Mommsen, p. 205; Malal, pp. 421.82–422.19; Theoph. a.m. 6051 pp. I 233.4–234.12.

"pious emperor" (εὐσεβὴς βασιλεύς) passed on horseback through the Charisios Gate in the northern part of the city walls, where he was ceremonially greeted by senators and the urban prefect. From there, the procession continued to the Church of the Apostles, the site of the imperial crypt; Justinian paused, prayed, and lit candles at the sarcophagus of his wife Theodora († 548). Then the procession moved again, now constantly being joined by further dignitaries, soldiers in parade uniform (with lights and wearing white mantles), and, naturally, the city's population. It proceeded toward the Capitolium and, from there, via the *Mése*, the main street, to the imperial palace. As Justinian crossed the magnificent gates of the palace complex (the *Chalke*), he was received to the sound of the ritual triumphal chant (ἔκραξεν τὸ θριαμβευτάλιον).[6] The *adventus* of 559 thus also incorporated elements of the ancient Roman triumph. And yet the ceremonial celebrations of the years 534 and 559 were fundamentally different. Of course, the same emperor stood at the center of events in both cases, but while the demonstrative adaptation of the ancient Roman past determined the profile of Justinian's triumph over the Vandals, his *adventus* in Constantinople is imbedded in religious symbolism that served to prove the piety of the emperor, the elites, and the people. Thus, this event also has a paradigmatic character: just as the triumph of 534, ushering in a new era, stands for the optimistic, vibrant adaptation of Roman tradition in Justinian's early years, the *adventus* of 559 represents a religiously driven fossilization bereft of any glimpse of earlier years and lacking any eager anticipation of the future.[7] The orientation of the emperor's actions and even the expectations and forms of articulation of Eastern Roman society had profoundly changed in the twenty-five years between 534 and 559. The once-heralded age of Justinian was now split into two different phases, thereby losing all coherence. The cause of this profound change lies in unforeseeable events that befell the Eastern Roman Empire especially in the years 540–42; coping with them initiated or accelerated transformations that enable us, at least in part, to analytically establish the transition from Late Antiquity to the Byzantine Middle Ages (on which, see below).

The experience of being at the mercy of unmanageable, utterly inexorable forces, of being overtaken by sudden developments and unanticipated series of events; awareness of the growing presence of the uncontrollable – in brief: a high number of what we call borderline experiences ("Kontingenzerfahrung") – profoundly influenced contemporary perceptions of current events in the

---

6   *De caerim.* append. ad 1, ed. Reiske, pp. 497.13–498.13 = ed. Haldon, *Constantine Porphyrogenitus*, pp. 138.707–140.723.
7   Cf. Meier, *Zeitalter*, p. 304f.; Leppin, *Justinian*, p. 320f.

6th century.[8] The initial cause was an unprecedented series of natural disasters and military catastrophes that overtook the Eastern Roman Empire and its population in the late 5th century. Earthquakes, fires, floods, volcanic eruptions, extreme weather and its subsequent crop failures, locust swarms, raids by foreign plunderers, wars, and devastating epidemics marked everyday life for decades. Strange northern lights, the appearance of comets, and solar eclipses were further associated with these disasters as ominous epiphenomena.[9] A chronologically predetermined (see below) sensitivity to unusual phenomena (which were seen as either punishing or warning acts of divine communication) spilled over into the practice of mentioning earthquakes that caused no damage whatsoever in historiographical works[10] and even occasionally in compiling outright disaster chronicles, such as the *Chronicon Edessenum* (after 540), listing the calamities of the city of Edessa (modern Şanlıurfa, Turkey), or the *Chronicle* of Joshua the Stylite composed in 507, recording the severe trials faced by Syria and Northern Mesopotamia in the years 494–506. But the wave of disasters in these decades cannot simply be dismissed as the result of literary stylization. There is no reason to dispute the historicity of most of the events mentioned in the sources, and some of them can be confirmed by modern scientific methods. Much discussion, for example, has recently revolved around an eighteen-month period of diminished sunlight in 536/37, which is attested across the entire northern hemisphere; it apparently led to at least one "summerless year" and may have caused severe crop failures across the Mediterranean.[11] While sometimes far-reaching consequences were attributed to this phenomenon (which was probably caused by a major volcanic eruption[12]) until the rise of Islam,[13] scholars today tend

---

8   The following remarks are essentially based on the findings of my monograph, Meier, *Zeitalter*.
9   A list of such events over the period 500–65 appears in Meier, *Zeitalter*, pp. 656–70. Cf. also Stathakopoulos, *Famine*, and the recent overview by Preiser-Kapeller, *Der lange Sommer*, pp. 29–89.
10   E.g., Malal. pp. 402.34–36; *Chron. Pasch.* p. I 629.10–20.
11   Cassiod. *var.* 12.25, ed. Th. Mommsen; Proc. BV 2.14.4–6; Joh. Lyd. *ostent.* 9c, ed. C. Wachsmuth; Ps.-Zach. 9.19, p. 370; [Joh. Eph.] in the *Chronicle of Zuqnîn* p. 65; Theoph. a.m. 6026 p. I 202.10–15; Kedren. 650 PG 121.710; Mich. Syr. 9.26, ed. Chabot; *Chron. ad ann. 1234* LXI, p. 157. On this event, see especially Stathakopoulos, "Reconstructing the Climate", pp. 251–55; Meier, *Zeitalter*, pp. 359–65; Arjava, "Mystery Cloud" (with further sources); Harper, *Fate*, pp. 251–54; Preiser-Kapeller, *Der lange Sommer*, pp. 29–33.
12   Other theories presume a comet or asteroid impact; the volcano theory, however, is currently more widely accepted; for discussion, cf. the overviews in Stathakopoulos, "Reconstructing the Climate", p. 252f., and Arjava, "Mystery Cloud", p. 77f.
13   Baillie, *Exodus*; Keys, *Catastrophe*.

to take a much more sober, relativizing view.[14] It is nonetheless very plausible that the famines caused by this dimming of the sun (which, again, are attested by literary sources[15]), which intensified a trend to global cooling (the so-called "Late Antique Little Ice Age" (LALIA, see below) may have facilitated the rapid advance of the plague in 541.[16]

If we cast a glance at the long reign of Justinian, it seems particularly to be characterized by devastating disasters and borderline experiences: this is the "Other Age of Justinian". Scholars have long struggled to perceive the dark side of a supposedly brilliant age and accept it as an integral part of the history of the 6th century. In 1996, for example, the historian J.A.S. Evans dedicated only a brief section to the plague in his *Age of Justinian*.[17] Only during the last two decades has a nuanced view gained ground. Today, the disasters that left such a long-lasting mark on the "Age of Justinian" and even on subsequent decades are no longer regarded as mere epiphenomena on the margins of "really" relevant history, but rather as events that stood at the center of contemporary attention and, precisely for that reason (and also on account of their demographic and material consequences), were key factors in initiating the transformation of Late Antiquity into the Early Middle Ages.[18] At any rate, no one today can seriously dispute the great significance of unforeseeable events for the historical development between the late 5th and the 7th centuries. And in the context of a methodologically sophisticated environmental history, this by no means entails subjecting historical events to exogenous determinism.

2 Catastrophic Events of the 6th Century

Although we can identify a nearly unbroken string of disasters extending from the late 5th century to the 7th, we also find particularly intense phases, veritable disaster clusters, during the reign of Justinian. For example, the Syrian metropolis Antioch was repeatedly struck by fires and earthquakes

---

14   Most recently, Arjava, "Mystery Cloud". But see also Harper, *Fate*, pp. 251–54 who points to the consequences of the event for the global climate.
15   References in Meier, *Zeitalter*, pp. 662–65; Stathakopoulos, "Reconstructing the Climate", pp. 265ff.
16   Haldon et al., "Climate", p. 123, however, correctly points out that no clear evidence of a connection between the atmospheric even of 536/37 and the outbreak of the plague has thus far been found.
17   Evans, *Age of Justinian*, pp. 160–65.
18   Cf. Meier, *Zeitalter*; Maas, *Companion*; Leppin, "(K)ein Zeitalter"; Leppin, *Justinian*; Little, *Plague*; Meier, *Geschichte*.

during the years 525–28. It was destroyed to such an extent that the contemporary Antiochene chronicler John Malalas described the city as "unusable" (ἄχρηστος).[19] In 548, "constant earthquakes", storms, Slavic raids, famines caused by irregular water levels of the Nile, and the killing of a mysterious sea monster (κῆτος) called "Porphyrios" led the people of Constantinople to speculate fearfully about the future.[20] Finally, in 557–59, a major earthquake (causing the dome of the Hagia Sophia to collapse, among other things), a devastating outbreak of plague, and the invasion of the Kutrigurs mentioned above shook the metropolis on the Bosporus.[21] The disaster cluster of the years 540–42, however, seems to have left the longest-lasting mark: contemporaries later interpreted a comet that appeared in the sky in 539 as heralding the catastrophe that immediately followed. Now the Kutrigurs plundered Thrace and Illyria, and individual bands advanced as far as the suburbs of Constantinople and even the Isthmus of Corinth in Greece. A Persian invasion in breach of the "eternal" peace proved, in 540, to be equally catastrophic, claiming Antioch, among other cities, among its victims. At the same time, the Gothic War, which contemporaries in 540 believed had been brought to a victorious conclusion, flared up again in Italy. Within the shortest timespan, most of the Eastern Roman conquests were lost. A protracted, resource- and energy-draining war ensued that ultimately delivered the Romans an impoverished, utterly exhausted province (and, even that, for only a few years). And, while repeated earthquakes in 540–41 demoralized the population of Constantinople, on top of all this ominous news, plague broke out in Egypt in 541 and began its horrific march across the Mediterranean world. The horror that now confronted the Romans knew no bounds. The plague reached Constantinople by fall of 541 at the latest and caused horrific damage.[22] While ancient sources give inconceivably high numbers of victims – Procopius first claims 5,000 and finally over 10,000 dead per day; according to John of Ephesus, imperial officials in Constantinople gave up counting the dead when they reached a total of 230,000 victims[23] – scholars have variously assessed

---

19   Meier, *Zeitalter*, p. 659f., with references. "Unusable": Malal. p. 346.14.
20   Earthquake: Malal. p. 410.49; storms: Theoph. a.m. 6040 p. I 226.4–7; cf. Malal. p. 410.50–53; Slavic raids: Proc. *BG* 3.29.1–3; Nile: Proc. *BG* 3.29.6–8; *HA* 18.39; "Porphyrios" and speculation about the future: Proc. *BG* 7.29.9–20; *HA* 15.37.
21   Earthquake in 557: Malal. pp. 419.55–66; 420.75–81; Agath. 5.3–9; [Joh. Eph.] in the *Chronicle of Zuqnîn* p. 117f.; 126f.; Theoph. a.m. 6050 pp. I 231.13–232.6; 232.27–233.3; plague 558: Malal. 420.71–74; Agath. 5.10; Theoph. a.m. 6050 p. I 232.13–115; Kutrigurs 559: see above, n. 5.
22   For details on the disasters in the years 540–42, cf. Meier, *Zeitalter*, pp. 307–41.
23   Proc. *BP* 2.23.1–2; [Joh. Eph.] in the *Chronicle of Zuqnîn* p. 87.

the demographic footprint of the plague.[24] But no one can reasonably doubt *whether* the plague, which became endemic after the initial outbreak in 541/42 and flared up again and again in different, regionally varying waves until the mid-8th century, represented a major demographic and economic caesura – even if it ultimately cannot be quantified.[25] A number of indications suggest that it also had considerable influence on cultural developments relevant to the history of mentalities.[26]

All these events occurred during a period for which significant climate deterioration has been documented. Available data indicates – albeit not without controversy and allowing for regional variation – that average temperatures over the period of *c*.500–850/1000 were lower than in previous centuries, while simultaneously humidity significantly increased – the consequences of the LALIA.[27] That in turn made the predominantly agrarian population, which largely relied on subsistence agriculture, particularly vulnerable to such phenomena, whereas under more favorable climatic conditions they would not have registered significant effects, somewhat like short-term weather anomalies. The *vulnerability* of society had thus increased.

3 "Vulnerability", "Resilience", and "Cultures of Disaster"

"Vulnerability" is more than a mere word in this context; it is a sociological concept that gives us insight into recurrent patterns in the way different societies at different times cope with disaster. It also helps us assess the forms and

---

24 Cf., for example, the conflicting conclusions of Wickham, *Framing*, p. 548f. and Evans, *Age of Justinian*, p. 160. A new discussion on the impact and consequences of the "Justinianic Plague" has come up since 2019, see the conflicting views of Mordechai et al., "Justinianic Plague"; Meier, "The Justinianic Plague: An 'Inconsequential Pandemic'?"; Sarris, "New Approaches".

25 In this sense, cf. Sarris, "Bubonic Plague"; Meier, "The Justinianic Plague: An 'Inconsequential Pandemic'?"; Sarris, "New Approaches".

26 This is my hypothesis in Meier, "Justinianic Plague". There I also discuss in greater detail the scholarly controversy over the significance of the plague for the transition between Antiquity and the Middle Ages. Cf. also the contributions in Little, *Plague*.

27 On the LALIA, see now Haldon et al., "Climate"; Büntgen/McCormick et al., "Cooling"; Harper, *Fate*; Izdebski/Mulryan, *Environment and Society*; Preiser-Kapeller, *Der lange Sommer*, pp. 29–33. Older research: Koder, "Historical Aspects"; Koder, "Climatic Change"; cf. Stathakopoulos, "Reconstructing the Climate", p. 250; Morrisson, "Peuplement", p. 194; Greater humidity in Late Antiquity: Izdebski, "Agriculture", who also notes that climatic variations (Izdebski rightly prefers the term "climate fluctuations" to general climate change) may have had very different consequences depending on the region affected. See also Telelis, *Meteorologika Phainomena*.

extent of the susceptibility of individual groups or societies to specific events or phenomena. Every society gradually learns over time to adapt to specific dangers that threaten it. Seaside village societies develop mechanisms to cope with floods, just as settlements near active volcanoes become experienced in dealing with eruptions, or cities near aggressive neighbors develop specific defensive measures, and so on. Societies establish a certain kind of "pain threshold" that determines their ability to cope – that is, their vulnerability – in the event of an earthquake, flood, or volcanic eruption. In this way, vulnerability gives us a tool to compare and thereby make at least approximate inferences about ancient societies for which we otherwise possess very few direct sources.

The concept of "resilience" complements that of vulnerability: resilience allows us to assess to what extent individual groups or societies can cope with disaster or adapt to external conditions so as to compensate for damage. If we analyze individual societies with respect to their vulnerability and resilience, we can make inferences about their respective disaster cultures, that is, about the mechanisms and modes of adaptation with which they react to recurrent threats. Often there emerges an idiosyncratic rhythm of disaster, collective coping, reconstruction, preparing for the unknown, and so on. Various sources allow us to recognize the existence of such disaster cultures also in Late Antiquity.[28] Disaster cultures were based on basic collective knowledge that was activated in the event of a disaster. This knowledge not only informed preexisting perceptual patterns (such as, for example, the widespread perception of catastrophic events in Late Antiquity as being punishment sent by God), but also shaped coping behavior. The basis for this collective knowledge, which supported the development of a society-stabilizing disaster culture, was largely undermined in the 6th century – greatly exacerbating the consequences of disasters and vastly increasing the vulnerability of the society affected. Fundamental coping mechanisms broke down. The resilience of the people in many areas significantly failed, and we are repeatedly confronted in the 6th and 7th century with societies on the brink of collapse.[29] The world order seemed to be coming undone.

---

28 On vulnerability and resilience: Hoffman/Oliver-Smith, *Catastrophe and Culture*; Bankoff/Frerks/Hilhorst, *Mapping Vulnerability*; Wisner et al., *At Risk*; cf. also the overview in Schenk, "Historical Disaster Research". For the concept of disaster cultures: Bankoff, *Cultures of Disaster*.

29 For example, during the mass hysteria in Constantinople 541/42 ([Joh. Eph.] in the *Chronicle of Zuqnîn* pp. 97–98) and in Amida ([Joh. Eph.] in the *Chronicle of Zuqnîn* pp. 104–06; cf. also p. 107: dated to the year 555/56 in contrast to the preceding accounts); [Joh. Eph.] *Vita Jacobi* PO 19.259–262; Mich. Syr. 9.32; *Chron. ad ann. 1234* LXII p. 157, with Ashbrook Harvey, "Asceticism").

Obviously, periods of intense misfortune and manifold catastrophes were nothing new. Why then did the disasters that struck after c.500 no longer fit into the established interpretive framework, thereby becoming particularly severe?

4   Eschatological Expectations of the Second Coming around 500 and the "Mentality Crisis" of the 6th Century

There is substantial evidence that very specific fears of the imminent end of the world became widespread around the year 500. These expectations of the Second Coming were by no means an esoteric, marginal phenomenon, but rather appear to have gripped large sections of the population. They represent the outcome of a long-term development that had commenced under the High Empire, the "delay" of the Parousia. The failure of the Second Coming of Christ to materialize as foretold in Early Christianity and the oppression Christians had endured in the 3rd century had revealed the necessity of establishing one's standpoint in a world history moving toward a clearly defined *eschaton*. The outcome of these reflections was the calculation of earthly time on a 6000-year continuum, with the birth of Christ occurring in the 5,500th year; that placed the Parousia or the end of the world in the year AD 500 after the lapse of 6,000 years. The years around AD 500 thus became eschatologically loaded, as did widespread expectations among contemporaries – who eagerly awaited a visible sign of the approaching end of the world.[30] Against this background, extraordinary disasters might indicate the Parousia and the arrival of the End of Days, especially if they came in numbers and were accompanied by other supposed indicators of the end of the world. The unforeseeable events that occurred around AD 500 were accordingly interpreted in precisely this way. This interpretation in turn strengthened the acute anticipation of the Second Coming, setting in motion an increasingly dynamic process. The series of extreme natural disasters and unusual natural phenomena that began precisely during these years virtually forced contemporaries to interpret them as the signs of the anticipated end of the world. And did not the reigning emperor moreover bear the name Anastasius, which unmistakably referred to the Greek word *anástasis* ("resurrection")?

Undoubtedly, the disasters that befell the Eastern Roman Empire in unusual frequency and severity after the early 6th century initially served an important function within prevailing contemporary interpretive patterns, insofar

---

[30]   On this phenomenon, see, for instance, Landes, "Millennium"; Magdalino, "History"; Brandes, "Anastasios"; Meier, *Zeitalter*; Meier, "Eschatologie".

as they seemed to confirm specific expectations; at first, it was easier to cope with them because expectation and experience coincided. In subsequent decades, however, a serious problem began to emerge, as contemporaries began to realize that the end of the world that everyone had expected had *not* come, while the disasters they suffered continued and even – especially in the years 540/42 – grew vastly more intense. Now expectation and experience diverged. The consequences – the collapse of the established conceptual framework and even chronology[31] – were fatal: the collective mental foundation of the Eastern Roman population was placed under immense pressure, threatening to result in a complete loss of identity and the general collapse of society.

This phenomenon – we might call it a collective "mentality crisis" – was in my opinion a key factor in the transformation of Roman Late Antiquity into the Byzantine Early Middle Ages. It confronted the Eastern Roman population with massive challenges; overcoming them may be considered one of the greatest achievements of the Eastern Roman Empire. It is no surprise that this process of consolidation came at a high price. The effort to overcome the existential threats of the 6th century thus structurally resembles the mechanisms that were used in the late 5th and early 6th century to contain a dangerous threat to the Eastern Roman monarchy (in this case, by accepting the growing sacralization of the imperial monarchy) and that enabled the Byzantines in the 7th and 8th centuries to emerge successfully from the physical struggle for existence (while accepting far-reaching structural changes to the society and administrative organization of the Empire). In sum, we see three stages of intensified transformation between the late 5th and the 7th/8th centuries that can help us analyze the transition from Antiquity to the Middle Ages in the Roman East. The price that Eastern Roman society had to pay to overcome the "mentality crisis" of the 6th century is hidden behind the term "liturgification".[32]

5 Consolidation through Liturgification

Averil Cameron has described liturgification as a complex process of social integration that enabled the population of the Eastern Roman Empire to adapt to changed external conditions without collapsing under the weight of the

---

31   Details in Meier, *Zeitalter*, pp. 443–81.
32   For this three-stage model, see Meier, "Ostrom-Byzanz".

challenges of the time.³³ The liturgification of all public communication created new poles of identification that could help anchor the people, enabling them to find a new place and orientation in a rapidly changing world. Liturgification, however, is not easy to document analytically. In the simplest terms, it can be described as the process whereby originally profane areas became invested with "the holy". Without going into the complex, ongoing discussion of this term, "the holy" should for now be understood merely as something that brought order and structure – in contrast to the profane, which represented chaos and randomness. It is easier to observe the liturgification that commenced in the late Justinianic period by considering its real consequences. These include – in particular, with respect to the early Justinianic period – the strikingly radical rejection of classicizing tendencies and demonstrative references to the Roman past. The abolition of the venerable annual consulship precisely in the year of the devastating plague, AD 541/42, marks an important caesura.³⁴ The ceremonial surrounding the emperor and his rare public appearances also underwent a process of sacralization (corresponding to the renewed sacralization of the emperor himself; on which, see below) that appears, for instance, in the involvement of the so-called circus factions in ceremonial contexts. The forms of general religious practice changed: we can observe a dramatic increase in the veneration of the Virgin Mary and the rise of icons (see below). Where we can also cautiously quantify religiosity – for example, the number of processions – there are further significant increases. In the latter half of the 6th century, new compilations of secular (*nómoi*) and ecclesiastical (*kanónes*) law, known since the 11th century as *nomocanons*, begin to appear, attesting to the blending of secular and sacral elements in the legal sphere. Even time and space now became sacrally charged to an unprecedented extent: especially in the latter half of the 6th century, the Byzantine liturgical year acquired several long-lasting features. A series of feasts and commemorations was created, and a growing number of processions defined new areas of the sacred in cities – and above all in the capital Constantinople. Transcendental civic patrons (icons, Mary, saints) took their place alongside – and soon in place of – traditional defense mechanisms that seemed to be overwhelmed or ineffective (e.g., garrisons, but also Holy Men). Constantinople itself transformed into the "residence" of the Mother of God, so much so that contemporaries in

---

33 Cameron, "Images", p. 4; 14f.; 24; 35. On the phenomenon of liturgification, see also Cameron, "Theotokos", pp. 80–82; 107f.; Meier, "Sind wir nicht alle heilig", with further literature (p. 133, note 1); Meier, "Liturgification".
34 For further details, see Meier, "Konsulat".

626 believed that she personally defended the city against the Avars. The city thus advanced to become a sacred space, and this holiness ultimately extended over the entire empire. The poet Corippus remarks in his panegyric for the accession of Justin II (565–78), "The Roman Empire is in the hands of God; it has no need of earthly weapons" (*res Romana Dei est, terrenis non eget armis*).[35] These new sacred protective powers also increasingly appeared in the conduct of war: in 591, Emperor Maurice demonstratively marched against the Avars under the sign of the cross; his general Philippicus carried an icon of Christ into battle against the Persians; and Heraclius set sail for Constantinople in 610 with an image of the Mother of God affixed to the mast and set out against the Persians in 622 with a relic of the cross. "Mary" became a watchword in the Roman army.[36] Since during the process of liturgification the sacred typically begins to pervade ever-greater areas and ceases to be limited to individual places or persons (e.g., Holy Men), the population of the Empire itself became a sacred society, a collective bulwark against external pressures. This perspective lies behind the identification of the last of the four world empires of the Old Testament prophecy of Daniel (Dan 2; 7) with the Macedonian Empire (and not the Roman), as appears in Kosmas Indikoleustes (c.550): the demise of the Macedonians is directly followed by the reign of Christ, which commences with his incarnation in Roman times.[37] The Roman Empire and the messianic empire of saints thus fuse into one. *All Romans* accordingly are holy, and the *res Romana*, which according to Corippus no longer requires earthly weapons, is in truth a *res Christiana*.

A glance at the historiography of the latter half of the 6th century and the first half of the 7th shows that this process of liturgification was not only a result of the severe disasters of the 6th century, but also was a consequence of their inexplicability after the anticipated end of the world failed to materialize.[38] These historiographical works reflect their authors' desperate and ultimately futile effort to find a causal framework that could explain and interpret the disasters. Their inability to offer plausible chains of events according to the postulates of classicizing pagan historiography since Thucydides ultimately led to the abandonment of this thousand-year-old historiographical form and

---

35   Coripp. *Laud. Iust.* 3.333, ed. Antès.
36   Maurice 591: Theophyl. Sim.5.16.11; Philippicus: Theophyl. Sim. 2.3; Theoph. a.m. 6078 p. I 255.13–19; Heraclius 610: Georg. Pisid. *Heracl.* 2.12–16; Theoph. a.m. 6102 p. I 298.15–17; Heraclius 622: Georg. Pisid. *Exp. Pers.* 2.252–55; "Mary" as a watchword: Theophyl. Sim. 5.10.
37   Kosm. Ind. 2.66–76, esp. 66 and 74–75, ed. Wolska-Conus, pp. 381–93.
38   For a full account of the following, see Meier, "Prokop".

its transformation into ecclesiastical history. Only the latter could somehow reconcile all these occurrences with God's providential plan. The development of classicizing historiography – that is, historiography according to the model of Herodotus, Thucydides, and Polybius – is highly significant: the cause that Procopius, one of the chief representatives of the genre, cites for the plague is the power of God; in doing so, he decisively makes an interpretive pattern of ecclesiastical historiography of his own.[39] Agathias, who desperately wrestled with the question of guilt, innocence, retaliation, and justice and was unwilling to accept interpretations based on divine punishment, because they could not sufficiently explain the suffering of the innocent, ultimately retreated to the minimalistic standpoint that the historian's task was merely to give an overview of events – thereby blatantly contradicting his earlier programmatic claim that such minimal historiography was *not* sufficient.[40] Agathias thus seems to base his work, which nonetheless revolves primarily around disasters, fear, and overcoming them, deliberately on a conceptual contradiction, thereby effectively destroying it; traditional historiography, with its emphasis on finding cause–effect relationships, no longer seems feasible for him. Only ecclesiastical historiography with its providential explanatory framework offers a way out. With Evagrius, we see particularly clearly how secular and ecclesiastical history gradually blur; this process is most explicit in the historiographical work of Theophylact Simocatta, which was composed in the reign of Heraclius (610–41) and covers the reign of Maurice (582–602). Every event in this work is subordinated to God's divine plan. Crises of explanation are no longer accepted. Human understanding is limited; God's plan is not always evident, but it cannot be doubted. Traditional, classicizing secular historiography had come to terms with this. It could no longer explain and interpret current events with the tools at its disposal and thus was swept away by liturgification – which in this case meant fusion with ecclesiastical historiography.

6 Liturgification and Accelerated Historical Change

As suggested above, liturgification is reflected especially strikingly by the increasingly widespread veneration of the Virgin Mary and icons. Both phenomena may ultimately derive from the disaster experiences of the population in the 6th century – the veneration of Mary primarily from the first wave of the

---

39 Proc. *BP* 2.22.2.
40 Agath. 5.10.7; 1.7.6–7.

plague in 541/42.[41] Veneration of the Mother of God represented an important aspect of Eastern Roman piety at least since the Council of Ephesus in 431, but it exploded in the wake of the plague.[42] It is significant that the people of Constantinople shouted "Mary" whenever they met a monk or clergyman (whom they viewed as responsible for the plague).[43] It was, moreover, precisely in the plague year 542 that Justinian decided to move the *Hypapante* (known in English as Candlemas or the Presentation of Jesus at the Temple) from February 14 to February 2. Changing the date of the feast went – broadly speaking – hand in hand with its transformation from what was originally a feast for Christ into one for Mary. It emerges from a Mary legend concerning the change that it explicitly intended to mitigate the plague – a move that soon appeared to have been so successful that the designated pope Gregory I, who himself had studied the local disaster culture of Constantinople for several years, copied it in Rome in 590 to counteract a devastating plague outbreak.[44] Yet Justinian not only attempted to respond to the rapidly rising popularity of the Mother of God by moving the *Hypapante*; he now also presented himself as a devout worshipper of Mary. In his panegyric, Procopius explicitly describes how much the building of churches for Mary – most famously, the *Nea* in Jerusalem consecrated in 543 – meant to Justinian.[45] The number of feasts for the Virgin Mary also dramatically increased in the 6th century.

Although Christians had initially rejected all forms of icon-worship as a relic of pagan practices, the picture changed dramatically in the middle of the 6th century – apparently under repeated pressure from unforeseeable disasters. Foreign attacks above all may have spurred the rise of icon-worship, although the plague also seems to have been relevant.[46] During the epidemic in 541–44, St. Theodore of Sykeon was allegedly cured of the disease by an icon.[47] Thereafter, venerated icons appeared everywhere: in 544 an icon of Christ supposedly saved Edessa from the Persians; in Kamulianai in Asia Minor, another icon of Christ appeared that soon miraculously reproduced itself. An icon of Mary from Sozopolis enjoyed great prestige, and there are accounts of further icons. Whole communities believed they were protected from foreign attacks by miracle-working icons, especially Edessa, the home of

---

41 A similar phenomenon was incidentally observed during the "Black Death" in the Late Middle Ages; cf. Bulst, "Heiligenverehrung".
42 The following is a summary of my reflections in Meier, *Zeitalter*, pp. 502–28.
43 [Joh. Eph.] in the *Chronicle of Zuqnîn*, pp. 97–98.
44 Meier, *Zeitalter*, pp. 570–86.
45 Proc. *aed.* 1.3.1.
46 The following is a summary of my reflections in Meier, *Zeitalter*, pp. 528–60.
47 Festugière (ed.), *Vie de Théodore de Sykéôn*, p. 7.

one of the most famous. The cities of the Empire thus gave substance to their belief that the traditional means of maintaining peace and order, especially imperial officials and troops, no longer afforded them adequate protection – a dangerous development that might lead to rivalry between the representatives of the emperor's authority and new, supernatural protectors, as well as to the dissociation of the center from the periphery, thereby intensifying regionalization tendencies. That none other than the capital Constantinople promoted this development by monopolizing the Mother of God as its patron and gradually becoming the destination of numerous transfers of relics and icons only complicated the situation. Important categories that had once constituted identities under the Roman Empire and held it together began to lose their cohesive force. The empire of "saints" that needed no earthly weapons now had to struggle with growing centrifugal forces in its midst.

We can observe these profound transformations in progress from the middle of the 6th century. They encompassed the *entire* Eastern Roman population, with the emperor at the top. Even though the emperor repeatedly stands out as an effective agent by introducing or moving feasts, building churches, transferring relics, and so on, it would be mistaken to view liturgification as a carefully orchestrated process. On the contrary, Justinian and his successors often merely reacted to situational expectations and demands, in turn planting the seeds for subsequent developments. In this way, a complex interplay arose that makes it difficult to speak of individual agency. Far-sighted strategic decisions were probably rare. In one respect, however, the emperor energetically attempted to keep the power of agency firmly in his hands: in the representation of his own person and his reign *vis-à-vis* a population shaken by disaster experiences and growing uncertainty, a population that increasingly vented its irritation in the form of criticism of the emperor, virtually forcing him to reconceptualize imperial rule.

When Procopius depicts Justinian in his *Secret History* as the prince of demons who was intent on annihilating mankind and therefore brought about disasters like the plague,[48] we certainly cannot regard this all-out attack on the emperor as representative of widespread popular opinion. The unending series of severe catastrophes nonetheless seems to have opened the door to attacks on the emperor. The emperor – and Justinian in particular – continued to postulate that he was chosen by God and ruled the Oecumene on His behalf.[49] In return, he naturally had to demonstrate, again and again, his exceptional piety as virtually the decisive qualification for his appointment – especially

---

48   Proc. *HA* 12.12–32; 18.
49   Cf. Leppin, *Justinian*.

in the capital Constantinople, where a mistrustful population apt to riot and rebel closely monitored the humble piety of the "orthodox" emperor, and where a consensual balance between the people, elite, and clergy underpinned the emperor's delicate position (the imperial monarchy "of the capital" / the "acceptance system" (*Akzeptanzsystem*).[50] In the 5th century, emperors like Theodosius II or Marcian stabilized their positions with virtuoso performances of piety and humility and even gave themselves greater room to maneuver. Sudden disasters could sometimes even help them do so. After an earthquake in 447, for instance, Theodosius II appeared as a humble penitent at the head of a procession of the people of Constantinople and thus warded off, as contemporaries believed, a "great threat such as was not since the beginning of the world" (ἀπειλὴ μεγάλη, οἵα οὐ γέγονεν ἀπ' ἀρχῆς), proving "the forbearance of God in his love for mankind" (τῆς τοῦ φιλανθρώπου θεοῦ μακροθυμίας).[51] The massive shocks to be overcome since the late 5th century, however, gradually overwhelmed this acceptance system – and may ultimately have caused piety to lose its central role as a virtue that stabilized imperial rule in the transition to the 7th century.

While references to contemporary criticism of the emperor under Justinian are rather reserved[52] – if we disregard for a moment Procopius' *Secret History* – and for the most part have to be inferred indirectly, from the mid-540s the amount of unrest in Constantinople increased significantly. We may plausibly infer that the situation became more difficult for the emperor from his effort to insulate his person and his position by repeatedly adding new sacral elements.[53] Justinian took this effort very far: he not only presented himself as a strict ascetic whose abstemiousness and selfless way of life placed him alongside prominent Holy Men,[54] but he also went a significant step further. After 540, there is an increasing number of signs that the emperor deliberately equated himself with Jesus Christ. A consular diptych from the year 540, for example, depicts the emperor and Christ on the same level – a message that had immense implications for contemporaries.[55] In Paul the Silentiary's *Ekphrasis* of the Hagia Sophia, recited at the turn of the year 562/63, Justinian becomes a transcendent figure bereft of all human emotion, at whose side

---

50 The fundamental work on this complex is Pfeilschifter, *Kaiser*.
51 *Chron. Pasch.* p. I 586.9–12; p. I 589.12–15.
52 Examples: Proc. *BV* 2.14.4–6; [Joh. Eph.] in the *Chronicle of Zuqnîn* p. 83. On the phenomenon, see Meier, *Zeitalter*, pp. 427–43.
53 The following is a summary of my reflections in Meier, *Zeitalter*, pp. 608–38 and Meier, "Liturgification".
54 Cf. Proc. *aed.* 1.7.7–12; *HA* 13.28–30; cf. 12.24–27. On this subject, see Leppin, *Justinian*, pp. 286–88.
55 Volbach, *Elfenbeinarbeiten*, p. 41 no. 33 Table 17.

Christ stands as "helper" (συνεργός).⁵⁶ Other sources indicate that Justinian presented his own body as a miracle-working relic in his own lifetime.⁵⁷

In another publication, I have proposed the term "hypersacralization" (*Hypersakralisierung*) to describe this unprecedented development in Roman history.⁵⁸ This term encompasses not only the emperor's efforts to insulate himself against attacks and criticism, as sketched above, but also takes into account the fact that he was compelled to maintain appropriate distance from his "subjects" (*subiecti*/ὑπήκοοι) – the term Justinian consistently used to designate the population – during this escalating process of liturgification, over the course of which the entire Eastern Roman population increasingly took on a sacral aura. His person and position became so sacrally loaded – or overloaded – that the paradigm of the exceedingly pious and therefore invulnerable ruler finally lost its persuasive force and failed. The first criticism of the exaltation of the emperor's body appears retrospectively in a remark made by the church historian Evagrius about Justinian's death, according to which Justinian was "invisibly wounded" and had destroyed his earthly life (ἀοράτως τρωθεὶς τὸν τῇδε κατέστρεψε βίον).⁵⁹ The fact that the emperor himself caught the plague, which reduced him to the level of countless members of the Roman population, may have spread doubt about the justification for his sacral exaltation; the mental illness of his successor Justin II, which broke out publicly in 573 and effectively forced him to abdicate, potentially had a similar effect. In his abdication speech, Justin described his extraordinary piety as a ruler and played on the part of the contrite sinner,⁶⁰ but it did him no good. Piety, moreover, was neither a relevant argument in the case of the bloody overthrow of Maurice (602) – although his piety was considered so exceptional that a Maurice legend quickly emerged after his death – nor could it prevent the brutal murder of Phocas (610). Instead, the exceptional brutality of the murder of these emperors in 602 and 610 seems to respond to a need to prove the vulnerability and earthliness of the emperor and his body.

7   The Path toward the 7th Century

Piety had largely lost its effect as a key means of stabilizing an emperor's reign by the year 600; we may attribute this fact to the gradual erosion of the

---

56 Paul. Silent. *Ekphr.* 6, ed. P. Friedländer.
57 References in Meier, "Liturgification".
58 Meier, "Liturgification".
59 Euagr. *HE* 4,41, ed. J. Bidez/L. Parmentier.
60 Cameron, "Abdication".

socio-political conditions in Constantinople that had sustained imperial rule as an acceptance system for over two centuries. They likewise succumbed to the pressure of change around the year 600. The disaster-driven hypersacralization of the emperor and its consequences since the mid-6th century, however, will have also played a prominent part in this development. It was certainly clear after the murder of Phocas in 610 that the imperial monarchy required a new foundation before it could continue to decide the fate of the *imperium Romanum* as a generally acknowledged authority – in particular during the existential threats faced *circa* 610–30 (Persian war) and Arabic attacks from 634 onwards. Phocas' successor Heraclius (610–41) seems to have successfully risen to the challenge. After various, apparently fruitless attempts to appear as an exceptionally pious emperor in the tradition of his predecessors, he did not merely adopt the logical response to the progressive erosion of the capital-based imperial monarchy by becoming the first Eastern Roman emperor to lead his army personally on campaign in over two hundred years in 622.[61] The desperate situation of the Empire, which had lost province after province to the Persians and stood on the brink of collapse, and his own personal situation as a usurper – whose initial position was extremely unstable and who had to counteract the structural parallels between his own usurpation and that of the "tyrant" Phocas, which were clear for all contemporaries to see[62] – virtually forced him to take this radical departure from what had become traditional conduct.

Heraclius also consistently strove to exalt his person and likewise made use of references to Jesus Christ – even to a far greater extent than Justinian. While Justinian had presented the supposed parallels in a way that assimilated him to Christ, Heraclius pushed the process as far as temporary identity between himself and Christ.[63] As a ruler who showed his physical presence also outside the capital, he moreover appears to have maintained a similar self-representation in the contested provinces. He thereby deliberately exploited expectations of the Second Coming, which enjoyed a resurgence at the beginning of the 7th century on account of military disasters, in order to construct a new imperial monarchy that I would call "messianic" insofar as it instrumentalized now widespread fears of the immediate end of the world to consolidate the empire and the monarchy. The eschatological implications of this "messianic" imperial monarchy appear most explicitly in the assumption of the title *basileus* for the first time by Heraclius and his son Constantine – in 629, immediately after

---

61 For the historical context, see Kaegi, *Heraclius*; Raum, *Szenen*; Viermann, *Herakleios*.
62 Cf. Olster, *Politics*.
63 For examples, see Meier, "Herakles".

the unexpectedly successful conclusion of the Persian War.[64] Even though the context and exact reasons for this step remain controversial, it seems evident to me that the emperor intended to tie his well-attested evocation of the Old Testament kingdom of David to general messianic-eschatological elements in conjunction with the return of the cross taken by the Persians from Jerusalem (630). Scholars plausibly conjecture that Heraclius thereby paralleled the restoration of the cross with King David's recovery of the Ark of the Covenant in order to place a New Covenant (with the Romans) alongside the Old Covenant; for this reason, he assumed the Davidic royal title *basileús*.[65] As "savior of the world" (*kosmorhýstes* – a term apparently created specifically for Heraclius),[66] the messianic ruler set about establishing a new order in a world shaken for decades by natural disasters, wars, and other catastrophes.

8 Concluding Remarks

In conclusion, we may ask what role exogenous factors – general climate deterioration and natural and military disasters – actually played in the transition from Antiquity to the Middle Ages; is the conventional epochal caesura the result of environmental change?

We probably cannot draw such direct, linear connections. On the one hand, change from one epoch to another is generally too complex a historical phenomenon to be attributed to a particular cause. On the other, natural events as such cannot bring about historical change. They become catastrophes only at the moment that they affect people: the involvement of people is what allows us to classify a specific phenomenon as a disaster; we are thus observing processes that are situated on the threshold between nature and culture and affect societies variously, depending on the level of each one's vulnerability. When a society, however, incorporates such phenomena more and more into its everyday life by developing a disaster culture, it becomes ever more problematic to speak of "natural" disasters. Eastern Roman disaster cultures reached the limits of their capacities in the 6th and 7th centuries. But this was also less a consequence of the high frequency and severity of the individual events than a consequence of the specific outlook with which they were received, which served as the basis of an established conceptual and coping framework. Only after

---

64   Konidaris, "Die Novellen des Kaisers Herakleios", pp. 33–106, here p. 84; on the date of the novel, see ibid. p. 58f.
65   Kresten, "Oktateuch-Probleme", p. 504, note 13; Kresten, "Herakleios", pp. 178–79.
66   Meier, "Herakles", p. 185.

disappointed expectations of the Second Coming lost their persuasive force did the disasters transform into catalysts for rapid historical change – albeit indirectly. The key change occurred in specific areas: in those overtaken by the unfolding "mentality crisis" and the reaction to it that we can trace to the mid-6th century, namely, liturgification as an overarching process of consolidation (the demographic and economic consequences, in contrast, were not ultimately insurmountable, despite their severity). To that extent, the disasters from the late 5th to the 7th century, as manifestations of dramatically worse external living conditions, indeed played a key part in the transformation of Late Antiquity into the Early Middle Ages, but attributing the complex social, cultural, and religious changes of these decades to them directly falls far short of an adequate explanation.

Bibliography

Primary Sources

Chronicon Paschale, ed. L. Dindorf, *Chronicon Paschale ad Exemplar Vaticanum*, vol. 1, Bonn 1832.

George of Pisidia, *Heraclias/Expeditio Persica*, ed. L. Tartaglia, *Carmi di Giorgio di Pisidia*, Turin 1998.

John of Ephesus, *Church History*, trans. W. Witakowski, *Pseudo-Dionysios of Tel-Mahre. Chronicle, Part III*, Liverpool 1996.

John Malalas, *Chronicle*, ed. I. Thurn, *Ioannis Malalae Chronographia*, Berlin/New York 2000.

Procopius, *Bellum Vandalicum*, ed. J. Haury (ed. corr. G. Wirth), *Procopii Caesariensis Opera Omnia*, vols. 1–4, Leipzig 1963 (vols. 1–3)/1964 (vol. 4).

Theophanes, *Chronicle*, ed. C. de Boor, *Theophanis Chronographia*, vol. 1, Leipzig 1883, repr. Hildesheim 1963.

Theophylactus Simocates, *History*, ed. C. de Boor/P. Wirth, *Theophylacti Simocattae Historiae*, Stuttgart ²1972.

Secondary Literature

Arjava, A., "The Mystery Cloud of 536 CE in the Mediterranean Sources", *Dumbarton Oaks Papers* 59 (2005), 73–94.

Ashbrook, H.S., "Asceticism in Adversity: An Early Byzantine Experience", *Byzantine and Modern Greek Studies* 6 (1980), 1–11.

Baillie, M., *Exodus to Arthur: Catastrophic Encounters with Comets*, London 2000.

Bankoff, G., *Cultures of Disaster. Society and Natural Hazards in the Philippines*, London 2003.

Bankoff, G./Frerks, G./Hilhorst, D. (eds.), *Mapping Vulnerability. Disasters, Development & People*, London/Sterling VA 2004.

Börm, H., "Justinians Triumph und Belisars Erniedrigung. Überlegungen zum Verhältnis zwischen Kaiser und Militär im späten Römischen Reich", *Chiron* 43 (2013), 63–91.

Brandes, W., "Anastasios ὁ δίκορος: Endzeiterwartung und Kaiserkritik in Byzanz um 500", *Byzantinische Zeitschrift* 90 (1997), 24–63.

Bulst, N., "Heiligenverehrung in Pestzeiten. Soziale und religiöse Reaktionen auf die spätmittelalterlichen Pestepidemien", in: A. Löther/U. Meier et al. (eds.), *Mundus in imagine. Bildersprache und Lebenswelten im Mittelalter. Festgabe für Klaus Schreiner*, Munich 1996, pp. 63–91.

Büntgen, U./McCormick, M., et al., "Cooling and Societal Change during the Late Antique Little Ice Age from 536 to around 660 AD", *Nature Geoscience* 9, 2016 [NGEO2652], 231–236.

Cameron, Av., "An Emperor's Abdication", *Byzantinoslavica* 37 (1976), 161–167.

Cameron, Av., "Images of Authority: Elites and Icons in Late Sixth-Century Byzantium", *Past & Present* 84 (1979), 3–35.

Cameron, Av., "The Theotokos in Sixth-Century Constantinople", *Journal of Theological Studies* 29 (1978), 79–108.

Evans, J.A.S., *The Age of Justinian. The Circumstances of Imperial Power*, London/New York 1996.

Haldon, J., et. al., "The Climate and Environment of Byzantine Anatolia: Integrating Science, History, and Archaeology", *Journal of Interdisciplinary History* 45.2 (2014), 113–161.

Harper, K., *The Fate of Rome. Climate, Disease & the End of an Empire*, Princeton/Oxford 2017.

Hoffman, S.M./Oliver-Smith, A. (eds.), *Catastrophe and Culture*, Santa Fe 2002.

Izdebski, A., "Why Did Agriculture Flourish in the Late Antique East? The Role of Climate Fluctuations in the Development and Contraction of Agriculture in Asia Minor and the Middle East from the 4th till the 7th C. AD", *Millennium* 8 (2011), 291–312.

Izdebski, A./Mulryan, M. (eds.), *Environment and Society in the Long Late Antiquity*, Leiden/Boston 2019.

Kaegi, W.E., *Heraclius. Emperor of Byzantium*, Cambridge 2003.

Keys, D., *Catastrophe: An Investigation into the Origins of the Modern World*, London 2000.

Koder, J., "Historical Aspects of a Recession of Cultivated Land at the End of the Late Antiquity in the East Mediterranean", *Paläoklimaforschung – Paleoclimate Research* 10 (1994), 157–167.

Koder, J., "Climatic Change in the Fifth and Sixth Centuries?", in: P. Allen/E. Jeffreys (eds.), *The Sixth Century. End or Beginning?*, Brisbane 1996, 270–285.

Kresten, O., "Oktateuch-Probleme: Bemerkungen zu einer Neuerscheinung", *Byzantinische Zeitschrift* 84/85 (1991/92), 501–511.

Kresten, O., "Herakleios und der Titel βασιλεύς", in: Varia VII (= Poikila Byzantina 18), Bonn 2000, pp. 178–179.

Landes, R., "Lest the Millennium be Fulfilled: Apocalyptic Expectations and the Pattern of Western Chronography 100–800 CE", in: W. Verbeke/D. Verhelst/A. Welkenhuysen (eds.), *The Use and Abuse of Eschatology in the Middle Ages*, Leuven 1988, pp. 137–211.

Leppin, H., "(K)ein Zeitalter Justinians – Bemerkungen aus althistorischer Sicht zu Justinian in der jüngeren Forschung", *Historische Zeitschrift* 284 (2007), 659–686.

Leppin, H., *Justinian. Das christliche Experiment*, Stuttgart 2011.

Little, L.K. (ed.), *Plague and the End of Antiquity. The Pandemic of 541–750*, Cambridge 2006.

Maas, M. (ed.), *The Cambridge Companion to the Age of Justinian*, Cambridge 2005.

Magdalino, P., "The History of the Future and Its Uses: Prophecy, Policy and Propaganda", in: R. Beaton/Ch. Roueché (eds.), *The Making of Byzantine History. Studies Dedicated to Donald M. Nicol*, Aldershot 1993, pp. 3–34.

McCormick, M., *Eternal Victory. Triumphal Rulership in Late Antiquity, Byzantium and the Early Medieval West*, Cambridge u.a. 1986, ND 1990.

Meier, M., "Das Ende des Konsulats im Jahr 541/42 und seine Gründe. Kritische Anmerkungen zur Vorstellung eines 'Zeitalters Justinians'", *Zeitschrift für Papyrologie und Epigraphik* 138 (2002), 277–299.

Meier, M., *Das andere Zeitalter Justinians. Kontingenzerfahrung und Kontingenzbewältigung im 6. Jahrhundert n. Chr.*, Göttingen ²2004.

Meier, M., "Sind wir nicht alle heilig? Zum Konzept des 'Heiligen' (sacrum) in spätjustinianischer Zeit", *Millennium* 1 (2004), 133–164.

Meier, M., "Prokop, Agathias, die Pest und das 'Ende' der antiken Historiographie. Naturkatastrophen und Geschichtsschreibung in der ausgehenden Spätantike", *Historische Zeitschrift* 278 (2004), 281–310.

Meier, M., "Eschatologie und Kommunikation im 6. Jahrhundert n. Chr. – oder: Wie Osten und Westen beständig aneinander vorbei redeten", in: Brandes, W./ Schmieder, F. (eds.), *Endzeiten. Eschatologie in den monotheistischen Weltreligionen*, Berlin/New York 2008, 41–73.

Meier, M., "Ostrom-Byzanz, Spätantike-Mittelalter. Überlegungen zum 'Ende' der Antike im Osten des Römischen Reiches", *Millennium* 9 (2012), 187–253.

Meier, M., "Herakles – Herakleios – Christus. Georgios Pisides und der kosmorhýstes", in: Leppin, H., (ed.), *Antike Mythologie in christlichen Kontexten der Spätantike*, Berlin/Munich/Boston 2015, 167–192.

Meier, M., "The 'Justinianic Plague': the Economic Consequences of the Pandemic in the Eastern Roman Empire and its Cultural and Religious Effects", *Early Medieval Europe* 24 (2016), 267–292.

Meier, M., "Liturgification and Hyper-Sacralization. The Declining Importance of Imperial Piety in Constantinople between the 6th and 7th Centuries AD", in: Lanfranchi, G.-B./Rollinger, R., (eds.), *The Body of the King. The Staging of the Body of the Institutional Leader from Antiquity to Middle Ages in East and West*, Padua 2016, 227–246.

Meier, M., "The Justinianic Plague: An 'Inconsequential Pandemic'? A Reply", *Medizinhistorisches Journal* 55 (2020), 172–199.

Meier, M., *Geschichte der Völkerwanderung. Europa, Asien und Nordafrika vom 3. bis zum 8. Jahrhundert n. Chr.*, Munich, ^{8}2021.

Mordechai, L. et al., "The Justinianic Plague: An Inconsequential Pandemic?", *PNAS* 116 (2019), 25546–25554.

Morrisson, C., "Peuplement, économie, et société de l'Orient byzantin", in: C. Morrisson (ed.), *Le monde byzantin I: L'Empire romain d'Orient (330–641)*, Paris 2004, pp. 193–220.

Olster, D.M., *The Politics of Usurpation in the Seventh Century: Rhetoric and Revolution in Byzantium*, Amsterdam 1993.

Pfeilschifter, R., *Der Kaiser und Konstantinopel. Kommunikation und Konfliktaustrag in einer spätantiken Metropole*, Berlin/Boston 2013.

Preiser-Kapeller, J., *Der lange Sommer und die kleine Eiszeit. Klima, Pandemien und der Wandel der Alten Welt von 500 bis 1500 n. Chr.*, Vienna 2021.

Raum, Th., *Szenen eines Überlebenskampfes. Akteure und Handlungsspielräume im Imperium Romanum 610–630*, Stuttgart 2021.

Sarris, P., "Bubonic Plague in Byzantium. The Evidence of Non-Literary Sources", in: Little, L.K. (ed.), *Plague and the End of Antiquity. The Pandemic of 541–750*, Cambridge 2006, 119–132.

Sarris, P., "New Approaches to the 'Plague of Justinian'", *Past & Present* 254 (2021), 315–346.

Schenk, G.J., "Historical Disaster Research. State of Research, Concepts, Methods and Case Studies", *Historical Social Research* 32.3 (2007), 9–31.

Stathakopoulos, D., *Reconstructing the Climate of the Byzantine World: State of the Problem and Case Studies*, in: J. Laszlovszky/P. Szabó (eds.), *People and Nature in Historical Perspective*, Budapest 2003, pp. 247–61.

Stathakopoulos, D., *Famine and Pestilence in the Late Roman and Early Byzantine Empire. A Systematic Survey of Subsistence Crises and Epidemics*, Aldershot 2004.

Telelis, I.G., *Meteorologika Phainomena kai Klima sto Byzantio*, Athens 2004.

Viermann, N., *Herakleios, der schwitzende Kaiser. Die oströmische Monarchie in der ausgehenden Spätantike*, Berlin/Boston 2021.

Volbach, W.F., *Elfenbeinarbeiten der Spätantike und des frühen Mittelalters*, Mainz ³1976.

Wickham, Chr., *Framing the Early Middle Ages. Europe and the* Mediterranean 400–800, Oxford 2005, repr. 2006.

Wisner, B./Blaikie, P./Cannon, T./Davis, I. (eds.), *At Risk. Natural Hazards, People's Vulnerability, and Disasters*, London/New York ²2008.

CHAPTER 15

The Medieval Climate Anomaly, the Oort Minimum, and Socio-Political Dynamics in the Eastern Mediterranean and the Byzantine Empire, 10th to 12th Century

Johannes Preiser-Kapeller

In memory of Ronnie Ellenblum (1952–2021)

∴

1 From the "Medieval Warm Period" to the "Medieval Climate Anomaly"[1]

The intellectual history of what was called the "Medieval Warm Period" began in 1959, when Hubert Lamb (1913–97), a pioneer of historical climatology, introduced the term for the time between the 10th and 13th centuries AD, based on his reading of medieval sources and the then-limited number of temperature reconstructions for England.[2] In 1964, using the same data, Lamb published an influential graph with the caption "temperatures (°C) prevailing in central England, 50 years averages", indicating that it represented rather rough estimates. Nevertheless, the suggestive power of the image, showing an impressive temperature mount of a "Medieval Warm Period" proved more influential than the caveats of Lamb.[3]

A further misinterpretation of the image was initiated when the Intergovernmental Panel on Climate Change (IPCC) in its *First Assessment Report* in 1990 used Lamb's graph for central England with the misleading caption "Schematic

---

1 For these two terms see also Pfister/Wanner, *Klima und Gesellschaft in Europa*.
2 Rohr/Camenisch/Pribyl, "European Middle Ages"; Summerhayes, *Palaeoclimatology*, p. 440; Pfister/Wanner, *Klima und Gesellschaft in Europa*, pp. 22–23.
3 Rohr/Camenisch/Pribyl, "European Middle Ages"; Summerhayes, *Palaeoclimatology*, p. 440.

diagrams of *global* temperature variations since the last thousand years".[4] This mistake has been repaired in all following IPCC assessment reports since 1996, which have presented much more refined and global temperature reconstructions. They illustrated that the scale and rate of modern-day global warming significantly excels the medieval one. Furthermore, the IPCC reports demonstrated that modern-day climate dynamics, in contrast to those in medieval times, cannot be explained by natural forcing only, but mainly emerge from the impact of human activities.[5]

Sceptics and deniers of anthropogenic climate change, however, remain unconvinced and prefer to use the now-outdated Lamb/IPCC graph of 1990. The same groups tend to maintain the traditional interpretation that the "Medieval Warm Period" fostered a "rise of the European civilization" with beneficial climatic conditions, when the Vikings colonized Greenland and wine was produced even in the north of England.[6] This serves their agenda in two ways: first, to demonstrate that the scale of modern-day global warming is not exceptional in comparison with the medieval one – and can be explained by natural fluctuations in the same way; and second, to argue that warm periods in general are beneficial for human societies, as they assume the medieval one generally was. To illustrate that earlier warm periods equalled or even excelled modern-day global warming, they use versions of the graph created by Lamb. Recently, Birgit Schneider has analysed in detail the various ways in which this and other images are used and abused in the debate on global warming. She demonstrates how deniers of anthropogenic climate change manipulated such graphs to obscure the actual rate and scale of the rise in global temperatures in the last decades by, for example, cutting off the curve at an earlier point in time.[7]

Based on an increasing number of proxy data,[8] recent scholarship has demonstrated nonetheless that the "Medieval Warm Period" between the 10th and 13th centuries AD was neither continuously warm nor "optimal" in Western

---

4   Summerhayes, *Palaeoclimatology*, p. 442.
5   Mathez/Smerdon, *Climate Change*, pp. 265–303; Summerhayes, *Palaeoclimatology*, pp. 442–43; Zalasiewicz/Williams, "Climate change through Earth history", pp. 59–61; Campbell, *The Great Transition*, pp. 36–38; Intergovernmental Panel on Climate Change, *Climate Change 2021*.
6   Summerhayes, *Palaeoclimatology*, p. 440.
7   Schneider, *Klimabilder*, pp. 235–82.
8   For an overview on these types of data see Mathez/Smerdon, *Climate Change*, pp. 229–38; Brönnimann/Pfister/White, "Archives of Nature and Archives of Societies"; Pfister/Wanner, *Klima und Gesellschaft in Europa*, pp. 16–20 and 118–31, as well as the relevant chapters in the present volume.

and Central Europe, not to mention other parts of the globe.[9] Therefore, they mostly resorted to the term "Medieval Climate Anomaly" (MCA). It marks a period of globally higher average temperatures than the preceding "Late Antique Cold Period" and the succeeding "Little Ice Age", but with strong differences in the regional manifestation of this global climate trend, and equally interrupted by decades of lower average temperatures, which can be connected to reduced solar activity, sometimes in combination with the atmospheric impacts of major volcanic eruptions (see below).[10]

2 Climate Oscillations, Proxy Data, and the Medieval Climate Anomaly

One factor in the temporal dynamics of the Medieval Climate Anomaly (and of global climate in general) were fluctuations in the sun's activity, which influenced the amount of solar irradiation (an essential form of energy input) that reached planet Earth. For solar activity, which correlates with the number of observable sunspots (with a higher number of these phenomena on the sun's surface indicating a higher amount of activity), a cyclic fluctuation of 11 years (the "Schwabe Cycle") has been observed. Further cycles at a longer term (such as the "Gleissberg Cycle" of between 70 and 100 years, for instance) contribute to the emergence of maxima and minima of solar activity over several decades. Systematic observations of sunspots are available from the 17th century AD onwards; for earlier periods, reconstructions of solar activity are based on the analysis of concentrations of isotopes of carbon and beryllium in ice cores and other proxies. The Medieval Climate Anomaly included two solar maxima between c.920 and 1020 as well as between c.1100 and 1200/50. Reduced solar activity (and therefore cooler global average temperatures), on the contrast, characterized the "Oort Minimum" (c.1010 to 1080), while the "Wolf Minimum" (c.1280 to 1345) already marked the transition from the Medieval Climate Anomaly to the "Little Ice Age".[11]

9   Adamson/Nash, "Climate History of Asia (Excluding China)". For a reconstruction of European summer temperatures, see for instance Luterbacher et al., "European summer temperatures".
10 Diaz et al., "Spatial and Temporal Characteristics"; Rohr/Camenisch/Pribyl, "European Middle Ages"; Summerhayes, *Palaeoclimatology*, pp. 442–48.
11 Usoskin, "A History of Solar Activity"; Lean, "Estimating Solar Irradiance since 850 CE", 135 and 142; Mathez/Smerdon, *Climate Change*, pp. 180–82; Summerhayes, *Palaeoclimatology*, pp. 455–64; Guiot et al., "Growing Season Temperatures"; Polovodova Asteman/Filipsson/Nordberg, "Tracing winter temperatures"; Cohen/Stanhill, "Changes in the

Large volcanic eruptions had short-term climatic effects. Eruptive ejections of aerosols caused atmospheric phenomena, which disquieted contemporary observers (such as the "dust veil" of the year AD 536 described in Greek and Latin sources[12]). They could contribute to cooler temperatures over several months due to the reduction of solar irradiation, but also other and regionally diverse climatic effects (decreased as well as increased temperatures, decreases as well as increases in precipitation). Thus, various forms of weather extremes could emerge from the atmospheric perturbations caused by volcanic eruptions. They could initiate short-term climatic fluctuations also during periods otherwise characterized by higher and more stable temperature conditions, as during the above-mentioned solar maxima, such as an eruption described in written sources and also identified by its chemical signature in ice cores from Greenland for the year 939 (possibly coming from the Eldgjá on Iceland), as well as a "cluster" of eruptions (maybe in Iceland and Japan) between 1108 and 1110 (see the reconstruction of European summer temperatures in these years in Fig. 15.1). Furthermore, large volcanic eruption could aggravate the effects of minima of solar activity; the huge eruption of 1257 (now attributed to Samalas on Lombok island in modern-day Indonesia) together with following volcanic events contributed on top of the incipient Wolf Solar Minimum to the transition towards the "Little Ice Age" in the late 13th century (see Fig. 15.1).[13]

The actual regional effects of solar and volcanic climate forcing depended on their impact on regular climate oscillations between oceans and continents. For weather conditions in western Afro-Eurasia, the Northern Atlantic Oscillations (NAO) plays a decisive role. Its dynamics are measured in an index of the differences in air pressure between the Icelandic Low and the high over the Azores (see map in Fig. 15.2). A high difference between these air-pressure regions (resulting in a positive NAO index) usually causes warmer and wetter weather in Western and Central Europe, but drier conditions in the Mediterranean. A low difference, in contrast, results in colder and drier weather in Western and Central Europe, but more humid conditions in the

---

 Sun's radiation", pp. 691–705; Dorman, "Space weather and cosmic ray effects", pp. 713–31 (with some interesting, but problematic attempts to directly correlate wheat prices in late medieval England and Europe with reconstructions of solar activity); Campbell, *The Great Transition*, pp. 37–38, 50–54.

12 See the chapter by Mischa Meier in the present volume.

13 Sigl, "Timing and Climate Forcing"; Guillet, "Climatic and societal impacts"; Büntgen et al., "Cooling and societal change"; Mathez/Smerdon, *Climate Change*, pp. 176–80; Summerhayes, *Palaeoclimatology*, pp. 466–68; Stenchikov, "The role of volcanic activity"; Riede, "Doing palaeo-social volcanology"; Campbell, *The Great Transition*, pp. 55–58; Wozniak, *Naturereignisse im frühen Mittelalter*, pp. 315–19; Pfister/Wanner, *Klima und Gesellschaft in Europa*, pp. 180–82.

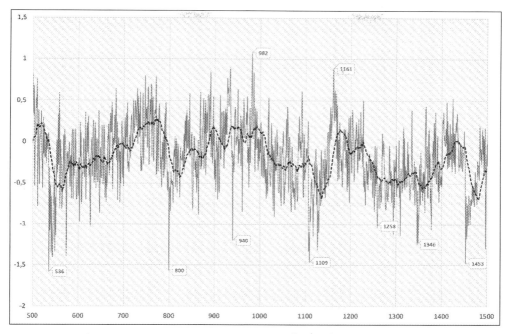

FIGURE 15.1   Average summer temperatures in Western and Central Europe AD 500–1500, (in comparison with the average AD 1960–1990) reconstructed on the basis of tree rings
DATA: LUTERBACHER ET AL., "EUROPEAN SUMMER TEMPERATURES"; GRAPH: J. PREISER-KAPELLER, OEAW, 2022

Mediterranean. For the more stable periods of the Medieval Climate Anomaly, such as around AD 950 or AD 1140, a predominantly positive NAO index was reconstructed, while weaker NAO effects have been identified during the Oort Solar Minimum in the mid-11th century.[14]

In the Mediterranean, however, a further "seesaw" of precipitation conditions was observed between the west and the east of the basin, with the former often affected by more arid conditions during positive NAO periods of the Medieval Climate Anomaly, while the latter, sometimes despite the impact of the NAO, experienced more humid ones. These differences can be connected to the impacts of further climate patterns on the Eastern Mediterranean: the so-called "North Sea–Caspian Pattern" (NCP) is defined by the pressure

14   Goosse et al., "The medieval climate anomaly in Europe"; Guiot et al., "Growing Season Temperatures"; Polovodova Asteman/Filipsson/Nordberg, "Tracing winter temperatures"; Lüning et al., "Hydroclimate in Africa"; Mathez/Smerdon, *Climate Change*, pp. 91–97; Summerhayes, *Palaeoclimatology*, pp. 437–38, 464–65; Campbell, The Great Transition, pp. 45–48; Pfister/Wanner, *Klima und Gesellschaft in Europa*, pp. 38–40.

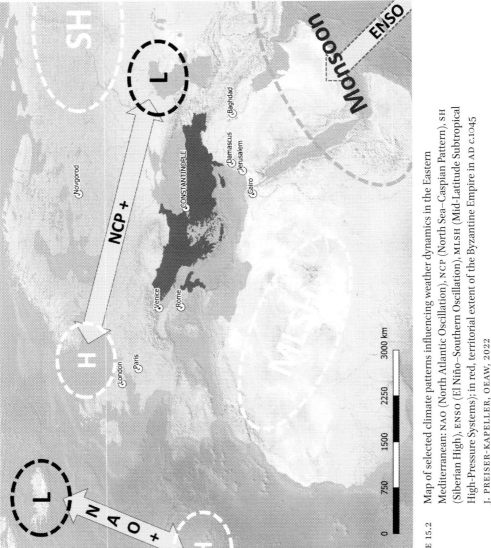

FIGURE 15.2 Map of selected climate patterns influencing weather dynamics in the Eastern Mediterranean: NAO (North Atlantic Oscillation), NCP (North Sea–Caspian Pattern), SH (Siberian High), ENSO (El Niño–Southern Oscillation), MLSH (Mid-Latitude Subtropical High-Pressure Systems); in red, territorial extent of the Byzantine Empire in AD c.1045

J. PREISER-KAPELLER, OEAW, 2022

difference between the North Sea and the Caspian Sea (see Fig. 15.2); a positive NCP brings cool and dry regional winter conditions to the central and eastern Mediterranean, while a negative NCP brings warm and wet ones. Furthermore, a strong Siberian High (see Fig. 15.2) could cause unusually cold airflow from Inner Eurasia to the eastern Mediterranean and the Middle East, contributing to otherwise rare phenomena such as snowfall and frost in Baghdad, which were described several times during the Oort Minimum of the 11th century (see below).[15]

A further oscillation pattern with even wider ranging impacts than the NAO is the El Niño–Southern Oscillation (ENSO), described as the interplay between an area usually characterized by low air pressure and warm water temperatures in the western Pacific (around modern-day Indonesia) and an area of high air pressure and cooler temperatures off the western coast of South America. These "usual" conditions characterize the "neutral" state of the Southern Oscillation. The "El Niño" state (usually observed around Christmas off the coast of Peru, hence the name) is characterized by cooler than normal conditions in the western Pacific and warmer ones in the eastern Pacific. Its counterpart, "La Niña", is characterized by warmer than normal water temperatures in the western Pacific warmer and cooler ones in the eastern Pacific. These different states of the Southern Oscillation bring about significant changes in the strength of winds and the distribution of precipitation from the ocean towards the continents. As the climatologists Mathez and Smerdon explain:

> El Niño commonly creates severe droughts in Australia, Indonesia, southern Africa, and the African Sahel (the southern borderland for the Sahara Desert stretching from Senegal in the west to Sudan in the east); weakens the South Asian monsoon; and brings increased winter precipitation to parts of North America. (...) La Niña similarly has significant global impacts. It causes droughts across the western United States and Mexico, brings heavy rain to northwestern Australia and Indonesia during the boreal (Northern Hemisphere) winter, and enhances the South Asian monsoon during the boreal summer.[16]

---

15 Roberts et al., "Palaeolimnological evidence"; Katrantsiotis, "Eastern Mediterranean hydroclimate reconstruction"; Kushnir/Stein, "Medieval Climate in the Eastern Mediterranean".
16 Mathez/Smerdon, *Climate Change*, pp. 71–73.

For the southwest of today's USA, recurring "megadroughts" during the 10th to 13th centuries, which have been reconstructed on the basis of tree rings and affected the Puebloan cultures (with the famous site of Mesa Verde in modern-day Colorado), have been connected with strong La Niña events, such as around AD 936, 1034, 1150 and 1253. A severe El Niño, in contrast, in the years around AD 1060, most probably affected precipitation conditions in East Africa (via the Monsoon system, see Fig. 15.2) and thereby contributed to a series of very low Nile floods in Egypt; it is equally reflected in proxy data from the Peruvian Andes.[17] Another sequence of low Nile floods around 1200 has been equally connected with a 30-year period of severe El Niños between AD 1180 and 1210, which accompanied a general change towards more arid conditions in the Eastern Mediterranean in the late 12th and early 13th centuries.[18]

3   The Time of the Medieval Climate Anomaly in the Byzantine Empire: "Economic Expansion" …

Thus, even across medieval Europe and the Mediterranean, not to mention other regions of the globe, nothing like a climatically coherent "Medieval Optimum" from the 10th to the 13th centuries can be identified from the palaeoclimatological data. Nevertheless, for Western and Central Europe, shorter periods (during the solar maxima, for instance) of on average more "beneficial" and stable temperature and precipitation conditions existed and were accompanied by significant demographic and economic growth.[19]

Similar phenomena of an "Economic Expansion in the Byzantine Empire" between 900 and 1200, especially since the publication of the monograph

---

17   Mathez/Smerdon, *Climate Change*, pp. 71–88 and 252–53 on the megadroughts in North America. For the dynamics of ENSO during the medieval centuries see Campbell, *The Great Transition*, pp. 38–45, and Grove/Adamson, *El Niño in World History*, pp. 5, 20, 51–53, also on the correlation with the Nile floods. On the latter, see equally Hassan, "Extreme Nile floods"; Zaroug/Eltahir/Giorgi, "Droughts and floods"; Nash et al., "African hydroclimatic variability"; Lüning et al., "Hydroclimate in Africa"; Kushnir/Stein, "Medieval Climate in the Eastern Mediterranean", p. 9–11; Henke/Lambert/Charman, "Was the Little Ice Age more or less El Niño-like than the Medieval Climate Anomaly".

18   Grove/Adamson, *El Niño in World History*, pp. 52–55; Nash et al., "African hydroclimatic variability"; Hassan, "Extreme Nile floods"; Nicholson, "A Multi-Century History of Drought".

19   Campbell, *The Great Transition*, pp. 58–86; Pfister/Wanner, *Klima und Gesellschaft in Europa*, pp. 274–84.

under this title by J.A. Harvey in 1989[20] (and in contrast to earlier scholarship, which linked the severe political crisis of Byzantium in the second half of the 11th century with an assumed economic one[21]), have been identified on the basis of written sources (such as the village tax charters from Mt. Athos, for instance) and an increasing number of archaeological evidence (coin finds, settlement numbers stemming from surveys such as in Laconia or Boeotia).[22] In the fundamental "Economic History of Byzantium" in 2002, the editor Angeliki E. Laiou (1941–2008) summed up the new consensus:

> Over the past few decades, the eleventh and twelfth centuries have been recognized as periods of economic growth, a judgment that goes counter to most of the earlier historiography. The main reason for the earlier perception, held by eminent historians, was that they saw Byzantium from the viewpoint of the state and considered that the military defeats and evident decline of the state in the late eleventh century, as well as the territorial retraction in the twelfth century, were paralleled by a decline in the economy. Instead, it has been recognized that, for the first time in Byzantine history, there was a disjunction between military and territorial developments on the one hand and economic activity on the other. (...) Finally, historians now look with a different eye at developments that in the past had been considered negatively: all devaluations [of the nomisma] had been thought bad, whereas now we differentiate between "devaluations of expansion" and those that result from a crisis; the large estate, once thought to signal and promote the collapse of Byzantium and its agrarian base, is now seen as a factor in economic expansion.[23]

Without doubt, the stabilization of the Byzantine frontiers *vis-à-vis* the Arabs in Eastern Asia Minor and the Bulgarians on the Balkans (respectively the conquest of the Arab Emirate on Crete in 961) under the so-called "Macedonian" dynasty founded by Emperor Basil I (867–86) allowed for a recovery of agricultural activities.[24] But especially the last aspect mentioned by Laiou (that is

---

20 Harvey, *Economic Expansion in the Byzantine Empire*. See also Harvey, "The Byzantine Economy in an International Context"; Preiser-Kapeller, "Byzantium 1025–1204", p. 65.
21 See, for instance, Svoronos, *Etudes sur l'organisation intérieure*, pp. 348–50 (originally published in 1966).
22 For an overview on the evidence especially for Greece see also Olson, *Environment and Society in Byzantium*, pp. 145–58.
23 Laiou, "The Byzantine Economy", p. 1150. See also Kaplan/Morrisson, "L'économie byzantine: perspectives historiographiques"; Prigent, "The Mobilisation of Fiscal Resources".
24 Kaldellis, *Streams of Gold*, p. 21; Olson, *Environment and Society in Byzantium*, pp. 144–45.

the role of the "large estates" in the agricultural dynamics of this time, as well as the actual scale of the economic growth) remain controversial; in 2008, for instance, Mark Whittow (1957–2017) argued:

> Rather than thinking of peasants needing to be forced onto the market and so launching an economic revolution, we should perhaps be thinking of a world where landowning aristocrats hijacked the fruits of pioneering peasant enterprise. (...) But if the economic revival of the middle Byzantine period was in fact driven from below, these vast estates might look more like a stifling of Byzantine economic enterprise. Did the great estates necessarily promote local and regional economic enterprise, or did they dampen such activity in favour of self-sufficiency and the provision of goods in kind to feed their dependents in the capital? Is the growth of Latin commerce a sign of the economic vitality of Byzantium, or rather a symptom of an economy where Byzantine traders were disadvantaged in favour of outsiders servicing the great estates?[25]

Recently, findings from palynology (pollen data) have confirmed an increase in agricultural cultivation for various regions of the Byzantine Empire from the late 9th century (Asia Minor) and 10th century (Southern Balkans) onwards after a significant decrease between the 6th and 8th centuries (see Figs. 15.4 and 15.5 for the case of cereals). They also indicate regional and local variations with regard to the increase in the cultivation of grain, olives and wine or a focus on pasturage and animal husbandry.[26] What this data cannot tell us, however, is whether the expansion of agriculture in the area around the pollen sites stemmed from the initiatives of communities of small-scale peasants, large noble or monastic estates, or imperial domains (or whether they tell us about the respective shares of these forms of economic organization in the growth).

Most recently, Alexander Olson in his study on oak and olive cultivation in the middle Byzantine period has renewed the argument that:

> greater pressure for surplus from elite figures led to economic and demographic growth, not the other way around. Put another way, the economic

---

25   Whittow, "The Middle Byzantine Economy", pp. 487–91. For an illuminating study on peasant strategies in pre-mechanized Mediterranean farming see Halstead, *Two Oxen Ahead*.
26   Izdebski/Koloch/Słoczyński, "Exploring Byzantine and Ottoman economic history"; Olson, *Environment and Society in Byzantium*, pp. 45–46, 65–71.

upsurge and agricultural intensification were the consequences of a more demanding elite rather than demographic growth.[27]

Furthermore, he identifies signs of slow agricultural growth and modest modifications of the landscape in the 10th- and 11th-century Aegean provinces; in his opinion, more significant economic dynamics only started in the late 11th century with:

> a Komnenian-led Byzantine state demanding more tax revenue, an emerging class of big landowners seeking rent, the presence of Italian merchants permitted to trade across the Aegean's waters, and peasants pressured to produce a surplus that garnered coins on the market.[28]

Surprisingly, in his otherwise excellent monograph, Olson largely ignored the earlier studies of the eminent historian of medieval Mediterranean trade and economy David Jacoby (1928–2018), who in one of his last papers on the Peloponnese summed up his earlier deliberations on 11th century agricultural dynamics, which suggest a different interpretation, at least for this region:

> It is commonly assumed that Italian merchants were the initiators of large-scale commercial exports of oil from the Peloponnese in the twelfth century. This proposition is rather implausible. It rests on skewed evidence – namely, the chance survival of a few Venetian charters and the absence of similar Byzantine documentation. (…) In short, there is good reason to believe that the export of foodstuffs from the Peloponnese and other provinces of the empire to Constantinople was likely initiated by large Byzantine landowners, merchants, and carriers, attentive to market demand. (…) We may safely assume, therefore, that [local archontes] encouraged the extension [of olive cultivation], both on their own demesne and on the peasants' land and that the peasants shared their market-oriented approach. The contention that Byzantine peasants produced surpluses only to pay their taxes in cash may be safely dismissed for the twelfth-century Peloponnese, even if correct for other Byzantine regions and other periods.[29]

---

27 Olson, *Environment and Society in Byzantium*, p. 197.
28 Olson, *Environment and Society in Byzantium*, p. 178.
29 Jacoby, "Rural Exploitation", pp. 237–38.

Also, the above-mentioned pollen data suggest the beginnings of significant agricultural growth already in the 10th and 11th centuries (see Fig. 15.4 and Fig. 15.5), a process intensified by Komnenian state activity and Italian merchants but not dependent on them to the extent suggested by Olson. Following Jacoby, we may assume a more complex interplay between the initiatives of large-, medium- and small-scale landowners and of the state (see also the illustrative example of the conflict between the monastery of Kolobou and the village of Siderokausia already of the year 995 below) – with shifting weights between these actors, however, as further discussed below. Yet, the share of climatic factors for these dynamics remains to be determined; Olson, for instance, sceptically, but – on the current basis of knowledge – legitimately states that:

> while I agree that climate change can have massive (even catastrophic) implications for people and plant life in various times and places, I privilege people's choices and botanical agency over climate as explanations for changes in the vegetative cover of the Aegean Basin.[30]

Nevertheless, recent studies, such as for Western Europe, have identified "beneficial" long-term climatic trends for the Byzantine territories during some periods of the Medieval Climate Anomaly based on proxy data. In 2016, Elena Xoplaki and her co-authors summed up the evidence on "the Medieval Climate Anomaly and Byzantium". They combined the above-mentioned evidence for economic and demographic growth in Byzantium between AD 850 and 1300 with new findings from palynology. Furthermore, they provided an overview on the "palaeoclimate evidence for the medieval Byzantine region", including "documentary textual evidence" (building on the pioneering work of Ioannis Telelis[31]) and "natural proxies" for the Balkans and Asia Minor. On this basis, they draw "potential links between climatic and societal changes that took place during specific periods in Byzantium", such as correlations between "a long-term trend towards wetter conditions in AD c.850–1000 in western Anatolia", and "stable and relatively warm-wet conditions in northern Greece AD 1000–1100", and periods of agricultural expansion in these regions (see the map in Fig. 15.3 for some proxy data sites).[32]

---

30 Olson, *Environment and Society in Byzantium*, pp. 13–14.

31 Esp. the systematic catalogue of meteorological phenomena described in Byzantine and other sources in Telelis, *Μετεωρολογικά φαινόμενα*. On this basis, a list (in English) with short entries was created for Haldon al., "The Climate and Environment of Byzantine Anatolia", pp. 154–60. See also Telelis, "Climatic fluctuations in the Eastern Mediterranean", pp. 167–207.

32 Xoplaki et al., "The Medieval Climate Anomaly and Byzantium", pp. 229–52. Also, the oxygen isotope data from Lake Nar in Cappadocia suggest a change towards a more humid

THE MEDIEVAL CLIMATE ANOMALY

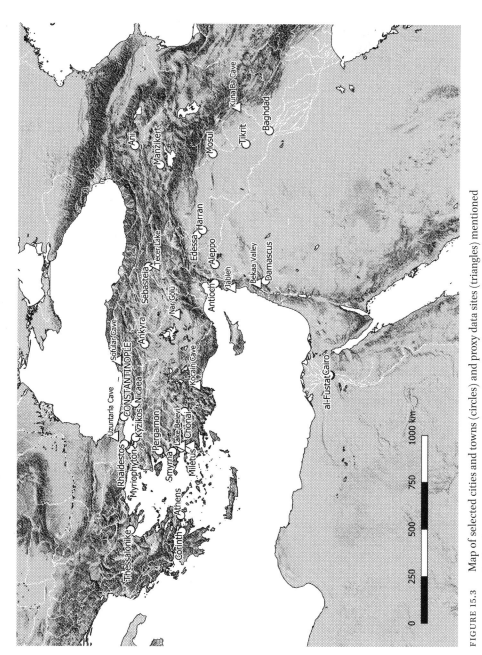

FIGURE 15.3 Map of selected cities and towns (circles) and proxy data sites (triangles) mentioned in the chapter
J. PREISER-KAPELLER, OEAW, 2022

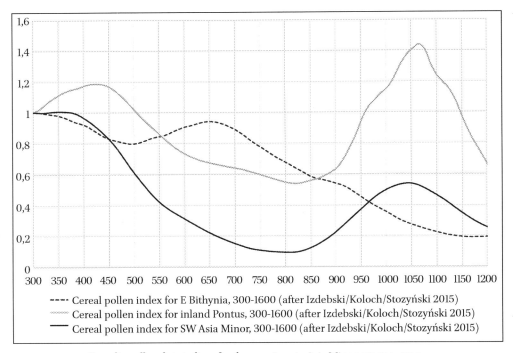

FIGURE 15.4   Cerealia pollen data indices for three regions in Asia Minor, AD 300–1200
DATA: IZDEBSKI/KOLOCH/SŁOCZYŃSKI, "EXPLORING BYZANTINE AND OTTOMAN ECONOMIC HISTORY"; GRAPH: J. PREISER-KAPELLER, OEAW, 2022

In the same volume, Alexandra Gogou and her co-authors provided additional evidence from the northern Aegean. Based on the analysis of a marine record from the Athos basin in Northern Greece, the authors reconstructed changes of sea-surface temperatures (SST) and other palaeo-environmental factors. Their data suggests a cooling trend from AD c.500 to 850, followed by a warming trend from AD c.850 to 950 in the Northern Aegean. Another positive trend of SST was identified from the end of the 11th century onwards, while the time from AD c.1250 to 1400 was, according to Gogou and her co-authors, characterized by "arid-like conditions", with another transition "towards more humid conditions" after AD c.1400.[33]

trend in the mid-9th century, see Woodbridge/Roberts, "Late Holocene climate"; Dean et al., "Palaeo-seasonality of the last two millennia".

33   Gogou et al., "Climate variability and socio-environmental changes". See also Olson, *Environment and Society in Byzantium*, pp. 13–14.

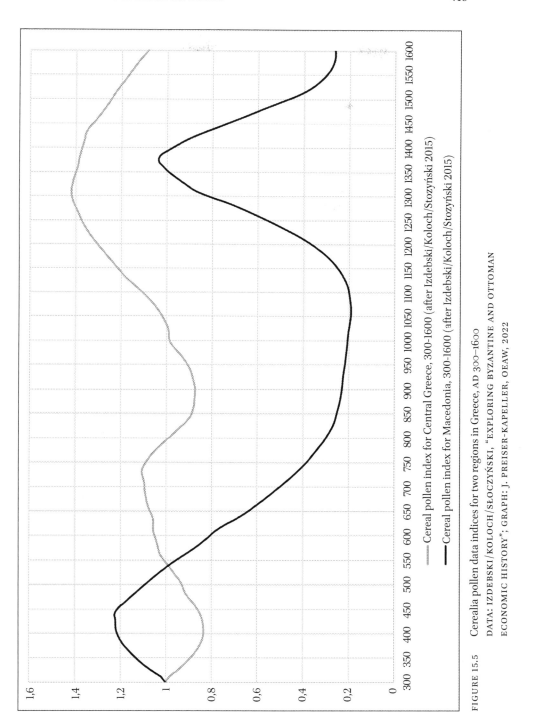

FIGURE 15.5   Cerealia pollen data indices for two regions in Greece, AD 300–1600
DATA: IZDEBSKI/KOLOCH/SŁOCZYŃSKI, "EXPLORING BYZANTINE AND OTTOMAN ECONOMIC HISTORY"; GRAPH: J. PREISER-KAPELLER, OEAW, 2022

More recent data from the southwestern Peloponnese published by Christos Katrantsiotis and his co-authors confirms these findings, with wetter conditions accompanying the transition to the Medieval Climate Anomaly in Southern Greece, with the period from 850 to 1050 reconstructed as relatively wet. The decades between c.1050 and 1150, however, were reconstructed as more arid.[34]

4   ... or a "Collapse of the Eastern Mediterranean"?

This later period partly overlaps with the already mentioned Oort Solar Minimum of the 11th century, which in general was characterized by cooler average temperatures and a higher number of weather extremes.[35] Proxy data such as those published by Katrantsiotis, as well as carbon isotope data from speleothems in the Kocain Cave in Southwestern Turkey and the Uzuntarla Cave in the European part of Turkey (see map in Fig. 15.3), indicate a general change towards cooler and more unstable conditions in the early 11th century.[36] In addition, written sources provide us with more or less detailed descriptions of weather anomalies and their sometimes catastrophic impacts in the form of harvest failures, rising prices and famines, accompanied by plagues of locusts or rodents and diseases among humans and animals (see below).

Based on some of these sources, Ronnie Ellenblum (1952–2021) in 2012 published a monograph on "The Collapse of the Eastern Mediterranean", which identified climate change as a prime mover for a political and economic "Decline of the East" (especially Abbasid/Buyid Mesopotamia, Fatimid Egypt and Byzantium) in the 11th century.[37] This counter-scenario to the above-mentioned notion of "Economic Expansion" has proven quite influential to this day,[38] despite strong criticism by several scholars of the rather monocausal and often insufficiently documented narrative of Ellenblum, including by myself.[39] Recently, the "collapse of the Eastern Mediterranean" has even

---

34   Katrantsiotis, "Eastern Mediterranean hydroclimate reconstruction".
35   Kushnir/Stein, "Medieval Climate in the Eastern Mediterranean", pp. 3, 11–12.
36   Göktürk, *Climate in the Eastern Mediterranean*, and most recently Jacobson et al., "Heterogenous Late Holocene Climate".
37   Ellenblum, *The Collapse of the Eastern Mediterranean*.
38   See for instance Kushnir/Stein, "Medieval Climate in the Eastern Mediterranean", pp. 11–12 (the authors refer to my earlier study ["A Collapse of the Eastern Mediterranean?"], which critically re-evaluated Ellenblum's book, on 20, n. 30, but did not take into consideration its findings), or Wozniak, *Naturereignisse im frühen Mittelalter*, pp. 493–94.
39   The review on Ellenblum's book by S. White in: *Mediterranean Historical Review* 28 (2013), pp. 70–72. Cf. also the reviews by S. Harris in: *Journal of Historical Geography* 42 (2013), pp. 218–19, by A. Izdebski in: *Annales ESC* 72 (2017), pp. 1168–70, and especially

been connected with the end of the "classical" period of Islam or an expanded "Long Late Antiquity" covering the entire first millennium AD.[40]

Ellenblum – deliberately – largely ignored the growing amount of natural scientific proxy data, which in his opinion could only record long-term trends, but not severe short-term shocks and supply shortfalls, which were only described in the written sources (what Christian Pfister has called the "archives of society"[41]). In his opinion, these shortfalls contributed to the destabilization of regimes in Baghdad, Cairo, or Constantinople or the collapse of infrastructures and communities.[42] Ellenblum's criticism is legitimate to a certain extent; several types of proxies such as pollen data from lake sediments often allow only for a reconstruction of dynamics at a time scale of centuries or several decades.[43] And even if tree rings or fine-graded sediments enable annual reconstructions of temperature or precipitation conditions, their spatial coverage or the seasonality of their signal (tree rings, depending on latitude and altitude, indicate precipitation mainly for the respective growing season, for instance) do not allow for a correlation with weather extremes described in written sources for other regions or times of the year.[44] However, so too the corpus of historiographical evidence is characterized by a highly unequal temporal and, especially, spatial resolution, so that the observation points of authors give us much more information on extreme events for the capitals of Baghdad, Cairo, and Constantinople and their environs than for other regions of the Abbasid/Buyid, Fatimid, or Byzantine empires.[45] Furthermore, descriptions

---

Preiser-Kapeller, "A Collapse of the Eastern Mediterranean?". See also Kaldellis, *Streams of Gold*, p. xxxi, who states: "Recent efforts to write narrative history from a climatological angle seem to be reductive and fail to explain Byzantine expansion in an age of supposed regional collapse".

40 Fowden, *Before and after Muḥammad*; Bauer, *Warum es kein islamisches Mittelalter gab*.
41 On the value of written evidence for the reconstruction of climates of the past and the problems of their interpretation see Brönnimann/Pfister/White, "Archives of Nature and Archives of Societies"; Pfister/Wanner, *Klima und Gesellschaft in Europa*, pp. 131–42; Nash, "Climate indices".
42 See also the posthumous publication Chipman/Avni/Ellenblum, "Collapse, affluence, and collapse", where it is stated already in the abstract: "Well-dated historical sources are the only way to follow the climatic and societal occurrences in a yearly resolution. No proxy data are sensitive enough to detect such changes and to reconstruct the historical and social processes that followed the climatic anomalies."
43 Izdebski/Koloch/Słoczyński, "Exploring Byzantine and Ottoman economic history".
44 Xoplaki et al., "Modelling Climate and Societal Resilience", for the unequal spatial distribution of proxies in the Eastern Mediterranean, as well as the relevant contribution in the present volume.
45 Grotzfeld, "Klimageschichte des Vorderen Orients"; Vogt et al., "Assessing the Medieval Climate Anomaly in the Middle East"; Xoplaki et al. "The Medieval Climate Anomaly and Byzantium", p. 239.

of meteorological phenomena (which in the tradition of antiquity include not only weather conditions but equally other celestial signs such as comets, meteors, or eclipses[46]) as well as epidemics and famines were included into histories and chronicles never as mere factual reports, but always serving narrative purposes. Often, they stem from a "moral meteorology", which attributes portents and catastrophes to the flaws and misdoings of individuals rulers, elites, or societies at large – of the past or present.[47] In addition, they were interpreted as harbingers of a king's fall or death or even the imminent end of the world (in the apocalyptic traditions of Judaism, Christianity, or Islam). In particular, the late 10th and early 11th century, with the turn of the first millennium since the birth of Jesus Christ, the 1000th anniversary of his crucifixion and resurrection (dated to around 1030) and other significant dates identified by studious calculators, provided several anchor points for such interpretative frameworks. Explicit in this regard are the historical works of the Byzantine Leo the Deacon (late 10th century) or the Armenian histories of Aristakēs Lastiverc'i (11th century) and Matthew of Edessa (12th century, see below).[48] The end-time atmosphere of their texts may have contributed to Ellenblum's development of the grim scenario of a "Collapse of the Eastern Mediterranean" in the 11th century.[49]

Furthermore, both the Byzantine Empire and the Fatimid Caliphate survived the 11th century, albeit on a modified and reduced power base; the written sources not only provide narratives of doom, but also hint at the resilience of societies and regimes, which, equally, could use crisis management as an opportunity to stabilise support and increase their legitimacy, at least from a symbolic point of view (see below). In addition, we have to contrast these short-term shocks with the undoubted long-term economic growth in 10th- to 11th-century Byzantium and Egypt, as documented in other forms of written sources (such as charters), archaeological evidence, and the increasing number of proxies such as pollen.[50]

---

46 Dagron, "Les diseurs d'événements"; Magdalino, "Astrology"; Tihon, "Astronomy".
47 For this term, see Elvin, "Who Was Responsible for the Weather". See also Burman, "The political ontology of climate change"; Pfister/Wanner, *Klima und Gesellschaft in Europa*, pp. 96–99.
48 Wozniak, *Naturereignisse im frühen Mittelalter*, pp. 715–31; Neville, *Guide to Byzantine Historical Writing*, pp. 124–25; Brandes, "Byzantine Predictions of the End of the World"; Andrews, *Matt'ēos Uṙhayec'i and His Chronicle*.
49 Ellenblum, *The Collapse of the Eastern Mediterranean*, p. 129.
50 On evidence of economic growth in Fatimid Egypt see Frantz-Murphy, "A New Interpretation of the Economic History of Medieval Egypt"; Frantz-Murphy, "Land Tenure in Egypt"; Mayerson, "The Role of Flax in Roman and Fatimid Egypt"; Udovitch, "International

In the following sections, we follow Ellenblum's lead to focus on the written sources for the 10th and 11th centuries, used (or more often not used) by Ellenblum, whose short chapter on Byzantium is relatively poorly documented when it comes to Byzantine historiography (as he himself acknowledged in personal communication), with a few passages from John Scylitzes, Scylitzes Continuatus, Michael Psellos, Michael Attaleiates, and Nicephorus Bryennios. Furthermore, he concentrated on the wars with the Pechenegs and Oghuz, so that not a single description of a climatic phenomenon from a Byzantine source is found in his chapter; characteristically, the few meteorological passages cited he took only from Matthew of Edessa.[51]

In addition to a close reading of relevant passages from Byzantine historiography, we try to find additional contemporary observations on climatic extremes from neighbouring regions of the Eastern Mediterranean and Middle East (with Telelis' ground-breaking catalogue once more serving as an indispensable guide[52]), but also Western Europe and China. Furthermore, historiography is augmented with information from imperial legislation and charters, as well as proxy data, if existing and significant. Thereby, we aim to put into perspective both Ellenblum's "collapse" as well as Harveys "economic expansion" through a more nuanced reconstruction of the short- and long-term results of the interplay between environmental and social dynamics.

5   The Winter of 927 as Short-Term Shock and the Long-Term Dynamics of Economic Growth and Socio-Political Changes in 10th- to 11th-Century Byzantium

As mentioned above, already during the more stable periods of the Medieval Climate Anomaly, such as the solar maximum between c.920 and 1000, short-term extremes left their traces in the sources. An often-discussed case is the "extreme winter" of AD 927/28. Already before, after the death of Tsar Simeon on 27 May 927, "the Bulgar nation was suffering a severe famine and a plague of locusts which was ravaging and depleting both the population and the

---

Trade"; Chipman/Avni/Ellenblum, "Collapse, affluence, and collapse", pp. 205–09. For Byzantium, see the evidence described above.

51   Ellenblum, *The Collapse of the Eastern Mediterranean*, pp. 123–46.
52   Telelis, Μετεωρολογικά φαινόμενα. See also now Telelis, "Byzantine Textual Sources". Ellenblum unfortunately did not use this systematic survey.

crops".[53] Then, in December 927, according to John Skylitzes (written in the late 11th century[54]):

> an intolerable winter suddenly set in; the earth was frozen for one hundred and twenty days. A cruel famine followed the winter, worse than any previous famine, and so many people died from the famine that the living were insufficient to bury the dead. This happened although the emperor [Romanos I Lakapenos] did his very best to relieve the situation, assuaging the ravages of the winter and the famine with good works and other aid of every kind.[55]

The winter of 927/28 – along the lines of Ellenblum's argument – illustrates the limits of the "archives of nature"; as Adam Izdebski, Lee Mordechai, and Sam White have pointed out, "no currently available palaeoclimate proxy confirms the occurrence of a strong winter cooling, or at least a potential increase in snowfall" exactly at the time of the winter of famine.[56] Isotope analyses for the Nar Gölü in Cappadocia (see map in Fig. 15.3) only hint at on average more snow-rich winters for the period from AD 921 to 1071 (which would also include the extreme winter of 927/28). Similarly, a long-term cooling trend can be observed in speleothem-data from the Kocain Cave in southwestern Anatolia (see Fig. 15.3).[57] We have, however, another observation on the severity of the winter 927/928 in the Chronography of Bar Hebraeus for Baghdad, who wrote that:

> there was a very bitterly cold winter again in Baghdad. It was so cold that the vinegar of the wine [the freezing point of five percent wine vinegar is -2 degrees Celsius] in the cellars and eggs, and oils, froze, and the trees withered.[58]

---

53   John Scylitzes, *Synopsis*, 18, ed. Thurn, pp. 222, 18–20; trans. Wortley, p. 215. Cf. also Telelis, Μετεωρολογικά φαινόμενα, N° 372. A chronological link of such calamities to the death of a ruler, however, is often used by medieval historians to underline the severity of the loss, see Wozniak, *Naturereignisse im frühen Mittelalter*, p. 576.

54   Neville, *Guide to Byzantine Historical Writing*, pp. 155–57.

55   John Scylitzes, *Synopsis*, 22, ed. Thurn, pp. 225, 90–95; trans. Wortley, p. 218. Cf. also Telelis, Μετεωρολογικά φαινόμενα, N° 373.

56   Izdebski/Mordechai/White, "The Social Burden of Resilience".

57   Woodbridge/Roberts, "Late Holocene climate"; Dean et al., "Palaeo-seasonality of the last two millennia". For the Kocain cave, see Göktürk, *Climate in the Eastern Mediterranean*, pp. 52–59, and most recently Jacobson et al., "Heterogenous Late Holocene Climate".

58   Bar Hebraeus, *Chronography*, trans. Budge, p. 155. See also Telelis, Μετεωρολογικά φαινόμενα, N° 373.

Latin sources speak about a "very great winter" in the Rhine region.[59]

Further information on the relief measures of Romanos I Lakapenos during the extreme winter can be found in the Chronicle attributed to Simon Logothetes (written in the 960s[60]): the emperor ordered the installation of wooden emergency shelters in the numerous porticos along the main streets of Constantinople to save the homeless from death by freezing; furthermore, money was collected in the churches for the needs of the poor, some of whom were also regularly fed in the imperial palace.[61]

The posteriority of Romanos I earned equal praise with another measure, which tackled a longer-term impact of the winter of famine seven years later: the novel of September 934 (with a probable first version issued already in 928/29[62]), which disposed that:

> from the previous first indiction (that is, from the advent or passage of the famine [during the winter of 927/28]), those illustrious persons, whom the present decree prescribes above be prohibited, who have come into control of hamlets or villages and have there acquired further properties either in part or in whole, are to be thence expelled, recovering the price they paid either from the original owners or from their heirs or relatives, or if these persons do not have the means, from the joint taxpayers, or even from the commune coming forward to return the price.[63]

This law was directed against those among the "powerful" (*dynatoi*),[64] who as owners or administrators of large estates "regard the poor as prey" and had abused their "indigence" as "opportunity for business instead of charity,

---

59   Newfield, *The Contours of Disease and Hunger*, p. 478 (N° 264); Wozniak, *Naturereignisse im frühen Mittelalter*, pp. 487–88.
60   Neville, *Guide to Byzantine Historical Writing*, pp. 118–21.
61   Symeon Magistros 136, 57 ed. Wahlgren, pp. 330, 434–331, 449. On the interpretation of this passage see Kresten, "Ἄρκλαι und τριμίσια", esp. 45–51; Dölger/Müller/Beihammer, *Regesten von 867–1025*, N° 616; Stathakopoulos, ">Philoptochos basileus<"; Morris, "The Powerful and the Poor", p. 18.
62   Dölger/Müller/Beihammer, *Regesten von 867–1025*, N° 620a.
63   Novels of the Macedonian emperors, ed. Svoronos, N° 3, p. 86, lns. 88–95; trans. McGeer, *The Land Legislation of the Macedonian Emperors*, p. 56; Dölger/Müller/Beihammer, *Regesten von 867–1025*, N° 628. See also Kresten, "Ἄρκλαι und τριμίσια", pp. 40–41; Kaplan, *Les hommes et la terre*, pp. 421–25.
64   The law lists "illustrious magistroi or patrikioi, [...] any of the persons honoured with offices, governorships, [...] civil or military dignities, [...] anyone [...] enumerated in the Senate, [...] officials or ex–officials of the themes, [...] metropolitans most devoted to God, archbishops, bishops, abbots, ecclesiastical officials, or supervisors and heads of pious or imperial houses", Novels of the Macedonian emperors, ed. Svoronos, N° 3, p. 84,

compassion, or kindness"; and "when they saw the poor oppressed by famine, they bought up the possessions of the unfortunate poor at a very low price, some with silver, some with gold, and others with grain or other forms of payment".[65] Such distress sales under the impact of the extreme winter of 927/28 and during the following years were to be annulled in order to restore small and medium-sized farmers to their property. "For their wellbeing", the law decreed,

> demonstrates the great benefit of its function – the contribution of taxes and the fulfilment of military obligations – which will be completely lost should the common people disappear. Those concerned with the stability of the state must eliminate the cause of disturbance, expel what is harmful, and support the common good.[66]

Earlier laws had already dealt with the growing influence of the *dynatoi* at the cost of the small free farmers, some of whom not only provided taxes, but also military service (the owner of *stratiotika ktemata*) to the state.[67] As Angeliki Laiou and Cecile Morrisson have pointed out, this process was also carried by dynamics from below; that is, with farmers preferring to sell their land to powerful elite neighbours and to work for them as tenants in order to profit from their protection and resources in cases of political unrest or – as in the aftermath of 927 – of crop failures and extreme events.[68] We may assume that this long-term trend started with the improvement of security and economic (as well as climatic) conditions in the 9th century, intensified with the imperial and economic expansion of the 10th and early 11th century, and heated up in the aftermath of short-term shocks such as in 927. Besides its actual socio-economic impact, the extreme winter of 927/28 (which also served as a reference point in later laws repeating and expending the regulations of Romanos I[69]) "was thus used as a way of understanding the reasons for the social transformation

---

  lns. 50–56; trans. McGeer, *The Land Legislation of the Macedonian Emperors*, pp. 54–55; Morris, "The Powerful and the Poor", 14.
65 Novels of the Macedonian emperors, ed. Svoronos, N° 3, pp. 83–86; trans. McGeer, *The Land Legislation of the Macedonian Emperors*, pp. 54–56.
66 Novels of the Macedonian emperors, ed. Svoronos, N° 3, p. 85, lns. 69–74; trans. McGeer, *The Land Legislation of the Macedonian Emperors*, p. 55.
67 Dölger/Müller/Beihammer, *Regesten von 867–1025*, N° 595; Kaldellis, *Streams of Gold*, pp. 10–11.
68 Laiou/Morrisson, *The Byzantine Economy*, p. 106. See also Kaplan, *Les hommes et la terre*, pp. 391–97.
69 Dölger/Müller/Beihammer, *Regesten von 867–1025*, N° 656 (March 947), N° 707e (966/967) N° 783 (January 996). See also Morris, "The Powerful and the Poor", pp. 5–6.

as it accelerated this process and brought it to contemporaries' attention."[70] In general, as Adam Izdebski, Lee Mordechai, and Sam White have analysed:

> the environmental stressor [of 927/28] – even if in physical terms it was not the harshest winter of the tenth century – impinged upon the complex web of crop ecologies, social relations, and the state's interests. Thus, it added new momentum to the extant social dynamic – that of officeholding elites accumulating wealth that allowed them to become an increasingly powerful social group within contemporary Byzantine society.[71]

Furthermore,

> from a broad perspective, (...) Byzantine society proved resilient, surviving the crisis caused by the long winter of 927/928. When seen from the point of view of specific social groups, however, the price for this resilience was a significant shift in the balance of socioeconomic relations.[72]

Most recently, however, Anthony Kaldellis has put into question such a "significant shift" in the balance of socio-economic relations and the traditional scenario of a conflict between landowning "magnates" and the imperial centre. He, by contrast, claims that:

> the emperors were threatened not by landowners but by army officers. Some were no doubt landowners, but there is no evidence that they were dangerous because of their property. (...) Instead, they were dangerous because they could subvert the loyalty of the armies.[73]

Kaldellis thus interprets the crisis of the 11th century as a "systemic crisis" of the usual (and usually often fragile) power arrangement of emperor, army, and state apparatus.

As a matter of fact, beyond the apparent support for the independence of farmers and especially soldier-farmers, the main aim of the laws of Romanos I

---

70 Izdebski/Mordechai/White, "The Social Burden of Resilience". See also Morris, "The Powerful and the Poor", 8–10; Sarris, "Large Estates and the Peasantry", pp. 446–47.
71 Izdebski/Mordechai/White, "The Social Burden of Resilience".
72 Izdebski/Mordechai/White, "The Social Burden of Resilience".
73 Kaldellis, *Streams of Gold*, pp. 13–15, also 224–28. For a similar interpretation also for elite rebellions in the late 12th century, see Olson, *Environment and Society in Byzantium*, pp. 209–10.

Lakapenos and his successors was the (re-)intensification of the access of the fiscus onto the fruits of the economic growth in the countryside. The same purpose served confiscations (also under the pretext of these new laws), reclaims of abandoned lands earlier made accessible for free to neighbouring peasants, and the creation of imperial domains in old and newly-conquered territories.[74] Furthermore, a close reading of jurisdiction of the 10th and early 11th centuries (such as the *Peira*) indicates that this new legislation was enforced during this period and also after the last of these "Macedonian" laws was issued by Emperor Basil II in 996.[75] Thus, Kaldellis is right to point out the still-strong institutional muscles of the Roman state against earlier notions of a "feudalization" of Byzantium. He claims that all significant means of power were still located within the imperial system and state apparatus and that the so-called "magnates of Asia Minor" were not able to challenge the emperor in Constantinople based on their new landed properties, but only due to their functions and prestige within the army and/or administration.[76]

A further reading of the laws of the Macedonian emperors, however, allows us to observe the actual interplay between the traditional allocation of rank and wealth within the army and administration and the growth and transmission of landed property within increasingly powerful noble clans. In AD 996, Emperor Basil II issued a law that he claimed to have based on his findings of conditions in the Anatolian provinces when travelling there. The emperor described the case of a man called Philokales, who:

> was originally one of the poor and the villagers, but afterwards one of the illustrious and wealthy, and who as long as he was among the lowly, he paid his taxes with his fellow villagers and did not interfere with them; but when God raised him to the title of *hebdomadarios*, then *koitonites*, and thereafter *protobestiarios*, in short order he took possession of the entire

---

74 Sarris, "Large Estates and the Peasantry", pp. 433–34; Kaldellis, *Streams of Gold*, pp. 147–48.
75 Morris, "The Powerful and the Poor in Tenth-Century Byzantium", p. 27; Magdalino, "Justice and Finance in the Byzantine State"; Gkoutzioukostas, "Administrative structures of Byzantium"; Prigent, "The Mobilisation of Fiscal Resources"; Dölger/Müller/Beihammer, *Regesten von 867–1025*, N° 688a (after October 960); Chitwood, *Byzantine Legal Culture*, pp. 83–86; *The Peira*, 8.1, 9.1–3, 9.9, 14.22, 15.10, 23.3, 40.12, 45.14, 51.9, 57, ed. Simon/Reinsch. pp. 50, 64, 66, 88, 98, 101, 182, 382, 440, 502, 542 and 708–09 (commentary on the legal definition of "dynatos"). This runs against Kaldellis' assumption that the laws of the Macedonian emperors were primarily "rhetoric" or "symbolic", see Kaldellis, *Streams of Gold*, pp. 17–18, 118–19. On the legislation of the Macedonian emperors see also Schminck, "Zur Einzelgesetzgebung".
76 Kaldellis, *Streams of Gold*, pp. 13–18.

village community and made it into his own estate; he even changed the name of the village.[77]

The promotion in the administration of the state thus provided Philokales with the means and influence to expand his landed property and to turn around completely the balance of power in his home region to his advantage. Furthermore, Emperor Basil II narrates how this interplay between rank and influence in the state apparatus and growing wealth and influence in the countryside worked even more for those "well-born" clans able to maintain and to transmit this combination of public office and private enrichment over generations ("for one hundred or even one hundred and twenty years"), such as the Phokas family.[78]

Even more efficient regarding the long-term transmission of wealth and privilege were monasteries, whose institutional arrangements did not depend on the fortunes of genealogy as lay families did from one generation to the next; they equally tended to infringe upon the customary rights of villages adjacent to their domains. In an early example from December 995 (also from the reign of Basil II), the monks of Kolobou (founded in 866 and later in 980 obtained by the Monastery of Iviron on Mt. Athos) near Hierissos tried to impede the inhabitants of the nearby village of Siderokausia from further usage of an area called Arsinikeia, where the villagers had been accustomed to pasture their animals, gather wood, harvest chestnuts and plant crops. Furthermore, the monastery's cattle had damaged the crops in the area of Kato Arsinikeia, which the villagers had cultivated.

> While Lower Arsinikeia, as mentioned, was once completely covered in woodland and trees, with canals dug to bring waters from the heights to operate the mills and make fertile the gardens and orchards, as well as the grazing lands for the beasts, the monks thought it would be a good idea to allow a multitude of animals loose there, which ruined the seeds that the Siderokausites living there had planted.

---

77   Novels of the Macedonian emperors, ed. Svoronos, N° 14, p. 203, lns. 51–58; trans. McGeer, *The Land Legislation of the Macedonian Emperors*, p. 119. Cf. Dölger/Müller/Beihammer, *Regesten von 867–1025*, N° 783; Morris, "The Powerful and the Poor", pp. 13–14.

78   Novels of the Macedonian emperors, ed. Svoronos, N° 14, p. 203, lns. 38–45; trans. McGeer, *The Land Legislation of the Macedonian Emperors*, p. 117. Cf. also Morris, "The Powerful and the Poor", 16–17; Whittow, "The Middle Byzantine Economy"; Cooper/Decker, *Life and Society in Byzantine Cappadocia*; Grünbart, *Inszenierung und Repräsentation*; Andriollo, *Constantinople et les provinces d'Asie Mineure*; Andriollo/Métivier, "Quel rôle pour les province"; Sarris, "Large Estates and the Peasantry", pp. 436–37.

The (informal) customary usage and significant modification of the landscape by a village community collided with the legal claims of an expanding monastic landowner. In this case, the judge decreed a division of the usage of the areas around Arsinikeia between Siderokausia and Kolobou, but in many similar cases, monastic institutions would be even more successful in enforcing their interests.[79]

For the lay families, however, Kaldellis is again right in his observation on the general fragility of elite status in Byzantium; in contrast to Western Europe, noble status and access to offices never became hereditary.[80] As John Haldon points out:

> Being a member of (Byzantine) elite was never (…) a fixed or determinate quantity – on the contrast, it was to occupy a position in a complex set of social and cultural relationships, in which position, status, and income remained both negotiable and fragile.[81]

Those families able to transmit wealth and power across generations "for one hundred or even one hundred and twenty years" (as Basil II has claimed) remained exceptional. In a statistical analysis of the material on elite families of the 10th to the 12th centuries collected in the study of Alexander Kazhdan and Silvia Ronchey, we observe a significant "turnover" of elite families during this period; out of 282 families in the sample, only four were able to maintain their status throughout the entire 228 years covered in the study and only ~15 per cent for more than 100 years. The vast majority lost elite status again after three or two generations – or even only one, with the 11th century showing an especially high "turnover".[82]

The potential effect of the fragility of elite status on political stability, however, may have been counterintuitive. As again John Haldon has pointed out, especially since the territorial shrinking of the Byzantine Empire in the 7th century due to the Arab expansion, Constantinople and the imperial apparatus had, even more than before, become the source of wealth and

---

79 *Actes d'Iviron* I, ed. Lefort/Oikonomidès/Papachryssanthou, N° 9, pp. 160–63. For a detailed discussion and English translation of this charter, see now Kaplan, "The Monasteries of Athos and Chalkidiki", pp. 72–77. See also Olson, *Environment and Society in Byzantium*, pp. 215–216 and 219 (who correctly remarks that "appropriation of a resource can generate as much societal pressure as resource depletion"); Smyrlis/Banev/Konstantinidis, "Mount Athos", pp. 41–42.

80 Kaldellis, *Streams of Gold*, pp. 3–4. Cf. also Barthélemy, "L'aristocracie franque".

81 Haldon, "Social élites, wealth, and power", p. 174.

82 Calculations based on data from Kazhdan/Ronchey, *L'aristocrazia bizantina*.

prestige. Thus, even more aspiring elite members and their descendants had to guarantee their access to either imperial favour or the imperial office itself, which increased the competition for the throne in Constantinople.[83] When the improved security situation and the territorial expansion of the empire from the late 9th century onwards allowed the "powerful" to entangle their revenues and prestige from the state with extension of their landed properties and influence in the countryside, there was even more to lose when a family lost access to the imperial system. Furthermore, leading members of the office-holding and landowning elite at times of minority of the heir to the throne of the Macedonian dynasty, starting with Romanos I Lakapenos (who ruled for Constantine VII) and continuing with Nikephoros II Phokas and John I Tzimiskes (for Basil II and Constantine VIII), served as co-emperors. Thereby, these clans had also tasted from the imperial office and were eager to maintain their grasp on it.[84]

As I have argued elsewhere, these observations correlate with more general theories from the field of institutional economic theory that suggest that also periods of economic growth can destabilize earlier elite arrangements due to the concomitant shift in the balances of power between factions and clans, as well as centres and peripheries. The long-term trend in the transformation of the Byzantine countryside, partly supported by periods of more stable and "beneficial" climatic conditions but also intensified by short-term shocks such as the winter of 927 (and a further "cluster of calamities", which we inspect on the following pages), thus contributed to increased competition for the imperial office in the Byzantine centre, which weakened its abilities to react to exogenous challenges and decreased the centre's integrative power for the peripheries.[85]

6   A Cluster of Calamities in the 960s and Regime Changes in Constantinople and Egypt

During the reign of Romanos I Lakapenos (920–944), another natural disaster seems to have started that plagued the empire for the following years until the reign of his namesake and grandson Romanos II (959–963). This was an epidemic of cattle:

---

83   Haldon, "Social élites, wealth, and power", p. 177.
84   Kaldellis, *Streams of Gold*, pp. 21–23, 42–44; Preiser-Kapeller, "Byzantium 1025–1204", pp. 65–66.
85   Preiser-Kapeller, *Der Lange Sommer und die Kleine Eiszeit*, pp. 128–29, 178–81.

> In those days [in the reign of Romanos II] the cattle disease was raging which had plagued the Roman empire for some time, a disease known as *krabra* that wastes and destroys bovines. They say that it originated in the days of Romanos [I] the Elder. It is said that when he was constructing a palace in which he gained relief from the summer heat close to the cistern of Bonos [in Constantinople], the head of a marble ox was found while the foundations were being dug. Those who found it smashed it up and threw it into the lime kiln; and from that time until this there was no interruption in the destruction of the bovine race in any land that was under Roman rule.[86]

Tim Newfield has collected parallel reports on an epizootic among cattle from Western Europe between 940 and 944 and suggests a possible connection of the outbreak and spread of the disease with climate anomalies in the aftermath of volcanic eruptions in 939/40 such as the one of the Eldgjá on Iceland.[87]

In the early reign of Romanos II, in October 960, so too a lack of grain and an increase in prices are reported for Constantinople, which the emperor tried to mitigate with the purchase of grain in "west and east".[88] Weather extremes may have contributed to this shortfall; we read about unusual cold and heavy rains during the (ultimately successful) Byzantine expedition against Arab Crete in 960/61.[89] In January 960, a lack of rain afflicted Baghdad (the 10th century in general is marked as on average more arid than preceding and following periods in the oxygen isotope data from the speleothems in Kuna Ba Cave in Northern Iraq, with the years between 960 and 986 being the driest of the second half of the 10th century, see Fig. 15.6); a plague of locusts devastated

---

86   John Scylitzes, *Synopsis*, Romanos II, 8, ed. Thurn, pp. 251–52; trans. Wortley, pp. 242–43. Schminck, "Zur Einzelgesetzgebung", 281, note 73 (arguing of a dating of the lack of grain to October 961). For further evidence, see also PmbZ N° 26834, note 17.

87   Newfield, "Early Medieval Epizootics"; Newfield, "Domesticates, disease and climate". See also Sigl, "Timing and Climate Forcing"; Wozniak, *Naturereignisse im frühen Mittelalter*, pp. 680–81. For references to climate extremes in the 940s in Egypt and Mesopotamia see also Telelis, Μετεωρολογικά φαινόμενα, N°s 376 and 377.

88   Theophanes Continuatus VI, 13, ed. Bekker, p. 479, 1–11. Telelis, Μετεωρολογικά φαινόμενα, nr 394; Teall, "The Grain Supply"; Kaldellis, *Streams of Gold*, p. 32. For references to extreme events and famines in neighbouring regions of Byzantium such as Armenia and Mesopotamia during the 950s see Matthew of Edessa, *History* I, 1, trans. Dostourian, p. 19; al-Maqrīzī, *Ighāthah*, trans. Allouche, p. 29; Bar Hebraeus, *Chronography*, trans. Budge, pp. 165 and 167; Telelis, Μετεωρολογικά φαινόμενα, N°s 388 and 391–93.

89   Telelis, Μετεωρολογικά φαινόμενα, N° 395; Kaldellis, *Streams of Gold*, pp. 34–38.

THE MEDIEVAL CLIMATE ANOMALY

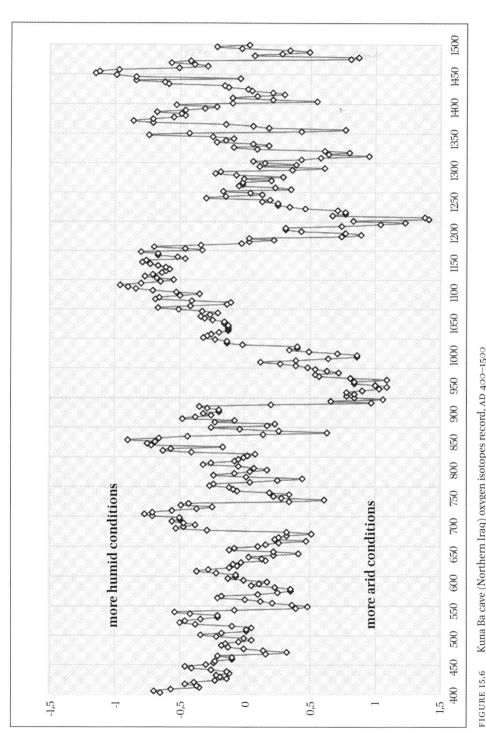

FIGURE 15.6   Kuna Ba cave (Northern Iraq) oxygen isotopes record, AD 400–1500
DATA: SINHA ET AL., "ROLE OF CLIMATE"; GRAPH: J. PREISER-KAPELLER, OEAW, 2022

the countryside of Iraq in March. In February 961, a strong hailstorm beset Baghdad, as it did in the following winter of 962/63.[90] In 963/64:

> there was a great famine in Cilicia [which also impeded some of the Byzantine campaigns in the area], and a great many of the people of the Arabs left and fled to Damascus. And there was also a severe famine in Aleppo, and in Harran and in Edessa.[91]

Around the same time, in 963 and 964, parts of Italy were affected by famine, while severe floods affected the provinces along the Yellow River in China between 964 and 968, thus illustrating the geographical dimensions of the climate anomalies in these years.[92]

Equally, 963 started a series of low Nile floods, which would continue until 969 and contributed to the downfall of the dynasty of the Iḫšīdiyūn, which had ruled over Egypt and Syria (more or less) independently from the Abbasid Caliph in Baghdad since 935. Especially, when Abū l-Misk Kāfūr, vizir and since 946 *de facto* ruler of the realm, died in 968:

> unrest increased and riots multiplied. Much strife between the soldiery and the commanders resulted in a great loss of human life. Markets were looted and several buildings were burned. The fear of the populace intensified: they lost their wealth and their spirits. Prices became high and it was difficult to find foodstuffs, to the point that one measure of wheat sold for one dinar.[93]

Eventually, in 969, an army of the Fatimid Caliph al-Muʿizz li-Dīn Allāh from North Africa under the command of Ǧauhar aṣ-Ṣiqillī invaded Egypt and brought the Iḫšīdiyūn regime to an end. With a strict regulation of the grain market, Ǧauhar mitigated the distress in al-Fusṭāṭ, which together with a return of adequate Nile floods from 971 onwards contributed to the acceptance of the new Fatimid rule in the country, which manifested itself in the building

---

90 Busse, *Chalif und Großkönig*, p. 387; Telelis, Μετεωρολογικά φαινόμενα, N° 396, 397. For the Kuna Ba data, see Sinha et al., "Role of climate".

91 Bar Hebraeus, *Chronography*, trans. Budge, p. 170. Telelis, Μετεωρολογικά φαινόμενα, N° 398; Hassan, "Extreme Nile floods".

92 Wozniak, *Naturereignisse im frühen Mittelalter*, p. 615 (with citation of sources); Kaldellis, *Streams of Gold*, pp. 46–47; Zhang, *The River, the Plain, and the State*, pp. 110–12; Mostern, *The Yellow River*, pp. 123–25.

93 al-Maqrīzī, *Ighāthah*, trans. Allouche, pp. 30–31. Telelis, Μετεωρολογικά φαινόμενα, N° 399. See also Chipman/Avni/Ellenblum, "Collapse, affluence, and collapse", p. 202.

of a new residential city to the north of al-Fusṭāṭ, al-Qāhira ("the Conquering"), i.e. Cairo.⁹⁴

The turbulences in the Iḫšīdiyūn territories during these years (together with the death of the Emir of Aleppo, Saif ad-Daula of the Hamdanid-dynasty, in 967) also eased the Byzantine expansion towards Cilicia (to which an Egyptian fleet was still sent in 965) and Northern Syria under Emperor Nikephoros II Phokas (963–69). His troops conquered Antioch in October 969, while severe rainfalls had enforced an abandonment of an earlier siege in December 966.⁹⁵ Yet also Byzantium was perturbed by portents and catastrophes, at least according to the apocalyptically inspired history of Leo the Deacon, who mentions an earthquake in northwestern Asia Minor in 967 and a severe storm and flooding in Constantinople and its environs on 21 June of the same year, so that:

> people wailed and lamented piteously, fearing that a flood like that fabled one of old was again befalling them. But compassionate Providence, which loves mankind, thrust a rainbow through the clouds, and with its rays dispersed the gloomy rain, and the structure of nature, returned again to its previous condition. It so happened that there was a later downpour, which was turbid and mixed with ashes (*tephra*), as in the soot from a furnace, and it seemed lukewarm to those who touched it.⁹⁶

Furthermore, on 22 December 968 "an eclipse of the sun took place", so that once more "people were terrified at the novel and unaccustomed sight, and propitiated the divinity with supplications, as was fitting". As Leo does not forget to mention, he was an eyewitness, since "at that time I myself was living in Byzantium, pursuing my general education".⁹⁷

In addition to these short-term portents and calamities, a shortage of grain of three or even five years duration reportedly troubled the population during the reign of Nikephoros II Phokas (963–69).⁹⁸ The causes for this famine

---

94   al-Maqrīzī, *Ighāthah*, trans. Allouche, pp. 30–31. Telelis, Μετεωρολογικά φαινόμενα, N° 399.
95   Telelis, Μετεωρολογικά φαινόμενα, N° 401; Kaldellis, *Streams of Gold*, pp. 28–29, 38–40, 46–49, 60–62.
96   Leo the Deacon, *History* IV, 9, ed. Hase, pp. 69–70; trans. Talbot/Sullivan, pp. 117–19. Telelis, Μετεωρολογικά φαινόμενα, N° 402; Wozniak, *Naturereignisse im frühen Mittelalter*, pp. 287–88 (on the earthquakes). The ashes could have been the result of an eruption of Vesuvius in 968, see Wozniak, *Naturereignisse im frühen Mittelalter*, pp. 329–30.
97   Leo the Deacon, *History* IV, 11, ed. Hase, p. 72; trans. Talbot/Sullivan, pp. 122–23. Telelis, Μετεωρολογικά φαινόμενα, N° 402; Wozniak, *Naturereignisse im frühen Mittelalter*, pp. 196, 216–17.
98   John Scylitzes, *Synopsis*, John I, 3, ed. Thurn, pp. 286, 48–56; trans. Wortley, pp. 273–74; Leo the Deacon, *History* VI, 8, ed. Hase, p. 103; trans. Talbot/Sullivan, pp. 152–53. Telelis, Μετεωρολογικά φαινόμενα, N° 406.

are not mentioned, but in the *History* of John Scylitzes we are informed that in May 968 "there were fierce, burning winds (...), which destroyed the crops, even the vines and trees, with the result that in the twelfth year of the indiction there was an intense famine".[99] A change towards more arid conditions in the late 960s, which continued until the early 11th century, is also indicated in the isotope data from the speleothems in the Sofular cave in northwestern Asia Minor (see Fig. 15.7).[100] In 968, Iraq, too, was affected by drought and famine.[101]

John Scylitzes further writes that:

> the emperor (who ought to have been concerned for his subjects' well-being) now shabbily sold the imperial grain, profiting from the misfortune of those in need, and he congratulated himself as though it were some great deed that, when [grain] was selling for one gold piece a bushel, he ordered it to be sold for two.

Nikephoros II Phokas' greed is contrasted with the munificence of the first "Macedonian" emperor, Basil I (867–86); in addition, Nikephoros II acquired a bad reputation due to a reduction in the weight of gold coins.[102] The low popularity of the emperor according to some modern scholars may also "partly explain the somewhat feeble public reaction to the murder of Nikephoros" by his relative John I Tzimiskes in December 969.[103] The new emperor "put an end to the relentless evil of famine by the importation of grain, which he collected quickly [and] with forethought from markets everywhere, stopping the spread of such a calamity"[104] – and thereby gaining popularity.

Thus, the famine crises of the 960s ended in 969[105] both in Egypt and in Byzantium to the accompaniment of a violent regime change, with the new rulers legitimizing their takeovers by more efficient crisis management.

---

99 John Scylitzes, *Synopsis*, Nikephoros II, 20, ed. Thurn, pp. 277, 37–43; trans. Wortley, p. 266.
100 Fleitmann et al., "Sofular Cave".
101 Busse, *Chalif und Großkönig*, p. 387.
102 John Scylitzes, *Synopsis*, Nikephoros II, 20, ed. Thurn, pp. 277–78; trans. Wortley, pp. 266–67. Dölger/Müller/Beihammer, *Regesten von 867–1025*, N° 702.
103 John Scylitzes, *Synopsis*, trans. Wortley, p. 267, n. 78. On the declining popularity of Nikephoros II Phokas and its causes, see also Kaldellis, *Streams of Gold*, pp. 51–54 and 63–64.
104 John Scylitzes, *Synopsis*, John I, 3, ed. Thurn, pp. 286, 48–56; trans. Wortley, pp. 273–74; Leo the Deacon, *History* VI, 8, ed. Hase, p. 103; trans. Talbot/Sullivan, pp. 152–153. Telelis, Μετεωρολογικά φαινόμενα, N° 406.
105 For parallel reports on weather extremes in Western Europe, see Newfield, *The Contours of Disease and Hunger*, p. 484 (N° 304).

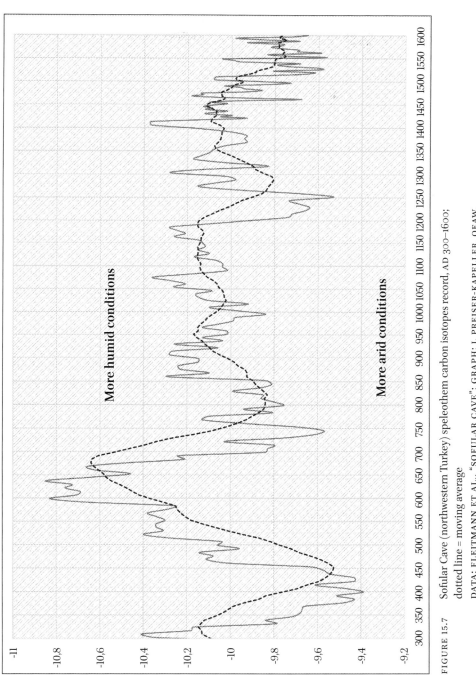

FIGURE 15.7 Sofular Cave (northwestern Turkey) speleothem carbon isotopes record, AD 300–1600; dotted line = moving average
DATA: FLEITMANN ET AL., "SOFULAR CAVE"; GRAPH: J. PREISER-KAPELLER, OEAW, 2022

In turn, the sources suggest that the severity of the supply shortfall did not depend on the strength of the environmental stressors alone, but equally on the decision-making of the earlier administrations. Thus, "climate" on its own did not topple the Iḫšīdiyūn or Nikephoros II. Nevertheless, the obviously tense economic situation may have contributed to a further intensification of the growth of large estates of the "powerful" in the Byzantine provinces; at least, Nikephoros II issued another five laws repeating and augmenting the legislation against the encroachments of *dynatoi* on the properties of their poorer neighbours. However, as mentioned above, these laws equally provided pretexts for the state to intervene in the (re-)distribution of the increasing pool of economic resources in the countryside for its very own material interests.[106]

7   The Turn of the Millennium and the Different Narratives on the Reign of Basil II

Two further laws for the "defence of the poor" were issued by Emperor Basil II (976–1025), whose reign, especially due to its military successes in the East and on the Balkans, is often seen as the apex of medieval Roman power.[107] His early reign between 976 and 989, however, was overshadowed by attempted military coups by two relatives of his predecessors Nikephoros II Phokas and John I Tzimiskes, namely Bardas Phokas and Bardas Skleros.[108] The succession of two bloody civil wars also contributed to the "apocalyptic" mood of the history of Leo the Deacon, who wrote that:

> many extraordinary and unusual events have occurred in novel fashion in the course of my lifetime: fearsome sights have appeared in the sky, unbelievable earthquakes have occurred, thunderbolts have struck and torrential rains have poured down, wars have broken out and armies have overrun many parts of the inhabited world, cities and whole regions have moved elsewhere, so that many people believe that life is now undergoing a transformation, and that the expected Second Coming (*deutera katabasis*) of the Savior and God is near, at the very gates.[109]

---

106   Novels of the Macedonian emperors, ed. Svoronos, Nos 8–12, pp. 151–84; trans. McGeer, *The Land Legislation of the Macedonian Emperors*, pp. 86–108. See also Sarris, "Large Estates and the Peasantry in Byzantium".
107   Kaldellis, *Streams of Gold*, p. xxviii.
108   Kaldellis, *Streams of Gold*, pp. 81–102.
109   Leo the Deacon, *History* I, 1, ed. Hase, p. 4; trans. Talbot/Sullivan, pp. 55–56.

For Basil II, this sequence of portents starts in Leo's text with a comet in August to October 975 (so still during the reign of John I), which "scholars of astronomy" misinterpreted as a sign of future victories, while according to Leo it foretold "bitter revolts, and invasions of foreign peoples, and civil wars, and migrations from cities and the countryside, famines and plagues and terrible earthquakes, indeed almost the total destruction of the Roman empire (...)".[110] Another "sinking" star in August 986 foreboded a defeat of Basil II's army against the Bulgarians.[111] The sighting of Halley's Comet between August and September 989, which was equally visible in other parts of Europe,[112] was followed by further military defeats and especially a devastating earthquake in Constantinople on 25 October 989, which even damaged Hagia Sophia. Leo adds that "harsh famines and plagues, droughts and floods and gales of violent winds (...), and the barrenness of the earth and calamities that occurred, all came to pass after the appearance of the star".[113] The reference to drought would find a counterpart in the isotope record from the Sofular cave in northwestern Asia Minor, which indicates the 990s as the driest decade in the entire 10th century (see Fig. 15.7).[114] Tree-ring data from modern-day Albania points to very cold conditions in that region in the early 990s.[115] Leo's history ends, however, shortly after this passage, and the author most probably died at some point before the year 1000. Thus, he did not witness the later military successes of Basil's II reign, especially his ultimate destruction of the Bulgarian Empire in 1018, which earned him the praise of later historians (since the 12th century as "Bulgar Slayer"), who also wrote under the impression of the severe crisis of the empire emerging under Basil's successors in the 11th century.[116] Therefore, we have little information on the further sequence of "harsh famines and plagues, droughts and floods and gales of violent winds" that Leo mentioned as underpinnings of his apocalyptic reading of Basil II's reign. John Scylitzes, for instance, informs us that, in 1010/11, "there was a most severe winter; every

110 Leo the Deacon, *History* x, 6, ed. Hase, p. 169; trans. Talbot/Sullivan, pp. 210–12.
111 Leo the Deacon, *History* x, 8, ed. Hase, p. 172; trans. Talbot/Sullivan, p. 214; Kaldellis, *Streams of Gold*, pp. 95–96. On this and other observations of this comet, see Wozniak, *Naturereignisse im frühen Mittelalter*, pp. 141–42.
112 Wozniak, *Naturereignisse im frühen Mittelalter*, pp. 106–07.
113 Leo the Deacon, *History* x, 10, ed. Hase, pp. 175–76; trans. Talbot/Sullivan, pp. 217–18. Kaldellis, *Streams of Gold*, p. 104. On the possible sighting of aurora borealis as one explanation for some of the celestial phenomena described by Leo, see Wozniak, *Naturereignisse im frühen Mittelalter*, p. 189.
114 Fleitmann et al., "Sofular Cave".
115 PAGES 2k Network consortium, Database.
116 Neville, *Guide to Byzantine Historical Writing*, pp. 124–25; Kaldellis, *Streams of Gold*, pp. 104–05.

river and lake was frozen, even the sea itself. And in January of the same year of the indiction a most awesome earthquake occurred; it continued to shake the earth until the ninth of March."[117] Yet, in contrast to the extreme winter of 927/28, Scylitzes does not mention any effects on agriculture, nor a famine.

Leo the Deacon, however, finds a counterpart in the equally apocalyptically inspired 12th-century Armenian chronicle of Matthew of Edessa:

> During the reign of Basil, the Greek emperor, and in the year 452 of the Armenian era [1003–04] a certain star, appearing in the form of fire, arose in the heavens, an omen of the wrath of God towards all living creatures and also a sign of the end of the world. There was a violent earthquake throughout the whole land, to such an extent that many thought that the day of the end of the world had arrived. Like the time of the flood all living creatures shook and trembled, and many fell down and died from fear of the intensity of this wrath. After this outpouring of God's wrath a plague (...) came upon the area and spreading through many regions, reached Sebasteia [modern-day Siwas, in Byzantine Cappadocia, where many Armenians lived, see Fig. 15.3]. This plague clearly manifested itself on men's bodies and, because of its harshness, many had no time to make their confession or take communion. Men and beast diminished from the land, and those remaining quadrupeds roamed about the countryside without anyone to take care of them.[118]

This information on an epidemic in the eastern provinces of the Byzantine Empire is not found in any Greek source, but it fits within a larger pattern of weather extremes and calamities affecting the Middle East in the years around the turn of the first millennium AD.[119] Again, Matthew of Edessa mentions that "it happened at the beginning of the year 446 of the Armenian era [997–98] that a certain comet arose in the heavens and it became visible with a horrible and dreadful appearance, bright and marvellous".[120] Around the same time, during the reign of the Fatimid Caliph al-Ḥākim (996–1021) in Egypt:

> a period of inflation occurred (...). It was caused by an insufficient level of the Nile, which reached only sixteen cubits and a few fingers. Prices rose

---

117 John Scylitzes, *Synopsis*, Constantine VIII, 2, ed. Thurn, p. 373, 3–11; trans. Wortley, p. 352. Telelis, *Μετεωρολογικά φαινόμενα*, N° 432.
118 Matthew of Edessa, *History* I, 46, trans. Dostourian, p. 43.
119 Some parallel observations exist for Western Europe, see Wozniak, *Naturereignisse im frühen Mittelalter*, pp. 494–96, 617–21.
120 Matthew of Edessa, *History* I, 41, trans. Dostourian, p. 41.

sharply and wheat was in high demand but was unattainable. The populace lived in a heightened state of fear, women were kidnapped in the streets, and the situation deteriorated. The price of bread reached one dirham for four ratls; then the situation eased when prices dropped.[121]

For the area of Baghdad, Bar Hebraeus reports for the winter of 998/99 that "severe frost took place (...), and thousands of the palm-trees (...) were destroyed. And those which remained only after very many years acquired straightness."[122] In 1002, first severe cold in March and then an exceptional flood of the Euphrates in April plagued Baghdad before:

> swarms of locusts appeared in the country of Mosul and in Baghdad and they became very numerous in Shiraz [in Iran]. They left no grass [in the fields] and no leaves on the trees and they even consumed the rolls of cloth which the fullers were bleaching; and of each roll of cloth the fuller was only able to give a rag to its owner. And there was a famine, and a measure of wheat was sold in Baghdad for one hundred and twenty gold dinars. And pillars of fire appeared in the heavens, from the north pole to the middle of the sky.[123]

Between 1005 and 1008, low Nile floods again caused shortages of food and a rise in grain and bread prices in Egypt, which Caliph al-Ḥākim and his officials tried to mitigate with price regulations and drastic measures (such as flogging and public parading) against millers, bakers, hoarders of grain and speculators suspected of taking advantage of the misery of the population – obviously with some success, since "prices decreased and harm was averted (...)".[124] Around the same time, in 1007, "snow fell in Baghdad", but the next harvest brought "great abundance" and low prices for wheat. But later, "violent black winds" in the area of Tikrīt to the northwest of Baghdad (see Fig. 15.3) "destroyed many

---

121 al-Maqrīzī, *Ighāthah*, trans. Allouche, p. 31. Telelis, Μετεωρολογικά φαινόμενα, N° 419–20; Hassan, "Extreme Nile floods".
122 Bar Hebraeus, *Chronography*, trans. Budge, pp. 181–82. Telelis, Μετεωρολογικά φαινόμενα, N° 421; Busse, *Chalif und Großkönig*, pp. 388–89.
123 Bar Hebraeus, *Chronography*, trans. Budge, p. 183. Busse, *Chalif und Großkönig*, p. 389.
124 al-Maqrīzī, *Ighāthah*, trans. Allouche, pp. 31–33. Telelis, Μετεωρολογικά φαινόμενα, Nos 424–27, 430–31; Hassan, "Extreme Nile floods"; Wozniak, *Naturereignisse im frühen Mittelalter*, p. 619.

houses and tore up very many palm-trees and olive-trees by the roots; and great ships were sunk in the Sea of Persia".[125] In 1010:

> swarms of locusts appeared in the country of Mosul, and the nomads raided the country on all sides, and there was also a great pestilence. And the famine waxed strong in the country of Khorasan [in eastern Iran] until one litre of bread was sold for a gold dinar.

People would even resort to cannibalism, Bar Hebraeus and other sources tell us.[126] Further reports on floods come from China for the period between 1000 and 1014.[127]

Thus, in comparison with Egypt, Mesopotamia, or Persia, despite the apocalyptic expectations of Leo the Deacon, the Byzantine Empire seems to have been less significantly affected during this cluster of extreme events at the turn of the first millennium, although we have to take into consideration that the latter historians of the 11th century were less eager to register catastrophes for the reign of Basil II than Leo was. For the late reign of Basil II, we learn from Armenian sources (interpreting this as another sign of divine wrath) that, in 1021/22, the emperor and his army encountered "violent snowstorms" and flooding during a campaign in Armenia (in the area east of Lake Van), which caused severe losses.[128] These extreme conditions could already be attributed to more turbulent climatic period connected with the Oort Solar Minimum (see above).

8   The Oort Solar Minimum and a Cluster of Disasters between 1025 and 1042

As mentioned above, the historians of the late 11th century wrote under the impression of a "decline" from the apex of Byzantine power under Basil II to

---

125 Bar Hebraeus, *Chronography*, trans. Budge, pp. 183–84. Telelis, Μετεωρολογικά φαινόμενα, Nos 428–29; Busse, *Chalif und Großkönig*, p. 389.

126 Bar Hebraeus, *Chronography*, trans. Budge, p. 185. Busse, *Chalif und Großkönig*, p. 389. Another plague of locusts occurred in Baghdad in 1018, see Bar Hebraeus, *Chronography*, trans. Budge, p. 185. In general, on the "topos" of cannibalism during famines see Wozniak, *Naturereignisse im frühen Mittelalter*, pp. 731–39.

127 Zhang, *The River, the Plain, and the State*, pp. 37, 110–12; Mostern, *The Yellow River*, pp. 142–44.

128 Aristakēs Lastiverc'i, *History*, ed. and trans. Bedrosian, pp. 46–49; Matthew of Edessa, *History* I, 51, trans. Dostourian, p. 47. Telelis, Μετεωρολογικά φαινόμενα, No 433; Kaldellis, *Streams of Gold*, pp. 131–33.

the almost fatal crisis of the 1070s (especially after the defeat at Manzikert 1071); thus, positive verdicts on the successors of the "Bulgar Slayer", including his brother Constantine VIII, are quite rare.[129] During his reign from 1025 to 1028, so John Scylitzes tells us:

> there was a severe drought; even unfailing springs and rivers dried up. The emperor Basil (II) used to spare the poor by not insisting that be paid on time, granting a delay or postponement to those who asked. When he died, two years' taxes were owing; these payments Constantine demanded immediately, and he also stipulated those taxes be paid on time for the three next years (for that is how long his reign lasted). By demanding five years' payments in three he ruined not only the poor (*penetes*) and indigent (*aporoi*) but also those who were well off.[130]

In the chronicle of John Zonaras (written in the 12th century[131]), the correlation between the stinginess of the emperor, the "ruin" of the poor and the drought is even more explicit:

> But since the taxes of two years had not been collected at the death of the Emperor Basil (he granted a deferment of the taxes in order to spare the taxpayers), those of the past and those of the three years of his reign he [Constantine VIII] demanded mercilessly, and that, although all the time of his reign there was drought, so that the poor perished.[132]

We may assume that, under these conditions, the pressure from above and from nature, together with dynamics from below (that is, farmers preferring to sell their land to powerful elite neighbours and to work for them as tenants in order to profit from their protection and resources in cases of political unrest, additional tax demands, or – as in the aftermath of 927 – of crop failures and extreme events), worked again for a further shift of the balance of power in the countryside.[133] As Anthony Kaldellis points out, however, the Christian Arab chronicler Yaḥyā of Antioch (11th century), by contrast, praised

---

129 Kaldellis, *Streams of Gold*, pp. 155–56; Preiser-Kapeller, "Byzantium 1025–1204", p. 60; Krallis, "Historiography as Political Debate".
130 John Scylitzes, *Synopsis*, Basil II and Constantine VIII, 34, ed. Thurn, pp. 347, 20–348, 1; trans. Wortley, p. 330. Telelis, Μετεωρολογικά φαινόμενα, N° 437. On identifying the "poor", see also Morris, "The Powerful and the Poor".
131 Neville, *Guide to Byzantine Historical Writing*, pp. 191–96.
132 Zonaras, *Epitome* 17, 10, ed. Büttner-Wobst, pp. 572–73.
133 Laiou/Morrisson, *The Byzantine Economy*, p. 106.

Constantine VIII "for remitting back taxes and not collecting them on abandoned land".[134]

The references to a drought during the reign of Constantine VIII, at least, find partial confirmation in similar reports on weather extremes and famines from neighbouring polities. Bar Hebraeus mentions a hailstorm in Baghdad in April 1026, while in the winter of 1026/27:

> there was an intense cold (...), and the banks of the Euphrates and Tigris were covered with ice, and the palm trees were destroyed. And in Baghdad men used to cross over the small canals on the frozen water, and the farmers were unable to sow seed.

Frost periods continued in 1027 and 1028.[135]

In Egypt, under Caliph al-Ḥākim's successor aẓ-Ẓāhir, there was an even greater hunger crisis already in the years 1023 to 1025, for which we also have precise information on the price increase (up to ten times the usual value), which the French scholar Thierry Bianquis (1935–2014) evaluated in an important study.[136] The contemporary chronicler al-Muṣābiḥī wrote:

> The water (of the Nile) sank incessantly and beyond measure; the lands were not flooded and the ground bore nothing. The people of al-Fusṭāṭ shouted and begged God for moisture. Many people from the city, men and children, went to the mountains with Korans to implore God for water. Bread became scarce in the markets; the masses crowded around the grain.[137]

In this time of need, a traditional ceremony turned out to be fatal: in February 1025, on the eve of the Islamic festival of sacrifice, which marks the climax of the pilgrimage season to Mecca, particularly extravagant food arrangements, which the next day were to be served at the caliph's banquet to his

---

134 Yaḥyā of Antioch, *Chronicle* 15, 71, trans. Pirone, p. 338: "He [Constantine VIII] annulled all claims for sums due from the subjects of the Roman country, what was demanded of them beyond what was due and what was usually collected from the imperial villages that had been destroyed, and from each of their neighbouring communities until they were rebuilt." Kaldellis, *Streams of Gold*, pp. 155–56.

135 Bar Hebraeus, *Chronography*, trans. Budge, p. 191. Telelis, Μετεωρολογικά φαινόμενα, Nº 439; Busse, *Chalif und Großkönig*, p. 390.

136 Bianquis, "Une crise frumentaire dans l'Égypte Fatimide", esp. pp. 100–01. See also Hassan, "Extreme Nile floods".

137 Cited after Halm, *Die Kalifen von Kairo*, p. 322.

exquisite selection of guests, were carried through the capital to present the splendour of the ruler's court. This time, however, such a display made clear to the starving masses the social and material distance between the palace and the rest of the city, and tensions in the population rose. For fear of revolts, not only the broad masses, but also some of the palace guards, including regiments recruited from African slaves, who also could not be fed as they would usually, were excluded from the banquet. But some of these soldiers entered the palace and according to al-Muṣābiḥī stormed the banquet with the words:

> "Hunger! We have more right to partake in our Lord's table!" (…) Then they attacked the food, fought and stole everything that was prepared: bread, roast meat and sweets; they stole plates, trays and bowls. Bad thing! They took 300 plates with them, and those present could hardly believe that they had escaped and got away with intact skin.[138]

Cairo and al-Fusṭāṭ experienced a multiple breakdown in the symbolic communication between rulers, court society, army, and people in these days. Acceptance for the regime dwindled to a dangerous extent.[139] Relief was finally brought by sufficient floods of the Nile, which allowed a return to the usual generosity of the caliph, especially towards his troops.[140]

In Byzantium, the drought of the reign of Constantine VIII, however, reportedly ended after his death with the coronation of Emperor Romanos III Argyros (1028–34), husband of Constantine's daughter Zoë; Skylitzes wrote: "In those days God caused an adequate amount of rain to fall and the crops were abundant, especially the olives."[141] Soon, however, celestial phenomena foretold havoc, and weather extremes and hardship followed:

> In October [1029], the thirty-first of that month, the fall of a star occurred, following a path from west to east, and on that day the Roman army suffered a severe defeat in Syria (…). And rain fell in torrents continuously until the month of March. The rivers overflowed and hollows turned into

---

138   Cited after Halm, *Die Kalifen von Kairo*, p. 322.
139   Oesterle, *Kalifat und Königtum*, pp. 160–62. Cf. also Halm, *Die Kalifen von Kairo*, pp. 319–24; Brett, *The Fatimid Empire*, pp. 163–64; Chipman/Avni/Ellenblum, "Collapse, affluence, and collapse", 202–03.
140   On the role of the military in Fatimid Egypt, see Sanders, "The Fāṭimid State, 969–1171", pp. 154–57.
141   John Scylitzes, *Synopsis*, Romanos III Argyros, 2, ed. Thurn, pp. 376, 77–78; trans. Wortley, p. 355. Telelis, Μετεωρολογικά φαινόμενα, N° 440; Olson, *Environment and Society in Byzantium*, p. 183.

lakes, with the result that nearly all the livestock was drowned, and the crops were levelled. This was the cause of a severe famine in the following year.[142]

The sequence of calamities continued two years later:

> On Friday, 28 July, at the second hour of the night, a star fell from south to north, lighting up the whole earth, and shortly afterwards there were reports of disasters afflicting the Roman empire (…). This year [1032] famine and pestilence afflicted Cappadocia, Paphlagonia, the Armeniakon theme and the Honoriad, so grave that the very inhabitants of the themes abandoned their ancestral homes in search of somewhere to live. The emperor [Romanos III Argyros] met them on his return to the capital from Mesanakata [in central Asia Minor, to which a campaign had let him[143]] and, unaware of the reason for this migration, obliged them to return home, providing them with money and the other necessities of life. And Michael, who was then governing the church of Ankyra, performed virtuous works, sparing nothing which might procure the survival of the victims of famine and pestilence. On Sunday, 13 August, at the first hour of the night, AM 6540, there was a severe earthquake. The emperor came into the capital and Helena, his former wife, having died, he distributed many alms on her behalf. In that year on 20 February [1033] a star traversed from north to south with noise and commotion. It was visible until 15 March, and there was a bow above it. On 6 March, third hour, there was an earthquake.[144]

Yet beyond the accumulation of portents and catastrophes, John Scylitzes uses these calamities to hint at the efforts of Romanos III (and a member of the church elite) to mitigate the need of those afflicted by famine, disease, and earthquakes.[145] This is also true for the last period of the emperor's reign:

---

142 John Scylitzes, *Synopsis*, Romanos III Argyros, 3, ed. Thurn, pp. 377, 4–12; trans. Wortley, p. 356.
143 Kaldellis, *Streams of Gold*, p. 163.
144 John Scylitzes, Synopsis, Romanos III Argyros, 10–12, ed. Thurn, pp. 385, 52–386, 81; trans. Wortley, pp. 364–365. See also Aristakēs Lastiverc'i, *History*, ed. and trans. Bedrosian, pp. 76–77 (dating the portent to 1033, but to the reign of Michael IV). Wozniak, *Naturereignisse im frühen Mittelalter*, p. 621; Dagron, "Quand la terre tremble".
145 Kaldellis, *Streams of Gold*, pp. 163–64.

On the seventeenth of February [1034], there was an earthquake and the cities of Syria suffered severely. (…) For some time, the eastern themes had been consumed by locusts, compelling the inhabitants to sell their children and move into Thrace. The emperor gave to every one of them three pieces of gold and arranged for them to return home. The locusts were finally carried away by a powerful wind, fell into the high sea off the Hellespont and perished. They were washed up onto the shore where they covered the sand of the beach. The emperor renovated the aqueducts which bring water into the city and also the cisterns which receive that water. He restored the leper house and every other hospice which had been damaged by the earthquake. In a word, every good work was his concern. But he was afflicted by a chronic disease; his beard and his hair fell out. It was said he had been poisoned by John, who later became *orphanotrophos*.[146]

The "good works" of Romanos III are contrasted with the intrigues of John, a eunuch at the court, who arranged for a love affair between his brother Michael and Empress Zoë. Thus, the empress reportedly supported a plot to get rid of her husband Romanos III by poisoning and murder, which allowed her to marry Michael [IV], who became the new ruler.[147] John, who held the office of *orphanotrophos*,[148] however, was the true power behind the throne, especially also since his brother suffered from severe illness (the description in the sources hints at epilepsy),[149] which John Skylitzes together with portents and calamities interpreted as signs of divine distaste for the new regime:

> But it was clearly shown from the outset that what had transpired was not pleasing to God. At the eleventh hour of Easter Day [14 April 1034] there was an unendurable hailstorm, so violent that not only the trees (fruit-bearing and otherwise) were broken down, but also houses and churches collapsed. Crops and vines were laid flat to the ground; hence there ensued a great shortage of all kinds of produce at that time. There was a falling star about the third hour of the night on the Sunday after

---

146 John Scylitzes, *Synopsis*, Romanos III Argyros, 17, ed. Thurn, pp. 389, 54–69; trans. Wortley, pp. 367–68. Cf. also Zonaras, *Epitome* 17, 12, ed. Büttner-Wobst, pp. 580–81. Wozniak, *Naturereignisse im frühen Mittelalter*, p. 576.
147 Preiser-Kapeller, "Byzantium 1025–1204", p. 61; Kaldellis, *Streams of Gold*, pp. 164–65. The rumours about the plot of Zoë also made it to Armenian sources, see Aristakēs Lastiverc‛i, *History*, ed. and trans. Bedrosian, pp. 66–69.
148 For this office, see Kazhdan, "Orphanotrophos".
149 Kaldellis, *Streams of Gold*, pp. 165–66.

Easter; the brilliance of its shining put all the stars into the shade and, for many, it looked like the rising sun. And the emperor [Michael IV] became possessed of a demon; those close to him, using fine phrases, called it a madness-causing disease, but it endured to the end of his life. He received no relief either by divine might or from doctors but was grievously tormented and tortured.[150]

To make his message clear, Skylitzes connects the renewed outbreak of the plague of locusts with a vision of a eunuch (meaning John, the Orphanotrophos, of course) who carries three sacks full of vermin:

The swarms of locusts which had expired (as we reported) on the sands of the shore of the Hellespont now spontaneously regenerated and overran the coastal regions of the Hellespont again, devastating the Thrakesion theme for three whole years. Then they appeared in Pergamon but perished there, as one of the bishop's servants saw beforehand in a vision (not a dream, for he was awake). It was as though he saw a eunuch dressed in white, of radiant appearance. [This apparition] was ordered to open and empty the first of three sacks lying before him, then the second and, after that, the third. He did as he was commanded; the first sack poured out snakes, vipers and scorpions; the second, toads, asps, basiliscs, horned serpents and other venomous creatures; the third, beetles, gnats, hornets and other creatures with a sting in the tail. The man stood there speechless; the bright apparition stood close to him and said: "These came and will come upon you because of your transgression of God's commandments and the desecration of the emperor Romanos which has taken place and the violation of his marriage bed." That is what happened so far.[151]

God also rejects any appeal for relief from another climatic calamity in 1036:

Because there was a drought and for six whole months no rain had fallen, the emperor's brothers held a procession, John carrying the holy *mandylion*, the Great Domestic the Letter of Christ to Abgar, the *protobestiarios* George the holy Swaddling Bands. They travelled on foot from the Great Palace to the church of the exceedingly holy Mother of God at Blachernae.

---

150 John Scylitzes, *Synopsis*, Michael IV, 2, ed. Thurn, pp. 393, 45–57; trans. Wortley, p. 371.
151 John Scylitzes, *Synopsis*, Michael IV, 4, ed. Thurn, pp. 394, 77–395, 94; trans. Wortley, p. 372. Krallis, "Historiography as Political Debate".

The patriarch and the clergy made another procession, and not only did it not rain but a massive hailstorm was unleashed which broke down trees and shattered the roof tiles of the city. The city was in the grip of famine so John purchased one hundred thousand bushels of grain in the Peloponnese and in Hellas; with this the citizens were relieved.[152]

With the last sentence, however, Skylitzes has to admit that some of the relief measures of his villain, John Orphanotrophos, proved effective – and we also learn that the drought affecting the environs of Constantinople did not prevent a surplus of harvest in central and southern Greece to be purchased for the capital.

In another episode reported by Scylitzes, so too the actions of Emperor Michael IV, who spent a long period of his reign in Thessalonike, where he hoped for a healing from his illness at the intervention of Saint Demetrios, are quite effective at mitigating a supply shortfall:

In AM 6546, sixth year of the indiction, there was an earthquake on 2 November [1037] about the tenth hour of the day, and the earth continued to tremble into and throughout the month of January [1038]. There was a famine in Thrace, Macedonia, Strymon and Thessalonike, right into Thessaly. When the clergy of Thessalonike accused Theophanes the Metropolitan of withholding their customary allowance, the emperor (who was staying there) tried admonishing him, urging him not to deprive the personnel of the church of the allowance stipulated in the law. When the bishop showed himself recalcitrant and inflexible, the emperor realised he would have to circumvent him with a subterfuge to punish his avarice. He therefore sent one of his servants to him requesting the loan of one kentenarion [100 pounds] until gold was delivered from Byzantium. The bishop denied with oaths that he had any more than thirty pounds on hand but the emperor did not let this stand in his way. He sent and scrutinised the man's treasury and found thirty-three kentenaria of gold. Out of this he paid the clergy what was owing to them since the first year of Theophanes' episcopate until the present hour: the rest he distributed to the poor. He expelled the metropolitan from the church and restricted him to an estate.[153]

---

152 John Scylitzes, *Synopsis*, Michael IV, 10, ed. Thurn, pp. 400, 39–49; trans. Wortley, pp. 377–78.
153 John Scylitzes, *Synopsis*, Michael IV, 13, ed. Thurn, pp. 402, 81–5; trans. Wortley, p. 379.

Otherwise, however, for Scylitzes the regime around Michael IV and John Orphanotrophos could not hope for divine forgiveness, and thus the sequence of calamities affecting them, and the empire continued:

> The emperor was still afflicted by the demon and, finding no relief, he sent two pieces of gold for each priest in all the themes and the islands, one for each monk. He also stood godfather at the baptism of new-born children, giving each one a single piece and four miliarisia, but none of this did him any good. In fact, the condition worsened and in addition he was afflicted by dropsy. That year there were continuous earthquakes and frequent heavy rainfalls while, in some of the themes there was such an epidemic of quinzy [*kynagches nosima*, maybe diphtheria] that the living were unable to carry away the dead. On 2 February, eighth year of the indiction, AM 6548 [1040], there was an appalling earthquake; other places and cities suffered too. Smyrna was a pathetic sight for its most beautiful buildings fell down and many of the inhabitants lost their lives.[154]

John Skylitzes is even more explicit in his "moral meteorology" in another passage:

> Most of the time the emperor Michael resided at Thessalonike where he frequented the tomb of the wondrously victorious martyr Demetrios in the sincere hope of finding relief from his illness. He had nothing whatsoever to do with affairs of state other than those which were absolutely necessary; the administration and the handling of public business rested entirely on John's shoulders and there was no imaginable form of impurity or criminality that he did not search out for the affliction and mistreatment of the subjects. It would be a Herculean task to list them all. Everybody living under this grievous tyranny persisted in interceding with the Deity, appealing for some relief. God frequently shook the earth; the inhabited world was assailed by awesome and fearful [portents]: comets appearing in the sky, storms of wind and rain in the air, eruptions and tremblings on earth. In my opinion, these things presaged the forthcoming unparalleled catastrophe for the tyrants.[155]

---

154 John Scylitzes, *Synopsis*, Michael IV, 18–19, ed. Thurn, pp. 405, 67–79; trans. Wortley, p. 381.
155 John Scylitzes, *Synopsis*, Michael IV, 21, ed. Thurn, pp. 408, 51–63; trans. Wortley, pp. 383–84. See also Kaldellis, *Streams of Gold*, p. 168. The long stays of Michael IV in Thessaloniki are also mentioned in Aristakēs Lastiverc'i, *History*, ed. and trans. Bedrosian, pp. 72–73.

Before the final act towards the ultimate punishments of "tyrants" can take place, further calamities affect the empire and the capital:

> There was a drought that year [1040], so severe that copious springs and ever-flowing rivers almost dried up. There was a fire at the Arsenal [in Constantinople] on 6 August and all the ships that were moored there were burnt together with their fittings.[156]

On 10 December 1041, Michael IV died.[157] John the Orphanotrophos, however, had taken precautions for this by introducing his nephew Michael to the court. He found the approval of Empress Zoë, who adopted him. Thus, Michael V acceded to the throne on the day after the death of his uncle.[158] Skylitzes, however, illustrates the shaky basis of this regime from the beginning:

> In the very same hour at which he received the diadem Michael [V] was afflicted with vertigo and swimming in the head. He almost fell over; they were only just able to revive him with sweet oils, perfumes and other aromatic substances. The earth was a-tremble throughout the four months of his reign.[159]

As a matter of fact, Michael V causes his own downfall within a few months by first exiling his uncle John, the actual mastermind of the rise of his family, to a monastery, and second by attempting to do the same with his adoptive mother, Empress Zoë. This in April 1042 led to a general rebellion in Constantinople, where large groups of the population were still loyal to the Macedonian dynasty of which Zoë and her sister Theodora were the last scions.[160] Michael V was toppled from the throne and eventually, together with his uncle John, blinded; Skylitzes finished his description of the "unparalleled catastrophe for the tyrants" with the sentence: "Michael fervently entreated that his uncle [John Orphanotrophos] be blinded before him because he was the cause and instigator of all the evils that had taken place and that is what happened."[161]

---

156 John Scylitzes, *Synopsis*, Michael IV, 24, ed. Thurn, pp. 411, 46–50; trans. Wortley, p. 386.
157 John Scylitzes, *Synopsis*, Michael IV, 29, ed. Thurn, pp. 415, 50–56; trans. Wortley, p. 390.
158 Kaldellis, *Streams of Gold*, pp. 174–75; Preiser-Kapeller, "Byzantium 1025–1204", p. 61.
159 John Scylitzes, *Synopsis*, Michael V, 1, ed. Thurn, pp. 417, 79–83; trans. Wortley, p. 392. Cf. also Michael Attaleiates, *History* 4, 9, ed. and trans. Kaldellis/Krallis, pp. 26–29.
160 Kaldellis, *Streams of Gold*, pp. 175–78.
161 John Scylitzes, *Synopsis*, Michael V, 2, ed. Thurn, pp. 420, 96–421, 2; trans. Wortley, pp. 395–96.

If read in continuation and in context (and not as single pieces of meteorological data), the narrative function of the descriptions of extreme events and calamities provided by John Skylitzes becomes clear. In contrast and beyond Skylitzes' interpretation, it is hard to estimate to what extent these portents and catastrophes undermined the legitimation of and support for the regime of John Orphanotrophos and his brother and nephew, especially since Skylitzes himself in two cases has to concede the effectiveness of relief measures of John and Michael IV.[162]

The clustering of meteorological extremes and calamities in the 1030s as such finds again confirmation in similar descriptions for neighbouring regions. The famine affecting the Byzantine provinces in Asia Minor in 1032/33 also raged further to the east in Armenia and Northern Mesopotamia, as Matthew of Edessa indicates:

> At the beginning of the year 481 of the era of the Armenian calendar [1032–33] there was a severe famine throughout the entire land. Many people died because of this famine, and many sold their women and children for want of bread. Because of the intensity of the hardships, whenever one spoke, he yielded up his soul. In this manner the land was consumed by famine.[163]

For Baghdad and wider regions of the Islamic world, catastrophe was equally foretold by a portent:

> And in the year four hundred and twenty-three of the Arabs (1031 AD) a woman in Baghdad gave birth (to a being) which was like an ill-formed serpent. He had the head of a man, and a mouth and a neck, and he was without hands and without feet. And, moreover, when he fell upon the ground, he spoke and said, 'Four years from now a famine shall make an end of the children of men, unless men, and women, and children, and the beasts go forth and weep before the Lord, so that He may make His rain to descend'. And when the Caliph heard this, he commanded that all the people should go outside [the city] and make supplication. And because many did not believe this report, very few went out. And in that year [1031–32] the water froze in Bagdad and the red sand descended as

---

162   Kaldellis, *Streams of Gold*, p. 168, on other sources indicating that Michael IV was relatively popular. See also Krallis, "Historiography as Political Debate".
163   Matthew of Edessa, *History* I, 60, trans. Dostourian, p. 55. Telelis, Μετεωρολογικά φαινόμενα, N° 443.

rain, and the trees were destroyed and produced no fruit at all the season. And there was so great a famine in the wilderness that the nomads who lived there ate their camels and their horses, and even their children. (…) And they were in tribulation not only because of the famine (or, want of food), but also through thirst which was due to the scarcity of water, and they came and camped by the rivers (or, canals) which were in the neighbourhood of the towns and villages. And there was a pestilence in India and in all Persia; forty thousand biers with dead men on them were taken out from Isfahan in one week. And in Baghdad also there was not a single house left in which there was not wailing. And in Mosul four thousand young men died of the disease of inflammation of the eye-lids.[164]

A disease, perhaps akin to the one reported for Byzantium for 1039/40 (maybe diphtheria), had raged in Baghdad a few years earlier in 1033/34, when heavy storms and rainfalls also affected Northern and Southern Mesopotamia (in general, the Kuna Ba isotope date from Northern Iraq indicates on average much more humid conditions when compared with the 10th century, see Fig. 15.6).[165] For 1037, Bar Hebraeus again reports snowfall in Baghdad, followed by an intense cold. Similar phenomena occurred in January 1039, followed by unusual heat in March and another frost period a few days later.[166] In 1042, hailstorms destroyed more than 30 villages around Baghdad.[167] For the years between 1042 and 1045, we read about famine in various regions of Western Europe.[168] Equally, in China, the 1030s and 1040s were plagued by various catastrophes such as droughts, floods, famine, earthquakes and epidemics among humans and animals, culminating in a extremely devastating flood of the Yellow River in 1048, followed by another famine and large movements of refugees.[169] Some of these global climate fluctuations, in addition to or as further effect of the impact of the Oort Solar Minimum, may have been connected to strong La Niña events identified also on the basis of proxies from South Asia and the Americas.[170]

164   Bar Hebraeus, *Chronography*, trans. Budge, pp. 193–94. Telelis, Μετεωρολογικά φαινόμενα, Nos 443, 444. Busse, *Chalif und Großkönig*, pp. 390–91.
165   Bar Hebraeus, *Chronography*, trans. Budge, p. 194. Telelis, Μετεωρολογικά φαινόμενα, Nos 445–446, 449–450. For the Kuna Ba data see Sinha et al., "Role of climate".
166   Bar Hebraeus, *Chronography*, trans. Budge, p. 199. Telelis, Μετεωρολογικά φαινόμενα, N° 456; Busse, *Chalif und Großkönig*, p. 391.
167   Bar Hebraeus, *Chronography*, trans. Budge, p. 200. Telelis, Μετεωρολογικά φαινόμενα, N° 461.
168   Wozniak, *Naturereignisse im frühen Mittelalter*, pp. 622–23.
169   Zhang, *The River, the Plain, and the State*, pp. 1–3, 100–02, 224–26; Mostern, *The Yellow River*, pp. 155–60, 166–68.
170   Campbell, *The Great Transition*, pp. 39–43.

9 Further Climatic Anomalies and the Migrations from the Steppes

Scylitzes continued his focus on portents to the reign of Constantine IX Monomachos (June 1042 to January 1055), the last husband of Empress Zoë, who died in June 1050:[171]

> Those were the first deeds of (Constantine IX) Monomachos in the tenth year of the indiction. On the eleventh of October, eleventh year of the indiction, AM 6551 [1042], a comet appeared travelling from east to west and it was seen shining during the whole month; it presaged the forthcoming universal disasters.[172]

We do not find, however, a similar density of meteorological phenomena and calamities as in the narrative of Skylitzes for the years 1025 to 1042. For September of 1043, the year in which Constantine IX also had to face a military rebellion and a surprise attack of the Rus on Constantinople, Skylitzes informs us, "a wind blew so violently that almost the entire fruit of the vine was destroyed".[173] A major disaster of meteorological and epidemiological character in Skylitzes "Synopsis" only hit Constantinople again towards the end of Constantine IX's reign in 1054:

> In the seventh and eighth years of the indiction the capital was visited by a plague; the living were unequal to the task of bearing away the dead. In the summer of the seventh year of the indiction [July–September 1054] there was a great hailstorm which caused many deaths, not only of animals but of men too. The emperor had an attack of gout, a familiar affliction for him, and was lying in the Mangana monastery which he had recently built. A further illness followed on the first one and he was near to death; the question of whom they should establish on the imperial throne was debated by those who held the highest positions in the palace.[174]

---

171   Kaldellis, *Streams of Gold*, pp. 180–81, 201; Preiser-Kapeller, "Byzantium 1025–1204", pp. 61–62, 64.
172   John Scylitzes, *Synopsis*, Constantine IX, 2, ed. Thurn, pp. 423, 56–424, 62; trans. Wortley, p. 399.
173   John Scylitzes, *Synopsis*, Constantine IX, 7, ed. Thurn, pp. 433, 38–39; trans. Wortley, p. 407. Telelis, Μετεωρολογικά φαινόμενα, Nº 462; Kaldellis, *Streams of Gold*, pp. 184–87.
174   John Scylitzes, *Synopsis*, Constantine IX, 7, ed. Thurn, pp. 477, 74–82; trans. Wortley, p. 445. Telelis, Μετεωρολογικά φαινόμενα, Nº 472. On the death of Constantine IX see also Michael Psellos, *Chronographia* VI, 201–203, ed. Reinsch, pp. 195–96.

Around the same time, extreme cold affected Armenia in 1054 and 1055,[175] while low Nile floods causes a "dearth of grain" in Egypt between 1052 and 1055, aggravated by speculations of members of the elite and even the Fatimid Caliph al-Mustanṣir (1036–94) himself.[176] The Fatimid government also asked for help from Constantine IX Monomachos. The emperor agreed after April 1054 to ship 400,000 *irdabb*, which is 2,700 tons of grain, to Egypt.[177] Yet the death of Constantine IX in January 1055 dashed all hopes by the Fatimid regime for support from Constantinople, since Empress Theodora, the sister of Zoë and last scion of the Macedonian dynasty, decided to cancel the deal.[178]

The dynamic vizir al-Yāzūrī, however, was able to convince Caliph al-Mustanṣir to end speculations in grain and in general to confine price rigging. As al-Maqrīzī indicates:

> al-Yāzūrī performed his task superbly for twenty months until the harvest of the crops two years later, which relieved the populace and ended inflation. People did not suffer in the least, thanks to his good administration. After the vizir [al-Yāzūrī] was killed [in March 1058], the state enjoyed neither righteousness nor stability. The affairs of the state were in disarray, and no praiseworthy or efficient vizir was appointed. The office of vizir became highly discredited.

This violent change of administration proved fatal in the next, even more severe supply crisis in Fatimid Egypt in the 1060s (see below).[179]

One cause for the decision of Empress Theodora to cancel the delivery of grain to Egypt was the advance of the Seljuks from Iran, who in 1055/56 took over control in Baghdad and replaced the Buyids as "protectors" and *de facto* rulers in Mesopotamia.[180] The upheavals connected to warfare and regime change between 1055 and 1060 were aggravated by plagues of insects and diseases, so that famine raged in Iraq, Syria, and Persia, while sickness affected Baghdad, where there were "great swarms of flies which polluted the air, and

---

175 Telelis, Μετεωρολογικά φαινόμενα, Nos 471 and 474.
176 al-Maqrīzī, *Ighāthah*, trans. Allouche, pp. 33–36. Telelis, Μετεωρολογικά φαινόμενα, Nos 469, 475; Hassan, "Extreme Nile floods".
177 Dölger/Wirth, *Regesten von 1025–1204*, N° 912; Miotto, *Ο ανταγωνισμός Βυζαντίου και Χαλιφάτου των Φατιμιδών*, pp. 251–52 (with reference to the Arabic sources); Halm, *Die Kalifen von Kairo*, pp. 381–82; Felix, *Byzanz und die islamische Welt*, pp. 119–20. Cf. in general Jacoby, "Byzantine Trade with Egypt", and for the imperial granaries Cheynet, "Un aspect du ravitaillement de Constantinople".
178 Dölger/Wirth, *Regesten von 1025–1204*, N° 929a.
179 al-Maqrīzī, *Ighāthah*, trans. Allouche, pp. 35–36. Telelis, Μετεωρολογικά φαινόμενα, N° 475.
180 Kaldellis, *Streams of Gold*, pp. 197–99, 215.

more than one third of the population perished". Bar Hebraeus even claims that within three months 1.65 million people died in Bukhara and within two months 236,000 in Samarkand (both unrealistic numbers); and "it is said that from the beginning of the world never there was such a plague as this".[181] While first raids of Seljuk and other Turkmen units perturbed Armenia and eastern Anatolia, the area, largely under Byzantine rule was, according to Matthew of Edessa plagued by a long severe winter in 1058, followed by drought, harvest failure and famine; "on the other hand, at the beginning of the next year there was plenteousness and abundance of all types of foodstuffs (...)".[182] This abundance, however, soon came to an end due to the increasing number of Seljuk and Turkmen advances towards Armenia, Anatolia, and Syria. In 1064 they even conquered the former royal Armenian capital of Ani (see Fig. 15.3) that since 1045 had been under Byzantine administration.[183]

One cornerstone of Ellenblum's scenario was the notion of climate-induced stress on the steppe nomads in Central Asia and resulting migration of Turkmen groups under the leadership of the Seljuk dynasty towards the south into Transoxania and Eastern Iran (Khorasan) in the 1040s. Ellenblum partly based his study on an earlier analysis of Richard Bulliet, who attributed the Seljuk invasion and the "decline" of the wealth of Eastern Iran (including the cotton "industry" which had expanded the centuries before) to a severe cold period (the "Great Chill") in the 11th century.[184] As a matter of fact, some natural scientific proxy datasets (one also cited by Bulliet) indicate severely arid and/or cold conditions during parts of the late 10th or early 11th century; they are, however, located at considerable distance from the areas of settlement of the Turkmen before their migrations. Furthermore, there is no overlap between the periods of the adverse climate conditions and the movements of the Seljuks to the south.[185]

Based on a systematic and detailed survey of the written sources and partly also of proxy data, three scholars recently and independently rejected the Bulliet–Ellenblum scenario; Jürgen Paul in 2016 wrote: "In all, the article rejects Bulliet's causation chain and proposes that the Ghuzz-Seljuq migration

---

181   Bar Hebraeus, *Chronography*, trans. Budge, p. 209. Telelis, Μετεωρολογικά φαινόμενα, N° 477; Busse, *Chalif und Großkönig*, pp. 391–92.
182   Matthew of Edessa, *History* II, 11, trans. Dostourian, p. 94. Telelis, Μετεωρολογικά φαινόμενα, Nos 478, 486 (with a wrong dating to the year 1068–1069).
183   Aristakēs Lastiverc'i, *History*, ed. and trans. Bedrosian, pp. 308–13; Beihammer, *Byzantium and the Emergence of Muslim-Turkish Anatolia*, pp. 27, 55, 111–15; Kaldellis, *Streams of Gold*, pp. 234–35; Preiser-Kapeller, "Byzantium 1025–1204", p. 63.
184   Bulliet, *Cotton, Climate, and Camels*. See also Koder, "Zeitenwenden".
185   See also Campbell, *The Great Transition*, pp. 48–49.

into Transoxiana was due to political reasons rather than induced by climate change."[186] Deborah Tor in 2018 stated that "this catastrophe was not due to 'climate, cotton and camels' [the title of Bulliet's book] – in fact, Khurāsān was doing very well until the 1150s – but to concrete human agency and action".[187] And most recently, Yoshua Frenkel (2019) confirmed that "the sources do not provide decisive evidence to support a meteorological interpretation as the prime explanation of the massive human movement across the Steppes/ Iranian frontier during the eleventh century".[188] Thus, although we find some references to climatic extremes and epidemics in Eastern Iran and Central Asia from Bar Hebraeus around the time of the Seljuk advance (see above), for instance, specialists on the region do not find sufficient evidence in the sources for a climate-induced migration and collapse scenario as proposed by Bulliet and Ellenblum, who otherwise argued for the primacy of historiography over proxy data.

The Byzantines, however, faced nomadic invaders from the Steppes not only in Anatolia, but equally at the Danube, as also prominently discussed in Ellenblum's chapter on Byzantium. The Pechenegs had controlled the steppes north of the Black Sea since the late 9th century, but since the 1030s were increasingly under pressure from new steppe formations in the east (the Oghuz and the Cumans) and the princedoms of the Rus in the north. Eventually, some groups crossed the Danube and after some devastating warfare came to an arrangement with Constantinople, which included the establishment of a semi-independent "Patzinakia" in modern-day Bulgaria, from where, however, raids to other provinces of empire and even involvement in Byzantine civil wars were undertaken. Only Alexios I Komnenos was ultimately able to defeat them and to avoid the emergence of an enduring Pecheneg polity in AD 1091.[189]

At this "front" we also find some references to extremely cold conditions, as in 1048, when:

> it was toward the end of autumn and winter about to begin, the sun being in Capricorn, when a very strong wind arose from the north so that the river [Danube] froze to a depth of fifteen cubits. All guard duties being relaxed, Tyrach [one leader of the Pechenegs] seized the opportunity for which he prayed: he crossed the Danube with all the Patzinaks

---

186 Paul, "Nomads and Bukhara".
187 Tor, "The Eclipse of Khurāsān".
188 Frenkel, "The Coming of the Barbarians".
189 Curta, "The Image and Archaeology of the Pechenegs"; Meško, "Pecheneg groups in the Balkans".

> [Pechenegs], eighty thousand in number they say. They installed themselves on the other side, razing and devastating everything they came across.[190]

We hear, however, also about disease among the newcomers from the Steppes:

> The enemy [the Pechenegs] were not yet used to these lands that were foreign to them and were afflicted by a pestilent disease; they were, moreover, not used to fighting against the Roman phalanxes. So they did not even attempt to raise up arms against them, but gave up as hostages their own rulers and commanders and thus pretended to have been subdued, obtaining a reprieve in this way.[191]

Yet while the Pechenegs were able to establish a durable presence in the Balkans,[192] weather and disease together with enemy attacks brought almost complete destruction to another group trying to cross the Danube in 1064/65 – the Oghuz (*Ouzoi* in Greek sources);[193] Michael Attaleiates wrote:

> Such was the state of his [Emperor Constantine X Dukas, r. 1059–67] preparation [for a campaign against the Oghuz] when messengers from those who had been dispatched to the Danube returned post-haste with the news that that nation had been utterly destroyed. For the captured generals had managed to escape their captivity and explained how this destruction had occurred, saying that the leaders of the Ouzoi had, at the instigation of the Roman authorities in the cities along the Danubian shores, embarked on ships and crossed the Danube, returning to their own lands. Among those who were left behind, however, a vast horde still, some were devastated by an epidemic disease and hunger and were only half alive, while others had been defeated by the Bulgarians and the Pechenegs who were in proximity and were utterly annihilated by iron and the hooves of horses and were even crushed by their own wagons. And so they were killed contrary to all human expectation and those who at one point thought that they would prevail over all others were now

---

190 John Scylitzes, *Synopsis*, Constantine IX, 7, ed. Thurn, pp. 458, 40–46; trans. Wortley, p. 429. Telelis, Μετεωρολογικά φαινόμενα, nr 467; Wozniak, *Naturereignisse im frühen Mittelalter*, p. 499; Kaldellis, *Streams of Gold*, pp. 192–94; Dölger/Wirth, *Regesten von 1025–1204*, N° 879c. Cold conditions between 1046 and 1048 are also indicated in tree-ring data from Albania, see PAGES 2k Network consortium, Database.
191 Michael Attaleiates, *History* 7, 2, ed. and trans. Kaldellis/Krallis, pp. 52–53.
192 Kaldellis, *Streams of Gold*, pp. 199–201.
193 Kaldellis, *Streams of Gold*, p. 236.

held in little regard. In fact, the reports were not far from the truth. (...) As for this Scythian nation, some crossed the Danube and were destroyed by a famine against which there was no recourse, for they had no food and no hope of foraging for it, as their land had neither been ploughed nor sown.[194]

Similar descriptions can be found in the continuation of Scylitzes' chronicle and the work of Zonaras.[195]

It is hard to tell whether the factors described as bringing about the defeat of the Oghuz had also originally motivated their decision to attempt a migration/invasion across the Danube into Byzantine territories, thus confirming Ellenblum's scenario at least for this region. A prevalence of rather unstable and extreme climatic conditions across parts of Southwestern Asia and the Eastern Mediterranean during the 1060s is again confirmed by parallel descriptions for Iraq and Egypt. In Baghdad, the months from October to December 1063, for instance, were characterized by "fierce heat", accompanied by "sickness and pestilence", while January 1064 brought "intense cold", with the Tigris frozen and snowfall.[196] Furthermore, severe floods plagued China in the 1060s, and droughts rages between 1068 and 1070. Together with the calamities in Western Afro-Eurasia, these phenomena hint at a larger-scale climate anomaly across Afro-Eurasia that, as mentioned above, was perhaps to be connected with strong El Niño events as also reconstructed from South American proxy data. It also affected precipitation conditions in East Africa in the headwaters of the Nile.[197]

10 The Great Calamity in Fatimid Egypt and the Byzantine Loss of Anatolia

Due to these precipitation shortfalls, Fatimid Egypt in the 1060s and early 1070s was plagued by a sequence of low Nile floods, aggravated by the instability of the regime after the death of Vizir al-Yāzūrī in March 1058 and its inability to

---

194 Michael Attaleiates, *History* 14, 9 and 12, ed. and trans. Kaldellis/Krallis, pp. 154–57 and 158–59.

195 John Scylitzes continuatus, *Chronicle*, ed. and trans. McGeer, pp. 64–65. See also Zonaras, *Epitome* 18, 9, ed. Büttner-Wobst, p. 680, and Wozniak, *Naturereignisse im frühen Mittelalter*, p. 658.

196 Bar Hebraeus, *Chronography*, trans. Budge, p. 216. Telelis, Μετεωρολογικά φαινόμενα, Ν[os] 481–82.

197 Hassan, "Extreme Nile floods"; Zaroug/Eltahir/Giorgi, "Droughts and floods"; Zhang, *The River, the Plain, and the State*, pp. 194–95; Mostern, *The Yellow River*, pp. 156–57, 168–70.

take efficient measures to mitigate the catastrophic supply shortfalls, not even for the core guard regiments of the Caliph. This contributed to the outbreak of civil war between competing factions of the army, which finally would even plunder the Caliphal palaces in Cairo, and an almost-collapse of Fatimid reign in Egypt. Al-Maqrīzī sums it up thus:

> During the reign of [Caliph] al-Mustanṣir occurred the famine that had an atrocious effect and left a horrid memory. It lasted seven years and was caused by the weakness of the [Caliph's] authority, the deterioration of the affairs of state, the usurpation of power by the military commanders, the continuous strife among the Bedouins, the failure of the Nile to reach its plenitude, and the absence of cultivation of the lands that had been irrigated. This began in 457/1064–65. It resulted in rising prices and increased famine and was followed by an epidemic. The lands remained uncultivated, and fear prevailed. Land and sea routes became unsafe, and travel became impossible without a large escort; otherwise, one would be exposed to danger.[198]

As the sequence of factors for the later so-called "Great Calamity" mentioned by al-Maqrīzī makes clear, he lists the shortfall of Nile floods as one cause among others, especially political and institutional ones. As we have read for earlier low Nile floods of the 11th century, the Fatimid governments had then been able to mitigate the distress of the population – in contrast to the 1060s; this failure dramatically further undermined the authority of the Caliph.[199] The salvation for the Fatimids came through still-loyal troops from the remaining bases on the coast of Palestine, which were under the command of the Armenian-born General Badr al-Ǧamālī. He marched to Cairo in January 1074 and was able to lure the rebelling commanders of the other regiments into a trap at a feast and had them all killed. In addition, he forced the merchants of grain and bakers to bring their hoarded stocks at low prices to the market of the capital by sheer physical threat, including the beheading of some of their representatives. Badr al-Ǧamālī (1074–94) and his son al-Afdal (1094–1121) held

---

198 al-Maqrīzī, *Ighāthah*, trans. Allouche, p. 37. Telelis, Μετεωρολογικά φαινόμενα, Nos 480, 484, 487; Hassan, "Extreme Nile floods".

199 Halm, *Die Kalifen von Kairo*, pp. 404–20; Ellenblum, *The Collapse of the Eastern Mediterranean*, pp. 151–55; Brett, *The Fatimid Empire*, pp. 201–06. In contrast, Chipman/Avni/Ellenblum, "Collapse, affluence, and collapse", 200–01, 204–05 and 210–11, propose a more or less climate-deterministic scenario, arguing that, in the face of low Nile floods, "the relative capacity or lack of ability of the central government in these circumstances had very limited influence on the state's fortunes".

the office of the vizir and the *de facto* power in Fatimid Egypt for almost the next 50 years.[200]

In any case, the "Great Calamity" would very much frustrate any coordinated Fatimid efforts to defend the provinces in Syria against the advance of the Seljuks from Mesopotamia. But also in Byzantine historiography, written with the "benefit" or "bias" of hindsight, the reigns of Constantine x Dukas and Romanos IV Diogenes seem inevitably to lead to the catastrophe of Manzikert in 1071 and the following loss of Asia Minor. This time, also Michael Attaleiates (writing in 1079/80[201]) resorts to celestial phenomena (including Halley's Comet in 1066, whose last sighting between August and September 989 Leo Deacon had mentioned as ill-omened, see above) and other portents as harbingers of imminent doom:[202]

> Before this year, in the month of September of the second indiction, on the twenty-third of that month [23 September 1063], during the second watch of the night, there was a sudden powerful earthquake, more frightening than any that had happened before, and it began in the western regions. It was so great in magnitude that it overturned many houses, leaving only a few undamaged. (...) In the regions of Macedonia, the coastal cities suffered more on that night than the others, I mean Rhaidestos and Panion and Myriophyton [see the map in Fig. 15.3], where whole sections of the walls collapsed to their very foundations along with many houses, and many people died. In the Hellespont, Kyzikos was especially struck, where the ancient Greek temple was also shaken and most of it collapsed. (...) From that time on and for two years earthquakes continued to occur sporadically at various times, leaving mortal men speechless in wonder. (...) After the two-year period, an earthquake occurred that was larger than the frequent aftershocks, but smaller than the initial one. It happened at Nicaea in Bithynia and brought almost total devastation and ruin to the place. Its most important and large churches – the one founded in honor of the Wisdom of the Word of God, which was also the cathedral, and the one of the Holy Fathers, where the Council of the most Holy and Orthodox Fathers against Areios confirmed its decisions and where Orthodoxy was proclaimed openly to shine brighter than the sun-those churches, then, were shaken and collapsed as did the walls of

---

200   al-Maqrīzī, *Ighāthah*, trans. Allouche, p. 39. Feldbauer, *Die islamische Welt*, pp. 361–62; Halm, *Kalifen und Assassinen*, pp. 17–86; Brett, *The Fatimid Empire*, pp. 210–15.
201   Neville, *Guide to Byzantine Historical Writing*, pp. 150–52.
202   Krallis, "Historiography as Political Debate".

the city along with many private dwellings. And on that day the shaking ceased. These events were earned by our sins and were surely caused by divine anger; but it seems also that they were a predictive sign of the invasion by that nation, which I mentioned, and its destruction, for in divine signs it is possible to glimpse not only the things that we have already spoken about but also some things to come. During the course of the month of May of the fourth indiction [1066], a bright comet [Halley's comet[203]] appeared after the sun had set, which was as large as the moon when it is full, and it gave the impression that it was spewing forth smoke and mist. On the following day it began to send out some tendrils and the longer they grew the smaller the comet became. These rays stretched toward the east, the direction toward which it was proceeding, and this lasted for forty days. From the month of October until the following May [1067], the emperor [Constantine X Dukas] was afflicted by illness, which wore him out and so he departed from this life.[204]

Similar descriptions and prophetic notions can be found in Skylitzes continuatus, who follows Attaleiates in these passages.[205]

In contrast to Egypt, however, we hear little about climatic extremes; only during the first campaign of Romanos IV Diogenes, who succeeded on the throne in January 1068 against the Seljuks in the East, we hear from Michael Attaleiates as eyewitness that the Byzantine army suffered cold conditions after it had crossed the Taurus mountains to the north in December 1068:

And proceeding through that country in this way and crossing over the Taurus mountains with his entire army, he [Romanos IV Diogenes] entered Roman territory. But the men marching with him, who were coming from a warm climate, suddenly found themselves in icy cold weather, with everything covered with frost. It was about the end of the month of December, and they felt the bitter cold. Thus it happened that horses, mules, and men, especially those whose bodies were not robust or

---

203 On observations of Halley's comet in 1066, which was even depicted on the famous Bayeux Tapestry, in other parts of Europe and the Mediterranean see Wozniak, *Naturereignisse im frühen Mittelalter*, pp. 107–12.
204 Michael Attaleiates, *History* 15, 1–7, ed. and trans. Kaldellis/Krallis, pp. 160–67.
205 John Scylitzes continuatus, *Chronicle*, ed. and trans. McGeer, pp. 64–67. See also Neville, *Guide to Byzantine Historical Writing*, p. 157; it is unclear if this continuation was written by John Skylitzes himself or by another (anonymous) author.

well clothed, froze to death in the sudden cold and had to be left on the road, a pitiable sight.[206]

Occasion to reflect on the enmity of both Seljuks and nature against empire is provided for Michael Attaleiates, however, when Turkmen raiders plundered the city of Chonai (see the map in Fig. 15.3) and its famous sanctuary of Archangel Michael in 1070:

> Even before these news became widely known, they heard more tidings to the effect that the Turks had taken by storm the city of Chonai and the very shrine of the Archgeneral [Michael], famous for its miracles and dedications, and that they had filled the place with slaughter and filth, and polluted the church with many outrages. Worst of all was this: the channels in the cavern that, ever since the ancient visitation and divine manifestation of the Archgeneral, funnel the rivers flowing past that area whose current is precipitous, turbulent, and swift, failed to protect the refugees who sought to escape from the danger in them. Instead – and this had never happened before – the water flooded, was then sucked down, and again disgorged. It drowned almost all the fugitives, submerging them under water even though they were on land. The news of this greatly depressed us, for it was as though these disasters were being caused by divine anger. Not only the enemy but the very forces of nature seemed to be fighting against us.[207]

---

206 Michael Attaleiates, *History* 17, 20, ed. and trans. Kaldellis/Krallis, pp. 218–19. Cf. also John Scylitzes continuatus, *Chronicle*, ed. and trans. McGeer, pp. 94–95. Telelis, Μετεωρολογικά φαινόμενα, Nº 485. There are parallel reports on a severe winter for Central Europe, see Wozniak, *Naturereignisse im frühen Mittelalter*, pp. 500–01.

207 Michael Attaleiates, *History* 19, 3–4, ed. and trans. Kaldellis/Krallis, pp. 256–57. On the event, see also Thonemann, *The Maeander Valley*, p. 93. This passage is also adapted by Scylitzes continuatus; he augments it, however, with some interesting observations on the differences between earlier Seljuk attacks on marginal provinces in the east with a non-orthodox population and the recent raids into the Byzantine-orthodox heartlands: "For in times previous so great an invasion and onslaught of foreign enemies and the decimation of the people living under Roman rule were taken to be the wrath of God, but it was directed against those heretics who inhabit Iberia and Mesopotamia as far as Lykandos and Melitene, as well as the adjacent Armenia, or the ones who practise the Judaic heresy of Nestorios and the Akephaloi. These lands are full of this sort of erroneous belief. But when the calamity affected the Orthodox, all those who practised the faith of the Romans were at a loss as to what to do, thinking that they had reached their limit of iniquity just as the Amorites had reached theirs, and believing that in these circumstances not only correct belief was required but also a life not at odds with faith. It followed that both the man who clearly erred with respect to belief and the man who stumbled and fell

The severe crisis of the empire in the aftermath of the defeat at Manzikert of 1071 in Attaleiates' narrative, however, largely unfolds without the "very forces of nature" – in a combination of civil wars, fights between independently acting warlords of Byzantine, Armenian, Norman, or Turkmen background, devastations of large areas and displacements of masses searching refuge in the capital, and a meltdown of state finances reflected in the debasement of the Byzantine gold coins, all aggravated by the incompetence or even viciousness of officials around the new young Emperor Michael VII Dukas (1071–78), especially the eunuch Nikephoritzes (in some aspects a narrative revenant of the eunuch John Orphanotrophos).[208]

In addition to his criticism of the regime of Michael VIII, Michael Attaleiates, however, did not abstain from other unhappy omens in his narrative:

> In that year a number of portents were observed in the City of Byzas [Constantinople]. A three-legged chicken was born as well as a baby with an eye on its forehead (and having a single eye at that) and the feet of a goat. When it was exposed in the public avenue in the area of Diakonissa, it uttered the cries of a human baby.[209] Two soldiers of the Immortals [a guard regiment] were struck by lightning in a public place close to the western walls of the City. Not only that but certain comets streaked

---

     into an imperfect way of life were subject to the same punishment. Whosoever practises this and teaches this is praised and blessed." John Scylitzes continuatus, *Chronicle*, ed. and trans. McGeer, pp. 108–09.

208 Krallis, *Michael Attaleiates and the Politics of Imperial Decline*, pp. 171–212; Krallis, "Historiography as Political Debate"; Kaldellis, *Streams of Gold*, pp. 248–54; Preiser-Kapeller, "Byzantium 1025–1204", pp. 63–64; Hendy, *Studies in the Byzantine Monetary Economy*, pp. 233–36, 509–12; Caplanis, "The Debasement of the 'Dollar of the Middle Ages'"; For the background to the "loss" of Anatolia, see now especially Beihammer, *Byzantium and the Emergence of Muslim-Turkish Anatolia*, pp. 9, 15, 388 and 390, who sums up: "The political situation of Byzantine Asia Minor from 1056 onwards was marked by serious tensions between centralizing tendencies and the gradual strengthening of regional powers backed by military forces. These consisted of seditious Byzantine aristocrats, foreign mercenary troops, Armenian noblemen, Arab and Kurdish emirs and many others. This process resulted in a fragmentation of state authority and the emergence of numerous, mostly short-lived, semi-independent local lordships of limited size. Political power, to a large extent, was regionalized. This is to say, that we are dealing not necessarily with a conflict between the Byzantine central government and Turkish invaders but with struggles and contentions within a complicated patchwork of local powers, in which the Turks intruded and eventually managed to prevail."

209 One is reminded of a similar portent reported by Bar Hebraeus for Baghdad in 1031, see Bar Hebraeus, *Chronography*, trans. Budge, pp. 193–94, and above. On portents in Attaleiates, see also Krallis, *Michael Attaleiates and the Politics of Imperial Decline*, pp. 205–10.

across the sky. Meanwhile, because the east was being wasted by the barbarians there who were ruining and subjecting it, large multitudes were fleeing those regions on a daily basis and seeking refuge in the Imperial City [Constantinople], so that hunger afflicted everyone, oppressing them because of the lack of supplies. When winter arrived, because the emperor [Michael VII Dukas] lacked generosity and was extremely stingy, he offered no succour from the imperial treasuries or any other form of provident welfare either to those in office or to the people of the City, and so each person wallowed in his own misery, nor did he hold out an abundant hand that could assist the poor and provide them with daily provisions, for it is through these means that the poor are normally supplied with necessities. There were many, indeed countless deaths every day, not only among the refugees but also among the people of the City [Constantinople], so that their dead bodies were heaped both in the so-called porticos and in open spaces, and they were carried on stretchers, each one of which was often stacked with five or six bodies piled up in a random heap. Everywhere you saw sad faces and the Reigning City [Constantinople] was filled with misery. The rulers did not let up on their daily injustices and illegal trials, but acted as though the Romans were not being afflicted by anything out of the ordinary, be it foreign war, divine wrath, or poverty and violence oppressing the people; it was with such nonchalance that they practiced all their tyrannical impieties. Every imperial scheme and plan, in fact, was preoccupied with some injustice against their own subjects, at the ingenious looting of their livelihoods and their resources for living.[210]

The reference to the porticoes reminds at least the modern reader of the winter of 927, when Romanos I Lakapenos used them as emergency shelter for the homeless of the capital, while now they served for the deposition of the bodies of victims of the famine that, according to Attaleiates, had been aggravated by the "nonchalance" and "tyrannical impieties" of the current government. Another example of Attaleiates for the aggravation or even causation of supply shortfalls by "imperial plans" is the establishment of the so-called *phoundax* by the *logothetes tou dromou* Nikephoritzes in the important grain market of Rhaidestos (see the map in Fig. 15.3) in Thrace. This, according to

---

210   Michael Attaleiates, *History* 26, 8–9, ed. and trans. Kaldellis/Krallis, pp. 384–87. See also John Scylitzes continuatus, *Chronicle*, ed. and trans. McGeer, pp. 162–65; Bar Hebraeus, *Chronography*, trans. Budge, p. 226. Wozniak, *Naturereignisse im frühen Mittelalter*, pp. 625–26.

Michael Attaleiates, contributed to a scarcity of food and an increase in prices in Constantinople, in turn raising resistance against the regime of the emperor.

> He [Nikephoritzes] thereby established a monopoly over this most essential of trade, that of grain, as no one was able to purchase it except from the *phoundax*. (...) For from that moment on they monopolized not only the grain carts (...) but also all other goods the circulated in the vicinity. (...) He, then, farmed out the phoundax for sixty pounds of gold, and enjoyed the proceeds, while everyone else was hard-pressed by a shortage not only of grain but of every other good. For the dearth of grain causes dearth in everything else, as it is grain that allows the purchase or preparation of other goods, while those who work for wages demand higher pay to compensate for the scarcity of food. (...) As a result of the emperor's planning or, rather, of Nikephoros's evil designs, grain was in short supply and abundance turned into dearth. The people's discontent increased.[211]

While Michael Attaleiates provides interesting observations on the impact of a price increase in basic foodstuffs on other economic sectors, we have to be aware that he is not necessarily a trustworthy rapporteur. During the reign of Michael VII Dukas, he had no qualms in cooperating with the regime and seeking favours from it; his highly critical narrative was written only after the downfall of Michael VII and Nikephoritzes, also to create an evil counterexample to the new emperor Nikephoros III Botaneiates (1078–81), to whom he dedicated his text. Furthermore, Michael Attaleiates himself was engaged in the grain trade at Rhaidestos as a landowner in the city's environs and proprietor of a landing place for cargo vessels in the capital and he was thus affected by the introduction of the *phoundax*, whose impact on the prices also arose from the decision by market actors such as Attaleiates to withhold their stocks of grain under these less profitable circumstances.[212]

Nevertheless, it seems plausible that a majority of the population in Constantinople held the regime of Michael VII Dukas responsible for the sorry

---

[211] Michael Attaleiates, *History* 25, 4–6, ed. and trans. Kaldellis/Krallis, pp. 366–73: For interpretations of this passage: Angold, *The Byzantine Empire*, pp. 122–23; Laiou/Morrisson, *The Byzantine Economy*, pp. 135–36; Laiou, "God and Mammon"; Dölger/Wirth, *Regesten von 1025–1204*, N° 996. See also John Scylitzes continuatus, *Chronicle*, ed. and trans. McGeer, pp. 146–47.

[212] Krallis, *Michael Attaleiates and the Politics of Imperial Decline*, pp. 20–29; Kaldellis, *Streams of Gold*, pp. 262–63; Krallis, "Historiography as Political Debate".

state of the empire and especially of the supplies of the capital, which lead to the eventual downfall of the government and the acceptance of Nikephoros III as emperor.²¹³ In contrast to Ellenblum's scenario, however, no "short-term climatic catastrophe" can be identified from the written sources as contributing either to the regime chance of 1078 or to the severe crisis of the Byzantine Empire in the 1070s or 1080s; on the occasion of another rebellion in the European provinces during the reign of Michael VII, we learn from Attaleiates that when the "summer was beginning (…) the fruit was still hanging unpicked from the trees", since people had fled from their farms due to ongoing warfare; therefore, "there was not small shortage of food in the Reigning City and the other western cities".²¹⁴ So there was a lack not of rain, temperature, or vegetation, but of security.

From neighbouring regions, we read that in 1074 in Syria the effects of ongoing warfare on the food situation around Damascus were aggravated by a plague of rodents, resulting in famine and disease.²¹⁵ More generally, however, Matthew of Edessa connects the "severe famine" which in 1079/80 "occurred throughout all the lands of the venerators of the cross, lands which are located on this side of the Mediterranean Sea" to the raids of the "bloodthirsty and ferocious Turkish nation", since they "interrupted the cultivation of land", causing a "shortage of food"; furthermore:

> the cultivators and laborers decreased due to the sword and enslavement, and so famine spread throughout the whole land. Many areas became depopulated, the Oriental peoples began to decline, and the country of the Romans became desolate; neither food nor security for the individual was to be found anywhere except in Edessa and its confines.²¹⁶

Again, we do not read about direct climatic factors. Baghdad, however, between November 1073 and February 1074, suffered from torrential winter rains and severe floods, destroying large areas in the east of the city.²¹⁷

---

213 Kaldellis, *Streams of Gold*, pp. 265–66; Preiser-Kapeller, "Byzantium 1025–1204", pp. 63–64.
214 Michael Attaleiates, *History* 26, 5, ed. and trans. Kaldellis/Krallis, pp. 378–81.
215 Bar Hebraeus, *Chronography*, trans. Budge, pp. 225–26.
216 Matthew of Edessa, *History* II, 73, trans. Dostourian, p. 143.
217 Bar Hebraeus, *Chronography*, trans. Budge, pp. 224–25. Telelis, Μετεωρολογικά φαινόμενα, Nº 491.

11 The Komnenian Dynasty, the End of the Oort Minimum and the Medieval Climate Anomaly in the Eastern Mediterranean in the 12th to 13th Century

In 1081, the elderly Nikephoros III Botaneiates was forced to step down from the throne in favour of the young Alexios I Komnenos;[218] the later pro-Komnenian historiography, especially the "Alexias" written down by Alexios' daughter Anna in the 1140s, celebrated him as saviour of the state, stabilizing the empire in terms of administration, finances and especially its borders, first on the Balkans, then in Asia Minor.[219] We have a contrary opinion in the 12th century history of Zonaras, who complained that Alexios I:

> did not behave with (the state's) institutions as common and as with public ones and did not consider himself their steward but their owner; he considered and named the palace his own house. (...) he offered the relatives and some servants public funds in whole wagonloads, and gave them ample annual allowances, so that they embraced themselves with great wealth.[220]

While earlier scholarship has followed this opinion and has characterized Alexios I's reign as a completion of the takeover of the state by the powerful families that had been struggling for access to the throne since the 10th century, or even as a decisive step toward a "feudalization" of Byzantium, recent research has demonstrated that Alexios I did not dissolve the "centralized" Roman polity of the past, but even strengthened existing instruments of the state's grasp onto taxes and properties created by the Macedonian legislation (see above). Thereby, the Byzantine government re-established the material basis to act as a great power also in the 12th century (especially in the reign of Alexios' I grandson Manuel I, 1143–80) with a radius of action still comparable with that of the assumed singular apex of Byzantine power in the early 11th century (under Basil II), ranging from Southern Italy to the Euphrates and from beyond the Danube (Hungary) to Egypt (the target of naval operations in the 1160s and 1170s).[221]

---

218 Kaldellis, *Streams of Gold*, pp. 269–70; Preiser-Kapeller, "Byzantium 1025–1204", pp. 64–65.
219 Neville, *Guide to Byzantine Historical Writing*, pp. 174–79; Kaldellis, *Streams of Gold*, pp. 287–301; Preiser-Kapeller, "Byzantium 1025–1204", pp. 67–70.
220 Zonaras, *Epitome* 18, 29, ed. Büttner-Wobst, p. 767. It is unclear if John Zonaras wrote his history also in response to Anna's *Alexias*, see Neville, *Guide to Byzantine Historical Writing*, p. 195.
221 Smyrlis, "Private property and state finances"; Smyrlis, "The Fiscal Revolution of Alexios I Komnenos"; Magdalino, *The Empire of Manuel I Komnenos*; Kaldellis, *Streams of*

Regarding climatic events, besides localized events such as stormy weathers on the sea between Greece and Southern Italy during warfare with the Normans in 1081 and 1085,[222] Anna Komnene for Alexios' reign refers to extreme conditions in the winter of 1090/91, when, after a defeat against the Pechenegs and due to a threat to the maritime supply lines of Constantinople by the fleets of the Turkish Emir Tzachas of Smyrna, the situation for Alexios I was already precarious:

> Things were not going well for Alexios either by sea or on land, and the severe winter did not help; in fact, the doors of houses could not be opened for the heavy weight of snow (more snow fell that year than anyone could remember in the past). Still, the emperor did all that he could by summoning mercenaries by letter from all quarters.[223]

This extreme winter overlaps with reports on climate anomalies such as severe winters and dry summers in Western Europe in the early 1090s, followed by famines and epidemics among humans and animals, which have been discussed as possible motivations for the mobility of laymen toward a "promised land", where "milk and honey flows" in the First Crusade after 1095.[224] For Northern Iraq, the Kuna Ba data indicates the years between 1085 and 1094 as the most humid ones in the entire 11th century (see Fig. 15.6).[225] In addition, very cold winters with heavy snowfall were reported for 1091 and 1093 in China, again demonstrating the wide range of these climate anomalies.[226]

For John Zonaras, by contrast, like earlier governments for Skylitzes or Attaleiates, so too the reign of Alexios I Komnenos in general was beclouded by portents and catastrophes:

> During the reign of this emperor [Alexios I Komnenos], there were many fires in different parts of the city [of Constantinople], and many of them the fire ravaged and destroyed. Once a very strong and violent wind blew

---

Gold, pp. 276–77; Preiser-Kapeller, "Byzantium 1025–1204", pp. 73–76; Olson, *Environment and Society in Byzantium*, pp. 193–94.

222 Telelis, Μετεωρολογικά φαινόμενα, Nos 494, 496–497.
223 Anna Komnene, *Alexias* VIII, 3, ed. Reinsch/Kambylis, pp. 241, 78–242, 84; trans. Sewter/Frankopan, p. 220. Telelis, Μετεωρολογικά φαινόμενα, No 502. Cold conditions are also indicated for Albania in the early 1090s in tree-ring data, see PAGES 2k Network consortium, Database.
224 i Monclús, "Famines sans frontiers", pp. 48–50; Wozniak, *Naturereignisse im frühen Mittelalter*, pp. 514–15, 533–34, 545, 627–28, 658–60, 685; Salvin, "Crusaders in Crisis"; Pfister/Wanner, *Klima und Gesellschaft in Europa*, pp. 172–74.
225 Sinha et al., "Role of climate".
226 Zhang, *The River, the Plain, and the State*, p. 156.

under this ruler during the springtime, which caused many structures to collapse. The statue, which was placed on the large round porphyry column on the Plakaton, fell down and killed many passers-by. The image, which broke and fell into many pieces when it fell, was of immense size and wonderful beauty. Another time a very heavy downpour broke out, just on the festive day of the chief apostles of Christ, Peter and Paul; it began late in the evening and lasted until the same hour of the following day without subsiding. At that time houses collapsed due to the rush of water, the valleys were filled with water and were in no way different from seas, and not a few people and many animals died.[227]

Again, the number of calamities and climatic events we find in a source also depends on its narrative intentions, such as its possible framing of an emperor's reign through the lens of "moral meteorology". Ellenblum was right that we cannot subordinate historiography to the primacy of the proxy data. However, we also cannot take its information on the frequency, severity, or impact of environmental stressors at face value. Nevertheless, written evidence from various points of observations (Constantinople, Baghdad, Cairo, Armenia) can allow us to "triangulate" actual clusters of climatic extremes across the Eastern Mediterranean and the Middle East (or with a glance at the rich "archives of society" in Western Europe or China even across Afro-Eurasia), as during the Oort Solar Minimum. In some cases, high-resolution proxies provide additional confirmation.

Regarding the interplay between environmental and socio-political dynamics, however, the texts we have inspected themselves often provide more complex lines of causation beyond mere linear climatic impacts on a society, hinting at the role of institutions and market actors for the mitigation or aggravation of a supply shortfall after a strong winter or a low Nile flood, for instance. And beyond the focus on "short-term climatic catastrophes" propagated by Ellenblum and his co-authors also in his last publications,[228] we have to consider the interplay between long-term trends in climate, agriculture, and society and singular shocks in order to provide convincing scenarios that do justice to both the possible fragility and the resilience of regimes and polities during the Medieval Climate Anomaly.

---

227 Zonaras, *Epitome* 18, 26, ed. Büttner-Wobst, pp. 755–56. Telelis, Μετεωρολογικά φαινόμενα, Nº 495.
228 Li/Shelach-Lavi/Ellenblum, "Short-Term Climatic Catastrophes"; Chipman/Avni/Ellenblum, "Collapse, affluence, and collapse".

After the end of the Oort Solar Minimum around 1080/90, more stable temperature and precipitation conditions returned in Western and Central Europe in the 12th century and first half of the 13th, of course not excluding short-term anomalies and calamities such as a "mega drought" in 1137.[229] "Beneficial" climate parameters can be reconstructed equally for parts of the Eastern Mediterranean in the 12th century; more humid conditions and an increase in human activity during the Crusader period have been identified in proxy data from the site of Jableh, then within the territory of the Principality of Antioch (see the map in Fig. 15.3). A similar increase in indicators of human agricultural activity can be seen in pollen data from the Southern Bekaa Valley in Lebanon. Besides these long-term trends, however, again written evidence documents the recurrence of severe droughts, famine, and plagues of locusts and rodents in the Crusader states especially also during the 12th century; but in general, the "Latin" regimes were able to cope with these situations better than in the 13th century, when also general political and military conditions had changed to their disadvantage.[230]

Equally, for the remaining Byzantine provinces on the Aegean, especially Greece, various types of evidence confirm the scenario of continued or even intensified 12th-century economic growth, be it the increase in the number of settlements mentioned in the documents of Mount Athos for the Chalkidike, the increase in the number of church buildings in Messenia from the 10th to 13th century or the increase in the monetary finds in Corinth or Athens.[231] Even the increase in the number of sites of Venetian commercial activity (as documented in the Chrysobulls of 1082 and 1198) especially in the provinces of the Southern Balkans can be interpreted as an indicator of economic growth

---

229 Goosse et al., "The medieval climate anomaly in Europe"; Sirocko/David, "Das mittelalterliche Wärmeoptimum"; Behringer, *Kulturgeschichte des Klimas*, pp. 103–15; i Monclús, "Famines sans frontiers"; Pfister/Wanner, *Klima und Gesellschaft in Europa*, pp. 175–84.

230 Kaniewski et al., "Medieval coastal Syrian vegetation patterns"; Kaniewski et al., "The Medieval Climate Anomaly and the Little Ice Age in Coastal Syria"; Hajar et al., "Environmental changes in Lebanon" (for the Southern Bekaa-Valley). Cf. also Redford, "Trade and Economy in Antioch and Cilicia". On famine and droughts in the Crusader states and their reactions to it, cf. Raphael, *Climate and Political Climate*, pp. 21–27, 56–94 and 191–93; Xoplaki et al., "Modelling Climate and Societal Resilience".

231 Kazhdan/Epstein, *Change in Byzantine Culture*, pp. 34–37; Angold, *The Byzantine Empire*, pp. 280–86; Laiou/Morrisson, *The Byzantine Economy*, pp. 91–96; Whittow, "The Middle Byzantine Economy", pp. 475–76; Curta, *Southeastern Europe in the Middle Ages*, pp. 323–27; Gerolymatou, Αγορές, έμποροι και εμπόριο, pp. 152–70; Bintliff, *The Complete Archaeology of Greece*, pp. 391–93 (with graphs); Izdebski/Koloch/Słoczyński, "Exploring Byzantine and Ottoman economic history"; Olson, *Environment and Society in Byzantium*, p. 196.

and demand – despite the long-term consequences these activities may have had.[232]

These long-term trends even continued when we can reconstruct another change in climatic conditions towards less "favourable" parameters in the Eastern Mediterranean and Middle East from the middle to the end of the 12th century onwards. In Cappadocia (now beyond the Byzantine borders), the oxygen isotope data from Lake Nar indicates a trend reversal towards more arid conditions had already begun in the early 11th century, with the driest period being in the 1180s (see Fig. 15.8).[233] For Northwestern Anatolia, proxy data (speleothems from the Sofular cave, see Fig. 15.7) documents a turn towards more arid conditions from the 1180s onwards, which continued until after the mid-13th century.[234] A similar pattern can be identified in a May–June precipitation reconstruction based on tree rings for the Northern Aegean (see Fig. 15.9).[235] In another precipitation reconstruction for Southwestern Anatolia for the years 1097 to 2000, the 70 years from 1195 to 1264 were identified as the driest period in the entire record (while the years 1098 to 1167 marked one of the most humid ones). An equal pattern can be found in speleothems from Thrace (Uzuntarla Cave, Turkey), in sediments of the Tecer Lake from Cappadocia (see the map in Fig. 15.3) or in the pollen data from the area of Antioch, with a shift towards drier conditions from the later 12th century onwards that overlapped with a severe famine in Syria between 1178 and 1181.[236] A similarly dry period is indicated in the Kuna Ba data from Northern Iraq, starting around 1165 and continuing until the mid-13th century (see Fig. 15.6).[237] Around 1180, a 30-year period of severe El Niño events began, and Egypt, now under Ayyubid rule, was hit by extremely low Nile floods in the years around 1200; the ensuing catastrophic famine and horrendous social phenomena that accompanied have been described by an eyewitness, the physician and historian ʿAbd

---

232   Lilie, *Handel und Politik*, esp. pp. 117–221 on the Italian presence in the cities in the Byzantine provinces; Laiou/Morrisson, *The Byzantine Economy*, pp. 141–47; Gerolymatou, Αγορές, έμποροι και εμπόριο, pp. 102–09; Whittow, "The Middle Byzantine Economy", pp. 476–77; Jacoby, "Venetian commercial expansion".

233   Woodbridge/Roberts, "Late Holocene climate"; Dean et al., "Palaeo-seasonality of the last two millennia".

234   Fleitmann et al., "Sofular Cave".

235   Griggs et al., "A regional high–frequency reconstruction".

236   Kuzucuoglu et al., "Mid- to late-Holocene climate change". A more detailed discussion and references to this evidence can be found in Preiser-Kapeller, "A Collapse of the Eastern Mediterranean?".

237   Sinha et al., "Role of climate".

THE MEDIEVAL CLIMATE ANOMALY

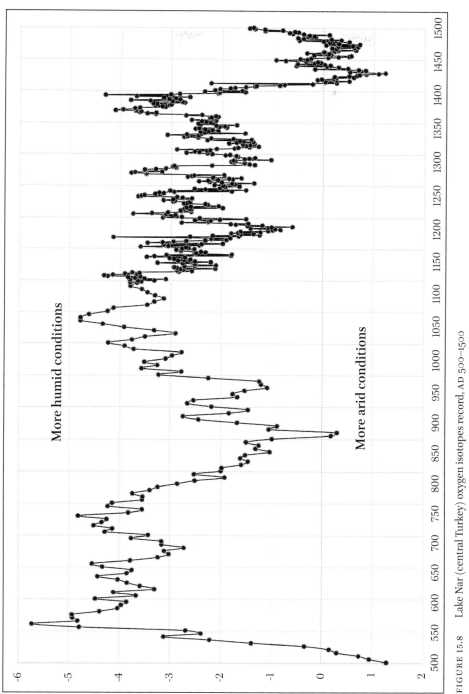

FIGURE 15.8 Lake Nar (central Turkey) oxygen isotopes record, AD 500–1500
DATA: WOODBRIDGE/ROBERTS, "LATE HOLOCENE CLIMATE"; GRAPH:
J. PREISER-KAPELLER, OEAW, 2022

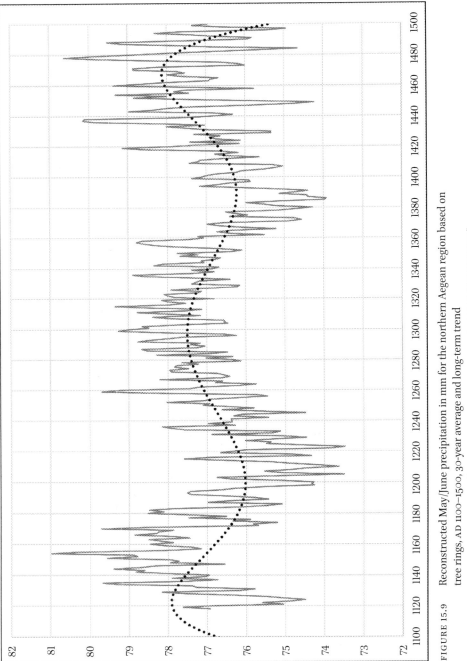

FIGURE 15.9 Reconstructed May/June precipitation in mm for the northern Aegean region based on tree rings, AD 1100–1500, 30-year average and long-term trend
DATA: GRIGGS ET AL., "A REGIONAL HIGH-FREQUENCY RECONSTRUCTION";
GRAPH: J. PREISER-KAPELLER, OEAW, 2022

al-Laṭīf from Baghdad, who spent these years in Egypt.[238] In various regions, these climatic changes to more unstable, arid and/or cold conditions continued beyond the mid-13th century into the general period of transition from the Medieval Climate Anomaly toward the "Little Ice Age" across Afro-Eurasia, which we have discussed for Byzantium in an earlier publication.[239]

12 Conclusion and Outlook

In sum, thus, from a palaeoclimatological perspective and synthesizing important parts of the archives of society and of nature, we encounter a rather short, temporarily and spatially incoherent "Medieval Climate Anomaly" in the Eastern Mediterranean, punctuated by recurring anomalies and extreme events, but nevertheless not necessarily causing "collapse" in Byzantium or neighbouring polities, but even correlating with a long-term "economic expansion", for certain times at least. What we lack to complete and further nuance this picture are in-depth regional studies, ideally again combining rich written evidence (especially charters) with archaeological and proxy data (for agricultural activities as well as temperature and precipitation conditions).

Recently, promising studies along these lines for the hinterlands of Ephesus (with pollen data from Lake Belevi, see Fig. 15.3)[240] and of Miletus (see Fig. 15.3, including pollen data from Bafa Gölü)[241] have been published. In addition to long-term trends, such regional archives can informs us also on short-term localized events as in a charter for Andronikos Dukas issued by his cousin Emperor Michael VII in 1073, by which he granted Andronikos a large domain in the Maeander delta plain near Miletus; we learn that one of the estates, Mandraklou, had been damaged by a flood of the river before, so that of the 185 modioi only 36 were cultivable now, while the rest was marshland.[242] Ultimately, a combination of these spatial levels of analysis may allow us to describe in more detail the resilience (or fragility) of the Byzantine Empire

---

238 Grove/Adamson, *El Niño in World History*, pp. 52–55; Nash et al., "African hydroclimatic variability". 'Abd al-Laṭīf al-Baġdādī, *Description of Egypt*, ed. and trans. Mackintosh-Smith, pp. 122–79. See also al-Maqrīzī, *Ighāthah*, trans. Allouche, pp. 41–42. Telelis, Μετεωρολογικά φαινόμενα, Nº 595–597; Hassan, "Extreme Nile floods".
239 Preiser-Kapeller/Mitsiou, "The Little Ice Age and Byzantium".
240 Stock et al., "Human–environment interaction in the hinterland of Ephesos".
241 Niewöhner et al., "The Byzantine Settlement History of Miletus"; Olson, *Environment and Society in Byzantium*, pp. 179–80.
242 Βυζαντινά έγγραφα της Μονής Πάτμου: Β', ed. Nystazopoulou-Pelekidou, Nº 50, lns. 270–74. Dölger/Wirth, *Regesten von 1025–1204*, Nº 994; Thonemann, *The Maeander Valley*, pp. 259–70, esp. 266, and 302–06, on the further development of Mandraklou.

in the face of climatic, epidemic, and other exogenous shocks through the dynamics of its rural and urban communities.[243]

...

Originally, Ronnie Ellenblum was invited to write the chapter on the Medieval Climate Anomaly for the present volume. His unexpected death in January 2021 made this impossible. The chapter is devoted to his memory and tries to engage critically (as Ronnie preferred) with his provocative and startling research on the period and region and his methodological approach to historical climatology;[244] in order to do justice to his arguments, the chapter is of unusual length. The chapter was finished within the framework of the project "Entangled Charters of Anatolia (1200–1300). Diplomacy, administration and world ordering during crisis in the transcultural mirror of governmental writing" (ENCHANT, FWF P-36403), funded by the Austrian Science Fund FWF.

Bibliography

Primary Sources

ʿAbd al-Laṭīf al-Baġdādī, *Description of Egypt*, ed. and trans. T. Mackintosh-Smith, *ʿAbd al-Laṭīf al-Baghdādī, A Physician on the Nile. A Description of Egypt and Journal on the Famine Years*, New York 2021.

Actes d'Iviron I, Des origines au milieu du XIᵉ siècle, ed. J. Lefort/N. Oikonomidès/ D. Papachryssanthou, Archives de l'Athos XIV, Paris 1985.

al-Maqrīzī, *Ighāthah*, trans. A. Allouche, *Mamluk Economics: A Study and Translation of al-Maqrīzī's Ighāthah*, Salt Lake City 1994.

Anna Komnene, *Alexias*, ed. D.R. Reinsch/A. Kambylis, *Annae Comnenae Alexias* (Corpus Fontium Historiae Byzantinae 40), Berlin 2001.

---

243 See for instance also the "Palaeo-Science and History" project of Adam Izdebski at the Max Planck-Institute for the Science of Human History in Jena, https://www.shh.mpg.de /1056512/byzres.

244 See especially Ellenblum, *The Collapse of the Eastern Mediterranean*, and the posthumous article Chipman/Avni/Ellenblum, "Collapse, affluence, and collapse". Ronnie Ellenblum's last lecture journey just at the time of the outbreak of the Covid-19 pandemic in Israel and Europe led him to Vienna in March 2020, when we had the last opportunity for a heated, but (as always) friendly debate on these issues. His planned talk on the resilience and fragility of societies of course caused even more interest at that time in 2020 and media attention, for instance also in Austrian TV: https://science.orf.at/stories/3200323/ [14 April 2020].

Anna Komnene, *Alexias*, trans. E.R.A. Sewter, *Anna Komnene, The Alexiad*, revised by P. Frankopan, London 2009.

Aristakēs Lastiverc'i, *History*, ed. and trans. R. Bedrosian, *Aristakes Lastivertc'i's History*, Traralgon 2020.

Bar Hebraeus, *Chronography*, trans. E.A.W. Budge, *The Chronography of Gregory Abû'l Faraj, the Son of Aaron, the Hebrew Physician, Commonly Known as Bar Hebraeus: Being the First Part of his Political History of the Word*, 2 vols., London 1932.

Βυζαντινά έγγραφα της Μονής Πάτμου: Β΄ Δημοσίων Λειτουργών, ed. M. Nystazopoulou-Pelekidou, Athens 1980.

John Scylitzes, *Synopsis*, ed. I. Thurn, *Ioannis Scylitzae Synopsis historiarum* (Corpus Fontium Historiae Byzantinae 5), Berlin 1973.

John Scylitzes, *Synopsis*, trans. J. Wortley, *John Skylitzes, A Synopsis of Byzantine History 811–1057*, with introductions by J.-Cl. Cheynet and B. Flusin and notes by J.-Cl. Cheynet, Cambridge 2010.

John Scylitzes continuatus, *Chronicle*, ed. and trans. E. McGeer, *Byzantium in the Time of Troubles. The Continuation of the Chronicle of John Skylitzes (1057–1079). Prosopographical Index and Glossary of Terms by J.W. Nesbitt*, Leiden 2020.

Leo the Deacon, *History*, ed. Ch. B. Hase, *Leonis diaconi Caloënsis Historiae libri X*, Bonn 1828.

Leo the Deacon, *History*, trans. A.-M. Talbot/D.F. Sullivan, *The History of Leo the Deacon. Byzantine Military Expansion in the Tenth Century*, Washington, D.C. 2005.

Matthew of Edessa, *History*, trans. A.E. Dostourian, *Armenia and the Crusades, Tenth to Twelfth Centuries. The Chronicle of Matthew of Edessa*, Lanham 1993.

Michael Attaleiates, *History*, ed. and trans. A. Kaldellis/D. Krallis, *Michael Attaleiates, The History*, Cambridge Mass. 2012.

Michael Psellos, *Chronographia*, ed. D.R. Reinsch, *Michaelis Pselli Chronographia*, 2 vols., Berlin 2014.

Novels of the Macedonian emperors, ed. N. Svoronos, *Les novelles des empereurs Macédoniens concernant la terre et les stratiotes. Introduction – edition – commentaires*. Édition posthume et index établis par P. Gounaridis, Athens 1994.

Novels of the Macedonian emperors, trans. E. McGeer, *The Land Legislation of the Macedonian Emperors* (Medieval Sources in Translation 38), Toronto 2000.

Symeon Magistros, ed. St. Wahlgren, *Symeonis Magistri et Logothetae Chronicon* (Corpus Fontium Historiae Byzantinae 44/1), Berlin 2006.

Theophanes Continuatus, ed. I. Bekker, *Theophanes continuatus, Joannes Cameniata, Symeon Magister, Georgius Monachus*, Bonn 1838.

The Peira, ed. D.R. Simon/D.R. Reinsch, Ἡ Πεῖρα – *Die Peira. Ein juristisches Lehrbuch des 11. Jahrhunderts aus Konstantinopel – Text, Übersetzung, Kommentar, Glossar* (Forschungen zur byzantinischen Rechtsgeschichte, Neue Folge 4), Berlin 2023.

Yaḥyā of Antioch, *Chronicle*, trans. B. Pirone, *Yaḥyā al-Anṭākī, Cronache dell'Egitto fāṭimide e dell'impero bizantino (937–1033)*, Bologna 2018.

Zonaras, *Epitome*, ed. Th. Büttner-Wobst, *Ioannis Zonarae Epitomae Historiarum Libri XIII–XVIII*, Bonn 1897.

Secondary Literature

Adamson, G.C.D./Nash, D., "Climate History of Asia (Excluding China)", in S. White/Ch. Pfister/F. Mauelshagen (eds.), *The Palgrave Handbook of Climate History*, London 2018, pp. 203–11.

Andrews, T.L., *Mattʿēos Uṙhayecʿi and His Chronicle. History as Apocalypse in a Crossroads of Cultures*, Leiden 2017.

Andriollo, L., *Constantinople et les provinces d'Asie Mineure, IXe–XIe siècle. Administration impériale, sociétés locales et rôle de l'aristocratie*, Paris 2017.

Andriollo, L./Métivier, S., "Quel rôle pour les province dans la domination aristocratique au XIe siècle?", in B. Flusin/J.-Cl. Cheynet (eds.), *Autour du Premier humanisme byzantin & des Cinq études sur le XIe siècle, quarante ans après Paul Lemerle* (Travaux et Mémoires 21/2), Paris 2017, pp. 505–30.

Angold, M., *The Byzantine Empire 1025–1204*, London 1997.

Barthélemy, D., "L'aristocracie franque du XIe siècle en constraste avec l'aristocratie byzantine", in B. Flusin/J.-Cl. Cheynet (eds.), *Autour du Premier humanisme byzantin & des Cinq études sur le XIe siècle, quarante ans après Paul Lemerle* (Travaux et Mémoires 21/2), Paris 2017, pp. 491–504.

Bauer, Th., *Warum es kein islamisches Mittelalter gab. Das Erbe der Antike und der Orient*, Munich 2018.

Behringer, W., *Kulturgeschichte des Klimas. Von der Eiszeit bis zur globalen Erwärmung*, Munich 2007.

Beihammer, A.D., *Byzantium and the Emergence of Muslim-Turkish Anatolia, ca. 1040–1130*, London/New York 2017.

Bianquis, Th., "Une crise frumentaire dans l'Égypte Fatimide", *Journal of the Economic and Social History of the Orient* 23 (1980), 67–101.

Bintliff, J., *The Complete Archaeology of Greece: From Hunter-Gatherers to the 20th Century AD*, Malden/Oxford 2012.

Brandes, W., "Byzantine Predictions of the End of the World in 500, 1000, and 1492 AD", in H.-C. Lehner (ed.), *The End(s) of Time(s). Apocalypticism, Messianism, and Utopianism through the Ages*, Leiden 2021, pp. 32–63.

Brett, M., *The Fatimid Empire*, Edinburgh 2017.

Brönnimann, St./Pfister, Ch./White, S., "Archives of Nature and Archives of Societies", in S. White/Ch. Pfister/F. Mauelshagen (eds.), *The Palgrave Handbook of Climate History*, London 2018, pp. 27–36.

Bulliet, R.W., *Cotton, Climate, and Camels. A Moment in World History*, New York 2009.

Büntgen, U., et al., "Cooling and societal change during the Late Antique Little Ice Age from 536 to around 660 AD", *Nature Geoscience* 9 (2016), 231–236, https://doi.org/10.1038/ngeo2652.

Burman, A., (2017) "The political ontology of climate change: moral meteorology, climate justice, and the coloniality of reality in the Bolivian Andes", *Journal of Political Ecology* 24 (1), 921–930.

Busse, H., *Chalif und Großkönig. Die Buyiden im Irak (945–1055)*, Beirut 2004.

Campbell, B.M.S., *The Great Transition. Climate, Disease and Society in the Late-Medieval World*, Cambridge 2016.

Caplanis, C., "The Debasement of the 'Dollar of the Middle Ages'", *The Journal of Economic History* 63/3 (2003), 768–801.

Cheynet, J.-Cl., "Un aspect du ravitaillement de Constantinople aux xe/xie siècles d'après quelques sceaux d'horreiarioi", *Studies in Byzantine Sigillography* 6 (1999), 1–26.

Chipman, L./Avni, G./Ellenblum, R., "Collapse, affluence, and collapse again: contrasting climatic effects in Egypt during the prolonged reign of al-Mustanṣir (1036–1094)", *Mediterranean Historical Review* 36:2 (2021), 199–215.

Chitwood, Z., *Byzantine Legal Culture and the Roman Legal Tradition, 867–1056*, Cambridge 2017.

Cohen, Sh./Stanhill, G., "Changes in the Sun's radiation: the role of wisespread surface solar radiation trends in climate change: dimming and brightening", in T.M. Letcher (ed.), *Climate Change. Observed Impacts on Planet Earth*, Amsterdam 2021, pp. 687–709.

Cooper, E./Decker, M., *Life and Society in Byzantine Cappadocia*, London 2012.

Curta, F., "The Image and Archaeology of the Pechenegs", *Stratum Plus Journal* 5 (2013), 203–34.

Curta, F., *Southeastern Europe in the Middle Ages, 500–1250*, Cambridge 2012.

Dagron, D., "Quand la terre tremble ...", in G. Dagron, *Idées byzantines*, vol. I, Paris 2012, pp. 3–22.

Dagron, G. "Les diseurs d'événements: Approche de l'astrologie orientale", in G. Dagron, *Idées byzantines*, vol. I, Paris 2012, pp. 23–52.

Dean, J.R., et al., "Palaeo-seasonality of the last two millennia reconstructed from the oxygen isotope composition of carbonates and diatom silica from Nar Gölü, central Turkey", *Quaternary Science Reviews* 66 (2013), 35–44.

Diaz, H.F., et al., "Spatial and Temporal Characteristics of Climate in Medieval Times Revisited", *Bulletin of the American Meteorological Society* 92/11 (2011), 1487–1500.

Dölger, F./Müller, A./Beihammer, A., *Regesten der Kaiserurkunden des oströmischen Reiches von 565 bis 1453. 1. Teil, 2. Halbband: Regesten von 867–1025*, Munich 2003.

Dölger, F./Wirth, P., *Regesten der Kaiserurkunden des oströmischen Reiches von 565 bis 1453. 1. Teil, 2. Halbband: Regesten von 1025–1204*, Munich 1995.

Dorman, L.I., "Space weather and cosmic ray effects", in T.M. Letcher (ed.), *Climate Change. Observed Impacts on Planet Earth*, Amsterdam 2021, pp. 711–68.

Ellenblum, E., *The Collapse of the Eastern Mediterranean. Climate Change and the Decline of the East, 950–1072*, Cambridge 2012.

Elvin, M., "Who Was Responsible for the Weather? Moral Meteorology in Late Imperial China", *Osiris 13, Beyond Joseph Needham: Science, Technology, and Medicine in East and Southeast Asia* (1998), 213–37.

Feldbauer, P., *Die islamische Welt 600–1250. Ein Frühfall von Unterentwicklung?*, Vienna 1995.

Felix, W., *Byzanz und die islamische Welt im früheren 11. Jahrhundert. Geschichte der politischen Beziehungen von 1001 bis 1055*, Vienna 1981.

Fleitmann, D., et al., "Sofular Cave, Turkey 50KYr Stalagmite Stable Isotope Data", *IGBP PAGES/World Data Center for Paleoclimatology Data Contribution Series* # 2009-132, online: https://www.ncei.noaa.gov/access/paleo-search/study/8637.

Fowden, G., *Before and after Muḥammad: The First Millennium Refocused*, Princeton 2014.

Frantz-Murphy, G., "A New Interpretation of the Economic History of Medieval Egypt: The Role of the Textile Industry 254–567/868–1171", *Journal of the Economic and Social History of the Orient* 24/3 (1981), 274–97.

Frantz-Murphy, G., "Land Tenure in Egypt in the First Five Centuries of Islamic Rule (Seventh-Twelfth Centuries AD)", *Proceedings of the British Academy* 96 (1999), 237–66.

Frenkel, Y., "The Coming of the Barbarians: Can Climate Explain the Saljūqs' Advance?", in L.E. Yang/H.-R. Bork/X. Fang/St. Mischke (eds.), *Socio-Environmental Dynamics along the Historical Silk Road*, Cham 2019, pp. 261–74.

Gerolymatou, M., *Αγορές, έμποροι και εμπόριο στο Βυζάντιο (9ος–12ος αι.)*, Athens 2008.

Gkoutzioukostas, A., "Administrative structures of Byzantium during the 11th century: officials of the imperial secretariat and administration of justice", in B. Flusin/J.-C. Cheynet (eds.), *Autour du Premier humanisme byzantin & des Cinq études sur le xie siècle, quarante ans après Paul Lemerle* (Travaux et mémoires 21/2), Paris 2017, pp. 561–80.

Gogou, A., et al., "Climate variability and socio-environmental changes in the northern Aegean (NE Mediterranean) during the last 1500 years", *Quaternary Science Reviews* 136 (2016), 209–28.

Göktürk, O.M., *Climate in the Eastern Mediterranean through the Holocene Inferred from Turkish Stalagmites*, Ph.D.-Thesis, University of Bern 2011.

Goosse, H., et al., "The medieval climate anomaly in Europe: Comparison of the summer and annual mean signals in two reconstructions and in simulations with data assimilation", *Global and Planetary Change* 84–85 (2012), 35–47.

Griggs, C., et al., "A regional high-frequency reconstruction of May–June precipitation in the north Aegean from oak tree rings, A.D. 1089–1989", *International Journal of Climatology* 27 (2007), 1075–89.

Grotzfeld, H., "Klimageschichte des Vorderen Orients 800–1800 A.D. nach arabischen Quellen", in R. Glaser/R. Walsh (eds.), *Historische Klimatologie in verschiedenen Klimazonen*, Würzburg 1991, pp. 21–44.

Grove, R./Adamson, G., *El Niño in World History*, London 2018.

Grünbart, M., *Inszenierung und Repräsentation der byzantinischen Aristokratie vom 10. bis zum 13. Jahrhundert*, Paderborn 2015.

Guillet, S., et al., "Climatic and societal impacts of a 'forgotten' cluster of volcanic eruptions in 1108–1110 CE", *Nature Scientific Reports* 10 (2020), online: https://doi.org/10.1038/s41598-020-63339-3.

Guiot, J., et al., "Growing Season Temperatures in Europe and Climate Forcings Over the Past 1400 Years", *PLoS ONE* 5(4) (2010), e9972. doi:10.1371/journal.pone.0009972.

Hajar, L., et al., "Environmental changes in Lebanon during the Holocene: Man vs. climate impacts", *Journal of Arid Environments* 74 (2010), 746–55.

Haldon, J.F., "Social élites, wealth, and power", in J. Haldon (ed.), *A Social History of Byzantium*, Malden/Oxford 2009, pp. 168–211.

Haldon, J.F., et al., "The Climate and Environment of Byzantine Anatolia: Integrating Science, History, and Archaeology", *Journal of Interdisciplinary History* 45,2 (2014), 113–61.

Halm, H., *Die Kalifen von Kairo: Die Fatimiden in Ägypten 973–1074*, Munich 2003.

Halm, H., *Kalifen und Assassinen: Ägypten und der Vordere Orient zur Zeit der ersten Kreuzzüge 1074–1171*, Munich 2014.

Halstead, P., *Two Oxen Ahead. Pre-Mechanized Farming in the Mediterranean*, Chichester 2014.

Harvey, J.A., *Economic Expansion in the Byzantine Empire 900–1200*, Cambridge 1989.

Harvey, J.A., "The Byzantine Economy in an International Context", *Historisch Tijdschrift Groniek* 39/171 (2006), 163–74.

Hassan, F.A., "Extreme Nile floods and famines in Medieval Egypt (AD 930–1500) and their climatic implications", *Quaternary International* 173–174 (2007), 101–12.

Hendy, M.F., *Studies in the Byzantine Monetary Economy c. 300–1450*, Cambridge 1985.

Henke, M.K./Lambert, F.H./Charman, D.J., "Was the Little Ice Age more or less El Niño-like than the Medieval Climate Anomaly? Evidence from hydrological and temperature proxy data", *Climate of the Past* 13 (2017), 267–301.

i Monclús, P.B., "Famines sans frontiers en Occident avant la 'conjuncture de 1300'. À propos d'une enquête en cours", in M. Bourin/J. Drendel/F. Menant (eds.), *Les disettes dans la conjuncture de 1300*, Rome 2011, pp. 37–86.

Intergovernmental Panel on Climate Change, *Climate Change 2021. The Physical Science Basis*, 7 August 2021, online: https://www.ipcc.ch/report/ar6/wg1/downloads/report/IPCC_AR6_WGI_Full_Report.pdf.

Izdebski, A./Koloch, G./Słoczyński, T., "Exploring Byzantine and Ottoman economic history with the use of palynological data: a quantitative approach", *Jahrbuch der Österreichischen Byzantinistik* 65 (2015), 67–110.

Izdebski, A./Mordechai, L./White, S., "The Social Burden of Resilience: A Historical Perspective", *Human Ecology* 46 (2018), 291–303.

Jacobson, M.J. et al., "Heterogenous Late Holocene Climate in the Eastern Mediterranean – The Kocain Cave Record From SW Turkey", *Geophysical Research Letters* 48 (2021), online: https://doi.org/10.1029/2021GL094733.

Jacoby, D., "Byzantine Trade with Egypt from the Mid-Tenth Century to the Fourth Crusade", *Thesaurismata* 30 (2000), 25–77.

Jacoby, D., "Venetian commercial expansion in the eastern Mediterranean, 8th–11th centuries", in: M. Mundell Mango (ed.), *Byzantine trade, 4th–12th centuries. The Archaeology of Local, Regional and International Exchange. Papers of the Thirty-Eighth Spring Symposium of Byzantine Studies, St. John's College, University of Oxford, March 2004*, Farnham/Burlington 2009, pp. 371–91.

Jacoby, D., "Rural Exploitation and Market Economy in the Late Medieval Peloponnese", in Sh.E.J. Gerstel (ed.), *Viewing the Morea. Land and People in the Late Medieval Peloponnese*, Washington, D.C. 2013, pp. 213–75.

Kaldellis, A., *Streams of Gold, Rivers of Blood. The Rise and Fall of Byzantium, 955 A.D. to the First Crusade*, Oxford 2017.

Kaniewski, D. et al., "Medieval coastal Syrian vegetation patterns in the principality of Antioch", *The Holocene* 21 (2011), 251–62.

Kaniewski, D., et al., "The Medieval Climate Anomaly and the Little Ice Age in Coastal Syria inferred from Pollen-derived Palaeoclimatic Patterns", *Global and Planetary Change* 78 (2011), 178–87.

Kaplan, M., *Les hommes et la terre à Byzance du VIᵉ au XIᵉ siècle: Propriété et exploitation du sol* (Byzantina Sorbonensia 10), Paris 1995.

Kaplan, M., "The Monasteries of Athos and Chalkidiki (8th–11th Centuries): A Pioneering Front?", *Medieval Worlds* 9 (2019), 63–81.

Kaplan, M./Morrisson, C., "L'économie byzantine: perspectives historiographiques", *Revue historique* 630/2 (2004), 391–411.

Katrantsiotis, Ch., et al., "Eastern Mediterranean hydroclimate reconstruction over the last 3600 years based on sedimentary n-alkanes, their carbon and hydrogen isotope composition and XRF data from the Gialova Lagoon, SW Greece", *Quaternary Science Reviews* 194 (2018), 77–93.

Kazhdan, A./Epstein, A.W., *Change in Byzantine Culture in the Eleventh and Twelfth Centuries*, Berkeley/Los Angeles/London 1985.

Kazhdan, A., "Orphanotrophos", in A. Kazhdan (ed.), *The Oxford Dictionary of Byzantium*, Oxford/New York 1991, pp. 1537–538.

Kazhdan, A./Ronchey, S., *L'aristocrazia bizantina dal principio dell'XI alla fine del XII secolo*, Palermo 1999.

Koder, J., "„Zeitenwenden". Zur Periodisierung aus byzantinischer Sicht", *Byzantinische Zeitschrift* 84/85 (1991/1992), 409–22.

Krallis, D., *Michael Attaleiates and the Politics of Imperial Decline in Eleventh-Century Byzantium*, Tempe 2012.

Krallis, D., "Historiography as Political Debate", in A. Kaldellis/N. Siniossoglou (eds.), *The Cambridge Intellectual History of Byzantium*, Cambridge 2017, pp. 599–614.

Kresten, O., "'Ἀρχλαι und τριμίσια. Lexikalisches zu den sozialen Maßnahmen des Kaisers Rhomanos I. Lakapenos im „Katastrophenwinter" 927/928", *Österreichische Akademie der Wissenschaften. Anzeiger der Philosophisch-Historischen Klasse* 137/2 (2002), 35–52.

Kuzucuoglu, C., et al., "Mid- to late-Holocene climate change in central Turkey: The Tecer Lake record", *The Holocene* 21/1 (2011), 173–88.

Kushnir, Y./Stein, M., "Medieval Climate in the Eastern Mediterranean: Instability and Evidence of Solar Forcing", *Atmosphere* 10 (2019), 29; doi:10.3390/atmos10010029.

Laiou, A.E., "God and Mammon: Credit, Trade, Profit and the Canons", in N. Oikonomides (ed.), *Byzantium in the 12th Century. Canon Law, State and Society*, Athens 1991, pp. 261–300.

Laiou, A.E., "The Byzantine Economy: An Overview", in A.E. Laiou (ed.), *The Economic History of Byzantium. From the Seventh through the Fifteenth Century*, Washington, D.C. 2002, pp. 1145–164.

Laiou, A./Morrisson, C., *The Byzantine Economy*, Cambridge 2007.

Lean, J.L., "Estimating Solar Irradiance Since 850 CE", *Earth and Space Science* 5 (2018), 133–49.

Li, Y./Shelach-Lavi, G./Ellenblum, R., "Short-Term Climatic Catastrophes and the Collapse of the Liao Dynasty (907–1125): Textual Evidence", *Journal of Interdisciplinary History* 49(4) (2019), 591–610.

Lilie, R.-J., *Handel und Politik zwischen dem byzantinischen Reich und den italienischen Kommunen Venedig, Pisa und Genua in der Epoche der Komnenen und der Angeloi (1081–1204)*, Amsterdam 1984.

Lüning, S., et al., "Hydroclimate in Africa during the Medieval Climate Anomaly", *Palaeogeography, Palaeoclimatology, Palaeoecology* 495 (2018), 309–22.

Luterbacher, J., et al., "European summer temperatures since Roman times", *Environmental Research Letters* 11 (2016) 024001, https://iopscience.iop.org/article/10.1088/1748-9326/11/2/024001.

Magdalino, P., "Justice and Finance in the Byzantine State, Ninth to Twelfth Centuries", in A.E. Laiou-Thomadakis/D. Simon (eds.), *Law and Society in Byzantium, Ninth–Twelfth Centuries. Proceedings of the Symposium on Law and Society in Byzantium, 9th–12th Centuries, May 1–3, 1992*, Washington, D.C. 1994, pp. 93–115.

Magdalino, P., *The Empire of Manuel I Komnenos (1143–1180)*, Cambridge 1993.

Magdalino, P., "Astrology", in A. Kaldellis/N. Siniossoglou (eds.), *The Cambridge Intellectual History of Byzantium*, Cambridge 2017, pp. 198–214.

Mathez, E.A./Smerdon, J.E., *Climate Change. The Science of Global Warming and our Energy Future*, New York 2018.

Mayerson, Ph., "The Role of Flax in Roman and Fatimid Egypt", *Journal of Near Eastern Studies* 56/3 (1997), 201–07.

Meško, M., "Pecheneg groups in the Balkans (ca. 1053–1091) according to the Byzantine sources", in F. Curta/B.-P. Maleon (eds.), *The Steppe Lands and the World beyond them. Studies in honor of Victor Spinei on his 70th birthday*, Iaşi 2013, pp. 179–205.

Miotto, M., *Ο ανταγωνισμός Βυζαντίου και Χαλιφάτου των Φατιμιδών στην Εγγύς Ανατολή και η δράση των ιταλικών πόλεων στην περιοχή κατά τον 10ο και τον 11ο αιώνα*, Thessaloniki 2008.

Morris, R., "The Powerful and the Poor in Tenth-Century Byzantium: Law and Reality", *Past & Present* 73 (1976), 3–27.

Mostern, R., *The Yellow River. A Natural and Unnatural History*, New Haven/London 2021.

Nash, D.J., et al., "African hydroclimatic variability during the last 2000 years", *Quaternary Science Reviews* 154 (2016), 1–22.

Nash, D.J., et al., "Climate indices in historical climate reconstructions: A global state-of-the-art", *Climate of the Past Discussions*, 2020, https://doi.org/10.5194/cp-2020-126.

Neville, L., *Guide to Byzantine Historical Writing*, Cambridge 2018.

Newfield, T., *The Contours of Disease and Hunger in Carolingian and early Ottonian Europe (c.750–c.950 CE)*, Doctoral dissertation, McGill University, Montreal 2010.

Newfield, T., "Early Medieval Epizootics and Landscapes of Disease: The Origins and Triggers of European Livestock Pestilences", in: S. Kleingärtner/T.P. Newfield/S. Rossignol/D. Wehner (eds.), *Landscapes and Societies in Medieval Europe East of the Elbe. Interactions Between Environmental Settings and Cultural Transformations*, Toronto 2013, pp. 73–113.

Newfield, T., "Domesticates, disease and climate in early post-classical Europe: the cattle plague of c.940 and its environmental context", *Post-Classical Archaeologies* 5 (2015), 95–126.

Nicholson, Sh.E., "A Multi-Century History of Drought and Wetter Conditions in Africa", in S. White/Ch. Pfister/F. Mauelshagen (eds.), *The Palgrave Handbook of Climate History*, London 2018, pp. 225–36.

Niewöhner, Ph., et al., "The Byzantine Settlement History of Miletus and Its Hinterland – Quantitative Aspects: Stratigraphy, Pottery, Anthropology, Coins, and Palynology, *Archäologischer Anzeiger* 2 (2016), 225–90.

Oesterle, J.R., *Kalifat und Königtum. Herrschaftsrepräsentation der Fatimiden, Ottonen und frühen Salier an religiösen Hochfesten*, Darmstadt 2009.

Olson, A., *Environment and Society in Byzantium, 650–1150. Between the Oak and the Olive*, Cham 2020.

PAGES 2k Network consortium, Database S1 – 11 April 2013 version: http://www.pages-igbp.org/workinggroups/2k-network.

Paul, J., "Nomads and Bukhara. A Study in Nomad Migrations, Pasture, and Climate Change (11th century CE)", *Der Islam* 93/2 (2016), 495–531.

Pfister, Ch./Wanner, H., *Klima und Gesellschaft in Europa. Die letzten tausend Jahre*, Bern 2021.

PmbZ: Lilie, R.J., et al., *Prosopographie der mittelbyzantinischen Zeit Online*, Berlin 1998–2013, https://doi.org/10.1515/pmbz.

Polovodova Asteman, I./Filipsson, H.L./Nordberg, K., "Tracing winter temperatures over the last two millennia using a north-east Atlantic coastal record", *Climate of the Past* 14 (2018), 1097–1118.

Preiser-Kapeller, J., "A Collapse of the Eastern Mediterranean? New results and theories on the interplay between climate and societies in Byzantium and the Near East, ca. 1000–1200 AD", *Jahrbuch der Österreichischen Byzantinistik* 65 (2015), 195–242.

Preiser-Kapeller, J., "Byzantium 1025–1204", in F. Daim (ed.), *History and Culture of Byzantium* (Brill's New Pauly 11), Leiden 2019, pp. 59–89.

Preiser-Kapeller, J., *Der Lange Sommer und die Kleine Eiszeit. Klima, Pandemien und der Wandel der Alten Welt von 500 bis 1500 n. Chr.*, Vienna 2021.

Preiser-Kapeller, J./Mitsiou, E., "The Little Ice Age and Byzantium within the Eastern Mediterranean, ca. 1200–1350: An Essay on Old Debates and New Scenarios", in M. Bauch/G.J. Schenk (eds.), *The Crisis of the 14th Century. Teleconnections between Environmental and Societal Change?*, Berlin 2020, pp. 190–220.

Prigent, V., "The Mobilisation of Fiscal Resources in the Byzantine Empire (Eighth to Eleventh Centuries)", in J. Hudson/A. Rodríguez (eds.), *Diverging Paths? The Shapes of Power and Institutions in Medieval Christendom and Islam*, Leiden 2014, pp. 182–229.

Raphael, S.K., *Climate and Political Climate. Environmental Disasters in the Medieval Levant* (Brill's Series in the History of the Environment 3), Leiden 2013.

Redford, S., "Trade and Economy in Antioch and Cilicia in the Twelfth and Thirteenth Centuries", in C. Morrisson (ed.), *Trade and Markets in Byzantium*, Washington, D.C. 2012, pp. 297–309.

Riede, F., "Doing palaeo-social volcanology: Developing a framework for systematically investigating the impacts of past volcanic eruptions on human societies using archaeological datasets", *Quaternary International* 499 (2019), 266–77.

Roberts, N., et al., "Palaeolimnological evidence for an east-west climate see-saw in the Mediterranean since AD 900", *Global and Planetary Change* 84–85 (2012), 23–34.

Rohr, Ch./Camenisch, Ch./Pribyl, K., "European Middle Ages", in S. White/Ch. Pfister/F. Mauelshagen (eds.), *The Palgrave Handbook of Climate History*, London 2018, pp. 247–63.

Salvin, Ph., "Crusaders in Crisis: towards the Re-Assessment of the Origins and Nature of the 'People's Crusade' of 1095–1096", *Imago Temporis. Medium Aevum* 4 (2010), 175–99.

Sanders, P.A., "The Fāṭimid State, 969–1171", in C.F. Petry (ed.), *The Cambridge History of Egypt. Volume 1, 640–1517*, Cambridge 1998, pp. 151–74.

Sarris, P., "Large Estates and the Peasantry in Byzantium, c. 600–1100", *Revue Belge de Philologie et d'Histoire / Belgisch Tijdschrift voor Filologie en Geschiedenis* 90 (2012), 429–50.

Schminck, A., "Zur Einzelgesetzgebung der „makedonischen" Kaiser", *Fontes Minores* 11 (2005), 269–323.

Schneider, B., *Klimabilder. Eine Genealogie globaler Bildpolitiken von Klima und Klimawandel*, Berlin 2018.

Sigl, M., et al., "Timing and Climate Forcing of Volcanic Eruptions for the Past 2,500 Years", *Nature* 523 (2015), 543–49.

Sinha, A., et al., "Role of climate in the rise and fall of the Neo-Assyrian Empire", *Science Advance* 5 (2019), online: https://advances.sciencemag.org/content/5/11/eaax6656/tab-pdf.

Sirocko, F./David, K., "Das mittelalterliche Wärmeoptimum (1150–1260 AD) und der Beginn der Kleinen Eiszeit (nach 1310 AD) mit ihren kulturhistorischen Entwicklungen", in: F. Daim/D. Gronenborn/R. Schreg (eds.), *Strategien zum Überleben. Umweltkrisen und ihre Bewältigung*, Mainz 2011, pp. 243–54.

Smyrlis, K., "Private property and state finances. The emperor's right to donate his subjects' land in the Comnenian period", *Byzantine and Modern Greek Studies* 33/2 (2009), 115–32.

Smyrlis, K., "The Fiscal Revolution of Alexios I Komnenos: Timing, Scope, and Motives", in B. Flusin/J.-C. Cheynet (eds.), *Autour du Premier humanisme byzantin & des Cinq études sur le xie siècle, quarante ans après Paul Lemerle* (Travaux et mémoires 21/2), Paris 2017, pp. 593–610.

Smyrlis, K./Banev, G./Konstantinidis, G., "Mount Athos and the economy of Chalkidike, tenth to fifteenth century", in *Η εξακτίνωση του Αγίου Όρους στον ορθόδοξο κόσμο: τα μετόχια – Mount Athos: Spreading the Light to the Orthodox World. The Metochia*, Thessaloniki 2015, pp. 35–59.

Stathakopoulos, D., "›Philoptochos basileus‹: Kaiserliche Armenfürsorge zwischen Rhetorik und Realität in Byzanz", in R. Lutz/H. Uerlings (eds.), *Zwischen Ausschluss und Solidarität. Modi der Inklusion/Exklusion von Fremden und Armen in Europa seit der Spätantike*, Frankfurt am Main 2008, pp. 165–80.

Stenchikov, G., "The role of volcanic activity in climate and global changes", in T.M. Letcher (ed.), *Climate Change. Observed Impacts on Planet Earth*, Amsterdam 2021, pp. 607–43.

Stock, F., et al., "Human-environment interaction in the hinterland of Ephesos – As deduced from an in-depth study of Lake Belevi, west Anatolia", *Quaternary Science Reviews* 244 (2020), online: https://doi.org/10.1016/j.quascirev.2020.106418.

Summerhayes, C.P., *Palaeoclimatology. From Snowball Earth to the Anthropocene*, Chichester 2020.

Svoronos, N., *Etudes sur l'organisation intérieure, la société et l'économie de l'Empire Byzantin*, London 1973.

Teall, J.L., "The Grain Supply of the Byzantine Empire, 330–1025", *Dumbarton Oaks Papers* 13 (1959), 87–139.

Telelis, I.G., *Μετεωρολογικά φαινόμενα και κλίμα στο Βυζάντιο*, 2 vols., Athens 2004.

Telelis, I.G., "Climatic fluctuations in the Eastern Mediterranean and the Middle East AD 300–1500 from Byzantine documentary and proxy physical paleoclimatic evidence – a comparison", *Jahrbuch der Österreichischen Byzantinistik* 58 (2008), 167–207.

Telelis, I.G., "Byzantine Textual Sources for Climatic and Environmental Developments", *Byzantine Symmeikta* 32 (2022), 17–41.

Thonemann, P., *The Maeander Valley. A Historical Geography from Antiquity to Byzantium*, Cambridge 2011.

Tihon, A., "Astronomy", in A. Kaldellis/N. Siniossoglou (eds.), *The Cambridge Intellectual History of Byzantium*, Cambridge 2017, pp. 183–97.

Tor, D., "The Eclipse of Khurāsān in the Twelfth Century", *Bulletin of the School of Oriental and African Studies* 81/2 (2018), 251–76.

Udovitch, A.L., "International Trade and Medieval Egyptian Countryside", *Proceedings of the British Academy* 96 (1999), 267–85.

Usoskin, I.G., "A History of Solar Activity over Millennia", *Living Reviews in Solar Physics* 10 (2013), 1, http://www.livingreviews.org/lrsp-2013-1.

Vogt, St., et al., "Assessing the Medieval Climate Anomaly in the Middle East: The potential of Arabic documentary sources", *PAGES news* 19/1 (2011), 28–29.

Whittow, M., "The Middle Byzantine Economy (600–1204)", in J. Shepard (ed.), *The Cambridge History of the Byzantine Empire, c. 500–1492*, Cambridge 2008, pp. 465–92.

Woodbridge, J./Roberts, N., "Late Holocene climate of the Eastern Mediterranean inferred from diatom analysis of annually-laminated lake sediments", *Quaternary Science Reviews* 30 (2011), 3381–392.

Wozniak, Th., *Naturereignisse im frühen Mittelalter. Das Zeugnis der Geschichtsschreibung vom 6. bis 11. Jahrhundert*, Berlin 2020.

Xoplaki, E., et al., "The Medieval Climate Anomaly and Byzantium: A review of the evidence on climatic fluctuations, economic performance and societal change", *Quaternary Science Reviews* 136 (2016), 229–52.

Xoplaki, E., et al., "Modelling Climate and Societal Resilience in the Eastern Mediterranean in the Last Millennium", *Human Ecology* 46 (2018), 363–79.

Zhang, L., *The River, the Plain, and the State: An Environmental Drama in Northern Song China, 1048–1128*, Cambridge 2016.

Zalasiewicz, J./Williams, M., "Climate change through Earth history", in T.M. Letcher (ed.), *Climate Change. Observed Impacts on Planet Earth*, Amsterdam 2021, pp. 49–65.

Zaroug, M.A.H./Eltahir, E.A.B./Giorgi, F., "Droughts and floods over the upper catchment of the Blue Nile and their connections to the timing of El Niño and La Niña events", *Hydrology and Earth System Sciences* 18 (2014), 1239–249.

CHAPTER 16

The Ecology of the Crusader States

Abigail Sargent

Crusading was, in many ways, an encounter across difference. Gathered from western Europe, travelling south, east, and north by land and by sea, Crusaders eventually found themselves in very foreign worlds. They were foreign linguistically, culturally, and religiously, but also ecologically. The Crusaders who went to the Holy Land left behind relatively cool and wet homelands, where the climate was regulated mostly by the vast Atlantic Ocean. By the time they reached Jerusalem, they were well within the bounds of a new landscape – much warmer, more arid, and regulated by not only the Atlantic but also tropical winds from the south.[1] Arriving in these lands, they not only conquered them, but also set up independent polities, known collectively as the Crusader States. Many scholars have investigated the ways in which Crusaders reacted when faced with a new culture. To what extent did they adapt and assimilate to their new homes? To what extent did they use their positions of power to change local culture or law?[2] These questions are fascinating, and the sources are suggestive though frustratingly inconclusive. They have, however, been asked mostly within the cultural, political, and religious sphere, while the environmental history of the Crusades has been largely ignored.[3]

The gap in the scholarship is surprising for several reasons. First, since crusading has sometimes been discussed by modern historians as a colonial or proto-colonial enterprise,[4] it might be expected that scholars would ask of it

---

1 McNeill, *The Mountains of the Mediterranean World*, pp. 14–15.
2 See for instance Kedar, "Latins and Oriental Christians in the Frankish Levant, 1099–1291", pp. 209–22; MacEvitt, *The Crusades and the Christian World of the East*; and Ciggaar/Davids/Teule (eds.), *East and West in the Crusader States*, which includes titles such as Ciggaar, "Manuscripts as Intermediaries: the Crusader States and Literary Cross-Fertilization", (pp. 131–52) and Jackson, "Some Considerations relating to the History of the Muslims in the Crusader States", (pp. 21–30).
3 A remarkable exception is Aleksander Pluskowski, ed., *Environment, Colonization, and the Baltic Crusader States* and *Ecologies of Crusading, Colonization, and Religious Conversion in the Medieval Baltic*.
4 For the strongest study from this position as regards the Latin East, see Prawer, *The Latin Kingdom of Jerusalem: European Colonialism in the Middle Ages*; see also J. Richard, "Une économie coloniale? Chypre et ses ressources agricoles au Moyen Age" *Byzantinische Forschungen* V (1977) 331–52. For an excellent overview of the problems with considering crusader states as

some of the same questions that Alfred Crosby and many others after him have asked about the ecological ramifications of colonial expansion (and about the role that the environment played in shaping it).[5] Granted, the Crusaders hardly had time to effect sweeping changes at the level of ecology, since they held most of their territory for only a few generations. Nevertheless, it is worth considering what changes the Franks attempted or unintentionally initiated, which may point to Frankish attitudes towards and understandings of their new environment.[6] The question is not unlike those about culture and law – to what extent did the Franks adapt themselves to their new lands, and to what extent did they expect conquered territories to adapt for them? Moments in history when powerful groups have been faced with new environments are interesting not only for their own sakes, but also for the light they can shed on human interactions with the environments around them because, like good experiments, they change select variables in the ordinary framework. Similarly and more mundanely, understanding the ecology of the land the crusaders walked into is an obvious and necessary step for understanding almost every other element of warfare, trade, society, and even cultural mentalities within the Crusader States.

The ecology of the Crusader States is not entirely neglected. Numerous articles and some books in fields related to ecology have begun to approach the topic.[7] Because ecology touches so many areas of life and society, some

---

medieval colonies, see the discussion recorded as Kedar, ed., "The Crusading Kingdom of Jerusalem – The First European Colonial Society? A Symposium", 341–66. Participants point to the emotional baggage that the term "colonial" carries for modern people, and the connotations that it draws of being subordinated to a particular mother country, being established in a land that is less technologically developed than the mother country, and being ruled by a segregated immigrant or itinerant population – none of which are fully supportable for the Latin East.

5 Crosby, *Ecological Imperialism*. Other examples include: Melville, *A Plague of Sheep*, and Cronon, *Changes in the Land*. Some of this work has begun to be done for the Baltic Crusades and for Cyprus; Pluskowski/Boas/Gerrard, "The Ecology of Crusading: Investigating the Environmental Impact of Holy War and Colonisation at the Frontiers of Medieval Europe", pp. 192–225; Pluskowski, ed., *Ecologies of Crusading, Colonization, and Religious Conversion in the Medieval Baltic*; Dietzel, *The Ecology of Coexistence and Conflict in Cyprus*.

6 Following common usage, "Frank" throughout will be used to denote all people from western Europe who came to the Eastern Mediterranean. It is more comprehensive than "Crusader", which refers only to people who had arrived specifically to fight, usually for a limited period of time.

7 See Ellenblum, *Frankish Rural Settlement in the Latin Kingdom of Jerusalem*; Avni/Porat/Avni, "Byzantine–Early Islamic Agricultural Systems in the Negev Highlands: Stages of Development as Interpreted through OSL Dating" pp. 332–46; Hill, "Decision Making at the Margins: Settlement Trends, Temporal Scale, and Ecology in the Wadi Al Hasa, West-Central Jordan", pp. 221–41; Issar/Zohar, *Climate Change: Environment and Civilization in the Middle East*.

relevant research – particularly studies of commerce or military histories – only addresses ecology incidentally. More germane are agricultural histories and archaeological studies, whose urban bias has been mitigated in recent years, especially in Israel.[8] Dedicated studies of climate also contribute to our understanding, although much of the work in this field (like some archaeology) investigates eons rather than centuries.[9] Further temporally-focused studies on climate, agriculture, and rural settlement are obviously desirable. At the moment, case studies also have potential to bring together information from these disparate types of history and to train attention on ecology.

The sources do not paint a uniform picture. The Crusader States, in their greatly varying extents, included land endowed with very diverse natural resources. The old triumvirate of grain, wine, and olive oil reigned supreme, and many villages kept flocks and herds, while nomadic or semi-nomadic herders of sheep and goats also used the grazing lands. This type of mixed agriculture was well-adapted to the hot and dry Mediterranean and Near Eastern climate.[10] Despite overarching commonalities, however, there were (and are) notable variations on this ecological and agrarian theme. In the north, the region around Apameia in Syria was famed from antiquity for its excellent pastures, which were well-watered by the slow, spreading Orontes River.[11] Crusaders making their way south along the coast from Acre complained about "tall grasses and great thorny bushes which troubled the footsoldiers and struck them in the face"; as they progressed, they could not find sufficient fodder for their animals.[12] In the Negev Highlands, farmers scratched out a living based on careful conservation and distribution of collected rainwater, while in the marshy Valley of Jezreel tropical fruits could be grown. Northern

---

8   Pluskowski et al. "The Ecology of Crusading", 202; Barbé, "Safed Castle and Its Territory: Frankish Settlement and Colonisation in Eastern Galilee during the Crusader Period;" Khamisy, "The Mount Tabor Territory under Frankish Control" p. 49, and "Western Upper Galilee under Crusader Rule;" Sinibaldi, "Settlement in the Petra Region during the Crusader Period". Ellenblum's archaeological work is a refreshing example of this shift, since he has written almost exclusively on the rural elements of the Latin East; Ellenblum, *Frankish Rural Settlement*, passim; see also his articles, for instance Ellenblum, "Who Built Qal'at Al-Ṣubayba?" pp. 103–12.

9   Here again more work has been done on modern Israel than elsewhere; MacDonald, "Climatic Changes in Jordan through Time", pp. 595–601. For the use of written documents to reconstruct climate, see St. Vogt/Glaser/Luterbacher et alii, "Assessing the Medieval Climate Anomaly in the Middle East: The potential of Arabic documentary sources", pp. 28–9.

10 Butzer, "The Islamic Traditions of Agroecology: Crosscultural Experience, Ideas and Innovations", p. 19.

11 Strabo, *The Geography of Strabo*, trans. Duane W. Roller (Cambridge: Cambridge University Press, 2014), 16.2.10.

12 Ambroise, *The History of the Holy War*, pp. 112, 130.

Transjordan was known for its grain and wine, but farther south pastoralism was more common, though a mix of the two predominated.[13] These regional variations were significant, and, within regions, changes in elevation led to substantial differences: a palynological study of the region around Lake Kinneret, not far from Jezreel (see Fig. 16.1), identified five vegetation zones determined largely by elevation. Below sea level, scrubby shrubs predominated, shading into steppe-forests, then evergreen oak and terebinth woodlands, followed by short, deciduous oaks, and finally steppic vegetation on the heights of the Hermon range.[14]

The writings of western travelers, whether coming on campaign or on pilgrimage, present a valuable opportunity to see this varied ecology through Frankish eyes. Pilgrims had, of course, been writing accounts of their travels for centuries, marveling at the holy sites and often finding time to comment on the landscapes they passed through.[15] For Crusaders, the landscape could have more than a passing interest. It frequently seemed to fight them, and occasionally to welcome or justify them. Ambroise, in his chronicle of the Third Crusade, showed particular sensitivity to the landscape and the weather as an opposing force – sometimes it rained so much that people and animals were swept away or sickened and died, at other times it was too hot and dry.[16] One of the dangers of any description of the Holy Land is the tenacity of the biblical tropes. No one is surprised to find the Promised Land to be flowing with literal or metaphorical milk and honey – on the contrary, they would have been surprised to find it otherwise. Sometimes it is hard to tell how much these expectations shaped travelers' vision and memories. Even suspiciously-glowing reports, however, can help to shape an image of the ecology both as it was and as it was understood by the Franks.[17] At other times, observation seems to have

---

13　Saidel, "On the Periphery of an Agricultural Hinterland in the Negev Highlands: Rekhes Nafha 396 in the Sixth through the Eighth Centuries C.E." p. 241. Even further south in the Negev, farmers used qanats to irrigate their crops; Avner/Magness, "Early Islamic Settlement in the Southern Negev", p. 46; Prawer, *Latin Kingdom of Jerusalem*, p. 363.

14　Baruch, "The Late Holocene Vegetational History of Lake Kinneret (Sea of Galilee), Israel", pp. 39–40.

15　For example, see Burchardus de Monte Sion, "Descriptio Terrae Sanctae", in *Peregrinatores medii aevi quatuor: Burchardus de Monte Sion, Ricoldus de Monte Crucis, Odoricus de Foro Julii, Wilbrandus de Oldenborg*, ed. J.C.M. Laurent (Leipzig: J.C. Hinrichs, 1873), p. 29.

16　Ambroise, *History of the Holy War*, pp. 135, 112. Even the "stinging worms and tarantulas" that came out at night to plague the righteous army caught his notice; p. 113.

17　The reports also gain credibility when they line up with similar descriptions by Muslim geographers; Walmsley, "Fatimid, Ayyubid and Mamluk Jordan and the Crusader Interlude", p. 517.

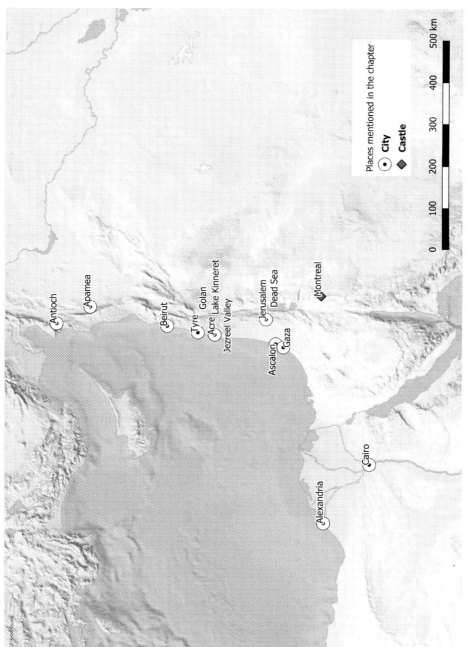

FIGURE 16.1   Localities mentioned in the chapter
DRAWN BY JOHANNES PREISER-KAPELLER, 2023

been too detailed to have sprung simply from recycled praise of the fertility of the land. For example, a pilgrim named Theoderich in the 1170s reported that, on a plain between Jerusalem and the Jordan, there was soil "fit for growing all manner of fruit" and, moreover, "ripe barley on the Monday after Palm Sunday."[18]

The picture painted by the sources is of an ecology that, while diverse, was fairly stable before the Crusaders arrived, and remained so under Frankish rule. The climate seems to have been mostly stable through the period. Focused studies have detected a slight drying trend beginning around AD 1400 and continuing to the present, while precipitation levels were higher during the rest of the Holocene (including the medieval period).[19] More recent analysis confirms that the Southern Levant was experiencing wetter conditions than average in the middle of the 13th century.[20] There may also have been a longer humid period in the Decapolis region between the 11th century and the end of the 13th.[21] At the same time, sites in Palestine were drier than average in the 11th century, directly before the coming of the Franks, while sites in northern Syria were more normal.[22] None of these data point to a violent rupture – the Crusaders and other human agents created what disruption they encountered.

Palynological studies, whose evidence reflect climatic changes as well as human activity, often work on time scales which are not useful for the medieval historian. When they do restrict their inquiry to the historical past, they confirm the image of a mostly-stable vegetation during the period of Frankish rule. For instance, the pollen core from Lake Kinneret mentioned above showed significant vegetation change at the end of the Roman period, when the uncultivated forest of evergreen oaks and terebinths returned.[23] The same vegetation structure remained from the 6th century until the 18th, despite some minor changes in the intervening period.[24] Similarly, palynology from

---

18 Theoderich, "Theoderich's Description of the Holy Places", p. 46.
19 MacDonald, "Climatic Changes", p. 599.
20 Xoplaki E. et al. "Modelling Climate and Societal Resilience in the Eastern Mediterranean in the Last Millennium".
21 Lucke et al., "The Abandonment of the Decapolis Region in Northern Jordan – forced by Environmental Change?", p. 79.
22 Preiser-Kapeller, "A Collapse of the Eastern Mediterranean? New Results and Theories on the Interplay between Climate and Societies in Byzantium and the Near East, Ca. 1000–1200 AD", p. 201.
23 Baruch, "Late Holocene Vegetational History", p. 46. This pattern is echoed in a more recently analyzed (and longer) pollen core from Lake Kinneret: Schiebel/Litt, "Holocene vegetation history of the southern Levant", pp. 583, 585, 588.
24 Baruch, "Late Holocene Vegetational History", p. 41. The radiocarbon dates that were obtained for Lake Kinneret (KIND4) in the 1970s and early 1980s relied on calibration

the Golan Heights just north and east of Lake Kinneret shows a precipitous decline in anthropogenic indicators – the types of pollen which tend to appear because of human activity, in this case largely olive pollen – in the 7th century, which were not recovered until the 19th century.[25] The Decapolis region, more suggestively, lost most evidence for human activity after the 10th century, not regaining it until the modern period. Evidently here, ecological change (spurred by or spurring social change) had occurred shortly before the coming of the Crusaders in the late 11th century.[26]

Because palynology reflects not only changes in uncultivated vegetation, but also in agriculture and in human management of the landscape, it can point to the types of agriculture that were being practiced in the region at the time of the First Crusade. It indicates that, for the most part, the same agriculture continued without major ruptures under Frankish rule. Many studies of agriculture from documentary or archaeological sources likewise point to relative stability in production and technique during the period. Such stability is both indicated and explained by the continuity of most of the agricultural producers. Cultivation seems to have been carried out mostly by native Christians and Muslims[27] – there was no reason for incoming Franks to quarrel with a peasant base who would extract value from the land and hand over at least some of it to their new lords. In a similar way, the Franks seem to have usually left estate administration in the hands of Syrian Christian dragomans, or the Muslim administrators who had worked under their predecessors.[28] The same attitude seems to have prevailed in the Frankish possessions in the

---

curves, which have since been updated several times. Moreover, in accordance with normal practice at the time, dates were only provided for the samples on which radiocarbon dating had been performed. For any samples in between, scholars had to estimate the dates based on simple distance from the dated samples. Normal practice now, in contrast, is to calibrate the radiocarbon dates and then use a mathematical function to create an age-depth model, estimating the dates for the other samples in the core, with their corresponding confidence intervals. When this modeling is carried out using cubic spline interpolation with two standard deviations for the confidence intervals (68 per cent probability; using Clam age-modeling software; see Table 16.1), the dates for the changes in vegetation actually mirror those in the Golan Heights. I thank Adam Izdebski for his help in re-calibrating the Lake Kinneret sediment profile.

25 Neumann et al., "Holocene Vegetation and Climate History of the Northern Golan Heights (Near East)", p. 340.
26 Lucke et al., "The Abandonment of the Decapolis Region", pp. 65, 78–9.
27 Prawer, *Latin Kingdom of Jerusalem*, p. 354.
28 Ellenblum, *Frankish Rural Settlement*, pp. 194–8; Riley-Smith, "The Survival in Latin Palestine of Muslim Administration", p. 16.

Morea, also won by crusade.[29] Notably, Frankish lords in the Levant (though not in the Morea) were apparently eager not only for the value of the rents, but specifically for the produce. At a time when lords in western Europe increasingly demanded cash instead of rents in kind, their brothers and nephews in the Latin East retained the old rents in kind. Sometimes they even seem to have maneuvered to ensure they received produce rather than other services or rents.[30]

In some regions, there is evidence that Franks may have spurred an intensification or extension of agriculture. Palynological evidence indicates greater agricultural activity around Antioch, a major and longstanding Frankish center in the Holy Land, from the 11th century through the end of the 13th. The increased production in the 11th century is obviously not attributable to the Franks, but their presence may have maintained pressure on the land through the middle of the 13th century.[31] The Franks also encouraged people to bring wasteland under cultivation by waiving tithes on such land.[32] (Unfortunately, much of the "wasteland" may have been the sites of seasonal villages integral to land-use schemes of the Levant and not as "wasted" as it at first appeared.)[33]

In most regions, however, there is no evidence of increased agricultural activity, and in some it seems to have declined.[34] Loss of agricultural land was usually associated with war. The coastal plain around Ascalon and Gaza had been important for producing wheat, but was destroyed in and around the First Crusade, and was not immediately productive.[35] Reports of the reconquest of fertile Transjordan by Salah ad-Din prove that villages and fields (destroyed by Crusaders) had been rebuilt – because his men destroyed them again.[36] Later conquests and raids by the Mamluks, especially in Galilee and the plains around Acre, destroyed productive land and forced the Franks to rely increasingly on a small strip of coastal plain – which was itself eventually either destroyed or wrested from them.[37] Even when land was functioning, the presence of the Franks could discourage trade and force reorientation of

---

29 Jacoby, "Rural Exploitation and Market Economy in the Late Medieval Peloponnese", pp. 213–75.
30 Riley-Smith, *The Knights Hospitaller in the Levant, c.1070–1309*, p. 178.
31 Kaniewski et al., "Medieval Coastal Syrian Vegetation Patterns in the Principality of Antioch", p. 251.
32 Riley-Smith, *Knights Hospitaller in the Levant*, p. 177.
33 Benvenisti, *The Crusaders in the Holy Land*, p. 216.
34 For no change, see for instance Neumann et al., "Northern Golan Heights", p. 340.
35 Prawer, *Latin Kingdom of Jerusalem*, p. 359.
36 Walmsley, "Fatimid, Ayyubid and Mamluk Jordan and the Crusader Interlude", p. 520.
37 Bronstein, *The Hospitallers and the Holy Land: Financing the Latin East, 1187–1274*, pp. 36, 38.

resources, as it did in the very southern parts of Jordan which had previously traded with Cairo and Damascus.[38]

Despite these disruptions, it is not surprising that the Franks should have had a relatively small impact on the overall ecology of the Levant. Most of the Crusader States were very short-lived, and the rulers were occupied with other things than agricultural reform, even had they been arrogant enough to attempt it. Moreover, the new environment they found themselves in was, in places, intractable. The 13th-century Arab geographer Yaqut al-Hamawi commented on the Judean Mountains, where much Frankish settlement was concentrated, that the land was terraced and difficult to cultivate – animal traction was impossible to use, and the ground had to be worked with hoes.[39] While such a situation might have been familiar to Franks from Italy or the south of France, for many it would have been a completely new type of agriculture, best left in the hands of those who understood it by long experience.

Most Franks seem to have adhered to this relatively "hands-off" attitude toward their environment. Some, however, saw it as a promising place when approached on its own terms. Some new villages were founded in the period of the Crusader States, evidently by Franks since they reflect a planned layout influenced by Frankish conceptions of village designs.[40] They look remarkably well-suited to their surroundings, sporting terraces and irrigation systems like their neighbors', and relying upon olive oil production and other respectably Levantine forms of agriculture.[41] But who inhabited these settlements? Were they simply redistributed populations of native Christians and Muslims? Certain scraps of evidence hint that they were not, and show that some inhabitants certainly came from elsewhere.[42] The passenger list of a vessel bound for Egypt during the campaign of Louis IX of France includes a large number of unattached people travelling east to settle in the land around Damietta, presumably providing the labor the king needed to set in motion plows he had brought on crusade expressly to place Egypt under solid and profitable control.[43] Louis IX's plows indicate that at least some Franks considered

---

38 Walmsley, "Fatimid, Ayyubid and Mamluk Jordan and the Crusader Interlude", p. 542.
39 Prawer, *Latin Kingdom of Jerusalem*, p. 360.
40 Ellenblum, *Frankish Rural Settlement*, p. 92; Davais, "A Seigneury on the Eastern Borders of the Kingdom of Jerusalem: The Terre de Suète", p. 91.
41 Ellenblum, *Frankish Rural Settlement*, pp. 46–50, 52, 91, 191.
42 Ellenblum, *Frankish Rural Settlement*, pp. 77, 281. See also Barbé, "Safed castle and its territory", pp. 72–4.
43 Kedar, "The Passenger List of a Crusader Ship, 1250: Toward the History of the Popular Element on the Seventh Crusade", pp. 270–71, 275–6.

imported technology to be necessary for full entrenchment in and possession of the conquered lands.

When Franks paid attention to the land (and were not founding whole villages) they put most of their effort into specialty crops. First, they favored the grapevine, cultivated for wine-production.[44] It was, of course, a familiar specialty crop from home and a familiar product. Vineyards quickly became prominent both in the land and in the imagination of the land. In some parts of the Levant, they came to stand for all agriculture in descriptions of prosperity, overshadowing grain fields and fruit trees.[45] Theoderich, the pilgrim noted above, describes a land that is "plenteous in vineyards."[46] Vineyards appear in charters as well, sometimes with evidence that they had been recently planted. For instance, when the Hospitallers entered a dispute over two vineyards near Acre, they happened to record in their cartulary that one of those vineyards had been planted by a Hospitaller knight.[47] Several grants in the same cartulary also included land specifically intended to become vineyards. So, when in 1152 the lord of Montréal gave the Hospitallers two castles east of the southern end of the Dead Sea, he mentioned several vineyards already included in the lands, as well as a plot "for planting vines."[48] This example comes from the Hospitallers' cartulary, but relatively poor farmers could hold vineyards as well.[49] The expansion of vineyards may have been instigated by the replacement of a Muslim elite with a Christian one. Vineyards and winepresses had not ceased to operate in the area during the period of Muslim rule before the Crusades, since many Muslims drank wine, and a large percentage of the population was still Christian.[50] Nevertheless, wealthy Christian rulers buying wine

---

44 Prawer, "Colonization Activities in the Latin Kingdom of Jerusalem", pp. 1098–107.
45 Prawer, "Colonization Activities", pp. 1098–9. I thank Tobias Hrynick for an introduction to viticulture in the Crusader States.
46 Theoderich, "Theoderich's Description of the Holy Places", p. 62.
47 Le Roulx, ed., *Cartulaire des Hospitaliers*, vol. 2, pp. 289–90.
48 Le Roulx, ed., *Cartulaire des Hospitaliers*, vol. 1, p. 160 no. 207. Thirteen years later, Baldwin of Mirabelle likewise gave the Hospitallers land that included vineyards, and some land for planting vines; ibid., vol. 1, p. 238. For more information on the conversion of other lands into vineyards, see Chalandon, ed., "Un diplome inedit d'Amaury I Roi de Jerusalem, en faveur de L'abbaye du Temple-Notre-Seigneur", vol. 8, p. 314.
49 Charters from the Church of the Holy Sepulcher seem to indicate that even upper-level peasantry might own vineyards; Bresc-Bautier, *Le Cartulaire du Chapitre du Saint-Sépulcre de Jérusalem*, pp. 115, 121. They were also certainly owned or leased by Syrian Christians, at least sometimes; ibid., pp. 69, 131.
50 Gil, *A History of Palestine, 634–1099*, pp. 170–72. Some dietary habits seem nevertheless to have been affected. Excavations at several sites, for example, show a sharp decline in discarded pig bones after the Arab conquest, and a corresponding rise after the coming of the Crusaders; Pluskowski et al., "Ecology of Crusading", p. 198.

for consumption and display (and endowing churches, which celebrated the Eucharist) may well have provided a more viable market for wine.[51] The evidence points to expanded vineyards, whatever the social or religious causes.

Even more striking than the expansion of vineyards is the cultivation of sugarcane, and the production of sugar, which the Franks embraced zealously not only in the Levant but also in Cyprus.[52] Sugarcane was already grown in the Levant when the Crusaders arrived, but unlike grapevines, it was not a familiar crop to the Franks. They brought a new fascination with the delectable product, and links to a largely unexploited market in Europe.[53] Individual Franks became involved in cultivating sugarcane, refining sugar, and exporting it; the most famous examples of this investment come, however, from groups like the Hospitallers, and the Venetians around Tyre.[54] Sugar production was not a simple thing to expand – the plants require much more substantial irrigation than other crops, and processing them is an arduous task. The sugar-mills that the Franks built in the Levant are still scattered in the landscape today.[55] Nevertheless, where this crop was concerned, the environmental challenges did not daunt the Franks.

The ecology of the Crusader States can be overwhelming to approach, because it is such a broad subject, touching many points of historical inquiry and requiring the use of paleoclimatic sources, which have sometimes been processed with a view to detecting the Little Ice Age rather than the fall of Acre. A fruitful way to begin to build a functional structure out of these scattered pieces is to address ecology through case studies, especially those that train the spotlight on natural pressure points. One such pressure point was the Franks' warhorses. In an unfamiliar environment, the Franks had to come up with modified strategies for feeding their mounts.

Horses were indispensable for Frankish warfare.[56] Knights – logistically and ideologically the backbone of the western medieval army – needed strong

---

51 Prawer, "Colonization Activities", p. 1105.
52 von Wartburg, "The archeology of sugar cane production: a survey of twenty years of research in Cyprus", pp. 305–35. For sugar in the medieval Mediterranean see especially Ouerfelli, *Le sucre*.
53 Galloway, "The Mediterranean Sugar Industry", pp. 180–81; Prawer, *Latin Kingdom of Jerusalem*, p. 364; Riley-Smith, "Survival of Muslim Administration", p. 9.
54 Riley-Smith, *The Feudal Nobility and the Kingdom of Jerusalem, 1174–1277*, p. 176; Richard, "Agricultural Conditions in the Crusader States", p. 256.
55 See for example Pringle, *Secular Buildings in the Crusader Kingdom of Jerusalem*, pp. 99–101.
56 For a vivid depiction of the ideological centrality of mounted knights and hand-to-hand combat (as opposed to the archery more often associated, in the west, with footsoldiers), see John of Joinville's assessment of the battle of Mansurah: "And know that this was a

warhorses, capable of carrying them into battle in full armor.[57] Each knight had multiple horses. He usually tried to have a remount available in case of injury, and if possible to keep riding, and baggage horses (or mules) for himself and his servant.[58] A reasonably well-endowed knight might thus hope to maintain at least five horses, two being warhorses. Though sergeants and other more minor fief-holders probably needed fewer horses, the animals were still essential for the men's function. Each horse, in turn, needed large quantities of good fodder.

The Levant presented the Franks with a new environment in which to keep their horses, but the species was certainly not foreign to the Levant. Parts of Syria had been raising horses since at least the Hellenistic period, and every major ruling power since then had used cavalry, and had needed to develop strategies for feeding the mounts.[59] All of them – including the Franks – fed

---

very fine feat of arms, for no one fired either a bow or a crossbow, but rather there were blows of maces and swords from the Turks and our men, who were all ensnarled with each other", Jean de Joinville, "The Life of Saint Louis", p. 202 (II, 6.229). See also Stone, "Technology, Society, and the Infantry Revolution of the Fourteenth Century", pp. 368–9, 375. John France, however, points out that historians have tended to overemphasize the importance of cavalry and unjustly minimize the essential role played by infantry throughout the period; France, "A Changing Balance: Cavalry and Infantry, 1000–1300", p. 155.

57 For descriptions of the armor of the period (which changed somewhat over time), see DeVries/Smith, *Medieval Military Technology*, pp. 66–74. The Old French continuation of William of Tyre, written sometime in the middle of the 13th century but recounting events in the late 12th, noted the changing styles of armor knights used, and its weight: "At that time [i.e. 1192] hardly anyone had a bacinet, shoulder pieces, pointed coif, grieves or a helm with a visor unless he were a king, a count or a great lord. Because they were lightly armed, if by some chance a knight or sergeant lost his horse he could manage on foot, may God be merciful! But now their armour is so tight and heavy that if a knight falls from his horse he can do nothing to help himself"; "The Old French Continuation of William of Tyre, 1184–97", p. 119.

58 John of Joinville describes the need for remounts incidentally at the battle of Mansurah: he was unhorsed, and fought on foot for a while, but eventually one of his squires brought one of John's spare horses, so that he could mount and go to the king; John of Joinville, "Life of Saint Louis", p. 202 (II, 6.229); Ayton, "Arms, Armour and Horses", p. 197; Pryor, "Introduction: Modelling Bohemond's March to Thessalonikē", p. 7. In the 1260s, the knights holding land in the lordship of Arsuf owed military service with four warhorses each. Riley-Smith, *Feudal Nobility*, p. 175; Le Roulx, ed., *Cartulaire des Hospitaliers*, vol. 3, pp. 6–7 (no. 2985).

59 See discussions in Dixon, *The Roman Cavalry*, and Bivar, "Cavalry Equipment and Tactics on the Euphrates Frontier", pp. 271–91; Hyland, *The Medieval Warhorse*, p. 108; France, *Perilous Glory*, pp. 100–103; Lev, "Infantry in Muslim Armies during the Crusades",

their horses grain, which ideally constituted between one third and one half of their daily nutrition.[60] Frankish horses seem to have required more grain than others, both because through breeding their bodies had come to require it, and because they were larger and heavier than the Muslims' horses.[61] Barley was the grain of choice for horse feeding, being hardier than wheat and cheaper, since it was less desirable as human food.[62] Though it seems counterintuitive to modern equestrian wisdom, most medieval European horses were stall-fed.[63] Alongside the grain, Muslims and Franks both used cut grass or other plants, which might be dried for storage before being fed to the horses. Horses did also graze, and even stabled horses kept in cities were put out to pasture at least occasionally, especially in the spring.[64]

The Frankish ruling class, then, had an ongoing need for large quantities of both grain and fodder. Viewed carefully, pollen records and documentary evidence provide hints as to how they may have acquired these when faced with the constraints of Levantine agriculture. A pollen core from Lake Kinneret shows suggestive changes during the period of Frankish rule that are potentially traceable specifically to grazing. These changes appear in the pollen percentages for "Trifolium-type", a meadow plant taxon that includes both clover and alfalfa. Ancient and medieval authors recognized the benefits of clover, alfalfa, and related plants as components of horse pasture, both for their heartiness as

pp. 191–3; Crone, "The 'Abbāsid Abnā' and Sāsānid Cavalrymen", pp. 17–18; Jandora, "Archers of Islam: A Search for 'lost' History", p. 112.

60 Gladitz, *Horse Breeding in the Medieval World*, p. 127; Haldon, "Roads and Communications in the Byzantine Empire: Wagons, Horses, and Supplies", p. 145. This percentage is far higher than modern recommendations. In a world always under the threat of famine – where, in northern Europe, returns of four or five to one on grain crops (of bushels harvested to bushels sown) was considered a good harvest, and the Egyptian returns of more than twenty to one were unbelievably rich – feeding horses grain illustrates the value of the animals; for harvest yields see Jordan, *The Great Famine*, p. 25. The exceptions were the herds maintained by nomads, like the Türkmen who had invaded the Levant shortly before the First Crusade, and the Mongols who helped to finish off the Crusader States in the 13th century. Both of these groups relied instead upon extensive grazing, moving their horses when grass in one area was used up. Their horses had not been bred to require grain; Hyland, *Medieval Warhorse*, p. 126; Peacock, *The Great Seljuk Empire*, p. 224.

61 Ayton, "Arms, Armour and Horses", p. 197, Hyland, *Medieval Warhorse*, p. 140. Ambroise echoes the astonishment of many of his compatriots at the marked differences between western and "Turkish" horses, which "seem to fly like swallows", and could not be caught by the larger, thicker western horses; Ambroise, *History of the Holy War*, p. 110.

62 Ambroise, *History of the Holy War*, p. 133; Pryor, "In Subsidium Terrae Sanctae", p. 134.

63 Pryor, "Modelling Bohemond's March", p. 15.

64 Hyland, *The Warhorse, 1250–1600*, p. 120; Gladitz, *Horse Breeding*, p. 188.

feed and their hardiness as plants.[65] Lorenzo Rusio, writing in Italy in the early 14th century, noted clover as an excellent crop for grazing, and also suggested that it was only necessary to sow it every three years, an important indication that good pasture was sometimes created rather than discovered.[66] Islamic authors recommended clover for horses, and there is evidence that it was commonly used as a pasture crop for the horses kept in Cairo.[67]

The pollen record for Trifolium-type in Galilee is at first glance counterintuitive. Though never dominant in the region, the plants appear to have maintained a fairly steady presence throughout the Roman and early medieval period. In the sample representing, probably, the middle of the Frankish period, the taxon completely disappears for the first time since the Hellenistic period.[68] By the time of the next pollen sample, from the late Middle Ages, Trifolium-type pollen had stabilized again at its previous level (see Figure 16.2).[69] The evidence, then, does not suggest that Franks were deliberately sowing land with pasture rich in Trifolium-type plants, as Lorenzo Rusio or the farmers around Cairo might have recommended. What it might suggest, however, is that they were putting their horses out to graze on the existing meadows and pastures, which contained these plants. Once there, the horses (who prefer such plants), selectively grazed them intensively enough to prevent them from dispersing sufficient pollen to appear in the lakebed sediment.[70] The horses would almost certainly have been encouraged to eat the plants before they could produce pollen, since pasture that had already bloomed was considered useless.[71]

---

65   Gladitz, *Horse Breeding*, pp. 186–7; Hyland, *Equus*, p. 92. Modern equestrian wisdom concurs: Thomas, *Storey's Guide to Raising Horses*, pp. 3, 48. Thomas also points out, however, that feeding solely clover or alfalfa is detrimental to horses' health, as their digestive systems require more roughage than the plants provide.

66   Laurentius Rusius, *La mascalcia di Lorenzo Rusio volgarizzamento del secolo 14., messo per la prima volta in luce da Pietro Delprato, aggiuntovi il testo latino per cura di Luigi Barbieri*, ed. Luigi Barbieri and Pietro Delprato (Bologna: Bologna Presso G. Romagnoli, 1867), 50.

67   Hyland, *Warhorse 1200–1500*, pp. 120–21.

68   Sample number 16, at a depth of 105 cm, and dated between AD 1173 and 1426. Note that the more recent analysis of another pollen core from Lake Kinneret did not differentiate Trifolium-type pollen; Schiebel/Litt, "Holocene Vegetation History of the Southern Levant", 583.

69   Sample number 17, at a depth of 80 cm, and dated between AD 1355 and 1581.

70   For horses' preference for such plants, see Thomas, *Storey's Guide to Raising Horses*, pp. 46–7.

71   Gladitz, *Horse Breeding*, pp. 189, 185, from Ibn al-Munhir and Ibn al-Awwan. Modern wisdom concurs, encouraging farmers to use pasture and cut hay before blossoms appear; Thomas, *Storey's Guide to Raising Horses*, pp. 46–7. Palynologists have indicated in other cases that overgrazing might reduce the ability of certain plants to flower, triggering the

THE ECOLOGY OF THE CRUSADER STATES

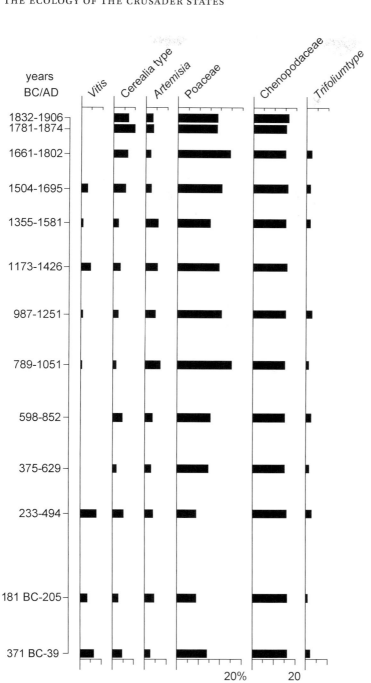

FIGURE 16.2 Pollen Variations: KIND4 (Sea of Galilee). Data for select pollen taxa from Baruch, "Late Holocene Vegetational History." Dates have been recalibrated as described above (note 23). See also Table 16.1

TABLE 16.1 Recalibrated dates for KIND4, using a cubic spline with 68 per cent certainty

Sample number	Depth (cm)	Min68 per cent	Max68 per cent	Best date BP (present=1950)	Accuracy Rate
21	12	44	118	82	5.29
20	20	76	169	124	5.44
19	37	148	289	219	5.74
18	59	255	446	350	6.13
17	80	369	595	482	6.5
16	105	524	777	650	6.94
15	130	699	963	828	7.38
14	156	899	1161	1026	7.84
13	180	1098	1352	1219	8.27
12	207	1321	1575	1449	8.74
11	223	1456	1717	1591	9.03
10	257	1745	2068	1907	9.63
9	279	1911	2321	2123	NA

Somewhat oddly, in Galilee, there is no indication in the pollen record for the expansion of grazing lands, which might appear through an increase in *Artemisia*, *Chenopodiaceae*, or *Gramineae*.[72] It appears that there, if the above hypothesis is correct, the Franks were exploiting the most nutritious meadows and pastures for their mounts, but were not so pressed as to expand pasture onto new land.[73] A different picture emerges for two other sites where pollen cores have been studied. In both the northern Golan Heights and the Principality of Antioch, slight increases in pollen from meadow and grassland plants may suggest an extension of pasture during the period of Frankish rule. In the Principality of Antioch, this rise is confined to the later Frankish period, after the loss of most of the Crusader States' good agricultural lands.[74] The

pollen's disappearance from the record. Bottema/Woldring, "Anthropogenic Indicators in the Pollen Record of the Eastern Mediterranean", p. 236.

72 Behre, "The Interpretation of Anthropogenic Indicators in Pollen Diagrams", p. 224.
73 For Frankish control of this area, see Khamisy "The Mount Tabor territory under Frankish control", p. 49, and Khamisy "Western Upper Galilee under crusader rule", *passim*.
74 Bronstein, *The Hospitallers and the Holy Land*, pp. 36, 38.

Franks seem to have been having more difficulty provisioning their remaining outposts, cities, and regions. In such a situation, they may well have put more pressure on the land immediately surrounding Antioch.

They also put more pressure on the West. The Latin Kingdom of Jerusalem was probably only self-sufficient in the middle of the 12th century – after that, it and the other Crusader States relied heavily on imported provisions, especially grain.[75] The quantity of grain sent from the west to the Crusader States is notable, and it is defined in the documents as both wheat and barley – presumably horse feed.[76] As Judith Bronstein has shown from the records of the Hospitallers, military orders organized their investments and rents in western lands partly in order to enable them to ship grain and other supplies to their houses in the Holy Land.[77] These documents, and others from the Kingdom of Sicily, demonstrate that southern Italy and Sicily were a major supplier.[78] Remarkably, as Sicily sent grain east, climatic conditions seemed to urge an opposite policy: in the middle of the 13th century the central Mediterranean was experiencing a drying trend, while the southern Levant remained wetter than average.[79] The Franks were clearly not simply responding to the dictates of ecology or climate, but were making their decisions with reference to a very human web of social, political, and economic relationships. Not infrequently, horses themselves were sent east as well, as replacements for those lost in battle.[80] The Franks do not seem to have been able (or perhaps did not find it to be necessary) to provide from their own lands all the fodder their horses needed, or to breed horses within their bounds.

The Frankish attitude towards horses and their fodder encapsulates what seems to have been a broader attitude towards the environment of the Crusader States. They did not attempt to revise the landscape or agrarian production along western European lines, as much later settlers and rulers from western

---

75 Richard, "Agricultural Conditions in the Crusader States", pp. 264–6; Raphael, *Environmental Disasters in the Medieval Levant*, p. 37; Bronstein, *The Hospitallers and the Holy Land*, pp. 64–5; Pluskowski et al., "Ecology of Crusading", p. 200.

76 Bronstein, *The Hospitallers and the Holy Land*, p. 98; Barber, "Supplying the Crusader States: The Role of the Templars", p. 325.

77 Bronstein, *The Hospitallers and the Holy Land*; see Chapter 2, "The Order in the West and Crises in the Latin East: The French Priories", pp. 64–102, which addresses Europe beyond France as well.

78 Barber, "Supplying the Crusader States", p. 326; Henri de Curzon, ed., *La règle du Temple* (Paris: Librairie Renouard, H. Laurens, 1886), pp. 314–15, clause 609; Bronstein, *The Hospitallers and the Holy Land*, p. 75.

79 Xoplaki et al., "Modeling climate and societal resilience".

80 Pryor, "In Subsidium", pp. 131–4.

Europe did in "Neo-Europes" like North America.[81] They were opportunistic where the ecology already coincided with their own needs or desires, and were willing to invest more effort when faced with the possibilities of trade: they grazed horses on rich pasture and intensified or expanded production of sugar and wine. Mostly, they recognized a well-functioning agriculture already in place, and found it prudent to exploit it as it stood, praise its fertility, and modify more malleable things like trade networks (as they imported large quantities of grain).[82] Though this strategy eventually broke down as the Crusader States shrank, it was replaced by a greater reliance upon imported provisions, which were increasingly subsidized by funds which also originated in the west.

Considering the ecology of the Crusader States begins to flesh out the history of those polities and the people who inhabited them – lords and peasants, Franks and Syrians. Besides providing a much-needed background, it uncovers unexpected, if shadowy, evidence for the attitudes and goals of the Franks themselves. The ecology of the Levant at that moment in time comprised in a significant way the world the Franks entered on crusade or as settlers. The Frankish response to their new environment demonstrates how the Franks were willing to adapt themselves to the unfamiliar land and adjust the land to suit their needs (or newfound desires). As the ecology is better understood, focused studies of the Franks' response to it and use of it will continue to illuminate not only the nature of these ephemeral polities, but also the ways the Franks viewed them and understood their place within a wider world.

Bibliography

Ambroise, *The History of the Holy War: Ambroise's Estoire de La Guerre Sainte*, trans. M. Ailes. Woodbridge, Suffolk, 2003.

Avner, U./Magness, J., "Early Islamic Settlement in the Southern Negev", *Bulletin of the American Schools of Oriental Research; Boston*, no. 310 (1998), 39–56.

Avni, G./Porat, N./Avni, Y., "Byzantine–Early Islamic Agricultural Systems in the Negev Highlands: Stages of Development as Interpreted through OSL Dating", *Journal of Field Archaeology* 38, no. 4 (2013), 332–46.

---

81 Alfred W. Crosby, *Ecological Imperialism*. Crosby's own explanation of the Crusader States' failure to thrive depends on the Franks' low population and susceptibility to malaria; pp. 64–6.

82 Butzer, "Islamic Traditions of Agroecology", p. 19; Richard, "Agricultural Conditions", pp. 259–60. Praise for fertility: Prawer, *Latin Kingdom of Jerusalem*, p. 365; Benvenisti, *Crusaders in the Holy Land*, p. 389 (citing Burchard of Mont Sion).

Ayton, A., "Arms, Armour and Horses", in M. Keen (ed.) *Medieval Warfare: A History*, Oxford 1999, pp. 186–208.
Barbé, H., "Safed Castle and Its Territory: Frankish Settlement and Colonisation in Eastern Galilee during the Crusader Period", in M. Sinibaldi/K. Lewis/B. Major/ J. Thompson (eds.), *Crusader Landscapes in the Medieval Levant: The Archaeology and History of the Latin East*, Cardiff 2016, pp. 55–79.
Barber, M.C. "Supplying the Crusader States: The Role of the Templars", in B. Kedar (ed.) *The Horns of Ḥaṭṭīn: Proceedings of the Second Conference of the Society for the Study of the Crusades and the Latin East, Jerusalem and Haifa, 2–6 July 1987*, Jerusalem 1992, pp. 314–26.
Baruch, U. "The Late Holocene Vegetational History of Lake Kinneret (Sea of Galilee), Israel", *Paléorient* 12, no. 2 (1986), 37–48.
Behre, K.-E., "The Interpretation of Anthropogenic Indicators in Pollen Diagrams", *Pollen et Spores* 23 (1981) 225–45.
Benvenisti, M., *The Crusaders in the Holy Land*, New York 1970.
Bivar, A.D.H. "Cavalry Equipment and Tactics on the Euphrates Frontier", *Dumbarton Oaks Papers* 26 (1972) 271–91.
Bottema, S./Woldring, H., "Anthropogenic Indicators in the Pollen Record of the Eastern Mediterranean", in S. Bottema/G. Entjes-Nieborg/W. van Zeist (eds.) *Man's Role in the Shaping of the Eastern Mediterranean Landscape*, Brookfield, VT, 1990, pp. 231–64.
Bresc-Bautier, G., *Le Cartulaire du Chapitre du Saint-Sépulcre de Jérusalem*, Paris 1984.
Bronstein, J., *The Hospitallers and the Holy Land: Financing the Latin East, 1187–1274*, Woodbridge, Suffolk, 2005.
Butzer, K.W., "The Islamic Traditions of Agroecology: Crosscultural Experience, Ideas and Innovations", *Cultural Geographies* 1, no. 1 (1994), 7–50.
Cartulaire général de l'ordre des Hospitaliers de S. Jean de Jérusalem (1100–1310), J. Delaville Le Roulx (ed.), 4 vols., Paris, 1894.
Ciggaar, K.N./Teule, H., eds., *East and West in the Crusader States. Context, Contacts, Confrontations III. Acta of the Congress Held at Hernen Castle in September 2000*, (Orientalia Lovaniensia Analecta, 125), Louvain, 2004.
Crone, P., "The 'Abbāsid Abnā' and Sāsānid Cavalrymen", *Journal of the Royal Asiatic Society (Third Series)* 8, no. 1 (April 1998), 1–19.
Cronon, W., *Changes in the Land: Indians, Colonists, and the Ecology of New England*, New York, 1983.
Crosby, A.W., *Ecological Imperialism: The Biological Expansion of Europe, 900–1900*, 2nd ed., (Studies in Environment and History), Cambridge, 2004.
Davais, C., "A Seigneury on the Eastern Borders of the Kingdom of Jerusalem: The Terre de Suète", in J.G. Schryver (ed.), *Studies in the Archaeology of the Medieval Mediterranean*, Leiden, 2010.

DeVries, K./Smith, R.D., *Medieval Military Technology*, 2nd ed., Toronto, 2012.

Dietzel, I. *The Ecology of Coexistence and Conflict in Cyprus: Exploring the Religion, Nature, and Culture of a Mediterranean Island*, Boston, 2014.

Dixon, K.R., *The Roman Cavalry: From the First to the Third Century AD*, London, 1992.

Ellenblum, R., "Who Built Qal'at Al-Ṣubayba?", *Dumbarton Oaks Papers* 43 (1989), 103–12.

Ellenblum, R., *Frankish Rural Settlement in the Latin Kingdom of Jerusalem*, Cambridge, 1998.

France, J., "A Changing Balance: Cavalry and Infantry, 1000–1300", *Revista de História das Ideias* 30 (2009), 153–77.

France, J., *Perilous Glory: The Rise of Western Military Power*, New Haven, 2011.

Galloway, J.H., "The Mediterranean Sugar Industry." *Geographical Review* 67, no. 2 (1977), 177–94.

Gil, M., *A History of Palestine, 634–1099*, Cambridge, 1992.

Gladitz, C., *Horse Breeding in the Medieval World*, Dublin, 1997.

Haldon, J.F., "Roads and Communications in the Byzantine Empire: Wagons, Horses, and Supplies", in J.H. Pryor (ed.), *Logistics of Warfare in the Age of the Crusades: Proceedings of a Workshop Held at the Centre for Medieval Studies, University of Sydney, 30 September to 4 October 2002*, Aldershot, 2006, pp. 131–58.

Hill, J.B., "Decision Making at the Margins: Settlement Trends, Temporal Scale, and Ecology in the Wadi Al Hasa, West-Central Jordan", *Journal of Anthropological Archaeology* 19, no. 2 (2000), 221–41.

Hyland, A., *Equus: The Horse in the Roman World*, London, 1990.

Hyland, A., *The Medieval Warhorse: From Byzantium to the Crusades*. Phoenix Mill, 1994.

Hyland, A., *The Warhorse, 1250–1600*, Stroud, 1998.

Issar, A./Zohar, M., *Climate Change: Environment and Civilization in the Middle East*, New York, 2004.

Jacoby, D., "Rural Exploitation and Market Economy in the Late Medieval Peloponnese," in: S.E.J. Gerstel (ed.), *Viewing the Morea: Land and People in the Late Medieval Peloponnese*, Washington D.C. 2013, pp. 213–75.

Jandora, J.W., "Archers of Islam: A Search for 'lost' History", *Medieval History Journal* 13, no. 1 (2010), 97–114.

Jean de Joinville, "The Life of Saint Louis", in C. Smith (trans.), *Chronicles of the Crusades*, London, 2009, pp. 136–336.

Jordan, W.C., *The Great Famine: Northern Europe in the Early Fourteenth Century*, Princeton, NJ, 1996.

Kaniewski, D./Van Campo, E./Paulissen, E./Weiss, H./Otto, T./Bakker, J./Rossignol, I./Van Lerberghe, K., "Medieval Coastal Syrian Vegetation Patterns in the Principality of Antioch", *The Holocene* 21, no. 2 (March 1, 2011), 251–62.

Kedar, B.Z., "Latins and Oriental Christians in the Frankish Levant, 1099–1291", in A. Kofsky/G.G. Stroumsa (eds.), *Sharing the Sacred: Religious Contacts and Conflicts in the Holy Land. First-Fifteenth Centuries CE*, 209–22, Jerusalem, 1998.

Kedar, B.Z., "The Passenger List of a Crusader Ship, 1250: Toward the History of the Popular Element on the Seventh Crusade", *Studi Medievali* 13, no. 1 (1972), 267–79.

Kedar, B.Z., ed., "The Crusading Kingdom of Jerusalem – The First European Colonial Society? A Symposium", in B.Z. Kedar, (ed.), *The Horns of Ḥaṭṭīn: Proceedings of the Second Conference of the Society for the Study of the Crusades and the Latin East, Jerusalem and Haifa, 2–6 July 1987*, Jerusalem, 1992, pp. 341–66.

Khamisy, R., "The Mount Tabor Territory under Frankish Control", in M. Sinibaldi/K. Lewis/B. Major/J. Thompson (eds.), *Crusader Landscapes in the Medieval Levant: The Archaeology and History of the Latin East*, Cardiff 2016, pp. 39–53.

Khamisy, R., "Western Upper Galilee under Crusader Rule", in A. Boas (ed.), *The Crusader World*, New York 2016, pp. 212–24.

Lev, Y./Pryor, J.H., "Infantry in Muslim Armies during the Crusades", in J. Pryor (ed.) *Logistics of Warfare in the Age of the Crusades: Proceedings of a Workshop Held at the Centre for Medieval Studies, University of Sydney, 30 September to 4 October 2002*, Aldershot, 2006, pp. 185–207.

Lucke, B./Schmidt, M./al-Saad, Z./Bens, O./Hüttl, R.F., "The Abandonment of the Decapolis Region in Northern Jordan – forced by Environmental Change?", *Quaternary International*, (Geochronology and Environmental Reconstruction: a Tribute to Glenn A. Goodfriend), 135, no. 1 (June 2005), 65–81.

MacDonald, B., "Climatic Changes in Jordan through Time", in B. MacDonald/R. Adams/P. Bienkowski (eds.), *The Archaeology of Jordan*, Sheffield, England, 2001, pp. 595–601.

MacEvitt, C., *The Crusades and the Christian World of the East: Rough Tolerance*, Philadelphia, 2008.

McNeill, J.R., *The Mountains of the Mediterranean World: An Environmental History*, Cambridge, 1992.

Melville, E.G.K., *A Plague of Sheep: Environmental Consequences of the Conquest of Mexico*, (Studies in Environment and History), Cambridge, 1994.

Neumann, F./Schölzel, C./Litt, T./Hense, A./Stein, M., "Holocene Vegetation and Climate History of the Northern Golan Heights (Near East)", *Vegetation History and Archaeobotany* 16, no. 4 (June 8, 2006), 329–46.

Ouerfelli, M., *Le sucre: production, commercialisation et usages dans la Méditerranée médiévale*, Leiden, 2008.

Peacock, A., *The Great Seljuk Empire*, (Edinburgh History of the Islamic Empires), Edinburgh, 2015.

Pluskowski, A., ed., *Environment, Colonization, and the Baltic Crusader States: Terra Sacra 1*, (Environmental Histories of the North Atlantic World 2), Turnhout, Belgium, 2019.

Pluskowski, A., ed., *Ecologies of Crusading, Colonization, and Religious Conversion in the Medieval Baltic: Terra Sacra II*, (Environmental Histories of the North Atlantic World 3), Turnhout, Belgium, 2019.

Pluskowski, A./Boas, A.J./Gerrard, C., "The Ecology of Crusading: Investigating the Environmental Impact of Holy War and Colonisation at the Frontiers of Medieval Europe", *Medieval Archaeology* 55, no. 1 (2011), 192–225.

Prawer, J., *The Latin Kingdom of Jerusalem: European Colonialism in the Middle Ages*, London, 1973.

Preiser-Kapeller, J., "A Collapse of the Eastern Mediterranean? New Results and Theories on the Interplay between Climate and Societies in Byzantium and the Near East, Ca. 1000–1200 AD", *Jahrbuch der österreichischen Byzantinistik* 65 (2015) 195–242.

Pringle, D., *Secular Buildings in the Crusader Kingdom of Jerusalem: An Archaeological Gazetteer*, Cambridge, 1997.

Pryor, J.H., "In Subsidium Terrae Sanctae: Exports of Foodstuffs and War Materials from the Kingdom of Sicily to the Kingdom of Jerusalem, 1265–1284", *Asian and African Studies* 22 (1988), 127–46.

Pryor, J.H., "Introduction: Modelling Bohemond's March to Thessalonikē", in J.H. Pryor (ed.) *Logistics of Warfare in the Age of the Crusades: Proceedings of a Workshop Held at the Centre for Medieval Studies, University of Sydney, 30 September to 4 October 2002*, Aldershot, 2006, pp. 1–24.

Raphael, K., *Climate and Political Climate: Environmental Disasters in the Medieval Levant*, (Brill's Series in the History of the Environment 3), Leiden, 2013.

Richard, J., "Une économie coloniale? Chypre et ses ressources agricoles au Moyen Age", *Byzantinische Forschungen* V (1977) 331–52.

Richard, J., "Agricultural Conditions in the Crusader States", in N. Zacour/H. Hazard (eds.), *A History of the Crusades, V: The Impact of the Crusades on the Near East*, Madison, Wisc., 1985, pp. 251–94.

Riley-Smith, J.S.C., *The Knights Hospitaller in the Levant, c.1070–1309*, New York, 2012.

Riley-Smith, J.S.C., *The Feudal Nobility and the Kingdom of Jerusalem, 1174–1277*, Hamden, Conn., 1973.

Riley-Smith, J.S.C., "The Survival in Latin Palestine of Muslim Administration", in P.M. Holt (ed.), *The Eastern Mediterranean Lands in the Period of the Crusades*, Warminster, 1977, pp. 9–22.

Saidel, B.A., "On the Periphery of an Agricultural Hinterland in the Negev Highlands: Rekhes Nafha 396 in the Sixth through the Eighth Centuries CE", *Journal of Near Eastern Studies* 64, no. 4 (2005), 241–55.

Schiebel, V./T. Litt, "Holocene Vegetation History of the Southern Levant Based on a Pollen Record from Lake Kinneret (Sea of Galilee), Israel", *Vegetation History and Archaeobotany* 27, no. 4 (2018), pp. 577–90.

Sinibaldi, M., "Settlement in the Petra Region during the Crusader Period: A Summary of the Historical and Archaeological Evidence", M. Sinibaldi/K. Lewis/B. Major/ J. Thompson (eds.), *Crusader Landscapes in the Medieval Levant: The Archaeology and History of the Latin East*, Cardiff 2016, pp. 81–102.

Stone, J., "Technology, Society, and the Infantry Revolution of the Fourteenth Century", *The Journal of Military History* 68, no. 2 (2004), 361–80.

Theoderich, "Theoderich's Description of the Holy Places", in A. Stewart (trans.), *Palestine Pilgrims' Texts Society*, London, 1896, vol. 5, 1–58.

Thomas, H.S., *Storey's Guide to Raising Horses: Breeding, Care, Facilities*, 2nd ed., North Adams, MA, 2009.

"Un Diplome Inedit d'Amaury I Roi de Jerusalem, En Faveur de L'abbaye Du Temple-Notre-Seigneur", Chalandon, F., (ed.) in *Revue de l'Orient Latin*, Paris, 1900, vol. 8, pp. 311–17.

Vogt, St./Glaser, R./Luterbacher J. et alii, "Assessing the Medieval Climate Anomaly in the Middle East: The potential of Arabic documentary sources", PAGES news 19/1 (2011), 28–29.

Walmsley, A., "Fatimid, Ayyubid and Mamluk Jordan and the Crusader Interlude", in B. MacDonald/R. Adams/P. Bienkowski (eds.), *The Archaeology of Jordan*, Sheffield, England, 2001, pp. 515–59.

von Wartburg, M.L., "The archeology of sugar cane production: a survey of twenty years of research in Cyprus", *The Antiquaries Journal* 81 (2001), 305–35.

Xoplaki, E./J. Luterbacher/S. Wagner/E. Zorita/D. Fleitmann/J. Preiser-Kapeller/ A. Sargent/S. White/A. Toreti/J. Haldon/L. Mordechai/D. Bozkurt/S. Akçer-Ön/ A. Izdebski, "Modelling Climate and Societal Resilience in the Eastern Mediterranean in the Last Millennium", *Human Ecology* 46, no. 3 (2018), 363–79.

CHAPTER 17

The Little Ice Age in the Eastern Mediterranean, 14th–17th Centuries

Sam White

1   Introduction

This chapter attempts to answer two questions about the environmental history of the late Byzantine Empire: First, did Byzantine lands experience a phase of climate that we could usefully label a "Little Ice Age" (LIA)? Second, if so, did it make a difference for many people in the empire or for the course of Byzantine history? This chapter will work backwards from a narrative of climate variability, extreme weather, and crisis in the late-16th- and 17th-century Ottoman Empire. That will help determine where to look for traces of a LIA and its possible impacts in the late Byzantine Empire. I will then try to extend the investigation of physical and written records into the 13th–15th centuries and discern a role for climate in late Byzantine history. The analysis here draws on written and physical evidence for temperature, precipitation, and land use discussed in chapters 2–4 of this volume, where readers can find further explanations of the underlying sources and methods.[1]

This contribution was first composed and submitted in 2014. From the evidence then available, I concluded that there was a climatic change affecting late-13th- and 14th-century Byzantine territories. However, it was difficult to distinguish the historical influence of that change amid the many problems facing the empire during its final two centuries, including the Black Death, civil wars, and foreign invasions. Since 2014, new paleoclimate and historical research has provided further insights into climatic variability, extreme

---

[1] See Haldon et al., "Climate and Environment of Byzantine Anatolia" for the state of the field at the time of writing (2014). For reviews of eastern Mediterranean climate history, see Finné et al., "Climate in the Eastern Mediterranean, and Adjacent Regions, during the Past 6000 Years – A Review" and Luterbacher et al., "A Review of 2000 Years of Paleoclimatic Evidence in the Mediterranean". For further reviews of the climate evidence, see Nicoll and Küçükuysal, "Emerging Multi-Proxy Records of Late Quaternary Palaeoclimate Dynamics in Turkey and the Surrounding Region"; Xoplaki et al., "The Medieval Climate Anomaly and Byzantium"; and Pfister et al., "Early Modern Europe".

weather, and socio-economic change in late Byzantine territories.[2] This research has mostly confirmed the previous conclusion, while also situating Byzantine history within a wider context of 14th-century climatic and historical change. Although we can identify impacts of extreme seasons and natural disasters, the available evidence does not provide clear indications of a climate-driven crisis. Nor, however, can that evidence rule out major impacts from climatic variability and change.

2   Defining the "Little Ice Age"

From the end of the last ice age around 11,700 years until the start of rapid man-made warming, human history took place within the relatively mild and steady climate of the Holocene interglacial. However, within the Holocene, glaciologists of the mid-20th century identified a "Little Ice Age" (LIA) of glacial readvances. Over time, climatologists borrowed this term to denote a period of cooling before c.1850 CE, which is especially evident in Northern Hemisphere summer temperature reconstructions. Different publications have placed its start anywhere from the 1250s to 1450s CE, and some have emphasized a period of more pronounced cooling from c.1560–1710.

As argued in a previous study, defining the LIA remains a challenge both for climatologists and for historians.[3] The precise onset of cooling depends on the region, season, and climate proxy. Multiple factors drove climatic change on different spatial and temporal scales. Over the long term, these forcings might have included orbital forcing, sunspot cycles, and an accelerating ice-albedo feedback loop. Yet recent research highlights the short-term effects of large volcanic eruptions, particularly during the coldest decades of the past millennium, including the 1250s, 1450s, 1590s–1600s, 1640s, and 1810s, and some of these extreme decades were separated by stretches of more or less average global temperatures.[4] Climatic oscillations such as the North Atlantic Oscillation and the El Niño Southern Oscillation also continued to create year-to-year and decade-to-decade variability and extreme events. Moreover, the human impacts of climatic variability and extreme weather depended on when and where they fell and how populations were exposed or vulnerable.

---

2   See Preiser-Kapeller and Mitsiou, "The Little Ice Age and Byzantium within the Eastern Mediterranean, ca. 1200–1350".
3   White, "The Real Little Ice Age".
4   See especially Sigl et al., "Timing and Climate Forcing of Volcanic Eruptions for the Past 2,500 Years".

Thus, defining the LIA is as much a matter of historical periodization as one of climate reconstruction. In this regard, this chapter asks not only whether Byzantine lands shared in the same climatic trends and extremes as other regions, but whether they endured significant climate change that helps define a distinct period in Byzantine history.

3 The Ottoman Crisis as an Example

Before answering these questions, it is essential to determine what LIA impacts in the eastern Mediterranean would look like and what kind of traces they might have left in physical and written records. Without such examples, it would be difficult if not impossible to assess which scenarios are plausible for late Byzantine history and whether or not we could find indications for them in our surviving sources. Fortunately, there is a growing body of research on the climate, society, and environmental history of the same region during the Ottoman period, for which there are more abundant climatic and archival records.[5] Following this research, we can better assess what kinds of climatic change would have produced what kinds of impacts, and where we might expect to see those events in sources covering the late Byzantine period. To illustrate events of the Ottoman era and their evidence, I will focus on a narrative of climate and crisis in late-16th and 17th-century Anatolia and the Aegean region, based on previous research.[6]

The backdrop to this crisis was a century and a half of imperial growth and conquest. By the late 1500s, Ottoman sultans ruled a territory comparable to the Eastern Roman Empire at is largest extent, the Ottoman capital held around half a million people, and the Ottoman military was easily the largest in Europe. The populations of Ottoman Anatolia and the southern Balkans increased rapidly, roughly doubling between the late 15th and late 16th centuries. Some of the fastest growth took place in semi-arid lands in inner Anatolia and the present Turkey–Syria–Iraq border region, where agriculture was often limited to a single crop of winter wheat or barley, supplemented by raising sheep. Many villages saw a rapid increase of small holdings and landless families. Moreover, the empire's systems for provisioning key commodities such as grain, timber, and sheep fell into difficulties, since population growth and resource pressures ate into the surplus of the countryside while major cities

---

5 E.g., Mikhail, *Under Osman's Tree*; Inal and Köse, *Seeds of Power: Explorations in Ottoman Environmental History*.
6 White, *The Climate of Rebellion in the Early Modern Ottoman Empire*.

and the military swelled in size, raising the demand for provisions. These problems became especially acute when the empire mobilized for military campaigns during frequent wars in the Mediterranean and on the Habsburg and Persian frontiers.[7]

From the 1560s to 1580s, a series of disasters tested the strength of the Ottoman imperial system. Several major droughts created significant shortages or famines in parts of the empire, which the administration could not always or completely allay through traditional relief measures. Food shortages sometimes combined with epidemic disease outbreaks, including bubonic plague, compounding the impact on rural populations and economies.[8] Major military campaigns and accompanying requisitions from the countryside frequently resulted in outbreaks of banditry.

Matters came to a head in the 1590s. The decade brought unusually cold winters across the Mediterranean, and from 1591 to 1596 Anatolia experienced one of its worst droughts of the past millennium. Numerous sources attest to famine across today's Turkey and surrounding regions. At the same time, the combination of cold and drought helped breed a panzootic (probably rinderpest) that decimated sheep and cattle from eastern Anatolia into central Europe.[9] Turning a natural disaster into a human catastrophe, the Ottomans embarked on another war with the Habsburg Empire in 1593, one that stretched on for fourteen years and involved heavy taxes and requisitions from already hungry Ottoman subjects. These demands, particularly for the dwindling number of Ottoman sheep to feed the army, were the apparent trigger for a provincial uprising known as the Celali Rebellion in 1596. With the Ottoman army locked in military stalemate on the northern frontier, the Celalis pillaged the Anatolian countryside for more than a decade, aggravating the prevailing famine and driving many villagers into flight. By the time imperial forces could broker peace with the Habsburgs and restore order in Anatolia and northern Syria, regions of the empire had been emptied of half or more of their population.[10]

---

7 For studies of Ottoman population and population pressure, see e.g., Hütteroth, *Laendliche Siedlungen im südlichen Inneranatolien*; Cook, *Population Pressure in Rural Anatolia, 1450–1600*; Erder, "Population Rise and Fall in Anatolia 1550–1620"; İslamoğlu and Faroqhi, "Crop Patterns and Agricultural Production Trends in Sixteenth-Century Anatolia"; Faroqhi, *Towns and Townsmen of Ottoman Anatolia*; Özel, "Population Changes in Ottoman Anatolia during the 16th and 17th Centuries".

8 For further discussion of Ottoman plague outbreaks, see Varlik, *Plague and Empire in the Early Modern Mediterranean World*.

9 White, "A Model Disaster".

10 On the Celali Rebellion see also Özel, "The Reign of Violence: The Celalis, c.1550–1700".

The turmoil persisted over the following decades. Factions in the capital including Janissary soldiers competed for political power while fending off rebellions in the provinces. The imperial government often failed to mobilize sufficient revenue and materiel for military campaigns, particularly during years of drought, severe winters, and poor harvests; and the resulting shortfalls resulted in military defeats and mutinies. Peasants fleeing hunger or violence sought refuge in towns and cities often lacking adequate infrastructure, contributing to disease outbreaks and a demographic drain. In the wake of rural depopulation, pastoral tribes made major inroads into former agricultural land, which made the abandonment of villages hard to reverse. The fall in the number of tax-paying subjects and rural revenue along with the debasement of coinage created fiscal and economic turmoil during the 17th century. To survive the crisis, the imperial government had first to resort to short-term tax-farming and eventually to alienate imperial land and powers to notables in the provinces.

This narrative of LIA crisis in the Ottoman Empire emerged in the 2010s only once it became possible to compare multiple types of evidence, including climate proxies in natural archives, various official Ottoman records, and narrative accounts from both Ottoman and European contemporaries. Tree-ring and paleolimnological studies largely agreed on the timing and magnitude of drought at the end of the 16th century, which provided independent backing for contemporary descriptions of parched fields and wells running dry.[11] Numerous studies of Ottoman cadastral surveys (*tahrir defterleri*) could be analyzed for a picture of population and land-use trends; petitions to the imperial divan (*mühimme defterleri*) indicated natural disasters and imperial responses; and various tax records indicated rural flight and urban problems from the late 16th to 17th centuries. Further corroboration of extreme weather and impacts emerged from matching descriptions in Ottoman and Armenian chroniclers and European travelogs and diplomatic dispatches. New sources – ranging from ecclesiastical correspondence to foundation records to probate inventories – have also revealed traces of climatic variability, extreme weather, and their impacts.[12] The narrative of climate and crisis thus emerged as the best explanation for a convergence of evidence from various independent sources.

---

11 Since White, *Climate of Rebellion*, additional studies have confirmed the severity of the 1590s drought and climate cooling during the late-16th–17th centuries – e.g., Roberts et al., "Palaeolimnological Evidence for an East–West Climate See-Saw in the Mediterranean since AD 900"; Touchan et al., "Dendroclimatology in the Eastern Mediterranean"; Cook et al., "Old World Megadroughts and Pluvials during the Common Era".

12 E.g., Orbay, "Financial Consequences of Natural Disasters in Seventeenth-Century Anatolia"; Coşgel and Ergene, "Inequality of Wealth in the Ottoman Empire: War, Weather, and

Before this evidence converged, historians had proposed plausible theories of economic and technological change to account for Ottoman crisis and transformation, without reference to environmental factors.[13] Even after Ottomanists discovered the first tree-ring studies demonstrating exceptional droughts in late 16th-century Anatolia, climate remained only one intriguing hypothesis among many for the outbreak of the Celali Rebellion.[14] Historians had other plausible ways to interpret references to extreme weather and natural disaster in Ottoman chronicles, such as metaphors of divine displeasure or political turmoil.[15]

Moreover, the Ottoman LIA did not leave consistent traces in all records, particularly in the types of records available for the Byzantine period. Regarding natural archives, there is little trace of this climatic event in speleothem studies or most low-resolution pollen studies. Because the political, economic, and demographic repercussions of the Ottoman crisis extended far beyond the regions and periods most affected by cold and drought, the evidence of land use and land cover change does not overlap neatly with evidence of climatic change. For example, a study of highly resolved sediments from Lake Çubuk (northwestern Anatolia) finds "an abrupt drop in cereal pollen concentration" from the early 1600s to c.1700, indicating the Celali Rebellion and its aftermath; yet the strongest indicators of *local* climate change come decades later.[16] Regarding written records, the amount of climate and weather information varies enormously depending on the author and type of source. Some chronicles and archival series include detailed accounts of drought, extreme cold, and famine, while others completely ignore these events. For example, only one Ottoman chronicler described the panzootic of the 1590s, which we know of mainly from Hungarian sources and a few incidental mentions in petitions to the divan. Certain chroniclers of the period did not even record the well-attested freezing of the Bosphorus in 1621.

Even with converging lines of evidence for a LIA crisis, questions of causation remain open. In terms of climate, a study comparing reconstructions to model simulations has found that volcanic forcing may explain the exceptional

---

 Long-Term Trends in Eighteenth-Century Kastamonu"; Stavrides, "Dearth in 19th-Century Cyprus: The Correspondence of the Metochia of the Holy Sepulchre".
13   E.g., İnalcık, "Military and Fiscal Transformation in the Ottoman Empire, 1600–1700".
14   This theory was first developed by Griswold, "Climatic Change: A Possible Factor in the Social Unrest of Seventeenth Century Anatolia".
15   As in Piterberg, *An Ottoman Tragedy*.
16   Ocakoğlu et al., "A 2800-Year Multi-Proxy Sedimentary Record of Climate Change from Lake Çubuk (Göynük, Bolu, NW Anatolia)".

cold of the 1590s–1600s but not the exceptional drought.[17] In terms of historical impacts, it seems fair to say that climatic extremes were highly necessary for at least the timing and severity of disasters in the Ottoman Empire – that is, but for the LIA it is hard to imagine such a crisis happening when it did and with such loss of life. Nevertheless, economic and technological factors cited by previous historians may have been sufficient to cause a different imperial crisis eventually. Moreover, the extreme events of the 1590s may not have resulted in crisis had it not been for the empire's ecological vulnerabilities, fragile provisioning systems, or ill-timed decision to go to war.

Therefore, the Ottoman example provides crucial lessons in the search for a Byzantine LIA and, for that matter, any hypothesis in Byzantine climate history. First, research should not start from an excessively high or low prior probability for major climate change and impacts in Byzantine territories. Climatic disasters and even crises are certainly a feature of eastern Mediterranean history. However, even the Ottoman crisis occurred during a particular ecological and political conjuncture. The plausibility of major LIA impacts in the Byzantine Empire thus depends on whether it presented comparable vulnerabilities to climatic change or extreme weather. Second, scholars should be cautious how they use evidence to update assessments of probabilities for climate events and impacts. Compared to the Ottoman period, the physical and written sources for Byzantine history are limited; and, as the Ottoman example shows, both natural archives and human archives were very inconsistent in recording even major events. Therefore, an absence of physical and written traces for climate change or disasters turns out to be a very weak indicator of climatic stability or societal resilience. Nor should researchers expect a neat fit between evidence of climatic events and environmental or societal transformation. Finally, even where there is clear correlation between climatic change and societal change, scholars should be careful about interpretation. The issue is not merely one of causation versus coincidence. The more important and difficult question is usually whether the climatic event was responsible for the *occurrence* of that change, or only for its *timing* or another aspect of the outcome.

4   Was There Significant Climate in Late Byzantine Territories?

With these lessons in mind, we can return to the questions at the start of the chapter, beginning with the evidence for climate change in late Byzantine

---

17   Xoplaki et al., "Modelling Climate and Societal Resilience in the Eastern Mediterranean in the Last Millennium".

territories. Staring in the 2000s, improvements in isotopic dating and mass spectrometry enabled researchers to obtain more precise, high-resolution information from various natural archives in the eastern Mediterranean. These include speleothems, corals, and lake sediments, as well as tree rings (which naturally have an annual resolution). The results should be handled with some caution, as it is not always possible to distinguish between temperature and precipitation signals, between signals and noise, and between natural and human environmental impacts in these proxies. Nevertheless, the quantity and quality of the evidence allow us to make informed hypotheses about climatic trends and events in the Eastern Mediterranean over the 14th and 15th centuries.

In general, physical records across the eastern Mediterranean indicate a shift from warmer, wetter climate in the 12th century to cooler, drier average conditions by c.1400. Many studies interpret this change as indicating a shift from a "Medieval Warm Period" to a LIA, as usually described for western Europe. However, the results vary by region and type of evidence. Some proxies indicate change as soon as the late 12th century, while others find no change until the end of the 14th century or later. In some records, particularly speleothems, there is scant indication of any LIA.[18]

The strongest evidence for a long-term regional climatic shift during the late Byzantine period comes from pollen, diatoms, biomarkers, isotope ratios, and trace elements in lake sediment and marine cores. In Anatolia, for the most part, "lake records show similar overall trends for the last 1100 years, with a shift to drier hydro-climatic conditions at AD 1350–1400, following a generally wetter phase during the MCA (AD 950 to 1300)."[19] However, a study of Tecer Lake (near Sivas) finds more arid conditions beginning as early as the 12th century, and no characteristic Little Ice Age climate until c.1550.[20] A study of pollen from

---

18   According to Luterbacher et al., "A Review of 2000 Years of Paleoclimatic Evidence in the Mediterranean", p. 107: "none of the three stalagmite records from Turkey strongly expresses the MCA [Medeival Climate Anomaly] or LIA [Little Ice Age]".

19   Roberts et al., "Palaeolimnological Evidence for an East–West Climate See-Saw in the Mediterranean since AD 900". Concurring assessment in Luterbacher et al., "Review of 2000 Years", pp. 111–12. For further studies, see England et al., "Historical Landscape Change in Cappadocia (central Turkey)"; Woodbridge and Roberts, "Late Holocene Climate of the Eastern Mediterranean Inferred from Diatom Analysis of Annually-Laminated Lake Sediments"; Jones et al., "A High-Resolution Late Holocene Lake Isotope Record from Turkey and Links to North Atlantic and Monsoon Climate"; Ocakoğlu et al., "A 2800-Year Multi-Proxy Sedimentary Record of Climate Change from Lake Çubuk (Göynük, Bolu, NW Anatolia)".

20   Kuzucuoğlu et al., "Mid- to Late-Holocene Climate Change in Central Turkey: The Tecer Lake Record".

Gravgaz Marsh in the western Taurus Mountains, Turkey, argues for a wetter Medieval Warm Period around AD 940–1280 followed by a dry Little Ice Age, when evidence of cereal cultivation disappears.[21] Nevertheless, these sources often provide stronger indications of cooling during the Ottoman period. For example, a 2016 study of a north Aegean core employing alkenone paleothermometry has concluded: "While the 14th and 15th centuries show steady [sea surface temperatures], the 16th century is characterized by significant fluctuations. A strong cooling of almost 1.5 degrees C is observed from the end of the 16th century to the beginning of the 18th century."[22]

Tree-ring studies have less skill at capturing long-term trends but shed more light on year-to-year and decade-to-decade variability and extremes. Most tree-ring growth in the region depends on spring and summer rainfall (also vital for the region's grain crops), and therefore most studies examine ring width as a proxy for rainfall between April and August. A tree-ring based precipitation reconstruction for the Aegean region – closely matching late Byzantine territory – finds evidence of extreme growing-season droughts in 1304 and 1333. Moreover, the tree-ring-based Old World Drought Atlas reveals that, even as northwestern Europe experienced extremely wet summers during the "Great Famine" of the 1310s, conditions around the Aegean were exceptionally dry.[23] In general, the tree-ring record indicates more extremes during the Ottoman period.[24] Other tree-ring studies have sought to capture temperature variability and trends. One such study has analyzed carbon isotopes in southwest Anatolian tree rings; it found a brief cooling during the mid- to late 1300s but no significant Little Ice Age cold until the late 16th century and 17th centuries.[25] Other studies have analyzed ring width in temperature-sensitive trees from mountains in surrounding regions. For example, a study from Calimani, Romania, finds a cool Little Ice Age from around 1370 to 1630.[26]

Luterbacher et al. (this volume) have used Bayesian hierarchical modeling to integrate disparate sources such as these to produce a best estimate of eastern Mediterranean temperatures over the past two millennia. According

---

21 Bakker et al., "Numerically Derived Evidence for Late-Holocene Climate Change and Its Impact on Human Presence in the Southwest Taurus Mountains, Turkey".
22 Gogou et al., "Climate Variability and Socio-Environmental Changes in the Northern Aegean (NE Mediterranean) during the Last 1500 Years".
23 Cook et al., "Old World Megadroughts and Pluvials during the Common Era".
24 Griggs et al., "A Regional High-Frequency Reconstruction of May–June Precipitation in the North Aegean from Oak Tree Rings, A.D. 1089–1989".
25 Heinrich et al., "Winter-to-Spring Temperature Dynamics in Turkey Derived from Tree Rings since AD 1125".
26 Popa and Kern, "Long-Term Summer Temperature Reconstruction Inferred from Tree-Ring Records from the Eastern Carpathians".

to this reconstruction, temperatures were unusually high at the start of the 1200s, then fell to roughly the long-term average during the first half of the century, with some particularly cold years following the Samalas eruption of 1257. However, there was no persistent cooling during the late 13th and 14th centuries. The coldest years and decades of the reconstruction follow major eruptions in the mid-15th, late 16th, and late 17th centuries.

Written records – the "archives of societies" – can complement this picture from the "archives of nature" by providing detailed information on specific weather events, natural hazards, and their human dimensions.[27] The written record for the Byzantine period is too sparse and discontinuous to provide a complete record of eastern Mediterranean climate. Nevertheless, historians such as Dionysios Stathakopoulos and Ioannis Telelis have compiled and analyzed incidents of extreme weather from hundreds of Byzantine sources, offering glimpses of extreme weather and impacts.[28] For example, observers recorded exceptional cold, snow, and hunger at the time of the Samalas eruption. The historical sources for the 14th century, while fewer than for other periods and covering a smaller geographical region, record an unusually high frequency of extreme cold events and severe winters in Byzantine territory, particularly during the 1340s and 1350s. Telelis maintains that these events would fit within a broader Little Ice Age pattern but has cautioned against drawing any firm conclusions from the limited historical evidence.[29] An analysis of Greek monastic records also notes severe winters in 1342, in 1402, and between 1425 and 1428. However, the same study finds these events were probably more frequent during the Ottoman period.[30]

Taken together, the balance of evidence suggests that there was likely a shift in climate during the last two centuries of the Byzantine Empire, with some

---

27   Brönnimann et al., "Archives of Nature and Archives of Societies".
28   Stathakopoulos, "Reconstructing the Climate of the Byzantine World: State of the Problem and Case Studies"; Stathakopoulos, *Famine and Pestilence in the Late Roman and Early Byzantine Empire*; Telelis, "The Byzantine Sources as Documentary Evidence for the Reconstruction of Historical Climate"; Telelis, "Medieval Warm Period and the Beginning of the Little Ice Age in the Eastern Mediterranean"; Telelis, "Historical-Climatological Information from the Time of the Byzantine Empire (4th–15th Centuries AD)"; Ioannis Telelis, "Weather and Climate as Factors Affecting Land Transport and Communications in Byzantium"; Telelis, "Climatic Fluctuations in the Eastern Mediterranean and the Middle East AD 300–1500 from Byzantine Documentary and Proxy Physical Paleoclimatic Evidence". See also the summary compiled in Haldon, "Climate and Environment of Byzantine Anatolia".
29   Telelis, "Climatic Fluctuations", p. 188.
30   Repapis et al., "A Note on the Frequency of Occurrence of Severe Winters as Evidenced in Monastery and Historical Records".

regional and temporal variation. We could reasonably label that change the start of a "Little Ice Age" in the Eastern Mediterranean – at least in contrast to the warmer conditions during the late 12th and early 13th centuries. There is nothing yet to suggest that this climatic change or accompanying weather extremes were as significant as those experienced by the Ottomans in the late 1500s and 1600s. A smaller climatic shift could still have been historically significant if the Byzantines were especially vulnerable to change or if there were particularly large or ill-timed weather events not captured in the physical or written records. Our analysis of Ottoman events and sources indicates that absence of evidence is not strong evidence of absence for local climate variability, extreme weather, or related disasters. Therefore, whether and how climate mattered for the late Byzantine Empire remains an open question, and one that depends on an assessment of Byzantine vulnerabilities and resilience. The following section can review only the essential evidence from current studies.

5 Did Climate Variability or Change Make a Difference in Late Byzantine History?

Coming to the question of climate impacts, late Byzantine Empire history presents some significant challenges. The documentary record is slight, although certain useful sources have survived that can provide unique information on population and economic history. Its territory was compact, having shrunk to a few lands around the Aegean, yet the empire was politically and geographically fragmented and challenged by neighboring powers. Historians face the difficult task of untangling the effects of climate from the effects of the empire's many other problems in an age when the Byzantines "seemed to live from crisis to crisis", as one historian has put it.[31] This period includes two civil wars, invasion by the Ottoman Turks, commercial rivalry from Italian states, and of course the Black Death. This section will examine both the direct evidence and the circumstantial case for climate impacts, while keeping in mind the bigger picture of events in Byzantine and European history.

Written sources offer scattered indications of impacts from extreme seasons and natural hazards, particularly during the early 14th century. Historical sources record famines in Constantinople during 1303–09, which would match well with the tree-ring evidence of a major drought in the Aegean region in 1304, as noted above. However, historical sources mostly blame the famine on the influx of refugees from Turkish raids in Anatolia and war with the Catalan

---

31   Nicol, *The Last Centuries of Byzantium*, p. 122.

company.³² Other sources describe weather impacts on transportation, such as roads blocked by heavy snow and ice, particularly during the harsh winters of 1299 and 1325–28. Heavy floods are attested for Thrace and Macedonia during 1341–43 and 1349–50. Yet it remains unclear whether these were exceptional conditions and whether they had a major impact on the Byzantine economy. Raúl Estangüi Gómez concludes: "In general, it is likely this unfavorable climate conjuncture added to the difficult conditions of the peasantry." However, his study gives a larger role to incursions by the Ottoman Turks, civil war, and insecurity in the countryside.³³

The case for more consequential climate impacts in the late Byzantine Empire turns on evidence for deepening economic difficulties and population pressure. A previous historiography associated the 13th and early 14th centuries with the strengthening grip of the wealthy and powerful on land and resources, rising economic inequalities, and a growing tax burden on the *paroikoi* (peasants).³⁴ A progressive debasement of the coinage from the mid-13th to early 14th centuries was interpreted as an indicator of economic and fiscal troubles as well.³⁵ Uniquely for this period, documents from Strymon (Greek Macedonia) have provided a detailed picture of landholdings and demography. On this basis, Angeliki Laiou-Thomodakis has argued for strong demographic growth in the medieval period leading to a "Malthusian bind by the late thirteenth-early fourteenth century, as the land constraint appears to have been reached, diminishing returns set in and, as a result, the economic condition of the population worsened."³⁶ In the first decades of the 1300s, birthrates fell, emigration rose, and regional population leveled off or declined amid signs of an economic crisis.

These conditions would have left the peasantry vulnerable to climatic fluctuations and extremes, such as the severe winters, floods, and heavy snows reported for Macedonia and Thrace during the 1320s and 1340s, particularly if these hazards affected the harvest or the health of livestock. Based on anecdotal evidence, the population and economy of Byzantine Anatolia had also begun to decline by the 14th century – although here it is difficult to distinguish

---

32 Table of famine and weather events in Haldon, "Climate and Environment", p. 160.
33 Estangüi Gómez, *Byzance face aux ottomans*, pp. 13–54.
34 E.g., Nicol, *Last Centuries*, pp. 109–10.
35 Cécile Morrisson, "Monnaie et finances dans l'Empire byzantin x^e–xive siècle".
36 See Laiou-Thomodakis, *Peasant Society in the Late Byzantine Empire*; Lefort, "Population et peuplement en Macedoine orientale"; and Laiou and Morrisson, *The Byzantine Economy*, pp. 90–91 (quoted).

environmental factors from political factors, including civil war and Ottoman incursions.[37]

In this historiography, the Black Death of the 1340s marked another turning point for the empire. "The countryside was depopulated and the agrarian economy became disarticulated, as did the entire economy. Land became worthless, and was not even taxed in the fifteenth century."[38] The sudden abandonment of agriculture – and possibly climatic events – apparently intensified soil erosion in Greece and Macedonia.[39] The wealthy and powerful were able to seize valuable land and resources freed up by the depopulation of the countryside, leaving the peasantry little better off than before.[40] Historical sources record another famine in western Anatolia, following a severe winter at the turn of the 15th century, indicating continued vulnerability to extreme weather.[41] While the imperial economy became disarticulated, agricultural production likely became more export-oriented and integrated into Italian trade networks.[42] On the other hand, it appears that the scarcity of labor drove up wages faster than prices, providing some Byzantine subjects with more purchasing power.[43]

Recent studies have also found signs of resilience in the Byzantine countryside throughout the last century of Byzantine rule. For instance, Estangüi Gómez identifies imperial measures to reverse the breakdown in communications and insecurity in the provinces, at least once the empire recovered from the crisis of the second civil war (1341–53).[44] In an archeological survey of island communities, Fontini Kandyli emphasizes villagers' "defensive strategies and community-building through shared experiences" that helped them deal with crisis.[45] In any case, there is little evidence for change in basic patterns of land use, such as adoption of new crop strains or a shift in sowing or harvest dates. Olive and fig trees, for instance, were planted in more or less the same regions as in the 20th century, suggesting no major long-term changes in the seasons.[46] In general, studies of cereal and arboreal pol-

37 Laiou, "The Agrarian Economy, Thirteenth–Fifteenth Centuries", p. 321.
38 Laiou and Morrisson, *Byzantine Economy*, p. 181.
39 Geyer, "Evolution of Land Use in the Byzantine World".
40 Laiou-Thomadikis, *Peasant Society*, pp. 208–9.
41 See the table of climate events in Haldon, "Climate and Environment".
42 Laiou, "Agrarian Economy", pp. 364–9.
43 Cheynet et al., "Prix et salaires à Byzance (x^e–xve siècle)".
44 Estangüi Gómez, *Byzance face aux Ottomans*.
45 Kondyli, *Rural Communities in Late Byzantium*.
46 Telelis, "Weather and Climate as Factors Affecting Land Transport and Communications in Byzantium"; Laiou-Thomodakis, *Peasant Society in the Late Byzantine Empire*, pp. 26–8.

len in the region do not indicate major changes during the late 13th or early 14th centuries – although our Ottoman example suggests that these may not be necessary evidence of a LIA crisis.[47] Contemporary sources from Turkish Anatolia give little or no indication of climate-driven famine either.[48]

Recent discussions in world environmental history have also emphasized a large-scale ecological conjuncture in the early 14th century, which Bruce Campbell has termed a "Great Transition" in climate, disease, and society.[49] Although initial research in the Great Transition emphasized events in northwestern Europe – including the extreme weather and Great Famine of the 1310s and the exceptional mortality and enduring socio-economic impacts of the Black Death – subsequent work has sought similar conjunctures throughout Europe and Asia. Strong evidence for a Great Transition in neighboring regions would render a similar outcome more plausible for the eastern Mediterranean as well. For instance, decades of population pressure, war, and poverty in the early 14th century might have weakened the immunities of Byzantine subjects, leaving them more susceptible to plague, as has been hypothesized for Englishmen who lived through the Great Famine.[50] Nevertheless, different regional studies have not yet found a consistent pattern of LIA impacts and increased vulnerability to epidemics across Europe and Asia – at least not consistent enough to justify presumptions about a Great Transition in the late Byzantine Empire absent further evidence.[51]

In short, there are grounds to continue investigations of climate, extreme weather, and societal impacts in the late Byzantine Empire. At the least, these territories experienced isolated meteorological disasters. The current evidence is not yet strong enough to exclude a larger role for climate change in the imperial crises, perhaps as a necessary condition of their timing or the severity of their impacts. However, unlike the Ottoman Empire of the late 16th and 17th centuries, there is presently no convergence of evidence for major climate-driven transformations in late Byzantine state or society.

---

47 Izdebski et al., "Exploring Byzantine and Ottoman Economic History with the Use of Palynological Data"; Xoplaki et al., "The Medieval Climate Anomaly and Byzantium".
48 On Turkish historical sources on food in 14th-century Anatolia, see Trépanier, *Foodways and Daily Life in Medieval Anatolia*.
49 Campbell, *The Great Transition*.
50 DeWitte and Slavin, "Between Famine and Death: England on the Eve of the Black Death".
51 Bauch and Schenk, *The Crisis of the 14th Century: Teleconnections between Environmental and Societal Change?*

6   Conclusion

Late Byzantine territories probably underwent cooling from the relatively high average temperatures of the late 12th and early 13th centuries. Certain periods, including the early 1300s, also brought recurring droughts and floods. However, it seems that both the strongest cooling and the most significant historical effects of the LIA came after the fall of Constantinople to the Ottomans. There are clearly grounds for further research into climatic changes, extreme weather, and their impacts in the late Byzantine Empire. Rising interest in climate change and continuous improvements in high-resolution paleoclimate reconstruction promise to produce new studies and new insights of interest to the region and period. At the least, we can anticipate a further shift in the way Byzantinists view climate, from a static backdrop in human affairs to a dynamic force in the empire's history.

The search for the LIA in the Byzantine Empire also offers broader lessons in the theory and methods of interdisciplinary history. Researchers must keep in mind that learning about the past is a task of *abductive* (i.e., explanatory) inference. It is a probabilistic reasoning from effects to causes – or more specifically, a reasoning from the traces left by past events and processes to a knowledge of the past itself. When we say a chronicle or inscription "tells us" that there was harvest failure and famine in Thrace seven centuries ago, we are saying that such harvest failure and famine is the best explanation for what we read in the chronicle or inscription. Similarly, when we say certain tree rings "tell us" that there was drought that year, we are saying that such a drought is the best explanation for the width of those rings. In theory, such inferences unite the methodologies of history and the historical sciences such as paleoclimatology, while demonstrating the power of an interdisciplinary approach. Many scenarios, after all, might explain *either* a written description of a long-ago drought and famine *or* a year of narrow tree rings: yet few scenarios can reasonably account for *both* traces at once. It is that convergence of evidence that gives us more certain knowledge of the past.[52]

Nevertheless, this work of abductive inference demands more than just gathering historical records: it demands knowledge of the causal processes – both physical and cultural – that produce traces within those records. As interdisciplinary investigations multiply their number and types of sources, they place ever greater demands on this causal understanding. Significant climate events were, in most cases, only imperfectly necessary or weakly sufficient to

---

52   See Douven, "Abduction" and Tucker, *Our Knowledge of the Past: A Philosophy of Historiography*.

produce traces in physical and written records. Similarly, most climate disasters were only imperfectly necessary or weakly sufficient to cause aspects of societal crises or transformation. Thus, researchers in interdisciplinary topics such as climate history – especially of the ancient or medieval world – cannot simply question "the evidence" and expect to find "proof" of climate change, crisis, adaptation, or resilience. Research must begin with carefully framed causal questions and scenarios, informed assessments of prior probabilities, and understanding of the likelihoods of finding traces (or not) in different archives of nature and societies.

Given the limits of the source material, it would be tempting to start from a prior assumption of either climate-driven crisis or resilience and then line up the evidence for and against. However, viewed from the perspective of the Ottoman LIA, it appears more logical to assign an intermediate prior probability to major climate change impacts in the late Byzantine Empire and to admit that the present evidence does not shift that balance of probabilities by much in either direction (though somewhat downwards for more catastrophic scenarios). Moving ahead, it is important that Byzantinists consider not only how each addition and refinement to the evidence weighs in that balance but also how wider historical perspectives and comparisons add to or subtract from the plausibility of different scenarios for crisis, impacts, and resilience.

Bibliography

Bakker, J. et al., "Numerically Derived Evidence for Late-Holocene Climate Change and Its Impact on Human Presence in the Southwest Taurus Mountains, Turkey," *The Holocene* 22 (2012), 425–38.

Bauch, M./Schenk, G.J., *The Crisis of the 14th Century, Teleconnections between Environmental and Societal Change?* Berlin 2019.

Brönnimann, S./Pfister, C./White, S., "Archives of Nature and Archives of Societies", in *The Palgrave Handbook of Climate History*, White, S./Pfister, C./Mauelshagen, F. (eds.) London 2018, pp. 27–36.

Campbell, B., *The Great Transition: Climate, Disease and Society in the Late-Medieval World* New York 2016.

Cheynet, J.-C. et al., "Prix et salaires à Byzance (x^e–xve siècle)", in *Hommes et richesses dans l'Empire byzantin*, Kravari, V./Lefort, J./ Morrisson, C. (eds.) Paris 1991, vol. 2, pp. 339–74.

Cook, E. et al., "Old World Megadroughts and Pluvials during the Common Era", *Science Advances* 1 (2015): e1500561.

Cook, M., *Population Pressure in Rural Anatolia, 1450–1600*, Oxford 1972.

Coşgel, M./Ergene, B., "Inequality of Wealth in the Ottoman Empire: War, Weather, and Long-Term Trends in Eighteenth-Century Kastamonu", *Journal of Economic History* 72 (2012), 308–31.

DeWitte, S./Slavin, P., "Between Famine and Death: England on the Eve of the Black Death – Evidence from Paleoepidemiology and Manorial Accounts", *Journal of Interdisciplinary History* 44 (2013), 37–60.

Douven, I., "Abduction", in Zalta, E. (ed.), *The Stanford Encyclopedia of Philosophy*, Stanford 2017, https://plato.stanford.edu/archives/sum2017/entries/abduction/.

England, A. et al., "Historical Landscape Change in Cappadocia (central Turkey): A Palaeoecological Investigation of Annually Laminated Sediments from Nar Lake", *Holocene* 18 (2008), 1229–45.

Erder, L. "Population Rise and Fall in Anatolia 1550–1620", *Middle East Studies* 15 (1979): 322–45.

Estangüi Gómez, R., *Byzance face aux Ottomans: Exercice du pouvoir et contrôle du territoire sous les derniers Paléologues (milieu XIVe–Milieu XVe siècle)*, Paris 2014.

Faroqhi, S., *Towns and Townsmen of Ottoman Anatolia*, New York 1984.

Finné, M. et al., "Climate in the Eastern Mediterranean, and Adjacent Regions, during the Past 6000 Years – A Review", *Journal of Archaeological Science* 38 (2011), 3153–73.

Geyer, B., "Evolution of Land Use in the Byzantine World", in Laiou, A. (ed.) *The Economic History of Byzantium*, Washington D.C. 2002, vol. 1, pp. 31–46.

Gogou, A. et al., "Climate Variability and Socio-Environmental Changes in the Northern Aegean (NE Mediterranean) during the Last 1500 Years", *Quaternary Science Reviews* 136 (2016), 209–28.

Griggs, C. et al., "A Regional High-Frequency Reconstruction of May–June Precipitation in the North Aegean from Oak Tree Rings, A.D. 1089–1989", *International Journal of Climatology* 27 (2007), 1075–89.

Griswold, W., "Climatic Change: A Possible Factor in the Social Unrest of Seventeenth Century Anatolia," in Lowry, H./Quataert, D. (eds.) *Humanist and Scholar: Essays in Honor of Andreas Tietze*, Istanbul 1993, pp. 37–57.

Haldon, J. et al., "The Climate and Environment of Byzantine Anatolia: Integrating Science, History, and Archaeology", *Journal of Interdisciplinary History* 45 (2014), 113–61.

Heinrich, I. et al., "Winter-to-Spring Temperature Dynamics in Turkey Derived from Tree Rings since AD 1125", *Climate Dynamics* 41 (2013), 1685–1701.

Hütteroth, W.-D., *Laendliche Siedlungen im südlichen Inneranatolien in den letzen vierhundert Jahren*, Göttingen, 1968.

İnal, O./Köse, Y., *Seeds of Power: Explorations in Ottoman Environmental History*, London 2019.

İnalcık, H., "Military and Fiscal Transformation in the Ottoman Empire, 1600–1700", *Archivum Ottomanicum* 6 (1980), 283–337.

İslamoğlu, H., and Faroqhi, S., "Crop Patterns and Agricultural Production Trends in Sixteenth-Century Anatolia", *Review* 2 (1979), 400–436.

Izdebski, A./Koloch, G./Słozyński, T., "Exploring Byzantine and Ottoman Economic History with the Use of Palynological Data: A Quantitative Approach", *Jahrbuch der österreichischen Byzantinistik* 65 (2015), 67–110.

Jones, M. et al., "A High-Resolution Late Holocene Lake Isotope Record from Turkey and Links to North Atlantic and Monsoon Climate", *Geology* 34 (2006), 361–64.

Kondyli, F., *Rural Communities in Late Byzantium: Resilience and Vulnerability in the Northern Aegean*, Cambridge 2022.

Kuzucuoğlu, C. et al., "Mid- to Late-Holocene Climate Change in Central Turkey: The Tecer Lake Record", *Holocene* 21 (2011), 173–88.

Laiou, A., "The Agrarian Economy, Thirteenth-Fifteenth Centuries," in Laiou, A. (ed.) *The Economic History of Byzantium*, ed. Angeliki Laiou, Washington D.C. 2002, vol. 1, pp. 311–75.

Laiou-Thomodakis, A., *Peasant Society in the Late Byzantine Empire*, Princeton 1977.

Laiou, A./Morrisson, C., *The Byzantine Economy*, Cambridge 2007.

Lefort, J., "Population et peuplement en Macedoine orientale," Kravari, V./Lefort, J./ Morrisson, C. (eds.) *Hommes et richesses dans l'Empire byzantin*, Paris 1991, vol. 2, 63–82.

Luterbacher, J. et al., "A Review of 2000 Years of Paleoclimatic Evidence in the Mediterranean," in Lionello, P. (ed.) *The Climate of the Mediterranean Region*, London 2012, 87–185.

Mikhail, A., *Under Osman's Tree: The Ottoman Empire, Egypt, and Environmental History*, Chicago 2017.

Morrisson, C., "Monnaie et finances dans l'Empire byzantin X^e–XIVe siècle," in Kravari, V./Lefort, J./ Morrisson, C. (eds.) *Hommes et richesses dans l'Empire byzantin*, Paris 1991, vol. 2, 291–315.

Nicol, D., *The Last Centuries of Byzantium, 1261–1453*, 2nd ed., New York 1993.

Nicoll, K./Küçükuysal, C., "Emerging Multi-Proxy Records of Late Quaternary Palaeoclimate Dynamics in Turkey and the Surrounding Region", *Turkish Journal of Earth Sciences* 21 (2012), 1–19.

Ocakoğlu, F. et al., "A 2800-Year Multi-Proxy Sedimentary Record of Climate Change from Lake Çubuk (Göynük, Bolu, NW Anatolia)", *The Holocene* 26 (2016), 205–21.

Orbay, K., "Financial Consequences of Natural Disasters in Seventeenth-Century Anatolia: A Case Study of the Waqf of Bayezid II", *International Journal of Turkish Studies* 15 (2009), 63–82.

Özel, O., "Population Changes in Ottoman Anatolia during the 16th and 17th Centuries: The 'Demographic Crisis' Reconsidered", *International Journal of Middle East Studies* 36 (2004), 183–205.

Özel, O., "The Reign of Violence: The Celalis, c.1550–1700," in Woodhead, C. (ed.) *The Ottoman World*, New York 2011, pp. 184–202.

Popa, I./Kern, Z., "Long-Term Summer Temperature Reconstruction Inferred from Tree-Ring Records from the Eastern Carpathians", *Climate Dynamics* 32 (2009), 1107–17.

Pfister, C., et al., "Early Modern Europe", in White, S./Pfister, C./Mauelshagen, F. (eds.) *The Palgrave Handbook of Climate History*, London 2018, pp. 265–95.

Piterberg, G., *An Ottoman Tragedy: History and Historiography at Play*, Berkeley 2003.

Preiser-Kapeller, J./Mitsiou, E., "The Little Ice Age and Byzantium within the Eastern Mediterranean, ca. 1200–1350: An Essay on Old Debates and New Scenarios", in Bauch, M./Schenk, G. (eds.) *The Crisis of the 14th Century: Teleconnections between Environmental and Societal Change?*, Berlin 2019, pp. 190–220.

Repapis, C. et al., "A Note on the Frequency of Occurrence of Severe Winters as Evidenced in Monastery and Historical Records from Greece during the Period 1200–1900 A.D.", *Theoretical and Applied Climatology* 39 (1989), 213–17.

Roberts, N. et al., "Palaeolimnological Evidence for an East–West Climate See-Saw in the Mediterranean since AD 900", *Global and Planetary Change* 84–85 (2012), 23–34.

Sigl, M. et al., "Timing and Climate Forcing of Volcanic Eruptions for the Past 2,500 Years", *Nature* 523 (2015), 543–49.

Stathakopoulos, D., "Reconstructing the Climate of the Byzantine World: State of the Problem and Case Studies," in Laszlovszky, J./Szabo, P. (ed.) *People and Nature in Historical Perspective*, Budapest 2003, pp. 247–61.

Stathakopoulos, D., *Famine and Pestilence in the Late Roman and Early Byzantine Empire*, Burlington 2004.

Stavrides, T., "Dearth in 19th-Century Cyprus: The Correspondence of the Metochia of the Holy Sepulchre," in *Studies on the History of Cyprus under Ottoman Rule*, Istanbul 2012, pp. 73–98.

Telelis, I., "The Byzantine Sources as Documentary Evidence for the Reconstruction of Historical Climate," in Frenzel, B. (ed.) *European Climate Reconstructed from Documentary Data: Methods and Results*, Stuttgart 1992.

Telelis, I., "Medieval Warm Period and the Beginning of the Little Ice Age in the Eastern Mediterranean: An Approach of Physical and Anthropogenic Evidence," in Belke, K. et al. (eds.) *Byzanz als Raum: zu Methoden und Inhalten der historische Geographie des östlichen Mittelmeerraumes*, Vienna 2000, pp. 223–243.

Telelis, I., "Historical-Climatological Information from the Time of the Byzantine Empire (4th–15th Centuries AD)", *History of Meteorology* 2 (2005), 41–50.

Telelis, I., "Weather and Climate as Factors Affecting Land Transport and Communications in Byzantium", *Byzantion* 77 (2007), 432–62.

Telelis, I., "Climatic Fluctuations in the Eastern Mediterranean and the Middle East AD 300–1500 from Byzantine Documentary and Proxy Physical Paleoclimatic Evidence – A Comparison", *Jahrbuch der österreichischen Byzantinistik* 58 (2008), 167–208.

Touchan, R./Meko, D./Anchukaitis, K., "Dendroclimatology in the Eastern Mediterranean," *Radiocarbon* 56 (2014), S61–68.

Trépanier, N., *Foodways and Daily Life in Medieval Anatolia: A New Social History*, Austin 2014.

Tucker, A., *Our Knowledge of the Past: A Philosophy of Historiography*, Cambridge, 2004.

Varlık, N., *Plague and Empire in the Early Modern Mediterranean World: The Ottoman Experience, 1347–1600*, Cambridge 2015.

White, S., *The Climate of Rebellion in the Early Modern Ottoman Empire*, Cambridge 2011.

White, S., "The Real Little Ice Age", *Journal of Interdisciplinary History* 44 (2014), 327–52.

White, S., "A Model Disaster: From the Great Ottoman Panzootic to the Cattle Plagues of Early Modern Europe," in Varlık, N (ed.) *Plague and Contagion in the Islamic Mediterranean*, Newark 2017, pp. 91–116.

Woodbridge, J./Roberts, N., "Late Holocene Climate of the Eastern Mediterranean Inferred from Diatom Analysis of Annually-Laminated Lake Sediments," *Quaternary Science Reviews* 30 (2011), 3381–92.

Xoplaki, E. et al., "The Medieval Climate Anomaly and Byzantium: A Review of the Evidence on Climatic Fluctuations, Economic Performance and Societal Change", *Quaternary Science Reviews* 136 (2016), 229–52.

Xoplaki, E. et al., "Modelling Climate and Societal Resilience in the Eastern Mediterranean in the Last Millennium", *Human Ecology* 46 (2018), 363–79.

Bibliography

Aldrich, Daniel P. 2012. *Building Resilience: Social Capital in Post-Disaster Recovery*. Chicago: University of Chicago Press.

Altuğ, K., *Arkeolojik Gezi Rehberi: Yeraltındaki İstanbul*, İstanbul Büyükşehir Belediyesi, İstanbul 2022.

Ambraseys, Nicholas. 2009. *Earthquakes in the Mediterranean and Middle East: A Multidisciplinary Study of Seismicity up to 1900*. Cambridge: Cambridge University Press.

Anagnostakis, I./Kolias, T./Papadopoulou, E. (eds), *Animals and Environment in Byzantium (7th–12th c.)*, Athens 2011.

Arentzen, Th./Burrus, V./Peers, G., *Byzantine Tree Life: Christianity and the Arboreal Imagination*, Cham 2021.

Asa Eger, A., *The Islamic-Byzantine Frontier. Interaction and Exchange among Muslim and Christian Communities*, London 2015.

Aufderheide, A./Rodríguez-Martín, C., *The Cambridge Encyclopedia of Human Paleopathology*, Cambridge 1998.

Baron, H./Daim, F. (eds), *A Most Pleasant Scene and an Inexhaustible Resource. Steps Towards a Byzantine Environmental History*, Mainz 2017.

Bauch, M./Schenk, G.J., *The Crisis of the 14th Century, Teleconnections between Environmental and Societal Change?* Berlin 2019.

Bodin, H./Hedlund R. (eds.), *Byzantine Gardens and Beyond*, Uppsala 2013.

Bourbou, C., *Health and Disease in Byzantine Crete (7th–12th Centuries AD)*, Surrey 2010.

Buikstra, J.E./Beck, L.A. (eds.), *Bioarchaeology: The Contextual Analysis of Human Remains*, Amsterdam 2006.

Büntgen, U., et al., "Cooling and societal change during the Late Antique Little Ice Age from 536 to around 660 AD", *Nature Geoscience* 9 (2016), 231–36, https://doi.org/10.1038/ngeo2652.

Campbell, B.M.S., *The Great Transition. Climate, Disease and Society in the Late-Medieval World*, Cambridge 2016.

Çeçen, K., *The longest Roman water supply line*, Istanbul 1996.

Crapper, M., "The Valens Aqueduct of Constantinople: Hydrology and Hydraulics", *Water History*, 12 (4) (2020), 427–448. DOI 10.1007/s12685-020-00254-4.

Crow, J. "'The City Thirsts', Water in Istanbul, Past, Present and Future", *Current World Archaeology* 117 (2023), 17–23.

Crow, J., "Waters for a Capital: Hydraulic infrastructure and use in Byzantine Constantinople", *Cambridge Companion to Constantinople*, (ed.) S. Bassett, Cambridge 2022, 67–86.

Crow, J., (Forthcoming), "Bridges on the Longest Roman Water Supply Line", in, *Crossing rivers in Byzantium and Beyond*, (eds.) G. Fingarova, A. Kulzer, *Byzantios: Studies in Byzantine History and Civilization*, Brepols.

Crow, J., "The Imagined Water Supply of Constantinople, New Approaches", in C. Zuckerman, J.-P. Sodini, C. Morrison (eds.) *Constantinople réelle et imaginaire. À la mémoire de Gilbert Dagron*, Travaux et Mémoires 22/1 (2018), 211–236.

Curtis, D.R., *Coping with Crisis. The Resilience and Vulnerability of Pre-Industrial Settlements*, Farnham 2014.

Della Dora, V., *Landscape, Nature, and the Sacred in Byzantium*, Cambridge 2016.

Ellenblum, E., *The Collapse of the Eastern Mediterranean. Climate Change and the Decline of the East, 950–1072*, Cambridge 2012.

Estangüi Gómez, R., *Byzance face aux Ottomans: Exercice du pouvoir et contrôle du territoire sous les derniers Paléologues (milieu XIVe–Milieu XVe siècle)*, Paris 2014.

Forchheimer, P. and Strzygowski, J., *Die Byzantinischen Wasserbehälter von Konstantinopel* Byzantinische Denkmäler 2, Vienna 1893.

Giorgi, E., *Archeologia dell'acqua a Gortina di Creta in età protobizantina*, Oxford 2016.

Grauer, A.L. (ed.), *A Companion to Paleopathology*, Chichester 2012.

Guidoboni, Emanuela. 1994. *Catalogue of Ancient Earthquakes in the Mediterranean Area Up to the 10th Century*. Rome: Istituto Nazionale di Geofisica.

Guidoboni, Emanuela, and Alberto Comastri. 2005. *Catalogue of Earthquakes and Tsunamis in the Mediterranean Area from the 11th to the 15th Century*. Rome: Istituto Nazionale di Geofisica e Vulcanologia.

Guidoboni, Emanuela, and John E. Ebel. 2009. *Earthquakes and Tsunamis in the Past: A Guide to Techniques in Historical Seismology*. Cambridge: Cambridge University Press.

Haldon, J.F., et al., "The Climate and Environment of Byzantine Anatolia: Integrating Science, History, and Archaeology", *Journal of Interdisciplinary History* 45,2 (2014), 113–61.

Halstead, P., *Two Oxen Ahead. Pre-Mechanized Farming in the Mediterranean*, Chichester 2014.

Hermann, A., "Der Nil und die Christen", *Jahrbuch für Antike und Christentum* 2 (1959), 30–69.

Hoffmann, R.C., *An Environmental History of Medieval Europe* (Cambridge Medieval Textbooks), Cambridge 2014.

Hofrichter, R. (ed.), *Das Mittelmeer: Geschichte und Zukunft eines ökologisch sensiblen Raums*, Berlin 2020.

Horden, P./Purcell, N., *The Corrupting Sea: A Study of Mediterranean History*, Malden – Oxford 2000.

Izdebski, A., *A Rural Economy in Transition. Asia Minor from Late Antiquity into the Early Middle Ages* (Journal of Juristic Papyrology, Supplement vol. 18), Warsaw 2013.

Izdebski, A., *Ein vormoderner Staat als sozio-ökologisches System. Das oströmische Reich 300–1300 n.Chr.*, Dresden 2022.

Izdebski, A./Koloch, G./Słoczyński, T., "Exploring Byzantine and Ottoman economic history with the use of palynological data: a quantitative approach", *Jahrbuch der Österreichischen Byzantinistik* 65 (2015), 67–110.

Kaplan, M., *Les hommes et la terre à Byzance du VIe au XIe siècle: Propriété et exploitation du sol* (Byzantina Sorbonensia 10), Paris 1995.

Koder, J., *Der Lebensraum der Byzantiner. Historisch-geographischer Abriss ihres mittelalterlichen Staates im östlichen Mittelmeerraum*, New edition, Vienna 2001.

Kondyli, F., *Rural Communities in Late Byzantium: Resilience and Vulnerability in the Northern Aegean*, Cambridge 2022.

Laiou, A.E. (ed.), *The Economic History of Byzantium. From the Seventh through the Fifteenth Century*, Washington, D.C. 2002.

Laiou, A./Morrisson, C., *The Byzantine Economy*, Cambridge 2007.

Larsen, C.S., *Bioarchaeology: Interpreting Behavior from the Human Skeleton*, Cambridge 1997.

Leppin, H., *Justinian. Das christliche Experiment*, Stuttgart 2011.

Lewis, M.E., *The Bioarchaeology of Children: Perspectives from Biological and Forensic Anthropology*, Cambridge 2007.

Littlewood, A./Maguire H. /Wolschke-Bulmahn J. (eds.), *Byzantine Garden Culture*, Washington D.C. 2002.

Lucke, B./Schmidt, M./al-Saad, Z./Bens, O./Hüttl, R.F., "The Abandonment of the Decapolis Region in Northern Jordan – forced by Environmental Change?", *Quaternary International*, (Geochronology and Environmental Reconstruction: a Tribute to Glenn A. Goodfriend), 135, no. 1 (June 2005), 65–81.

Luterbacher, J., et al., "A Review of 2000 Years of Paleoclimatic Evidence in the Mediterranean", in P. Lionello (ed.), *The Climate of the Mediterranean region: from the past to the future*, Amsterdam 2012, pp. 87–185.

Maas, M. (ed.), *The Cambridge Companion to the Age of Justinian*, Cambridge 2005.

Maguire, H., *Earth and Ocean: the Terrestrial World in Early Byzantine Art* (Monographs on the Fine Arts Sponsored by the College Art Association of America 43), University Park 1987.

Maguire, H., *Nectar and Illusion, Nature in Byzantine Art and Literature*, New York 2012.

Mango, C., *Le développement urbain de Constantinople (IVe–VIIe siècles)*. 3rd ed. Paris 2004.

McCormick, M., et al., "Climate Change during and after the Roman Empire: Reconstructing the Past from Scientific and Historical Evidence", *Journal of Interdisciplinary History* 43,2 (2012), 169–220.

McNeill, J.R., *The Mountains of the Mediterranean World. An Environmental History*, Cambridge 1992.

Meier, M., *Das andere Zeitalter Justinians. Kontingenzerfahrung und Kontingenzbewältigung im 6. Jahrhundert n. Chr.*, Göttingen ²2004.

Olson, A., *Environment and Society in Byzantium, 650–1150. Between the Oak and the Olive*, Cham 2020.

Ortner, D.J., *Identification of Pathological Conditions in Human Skeletal Remains*, San Diego 2003.

Pfister, Ch./Wanner, H., *Climate and Society in Europe. The Last Thousand Years*, Bern 2021.

Pickett, J., "Hydraulic Landscapes of Roman and Byzantine cities", in G. Farhat, (ed.) *Landscapes of preindustrial urbanism*, Washington 2020, pp. 115–143.

Pickett, J., "Water and social relationships in early Byzantine neighbourhoods", in F. Kondyli, and B. Anderson, (eds) *The Byzantine Neighbourhood, Urban space and political action*, London, 2022, pp. 125–152.

Pluskowski, A., ed., *Environment, Colonization, and the Baltic Crusader States: Terra Sacra I*, (Environmental Histories of the North Atlantic World 2), Turnhout, Belgium, 2019.

Pluskowski, A., ed., *Ecologies of Crusading, Colonization, and Religious Conversion in the Medieval Baltic: Terra Sacra II*, (Environmental Histories of the North Atlantic World 3), Turnhout, Belgium, 2019.

Pluskowski, A./Boas, A.J./Gerrard, C., "The Ecology of Crusading: Investigating the Environmental Impact of Holy War and Colonisation at the Frontiers of Medieval Europe", *Medieval Archaeology* 55, no. 1 (2011), 192–225.

Preiser-Kapeller, J., "A Collapse of the Eastern Mediterranean? New Results and Theories on the Interplay between Climate and Societies in Byzantium and the Near East, Ca. 1000–1200 AD", *Jahrbuch der österreichischen Byzantinistik* 65 (2015) 195–242.

Preiser-Kapeller, J., *Der Lange Sommer und die Kleine Eiszeit. Klima, Pandemien und der Wandel der Alten Welt von 500 bis 1500 n. Chr*, Vienna 2021.

Preiser-Kapeller, J./Mitsiou, E., "The Little Ice Age and Byzantium within the Eastern Mediterranean, ca. 1200–1350: An Essay on Old Debates and New Scenarios", in M. Bauch/G.J. Schenk (eds.), *The Crisis of the 14th Century. Teleconnections between Environmental and Societal Change?*, Berlin 2020, pp. 190–220.

Raphael, S.K., *Climate and Political Climate. Environmental Disasters in the Medieval Levant* (Brill's Series in the History of the Environment 3), Leiden 2013.

Reynolds, D. "Rethinking Palestinian Iconoclasm", *Dumbarton Oaks Papers* 71 (2017), 1–64.

Rife, J.L., *Isthmia. Vol. IX. The Roman and Byzantine Graves and Human Remains*. (The American School of Classical Studies), Athens 2012.

Schiebel, V./T. Litt, "Holocene Vegetation History of the Southern Levant Based on a Pollen Record from Lake Kinneret (Sea of Galilee), Israel", *Vegetation History and Archaeobotany* 27, no. 4 (2018), pp. 577–90.

Sigl, M., et al., "Timing and Climate Forcing of Volcanic Eruptions for the Past 2,500 Years", *Nature* 523 (2015), 543–9.

Sintubin, Manuel. 2011. "Archaeoseismology: Past, Present and Future." *Quaternary International*, Earthquake Archaeology and Paleoseismology, 242 (1): 4–10. https://doi.org/10.1016/j.quaint.2011.03.056.

Smith, Keith. 2013. *Environmental Hazards: Assessing Risk and Reducing Disaster*. New York: Routledge.

Snyder, J.R., "Manipulating the Environment: the impact of the construction of the Water Supply of Constantinople", in, H. Baron and F. Daim, (eds.) *A Most Pleasant Scene and an Inexhaustible Resource? Steps Towards Environmental History of the Byzantine Empire*, Byzanz zwischen Orient und Okzident Mainz 2017, pp. 169–185.

Squatriti, P., *Landscape and Change in Early Medieval Italy: Chestnuts, Economy, and Culture*, Cambridge 2013.

Stathakopoulos, D., *Famine and pestilence in the late Roman and early Byzantine Empire: a systematic survey of subsistence crises and epidemics*, Ashgate 2004.

Stathakopoulos, D., *Reconstructing the Climate of the Byzantine World: State of the Problem and Case Studies*, in: J. Laszlovszky/P. Szabó (eds.), *People and Nature in Historical Perspective*, Budapest 2003, 247–261.

Stodder, A.L./Palkovich, A.M., *The Bioarchaeology of Individuals. Bioarchaeological Interpretations of the Human Past: Local, Regional, and Global*, Gainesville 2012.

Talgam, R., *Mosaics of Faith: Floors of Pagans, Jews, Samaritans, Christians, and Muslims in the Holy Land*, Jerusalem 2014.

Tarlow, S./Nilsson Stutz, L. (eds.), *The Oxford Handbook of the Archaeology of Death*, Oxford 2013.

Telelis, I, "Environmental History and Byzantine Studies: a Survey of Topics and Results", in: Kolias, T. /Pitsakis, K. (eds), *Aureus. Volume dedicated to Professor Evangelos K. Chrysos*, Athens 2014, pp. 737–60.

Telelis, I., "Medieval Warm Period and the Beginning of the Little Ice Age in the Eastern Mediterranean: An Approach of Physical and Anthropogenic Evidence," in Belke, K. et al. (eds.) *Byzanz als Raum: zu Methoden und Inhalten der historische Geographie des östlichen Mittelmeerraumes*, Vienna 2000, pp. 223–243.

Telelis, I.G., "Climatic fluctuations in the Eastern Mediterranean and the Middle East AD 300–1500 from Byzantine documentary and proxy physical paleoclimatic evidence – a comparison", *Jahrbuch der Österreichischen Byzantinistik* 58 (2008), 167–207.

Telelis, I.G., Μετεωρολογικά φαινόμενα και κλίμα στο Βυζάντιο, 2 vols., Athens 2004.

Thomson, J.L./ Alfonso-Durruty, M.P./Crandall, J.J. (eds.), *Tracing Childhood. Bioarchaeological Investigations of Early Lives in Antiquity*, Gainesville 2014.

Wallace-Hadrill, D.S., *The Greek Patristic View of Nature*, New York 1968.

Ward, K., Smith, S., Crapper, M., "Using the Byzantine water supply of Constantinople to examine modern concepts of sustainability", in *Sustainable Water Engineering 2020* S. Charlesworth/C. Booth/K. Adeyeye, (eds.) Amsterdam 2021, pp. 13–30.

White, S., *The Climate of Rebellion in the Early Modern Ottoman Empire*, Cambridge 2011.

White, S./Pfister, C./Mauelshagen, F. (eds.) *The Palgrave Handbook of Climate History*, London 2018.

Wickham, Chr., *Framing the Early Middle Ages. Europe and the* Mediterranean 400–800, Oxford 2005, repr. 2006.

Winiwarter, V./Knoll, M., *Umweltgeschichte: eine Einführung*, Cologne 2007.

Wozniak, Th., *Naturereignisse im frühen Mittelalter. Das Zeugnis der Geschichtsschreibung vom 6. bis 11. Jahrhundert*, Berlin 2020.

Xoplaki, E. et al., "The Medieval Climate Anomaly and Byzantium: A Review of the Evidence on Climatic Fluctuations, Economic Performance and Societal Change", *Quaternary Science Reviews* 136 (2016), 229–52.

Xoplaki, E., et al., "Modelling Climate and Societal Resilience in the Eastern Mediterranean in the Last Millennium", *Human Ecology* 46 (2018), 363–79.

Index of Place Names

Abant Gölü 66
Ablada 116
Abydos 362, 369–171
Acıçay River 282
Acre 128, 236, 491, 496, 498–499
Adatepe 288
Adrianople (Edirne) 126, 208
Aegean Sea 17, 29, 39n, 50, 50n, 126–128, 206, 346–354, 357–358, 360–361, 361n, 362–363, 366–373, 415–416, 418, 471
Aegina 351, 353
Africa 12, 28, 30, 46–47, 50, 118, 124, 142, 146–147, 150, 153, 162n, 349, 353, 411, 412n, 475n
Agathonisi 352
Agioi Apostoloi (Thessalonike) 220, 449–450
Agios Efstratios 351
Ağlasun 257n, 259, 259n, 264
Aila ('Aqaba) 240
Ain-Témouchent (Algeria) 185
Alaca 279
Alagöz 279
Ałbag 320
Albania 38n, 40n, 44, 48, 64, 96, 96n, 439, 458n, 469n
Aleppo 124, 128, 434–435
Alexandria (Egypt) 124, 128, 183, 191, 203, 206, 235, 239
al-Fusṭāṭ 434, 435, 444–445
Algeria 129, 129n, 185
Alibey Dere (Hydrales river) 207–208, 212
Alikianos 90–91, 93, 98
Alimia 352
Allonissos 351
Alps 37n, 38n, 45, 49, 296n
Ałtamar 321–322, 324–325
Amaseia (Amasya) 278–279, 283, 299, 299n, 301
Amida 116, 236, 388n
Amisus (Samsun) 279
Amorgos 351, 364
Amorion/Amorium 302
Anafi 351
Anastasian Wall 208, 210
Anatolia 11n, 17, 39n, 40–41, 42n, 52n, 64, 71, 73–76, 143n, 162n, 167, 169, 210,
229–230, 230n, 231, 254, 257, 266–267, 268n, 278–279, 283–285, 287–288, 293, 295, 299–302, 317, 336, 416, 424, 428, 456–457, 459, 464n, 472, 476, 514–515, 517, 519, 520, 522–525
Ancient Forum (Thessalonike) 220
Androna (al-Andarin) 237
Andros 351, 353, 365, 370
Ani 318, 320, 336, 456
Ankara (Ankyra) 278, 446
Antikythira 352
Antinoe (Egypt) 186
Antioch (Syria) 116, 120, 128, 167, 168, 172n, 173, 203, 219, 230, 236–237, 385–386, 435, 443, 471–472, 496, 504–505
Antiparos 351
Apameia 491
Aphrodisias 353
Aphrodito (Egypt) 186
Apulia 9
Aqua Augusta 210, 210n
Aqueduct of Hadrian 207, 214–215
Aqueduct of Valens 212, 214, 215–216
Arabia 162n, 234, 237–238, 242–243
Araxes 313n, 314, 319, 321, 330, 336
Arcn 320
Arctic 12
Areopolis (Rabbat-Moab) 240
Argolic Gulf 351, 356
Argolid 356, 358, 360
Arkoi 352
Armenia 17, 308, 314–321, 328, 330, 334–336, 432n, 442, 452, 455–456, 463n, 464, 470
Armeniakon 278, 446
Ar-Raqqah (Callinicum) 241
Arsinikeia 429–430
Arzanene 235
Ascalon 128, 496
Asia Minor 116–117, 119, 120–122, 124, 126–127, 141–142, 146–147, 149–152, 162, 230, 235, 299n, 300, 300n, 301, 347, 358, 363, 366n, 368, 370, 394, 413–414, 416, 418, 428, 435–436, 439, 446, 452, 461, 464n, 468
Assyria 313–314, 316

Athens 127, 471
Astypalaia 352
Atlantic Ocean 8, 12, 35, 408, 489
Attica 351, 353, 361
Australia 411
Austria 8
Avkat Dağı 279
Ayia Roumeli 356
Azerbaijan 308, 330–331
Azores 408

Baalbek 236
Bafa Gölü 475
Baghdad 124, 128, 411, 421, 424, 432, 434, 441, 442n, 444, 452–453, 455, 459, 464n, 467, 470, 475
Balık Gölü (Lake Gaylatu) 330
Balkans 11n, 30, 39, 50, 64, 75, 121–122, 129, 147, 150, 162n, 219, 235, 351, 357, 368, 413–414, 416, 438, 458, 468, 471, 514
Ballıgerme (Thrace) 209–210
Barbalissos (Maskanah) 239, 241
Basilica cistern (Yerebatan Saray) 214–215, 218
Basra 236, 239
Beirut 168n, 172n, 239
Bekaa Valley 471
Bereket Basin 229, 26261, 263–264
Berenike 142, 148, 150, 153, 153n, 156
Beyşehir 253, 264, 288, 295
Bezabde (Cizre) 236
Binbirdirek (Constantinople) 217
Binkılıç (Thrace) 209
Bithynia 9, 73–76, 285, 301, 418, 461
Blachernae (Constantinople) 448
Black Sea 30, 153–154, 204, 206–208, 279, 301, 302n, 346, 351, 357, 361, 382, 457
Boeotia 347, 351, 413
Bolu 287
Bosporus 141, 204, 346, 386
Bozdğan Kemer 208, 216
Bryas 219
Bukhara 456
Bulgaria 204, 336, 439, 457
Butrint 44, 64, 96
Büyük 288
Büyükgerme (Thrace) 209
Büyükoz River 282

Byblos 239
Byzye (Vize) 209

Çadır Höyük 299
Caesarea maritima 169
Caffa (Crimea) 125
Çagēçor River (Vararak) 328
Cairo 47, 124, 128, 421, 435, 445, 460, 470, 497, 502
Çakır Dağı 279
Calimani (Romania) 520
Campagna 210
Çanakkale 351
Candia (Crete) 127
Çankırı 282–283, 287, 295
Cap Maleas 362
Cappadocia 71, 116, 279, 287, 293, 296–297, 300, 317, 319, 334–335, 416n, 424, 440, 446, 472
Caričin Grad 157–158
Carthage 152–153, 203, 235
Caspian Sea 409–411
Caucasia 311, 317, 319, 321n, 326–327, 331
Central Europe 28, 47–48, 75n, 154–155, 407–409, 412, 463n, 471, 515
Cerigo 127
Chalki 352, 354
Chalkida 351
Chalkidiki 351
Chile 84
China 112, 203, 423, 434, 442, 453, 459, 469–470
Chios 127, 351, 353, 357, 360, 364–365, 366n, 369–371
Chonai 463
Chora Monastery (Constantinople) 220
Chora Sfakion 356
Choriatis Springs (near Thessalonike) 220
Church of the Apostles (Constantinople) 194–195, 383
Cilicia 116, 434, 435, 471n
Circesium (Al-Busayrah) 242
Cistern of Asper (Constantinople) 217
Clermont 190
Çöl Gölü 287, 295–296, 298
Cold Cistern, Hippodrome (Constantinople) 218
Colorado 412

INDEX OF PLACE NAMES   541

Column of Marcian (Constantinople)   216
Constantinian Walls   204, 213
Constantinople   17, 44, 49–51, 72, 74, 116,
    119–128, 151, 155, 167–168, 173, 182, 193,
    203, 205, 207–208, 210–211, 213–214, 217,
    218n, 220, 222, 227, 253, 263, 268–271,
    281–283, 286, 288n, 291–292, 294–296,
    298, 415, 421, 425, 428, 430–432, 435,
    439, 449, 451, 454–455, 457, 464–466,
    469–470, 522, 526
Corfu   127
Corinth   353, 356–357, 370, 386, 471
Çorum   279–285, 287, 295, 298, 299n, 301
Çorum Çat suyu (Derinçay)   282
Çorum River   279
Crete   93–94, 99, 123, 126–127, 142, 144n, 147,
    184, 346–347, 349, 351–352, 354, 356,
    363–365, 369–371, 372, 413, 432
Crimea   125, 173
Čuaš   321
Cyclades   351–352, 363, 368–370
Cyprus   41, 98, 126–127, 173, 235, 356,
    369–370, 499

Dağyenice (Thrace)   208
Dalmatia   151–152
Damascus   46, 128, 239, 243, 434, 437, 497
Damietta   497
Danamandıra   208
Danube   142, 145–147, 150–152, 154, 157, 189,
    457–459, 468
Dardanelles   346, 351, 357, 370
Darmstadt   197–198
Dead Sea   148, 153, 196–197, 229–233, 498
Decapolis   494–495
Dehes   232
Delice River   282
Delos   351
Demiyurt   288
Denmark   8
Dia   371
Diakopene   298
Dobruja   142
Dodecanese   352
Doni Çayi   315
Donousa   352
Düğer river   256
Dvin   320
Dyrrachion   368, 370

East Africa   47, 124, 412, 459
Edessa   118, 236, 335, 384, 394, 434, 467
Edirne Kapı   208
Efendik River   279
Eğerli mountains   279
Egypt   46–47, 119–124, 129, 131, 142, 145,
    153, 162, 183–186, 190, 197, 206, 239,
    245–246, 386, 412, 420, 422, 431, 432n,
    434, 436, 440–442, 444, 445n, 455,
    459–462, 468, 472, 475, 496
Ein Gedi   232–235
Ējmiacin   328
el Haouria (Tunisia)   185, 196
Elaphonissos   352
Eldgjá (volcano)   408, 432
Eleutherna   96
Elmalı   279
En Boqeq   148, 153
England   85, 405–406, 408n
Engusner Çayi   322
Ephesus   475
Epidauros   352, 356, 370
Epirus   126
Eretria   353
Ergene (Thrace)   209, 218
Eschati   352
Eski Acıgöl   44, 287
Ethiopia   47
Euboea   126, 347, 351, 353–354, 361, 363
Euchaïta (Beyözü)   17, 278–279, 298–299,
    301, 302–303
Euphrates   148, 151, 155, 189, 191–192,
    241–243, 314, 441, 444, 468
Euripus   361

Famagusta   127
Farmakonisi   352
Faruk Bendi   322, 327
Ferhat Canal   330
Fertile Crescent   36
Fildamı Reservoir (Constantinople)   221
Filotas   97
Folegandros   351
Forest of Belgrade   207, 212, 214
Forum of Constantine (Constantinople)
    215–216, 218n
Forum of Theodosius   215
Forum Tauri (Constantinople)   215–216,
    218n

Fournoi 352, 371
France 6, 9, 13, 16, 497, 505n

Galata (Pera) 126, 127
Galatia 116
Galilee 183, 491, 496, 502, 504
Ganges 189
Gaul 190
Gaza 190–191, 496
Genoa 131
Gerasa 191
Germany 8
Ghab valley 230, 250
Gioura 351
Golan 230, 246, 495, 504
Gölcük (Sardis) 293
Golden Horn 208, 214
Gravgaz marsh 260–261, 263–264, 520
Great Britain 8
Great Palace (Constantinople) 214, 449
Greece 14, 28, 30, 41, 43–46, 63, 75–76, 94–95, 96n, 116–117, 126–127, 129, 146, 151, 167, 191, 347, 356, 358, 361, 372, 386, 413n, 416, 418–420, 449, 469, 471, 524
Greenland 287, 406, 408
Grotta Savi (SE Alps) 45, 49
Gulf of Almyros 352
Gulf of Çandarlı 351
Gulf of Cassandra 351
Gulf of Chania 352
Gulf of Corinth 356–357
Gulf of Dikili 351
Gulf of Edremit 351
Gulf of Euboea 351
Gulf of Fethiye 352
Gulf of Gökova 352
Gulf of Güllük 352
Gulf of Herakleion 352
Gulf of Hisarönü 352
Gulf of İzmir 351
Gulf of Karaağaç 352
Gulf of Kavala 351
Gulf of Kazıklı 352
Gulf of Kuşadası 351
Gulf of Laconia 352
Gulf of Limira 352
Gulf of Marmaris 352
Gulf of Messara 352

Gulf of Mirabellou 352
Gulf of Petalioi 351
Gulf of Sömbeki 352
Gulf of Souda 352
Gulfs of Epidauros 352
Gyali 352
Gyaros 352
Gytheion 356

Hadamakert (Başkale) 320
Hadrianopolis 302
Hagia Sophia (Constantinople) 193–194, 215, 386, 396, 439
Haiti 162–163
Halassarna (Kos) 354, 357
Halik (Siwnikʿ) 328–329
Hallabat 243
Halys (Kızılırmak) 282
Harran 434
Hebdomon (Constantinople) 221
Hejaz 46
Hellas 369, 449
Hellespont 447–448, 461
Herakleia at Latmum 353, 371
Hermon 492
Hierissos 429
Hippodrome (Constantinople) 214, 218–219, 381
Hisn Maslama (Madinat al-Far) 241
Homs (Emesa) 128, 236
Hoşap Valley 311
Hydra 351

Iassos 353
Iberian Peninsula 244
Iceland 408, 432
Ikaria 352–352, 354
Ilgaz 279
Illyria 386
Illyricum 116
Imbros (Gökçeada) 347, 351
India 189, 234, 453
Indian Ocean 162
Indonesia 408, 411
Ionian Islands 126–127
Ionian Sea 127–128, 360
Ios 351, 371
Irakleia 352
Iran 44, 331, 337, 441, 442, 455–357

INDEX OF PLACE NAMES

Iraq   44, 46–47, 231, 236, 241–243, 245,
    432–434, 436, 453, 455, 459, 469, 472, 514
Iris (Yeşilırmak)   279, 282
Israel   45, 167–168, 191, 196, 229, 237, 240,
    476n, 491
Issyk Kul (Kyrgyzstan)   125
Isthmus of Corinth   386
Italy   16, 42, 44–45, 50, 72, 123, 141–142,
    146–147, 150, 152, 386, 434, 468–369,
    497, 502, 505
Iviron (Monastery)   429

Jableh   471
Japan   162, 408
Jazira   245
Jerusalem   124, 197, 232, 321, 394, 399, 489,
    494, 505
Jezreel Valley   491
Jordan   87, 152, 191–192, 194, 196, 237, 240,
    497, 501n
Jordan (river)   148, 155, 186–188, 190, 197, 494
Judaean Hills   230

Kalymnos   352
Kamulianai   394
Karadağ   279
Karaman Dere   208
Karatepe (Thrace)   210
Karmir river   321
Karpathos   352, 364, 370
Kars   320
Karystos   353
K'asal River   327
Kasirin (Dibsi Faraj?)   239
Kassos   352
Kastellorizo   352
Kavak   279
Kaystros   360
Kaz   287–288, 291, 293
Kea   351
Keçigerme (Thrace)   209
Kemerburgaz (Thrace)   212
Kephallenia   368–369
Keşiş Gölü (Lake Rusa)   313
Keslik   279
Khabur   242
Khorasan   236, 442, 456
Khuzistan   242
Kimolos   351, 353

Kinaros   352
Kırkçeşme (Thrace)   214
Kırklar Dağı   279
Kırlar   279
Kocain Cave   45, 420, 424, 424n
Kolobou (Monastery)   416, 429–430
Kolumbo   353
Köroğlu   279
Korone   126–128
Kos   352–354, 357, 366n, 370
Köse Mountains   279
Kosmosoteira Monastery   182
Kotom   324
Koufonisia   352
Kranae Island   356
Küçük Akgöl   288
Küçükyalı   219, 221–222
Kufa   236, 239
Kumarlidere (Thrace)   209
Kuna Ba Cave   432–432, 472
Kurşunlugerme (Thrace)   209
Kyra-Panagia (Gymnopelagesio)   351, 364
Kyrgyzstan   125
Kythira   352
Kythnos   351
Kyzikos   369, 461

L'Aquila   173
Laconia   352, 356, 364, 413
Lâdik   287–288, 292–293
Lago Alimini Piccolo   72
Lago di Pergusa   44, 72
Lake Albert   47
Lake Belevi   475
Lake Birkat Ram   230
Lake Burdur   256
Lake Gölhisar   45, 229
Lake Orchid   44
Lake Urmia   337
Lake Van   40, 45, 64, 268, 300, 308, 310–311,
    313n, 314–315, 317–322, 324, 324n,
    325–327, 329, 331–337, 442
Lake Victoria   47
Languedoc   7
Laodicea (Latakia)   239
Lebanon   45, 471
Lemnos   126–127, 351
Leptiminus   153
Leros   352

Lesbos (Lesvos)   351, 353–354, 363, 364, 370
Levant   17, 41, 95, 146, 150, 155–156, 162,
   172–173, 227, 229–231, 234–239, 241,
   243–246, 266, 300, 371, 494, 496–497,
   499–500, 501n, 505–506
Levitha   352
Libya   147, 153, 352n
Libyan Sea   352
Lipsoi   352
Lombok   408
London   203
Loutra (Samothrace)   354
Luka Dere (Thrace)   210
Lycia   73

Macedonia   9, 44, 75–76, 351, 360–362, 392,
   419, 449, 461, 523–524
Madaba (Jordan)   191, 194–197
Madina   242
Maeander   475
Maghreb   245
Makronisos   352
Malian Gulf   356, 360
Mampsis   240
Mandraklou   475
Mangana monastery   454
Mani   364
Marakan   336, 443, 461, 464
Marathos   352
Marib Dam   238
Mecca   128, 444
Mecitözü Çayı   279n, 282
Mecitözü valley   279, 301
Melen   287–288
Menua Canal   311, 314, 316, 330, 337
Mesa Verde   412
Mesanakata   446
Mese (Constantinople)   209, 215–216
Mesoamerica   203
Mesopotamia   119–124, 131, 227, 234, 236,
   239, 241–243, 314, 284, 420, 432n, 442,
   452–453, 455, 461, 436n
Messene   97
Methana   353
Methone   126–128
Mexico   411
Miletus   72, 475
Milos   351, 353–354
Monastery of Satyros   219

Monemvasia   363
Montaillou   7
Montréal   498
Morea (Peloponnese)   496
Mosul   128, 441–442, 453
Mount Artos (Çadır Dağı)   322
Mount Athos   126, 154, 365, 471
Mount Çagēçor   328
Mount Smolikas   41
Mount Varag (Erek Dağı)   321–322
Mughan Steppe   330–331
Mykonos   351
Mylasa   353
Myra   362
Myrelaion (Constantinople)   219
Myriophyton   461
Myrtoan Sea   351–352

Naples   6
Nar Gölü   45, 287, 293, 295–298, 317, 334, 424
Naupaktos   369
Naxčawan   320
Naxos   13, 351, 353, 370–371
Nazianzus   182
Negev   148, 155, 157, 234, 238, 240, 246, 491
Negroponte   127
Nessana (Niṯzana, Israel)   237, 240
New Zealand   163
Nicaea   461
Nicomedia   173
Nicopolis ad Istrum   142, 157
Nicosia (Cyprus)   127
Nile   44, 47, 124, 141, 148, 154–156, 183–186,
   189, 190–191, 386, 412, 434, 440–441,
   444–445, 455, 459–460, 470, 472
Nimos   352
Nisyros   352–354
Norik (Siwnikʿ)   328–329
North Africa   28, 30, 46–47, 50, 142, 146–147,
   150, 153, 245, 352n, 356, 381, 411, 434
North Sea   409–411
Northern Europe   28, 118, 501n
Northern Sporades   351, 364

Octagon (Thessalonike)   220
Ohrid   190
Oran (Algeria)   129
Orontes River   11
Ostan (Gevaş)   320–324

INDEX OF PLACE NAMES   545

Otranto   72
Oxyrhynchus   184

Pacific Ocean   12, 411
Pagasetic Gulf   351
Palace of Antiochus (Constantinople)   219
Palaestina Salutaris   240
Palestine   44, 46–47, 116–117, 119–123, 131, 142, 147, 149n, 152–153, 172, 184, 192, 197, 230, 236, 237, 240–241, 246, 460, 494
Pamphylia   221
Panion   461
Pantokrator Monastery (Zeyrek Camii, Constantinople)   220
Paphlagonia   278, 285, 301, 446
Paris   203
Paros   352–353, 363, 366n
Partaw   320
Patmos   352
Patras   127
Pazarli (Thrace)   209–210, 218
Peloponnese   116, 126–128, 142, 147, 147n, 191, 349, 351–352, 356, 361, 366n, 415, 420, 449
Pelusium (Egypt)   119
Pergamon (Pergamum)   363, 448
Peristera   351
Persia   116, 124, 235, 237–239, 241, 243, 245, 314, 317, 442, 453, 455, 515
Peru   411
Petra   194, 237, 240
Peyniryemez   299
Phaeno, modern Khirbet Fayan   87
Phazemonitis   298
Phbow (Egypt)   116
Pherrai   182
Phoenicia   236
Phygela   371
Pınarca   208
Pindus Mountains   41
Pinios   360
Pisidia   73, 75–76, 256
Poland   64, 79
Poros   351
Portugal   6
Priene   353
Proikonessos   370
Provence   7
Pserimos   352

Pyrenees   8
Pythagorion (Samos)   360

Qasr al-Hayr al-Gharbi   243
Qasr al-Hayr al-Sharqi   243
Qusayr Amra   243

Ragusa (Dubrovnik)   127
Ravenna   186–188
Red Sea   142, 148, 153–154, 155, 155n, 156, 246
Rhaidestos   461, 465–466
Rhodes   126, 165n, 352–353, 363–365, 367, 369–371
Rhodope   361
Romania   46, 368, 520
Rome   42, 203–204, 207, 211, 211n, 212, 227, 317, 394
Rusafa   243

Sagalassos   17, 89n, 142, 144n, 147, 149n, 230, 251–271
Sahel   411
Salamis   173
Salamis (Cyprus)   351
Samalas (volcano)   408, 521
Samarkand   456
Samos   351–352, 360, 365, 366n, 369–371
Samothrace   351, 354
Sarakino   351
Sardis   293, 353
Saria   352
Saronic Gulf   351
Saronic Islands   351
Sawad   242
Scandinavia   85, 296n
Scylax (Çekerek)   282
Sea of Galilee (Lake Kinneret)   155, 233, 492, 494–495, 501, 502n, 503
Sea of Marmara   204, 207, 219, 346, 363, 382
Sebasteia (Sivas)   282, 296–297, 335, 440, 519
Senegal   411
Sepphoris   183
Serbia   157
Serifos   352, 354
Sétif (Algeria)   185
Seyfe   288
Shiraz   441
Siberia   410–411
Sicily   6, 44, 70, 72, 173, 206, 356, 505

INDEX OF PLACE NAMES

Siderokausia   416, 429–430
Sidon   128, 239
Sifnos   352, 354
Sigeion   362
Sikinos   352
Singara   236
Singitic Gulf   351
Sinope   279, 302n
Sistan   236
Siwnik‛   328–329
Skantzoura   351
Skiathos   351
Skopelos   351
Skyros   351, 353
Slovakia   48
Smyrna   370, 450, 469
Šnhērik (Siwnik‛)   328–329
Sofular Cave   45, 287, 436
Soğanlı – Ilyas Tepesi   256
Soreq Cave   45, 229
Sourtara   94
South Africa   12, 411
South America   411, 459
Southeast Asia   234
Southeastern Europe   36, 357
Southern Italy   72, 142, 146–147, 150, 468–469, 505
Southern Sporades   352
Sozopolis   394
Spain   6, 243, 356
Spetses   351
St. Petersburg   199
Strandja hills   204, 208
Strongyli   352
Strymon   360, 449, 523
Strymon river   365
Strymonian Gulf   351
Sudan   411
Sungurlu   279, 282
Sykeon   394
Symi   352
Synnada   299
Syria   44–47, 116, 119–124, 131, 142, 147, 150, 152–153, 162n, 230, 232, 234–240, 245, 384–385, 434–435, 445, 447, 455–456, 461, 467, 472, 491, 494, 500, 514–515
Syrna   352
Syros   352–353

Ta Christiana   371
Ta Peukia/Pefkia   371
Tabgha   191
Talas (Thrace)   209
Tarōn   335
Tat‛ev Monastery   328
Tatlı   288
Taurus Mountains   25, 462, 520
Tecer Gölü   296–298
Tegea (Peloponnese)   191–192
Telendos   352
Tell Hesban   142, 146n, 148, 152
Tenedos (Bozcaada)   347, 351, 371
Teos   353
Terkos Lake   208
Tezgâhçılar Kubbesi   214
Thasos   366n
Thebes (Egypt)   116
Thebes (Greece)   370
Theodosian Walls   204, 209, 213
Thera (Santorini)   371
Thessaloniki   17, 126–127, 168, 188, 203, 220–222, 363, 370, 450n
Thessaly   360, 449
Thrace   119, 124, 126–127, 182, 205, 208, 209, 209n, 210, 351, 386, 447, 449, 465, 472, 523, 526
Thrakesion   448
Thyrsos (Peloponnese)   191
Tiber   42, 44
Tigris   189, 191–192, 242, 444, 459
Tikrīt   441
Tilos   352
Tinos   352–353
Tivrik   128
Toprakkale (Rusahinili)   313
Transjordan   492, 496
Transoxania   456
Trebizond   126–127
Tripoli (Lebanon)   239, 370
Tristomon   362
Troad   353
Tunisia   185, 196
Turkey   28, 30, 44–46, 49, 63–64, 66–67, 69, 89n, 144n, 219, 229, 251, 253, 267, 279, 283–284, 287–288, 293, 295, 298, 308, 318, 347, 352, 357, 384, 420, 437, 472–473, 514–515, 520

Tuzla   288
Tyre   236, 499

Ultan Qalası (Azerbaijan)   330
Umm al-Rasas (Jordan)   192, 194
United States of America (USA)   4, 411
Unkapanı (Constantinople)   221
Upper Zohar   148, 149n, 157
Urartu   311, 315–316, 322, 326, 330, 332
Urlu   279
Uzuntarla Cave   45, 420, 472

Van (Tušpa)   45, 64, 308, 310–317, 320–322, 326, 327, 330–331, 334, 336–337
Vaspurakan   316–317, 317n, 318–321, 328, 330, 334–336
Veh-Ardashir   236
Venice   128, 131
Vlatadon Monastery (Thessalonike)   220

Xerias   360
Xotan (Siwnikʻ)   328–329

Yali   353
Yavuz Sultan Selim Camii (Constantinople)   217
Yellow River (China)   434, 453
Yemen   46
Yeniçağa   287–288, 290, 293
Yiali   354

Zela   279
Zeugma   148
Zeuxippus Baths (Constantinople)   214
Ziata   236
Zonguldak   287
Zuartʻnocʻ   327

Index of Names

Abū l-Misk Kāfūr 434
Abul al-ʿAbbas al-Saffah 242
Agathias 393
Akçer-Ön, Sena 45
al-Afdal 460
al-Maqrīzī 455, 460
al-Muṣābiḥī 444–445
al-Mustanṣir 455, 460
al-Muʿizz li-Dīn Allāh 434
al-Walid 242
al-Yāzūrī 455, 459
Alexios I Komnenos 368–369, 457, 468–469
Alizadeh, Karim 330
Altuğ, Kerim 216
Ambroise 492
Anastasios of Sinai 182
Anastasius 217–291, 389
Anderson, John G.C. 301
Andrew of Crete 184, 186
Andronikos III Palaiologos 117
Angel, J. Lawrence 91
Anna Komnene 468–469
King, Anthony 145–148
Antoninus Pius 255
Arcruni, Gagik 321–322, 324–325, 328, 336
Arcruni, Tʿovma 315, 321–322, 324, 326, 335–336
Arcruni, Yovhannēs-Senekʿerim 335–336
Aristakēs Lastivercʿi 422
Artabasdus 213
Attaleiates, Michael 423, 458, 461–463, 463n, 464–467, 469
Avitus 189
aẓ-Ẓāhir 444

Badr al-Ǧamālī 460
Baker, Julian 373
Bakker, Johan 17
Baladhuri 242
Banaji, Jairus 239, 242
Bar Hebraeus 424, 441–442, 444, 453, 456–457, 464n
Bar-Matthews, Miryam 45
Bardas Phokas 438
Bardas Skleros 438
Bardill, Jonathan 216

Barlas Şimşek, Funda 332–333
Baron, Henriette 17, 88
Basil I 413, 436
Basil II (the Great) 182, 210, 335, 428–431, 438–440, 442–443, 468
Belisarius 369, 381–382
Bianquis, Thierry 444
Sergius 194
Blaauw, Martin 67
Bourbou, Chryssi 17
Braudel, Fernand 6–7, 12–14, 15n, 16
Brickley, Megan B. 94
Bronstein, Judith 505
Bugha "the Elder" 319
Bulliet, Richard 456–457
Butzer, Karl W. 245

Çağatay, M. Namik 332–333
Caliph al-Ḥākim 440–441, 444
Cameron, Averil 15, 390
Campbell, Bruce 525
Camuffo 42, 44
Chatzipetros, Alexandros 355
Cheng, Haii 45
Choricius 190–191
Christ (Jesus Christ) 186–190, 321, 389, 392, 394, 396–398, 422, 470
Chrysobulls 471
Columbus, Christopher 5
Constantine 207, 216, 398
Constantine Manasses 182
Constantine V 210, 213, 219
Constantine VII Porphyrogennitus 366, 382, 431
Constantine VIII 210, 431, 443–445
Constantine IX (Monomachos) 454–455
Constantine X Doukas 458, 461–462
Constantius II 117, 207, 208
Cook, Edward 46
Cook, Benjamin I. 46
Corippus 392
Crapper, Martin 218
Cronon, William 5
Crosby, Alfred 5, 490
Crow, James 17
Cyril of Jerusalem 185

INDEX OF NAMES

Daniel 392
Danladi, Ilya B. 45
Dauphin, Cluadine 231
De Mussi 125
Dean, Jonathan 45
Decker, Michael 17
Dioscorus of Aphrodito 186

Eastwood, Warren 17, 45, 86
Eleutherios 278
Ellenblum, Ronnie 2, 405, 420–424, 456–457, 459, 470, 476, 476n, 491n
Enzi 42, 44
Esper, Jan 41
Estangüi Gómez, Raúl 523–524
Eusebius 232
Evagrios 120
Evagrius 393, 397
Evans, James A.S. 385
Ezekiel 189

Finné, Martin 36
Firmicus Maternus 184
Fleitmann, Dominik 17, 45
Flohr, Pascal 46
Francke, Alexander 44
Frenkel, Yoshua 457
Frisia, Silvia 45
Frogley, Michael R. 45
Frontinus 212

Gaba, Erik 348
Ǧauhar aṣ-Ṣiqillī 434
Gelimer 381
George of Pisidia 182
Glick, Thomas 244
Gogou, Alexandra 50, 418
Göktürk Ozan Mert 45
Gowland, Rebecca 85
Greenwood, Tim 328, 335
Gregory of Nazianzus 182
Grigor-Derenik 321
Grove, Alfred 14

Habakkuk 189
Hadrian 207, 212
Haldon, John 17, 71, 74, 86, 231, 430
Hall, Peter 203, 222
Halstead, Paul 330

Harvey, Alan J. 413, 423
Heinrich, Ingo 46, 49
Heraclius 235, 254n, 392–393, 398–399
Hermogenes 182
Herodotus 316, 393
Hewsen, Robert H. 317
Hill, Donald 244
Hirschfeld, Yizhar 233, 235
Hisham b. Abd al-Malik 241–242
Horden Peregerine 12–16
Hunger, Herbert 9
Huntington, Ellsworth 4, 234
Hysechios 209

Ibn Wahshiyya 244
Ignatios 219
Isaac Comnenus 182
Izdebski Adam 17, 88, 131, 271, 418–419, 424, 427, 495n

Jacobson Matthew J. 37, 45
Jacoby, David 414–16
Jeffreys, Elisabeth M. 371
John 186
John Chrysostom 363
John France 500n
John I Tzimiskes 431, 436, 438–439
John of Damascus 239
John of Ephesus 386
John of Jerusalem 185
John of Joinville 499n–500n
John Scylitzes 423–424, 436, 439–440, 443, 446–447, 449–451, 454, 459, 463n
John the Almsgiver 235
John Zonares 443, 459, 468–469
Joshua the Stylite 384
Justin II 392, 397
Justinian 206, 212, 218, 370, 381–383, 385, 394–398

Kaldellis, Anthony 427–428, 428n, 430, 443
Kaniewski, David 45, 271
Kantakouzenos 125
Kaplan, Michel 9n
Kaptijn, Eva 17
Ward, Kate 214, 217
Katholikos Nersēs III Šinoł 327
Katholikos Nersēs V 328
Katholikos Yovhannēs Drasχanakertcʻi 327

Katholikos Yovhannēs Drasxanakertc'i 327
Katrantsiotis, Christos 44, 420
Kazhdan, Alexander 430
Kekaumenos 368
Khusrow II 236
King David 399
Klippel, Lara 41, 46
Koder, Johannes 10–11, 71, 213, 367
Koloch, Grzegorz 418–419
Kondrashov, Dmitri 44
Konstantinianos 370
Konter, Oliver 41
Kosmas 369
Kosmas Indikoleustes 392
Kotsakis, Kostas 346
Kuzucuoglu, Catherine 44

Labuhn, Inga 36
Lacey, Jack H. 44
Laiou, Angeliki 413, 426, 523
Lamb, Hubert 8, 405–406
Lamy, Frank 45
Le Roy Ladurie, Emmanuel 7–8
Lefort, Jacques 9
Lemcke, Genry 331–332, 334
Leng, Melanie J. 44
Leo III 353
Leo of Tripoli 370
Leo the Deacon 422, 435, 438–439, 440, 442, 461
Leo VI 155, 222, 369
Leo, the bishop of Synnada 299
Lewis, Mary E. 85
Libanius 184
Linke, Julia 313
Liutprand of Cremona 368
Longinus 209
Lorenz, Edward 112
Louis IX 497
Luterbacher, Jürg 17, 40, 47–48, 409, 520

Magistros, Thomas 363
Magny, Michel 45
Maguire, Henry 17, 86
Malalas, John 386
Malamut, Elisabeth 364
Mango, Cyril 371
Mansur 239
Manuel I 468
Marcian (bishop of Gaza) 190

Marcian (emperor) 117, 396
Martin, Jean-Marie 9
Mais, Alessia 62, 70, 7
Maslama b. 'Abd al-Malik 241
Matthew of Edessa 335, 422–423, 440, 452, 456, 467
Maurice 233, 235, 292, 392–393, 397
Mauropous, John 278, 298–299
Maximus Confessor 235
McCormick, Michael 14, 218
McNeill, John 13–14
Meier, Mischa 17, 87
Mensforth, Robert 94
Menua of Urartu 311, 313
Merchant, Carolyn 5
Meslem (Maslama) 240, 242
Michael Glykas 182
Michael IV 446–452
Michael V 551
Michael VII Dukas 464–466, 475
Michael VIII 464
Mitchell, Piers D. 98
Moḥammad-Reżā-Šāh Pahlavī 331
Mohammed 206
Mordechai, Lee 17, 86, 424, 427
Morellon 44
Morrisson, Cecile 426
Movsēs Xorenac'i 316
Mu'awiya 236, 239
Mxit'ar Goš 329

Nicephorus Bryennios 423
Nikephoros II Phokas 368, 369, 431, 436, 438
Nikephoritzes 464–466
Nikephoros Gregoras 125
Nikephoros III Botaneiates 466
Nomikou, Paraskevi 348

Ocakoğlu, Faruk 45
Olson, Aleander 414–416
Orland, Ian J. 45
Orphanotrophos, John 449–452, 464

Paul the Silentiary 193, 396
Paul, Jürgen 456
Paulissen, Etienne 271
Peter Chrysologus 187–188
Pfister, Christian 8, 17, 421
Philip II 6

INDEX OF NAMES   551

Philippicus   392
Philokales   428–429
Phocas   397–398
Poblome, Jeroen   17, 270
Polybius   393
Preiser-Kapeller, Johannes   17, 43, 131, 318, 333, 359, 493
Procopius   206–207, 369, 382, 386, 393–396
Procopius of Gaza   199
Prodomos, Theodoros   118
Pryor, John   371
Psellos, Michael   118, 423
Psellos, Styliane   118
Purcell, Nicholas   12–16
Pʻilippē (Prince)   329
Pʻilippē (Lord)   328

Quennet, Grégory   1
Qusta ibn Luqa   243

Rackham, Olivier   14
Raphael, Sarah Kate   46, 173
Repapis, C.   43
Roberts, Neil   44
Romanos (poet)   190
Romanos I Lakapenos   424–428, 431–432, 465
Romanos II   431
Romanos II   431–432
Romanos III Argyros   445–447, 448
Romanos IV Diogenes   336, 461–462
Romanus Lecapenus   219
Ronchey, Silvia   430
Ruggeri, Francesca   205, 218
Rusa II   313–315
Rusio, Lorenzo   502

Sadori, Laura   44
Saif ad-Daula   435
Barbarian (*Hagios Barbaros*), St.   372
Demetrios, St.   449
Salah ad-Din   498
Samuel of Ani   318
Sargent, Abigail   17
Schilman, Bettina   45
Schneider, Brigit   406
Schönbein, Johannes   44, 46
Sebēos   327
Semiramis (Queen)   315–316, 322, 324

Sennacherib   316
Shapur II   236
Sharifi, Arash   44
Shaw, Beth   245
Sidonius Apollinaris   190
Simon Logothetes   425
Słoczyński, Tymon   418–419
Spyros, Pavlides   355
Squatriti, Paolo   15–16
Stathakapoulos, Dionysios   131, 521
Stepʻannos Ōrbēlean   328–329
Stevens, Lora R.   44
Strabo   298, 301–302, 316
Sturm, Michael   331–332, 334
Sultan Tullup (Toġrïl)   336
Synesius of Cyrene   367

Telelis, Ioannis   11, 11n, 42–44, 49, 86, 131, 416, 423, 521
Themistius   207
Theoderich   494, 498
Theodora (empress)   383, 451, 455
Theodore of Sykeon, St.   394
Theodore Tiro, St.   278
Theodosius   212
Theodosius II   396
Theophanes   213, 371–372, 449
Theophanes Continuatus   364
Theophanes the Confessor   371
Theophylact Simocatta   393
Theosodius   208
Thomas   194
Thucydides   392–393
Tiberius   235
Tor, Deborah   457
Toufic, Fahd   244
Tsar Simeon   423
Tsiamis, Costas   17, 87
Tyrach   457
Tzachas of Smyrna   370, 469

Ülgen, Umut B.   45

Veikou, Myrto   17
Verstraeten, Gert   271
Vogt, Steffen   44, 46

Waelkens, Marc   270–271
Walker, Phillip L.   92
Warken, Sophie Friederike   46

Watson, Adrew 244
Western, A. Gaynor 85
White, Sam 17, 424, 427
Whittow, Mark 414
Wick, Lucia 45, 331–332, 334
Widell, Magnus 47
William Henry Samuel Jones 4, 36, 297
Wilson, Andrew 245
Wittfogel, Karl August 326
Worster, Donald 4, 14

Xerxes 314
Xoplaki, Elena 17, 36, 43–44, 49, 52, 231, 416

Yaḥyā of Antioch 443, 444n
Yakob of Siwnikʻ 328
Yaqut al-Hamawi 497
Yovhannēs-Senekʻerim Arcruni 335

Zanchetta, Giovanni 44–45
Zarui Pogossian 319
Zeno 117, 211–212
Zimansky, Paul 326, 335
Zoë 445, 447, 451, 454–455
Zonaras, John 443, 459, 468–469

ʻAbd al-Laṭīf 472–475

Printed in the United States
by Baker & Taylor Publisher Services